And thousands more easily misspelled, important capitalized words and names are listed in this unique, extraordinarily comprehensive speller. Nowhere else can you find the variety of subject areas, vast number of entries, and contemporary items included in this indispensable reference. It is an invaluable resource for anyone who requires accuracy and precision when using the written word.

THE PERSONS, PLACES, AND THINGS SPELLING DICTIONARY

THE PERSONS, PLACES, AND THINGS SPELLING DICTIONARY

William C. Paxson

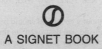

A SIGNET BOOK

This dictionary includes words that are or are asserted to be trademarks or service marks but neither the inclusion nor exclusion of the symbols ™ or ˢᴹ implies that particular words have acquired, or failed to acquire, proprietary status for legal purposes.

SIGNET
Published by the Penguin Group
Penguin Books USA Inc., 375 Hudson Street,
New York, New York 10014, U.S.A.
Penguin Books Ltd, 27 Wrights Lane,
London W8 5TZ, England
Penguin Books Australia Ltd, Ringwood,
Victoria, Australia
Penguin Books Canada Ltd, 10 Alcorn Avenue,
Toronto, Ontario, Canada M4V 3B2
Penguin Books (N.Z.) Ltd, 182–190 Wairau Road,
Auckland 10, New Zealand

Penguin Books Ltd, Registered Offices:
Harmondsworth, Middlesex, England

First published by Signet, an imprint of Dutton Signet,
a division of Penguin Books USA Inc.

First Printing, April, 1994
10 9 8 7 6 5 4 3 2 1

Contents

Contents

Acknowledgments

My many thanks go to my wife, Diana, for doing much of the typing and for valuable suggestions concerning the style and content of entries; to the publisher's editorial staff, for helping me finish what I started; and to the staff of The Library, California State University, Sacramento, for operating an excellent research facility.

Introduction

Content

How this book will help you. This book will help you spell the name or title of a popular or prominent person, place, or thing. The book contains many terms not found in desk or unabridged dictionaries. This is a partial list of the spellings:

- *Persons*. Heroes and villains; stars of the entertainment world; statesmen and politicians; given names
- *Places*. Continents; bodies of water; nations; cities; mountains; tourist attractions
- *Things*. Abstract ideas; organizations; scientific and technical terms; books, movies, plays, and works of art

Basically, the book is a guide to the spelling of the most commonly encountered terms that contain capital letters. Most of the content consists of capitalized nouns, along with an occasional capitalized adjective or verb.

Sources of entries. The book contains 50,000 entries derived from three categories of sources. One category is made up of lists bearing titles such as "Highest," "Longest," or "Most Notable"; these lists appear in atlases and encyclopedias. The second category consists of popular media contemporary with the period 1992 through early 1993. The third category consists of general and specialized reference works.

Entries were selected by a process that, although subjective, was planned to include a great variety of entries that would be useful to a large number of readers. If an entry was on a most-popular or best-known list or if the entry was an item in a major reference work, that entry had a good chance of being included. Similarly, if an entry was repeatedly newsworthy, as shown in *Facts on File* or *The New York Times Index*, that entry also had a good chance of being included.

An appendix presents guidelines for dividing words at the end of a line.

Accuracy of the spellings. Spellings were taken from and checked against a variety of sources; principal sources are listed in the book's References. In some cases, the sources did not agree on an entry's capitalization, punctuation, or spelling.

Some of the discrepancies were not errors but were instead caused by different approaches to converting foreign expressions into English. In cases such as these, synonymous forms and variant spellings are shown. See Style of Entries, below.

Other discrepancies existed because of errors in the reference works. When errors were encountered, a consensus spelling was adopted for use here. As more appropriate spellings come to light, they will be used in later editions of the book.

Limitations. The assumptions underlying this book are that readers know the definitions of terms that they are looking up and that they are using the book to check the spelling of a term. Accordingly, the book does not define terms other than to provide information pertaining to spelling.

In addition, the book is a guide to the spelling of uppercased terms and does not show corresponding lowercased terms. As an example, "Anchorage," the city in Alaska, is shown, but "anchorage," a place to anchor a boat, is not.

Neither does the book establish matters of style pertaining to the use of italics or quotation marks for items such as titles of books, works of art, or foreign words. Different styles exist for the use of these devices, and any attempt by a dictionary to establish a style could place the dictionary in conflict with the different styles.

Matters of style are best resolved by consulting a style manual for the appropriate profession.

Style of Entries

Description of entries. An entry can consist of three parts: a main term, shown in (1) below; any spelling variants or unusual plurals, shown in (2) below; and supplemental information, shown in brackets in (3) below.

(1) Arapahoe Community College
(2) Arapaho *or* Arapahoe, *n.*, *pl.* Arapaho *or* Arapahos *or* Arapahoe *or* Arapahoes
(3) AFLAC Inc. [*form.* American Family Corporation]

In giving variants, when only part of an entry changes, only the part that changes is shown.

Christian socialism *occas.* Socialism
Christian socialist *occas.* Socialist

Note: For information on abbreviations used in this dictionary, see the section immediately following this introduction.

Spelling and spelling variants. The main term shows the preferred spelling. Here *preferred spelling* refers to a spelling that is most commonly seen in edited, professional writing.

When a spelling variant is labeled *or*, either spelling is commonly used. However, when variants separated by *or* are out of alphabetical order, there could be a *slight* preference for the first spelling. Other spelling variants are introduced with terms such as *often* or *occas.* (occasionally).

The safest thing to do is to use the first spelling listed.

The first spelling is generally the one that is most acceptable to editors, teachers, and writers.

The expression *var. of* labels a spelling that is sometimes less commonly seen than the preferred spelling.

Supplemental information. Some entries contain brief supplemental comments. The comments are meant to help readers sort out the differences between confusing spellings. As an example, this pair of entries is annotated to show the different spellings of two presidents whose names are easily confused:

Adams, John [2d president]
Adams, John Quincy [6th president]

For similarly spelled communities, the state abbreviations are shown in brackets:

Oroville [* CA; WA]
Orrville [* OH]

Note: The asterisk (*) stands for a geographical or political entity such as a region, city, town, or village. As used in the example above, the asterisk indicates that there are communities named Oroville in California and Washington and a community named Orrville in Ohio.

Same meaning, different spelling. Many persons, places, and things are known by more than one name. The book shows the various names, but with no cross-references. Accordingly, you will find entries for

Kriss Kringle
Nicholas, Saint
Santa Claus

Same spelling, different meaning. Only one spelling is shown when different items are spelled identically. As an example, only one entry is shown for *Humperdinck, Engelbert,* a name used by both a German composer and a popular singer.

Along these same lines, given names are shown for numbered personages such as Henry V, Henry VI, Henry VII, and Henry VIII, but the roman numerals are not suffixed.

Capitalization. Where a distinctive style of capitalization is established by the reference works, that style is retained here. Otherwise, first and last words are capitalized as are all other words except articles, coordinate conjunctions, and prepositions. For the capitalization practices of a particular profession, consult that profession's style manual.

Punctuation. Punctuation follows the style of the original. When the references do not agree on a style, punctuation is according to standard editorial practice as best exemplified in the *Chicago Manual of Style* (University of Chicago Press, 1982).

Brackets or parentheses? Some entries, especially those of businesses and associations, use parentheses as part of their official forms, as shown in (1) below. Accordingly, brackets, instead of parentheses, are used for editorial insertions, as shown in (2).

(1) El Paso LNG Company (El Paso Tanker Companies)
(2) [San Antonio] Express News

Personal names. Personal names are shown as they are written in popular usage. As an example, Frank Sinatra is shown as *Sinatra, Frank*, not *Sinatra, Francis Albert*. The only titles shown are those such as *Sir* or *Cardinal*, which are considered a permanent part of a person's name.

Brand names. A brand name is identified with the trademark symbol™ or the service mark symbolˢᴹ. Use of the symbol does not mean that the product or service is registered with the United States Patent and Trademark Office.

The symbol is present solely to identify an entry thought to be a brand name. Owners of trademarks are obliged to use special symbols with them—an *R* or *TM* within a circle—in their advertisements; if they don't, they may lose exclusive right to use the mark.

The general writing public is under no obligation to use such special symbols. Accepted practice is to capitalize the first letter of the brand name, just as any other proper name would be capitalized.

Abbreviations. Titles and names are not abbreviated unless strong evidence in the references indicates that the official style uses an abbreviation.

Alphabetization

General. Alphabetization is letter by letter. The only inverted entries are those of contemporary, Westernized personal names. Names prefixed with *Mac* are alphabetized with other entries beginning with *Mac*; names prefixed with *Mc* are alphabetized with other entries beginning with *Mc*. *Saint* spelled out is alphabetized with entries beginning with *Sa*; the abbreviation *St.* is alphabetized with entries beginning with *St*.

The list below shows the style of alphabetization:

Lake Saint Clair
Lakes of Killarney
MacArthur, Douglas
Madeira Island
McKinley, William
Saint Croix Island
Saskatchewan
St. John, Jill

Single-word entries are alphabetized before inverted ones, inverted entries before noninverted entries:

Dayton
Dayton, Jonathan
Daytona Beach

Numbered persons such as saints come before persons known by family names.

Louis
Louis IX, Saint
Louis, Joe

The following items are ignored for the purposes of alphabetizing: titles such as *Sir* and *Madam*; diacritical marks; any punctuation marks that are part of the entry; and labels such as *occas.*, *or*, or *n.*, *pl.*

A symbol such as the & is alphabetized by the spelling of its meaning, *and*, not by its own spelling, *ampersand*.

Position of articles. Introductory articles in entries in English are placed at the end, and alphabetization is by key word. In entries in languages other than English, alphabetization is as the term is generally known, regardless of the position of articles.

El Paso
La Prensa
New York Times, The

Personal names. Personal contemporary, Westernized names are inverted and alphabetized last name first; personal names in languages such as Chinese and Japanese are generally not inverted unless they are contemporary names. Spanish names, names with particles, and unusual names are alphabetized according to the traditional or prevailing style.

Saints are alphabetized by their first names:

Thomas à Becket, Saint
Thomas Aquinas, Saint

Members of royalty are alphabetized by title or as they are familiarly known:

Chief Sitting Bull
Cleopatra
Prince Charles

Numerals. Numerals are alphabetized as though they were spelled out.

CH-53E Super Stallion
CH-47 Chinook
CH-46 Sea Knight

Abbreviations

adj. adjective
AK Alaska
aka also known as
AL Alabama
AR Arkansas
AS American Samoa
AZ Arizona
c. circa (about)
CA California
CM Northern Mariana
  Islands
CO Colorado
CT Connecticut
CZ Canal Zone
DC District of
  Columbia
DE Delaware
fem. feminine
FL Florida
form. formerly
GA Georgia
GU Guam

HI Hawaii
IA Iowa
ID Idaho
IL Illinois
IN Indiana
KS Kansas
KY Kentucky
LA Louisiana
MA Massachusetts
masc. masculine
MD Maryland
ME Maine
MI Michigan
MN Minnesota
MO Missouri
MS Mississippi
MT Montana
n. noun
NC North Carolina
ND North Dakota
NE Nebraska
NH New
Hampshire
NJ New Jersey
NM New Mexico
NV Nevada
NY New York
occas. occasionally

OH Ohio
OK Oklahoma
OR Oregon
PA Pennsylvania
pl. plural
PR Puerto Rico
RI Rhode Island
SC South Carolina
SD South Dakota
sing. singular
SM service mark
TM trademark
TN Tennessee
TT Trust Territory
of the Pacific
TX Texas
UT Utah
v. verb
VA Virginia
var. of variant
spelling
VI Virgin Islands
VT Vermont
WA Washington
WI Wisconsin
WV West Virginia
WY Wyoming

*   The asterisk (*) stands for a geographical or political entity such as
    a region, city, town, or village. As used in the example below, the
    asterisk indicates that there are communities named Abingdon in
    Illinois and Virginia.

    Abingdon [* IL; VA]

A

AAA World
Aachen
Aakjaer, Jeppe
Aalborg *or* Ålborg
Aalto, Alvar
Aames, Willie
A & P supermarket
A & W Beverages, Inc.
A & W Restaurants, Inc.
Aar *or* Aare
Aaron
Aaron, Henry
Aaron, Tommy
Aaron Brothers Art Marts
Aaron Burr Association
Aaronic
Aaronical
Aaronite
Aaron's beard
Aaron Spelling Productions, Inc.
Aaron's rod
AARP Bulletin
A-axis, *n., pl.* A-axes
Abaco and Cays
Abadan

Ābādān Island
Abaddon
ABA Journal
Abarbanel *var. of* Abrabanel, Isaac
Abarbanel *var. of* Abrabanel, Judah
A battery
Abba
Abbado, Claudio
Abbas
ABB Asea Brown Boveri Ltd.
Abbassid dynasty
Abbe, Cleveland
Abbe, Ernst
Abbe, Robert
Abbe condenser
Abbe number
Abbe sine condition
Abbe's sine
Abbeville
Abbeville Press, Inc.
Abbevillian *occas.* Abbevilliean
Abbey, Edwin Austin
Abbey of Saint Bavon
Abbey Theatre

AB Bookman's Weekly
Abbot, Charles Greeley
Abbott, Berenice
Abbott, Bud
Abbott, Edith
Abbott, George
Abbott, Grace
Abbott, Jacob
Abbott, Lyman
Abbott, Philip
Abbott and Costello
Abbott and Costello Fan Club
Abbott Laboratories
Abbott Laboratories Fund
ABC Afterschool Special
ABC books
ABC News
ABC News Nightline
ABC Radio Networks
ABC soil
ABC Sports
ABC's Wide World of Sports
ABC Technical and Trade School

ABC Weekend
  Special, The
ABC World News
  This Morning
Abderhalden, Emil
Abduction from the
  Seraglio, The
Abdul, Paula
Abdul-Jabbar, Kareem
Abdullah, Sheik
  Muhammad
Abdullah ibn Buhaina
Abdullah ibn Husayn
Abedi, Agha Hasan
Abednego
Abel
Abel, I. W.
Abel, Niels H.
Abel, Rudolf
Abelard, Peter
Abelard and Heloise
AB Electrolux
abelian *often* Abelian
  group
Abe Lincoln in Illinois
Abell, Kjeld
Abelson, P. H.
Abenaki *occas.*
  Abnaki *n., pl.*
  Abenaki *or*
  Abenakis
Abercrombie, Sir
  Patrick
Abercrombie and
  Fitch
Abercromby, James
Abercromby, Sir
  Ralph
Aberdeen
Aberdeen Angus

Aberdeen Proving
  Ground
Aberdeenshire
Aberdeen terrier
Aberdeen University
Abernathy, Ralph
  David
Abide with Me
Abidjan
Abie's Irish Rose
Abigail
Abilene
Abilene Christian
  University
Abingdon [* IL; VA]
Abington [* MA; PA]
Abitibi Lake
Abiti Game Reserve
Abiti River
Abnaki *var. of*
  Abenaki, *n., pl.*
  Abnaki *or* Abnakis
Abner
Abney level
ABO blood groups
A-bomb
Abominable Snowman
  occas. abominable
  snowman
Abosch, David T.
ABO system
Abou Ben Adhem
Abrabanel *or*
  Abarbanel *or*
  Abravanel, Isaac
Abrabanel *or*
  Abarbanel *or*
  Abravanel, Judah
Abraham
Abraham, F. Murray

Abraham Baldwin
  Agricultural
  College
Abraham Lincoln
  Birthplace National
  Historic Site
Abraham's bosom
Abramovitz, Max
Abrams, Creighton W.
Abravanel *var. of*
  Abrabanel, Isaac
Abravanel *var. of*
  Abrabanel, Judah
Abruzzi
Abruzzi, Luigi
Absalom
Absalom, Absalom!
Absalom and
  Achitophel
Absaroka
Absaroka Range
Abscam scandal
Absecon Beach
Absecon Inlet
Absinthe Drinkers,
  The
Abū Bakar [sultan of
  Johore]
Abū Bakr [1st caliph
  of Mecca]
Abu Dhabi
Abuja
Abundant Wildlife
  Society
Abu Simbel
Abyssinia
Abyssinian
Abyssinian banana
Abyssinian Church
Abyssinian well
Abzug, Bella
Acacia

Academic American Encyclopedia

Academic Festival Overture

Academic Press, Inc.

Academy Award

Academy of American Poets

Academy of Ancient Music

Academy of Art College

Academy of Motion Picture Arts and Sciences

Academy of Music

Academy of Natural Sciences

Academy of Political Science

Academy of Saint Martin-in-the-Fields

Academy of Television Arts and Sciences

Academy of the New Church

Acadia [old name for Nova Scotia; see also Arcadia]

Acadian

Acadia National Park

Acadian flycatcher

Acadia University

Acanthocephala

Acapulco

Acapulco gold

Acarigua

Accademia della Crusca

Accion International

Accius, Lucius

Accor

Accra

Accra Kotoka International Airport

Accuracy in Media, Inc.

AC/DC or A.C./D.C. [bisexuality]

AC/DC [musical group]

AC Delco 500

Ace, Goodman

Ace, Jane

Ace, Johnny

Ace Award

Ace Books

Achab var. of Ahab [a king of Israel]

Achaea

Achaean or Achaian

Achaean League

Achaemenes

Achaemenian

Achaemenid, n., pl. Achaemenidae or Achaemenids

Achaemenid dynasty

Achebe, Chinua

Achernar

Acheron

Acheson, Dean

Achille Lauro

Achilles

Achilles' or Achilles heel

Achilles reflex

Achilles occas. Achilles' tendon

Acker, Sharon

Acker Peak

Ackroyd, David

ACME Features Syndicate

A. C. Nielsen Company

Acoma

Acoma pueblo

Aconcagua

Acoustical Society of America

Acrea moth

Acrobat Family

Acrocorinthus

Acropolis

Acropolis Museum

Across the Board

Acrux

Acta

Acta Apostolicae Sedis

Acta Santorum

Acting Company, The

Action Comics

Action for Children's Television

Action on Smoking and Health

Actium

Active 20–30 Association of the United States and Canada

act of God

Act of Parliament clock

Act of Toleration

Act of Uniformity

Acton

Acton, John Emerich Edward Dalberg

Acton, Sir John Francis Edward

Actor Bando Hikosaburo III and the Actor Iwan Hanshiro IV, The

Actors' Equity Association

Actors' Fund of America

Actors Studio, Inc.

Actors Theatre of Louisville

Acts of the Apostles

Acts Satellite Network

ACT UP

Acuff, Roy

Acuson Corporation

Ada

Adair, Paul "Red"

Adalbert or Adelbert, Saint

Adam

Adam, Adolphe Charles

Adam, James

Adam, Juliette

Adam, Lambert Sigisbert

Adam, Nicholas Sebastian

Adam, Robert

Adam and Eve [biblical characters]

Adam-and-Eve [orchid]

Adam Ant

Adamawa Massif

Adam Bede

Adamic

Adamic, Louis

Adamical

Adamite

Adamitic

Adamitical

Adam of Bremen

Adams

Adams, Abigail

Adams, Alice

Adams, Andy

Adams, Ansel

Adams, Brooke

Adams, Bryan

Adams, Charles Francis

Adams, Don

Adams, Edie

Adams, Franklin Pierce

Adams, Henry

Adams, Herbert Baxter

Adams, James Truslow

Adams, Joey

Adams, John [2d president]

Adams, John Couch

Adams, John Quincy [6th president]

Adams, Julie

Adams, Lee

Adams, Léonie Fuller

Adams, Louisa Johnson

Adams, Mason

Adams, Maude

Adams, Oleta

Adams, Pepper

Adams, Samuel

Adams, Samuel Hopkins

Adam's ale

Adam's apple

Adam's Bridge

Adams Communications

Adam Smith's Money World

Adams National Historic Site

Adam's needle

Adamson, Joy

Adam's Peak

Adams State College

Adams-Stokes disease

Adams-Stokes syndrome

Adam-12

Adana

ADAPSO—The Computer Software and Services Industry Association

Adar

Adar Sheni

Adcock antenna

ADC Telecommunications, Inc.

Adda

Addams, Charles Samuel

Addams, Jane

Addams Family, The

Adderley, Cannonball

Addington, Henry

Addis Ababa

Addis Ababa Bole International Airport

Addison
Addison, Adele
Addison, Joseph
Addison, Thomas
Addisonian
Addison's anemia
Addison's disease
Addison-Wesley
  Publishing
  Company, Inc.
Addled Parliament
Addressograph™
Ade, George
Adelaide
Adelaide, Saint
Adelaide Island
Adelaide Peninsula
Adelard of Bath
Adele
Adélie Coast
Adélie Land
Adélie penguin
Adeline
Adelphi University
Aden
Adenauer, Konrad
Adeodatus II, Saint
Adeste Fidelis
Adham, Kamal
Adige River
Adirondack chair
Adirondack
  Community College
Adirondack [Indian],
  n., pl. Adirondack
  or Adirondacks
Adirondack Life
Adirondack Mountain
  Club

Adirondack
  Mountains
Adirondack Park
Adirondacks, the
Adirondack skiff
Adjani, Isabelle
Adlai
Adler, Alfred
Adler, Cyrus
Adler, Elmer
Adler, Felix
Adler, Jacob P.
Adler, Kurt
Adler, Kurt Herbert
Adler, Larry
Adler, Luther
Adler, Mortimer J.
Adler, Peter Herman
Adler, Richard
Adler, Stella
Adlerian
Adler Planetarium
Administrative
  Conference of the
  United States
Administrative Law
  Review
Administrative
  Management
  Society
Administrator,
  Environmental
  Protection Agency
Administrator,
  National
  Aeronautics and
  Space
  Administration
Admirable Crichton,
  The
Admiral Cruises

Admiral Graf Spee
Admiralty Island
Admiralty Island
  National Monument
Admiralty Islands
Admiralty mile
Admission Day
Adobe Systems, Inc.
Adolf of Nassau
Adolph Coors
  Company
Adolphus, The
Adolphus, Gustavus
Adonai occas. Adonoy
Adonis
Adoration of the
  Lamb, The
Adoration of the Magi
Adoration of the
  Shepherds
Adoree, Renee
Adorno, Theodore
  Wiesengrund
Adoula, Cyrille
Adrenalin™
Adriamycin™
Adrian
Adrian III, Saint
Adrian, Edgar
  Douglas
Adrian, Gilbert
Adrian College
Adrianople red
Adriatic Sea
Adrienne
Adult Basic Education
Advanced Micro
  Devices, Inc.
Advanced Tactical
  Aircraft

Advanced Tactical
 Fighter

Advanced
 Telecommunica-
 tions Corporation

Advance News
 Service, Inc.

Advance Publications,
 Inc.

Advent

Advent Christian
 Church

Adventism

Adventist

Adventist Book
 Center

Advent Sunday

Adventure Road

Adventures of
 Buckaroo Banzai,
 The

Adventures of
 Huckleberry Finn,
 The

Adventures of Ozzie
 and Harriet, The

Adventures of
 Pinocchio, The

Adventures of
 Superboy, The

Adventures of
 Superman, The

Adventures of Tom
 Sawyer, The

Advertising Age

Advertising Council

Advise and Consent

Advocacy Institute

Advocates, The

Adweek

Aegean

Aegean Bronze Age

Aegean Islands

Aegean Sea

Aegina Island

Aeginetan Marbles

Aelfric

Aeneas

Aeneid

Aeolian, *n.* [native or
 inhabitant of
 Aeolis]

aeolian *often* Aeolian,
 adj. [of or
 pertaining to
 Aeolus]

Aeolian Chamber
 Players

Aeolian Islands [*now*
 Lipari Islands]

Aeolian mode

Aeolic

Aeolis [ancient
 country]

Aeolus [Greek god of
 the winds]

Aer Lingus

Aerobics and Fitness
 Association of
 America

Aerobics and Fitness
 Foundation of
 America

Aeroflot

Aerolíneas Argentinas

Aeromexico

Aeronica

Aero Peru

Aerosmith

Aerospace
 Engineering

Aerospace Industries
 Association of
 America

Aero-Space Institute

Aerospace Medical
 Association

Aerospatiale Group

Aerovias de Mexico

Aeschines

Aeschylus

Aesop

Aesopian *occas.*
 Aesopic

Aesop's fables

Aesthetic Movement

Aetna Life and
 Casualty Company

Aetna Life and
 Casualty
 Foundation, Inc.

Aetna Life Insurance
 and Annuity
 Company

Aetna Life Insurance
 Company

Aetna Personal
 Security Insurance
 Company

Aetolia

Aetolian League

Affair of the Diamond
 Necklace

Affiliated
 Publications, Inc.

Affiliated Publishers,
 Inc.

Affleck, Thomas

Affluent Society, The

Afghan

Afghan hound

Afghanistan

Afghanistan Relief
 Committee

Afghan War

A-5 Vigilante

AFLAC Inc. [*form.* American Family Corporation]

A-4 Skyhawk

A-frame house

A-frame tent

Africa

Africa Fund

African

Africana

African-American

African-American Dance Ensemble

African-American Institute

African-American music

African cherry orange

African daisy

Africander *or* Afrikander [cattle; *see also* Afrikaner]

African Development Bank

African Development Foundation

African dominoes

African elephant

African Enterprise

Africa News Service

African gray parrot

Africanism

Africanist

African lily

African lion hound

African mahogany

African marigold

African Methodist Episcopal Church

African Methodist Episcopal Zion Church

African millet

African National Congress

Africanness

African Orthodox Church

African sleeping sickness

African trypanosomiasis

African Universal Church

African violet

African Wildlife Foundation

African woodbine

African yellowwood

Africare

Africa Watch

Afrikaans

Afrika Korps

Afrikaner [people; *see also* Africander]

Afrikanerism

Afrikaner Resistance Movement

Afro [hairstyle]

Afro- [combining form]

Afro-American

Afro-American music

Afro-Asian

Afro-Asiatic

Afrocentric

Afro-Cuban jazz

AFS Intercultural Programs

Afternoon of a Faun, The

Agadez *or* Agadès

Agadir

Aga Khan

Agamemnon

Agana

Agapetus I, Saint

Agar, John

Agassi, Andre

Agassiz, Alexander

Agassiz, Elizabeth

Agassiz, Louis

Agate Fossil Beds National Monument

Agatha

Agatha, Saint

A. G. Edwards, Inc.

Agee, James

Agena

Agence France-Presse

Agency, The

Agency for International Development

Agency-Rent-a-Car, Inc.

Agent 007

Agent Orange

Age of Aquarius

Age of Fable, The

Age of Metternich

Age of Reason [historical period]

Age of Reason, The [pamphlet by T. Paine]

Ager, Milton

Aggadah, *n., pl.* Aggadoth

Aggiornamento *or* aggiornamento

Agincourt

Agnes

Agnes, Saint

Agnesi, Maria Gaetana

Agnes Scott College

Agnew, David Hayes

Agnew, Spiro

Agnewism

Agnon, Shmuel Yosef

Agnos, Art

Agnus Dei

Agony and the Ecstasy, The

Agra

Agrarian Leader Zapata

AgriAmerica Network

Agricola, Georgius

Agricola, Gnaeus Julius

Agricultural Engineering

Agricultural Hall of Fame

Agricultural History Society

Agricultural Implement Workers of America

Agricultural Outlook

Agricultural Stabilization and Conservation Service

Agrinet Farm Radio Network

Agrippa, Marcus

Agrippina the Elder

Agrippina the Younger

Agronsky, Martin

Agua Caliente

Agua Caliente Race Track

Aguascalientes

Aguecheek, Sir Andrew

Aguinaldo, Emilio

Agulhas Current

Agutter, Jenny

Agway Inc.

Ahab [ship's captain in *Moby Dick*]

Ahab *or* Achab [a king of Israel]

Ahaggar

A. H. Belo Corporation

Ahern, James

Aherne, Brian

AH-58D Warrior

Ahlin, Lars

Ahmanson Theatre

Ahmedabad *or* Ahmadabad

Ahmedabad Airport

Ahnfelt's seaweed

AH-1 HueyCobra

AH-1 SeaCobra

AH-1 SuperCobra

AH-1 Viper

A-horizon

Ahriman

AH-6 Defender

AH-64 Apache

Ahura Mazda

Ahwaz

Ah! Wilderness

AIAA Journal

Aïda

Aid Association for Lutherans

AIDS Action Council

Aids Coalition to Unleash Power

AIDS-related complex

AIDS virus

Aid to Families with Dependent Children

Aiello, Danny

AIESEC-United States, Inc.

Aiken

Aiken, Conrad

Aiken, Howard H.

Aiken, Joan

Aiken Technical College

Ailes, Roger

Ailey, Alvin

Aimee, Anouk

AIM Report

Aims Community College

Ainsworth, William

Ain't Misbehavin'

Ainu, *n.*, *pl.* Ainu *or* Ainus

Aïr

Air Afrique

Air America

Air and Space/ Smithsonian Magazine

Air and Waste Management Association

Air and Water Technologies Corporation

Air Antilles

Airbus

Airbus Industrie

Air Canada
Air China
Air Combat Command
Air Conditioning
    Contractors of
    America
Aircraft Owners and
    Pilots Association
Aire
Airedale
Airedale terrier
Air Express
    International
    Corporation
Air Force Aid Society
Air Force Association
Air Force Cross
Air Force Institute of
    Technology
Air Force Magazine
Air Force Materiel
    Command
Air Force One
Air Force Sergeants
    Association
Air Force Space
    Museum
Air Force Times
Air France
Air Gabon
Air Guadeloupe
Air India
Air Jamaica
Air Line Employees
    Association
Airline of the Virgin
    Islands, Ltd.
Air Line Pilots
    Association
Air Malawi Ltd.
Air Malta

Airman's Medal
Air Medal
Air Micronesia, Inc.
Air Mobility
    Command
Air National Guard
Air New Zealand Ltd.
Air Niugini
Air Pacific Ltd.
Air Panama
    International
Airplane!
Airplane II: The
    Sequel
Airport
Airport 1975
Airport '77
Air Products and
    Chemicals, Inc.
Air Products
    Foundation
Air Supply
Air Tanzania
    Corporation
Air Traffic Control
    Association
Air Training
    Command
Air Transport
    Association of
    America
Airy, Sir George
Airy disc
AISI steel
Aisne River
Aitken, Robert Grant
Aiwa Company Ltd.
Aix-en-Provence
Aix-la-Chapelle
Ajaccio
Ajax

Ajax Mountain
Ajax Telamon
Ajax the Greater
Ajax the Lesser
Ajman
Akan, *n.*, *pl.* Akan *or*
    Akans
Akbar the Great
Akela
Akeley, Carl
AK-47 assault rifle
Akhenaton *occas.*
    Ikhnaton
Akhmatova, Anna
Akiba ben Joseph
Akins, Claude
Akins, Zoë
Akita
Akiyama, Kazuyoshi
Akkadian
Aklavik
Akron
Akron Beacon Journal
Aksakov, Sergey
Ak-Sar-Ben Coliseum
Ak-Sar-Ben Field
Akutagawa
    Ryunosoke
Akzo America
    Foundation
Akzo America, Inc.
Alabama
Alabama Agricultural
    and Mechanical
    University
Alabama Aviation and
    Technical College
Alabama Christian
    School of Religion
Alabama Claims

Alabama Fan Club
Alabama Heritage
Alabaman *or* Alabamian
Alabama Power Company
Alabama Space and Rocket Center
Alabama State University
Alabama State University Hornets
Ala Dagh Mountains
Aladdin
Aladdin and the Wonderful Lamp
Aladdin's lamp
Aladdin's ring
Alagnak Wild River
Alai
Al-Alamein *or* El-Alamein
Alamance
Alamance Community College
Alameda
Alameda Coast Guard Support Center
Alameda Naval Air Station
Alameda-Oakland Tunnel
Alamo, the
Alamo Community College District Central Office
Alamogordo
Alamogordo Dam
Alamo Heights
Alamo Rent A Car
Alamosa

Alan
Al-Anon
Al-Anon Family Group Headquarters
Al Aqabah
Alar™
Alarcón, Hernando de
Alarcón, Pedro Antonio de
Alarcón y Mendoza, Juan Ruiz de
Alaric
Alaska
Alaska Air Group, Inc.
Alaska Airlines, Inc.
Alaska Bible College
Alaska cedar
Alaska Coalition
Alaska cod
Alaska Current
Alaska-Hawaii Standard Time
Alaska *or* Alaskan Highway
Alaska History
Alaska Junior College
Alaskan
Alaskan Air Command
Alaska Native Claims Settlement Act
Alaskan Daylight Time
Alaskan malamute
Alaskan orchis
Alaska North Slope
Alaska Pacific University
Alaska Peninsula
Alaska pipeline

Alaska pollock
Alaska Quarterly Review
Alaska Railroad
Alaska Range
Alaska Standard Time
Alaska's Wildlife
Alaska time
Alateen
Alban, Saint
Albanese, Licia
Albania
Albanian
Albanian Orthodox Archdiocese in America
Albany
Albany College of Pharmacy of Union University
Albany Congress
Albany Firebirds
Albany International Corporation
Albany Law School of Union University
Albany Marine Corps Logistics Base
Albany Medical College
Albany Plan of Union
Albany Regency
Albany State College
Albee, Edward
Albemarle
Albemarle Sound
Albéniz, Isaac
Alberghetti, Anna Maria
Albers, Josef
Albert

Albert, Carl
Albert, Eddie
Albert, Edward
Alberta
Alberta Plain
Albert Canal
Alberti, Domenico
Alberti, Leon Battista
Alberti, Rafael
Alberti bass
Albertina Collection
Albertinelli, Mariotto
Albert Lea
Albert Memorial
Albert Nyanza
Alberto-Culver
  Company
Albert of Brandenburg
Albertson, Frank
Albertson, Jack
Albertson, Joseph
  Albert
Albertson's, Inc.
Albert's Son
Albert the Bear
Albertus Magnus,
  Saint
Albertus Magnus
  College
Albertville [*now*
  Kalemi]
Albigenses
Albigensian
Albigensian Crusade
Albigensianism
Albion
Albion College
Ålborg *or* Aalborg
Albright, Ivan
Albright, Jacob

Albright, Lola
Albright, Tenley
Albright, William
Albright College
Albrook Air Force
  Base
Albuquerque
Albuquerque, Alfonso
  de
Albuquerque
  International
  Airport
Albuquerque Journal
Albuquerque
  Technical-
  Vocational Institute
Alburn Bureau
Alcaeus
Alcaic
Alcamenes
Alcan Aluminum Ltd.
Alcan Highway
Alcatel Alsthom
Alcatraz
Alcatraz prison
Alcazar
Alcibiades
Alcoa Foundation
Alcoa Hour, The
Alcoa Theatre
Alcoholics
  Anonymous
Alcoholics
  Anonymous World
  Services
Al Collins Graphic
  Design School
Alcorn State
  University
Alcorn State
  University Braves

Alco Standard
  Corporation
Alcott, Amy
Alcott, Bronson
Alcott, Louisa May
Alcuin *or* Albinus
Alda, Alan
Alda, Frances
Alda, Robert
Aldabra Islands
Aldan
Aldan Mountains
Aldebaran
Aldeburgh Festival
Aldegrever, Heinrich
Alden, John
Alden, Norman
Alden, Priscilla
Alder, Kurt
Alderney
Aldershot
Alderson-Broaddus
  College
Aldhelm, Saint
Aldington, Richard
Aldis lamp
Aldiss, Brian
Aldrich, Bess
Aldrich, Henry
Aldrich, Nelson
Aldrich, Thomas
  Bailey
Aldrich Family, The
Aldridge, Ira
Aldrin, Buzz
Aldus Corporation
Aleichem, Shalom *or*
  Sholem
Aleixandre, Vicente

Alemán, Mateo
Alemán, Miguel
Alemanni
Alemannic
Alembert, Jean le
  Rond
Alençon
Alençon lace
Aleppo
Aleppo gall
Aleppo grass
Alessandria
Alessandro, Victor
Aleut
Aleutian
Aleutian Current
Aleutian Islands
Aleutian low
Aleutian Range
Aleutian Trench
Aleutian Trough
Alex
Alexander
Alexander I, Saint
Alexander, Franz
Alexander, Grover
  Cleveland
Alexander, Sir Harold
Alexander, Hartley
  Burr
Alexander, Jane
Alexander, Jason
Alexander, Jerome
Alexander, John
  White
Alexander, Lloyd
Alexander, Norman E.
Alexander, Samuel
Alexander, Shana

Alexander, William
Alexander and
  Alexander Services,
  Inc.
Alexander and
  Baldwin, Inc.
Alexander
  Archipelago
Alexander Bay
Alexander City
Alexander Graham
  Bell Association for
  the Deaf
Alexander Graham
  Bell National
  Historic Park
Alexander Hamilton
  Life Insurance of
  America
Alexander Island
  [*form.* Alexander I
  Island]
Alexander Nevsky
Alexander of
  Aphrodisias
Alexander of Hales
Alexander's Battle
  against Darius
Alexander Severus
Alexanderson, Ernst
Alexander's Ragtime
  Band
Alexander technique
Alexander the Great
Alexandra
Alexandra Feodorovna
Alexandre, Vincent
Alexandria
Alexandrian
Alexandrian Library
Alexandrian senna

Alexandria Technical
  College
alexandrine *often*
  Alexandrine
Alexandrine rat
Alexian brother
Alexis
Alexis Hotel
Alexius
Alexius of Edessa,
  Saint
Alfa-Romeo
  Distributors of
  North America
Al Fatah
al-Fayumi, Saadia ben
  Joseph
Alfie
Alfieri, Vittorio
Alfonsine *or*
  Alphonsine tables
Alfonso
Alfonso the Wise
Alfred
Alfred, Lord Tennyson
Alfred Adler Institute
  of Chicago
Alfred A. Knopf Inc.
Alfred Hitchcock
  Hour, The
Alfred Hitchcock
  Presents
Alfred Hitchcock's
  Mystery Magazine
Alfred Lunt and Lynn
  Fontanne
Alfred the Great
Alfred University
Al Fujayrah
Alfvén wave
Algardi, Alessandro

Algaroth powder
Algeciras
Algeciras Conference
Algemene Bank Nederland
Alger, Horatio
Algeria
Algerian
Algerian stripe
Algerine
Algerine War
Algernon
Algiers
Algiers El-Djazair Houari Boumedienne International Airport
Algoa Bay
Algol
Algónkian
Algonkian system
Algonquian *occas.* Algonquin *or* Algonkian *or* Algonkin [a stock of Indian languages spoken in much of eastern United States; Indian people who speak Algonquian languages]
Algonquin *occas.* Algonquian *or* Algonkian *or* Algonkin [dialect of Ojibwa Indians]
Algonquin *or* Algonquian *or* Algonkian *or* Algonkin [an Indian people of the

Ottawa River valley]
Algonquin Hotel
Algonquin Park
Algonquin Peak
Algonquin Round Table
Algren, Nelson
Alhambra [citadel of the Moorish kings in Spain; * CA]
Alhambra, The [book]
Alhambresque
Ali, Muhammad [boxer; *form.* Cassius Clay; *see also* Muhammad Ali]
Alia Communication Network
Ali Akbar, Syed Z.
Ali Baba
Ali Baba and the Forty Thieves
Alibates Flint Quarries National Monument
Alice
Alice blue
Alice Lloyd College
Alice's Adventures in Wonderland
Alice's fern
Alice Springs
Alice's Restaurant
Alice Tully Hall
Alicia
Alien
Alien³
Alien and Sedition Acts
Alien Registration Act

Aliens
Alighieri, Dante
A-line dress
Ali Paşa *occas.* Pasha
Aliquipa
Alison
Alitalia
Al Jizah *or* Al Giza
Alki Point
All about Eve
Allah
Allahabad
all-American
All-American Bowl
All-American Canal
All-American City
All-American Soap Box Derby
Allan
Allan-a-Dale
Allan Hancock College
Allan Mountain
Allatoona Dam
Allatoona Pass
Allbritton, Joe Lewis
All Creatures Great and Small
All Dogs Go to Heaven
Allegany Community College
Alleghenies, the
Allegheny
Allegheny and Western Railway Company
Allegheny barberry
Allegheny College

Allegheny Commuter Airlines, Inc.

Allegheny County Airport

Allegheny Front

Allegheny Heights

Allegheny Ludlum Corporation

Allegheny *occas.* Alleghany Mountains

Allegheny National Forest

Allegheny Paper Shredders Corporation

Allegheny Plateau

Allegheny Portage Railroad National Historic Site

Allegheny Power System, Inc.

Allegheny spurge

Allegheny vine

Allegory of the Marriage of Frederick Barbarossa and Beatrice of Burgundy

Alleluia *var. of* Hallelujah

Allen

Allen, Barbara

Allen, Charles, Jr.

Allen, Debbie

Allen, Ethan

Allen, Forest Phog

Allen, Fred

Allen, Frederick Lewis

Allen, George

Allen, Gracie

Allen, Grant

Allen, Herbert Anthony

Allen, Hervey

Allen, Ira

Allen, Joan

Allen, Karen

Allen, Marcus

Allen, Marty

Allen, Mel

Allen, Nancy

Allen, Paul Gardner

Allen, Peter

Allen, Rex

Allen, Rex, Jr.

Allen, Richard

Allen, Scott

Allen, Steve

Allen, Tim

Allen, Viola Emily

Allen, William

Allen, Woody

Allenby, Edmund Henry Hynman

Allen County Community College

Allendale

Allende, Ignacio

Allende Gossens, Salvador

All-England Championships

All-England Lawn Tennis and Croquet Club

Allen Park

Allen's Alley

Allen screw

Allentown

Allentown College of St. Francis de Sales

Allentown Morning Call, The

Allen University

Allen™ wrench

Allergan, Inc.

Alley, Kirstie

Alley-Oop

Alley Theatre

All Fools' Day

All God's Chillun Got Wings

Allgood, Sara

Allhallowmas

All Hallows' Day

Alliance

Alliance for Progress

Alliant Techsystems Inc.

Allianz AG Holding

Allied Bank Plaza

Allied Feature Syndicate

Allied-Lyons

Allied-Signal Foundation

Allied-Signal Inc.

Allied Van Lines

Alligator Lake

Alligator Point

Alligator River

Alligator Swamp

Alliluyeva, Svetlana

Allingham, Margery

All in the Family

All I Really Need to Know I Learned in Kindergarten

Allison

Allison, Bobby

Allison, Davey

Allison, Fran

Allman, Duane

Allman, Gregg

Allman Brothers Band, The

All My Children

All Nippon Airways Company, Ltd.

All-Pro Auto Parts 500

All Quiet on the Western Front

All Saints Church

All Saints' Day [form. Hallowmas]

All Souls' Day

All-Star Baseball Game

Allstar Inn

Allstate Foundation

Allstate Insurance Company

Allstate Life Insurance Company

Allston, Washington

All's Well That Ends Well

ALLTEL Corporate Communications

ALLTEL Corporation

All the King's Men

All Things Considered

All-Union Party Congress

Allyn and Bacon, Inc.

Allyson, June

Alma

Alma-Ata [now Almaty]

Alma College

Almaden Air Force Station

Almagro, Diego de

Almanach de Gotha

ALM Antillean Airlines

Alma-Tadema, Sir Lawrence

Almaty [form. Alma-Ata]

Almeida, Laurindo

Almeida Garrett, João Batista de

Almería

Almerían

Almighty, the

Almighty Dollar, The

Almohad dynasty

Almoravid dynasty

Aloha Airlines, Inc.

Aloha Bowl

Aloha Oe

Alonso, Alicia

Alonso, Dámaso

Alonso, Maria Conchita

Alonso, Odon

Alouette

Aloysius

Aloysius, Saint

Alpena

Alpena Community College

Alpert, Herb

Alpes-de-Hautes-Provence

Alpes-Maritimes

Alpha and Omega

Alpha Beta store

Alpha Centauri

Alpha Chi Omega

Alpha Chi Rho

Alpha Crucis

Alpha Delta Gamma

Alpha Delta Phi

Alpha Delta Pi

Alpha Epsilon Phi

Alpha Epsilon Pi

Alpha Gamma Delta

Alpha Gamma Rho

Alpha Gamma Sigma

Alpha Kappa Alpha

Alpha Kappa Lambda

Alpha Kappa Psi

Alpha Lambda Delta

Alpha Omicron Pi

Alpha Phi

Alpha Phi Alpha

Alpha Phi Delta

Alpha Phi Omega

Alpha Sigma Alpha

Alpha Sigma Phi

Alpha Sigma Tau

Alpha Tau Omega

Alpha Xi Delta

Alphonse

Alphonsine var. of Alfonsine tables

Alphonsus Liguori, Saint

Alpine often alpine

Alpine catchfly

Alpine currant

Alpine ibex

Alpine poppy

Alpine savory

Alpine wallflower

Alpo Petfoods, Inc.

Alps
Alsace
Alsace-Lorraine
Alsace-Lorrainer
ALSAC-Saint Jude Children's Research Hospital
Alsatian
Al Sirat
Alsop, Joseph
Alsop, Marin
Alsop, Richard
Alston, Walter
Alta California
Altadena
Altai
Altaic
Altair
Altamira
Altamont
Alta Peak
Altdorfer, Albrecht
Alternate View Network
Alternative Press Center
Altman, Jeff
Altman, Robert
Altmeyer, Jeannie
Alton
Altoona
Altrusa International
Alturas
Altus
Altus Air Force Base
Aluminum, Brick and Glass Workers International Union
Aluminum Company of America

Alundum™
Alvarado, Alonso de
Alvarado, Juan Bautista
Alvarado, Pedro de
Alvarez, A.
Alvarez, José
Alvarez, Luis Walter
Alvarez Quintero, Joaquin
Alvarez Quintero, Serafin
Alvaro, Corrado
Alvernia College
Alverno College
Alvin
Alvin Ailey American Dance Theater
Alvin Ailey Repertory Ensemble
Alvin and the Chipmunks
Alvin Community College
Always
Always on My Mind
Alworth, Lance
Alwyn, William
Alyce clover
Alyeska Pipeline Service Company
ALZA Corporation
Alzado, Lyle
Alzheimer, Alois
Alzheimer's Association
Alzheimer's disease
Alzheimer's Disease and Related Disorders Association

Alzheimer's Disease International
Alzheimer's Disease Research Program
Amadeus
Amadeus Quartet
Amadis of Gaul
Amado, Jorge
Amagasaki
Amahl and the Night Visitors
Amakusa Islands
Amalekite
Amalgamated Clothing and Textile Workers Union
Amalgamated Transit Union
Amalric
Amalric of Bena
Amami Islands
Amana Church Society
Amana Colonies
Amana Society
Amanda
Aman Folk Ensemble
Amanist
Amanite
Amarcord
Amargosa
Amargosa Range
Amarillo
Amarillo College
Amateur Athletic Union of the United States
Amateur Chamber Music Players

Amateur Hockey Association of the United States

Amateur Magicians Association Worldwide

Amateur Orchid Growers Society

Amateur Radio Relay League

Amateur Radio Satellite Corporation

Amateur Skating Union of the United States

Amateur Softball Association of the United States

Amateur Trapshooting Association

Amati, Andrea

Amati, Antonio

Amati, Girolami

Amati, Nicolò

Amati violin

Amato, Giuliano

AMAX Foundation

AMAX, Inc.

Amazing Grace

Amazing Kreskin, The

Amazing Spiderman, The

Amazing World of Kreskin

Amazon

Amazon ant

Amazon Basin

Amazonia

Amazonian

Amazon rain forest

Amazon River

Ambassador West Hotel

Amber

Amber University

Ambler, Eric

Amboina

Ambrose

Ambrose, Saint

Ambrose Channel

Ambrosiana Picture Gallery

Ambrosian chant

Ambrosian Library

AMC Cancer Research Center

Amchitka

Amdahl Corporation

Ameche, Don

Ameche, Jim

Amelia

Amelia Island

Amen

Amendment VIII *occas.* 8 [to the Constitution]

Amendment XVIII *occas.* 18 [to the Constitution]

Amendment XI *occas.* 11 [to the Constitution]

Amendment XV *occas.* 15 [to the Constitution]

Amendment V *occas.* 5 [to the Constitution]

Amendment IV *occas.* 4 [to the Constitution]

Amendment XIV *occas.* 14 [to the Constitution]

Amendment IX *occas.* 9 [to the Constitution]

Amendment XIX *occas.* 19 [to the Constitution]

Amendment I *occas.* 1 [to the Constitution]

Amendment VII *occas.* 7 [to the Constitution]

Amendment XVII *occas.* 17 [to the Constitution]

Amendment VI *occas.* 6 [to the Constitution]

Amendment XVI *occas.* 16 [to the Constitution]

Amendment X *occas.* 10 [to the Constitution]

Amendment XIII *occas.* 13 [to the Constitution]

Amendment III *occas.* 3 [to the Constitution]

Amendment XII *occas.* 12 [to the Constitution]

Amendment XX *occas.* 20 [to the Constitution]

Amendment XXI *occas.* 21 [to the Constitution]

Amendment XXII *occas.* 22 [to the Constitution]

Amendment XXIII *occas.* 23 [to the Constitution]

Amendment XXIV *occas.* 24 [to the Constitution]

Amendment XXV *occas.* 25 [to the Constitution]

Amendment XXVI *occas.* 26 [to the Constitution]

Amendment II *occas.* 2 [to the Constitution]

Amenemhet

Amen glass

Amenhotep *or* Amenhophis

Amerada Hess Corporation

Amerasian

America

America First Party

Americaine™

America-Mideast Educational and Training Services

American

Americana

American abscess root

American Academy and Institute of Arts and Letters

American Academy in Rome

American Academy of Actuaries

American Academy of Advertising

American Academy of Allergy and Immunology

American Academy of Art

American Academy of Arts and Sciences

American Academy of Dramatic Arts

American Academy of Dramatic Arts—West

American Academy of Environmental Engineers

American Academy of Facial Plastic and Reconstructive Surgery

American Academy of Family Physicians

American Academy of Family Physicians Foundation

American Academy of Forensic Sciences

American Academy of Mechanics

American Academy of Nursing

American Academy of Ophthalmology

American Academy of Orthopedic Surgeons

American Academy of Otolaryngology

American Academy of Pediatrics

American Academy of Political and Social Science

American Academy of Religion

American Accounting Association

American Aging Association

American Agricultural Economics Association

American Airlines, Inc.

American Alliance for Health, Physical Education, Recreation and Dance

American aloe

American Alpine Club

American Amateur Baseball Congress

American Amateur Karate Federation

American Anthropological Association

American Antiquarian Society

American Anti-Vivisection Society

American apple

American Arbitration Association

American architecture

American Armenian International College

American art

American Assembly of Collegiate Schools of Business

American Association for Adult and Continuing Education

American Association for Affirmative Action

American Association for Clinical Chemistry

American Association for Counseling and Development

American Association for Gifted Children

American Association for State and Local History

American Association for the Advancement of Science

American Association for the Study of the United States in World Affairs

American Association for World Health

American Association of Advertising Agencies

American Association of Botanical Gardens and Arboreta

American Association of Cereal Chemists

American Association of Classified School Employees

American Association of Community and Junior Colleges

American Association of Engineering Societies

American Association of Individual Investors

American Association of Law Libraries

American Association of Motor Vehicle Administrators

American Association of Museums

American Association of Oral and Maxillofacial Surgeons

American Association of Pathologists

American Association of Petroleum Geologists

American Association of Petroleum Landmen

American Association of Professors of Yiddish

American Association of Rabbis

American Association of Retired Persons

American Association of School Administrators

American Association of Teachers of French

American Association of Teachers of German

American Association of Teachers of Spanish and Portuguese

American Association of University Professors

American Association of University Women

American Association of Zoological Parks and Aquariums

American Astronautical Society

American Astronomical Society

American Atheists, Inc.

American Automobile Association

American Ballet Theatre

American Bandstand

American Bankers Association

American Bankruptcy Institute

American Baptist Association

American Baptist Churches in the United States of America

American Baptist College

American Baptist Seminary of the West

American Bar Association

American Baseball Fans Association

American Battle Monuments Commission

American Battleship Association

American Beauty rose

American Bed-and-Breakfast Association

American Bell Telephone Company

American Bible Society

American bison

American bittern

American Bloodhound Club

American Board of Obstetrics and Gynecology

American Board of Quality Assurance and Utilization Review

American Bodybuilders Association

American bond

American Book Review

American Booksellers Association

American Bowling Congress

American Brands, Inc.

American Brass Quintet

American Bridge Association

American Broadcasting Companies, Inc.

American brooklime

American Brotherhood for the Blind

American Buddhist Movement

American buffalo

American Bus Association

American Business Network

American Business Real Estate and Law Association

American Business Women's Association

American Camellia Society

American Camping Association

American Cancer Society

American Carpatho-Russian Orthodox Greek Catholic Church

American Cat Fanciers Association

American Catholic Historical Society

American Cemetery Association

American Ceramic Society

American chair

American Chamber of Commerce—United Kingdom

American chameleon

American Checker Federation

American cheese

American Chemical Society

American Chess Foundation

American chestnut

American Chiropractic Association

American Civil Liberties Union

American Civil War

American Classical League

American cloth

American Coalition for Traditional Values

American cockroach

American College [* AZ]

American College, The [* PA]

American College for the Applied Arts

American College of Medical Technologists

American College of Obstetricians and Gynecologists

American College of Physicians

American College of Surgeons

American College Testing Program

American Colonization Society

American Commercial Collectors Association

American Committee on Africa

American Community Cultural Center Association

American Composers Alliance

American Composers Orchestra

American Concrete Institute

American Congress on Surveying and Mapping

American Conservatory of Music

American Conservatory Theatre

American Continental Corporation

American Contract Bridge League

American copper

American Correctional Association

American cotton

American Council for Judaism

American Council for Nationalities Service

American Council for the Arts

American Council of Learned Societies

American Council of the Blind

American Council on Alcohol Problems

American Council on Consumer Interests

American Council on Education

American Council on Schools and Colleges

American Council on Science and Health

American Council to Improve Our Neighborhoods

American Courtroom Network

American cowslip

American crab

American cranberry

American Cryptogram Association

American Cyanamid Company

American Dairy Goat Association

American Dance Theater

American Defense Preparedness Association

American Demographics

American Dental Association

American Diabetes Association

American Dialect Society

American Diesel and Automotive College

American Directoire

American Dream *occas.* American dream

American Eagle [airline]

American eagle [bird]

American Economic Association

American Educational Research Association

American Education Week

American Egg Board

American Electric Power Company, Inc.

American Electroplaters' and Surface Finishers' Society

American elm

American Empire furniture

American English

American Enterprise Institute

American Episcopal Church

American Ethical Union

American Evangelistic Association

American Expeditionary Forces

American Express Card, The

American Express Company

American Express Corporate Card

American Express Credit Corporation

American Express Foundation

American Express Travelers Cheques™

American Ex-Prisoners of War

American Falls

American Family Corporation [*now* AFLAC Inc.]

American Family Life Assurance of Columbia

American Farm Bureau Federation

American Farmland Trust

American Federation of Arts

American Federation of Astrologers

American Federation of Aviculture

American Federation of Government Employees

Amercan Federation of Grain Millers

American Federation of Labor and Congress of Industrial Organizations

American Federation of Musicians of the United States and Canada

American Federation of Small Business

American Federation of State, County and Municipal Employees

American Federation of Teachers

American Federation of Television and Radio Artists

American Field Service

American Film Institute

American Film Institute—Center for Advanced Film and Television Studies

American Financial Corporation

American Financial Services Association

American Fishing Tackle Manufacturers Association

American flagfish

American Football Conference

American Footwear Industries Association

American Forest Council

American Forestry Association

American Fork

American Foundation for AIDS Research

American Foundation for the Blind

American Foundrymen's Society

American foxhound

American Friends Service Committee

American Frozen Food Institute

American Fund for Dental Health

American Fur Company

American Gas Association

American Gem Society

American General Corporation

American General Life and Accident

American Genetic Association

American Geographical Society

American Geological Institute

American Geriatrics Society

American Gladiators

American globeflower

American Gold Star Mothers

American Gothic

American Graduate School of International Management

American Greetings Corporation

American Group Psychotherapy Association

American Guild of Musical Artists

American Guild of Organists

American Guild of Variety Artists

American Gynecological and Obstetrical Society

American Harp Society

American Hawaii Cruises

American Health Assistance Foundation

American Health: Fitness of Body and Mind

American Health Properties, Inc.

American Heart Association

American Helicopter Society

American Heritage

American Heritage Dictionary of the English Language, The

American Hiking Society

American Historical Association

American holly

American Home Economics Association

American Home Products Corporation

American Honda Foundation

American Honda Motor Company, Inc.

American hornbeam

American Horse Council

American Horse Protection Association

American Horse Shows Association

American Horticulture Society

American Hospital Association

American Hotel and Motel Association

American Humane Association

American Humanics

American Humanist Association

American Hunter

American Independent Party

American Indian

American Indian Bible College

American Indian Day

American Indian Graduate Center

American Indian languages

American Indian Movement

American Indian Scholarships, Inc.

American Information Technologies Corporation

American in Paris, An

American Institute for Cancer Research

American Institute for Foreign Study

American Institute of Aeronautics and Astronautics

American Institute of Architects

American Institute of Business

American Institute of Certified Public Accountants

American Institute of Chemical Engineers

American Institute of Chemists

American Institute of Commerce

American Institute of Design

American Institute of Graphic Arts

American Institute of Industrial Engineers

American Institute of Mining, Metallurgical and Petroleum Engineers

American Institute of Nutrition

American Institute of Parliamentarians

American Institute of Physics

American Institute of Steel Construction

American Institute of Wine and Food

American Insurance Association

American International Automobile Dealers Association

American International Building

American International College

American International Group, Inc.

American International Syndicate

American ipecac

American Iron and Steel Institute

Americanism

Americanist

American Isuzu Motor Company

American ivy

Americanization

Americanize, *v.* Americanized, Americanizing

American Jewish Committee

American Jewish Congress

American Jewish Historical Society

American Judicature Society

American Judo Association

American Junior Quarter Horse Association

American Kennel Club

American kestrel

American Kidney Fund

American Labor Party

American Lane

American language

American Law Enforcement Officers Association

American League of Professional Baseball Clubs

American Legion

American Legion Auxiliary

American Legion Auxiliary National News

American Legion Baseball

American Legion Magazine

American leopard

American Leprosy Foundation

American Leprosy Missions

American Library Association

American Life Insurance Company

American linden

American Liver Foundation

American lotus

American Lung Association

American lungwort

American Lutheran Church, The

American Maize-Products Company

American Management Association

American Maritime Officers Service

American Marketing Association

American marten

American Mathematical Society

American Medical Association

American Medical International, Inc.

American Medical Record Association

American Mental Health Fund

American Merchant Marine Library Association

American Merchant Marine Veterans

American Meteorological Society

American Mideast Educational and Training Services

American Ministerial Association

American Montessori Society

American Motorcyclist

American Motorcyclist Association

American Motors Corporation

American Movie Classics

American mulberry

American Museum of Immigration

American Museum of Natural History

American Music Award

American Music Center

American Musicological Society

American Music Scholarship Association

American Narcolepsy Association

American National Bank and Trust Company of Chicago Foundation

American National Corporation

American National Insurance Company

American National Standards Institute

American National Theatre and Academy

American Natural Resources Company

American Near East Refugee Aid

American Negro spirituals

Americanness

American Newspaper Publishers Association

American Ninja

American Ninja 2: The Confrontation

American Nobel Laureate Center

American Nuclear Society

American Numismatic Association

American Numismatic Society

American Nurses' Association

Americano, *n.*, *pl.* Americanos

American Opera Center

American Opinion Bookstore

American Optometric Association

American Orchid Society

American organ

American Oriental Society

American Ornithologists' Union

American ORT Federation

American Osteopathic Association

American ostrich

American Paper Institute

American Parkinson's Disease Association

American Party

American Petroleum Institute

American Pharmaceutical Association

American Pharmaceutical Company

American Philatelic Society

American Philological Association

American Philosophical Association

American Philosophical Society

American Physical Society

American Physical Therapy Association

American Physiological Society

American Phytopathological Society, The

American Place Theatre

American plan

American Planning Association

American Playhouse

American Poetry Review

American Polar Society

American Political Items Collectors

American Political Science Association

American Postal Workers Union

American Powder Metallurgy Institute

American Power Boat Association

American President Companies, Ltd.

American Printing House for the Blind

American Professional Soccer League

American Psychiatric Association

American Psychoanalytic Association

American Psychological Association

American Public Radio

American Public Transit Association

American Public Welfare Association

American Quarter Horse Association

American Quarternary Association

American Quilter's Society

American Rabbit Breeders Association

American Radio Company

American Radio Networks

American Radio Relay League

American Railway Express Company

Amerian Railway Union

American Red Cross

American Refugee Committee

American Re-Insurance Company

American Rescue Workers

American Revised Version of the Bible

American Revolution

American Revolution Bicentennial Administration

American Rifleman

American rig

American River

American River College

American Road and Transportation Builders' Association

American Rose Society

American Royal Center, Kemper Arena

American Royal Livestock, Horse Show and Rodeo

American Running and Fitness Association

American sable

American saddle horse

American Samoa

American Samoa Community College

American Samoa National Park

American Savings and Loan Association of Florida

American Savings Bank

American School Counselor Association

American Schools of Professional Psychology

American Scientist

American Security Bank

American senna

Americans for Democratic Action

Americans for Human Rights and Social Justice

Americans for Indian Opportunity

American Shakespeare Festival Theatre and Academy

American Shore and Beach Preservation Association

American Sign Language

American smoke tree

American Social Health Association

American Society for Biochemistry and Molecular Biology

American Society for Engineering Education

American Society for Hospital Marketing and Public Relations

American Society for Industrial Security

American Society for Metals

American Society for Microbiology

American Society for Personnel Administration

American Society for Philatelic Pages and Panels

American Society for Public Administration

American Society for Quality Control

American Society for Testing and Materials

American Society for Theatre Research

American Society for the Prevention of Cruelty to Animals

American Society of Agricultural Engineers

American Society of Agronomy

American Society of Allied Health Professions

American Society of Appraisers

American Society of Association Executives

American Society of Bookplate Collectors and Designers

American Society of Brewing Chemists

American Society of Certified Life Underwriters

American Society of Chartered Life Underwriters and Chartered Financial Consultants

American Society of Cinematographers

American Society of Civil Engineers

American Society of Clinical Pathologists

American Society of Composers, Authors and Publishers

American Society of Criminology

American Society of Design Engineers

American Society of Dowsers

American Society of Geolinguistics

American Society of Heating, Refrigerating and Air-Conditioning Engineers

American Society of Indexers

American Society of Interior Designers

American Society of International Law

American Society of Journalists and Authors

American Society of Landscape Architects

American Society of Magazine Editors

American Society of Magazine Photographers

American Society of Mechanical Engineers

American Society of Naval Engineers

American Society of Newspaper Editors

American Society of Notaries

American Society of Parasitologists

American Society of Pension Actuaries

American Society of Photogrammetry and Remote Sensing

American Society of Plastic and Reconstructive Surgeons

American Society of Plumbing Engineers

American Society of Questioned Document Examiners

American Society of Safety Engineers

American Society of Traffic and Transportation

American Society of Transportation and Logistics

American Society of Travel Agents

American Society of Zoologists

American Sociological Association

American Sokol Organization

American Spanish

American Speech-Language-Hearing Association

American Sportscasters Association

American Sportsman, The

American Staffordshire terrier

American Standard Foundation

American Standard Inc.

American Standard Version of the Bible

American Statistical Association

American Stock Exchange Composite List

American Stock Exchange, Inc.

American Stores Company

American String Teachers Association

American Sunbathing Association

Americans United for Life

Americans United for Separation of Church and State

Americans with Disabilities Act

American Symphony Orchestra

American Symphony Orchestra League

American Technical College for Career Training

American Technical Institute

American Telecommunications Corporation

American Telephone and Telegraph Company

American Television and Communications Corporation

American Textile Manufacturers Institute

American Theatre Critics Association

American Theatre Organ Society

American Theatre Wing

American Theological Library Association

American Tobacco Company, The

American Topical Association

American Tragedy, An

American Trans Air, Inc.

American Translators Association

American Trucking Associations

American trypanosomiasis

American twist

American Unitarian Association

American United Life Insurance Company

American University

American University Eagles

American University of Beirut

American University of Puerto Rico

American upland cotton

American Veterans Committee

American Veterinary Medical Association

American Veterinary Medical Association Journal

American Vocational Association

American Volunteer Group

American Walking Association

American War Mothers

American War of Independence

American Waste Services, Inc.

American Watercolor Society

American Water Resources Association

American Water Ski Association

American Water Ski Educational Foundation

American water spaniel

American Water Works Association

American Water Works Company, Inc.

American wayfaring tree

American Way Features

American Welding Institute

American Welding Society

American West, The

American Whippet Club

American white hellebore

American wigeon

American wirehair cat

American Women in Radio and Television

American woodbine

American wormseed

American Youth Hostels

American Zionist Youth Foundation

Americares Foundation, Inc.

Américas

America's Cup

America's Cup Organizing Committee

America's Cup Syndicate

America's Dairy Farmers

America's Funniest Home Videos

America's Funniest People

America's Future, Inc.

America's Most Wanted

Americas Review, The

America's Rhine

America's Value Network

America the Beautiful

America the Beautiful Fund

America West Airlines, Inc.

America West Airlines Magazine

Americus

AmeriFirst Federal Savings Bank

Amerind

Amerindian

Amerindic

Ameritech Corporation

Ameritech Foundation

Ameritrust Company

Ameritrust Corporation

Ames

Ames, Ed

Ames, Ezra

Ames, Gene

Ames, Joe

Ames, Leon

Ames, Oakes

Ames, Vic

Ames, Winthrop

Ames Brothers, The

Amesbury

Ames Department Stores, Inc.

Ames-Dryden Flight Test Facility

Ames Research Center

Ames Test

AMETEK Foundation

AMETEK, Inc.

Amgen Inc.

Amharic

Amherst

Amherst, Jeffrey

Amherst College

Amicalola Falls

Amici, Giovanni Battista

Amici prism

Amiens

AmigaWorld

Amilcar Cabral International Airport

Amin, Idi

Amindivi Islands

Amis, Sir Kingsley

Amish

Amish Mennonites

Amistad National Recreation Area

Amityville

Amityville Horror, The

Amityville II: The Possession

Amman [capital of Jordan; see also Ammon]

Ammanati, Bartolommeo

Ammann, Othmar Herman

Ammianus, Marcelinus

Ammon [ancient country; see also Amman]

Ammonite

Ammonitish

Amnesty International

Amnesty International of the United States of America

Amoco Building

Amoco Canada Petroleum Company, Ltd.

Amoco Chemical Company

Amoco Company

Amoco Corporation

Amoco Gas Company

Amoco Oil Company

Amoco Pipeline Company

Amoco Production Company

Amon Carter Museum of Western Art

Amory, Cleveland

Amos

Amos, John

Amos 'n' Andy

Ampère, André-Marie

Ampère's law

Amperian

Ampersand Communications

AMP Foundation

Amphityron 38

AMP Inc.

Amram, David

AMR Corporation

AmSouth Bancorporation

AmSouth Bank

Amsted Industries Foundation

Amsted Industries Inc.

Amsterdam

Amsterdam, Morey

Amsterdam Airport
  Schiphol

Amsterdam-Rhine
  Canal

Amsterdam-Rotterdam
  Bank

Amtrak

[Amtrak *or* Amtrak's]
  Auto Train

[Amtrak *or* Amtrak's]
  Broadway Limited

[Amtrak *or* Amtrak's]
  California Zephyr

[Amtrak *or* Amtrak's]
  Capitol

[Amtrak *or* Amtrak's]
  Capitol Limited

[Amtrak *or* Amtrak's]
  Cardinal

[Amtrak *or* Amtrak's]
  City of New
  Orleans

[Amtrak *or* Amtrak's]
  Coast Daylight

[Amtrak *or* Amtrak's]
  Coast Starlight

[Amtrak *or* Amtrak's]
  Crescent

[Amtrak *or* Amtrak's]
  Desert Wind

[Amtrak *or* Amtrak's]
  Empire Builder

[Amtrak *or* Amtrak's]
  International

[Amtrak *or* Amtrak's]
  Metroliner

[Amtrak *or* Amtrak's]
  Montrealer

[Amtrak *or* Amtrak's]
  Mount Rainier

[Amtrak *or* Amtrak's]
  Palmetto

[Amtrak *or* Amtrak's]
  Pennsylvanian

[Amtrak *or* Amtrak's]
  Pioneer

[Amtrak *or* Amtrak's]
  Silver Crescent

[Amtrak *or* Amtrak's]
  Silver Meteor

[Amtrak *or* Amtrak's]
  Silver Star

[Amtrak *or* Amtrak's]
  Southwest Chief

[Amtrak *or* Amtrak's]
  Sunset Limited

[Amtrak *or* Amtrak's]
  Texas Eagle

[Amtrak *or* Amtrak's]
  Zephyr

Amu Darya

Amundsen, Roald

Amundsen-Scott
  Station

Amundsen Sea

Amur

Amur cork tree

Amur lilac

Amusement and
  Music Operators
  Association

Amusement Features
  Syndicate

AMVETS—American
  Veterans of World
  War II, Korea and
  Vietnam

AMVETS Auxiliary

AMVETS National
  Service Foundation

Amway Corporation

Amwest Savings
  Association

Amy

Amyotrophic Lateral
  Sclerosis
  Association

Amytal™

Anabaptism

Anabaptist

Anacapa Islands

Anacletus, Saint

Anacomp, Inc.

Anaconda

Anaconda Company

Anaconda Mountain

Anacortes

Anacostia

Anacostia Naval Air
  Station

Anacostia River

Anacreon

Anacreontic

Anadarko Petroleum
  Corporation

ANAD—National
  Association of
  Anorexia Nervosa
  and Associated
  Disorders

Anadyr *or* Anadir

Anadyr Range

Ana G. Méndez
  Educational
  Foundation

Anaheim

Anaheim Stadium

Analects of
  Confucius, The

Analog Devices, Inc.

Analog Science
  Fiction/Science Fact

Analytical Cubism
  occas. analytical
  cubism

Ananda

Anantapur

Anasazi, *n.*, *pl.*
Anasazi

Anastasia

Anastasia, Albert

Anastasia,
Nikolaievna
Romanov

Anastasius I, Saint

Anatolia

Anatolian

Anatolian languages

Anatomy of
Melancholy, The

Anaxagoras

Anaxagorean

Anaximander

Anaximandrian

Anaximenes of
Lampsacus

Anaximenes of
Miletus

Anaza

Anchorage

Anchorage Daily
News

Anchorage
International
Airport

Anchorage Times, The

Anchor Glass
Container
Corporation

Anchor Savings Bank

Anchors Aweigh

Ancient and Illustrious
Order Knights of
Malta

Ancient and Mystical
Order of the Rosae
Crucis

Ancient Arabic Order
of Nobles of the
Mystic Shrine

Ancient Egyptian
Arabic Order
Nobles of the
Mystic Shrine

Ancient Free and
Accepted Masons

Ancient of Days

Ancient Order of
Hibernians

Ancilla College

Andalusia

Andalusian

Andaman and Nicobar
Islands

Andamanese

Andaman Islands

Andaman Sea

Andean

Andean Common
Market

Andean condor

Andean deer

Andean Group

Anders, William

Andersen, Fred

Andersen, Hans
Christian

Andersen, Hans Jacob

Anderson

Anderson, Bill

Anderson, Brad

Anderson, Carl David

Anderson, Eddie

Anderson, Harry

Anderson, Ian

Anderson, Jack

Anderson, John

Anderson, Dame
Judith

Anderson, Ken

Anderson, Kevin

Anderson, Laurie

Anderson, Leroy

Anderson, Loni

Anderson, Lynn

Anderson, Margaret

Anderson, Marian

Anderson, Maxwell

Anderson, Melissa
Sue

Anderson, Richard

Andreson, Sherwood

Anderson, Sparky

Anderson College

Anderson Ranch Dam

Anderson University

Andersonville

Andersonville
National Historic
Site

Andersonville Prison

Andersson, Bibi

Andes

Andes glow

Andes lightning

Andhra Pradesh

Andorra

Andorran

Andover

Andover College

Andover Newton
Theological School

Andrássy, Julius

Andre, Carl

André, John

Andrea

Andrea del Sarto

Andrea Doria

Andreanof Islands

Andreas, Dwayne
Orville

Andreev, Andrei
Andreevich

Andress, Ursula

André the Giant

Andretti, Mario

Andretti, Michael

Andrew

Andrew, Saint

Andrew College

Andrew Jergens
Company, The

Andrew Johnson
National Historic
Site

Andrews, Anthony

Andrews, Charles
McLean

Andrews, Dana

Andrews, Julie

Andrews, Laverne

Andrews, Maxine

Andrews, Patti

Andrews, Roy
Chapman

Andrews Air Force
Base

Andrews Sisters

Andrews University

Andrew W. Mellon
Foundation

Andreyev, Leonid
Nikolayevich

Androcles

Androcles and the
Lion

Andromache

Andromeda

Andromeda Galaxy

Andromeda strain
[fictitious
microorganism]

Andromeda Strain,
The [book; movie]

Andronicus

Andropov, Yuri

Andros, Sir Edmund

Androscoggin

Androuet du Cerceau,
Baptiste

Androuet du Cerceau,
Jacques

Androuet du Cerceau,
Jean

Andy Capp

Andy Griffith Show,
The

Andy Griffith Show
Rerun Watchers
Club, The

Andy Warhol Museum

Andy Williams Show,
The

Angara

Angara Shield

Angela

Angela Merici, Saint

Angeleno, *n.*, *pl.*
Angelenos

Angeles National
Forest

Angel Falls *occas.*
Fall [Venezuela]

Angelico, Fra

Angelina College

Angelina National
Forest

Angel Island

Angell, Sir Norman

Angel of Death

Angelo State
University

Angelou, Maya

Angels: God's Secret
Agents

Angel Street

Angels We Have
Heard on High

Angelus [devotion]

Angelus, The
[painting]

Angelus bell

Angelus dynasty

Angevin

Angilbert, Saint

Angkor

Angkor Thom

Angkor Wat *or* Vat

Angles

Anglia

Anglican

Anglican chant

Anglican Church

Anglican Communion

Anglicanism

Anglican Orthodox
Church

Anglicism

Anglicist

Anglicization

Anglicize, *v.*
Anglicized,
Anglicizing

Anglin, Margaret

Anglo, *n.*, *pl.* Anglos
[white person of
non-Latin descent]

Anglo- [combining
form]

Anglo-American

Anglo-American cooperation

Anglo American Corporation

Anglo-Americanism

Anglo-Australian

Anglo-Catholic

Anglo-Catholicism

Anglo-Catholic movement

Anglo-Egyptian Sudan

Anglo-French

Anglo-Frisian

Anglo-Gallic

Anglo-Indian

Anglo-Irish

Anglo-Latin

Anglomania

Anglomaniac

Anglo-Norman

Anglo-Norman literature

Anglophile *occas.* Anglophil

Anglophilia

Anglophiliac

Anglophilic

Anglophobe

Anglophobia

Anglophobic

Anglo-Saxon

Anglo-Saxon Chronicle, The

Anglo-Saxon literature

Anglo-Venetian glass

Angola [*form.* Portuguese West Africa]

Angolese, *n.*, *pl.* Angolese

Angora cat

Angora goat

Angora rabbit

Angora wool

Angoumois

Angoumois grain moth

Angst

Ångström, Anders Jonas

Angstrom, Rabbit

angstrom *occas.* Angstrom unit

Anguier, François

Anguier, Guillaume

Anguier, Michel

Anguilla

Angus

Angus cattle

Anhalt, Frederik von

Anheuser-Busch Companies, Inc.

Anheuser-Busch Foundation

Anheuser-Busch, Inc.

Aniakchak

Aniakchak National Monument

Aniakchak National Preserve

Anicetus, Saint

Animal, The

Animal Farm

Animal Legal Defense Fund

Animal Protection Institute of America

Animals, The

Animals' Voice Magazine, The

Animal Welfare Institute

Animal World

Anishinabe

Anjou

Anjou pear

Anka, Paul

Ankara

Ankara Archeological Museum

Ankara Esenboga International Airport

Ann

Anna

Anna Christie

Anna Ivanovna

Anna Karenina

Anna Leopoldovna

Annam

Anna Maria College

Annamese, *n.*, *pl.* Annamese

Annamese Cordillera

Annapolis

Annapolis Convention

Annapolis Royal

Annapurna *or* Anapurna

Ann Arbor

Anne

Anne, Saint

Anne Arundel Community College

Annelida

Annenberg, Walter

Anne of Austria

Anne of Bohemia

Anne of Brittany

Anne of Cleves

Anne of Denmark

Anne of France

Anne of Green Gables

Annie

Annie Get Your Gun

Annie Hall

Annie Laurie

Annie Oakley, n., pl. Annie Oakleys [free ticket]

Annie's Book Stop

Anniston

Anniston Army Depot

Ann-Margret

Anno, Mitsumasa

anno Domini

Anno Hejirae

Annunciation [church festival]

Annunciation, The [painting]

Annunciation lily

Anointing of the Sick

Anoka

Anoka-Ramsey Community College

Another Bad Creation

Another 48 Hours

Another World

Anouilh, Jean

ANR Foundation

Ansara, Michael

Ansbach or Anspach

Anschauung

Anschluss

Anschutz, Philip Frederick

Anselm of Canterbury, Saint

Anselm II of Lucca, Saint

Ansermet, Ernest

Anshan

Anson

Anson, Cap

Anson Community College

Ansonia

Anspach, Susan

Antabuse™

Antananarivo

Antarctic

Antarctica

Antarctic Circle

Antarctic Circumpolar Current

Antarctic Continent

Antarctic Ocean

Antarctic Peninsula [form. Palmer Peninsula]

Antarctic Treaty

Antarctic Zone

Antares

Antelami, Benedetto

Antelope Peak

Antelope Range

Antelope Valley College

Antenor

Anterus, Saint

Antheil, George

Anthemius of Thales

Anthony

Anthony, Barbara Cox

Anthony, Earl

Anthony, Piers

Anthony, Ray

Anthony, Susan B.

Anthony Adverse

Anthony Claret, Saint

Anthony or Antony of Egypt, Saint

Anthony or Antony of Padua, Saint

Anthrax

Anthroposophical Society

Anthroposophical Society in America

anti-Arab

Antibes

anti-Catholic

anti-Catholicism

Antichrist [person or power]

Antichrist, The [book]

anti-Christian

anti-Christianity

Anti-Comintern Pact

Anti-Corn-Law League

Anti-Defamation League of B'Nai B'rith, The

anti-English

Antietam campaign

Antietam Creek

Antietam National Battlefield

Antietam National Cemetery

Anti-Federalism

Anti-Federalist

Anti-Federal Party

anti-French

anti-German

Antigone

Antigonus

Antigua

Antigua and Barbuda
Antigua Guatemala
Antigua Island
Antiguan
anti-Japanese
anti-Jewish
Anti-Lebanon
Antillean
Antilles
Antilles Current
Antillian College
Antimachus
Anti-Mason
Anti-Masonic
Anti-Masonic Party
Anti-Masonry
anti-Nazi
anti-Negro
Antioch
Antiochan Orothodox
  Christian
  Archdiocese of
  North America
  [*form.* Syrian
  Antiochan
  Orthodox
  Archdiocese]
Antioch College
Antiochian
Antioch Review
Antioch University
Antiochus
Antiquarian
  Booksellers
  Association of
  America
Antique Airplane
  Association
Antique Automobile
  Club of America

Antiques Dealers'
  Association of
  America
Antirent War
Anti-Saloon League of
  America
anti-Semite
anti-Semitism
anti-Soviet
Antisthenes
anti-West
anti-Western
anti-Zionist
Antofagasta
Antoinette, Marie
Anton, Susan
Antonelli Institute of
  Art and
  Photography
Antonello de Messina
Antoninus, Saint
Antoninus Pius
Antonio
Antonio María Claret,
  Saint
Antonioni,
  Michelangelo
Antony, Mark *or* Marc
Antony and Cleopatra
Antophyta
Antwerp
Antwerp blue
Antwerp Deurne
  Airport
[Antwerp] Fine Arts
  Museum
Antwerp hollycock
Anubis
Anvers
Anxiety Disorders
  Association of
  America

Anza, Juan Bautista de
Anzac
Anzengruber, Ludwig
Anzio
ANZUS Pact
ANZUS Treaty
A-OK
Aon Corporation
A-1 *or* A 1 *or* A-one
  or A one
Aon Foundation
Apache, *n., pl.* Apache
  or Apaches
Apache Corporation
Apache-Sitgreaves
  National Forest
Apalachee Bay
Apalachia Dam
Apalachicola
Apalachicola Bay
Apalachicola National
  Forest
Apalachicola River
Aparicio, Luis
Apartment, The
Apelles
Apennines
Apennine Tunnel
Apgar, Virginia
Apgar score
Apgar test
Aphrodite
Aphrodite of Melos
A Place for Us
AP Network News
Apocalypse Now
Apocrypha, The
Apollinaire,
  Giullaume
Apollinarianism

Apollinaris Sidonius
Apollo
Apollo Belvedere
Apollodorous
Apollodorous of
  Athens
Apollodorous of
  Damascus
Apollonian
Apollonius
Apollonius of Perga
Apollonius of Rhodes
Apollonius of Tralles
Apollonius of Tyana
Apollonius the
  Athenian
Apollo-Saturn
Apollo-Soyuz
Apollo space program
Apollo Theatre
Apostle Islands
Apostle Islands
  National Lakeshore
Apostle pitcher
Apostles' Creed
Apostleship of Prayer
Apostle spoon
Apostolic Christian
  Church
Apostolic Christian
  Churches of
  America
Apostolic Church
Apostolic
  Constitutions
Apostolic Faith
Apostolic Fathers
Apostolic See
A power supply
Appalachia

Appalachian
Appalachian America
Appalachian Bible
  College
Appalachian
  Consortium
Appalachian Folk
  Festival
Appalachian Mountain
  Club
Appalachian
  Mountains
Appalachian National
  Scenic Trail
Appalachian Regional
  Commission
Appalachian Spring
Appalachian State
  University
Appalachian State
  University
  Mountaineers
Appalachian tea
Appachalian Trail
Appalachian Trail
  Conference
Appaloosa
Appel, Karel
Appenzell
Appenzell Inner
  Rhodes
Appenzell Outer
  Rhodes
Appian
Appiani, Andrea
Appian Way
Appii forum
Appistoki Peak
Applause
Apple Bank for
  Savings
Appleby, John Francis

Apple Computer, Inc.
Apple™ computers
  and software
Applegate, Christina
Applegate, Jesse
Applegate Peak
Apple Macintosh™
  computer [see also
  McIntosh apple]
Appleseed, Johnny
Appleton
Appleton, Daniel
Appleton, Sir Edward
  Victor
Appleton, Victor
Appleton layer
Appleton Papers, Inc.
Applied Biosystems
Applied Materials,
  Inc.
Appling, Luke
Appomattox
Appomattox Court
  House
Appomattox Court
  House National
  Historical Park
April
April fool
April Fools' Day
April showers
A-proposition
APS Foundation
Apuleius, Lucius
Apure
Apurímac
Aqaba
Aqua-Lung™
Aquarian
Aquarian Foundation

Aquarius
Aqueduct Race Track
Aquila
Aquila Ponticus
Aquinas College
Aquinas Institute of Technology
Aquinas Junior College
Aquino, Benigno S., Jr.
Aquino, Corazon
Aquitaine
Arab
Arab Bank for Economic Development in Africa
Arab Fund for Economic and Social Development
Arabia
Arabian
Arabian American Oil Company
Arabian camel
Arabian coffee
Arabian Desert
Arabian horse
Arabian Horse Owners Foundation
Arabian jasmine
Arabian music
Arabian Nights Entertainments, The
Arabian Peninsula
Arabian primrose
Arabian Sea
Arabic
Arabic alphabet
Arabic languages

Arabic literature
Arabic numeral
Arab-Israeli
Arab-Israeli Six-Day War
Arab-Israeli Wars
Arabist
Arable, Fern
Arab League
Arab Monetary Fund
Arab Organization of May 15
Arab Palestine
Arachne
Arachnophobia
Arafat, Yasser *or* Yasir
Arafura Sea
Aragon
Aragon, Louis
Aragonese, *n., pl.* Aragonese
ARA Group, Inc., The
Araguaia
Arāk
Arakan Yoma
Araks
Aral Sea
Aramaean
Aramaic
Aramaic alphabet
Aramco
Aran
Aran Islands
Aransas Bay
Aransas National Wildlife Refuge
Aransas Pass
Arapaho *or* Arapahoe, *n., pl.* Arapaho *or* Arapahos *or*

Arapahoe *or* Arapahoes
Arapahoe Community College
Arapahoe Peak
Arapaho National Forest
ARA Services
Araucanian *occas.* Araucan
Arawak, *n., pl.* Arawak *or* Arawaks
Arbitron
Arbitron ratings
Arbor Day
Arbuckle, Fatty
Arbuckle Mountains
Arbus, Diane
Arbuthnot, John
Arcadelt, Jacob
Arcadia [* CA; FL; LA; WI; Greece; *see also* Acadia]
Arcadia Feature Syndicate
Arcadian
Arcadian hind
Arcadian stag
Arcaro, Eddie
Arc de Triomphe
Archaeological Institute of America
Archaeological Museum of La Serena
Archaeological Museum of the American University of Beirut
Archangel *or* Arkhangelsk
Archangel Gabriel

Archbishop and Metropolitan of the Roman Province

Archbishop of Canterbury

Archbishop of Canterbury and Primate of All England

Archbishop of Canterbury's Degrees

Archeozoic *occas.* Archaeozoic

Archer, Anne

Archer, George

Archer, Harry

Archer, Lew

Archer, William

Archerd, Army

Archer Daniels Midland Company

Archer Daniels Midland Foundation

Arches National Park

Archibald, Nate

Archie Bunker's Place

Archimedean

Archimedes

Archimedes' principle

Archimedes' screw

Archipenko, Alexander *or* Alexandr

Architectural Digest

Arch of Constantine

Arch of Titus

archy and mehitabel

Arcimboldo, Giuseppe

Arco Arena

Arco Chemical Company

Arco Foundation

Arco Oil and Gas Company

Arco Pipe Line Company

Arcosanti

Arctic

Arctic Archipelago

Arctic Circle

Arctic Coastal Plain

Arctic daisy

Arctic National Wildlife Refuge

Arctic North Slope

Arctic Ocean

Arctic Red River

Arctic Regions

Arctic Zone

Arcturus

Ardashir

Arden, Elizabeth

Arden, Eve

Arden, John

Ardennes

Ardennes Mountains

Ardizzone, Edward

Ardmore

Ardolino, Emile

Arecibo

Arecibo Ionospheric Observatory

Arena Chapel

Arena Football League

Arena Stage, The

Arendt, Hannah

Arens, Moshe

Arensky, Anton

Ares [Greek mythological god of war; *see also* Aries]

Aretino, Pietro

Arezzo

Argall, Sir Samuel

Argand, Aimé

Argand, John Robert

Argand burner

Argand diagram

Argand lamp

Argand plane

Argelander, Friedrich

Argenteuil

Argentina

Argentine

Argentine ant

Argentine cloth

Argento, Dominick

Argo

Argonaut

Argonne

Argonne Forest

Argonne National Laboratory

Argos [ancient city-state]

Argus [mythological giant]

Argus-eyed

Argyll

Argyll, Archibald Campbell

Argyll, John Campbell

Argyllshire

Argyros, George Leon

Århus *or* Aarhus

Ariadne

Ariane

Arias Sánchez, Oscar

Ariel

Aries [constellation; 1st sign of the zodiac; see also Ares]

Arikara

Arikha, Avigdor

Arimathea occas. Arimathaea

Ariosto, Ludovico

Arison, Ted

Aristarchus of Samos

Aristarchus of Samothrace

Aristide, Jean Bertrand

Aristide Bruant

Aristides, Saint

Aristophanes

Aristophanes of Byzantium

Aristotelian or Aristotelean

Aristotelianism

Aristotelian logic

Aristotle

Aristotle, Christina

Aristotle Contemplating the Bust of Homer

Aristotle's lantern

Aristoxenus of Tarentum

Arius

Arizona

Arizona Bank Charitable Foundation

Arizona Biltmore Resort and Conference Center

Arizona College of the Bible

Arizona cypress

Arizona Daily Star, The

Arizona Highways

Arizona Museum of Science and Technology

Arizonan occas. Arizonian

Arizona Public Service Company

Arizona Republic, The

Arizona ruby

Arizona-Sonora Desert Museum

Arizona State University

Arizona State University Sun Devils

Arizona Veterans Exposition Center

Arizona Veterans Memorial Coliseum

Arizona Veterans Memorial Coliseum and Exposition Center

Arizona Western College

Ark, Joan Van

Arkadelphia

Arkansan

Arkansas

Arkansas Baptist College

Arkansas City

Arkansas College

Arkansas Democrat

Arkansas Gazette

Arkansas Post

Arkansas Post National Memorial

Arkansas Radio Network

Arkansas River

Arkansas River Navigation System

Arkansas State University

Arkansas State University Indians

Arkansas Technological University

Arkansas Traveler

Arkhangelsk var. of Archangel

Arkie

Arkin, Alan

Arkla, Inc.

Ark of the Convenant

Arkwright, Sir Richard

Arlberg

Arlberg technique

Arledge, Roone

Arlen, Harold

Arlen, Michael

Arlen, Richard

Arlésienne

Arlington

Arlington Baptist College

Arlington Heights

Arlington House

Arlington House National Memorial

Arlington International Racecourse

Arlington Memorial Bridge

Arlington National Cemetery

Arlington Stadium

Arliss, George

Armada chest

Armageddon

Armagh

Armagnac

Armagnac brandy

Armagnacs and Burgundians

Armani, Giorgio

Armatrading, Joan

Armbruster, Robert

Armco Foundation

Armco Inc.

Armed Forces Communications and Electronics Association

Armed Forces Day

Armed Forces Radio

Armed Forces Staff College

Armenia [form. Armenian Soviet Socialist Republic]

Armenian

Armenian Church

Armenian language

Armenian literature

Armenian Soviet Socialist Republic [now Armenia]

Armentières

Armetta, Henry

Arminian

Arminianism

Arminius

Arminius, Jacobus

Armistead, George

Armistead, Lewis Addison

Armistice Day [now Veterans Day]

Armitage, Kenneth

Armory Show

Armour, Philip D.

Armour and Company

Arms, John Taylor

Arms, Russell

Arms and the Man

Arms Control and Disarmament Agency

Armstrong, Edwin Howard

Armstrong, Hamilton Fish

Armstrong, Harry

Armstrong, Henry

Armstrong, John

Armstrong, Louis Satchmo

Armstrong, Neil

Armstrong, R. G.

Armstrong, Samuel Chapman

Armstrong Circle Theater

Armstrong College

Armstrong-Jones, Antony

Armstrong State College

Armstrong World Industries, Inc.

Army and Air Force Mutual Aid Association

Army Command and General Staff College

Army Emergency Relief

Army Magazine

Army-McCarthy Hearings

Army-Navy Football Game

Army of Northern Virginia

Army of the United States

Army Post Office

Army Times

Army War College

Arnaz, Desi

Arnaz, Desi, Jr.

Arnaz, Lucie

Arne, Thomas Augustine

Arnel™

Arness, James

Arnett, Peter

Arnhem

Arnhem Land

Arno

Arno, Peter

Arnold, Benedict

Arnold, Eddy

Arnold, Henry Hap

Arnold, Malcolm

Arnold, Matthew

Arnold, Roseanne Barr

Arnold, Thomas [English educator]

Arnold, Tom [entertainment personality]

Arnold Air Force Base

Arnold of Brescia

Arnoldson, Klas

Arnolfini and His Bride

Arnolfinis, The

Arnolfo di Cambio

Arnon

Arno Valley

Arnulf

Aroostook

Aroostook War

Around the World in Eighty Days [book]

Around the World in 80 Days [movie]

Arp, Jean or Hans

Arquette, Cliff

Arquette, Lewis

Arquette, Rosanna

Arrangement, The

Arrau, Claudio

Arrested Development

Arrhenius, Svante August

Arrillaga, John

Arrow, Kenneth Joseph

Arrowhead Community College

Arrowhead Stadium

Arrow, Inc.

Arrow Lakes

Arrow Peak

Arrowsmith, Aaron

Arrowsmith, John

Arroyo, Martina

Arroyo Grande

Arsenic and Old Lace

Arsenio Hall Show, The

Arsonval, Arsène

Art Academy of Cincinnati

Art Advertising Academy

Artaud, Antonin

Artaxerxes

Art Center College of Design

Art Dealers Association of America

Artemis

Artemision

Art Ensemble of Chicago

Artesia

Artful Dodger

Art Gallery of Greater Victoria

Art Gallery of New South Wales

Art Gallery of Ontario

Art Gallery of South Australia

Arthritis Foundation

Arthropoda

Arthur

Arthur, Bea

Arthur, Chester A.

Arthur, Jean

Arthur, Julia

Arthur, Timothy Shay

Arthur Andersen and Company

Arthur D. Little Management Education Institute

Arthur Godfrey and His Friends

Arthur Godfrey Show, The

Arthur Godfrey Time

Arthurian

Arthurian legend

Arthur Kill

Arthur M. Sackler Gallery

Arthur Murray Party, The

Arthur Peak

Articles of Confederation

Articles of War [now Uniform Code of Military Justice]

Art Information Center

Art Institute of Atlanta

Art Institute of Boston

Art Institute of Chicago

Art Institute of Dallas

Art Institute of Fort Lauderdale

Art Institute of Houston

Art Institute of Philadelphia

Art Institute of Pittsburgh

Art Institute of Seattle, The

Art Institute of Southern California

Artists and Writers Syndicate

Artist's Magazine, The

Artist's Studio, The

Art Linkletter's House Party

Art Museum of Düsseldorf

Art Museum of the Socialist Republic of Romania

Art News

Art Nouveau *occas.* art nouveau

Art of Love, The

Artoo Detoo

Art Ross Trophy

Arts and Entertainment Network

Arturo Merino Benítez International Airport

Artweek

Artzybasheff, Boris

Artzybashev, Mikhail Petrovich

Aruba

Aru Islands

Arval Brothers

Arvin

Arvin Foundation

Arvin Industries, Inc.

Aryan

Aryan Brotherhood

Aryan myth

Aryan Nations

Asa

Asahi Shimbun

Asama-yama

Asarah Betebet *occas.* Betevet

ASARCO Inc.

Asben *var. of* Azben

Asbury, Francis

Asbury, Herbert

Asbury College

Asbury Park

Asbury Park Press

Asbury Theological Seminary

Ascari, Alberto

Ascension

Ascension Day

Ascension Island

Asch, Sholem *or* Shalom

Ascheim-Zondek test

Aschoff, Ludwig

Aschoff body

Asclepius

Ascot Gold Cup

A-7 Corsair

A-7 Corsair II

Ash, Mary Kay

Ashanti

Ashanti [people], *n., pl.* Ashanti *or* Ashantis

Ashbery, John

Ashburner, Charles Edward

Ashbury *occas.* Ashberry metal

Ashcan School

Ashcroft, Dame Peggy

Ashe, Arthur

Asheboro

Asheville

Asheville-Buncombe Technical Community College

Ashford, Evelyn

Ashikaga

Ashikaga shogunate

Ashikaga shoguns

Ashkenazi, *n., pl.* Ashkenazim

Ashkenazy, Vladimir

Ashkhabad

Ashland

Ashland Community College

Ashland Oil Foundation

Ashland Oil, Inc.

Ashland Pipe Line Company

Ashland University

Ashley

Ashley, Elizabeth

Ashley, Laura

Ashley, William Henry

Ashley National Forest

Ashman, Howard

Ashmole, Elias

Ashmolean Museum

Ashoka: Innovators for the Public

Ashokan Dam

Ashokan Reservoir

Ash Shariqah

Ashtabula

Ashton, Alan C.

Ashton, Sir Frederick

Ashton-Drake Galleries, The

Ashton-Warner, Sylvia

Ash Wednesday

Asia

Asia and Pacific Council

Asia Foundation, The

Asiago cheese

Asia Minor

Asian

Asian Art and Culture Center

Asian Art and Culture
 Center/Avery
 Brundage
 Collection
Asian cholera
Asian Development
 Bank
Asian flu
Asianic
Asian influenza
Asian Wall Street
 Journal Weekly
Asia Society, The
Asiatic
Asiatic beetle
Asiatic cholera
Asiatic elephant
Asiatic flu
Asiatic globeflower
Asiatic influenza
AsiaWeek
As I Lay Dying
Asimov, Isaac
Asir
As Is
A-6 Intruder
A-16 Fighting Falcon
Asmara
ASM International
Asner, Ed
Asnuntuck
 Community College
Aso-san
Aspen
Aspen Butte
Aspen Hill
Aspen Music Festival
Asperges
Aspin, Les
Aspira of America,
 Inc.

aspirin [American
 usage]
Aspirin™ [Canadian
 usage]
Asquith, Herbert H.
Assad, Hafez al-
Assam
Assamese, *n., pl.*
 Assamese
Assante, Armand
Assassin
Assateague Island
Assateague Island
 National Seashore
Assemblies of God
Assemblies of God
 Church
Assemblies of God
 Theological
 Seminary
Assembly of Notables
Assidean *occas.*
 Assidaean
Assiniboine River
Assiniboin *or*
 Assiniboine
 [Indian], *n., pl.*
 Assiniboin *or*
 Assiniboins *or*
 Assiniboine *or*
 Assiniboines
Assisi
Associated Builders
 and Contractors
Associated Features
Associated Humane
 Societies
Associated Milk
 Producers, Inc.
Associated Press, The
Associated Press
 Broadcast Services

Associated Press
 Radio Network
Associated YM-
 YMHAs of Greater
 New York
Associate Justice of
 the Supreme Court
Associate Reformed
 Presbyterian Church
 (General Synod)
Association, The
Association for
 Business
 Communication
Association for
 Childhood
 Education
 International
Association for
 Clinical Pastoral
 Education
Association for
 Communication
 Administration
Association for
 Computing
 Machinery
Association for
 Information and
 Image Management
Association for
 Information
 Management
Association for
 Investment
 Management and
 Research
Association for
 Manufacturing
 Technology
Association for
 Quality and
 Participation

Association for Retarded Citizens of the United States

Association for Spiritual Awareness

Association for Systems Management

Association for the Advancement of Creative Musicians

Association for the Education and Rehabilitation of the Blind and Visually Impaired

Association for the Study of Afro-American Life and History

Association for Voluntary Surgical Contraception

Association Montessori Internationale

Association of Amateur Astronomers

Association of Amateur Magicians

Association of American Colleges

Association of American Geographers

Association of American Publishers

Association of American Railroads

Association of American Universities

Association of Author's Representatives

Association of Baptists, Duck River (and Kindred)

Association of Brewers

Association of Conservation Engineers

Association of Energy Engineers

Association of Engineering Geologists

Association of Flight Attendants

Association of Former Intelligence Officers

Association of Free Lutheran Congregations

Association of Governing Boards of Universities and Colleges

Association of International Colleges and Universities

Association of Iron and Steel Engineers

Association of Junior Leagues International

Association of Legal Administrators

Association of Management Consulting Firms

Association of Military Surgeons of the United States

Association of Multiethnic Americans

Association of National Advertisers

Association of Old Crows

Association of Professional Ball Players of America

Association of Publicly Traded Companies

Association of Records Managers and Administrators

Association of Southeast Asian Nations

Association of State and Interstate Water Pollution Control Administrators

Association of Tennis Professionals

Association of Theatrical Press Agents and Managers

Association of Theological Schools in the United States and Canada

Association of the Sons of Poland

Association of the United States Army

Association of Trial Lawyers of America

Association of Vacuum Equipment Manufacturers

Association of Vineyard Churches

Association of Volleyball Professionals

Association on American Indian Affairs

Association Pro-Human Rights

Assumption College

Assumption College for Sisters

Assumptionist

Assumption of Mary

Assumption of the Virgin

Assyria

Assyrian

Assyrian art

Assyrian Church

Assyrian language

Assyrian religion

Assyriological

Assyriologist

Assyriology

Astaire, Adele

Astaire, Fred

Astell, Mary

Asterisk Features

As the World Turns

Asthma and Allergy Foundation of America

Asti

Astin, John

Astin, Patty Duke

Astispumante *occas.* Asti Spumante

Astley, Rick

Aston Hotel

Aston Magna Foundation for Music

Aston Resort

Astor, John Jacob

Astor, Lady

Astor, Mary

Astor, William Backhouse

Astor, William Waldorf

Astoria

Astoria Federal Savings and Loan Association

Astor Place

Astor Place Riots

Astounding Science Fiction

Astrakhan

AST Research, Inc.

Astrolabe Bay

Astrology

Astronomical Almanac, The

AstroTurf™

AstroWorld

AstroWorld, WaterWorld-Six Flags

Asturian

Asturias

Asturias, Miguel Ángel

Asunción

A supply

Aswān

Aswān Dam

Aswān High Dam

As You Like It

Atabrine™

Atacama Desert

Atahualpa

Atakapa, *n., pl.* Atakapa *or* Atakapas

Atalanta

AT & T Bell Laboratories

AT & T Capital Corporation

AT & T Corporate Center

AT & T Foundation

AT & T Information Systems Inc.

AT & T Pebble Beach National Pro-Am

Atari Corporation

Atascadero

Atatürk, Kemal

Atbara

Atchafalaya

Atchafalaya Bay

Atchison

Atchison, David Rice

Atchison, Topeka and Santa Fe Railway Company

A. T. Cross Company

A Team, The

Ateneum Art Museum

A-10 Thunderbolt

Athabasca *occas.* Athabaska

Athabascan

Athabasca Pass

Athanasian

Athanasian Creed

Athanasius the Athonite, Saint

Athanasius the Great, Saint

Athapaskan *or*
Athapascan *or*
Athabascan *or*
Athabaskan

Atheist Association

Athena *or* Athene

Athenaeum *or*
Atheneum

Athenaeum of Ohio

Athenaeum of
Philadelphia

Athenaeus

Athenagoras

Atheneum *or*
Athenaeum

Athenian

Athens

Athens Airport

Athens Area Technical
Institute

Athens State College

Atherton, Gertrude

Atherton, William

Athi

Athletic Equipment
Manufacturers
Association

Athletics Congress of
the United States of
America

Athol

Athos

A-3 Skywarrior

ATI Career Training
Center

Atka mackerel

Atkins, Chet

Atkins, Tom

Atkinson, Brooks

Atkinson, Eleanor

Atlanta

Atlanta Army Depot

Atlanta Braves

Atlanta campaign

Atlanta Christian
College

Atlantacism

Atlantacist

Atlanta Civic Center

Atlanta College of Art

Atlanta Constitution,
The

Atlanta Country Club

Atlanta Falcons

Atlanta-Fulton County
Stadium

Atlanta Gas Light
Company

Atlanta Golf Classic

Atlanta Hawks

Atlanta International
Raceway

Atlanta Journal, The

Atlanta Journal-
Constitution, The

Atlanta Metropolitan
College

Atlanta Naval Air
Station

Atlanta Rhythm
Section

Atlanta Symphony
Orchestra

Atlanta University
Center

Atlantean

Atlantic, The

Atlantic Cable

Atlantic Center (IBM)

Atlantic Charter

Atlantic Christian
College

Atlantic City

Atlantic City
International
Airport

Atlantic Coast
Airlines

Atlantic Coastal Plain

Atlantic Coast
Conferences

Atlantic Community
College

Atlantic Council of
the United States,
Inc., The

Atlantic croaker

Atlantic Daylight
Time

Atlantic Energy, Inc.

Atlantic Financial
Savings

Atlantic Highlands

Atlantic Intracoastal
Waterway

Atlantic Monthly
Company, The

Atlantic Monthly
Press, The

Atlantic Ocean

Atlantic Peak

Atlantic Provinces

Atlantic puffin

Atlantic Richfield
Company

Atlantic Southeast
Airlines, Inc.

Atlantic Standard
Time

Atlantic Starr

Atlantic Symphony
Orchestra

Atlantic Ten
Conference

Atlantic Union
  College
Atlantic World
  Airways Inc.
Atlantis
Atlas
Atlas, Charles
Atlas Mountains
Atlas Van Lines, Inc.
Atlin Lake
Atmospheric
  Laboratory for
  Applications and
  Science
Atomic Age
Atomic Energy
  Commission
Atoms for Peace
AT-6 Texan
Attalus
Attenborough, Sir
  David
Attenborough, Sir
  Richard
At the Milliner's
At the Movies
Attica
Attica Correctional
  Facility
Attic base
Attic faith
Attic Greek
Atticism *occas.*
  atticism
Attic salt
Attic wit
Attila
Attleboro
Attlee, Clement
Attorney General of
  the United States

Attu
Attucks, Crispus
Atwater
Atwater, Lee
A-20 Havoc
A-26 Invader
Atwill, Lionel
Atwood, Margaret
Auber, Daniel
Auberjonois, René
Aubervilliers
Aubrey, John
Auburn
Auburn Dam
Auburn University
Auburn University at
  Montgomery
Auburn University
  Tigers
Aubusson rug
Aucassin and
  Nicolette
Auchincloss, Louis
Auchinleck, Sir John
Auckland
Auckland City Art
  Gallery
Auckland
  International
  Airport
Auckland Islands
Auden, W. H.
Audi of America Inc.
Audubon
Audubon, John James
Audubon's warbler
Auel, Jean M.
Auer, Leopold
Auer, Mischa
Auerbach, Berthold

Auerbach, Red
auf Wiedersehen
Augean
Augean stables
Auger effect
Auger shower
Augsburg
Augsburg Cathedral
Augsburg College
Augsburg Confession
Augsburg Fortress
  Publishers
August
Augusta
Augusta College
Augusta College
  Jaguars
Augustan
Augustana College
Augustan Age
Augusta National Golf
  Club
Augustan Confession
Augusta Technical
  Institute
Augustine, Saint
Augustine of
  Canterbury
Augustine of Hippo,
  Saint
Augustinian
Augustinianism
Augustinian of the
  Assumption
Augustus
Aulby, Mike
Auld Lang Syne
Aulic Council
Aumont, Jean Pierre

Aunt Emma's Cope
  Book
Auntie Mame
Aunt Jemima
Aunt Jemima doll
Aunt Sally, *n.*, *pl.*
  Aunt Sallies *or*
  Aunt Sallys
Aunt Tom
Aurelian
Aurelian Wall
Aureomycin™
Au Revoir les Enfants
Auriol, Vincent
Aurora
Aurora University
Ausable
Ausable Chasm
Auschwitz
Aussie
Austen, Jane
Austerlitz
Austin
Austin, Alfred
Austin, Gene
Austin, John
Austin, Mary
Austin, Moses
Austin, Patti Duke
Austin, Stephen Fuller
Austin, Tracy
Austin American-
  Statesman
Austin College
Austin Community
  College
Austin Company, The
Austin friar
Austin-Healey
Austin Lake

Austin Peay State
  University
Austin Peay State
  University
  Governors
Austin Presbyterian
  Theological
  Seminary
Australasia
Australasian
Australia
Australia and New
  Zealand Banking
  Group, Ltd.
Australia antigen
Australia Day
Australian
Australian aborigine
Australian Airlines
  Ltd.
Australian Alps
Australian and New
  Zealand Army
  Corps
Australian Antarctic
  Territory
Australian ballot
Australian bear
Australian bluebell
  creeper
Australian Capital
  Territory
Australian cattle dog
Australian crawl
Australian English
Australia-New
  Zealand-United
  States Treaty
Australian fan palm
Australian kelpie
Australian literature
Australian Open

Australian pea
Australian pine
Australian Rules
  football
Australian rye grass
Australian tea tree
Australian terrier
Austral Islands
Australoid
Australopithecine
Australorp
Austria
Austria-Hungary
Austrian
Austrian Airlines
Austrian brier
Austrian Tyrol
Austro-Hungarian
Austro-Hungarian
  Monarchy
Austronesia
Austronesian
Austro-Prussian War
Authenticated News
  International
Authorized Version of
  the Bible
Authors Guild, Inc.,
  The
Authors League of
  America
Autism Society of
  America
Autobahn
Autobiography of
  Alice B. Toklas
Autodesk, Inc.
Autolycus
Automat
Automatic Data
  Processing, Inc.

Automobile License Plate Collectors' Association

Automobile Racing Club of America

Automotive Hall of Fame

Auto Page Syndicate

Auto-Train Corporation

AutoWeek

Autry, Alan

Autry, Gene

Autumn Sea

Autumn Sonata

Auvergne

Auvergne Mountains

Avalon

Avalon, Frankie

Avalon Peninsula

Avaz International Dance Theatre

Avco Financial Services, Inc.

Avedon, Richard

AV-8A Harrier

AV-8B Harrier II

Ave Maria

Aventine Hill

Avenue, The

Avenue des Champs Élysées

Avenue of the Americas

Average White Band, The

Averback, Hy

Averett College

Averill, Earl

Avernus Lake

Averroës

Avery, Alice O'Neill

Avery, Milton

Avery, Richard Jerome

Avery, Samuel Putnam

Avery, Tex

Avery Dennison Corporation

Avery Fisher Hall

Avery Island

Avianca

Aviateca

Aviation Week and Space Technology

Avignon

Avila College

Avildsen, John

Avis Inc.

Avnet, Inc.

Avogadro, Amedeo

Avogadro's *or* Avogadro constant

Avogadro's *or* Avogadro law

Avogadro's *or* Avogadro number

Avon

Avon Books

Avondale

Avondale Industries, Inc.

Avon Lake

Avon Park

Avon Park Air Force Base

Avon Park Air Force Range

Avon Products Foundation

Avon Products, Inc.

Awami League

Awana Clubs International

Away in a Manger

Ax, Emanuel

Axel Heiberg Island

Axis

Axis Powers

Axminster carpet

Axthelm, Peter M.

Axton, Hoyt

Aydelotte, Frank

Ayer, A. J.

Ayer, Francis W.

Ayers Rock

Aykroyd, Dan

Aymara, *n., pl.* Aymara *or* Aymaras

Aymaran

Ayr

Ayres, Agnes

Ayres, Lew

Ayrshire

Ayrshire cattle

Ayub Khan

Ayub Khan, Mohammad

Azanian Peoples' Organization

Azben *or* Asben

Azcapotzalco

Azerbaijan [*form.* Azerbaijan Soviet Socialist Republic]

Azerbaijani

Azerbaijanian

Azerbaijan Soviet Socialist Republic [*now* Azerbaijan]

Azeri

Azilian Cavern

Aziz, Tariq
Aznavour, Charles
Azores
Azores high
Aztec

Aztec marigold
Aztec Ruins National
  Monument
Aztec two-step

Azusa
Azusa Pacific
  University
Azzolina, Mark S.

B

Baade, Walter
Baal, *n.*, *pl.* Baalim
Baalbek
Baalish
Baalism
Baalist
Baalite
Ba'al Shem Tov
Baarlam and Josaphat
Babangida, Ibrahim
Babangida, Maryam
Babar *var. of* Babur
Babar the Elephant
Babbage, Charles
Babbit
Babbitt, Bruce
Babbitt, George F.
Babbitt, Harry
Babbitt, Irving
Babbitt, Milton
Babbitt, Natalie
Babbitt metal
Babbittry *often*
 Babbitry *occas.*
 babbittry *or*
 babbitry
Babcock, Barbara
Babcock and Wilcox
 Company, The

Babel
Babel, Isaac
Babelic
Babelism
Bab el Mandeb
Babe Ruth Baseball
Babe Ruth League
Babes
Babes in Arms
Babes in Toyland
Babe the Blue Ox
Babette
Babette's Feast
Babeuf, François Noël
Babilonia, Tai
Babinski, Joseph
 François Felix
Babinski *or* Babinski's
 reflex
Babinski *or* Babinski's
 sign
Babism
Babist
Babite
Babi Yar
Babson, Roger Ward
Babson College
Babur *occas.* Babar
Babuyan Islands

Baby Bell
Babyface
Baby Jesus
Baby Jogger™
Babylon
Babylonia
Babylonian
Babylonian art
Babylonian captivity
Babylonish
Baby Roo
Baby Snooks
Bacall, Lauren
Bacardi
Bacardi and Company
 Ltd.
Bacardi Imports, Inc.
Bacchae
Bacchanalia
Bacchelli, Riccardo
Bacchic
Bacchus
Bacchus and Ariadne
Bacchuslike
Bacchus of the United
 States
Bacchylides
Bach, Alice

69

Bach, Carl Philipp
Emanuel

Bach, Catherine

Bach, Johann
Christian

Bach, Johann
Christoph Friedrich

Bach, Johann
Sebastian

Bach, Richard

Bach, Wilhelm
Friedemann

Bacharach, Burt

Bache, Jules Sermon

Bache, Richard

Bacheller, Irving

Bachelor Father

Bachelor of Arts

Bachelor of Fine Arts

Bachelor of Laws

Bachelor of Music

Bachelor of Science

Bache Peninsula

Bachman, Richard

Bachman-Turner
Overdrive

Bach revival

Bach rock

Bach system

Bach trumpet

Bacitracin™

Back, Ernst

Back Bay

Backbone Mountain

Backer Spielvogel
Bates Worldwide
Inc.

Backhaus, Wilhelm

Backpacker

Back River

Back to the Future

Back to the Future
Part III

Back to the Future
Part II

Backus, Jim

Bacon, Francis [artist]

Bacon, Sir Francis
[author]

Bacon, Henry

Bacon, Kevin

Bacon, Nathaniel

Bacon, Peggy

Bacon, Roger

Bacone College

Baconian

Baconianism

Baconian method

Baconian theory

Bacon's Rebellion

Bactria occas.
Bactriana

Bactrian camel

Bad Axe

Bad Company

Baden

Baden-Baden

Baden-Powell, Sir
Robert

Baden-Württemberg

Bader Field

Badge of Military
Merit

Badger Pass

Bad Godesburg

Bad Homburg

Bad Ischi

Bad Kreuznach

Bad Lands

Badlands National
Park

Bad Nauheim

Bad Reichenhall

Badrinath

Baedeker, Karl

Baedeker™
guidebook

Baer, Bugs

Baer, Max

Baer, Max, Jr.

Baer, Parley

Baez, Joan

Baffin, William

Baffin Bay

Baffin Island [form.
Baffin Land]

Baffin Island National
Park

Bagdasarian, Ross

Bagehot, Walter

Baggetta, Vincent

Baggins, Bilbo

Baggins, Frodo

Baghdad or Bagdad

Baghdad International
Airport

Baghdad Pact

Baghdad Railway

Bagheera

Bagley, William
Chandler

Bagnold, Enid

Bagritski, Eduard

Baguio

Baha'i Allah or
Bahaullah

Baha'i House of
Worship

Baha'i [people], n., pl.
Baha'is

Baha'i [religion; *see also* Bahia]
Baha'ism
Baha'ist
Baha'i temple
Bahama Banks
Bahama grass
Bahama Islands
Bahamas, the
Bahasa Indonesia
Bahia [Brazilian state; *see also* Baha'i]
Bahía Blanca
Bahía Grande
Bahia grass
Bahrain *occas.* Bahrein
Bahraini
Bahrain International Airport
Bahrain Museum
Baikal Mountains
Bailey, Anne
Bailey, Deford
Bailey, Sir Donald
Bailey, F. Lee
Bailey, Gamaliel
Bailey, Liberty Hyde
Bailey, Mildred
Bailey, Nathan
Bailey, Pearl
Bailey, Razzy
Bailey bridge
Baily, Edward Hodges
Baily, Francis
Baily's beads
Bain, Alexander
Bain, Barbara
Bain, Conrad

Bainbridge
Bainbridge, William
Bainbridge College
Bainter, Fay
Baio, Scott
Baird, John Logie
Baird Mountains
Baire category theorem
Bais Medrash L'Torah Rabbinical College
Baizerman, Saul
Baja, the
Baja California
Baja California Norte
Baja California Sur
Bajer, Fredrik
baked Alaska
Bakelite™
Baker, Anita
Baker, Carroll
Baker, Chet
Baker, Diane
Baker, George Fisher
Baker, George Pierce
Baker, Ginger
Baker, Home Run
Baker, James A.
Baker, Janet
Baker, Joe Don
Baker, Josephine
Baker, LaVern
Baker, Ray Stannard
Baker, Russell
Baker, Sir Samuel White
Baker and McKenzie
Baker College
Baker-Finch, Ian

Baker Hughes Inc.
Baker Island
Baker Lake
Baker-Nunn camera
Baker-Nunn satellite-tracking camera
Bakersfield
Bakersfield College
Bakers Square
Baker Street
Baker Street Irregulars
Baker University
Baker v. Carr
Bakery, Confectionery and Tobacco Workers' International Union
Bakery Equipment Manufacturers Association
Bakhtiari
Bakker, Jim
Bakker, Tammy Faye
Bakst, Léon
Baku [*now* Baky]
Bakula, Scott
Bakunin, Mikhail
Baky [*form.* Baku]
Balaam
Balaamite
Balaamitical
Balaguer, Joaquín
Balakirev, Mili Alekseevich
Balaklava *occas.* Balaclava
Balanchine, George
Balante, *n., pl.* Balante *or* Balantes
Bala Shem Tov
Balbo, Cesare

Balbo, Italo

Balboa [* Panama; see also Bilbao]

Balboa, Vasco Núñez de

Balboa Heights

Balbuena, Bernardo de

Balch, Emily Greene

Balchen, Bernt

Balch Springs

Baldface Mountain

Bald-Headed Men of America

Bald Mountain

Baldovinetti, Alesso or Alessio

Baldung, Hans

Baldwin

Baldwin, Alec

Baldwin, Hanson

Baldwin, James

Baldwin, James Mark

Baldwin, Matthias William

Baldwin, Stanley

Baldwin, William

Baldwin Library

Baldwin Park

Baldwin Piano and Organ Company

Baldwin-Wallace College

Balearic

Balearic Islands

Balen, Hendrik van

Balenciaga, Cristóbal

Balewa, Sir Abubakar Tafawa

Balfe, Michael William

Balfour, Arthur James

Balfour, Francis Maitland

Balfour, Sir James

Balfour Declaration

Bal Harbour

Bali

Balikpapan

Balin, Ina

Balin, Marty

Balinese, n., pl. Balinese

Balinese cat

Balinese music

Baliol or Balliol, Edward de

Baliol or Balliol, John de

Balkan

Balkan Entente

Balkanite

Balkanization

Balkanize, v. Balkanized, Balkanizing

Balkan League

Balkan Mountains

Balkan Pact

Balkan Peninsula

Balkans, the

Balkan States

Balkan Wars

Ball, Ernest

Ball, Lucille

Ball, Thomas

Balla, Giacomo

Ballad of Reading Gaol

Balladur, Edouard

Ballantine™ Books

Ballantine Books, Inc.

Ballarat

Ballard, Florence

Ballard, Hank

Ballard, J. G.

Ballard, Kaye

Ball Corporation

Balleek ware

Ballesteros, Seve

Ballet Folklórico de Mexico

Ballet Hispanico of New York

Ballet Russe de Monte Carlo

Ballets Russes

Ballet Theatre Foundation

Balliol var. of Baliol, Edward de

Balliol var. of Baliol, John de

Balliol College

Ballistic Missile Early Warning System

Ball™ jar

Ball Mason™ jar

Ballmer, Steven Anthony

Ballou, Adin

Ballou, Hosea

Ballou, Hosea, II

Balls Bluff

Ball State University

Ball State University Cardinals

Ballston Spa

Ballwin

Bally Manufacturing Corporation

Bally's

Balmain, Pierre
  Alexander
Balmain fashions
Balmer, Johann
Balmer series
Balmer's formula
balm of Gilead
Balmont, Konstantin
  Dmitriyevich
Balmoral Castle
Balmoral Park Race
  Track
Balsam, Martin
balsam of Peru
balsam of Tolú
Balsas River
Balter, Alan
Balthazar
Balthus
Baltic
Baltic International
  Airlines
Baltic languages
Baltic provinces
Baltic Sea
Baltic Shield
Baltic States
Baltimore
Baltimore, Lord
Baltimore and Ohio
  Railroad Company
Baltimore and Ohio
  Railroad Museum
Baltimore chop
Baltimore clipper
Baltimore Gas and
  Electric Company
Baltimore Gas and
  Electric Company
  Foundation
Baltimore heater

Baltimore Hebrew
  University
Baltimore
  International
  Culinary College
Baltimore Maritime
  Museum
[Baltimore] Memorial
  Stadium
Baltimore Museum of
  Industry
Baltimore Oriole
  [baseball player]
Baltimore oriole [bird]
[Baltimore] Sun, The
Baltimore Symphony
  Orchestra
Baltimore-Washington
  International
  Airport
Balto-Slavic
Baluchi, *n., pl.*
  Baluchi *or* Baluchis
Baluchistan *occas.*
  Beluchistan
Balzac, Honoré de
Balzac, Jean Louis
  Guez de
Bamako
Bambaata, Afrika
Bambara, *n., pl.*
  Bambara *or*
  Bambaras
Bamberg
Bamberg Symphony
  Orchestra
Bambi
Bamboo Curtain
Bamm Bamm
Banacek
Banach, Stefan
Banach space

Bananarama
Banbury
Banbury bun
Banbury cake
Banbury tart
Banca Commerciale
  Italiana
Banca Nazionale del
  Lavoro
Banchs, Enrique
Banco Bilbao Vizcaya
Banco di Napoli
Banco di Roma
Banco do Brasil
Banco Espanol de
  Credito
Banco Nazionale del
  Lavoro
Banc One Corporation
Banco Popular de
  Puerto Rico
Bancorp Hawaii, Inc.
Bancroft, Anne
Bancroft, Dave
Bancroft, Edward
Bancroft, George
Bancroft, Hubert
  Howe
Band, The
Banda, Hastings
  Kamazu
Bandag, Inc.
Band-Aid™
Banda Islands
Banda Oriental
Bandaranaike,
  Sirimavo
Bandaranaike,
  Solomon West
  Ridgeway Dias
Banda Sea

Bandelier, Adolph Francis Alphonse

Bandelier National Monument

Bandello, Matteo

Banderas, Antonio

Bandimere Speedway

Bandinelli, Baccio *or* Bartolommeo

Bands of America

Bandung

Bandung Conference

Bandy, Moe

Banerjea, Sir Surendranath

Banff

Banff Centre School of Fine Arts

Banff National Park

Banfshire

Bang, Bernhard L. F.

Bangalore

Bangka

Bangkok

Bangkok International Airport

[Bangkok] National Museum

Bangladesh [*form.* East Pakistan]

Bangladeshi *n., pl.* Bangladeshis

Bangor

[Bangor] Daily News

Bangorian Controversy

Bangor International Airport

Bangor Naval Submarine Base

Bangor Theological Seminary

Bangs, John Kendrick

Bang's disease

Bangui *occas.* Bangi

Bangui-Mpoko International Airport

Bangweulu

Banja Luka

Banjarmasin *or* Bandjarmasin

Banjul

Banjul Yundum International Airport

Bank Administration Institute

BankAmerica Corporation

BankAmerica Foundation

Bankers Life Company

Bankers Trust Company

Bankers Trust New York Corporation

Bank for International Settlements

Bankhead, John Hollis

Bankhead, Tallulah

Bankhead, William Brockman

Bankhead National Forest

Bank Melli Iran

Bank of America

Bank of America Arizona

Bank of America National Trust and Savings Association

Bank of Boston Corporation

Bank of Boston Corporation Charitable Foundation

Bank of California

Bank of Canada

Bank of China

Bank of China Tower

Bank of Credit and Commerce International

Bank of England

Bank of Hawaii

Bank of Ireland

Bank of Italy

Bank of Japan

Bank of Montreal

Bank of New England

Bank of New England Corporation

Bank of New England Corporation Foundation

Bank of New York, The

Bank of New York Company, Inc., The

Bank of Nova Scotia

Bank of Seoul

Bank of the United States

Bank of Tokyo, Ltd.

Bank of Tokyo Trust Company

Bank of Yokohama, Ltd.

Bank One, Texas

Banks, Dennis

Banks, Ernie

Banks, Jonathan

Banks, Sir Joseph

Banks, Leslie

Banks, Nathaniel Prentiss

Banks, Thomas

Bank Saderat Iran

Banks Island

Banks' rose

Bank Street College of Education

Bank Western

Bannack

Banneker, Benjamin

Banning

Bannister, Sir Roger

Bannock

Bannockburn

Bannon, Jack

Banns of Marriage

Banque Bruxelles Lambert

Banque Indosuez

Banque Nationale de Paris

Banque Paribas

Banquet of Officers of the Civic Guard of Saint George at Haarlem, 1616

Banquo

Banta Corporation

Bantam™ Books

Bantam Books, Inc.

Bantam/Britannica™

Bantam Classics™

Bantam Doubleday Dell Publishing Group, Inc.

Bantam work

Banthine™

Banting, Sir Frederick Grant

Bantingism

Bantry Bay

Bantu, n., pl. Bantu or Bantus

Bantu languages

Bantustan

Banville, Théodore de

Bao Dai

Baoudjakdji, Millicent V.

Baptist

Baptist Bible College

Baptist Bible College and Seminary

Baptist Bible Fellowship International

Baptist Book Store

Baptist College at Charleston

Baptist College Buccaneers

Baptist General Conference

Baptistic

Baptist Life Association

Baptist Missionary Association of America [form. North American Baptist Association]

Baptist Missionary Association Theological Seminary

Baptist World Alliance

Bara, Theda

Baraba Steppe

Barabbas

Baraboo

Baradla Caves

Baraka, Amiri

Baranof Island

Baranov, Aleksander or Aleksandr

Barataria Bay

Barat College

Bar at the Folies Bergere

Barbadian

Barbados

Barbados aloe

Barbados cherry

Barbados flower fence

Barbados gooseberry

Barbados nut

Barbados pride

Barbados royal palm

Barbara

Barbara, Saint

Barbara Bush Foundation for Family Literacy

Barbarella

Barbareschi, Luca

Barbarossa

Barbarossa, Frederick

Barbary

Barbary ape

Barbary Coast

Barbary sheep

Barbary States

Barbeau, Adrienne

Barber, Red

Barber, Samuel

Barbera

Barbera, Joseph R.

Barber Institute of Fine Arts

Barber of Seville, The
Barber-Scotia College
Barber Shop, The
Barbers Point
Barbers Point Naval
  Air Station
Barberton
Barbie, Klaus
Barbie™ doll
Barbie-doll syndrome
Barbirolli, Sir John
Barbizon
Barbizon school
Barbon, Praise God
Barbour, John
Barbuda
Barbusse, Henri
BarcaLounger™
Barcelona
Barcelona Airport
Barcelona chair
Barclay College
Barclay de Tolly,
  Mikhail
Barclays
Barclays Bank
Barclays Bank of New
  York
Bard College
Bardeen, John
Bard of Avon
Bardolino
Bardot, Brigitte
Bardstown
Bare, Bobby
Barea, Arturo
Barefoot in the Park
Barenboim, Daniel
Barents, Willem

Barents Island
Barents Sea
Baretta [television
  series; see also
  Beretta]
Bargello National
  Museum
Bargello Palace
Barger, Sonny
Bar Harbor
Baring, Alexander
Baring, Evelyn
Baring, Maurice
Barker, Bob
Barker, Eugene
  Campbell
Barker, George
Barker, James Nelson
Barkin, Ellen
Barking Abbey
Barkley, Alban W.
Barkley, Charles
Barksdale Air Force
  Base
Barlach, Ernst
Barlick, Al
Barlow, Joel
Barlow's disease
Barmecidal
Barmecide
Barnabas, Saint
Barnaby Jones
Barnaby Rudge
Barnard, Christiaan
Barnard, Edward
  Emerson
Barnard, Frederick
  Augustus Porter
Barnard, George Grey
Barnard, Henry

Barnard College
Barnardo, Thomas
Barnardo Home
Barnard's star
Barnburners
Barnegat Bay
Barnes, Clive
Barnes, Djuna
Barnes, Harry Elmer
Barnes, William
Barnes & Noble™
  Books
Barnes & Noble
  Bookstore
Barnesboro
Barnes Group, Inc.
Barnesville
Barnet, Charlie
Barnett Bank of South
  Florida
Barnett Banks Inc.
Barnett Charities Inc.
Barneveldt, Jan van
  Olden
Barney, Joshua
Barney Google
Barney Miller
Barneys New York
Barney the Dinosaur
Barney the Dragon
Barnstable
Barnum, P. T.
Barocci or Baroccio,
  Federigo
Baroda Museum and
  Picture Gallery
Baroid Corporation
Baroja y Nessi, Pio
Barolo occas. baralo
  wine

Baron, Michel

Baron, Salo
  Wittmayer

Baronius, Caesar

Baron of Strathcona
  and Mount Royal

Barons' War

Barr, Alfred Hamilton,
  Jr.

Barr, Amelia Edith

Barr, Murray
  Llewellyn

Barrack-Room Ballads

Barranquilla

Barrault, Jean Louis

Barr body

Barre

Barren Grounds

Barres, Maurice

Barrett, Majel

Barrett, Rona

Barretts of Wimpole
  Street, The

Barrie, Barbara

Barrie, Sir James M.

Barrie, Mona

Barrie, Wendy

Barrier Reef

Barrington

Barrios, Eduardo

Barris, Chuck

Barron, Clarence
  Walker

Barron's

Barron's Educational
  Series, Inc.

Barron's National
  Business and
  Financial Weekly

Barrow

Barrow, Clyde

Barrow, Edward G.

Barrow, Sir John

Barrows, Sydney

Barry, Sir Charles

Barry, Dave

Barry, Gene

Barry, John

Barry, Marion

Barry, Philip

Barry, Rick

Barrymore, Diana

Barrymore, Drew

Barrymore, Ethel

Barrymore, John

Barrymore, Lionel

Barrymore, Maurice

Barry University

Barstow [* CA; see
  also Bartow]

Barstow College

Barstow Marine Corps
  Logistic Base

Bartered Bride, The

Barth, John

Barth, Karl

Barthelme, Donald

Barthelmess, Richard

Barthelmy, Sidney K.

Barthes, Roland

Barthian

Barthianism

Bartholdi, Frédéric
  Auguste

Bartholin, Kaspar

Bartholin, Thomas

Bartholin's gland

Bartholomew

Bartholomew, Dave

Bartholomew, Freddie

Bartholomew, Saint

Barthou, Louis

Bartlesville

Bartlesville Wesleyan
  College

Bartlett, Bonnie

Bartlett, John

Bartlett, Josiah

Bartlett, Paul Wayland

Bartlett, Robert
  Abram

Bartlett, Vernon

Bartlett pear

[Bartlett's] Familiar
  Quotations

Bartók, Béla

Bartolommeo, Fra

Bartolozzi, Francesco

Barton, Clara

Barton, Sir Derek

Barton, Sir Edmund

Barton, Elizabeth

Barton, James

Barton College

Barton County
  Community College

Bartow [* FL; see
  also Barstow]

Bartram, John

Bartram, William

Bartramian sandpiper

Barty, Billy

Baruch

Baruch, André

Baruch, Bernard M.

Baruch College

Barye, Antoine Louis

Baryshnikov, Mikhail

Barzini, Luigi

Barzun, Jacques

Baseball Digest
Baseball Weekly
Base Exchange
Basehart, Richard
Basel *occas.* Basle
Basel-Land
Basel-Mulhouse
  Airport
Basel-Stadt
basenji *occas.* Basenji
BASF Corporation
Bashford, Wilkes
Bashir, Omar Hassan
  Ahmed al-
Basic Books, Inc.
Basic English
Basic Institute of
  Technology
Basie, Count
Basil
Basil, Saint
Basilan Islands
Basilan Strait
Basilian
Basilian monk
Basilica of Our Lady
  of Peace
Basilica of Saint John
  Lateran
Basilica of Saint Mark
Basilica of Saint Mary
  Major
Basilica of Saint
  Paul's-outside-
  the-Walls
Basil the Great, Saint
Basinger, Kim
Basin Street
Basin Street Blues
Baskerville, John

Basketball Digest
Basketball Weekly
Basket Maker
Basket of Apples
Baskin, Leonard
Basle *var. of* Basel
Basle Fine Arts
  Museum
Basque
Basque language
Basque Provinces
Basque shirt
Basra *or* Al-Basrah
Bas-Rhin
Bass, Anne Hendricks
Bass, Edward Perry
Bass, Lee Marshall
Bass, Robert Muse
Bass, Sam
Bass, Sid Richardson
Bassano, Francesco
Bassano, Giambattista
  da Ponte
Bassano, Girolamo da
  Ponte
Bassano, Jacopo
Bassano, Leandro
Basse-Alpes
Basse-Normandie
Basses-Pyrénées
Basset Ali al-Megrahi,
  Abdel
Basse-Terre [island;
  port on this island]
Basseterre [port on
  Saint Christopher
  Island]
Bassett, John Spencer
Bassett Furniture
  Industries, Inc.

Bassey, Shirley
BASS, Inc.
Bassist College
Basso, Hamilton
Bass Strait
Bastian, Adolf
Bastian, Bruce W.
Bastidas, Rodrigo de
Bastille
Bastille Day
Bastogne
Bastrop
Basuto, *n., pl.* Basuto
  or Basutos
Basutoland [*now*
  Lesotho]
Bataan
Bataan Death March
Bataan Peninsula
Batangas
Batan Islands
Bâtard-Montrachet
Batavia
Batavia Downs
Bateman, Jason
Bateman, Justine
Bates, Alan
Bates, H. E.
Bates, Henry Walter
Bates, Katherine Lee
Bates, Kathy
Bates, Norman
Batesburg
Bates College
Batesian mimicry
Bates Shoe Company
Batesville
Bath
Bath brick

Bath bun

Bath chair

Bath Festival

Bathinette™

Báthory, Christopher

Báthory, Elizabeth

Báthory, Gabriel

Báthory, Sigismund

Báthory, Stephen

Bathsheba

Bathsheba Bathing

Baths of Caracalla

Baths of Diocletian

Bath stone

Bathurst

Bathurst Island

B.A.T. Industries

Batista y Zaldivar, Fulgencio

Batman

Batman Returns

Bat Masterson

Baton Rouge

Battelle Memorial Institute

Batten, Frank, Sr.

Battersea

Battersea Park

Battery, The

Battle, Kathleen

Battle above the Clouds

Battle Creek

Battleground National Cemetery

Battle Hymn of the Republic

Battle Mountain Gold Company

Battle of Actium

Battle of Agincourt

Battle of Al-Alamein or El-Alamein

Battle of Antietam

Battle of Arbela

Battle of Assundun

Battle of Austerlitz

Battle of Balaklava

Battle of Belfort

Battle of Belleau Wood

Battle of Bemis Heights

Battle of Blenheim

Battle of Borodino

Battle of Brandywine

Battle of Britain

Battle of Brunanburh

Battle of Buena Vista

Battle of Bull Run

Battle of Bunker Hill

Battle of Calderón Bridge

Battle of Camden

Battle of Cape Matapan

Battle of Cerro Gordo

Battle of Châllons-sur-Marne

Battle of Chancellorsville

Battle of Chapultepec

Battle of Chattanooga

Battle of Chickamauga

Battle of Churubusco

Battle of Cold Harbor

Battle of Constantinople

Battle of Copenhagen

Battle of Coral Sea

Battle of Corregidor

Battle of Crécy

Battle of Dien Bien Phu

Battle of Dogger Bank

Battle of El-Alamein var. of Battle of Al-Alamein

Battle of Fallen Timbers

Battle of Fehrbellin

Battle of Fishes

Battle of Five Forks

Battle of Flodden Field

Battle of Fort Henry

Battle of Fredericksburg

Battle of Germantown

Battle of Gettysburg

Battle of Glendale

Battle of Guadalcanal

Battle of Guilford Courthouse

Battle of Hampton Roads

Battle of Hastings

Battle of Heligoland Bight

Battle of Hobkirks Hill

Battle of Höchstädt

Battle of Horseshoe Bend

Battle of Jutland

Battle of Kings Mountain

Battle of Kulikovo

Battle of Lake Champlain

Battle of Lake Erie

Battle of Lepanto

Battle of Lexington

Battle of Leyte Gulf

Battle of Long Island

Battle of Lookout
Mountain

Battle of Lundy's
Lane

Battle of Malplaquet

Battle of Manassas

Battle of Manila Bay

Battle of Marathon

Battle of Marengo

Battle of Marignano

Battle of Messines

Battle of Metaurus

Battle of Midway

Battle of Missionary
Ridge

Battle of Mobile Bay

Battle of Monmouth

Battle of
Moraviantown

Battle of Navarino

Battle of New Orleans
[military
engagement]

Battle of New
Orleans, The [song]

Battle of Oriskany

Battle of Orléans

Battle of Palo Alto

Battle of Palo Duro
Canyon

Battle of Perryville

Battle of Pittsburg
Landing

Battle of Plassey

Battle of Point
Pleasant

Battle of Poitiers

Battle of Poltava

Battle of Port Said

Battle of Princeton

Battle of Pyramids

Battle of Quebec

Battle of Queenston
Heights

Battle of Querétaro

Battle of Ramillies

Battle of Resaca de la
Palma

Battle of San Jacinto

Battle of San Juan Hill

Battle of San Pietro,
The

Battle of San Romano,
The

Battle of Santiago

Battle of Saratoga

Battle of Sedan

Battle of Sempach

Battle of Seven Oaks

Battle of Seven Pines

Battle of Shiloh

Battle of Soissons

Battle of Solferino

Battle of Spotsylvania
Courthouse

Battle of Stalingrad

Battle of Suchow

Battle of Syracuse

Battle of Teutoburg
Forest

Battle of the Alamo

Battle of the Argonne

Battle of the Books,
The

Battle of the Bulge

Battle of the Dunes

Battle of the Falaise
Gap

Battle of the Falkland
Islands

Battle of the Herrings

Battle of the Little
Bighorn

Battle of the Marne

Battle of the
Philippine Sea

Battle of the Sea of
Japan

Battle of the Seven
Days

Battle of the Somme

Battle of the Spanish
Armada

Battle of the Spurs

Battle of the Thames

Battle of the White
Hill

Battle of the
Wilderness

Battle of Ticonderoga

Battle of Tippecanoe

Battle of Tours

Battle of Trafalgar

Battle of Trasemino

Battle of Trenton

Battle of Tsushima

Battle of Valcour
Island

Battle of Valmy

Battle of Verdun

Battle of Vicksburg

Battle of Vimy Ridge

Battle of Washita

Battle of Waterloo

Battle of Wounded
Knee

Battle of Yorktown

Battle of Ypres

Battles of Lexington
and Concord

Batton Lash

Batu Khan

BATUS, Inc.

Bat Yam

Baudelaire, Charles

Bauder Fashion
College

Baugh, Harold

Baugh, Sammy

Bauhaus

Bauhaus style

Baum, L. Frank

Baum, Vicki

Baum, William
Cardinal

Baumé, Antoine

Baumé hydrometer

Baumeister, Willi

Baumé scale

Bausch & Lomb Inc.

Bavaria

Bavarian

Bavarian Alps

Bavarian cream

Bax, Sir Arnold

B-axis, *n.*, *pl.* B-axes

Baxter, Anne

Baxter, Les

Baxter, Richard

Baxter, Warner

Baxter Foundation

Baxter International
Inc.

Baxter Springs

Bayamo [* Cuba]

Bayamón [* Puerto
Rico]

Bayamón Central
University

Bayar, Celâl

Bayard

Bayard, James Ashton

Bayard, Pierre Terrail

Bay Area Rapid
Transit System

Bay City

Bay City Rollers, The

Bay De Noc
Community College

Bayer

Bayerische
Hypotheken-und
Wechsel-Bank

Bayerische
Landesbank
Girozentrale

Bayerische Motoren
Werke

Bayerische
Vereinsbank

Bayer Mobay
Foundation

Bayer process

Bayer USA Inc.

Bayes, Nora

Bayes, Thomas

Bayesian statistics

Bayes' rule

Bayeux

Bayeux tapestry

Bay Islands

Bayle, Pierre

Baylor, Elgin

Baylor, Robert

Baylor College of
Dentistry

Baylor College of
Medicine

Baylor University

Baylor University
Bears

Bay Meadows

Bay Minette

Bay of Bengal

Bay of Billows

Bay of Biscay

Bay of Campeche

Bay of Dew

Bay of Fundy

Bay of Naples

Bay of Pigs

Bay of Pigs invasion

Bay of Quinte

Bay of Setúbal

Bay of Vigo

Bay of Whales

Bayonne

Bayonne Bridge

Bayonne Military
Ocean Terminal

Bayou Goula

Bayou Macon

Bayou Teche

Bay Path College

Bay Psalm Book

Bayreuth

Bayreuth Festival

Bay Ridge Christian
College

Bay Saint Louis

Bay Shore

Bay State

Bay State College

Bay Stater

Baytown

Bay Village

Bayville

Bazin, René François
Baziotes, William
B battery
BBC Symphony Orchestra
BBDO Worldwide Inc.
B.C. [comic strip]
BCE Inc.
B cell
BC soil
B. Dalton Bookseller
Beach, Mrs. H. H. A.
Beach, Moses Yale
Beach, Rex
Beach Boys, The
Beachwood
Beachy Amish Mennonite Churches
Beachy Head
Beacon
Beacon Hill
Beadle, Erastus Flavel
Beadle, George Wells
Beadle, Irwin
Beadle's dime novels
Beagle Channel
Beaker folk
Beal, John
Beal College
Beale, Edward Fitzgerald
Beale Air Force Base
Beale Street
Beals, Jennifer
Beamon, Bob
Bean, Alan
Bean, Leon Leonwood
Bean, Orson

Bean, Judge Roy
Beany and Cecil
Beard, Charles Austin
Beard, Daniel Carter
Beard, Mary
Bearden, Romare
Beardsley, Aubrey Vincent
Beardstown
Bear Flag Republic
Bear Flag Revolt
Bear Island
Bear Lake
Bear Mountain
Béarnaise *often* béarnaise sauce
Bear River
Bear Stearns Companies Inc., The
Bear Went over the Mountain, The
Beasley, Allyce
Beastie Boys
Beat Generation *often* beat generation
Beatitudes
Beatlemania
Beatles, The
Beatnik *often* beatnik
Beaton, Sir Cecil
Beatrice
Beatrice and Benedict
Beatrice Company
Beatrice Foundation
Beatrice/Hunt-Wesson
Beat the Clock
Beattie, Ann
Beattie, James
Beatty, Clyde
Beatty, David

Beatty, Ned
Beatty, Warren
Beaufort
Beaufort, Sir Francis
Beaufort County Community College
Beaufort Marine Corps Air Station
Beaufort *occas.* Beaufort's scale
Beaufort Sea
Beauharnais, Eugénie Hortense de
Beauharnais, Joséphine de
Beaujolais
Beaujolais [wine], *n.*, *pl.* Beaujolaises
Beaumarchais, Pierre Augustin Caron de
Beaumont
Beaumont, Francis
Beaumont, Hugh
Beaumont, William
Beauport
Beauregard, Pierre Gustave Toutant de
Beautiful British Columbia
Beauty and the Beast
Beauty with Fan and Parasol
Beauvais
Beauvoir, Simone de
Beaux, Cecilia
Beaux Arts
Beaux Arts Trio
Beaverboard™
Beaverbrook, Lord
Beaver College
Beaver Dam

Beaver Falls

Beaverhead National Forest

Beaver Indian

Beaver Island

Beavers, Louise

Beaverton

BeBe and CeCe Winans

Bebel, Ferdinand August

Bebe Miller and Company

Beccafumi, Domenico di Pace

Bechet, Sidney

Bechtel, Stephen Davison, Jr.

Bechtel Foundation

Bechtel Group, Inc.

Bechtle, Robert

Bechuana, *n.*, *pl.* Bechuanas *or* Bechuana

Bechuanaland [*now* Botswana]

Beck, C. C.

Beck, Dave

Beck, John

Beck, Julian

Becker, Boris

Becker, Carl Lotus

Becker, George Ferdinand

Becker, Howard Paul

Becker College

Becket

Beckett, Samuel

Beckford, William

Beckley

Beckley, Jake

Beckley College

Beckman Instruments, Inc.

Beckmann, Max

Beckwourth, James P.

Bécquer, Gustavo Adolfo

Becquerel, Alexandre Edmond

Becquerel, Antoine César

Becquerel, Antoine Henri

Becquerel effect

Becquerel ray

Becton, Dickinson and Company

Bedaux, Charles Eugène

Bedaux point

Bedaux point system

Bedaux system

Beddoes, Thomas Lovell

Bede, Saint

Bede, Venerable

Bedelia, Bonnie

Bedford

Bedford, Brian

Bedford, David

Bedford, Sybille

Bedford Beds

Bedford cord

Bedford Heights

Bedfordshire

Bedford-Stuyvesant

Bedivere, Sir

Bedlam

Bedlington

Bedlingtonshire

Bedlington terrier

Bedloe's Island [*now* Liberty Island]

Bedouin, *n.*, *pl.* Bedouin *or* Bedouins

Bee, Molly

Beebe, Charles William

Beebe, Lucius

Beech Aircraft Corporation

Beech Aircraft Foundation

Beecham, Sir Thomas

Beechcraft

Beecher, Catharine Esther

Beecher, Henry Ward

Beecher, Lyman

Beechey, Frederick William

Beech Grove

Beechman, Laurie

Bee County College

Beefeaters

Beefheart, Captain

beef Stroganoff

beef Wellington

Bee Gees, The

Beelzebub

Beene, Geoffrey

Beer, August

Beer, Thomas

Beerbohm, Sir Max

Beer Can Collectors of America

Beer Hall Putsch

Beer-Nuts™

Beers, Clifford Whittingham

Beersheba

Beer's law

Beery, Noah

Beery, Noah, Jr.

Beery, Wallace

Beeson, Jack

Beethoven, Ludwig van

Beethoven Satellite Network

Beethovian

Beetle Bailey ·

Beetlejuice [movie; see also Betelgeuse]

Beeville

Begas, Karl

Beggar's Opera, The

Begin, Menachem

Begley, Ed

Begley, Ed, Jr.

Beham, Barthel

Beham, Hans Sebald

Behan, Brendan

Behar, Joy

Behistun or Bisutin Inscription

Behrens, Peter

Behring, Emil Adolf von

Behring, Kenneth Eugene

Behrman, S. N.

Beiderbecke, Bix

Beiersdorf

Beijing [form. Peking]

Beijing Capital International Airport

Beilan Pass

Beirut occas. Bayrut

Beirut International Airport

Beissel, Johann Conrad

Bekins Van Lines Company

Bela

Bela Fleck and the Fleckstones

Belafonte, Harry

Belafonte-Harper, Shari

Bel Age hotel

Bel-Air hotel

Bel and the Dragon

Belarus or Byelarus [form. Byelorussian Soviet Socialist Republic]

Belarussian

Belasco, David

Belasco Theater

Belatrix

Belau

Belaúnde, Fernando

Belaya

Belch, Sir Toby

Belcher Islands

Belém

Belfast

Belfast International Airport

Belfer, Arthur Bejer

Belfer, Robert

Belfort

Belgaum

Bel Geddes, Barbara

Bel Geddes, Norman

Belgian

Belgian Congo [now Zaire]

Belgian griffon

Belgian hare

Belgian horse

Belgian literature

Belgian Malinois

Belgian sheepdog

Belgian Tervuren

Belgian truss

Belgic

Belgium

[Belgium] Royal Museum of Art and History

Belgrade

[Belgrade] Gallery of Frescoes

Belgrade National Museum

Belgravia

Belgravian

Belhaven College

Belial

Belisarius

Belitung

Beliveau, Jean

Belize [form. British Honduras]

Belizean

Belize City

Belize River

Belk Foundation Trust

Belknap Peak

Belk Store Services Inc.

Bell

Bell, Acton

Bell, Alexander Graham

Bell, Alexander Melville

Bell, Clive

Bell, Cool Papa

Bell, Currer

Bell, Ellis

Bell, Gertrude
  Margaret Lowthian

Bella Coola

Bellaire

Bellamy, David

Bellamy, Edward

Bellamy, Howard

Bellamy, Joseph

Bellamy, Ralph

Bellamy Brothers, The

Bell and Howell
  Company

Bell and Howell
  Foundation

Bellarmine College

Bell Atlantic
  Charitable
  Foundation

Bell Atlantic
  Corporation

Bellatrix

Bellay, Joachim du

Bell Biv Devoe

Belleau Wood

Belle Chase Naval Air
  Station

Belleek china

Belleek porcelain

Belleek ware

Bellefontaine

Bellefontaine
  Neighbors

Bellefonte

Belle Fourche

Belle Fourche Dam

Belle Fourche
  Reservoir

Belle Glade

Belle Isle

Belle Meade

Belle Plaine

Bellerophon

Bellerophontic letter

Belleville

Belleville Area
  College

Belleville spring

Bellevue

Bellevue College

Bellevue Community
  College

Bellevue Hospital

Bellflower

Bell for Adano, A

Bell Gardens

Bell Helicopter
  Textron, Inc.

Belli, Melvin

Bellin College of
  Nursing

Bellingham

Bellingham Bay

Bellingshausen,
  Fabian Gottlieb von

Bellingshausen Sea

Bellingshausen Station

Bellini, Gentile

Bellini, Giovanni

Bellini, Jacopo

Bellini, Vincenzo

Bellisario, Donald P.

Bell Island

Bell Laboratories

Bellmead

Bellmore

Bello, Andrés

Belloc, Hilaire

Bell of Pennsylvania

Bellona

Bellonian

Bellotto, Bernardo

Bellow, Saul

Bellows, George

Bellows, Henry
  Whitney

Bellows Air Force
  Station

Bell *occas.* Bell's
  purchase

Bells for John
  Whiteside's
  Daughter

bells of Ireland

Bell Song

BellSouth Corporation

BellSouth Foundation

Bell's palsy

Bell Telephone
  Company

Bell Telephone Hour,
  The

Bellwood

Bell X-1

Belmar

Belmondo, Jean Paul

Belmont

Belmont, August

Belmont Abbey
  College

Belmont College

Belmonte, Juan

Belmont Park

Belmont Park Race
  Track

Belmont Stakes

Belmont Technical
  College

Belo Horizonte

Beloit

Beloit College

Belorussian *or* Byelorussian Soviet Socialist Republic [*now* Belarus *or* Byelarus]

Bel Paese cheese

Bel-Rea Institute of Animal Technology

Bel-Ridge

Belsen

Belshazzar

Beltane

Belt Mountains

Belton

Beltrami, Eugenio

Beltsville

Beltsville swine

Beluchistan *var. of* Baluchistan

Belushi, James

Belushi, John

Belvedere [Vatican court; * CA]

Belvidere [* IL; NJ]

Bely, Andrei

Belzoni

Belzoni, Giovanni Battista

Bemba, *n.*, *pl.* Bemba *or* Bembas

Bemelmans, Ludwig

Bemidji

Bemidji State University

Bemis, Samuel Flagg

Bemis Company Foundation

Bemis Company Inc.

Benaderet, Bea

Benadryl™

Benaiah

Benaki Museum

Ben Ali, Zine el-Abidine

Benares

Benatar, Pat

Benavente y Martínez, Jacinto

Ben Bella, Ahmed

Benbow, John

Bence-Jones, Henry

Bence-Jones protein

Bench, Johnny

Benchley, Nathaniel

Benchley, Peter

Benchley, Robert

Benckiser Consumer Products Inc.

Bend

Benda, Julien

Benda, Wadyslaw Theodor

Ben Davis apple

benday *often* Benday *or* Ben Day process

Bender Gestalt test

Bendix, Vincent

Bendix, William

Bendix Corporation

Benecke, Tex

Benedetto da Majano

Benedicite

Benedict

Benedict II, Saint

Benedict, Dirk

Benedict, Ruth

Benedict, Saint

Benedict, Stanley Rossiter

Benedict College

Benedictine

Benedictine College

benedictine *occas.* Benedictine liqueur

Benedictine monk

Benedictine nun

Benedictine Order

Benediction of the Blessed Sacrament

Benedict of Nursia, Saint

Benedict's solution

Benedict's test

Benedict the Black, Saint

Benedictus

Beneficial Corporation

Beneficial Foundation

Bene *or* Beni Israel

Benelux Economic Union

Benelux nations

Benemid™

Beneš, Edvard

Benét, Stephen Vincent

Benét, William Rose

Benetton Group

Benevento

Benevolent and Protective Order of Elks

Ben Franklin store

Bengal

Bengal catechu

Bengalee [native or resident of Bangladesh]

Bengalese, *n.*, *pl.* - Bengalese [native

or resident of
Bengal]

Bengali [native or
resident of Bengal]

Bengal light

Bengal quince

Bengal rose

Bengal tiger [animal]

Bengal Tigers [British
regiment]

Benghazi *occas.*
Bengasi

Benghazi Benina
Airport

Benglis, Lynda

Benguela Current

Ben-Gurion, David

Ben-Gurion Airport

Ben Hur

Benicia

Benin [*form.*
Dahomey]

Benin City

Beninese, *n., pl.*
Beninese

Bening, Annette

Beni River

Benito Cereno

Benjamin

Benjamin, Asher

Benjamin, Judah
Philip

Benjamin, Richard

Benjamin Books

Benjamin Franklin
Stamp Club

Benjaminite

Benjamin of Tudela

Benjamite

Benji

Ben Lomond

Benn, Gottfried

Bennett, Arnold

Bennett, Constance

Bennett, Floyd

Bennett, Harve

Bennett, James
Gordon

Bennett, Jill

Bennett, Joan

Bennett, Michael

Bennett, Richard

Bennett, Richard
Bedford

Bennett, Richard
Rodney

Bennett, Robert
Russell

Bennett, Tony

Bennett, William
Gordon

Bennett, William J.

Bennett College

Bennettsville

Ben Nevis

Bennington

Bennington College

Benno, Saint

Benny, Jack

Benny Goodman
Orchestra

Benoit, David

Benoit, Joan

Benoît, Pierre

Benrus Watch
Company Inc.

Bensenville

Benson

Benson, Craig

Benson, Ezra Taft

Benson, Frank Weston

Benson, George

Benson, Ray

Benson, Robby

Bent, Charles

Bent, William

Bentham, Jeremy

Benthamic

Benthamism

Benthamite

Bentley

Bentley, Eric

Bentley, Phyllis

Bentley, Richard

Bentley College

Bentleyville

Benton

Benton, Barbi

Benton, Brook

Benton, Thomas Hart

Benton Harbor

Benton Heights

Bentonville

Bentsen, Lloyd

Bent's Fort

Bent's Old Fort
National Historic
Site

Benue

Benvenuto Cellini

Ben Yehudda, Eliezer

Benz, Carl Friedrich

Benzedrex™

Benzedrine™

Benzell, Mimi

Ben-Zvi, Itzhak

Beothuk

Beowulf

Beradino, John

Béranger, Pierre Jean de

Berber

Berbera

Berbick, Trevor

Berchtesgaden

Bercy sauce

Berdyaev, Nicolai

Berea

Berea College

Berean

Berean Bible Fellowship

Berean Bookstore

Berean College

Berechiah

Beregovoy, Pierre

Berenger, Tom

Berenice

Berenice's Hair

Berenson, Bernard

Berenstain, Jan

Berenstain, Stan

Berenstain Bears, The

Beresford, Charles William

Beretta U.S.A. Corporation

Beretta U.S.A.™ firearms [see also Baretta]

Berezina

Berg, Alban

Berg, Gertrude

Berg, Patty

Bergdorf Goodman

Bergen

Bergen, Candice

Bergen, Edgar

Bergen, Polly

Bergen-Belsen

Bergen Brunswick Corporation

Bergen Community College

Bergenfield

Berger, Senta

Berger, Thomas

Berger, Victor Louis

Bergerac, Cyrano de

Bergerac, Jacques

Bergin, Patrick

Bergman, Hjalmar

Bergman, Ingmar

Bergman, Ingrid

Bergson, Henri

Bergsonian philosophy

Bergsonism

Bergstrom Air Force Base

Beria or Beriya, Lavrenty

Berigan, Bunny

Bering, Vitus

Bering Daylight Time

Bering Island

Bering land bridge

Bering Land Bridge National Preserve

Bering Sea

Bering Sea Fur-Seal Controversy

Bering Standard Time

Bering Strait

Bering time

Berio, Luciano

Beriosova, Svetlana

Berisha, Sali

Beriya, Lavrenty var. of Beria, Lavrenty

Berkeleian or Berkeleyan

Berkeleianism

Berkeleian philosophy

Berkeley [* CA; see also Berkley]

Berkeley, Busby

Berkeley, George

Berkeley, Sir Lennox

Berkeley, Sir William

Berkeley College of Business

Berkeley College of Westchester, The

Berkeley School of Long Island, The

Berkeley School of New York, The

Berklee College of Music

Berkley [* MI; see also Berkeley]

Berkley, William Robert

Berkley™ Books

Berkley Publishing Group

Berkman, Alexander

Berkshire

Bershire Community College

Berkshire Festival

Berkshire Hathaway Inc.

Berkshire Hills

Berkshire Music Center

Berkshires, the

Berkshire swine

Berle, Adolf

Berle, Milton
Berlin
Berlin, Irving
Berlin, Sir Isaiah
Berlin airlift
Berlin blockade
Berlin Decree
Berliner
Berliner, Emile
Berliner Ensemble
Berlinger, Warren
[Berlin] National Gallery
Berlin Philharmonic Orchestra
Berlin procelain
Berlin-Schonefeld Airport
[Berlin] State Museums of the Foundation for Prussian Treasures of Culture
Berlin Tegel Airport
Berlin Tempelhof Airport
Berlin Wall
Berlin wool
Berlioz, Hector
Berlitz International Inc.
Berlitz Language Center
Berman, Eugène
Berman, Lazar
Berman, Shelley
Bermejo *occas.* Vermejo
Bermuda
Bermuda Airport
Bermuda bag

Bermuda buttercup
Bermuda chub
Bermuda collar
Bermuda cutter
Bermuda grass
Bermuda high
Bermuda Hundred
Bermuda Islands
Bermuda lily
Bermudan *or* Bermudian
Bermuda onion
Bermuda palmetto
Bermuda rig
Bermudas, the
Bermuda shorts
Bermuda Star Line
Bermuda Triangle
Bern *occas.* Berne [* Switzerland; *see also* Berne]
Bernadette of Lourdes, Saint
Bernadotte, Jean Baptiste Jules
Bernalillo
Bernanos, Georges
Bernard
Bernard, Claude
Bernard, Crystal
Bernardi, Herschel
Bernardin, Joseph Louis Cardinal
Bernardin de Saint-Pierre, Jacques
Bernardine
Bernardine of Siena, Saint
Bernard of Clairvaux, Saint
Bernard of Cluny

Bernard of Menthon, Saint
Bernard of Montjoux, Saint
Bernardsville
Berne [* IN; *see also* Bern]
Berne *var. of* Bern [* Switzerland; *see also* Bern]
Berne, Eric
Berne Museum of Fine Arts
Bernese, *n.*, *pl.* Bernese
Bernese Alps
Bernese mountain dog
Bernhard, Sandra
Bernhard of Saxe-Weimar
Bernhardt, Robert E.
Bernhardt, Sarah
Bernice
Bernie, Ben
Bernina
Bernina Pass
Berninesque
Bernini, Gianlorenzo
Bernoulli, Daniel
Bernoulli, Jacques
Bernoulli, Jean
Bernoullian
Bernoulli distribution
Bernoulli effect
Bernoulli equation
Bernoulli's lemniscate
Bernoulli's principle
Bernoulli trials
Bernsen, Corbin
Bernstein, Carl

Bernstein, Elmer

Bernstein, Leonard

Bernstein, Theodore M.

Berra, Yogi

Berrigan, Daniel

Berrigan, Philip

Berry, Chuck

Berry, Jack Monteith, Sr.

Berry, Jim

Berry, John William, Sr.

Berry, Ken

Berry, Martha McChesney

Berry, Raymond

Berry College

Berryman, John

Bertelsmann

Bertillon, Alphonse

Bertillon system

Bertinelli, Valerie

Berto, Giuseppe

Bertoia, Harry

Bertolucci, Bernardo

Berwick

Berwickshire

Berwyn

Beryl

Berzelius, Jöns Jakob

Besançon

Besant, Annie

Besant, Sir Walter

Besier, Rudolf

Bessarabia

Bessarabian

Bessel, Friedrich Wilhelm

Bessel function

Bessel method

Bessemer

Bessemer, Sir Henry

Bessemer City

Bessemer converter

Bessemer process

Bessemer State Technical College

Bessemer steel

Best-in-Show

Best Little Whorehouse in Texas, The

Best Products Company, Inc.

Best Products Foundation

Best's Review, Life/Health Insurance Edition

Best's Review, Property/Casualty Insurance Edition

Best Western hotel

Best Western motel

Best Years of Our Lives, The

Beta Alpha Psi

Beta Beta Beta

Beta Carotene

Beta Centauri

Beta Crucis

Beta fiber

Beta Gamma Sigma

Betamax™

Betancourt, Rómulo

Beta Sigma Phi

Beta Sigma Psi

Beta Theta Pi

Betelgeuse [star; see also Beetlejuice]

Bethany

Bethany Bible College

Bethany College

Bethany Lutheran College

Bethany Theological Seminary

Beth Benjamin Academy of Connecticut

Bethe, Hans Albrecht

Bethel

Bethel College

Beth-El College of Nursing

Bethel Theological Seminary

Bethesda

Bethesda National Naval Medical Center

Beth Hamedrash Shaarei Yosher Institute

Beth Hatalmud Rabbinical College

Beth Hillel

Bethlehem

Bethlehem Bach Choir

Bethlehem Bach Festival

Bethlehem sage

Bethlehem Steel Corporation

Bethlem Royal Hospital

Bethmann-Hollweg, Theobald von

Beth Medrash Emek Halacha Rabbinical College

Beth Medrash Govoha

Bethnal Green

Bethpage

Beth Shammai

Bethune, Mary McLeod

Bethune-Cookman College

Bethune-Cookman College Wildcats

Betjeman, Sir John

Bette Davis Eyes

Bettelheim, Bruno

Bettendorf

Bettenhausen, Tony

Better Boys Foundation

Better Business Bureau

Better Chance, Inc., A

Better Government Association

Better Homes and Gardens

Better Homes and Gardens New Cook Book

Betterton, Thomas

Better World Society

Betti, Ugo

Betty Ford Center

Betz Laboratories, Inc.

Beulah

Bevan, Aneurin

Beveridge, Albert Jeremiah

Beveridge, Sir William Henry

Beveridge plan

Beverly

Beverly, Robert

Beverly Enterprises

Beverly Heritage Hotel, The

Beverly Hillbillies, The

Beverly Hills

Beverly Hills Cop

Beverly Hills Cop II

Beverly Hills Diet, The

Beverly Hills Hotel

Beverly Hills 90210

Beverly Hilton

Bevilacqua, Anthony Cardinal

Bevin, Ernest

Bevis of Hampton

Bewick, Thomas

Bewitched

Bexley

Bey, Turhan

Beyazid

Beyond War Foundation

Bezae

Béziers

B. F. Goodrich Company, The

B-58 Hustler

B-50 Superfortress

B-52's [musical group]

B-52 Stratofortress

B-45 Tornado

B-47 Stratojet

B-girl

Bhabha, Homi J.

Bhagavad-Gita

Bhaktivedanta, A. C.

Bhattacharya, Bhabhani

Bhave, Vinoba

BHC Communications, Inc.

Bhili

Bhils

Bhopal

B-horizon

Bhutan

Bhutanese, *n., pl.* Bhutanese

Bhutto, Benazir

Bhutto, Zulfikar Ali

Biafra

Biafra, Jello

Biafran

Bialik, Chaim Nachman

Bianchi, Kenneth

Biarritz

Bibb, John

Bibb lettuce

Bibescu, Barbu

Bibescu, George

Bibiena, Allessandro

Bibiena, Antonio

Bibiena, Carlo

Bibiena, Ferdinando Gallo da

Bibiena, Francesco

Bibiena, Giovanni

Bibiena, Giuseppe

Bible

Bible-basher

Bible Belt

Bible Bookstore

Bible Christian Union

Bible Church of Christ

Bible class

Bible Holiness Movement

Bible League

Bible paper

Bible school

Bible Society

Bible-thumper

Bible Way Church of Our Lord Jesus Christ Worldwide

Biblia Pauperum

biblical *occas.* Biblical

Biblical Hebrew

Biblical Latin

Biblical Theological Seminary

Biblicism

Biblicist

Biblicistic

Bibliographical Society of America

Bibliothèque Nationale

Biblist

Bibulus

BIC Corporation

Bickerstaff, Isaac [fictitious person]

Bickerstaffe, Isaac [Irish playwright]

Bickertonite

Bickford, Charles

Bicycle Federation of America

Bicycle Manufacturers Association of America

Bicycle Thief, The

Bicycling

Bidault, Georges

Biddeford

Biddle, Francis

Biddle, George

Biddle, James

Biddle, John

Biddle, Nicholas

Biden, Joseph

Bidwell, John

Biedermeier

Biedermeier, Gottlieb

Biedermeier style

Bielefeld

Bien Hoa

Bienville, Sieur de

Bienville National Forest

Bierce, Ambrose

Bierstadt, Albert

Big Apple, the

Bigard, Barney

Bigart, Homer

Big Band era

Big Band sound

Big Bang *occas.* big bang

Big Bang theory *occas.* big bang theory

Big Bear Lake

Big Bear Solar Observatory

Big Belt Mountains

Big Ben

Big Bend Community College

Big Bend National Park

Big Bertha

Big Bird

Big Black Mountain

Big Board *occas.* big board

Big Bopper, The

Big Brother

Big Brotherism

Big Brothers/Big Sisters of America

Big C

Big Cypress National Preserve

Big Daddy

Big Diomede

Big Dipper

Bigelow, John

bigfoot *often* Bigfoot

Biggers, Earl

Biggs, E. Power

Big Hole National Battlefield

Bighorn

Bighorn Canyon National Recreation Area

Bighorn Lake

Bighorn Mountains

Bighorn National Forest

Bight of Benin

Bight of Biafra

Biglow Papers

Big Money, The

Big Muddy [nickname for Mississippi River]

Big Muddy River [IL waterway]

Big Payoff, The

Big Picture, The

Big Rapids

Big River

Big Sioux

Big Sky, The

Big Sleep, The

Big South Fork National River and Recreation Area

Big Spring

Big Stone Lake

Big Story, The

Big Sur

Big Sur River

Big Ten Conference

Big Thicket National Preserve

Big Three automakers

Big Top

Big Town

Big Valley, The

Big West Conference

Big Wichita Dam

Bihar

Bihari

Bihzad, Kamal ad-Din

Bikecentennial: The Bicycle Travel Association

Bikel, Theodore

Bikers against Manslaughter

Bikini

Biko, Steven

Biko Affair

Bikol, *n.*, *pl.* Bikol *or* Bikols

Bilac, Olavo

Bilauktaung

Bilbao [* Spain; *see also* Balboa]

Bilbeishi, Munther

Bildt, Carl

Bildungsroman

Biletnikoff, Fred

Bill, Tony

Bill Bailey, Won't You Please Come Home?

Bill Baird Puppets

Billboard Magazine

Bill Cosby Show, The

Billerica

Bill Haley and the Comets

Billings

Billings, Josh

Billings, Warren K.

Billings, William

Billingsgate

Billingsley, Barbara

Billingsley, Sherman

Billionaire Boys Club

Billiton

Bill Moyers' Journal

Bill of Rights

Bill T. Jones/Arnie Zane and Company

Bill Williams Mountain

Billy Budd [book; movie; opera]

Billy Budd, Foretopman [book]

Billy Graham Center

Billy Graham Crusades

Billy Graham Evangelistic Association

Billy the Kid

Biloxi

Biltmore

Bimini

Bimini Islands

Biminis, the

Binchois, Giles

Binet, Alfred

Binet scale

Binet-Simon scale

Binet-Simon test

Binet test

Bing, Sir Rudolph

Bing cherry

Binger, Virginia McKnight

Bingham, Caleb

Bingham, George Caleb

Bingham, Hiram

Bingham Canyon

Binghamton [*not* Binghampton]

Binh Dinh

Binns, Edward

Binyon, Lawrence

Bío Bío

Biogen, Inc.

Bioko Island

Biola University

Biomet, Inc.

Bion

Biondi, Matt

Bionic Woman, The

Biosphere II

Biospherian

Birch, John M.

Birch, Thomas

Bircher *or* John Bircher

Birches *or* John Birches

Birchism *or* John Birchism

Birchite *or* John
  Birchite
Bird, Larry
Bird in Space
Birdman of Alcatraz
Bird of Paradise
Bird on a Wire
Birdseye, Clarence
Birds Eye™ frozen
  foods
Bird Watcher's Digest
Birkenhead
Birkenhead, Frederick
Birket Qarun
Birman
Birmingham
Birmingham
  International
  Airport
Birmingham Museum
  and Art Gallery
Birmingham News
Birmingham Royal
  Ballet
Birmingham-Southern
  College
Birmingham
  University
Birnbaum, Stephen
Birnbaum Travel
  Guides™
Birney, David
Birney, James
  Gillespie
Birney, Meredith
  Baxter
Birrell, Augustine
Birthday
Birth of a Nation, The
Birth of Tragedy, The
Birth of Venus, The

Birthright, Inc.
Bisayan
Bisbee
Biscayne Bay
Biscayne Dog Track
Biscayne Key
Biscayne National
  Park
Bishop, Bonnie Lou
Bishop, Elizabeth
Bishop, Hazel
Bishop, Isabel
Bishop, Isabella Lucy
Bishop, Joey
Bishop, John Peale
Bishop, Morris
Bishop Clarkson
  College
Bishop of Rome
Bishop's Lodge Guest
  Ranch
Bishop's ring
Bishop State
  Community College
Bishop's University
Bishops' Wars
Bismarck
Bismarck, Otto von
Bismarck Archipelago
Bismarck herring
Bismarckian
Bismarck Range
Bismarck Sea
Bismarck State
  College
Bisoglio, Val
Bissau
Bissau Airport
Bissell, George Henry

Bissell, Melville
  Reuben
Bissell, Richard
Bissell, Whit
Bisset, Jacqueline
Bisutin *var. of*
  Behistun Inscription
Bitter Lakes
Bitterroot
Bitterroot National
  Forest
Bitterroot Mountains
Bitterroot Range
Bitterroot Tunnel
Bixby, Bill
Biya, Paul
Bizerte
Bizet, Georges
BIZ NET
Bjoerling, Jussi
Björnson, Björnstjerne
Blacher, Boris
Black, Clint
Black, Hugo
Black, Karen
Black, Shirley Temple
Black American music
Black & Decker
  Corporation, The
Black and Tan
Black Angus
Black Artists Group
Blackbeard
Black Beauty
Black Belt *occas.*
  black belt
Blackboard Jungle
  [movie]
Blackboard Jungle,
  The [book]

Blackburn

Blackburn, Joseph

Blackburn College

Blackburnian warbler

Black Business Alliance

Black Canyon of the Colorado

Black Canyon of the Gunnison

Black Canyon of the Gunnison National Monument

Black Country

Black Crowes, The

Black Dahlia

Black Death

Black Douglas

Black English

Black Enterprise

Black Entertainment Television

Blackett, Patrick Maynard Stuart

black-eyed Susan

Blackfeet Community College

Blackfoot

Blackfoot [Indian], *n.*, *pl.* Blackfoot *or* Blackfeet

Blackfoot Mountain

Blackfoot River

Blackfoot River Reservoir

Black Forest

Black Forest cake

Black Friar

Blackfriars Theatre

Black Friday

Black Hand

Black Hawk College

Blackhawk Technical College

Black Hawk War

Black Hills

Black Hills National Forest

Black Hills State University

Black Hole of Calcutta

Black Journal

Black Lung Association

Blackman, Honor

Black Maria

Black Mass

Blackmer, Sidney

Black Monday

Black Monk

Black Mountain poets

Black Mountains

Blackmun, Harry Andrew

Blackmur, R. P.

Black Music Hall of Fame and Museum

Black Muslim

Black Oak Arkansas

Black Panther

Black Panther Party

Black Perspective on the News

Black Plague

Black Pope

Black Press Service, Inc.

Black Prince

Black River

Black River Falls

Black Rock Desert

Black Rod

Black Russian

Black Sabbath

Black Sampson

Blacksburg

Black Sea

Black September

Blackshirt

Black's Law Dictionary

Black Sox Scandal

Black speech

Blackstone

Blackstone, Harry, Jr.

Blackstone, Sir William

Black Stream

Black Tom

Black Tom Island

Black Velvet *occas.* black velvet [cocktail]

Black Virgin

Black Volta

Blackwall frigate

Blackwall hitch

Black Warrior

Black Watch

Blackwell, Alice Stone

Blackwell, Elizabeth

Blackwell, Henry Brown

Blackwell, Otis

Blackwood, English

Blackwood, Nina

Black X

Bladen Community College

Bladerunner™ roller blades

Blades, Ruben

Blaeu, Willem Janszoon

Blagoveschensk

Blaine, James G.

Blaine, Vivian

Blair

Blair, Betsy

Blair, Bonnie

Blair, Henry

Blair, Janet

Blair, Linda

Blair Junior College

Blairsville

Blaise or Blaize, Saint

Blake

Blake, Amanda

Blake, Eubie

Blake, Nicholas

Blake, Robert

Blake, William

Blakelock, Ralph Albert

Blakely

Blakely, Susan

Blakely Features Syndicate

Blakeney, Sir Percy

Blam

Blanc, Jean Joseph

Blanc, Louis

Blanc, Mel

Blanca Peak

Blanchard, Doc

Blanchard, Jack

Bland, Bobby

Blanda, George

Bland-Allison Act

Blanding, Sarah G.

Blanton, Billy

Blanton, Jimmy

Blanton's Junior College

Blarney

Blarney Castle

Blarney stone

Blasco Ibáñez, Vincente

Blashfield, Edwin Holland

Blasket Islands

Blass, Bill

Blau, Joseph Leon

Blaustein, Morton K.

Blavatsky, Helena Petrovna

Bleak House

Bledsoe, Jules

Bledsoe, Tempestt

Blegen, Judith

Blenheim

Blenheim Park

Blenheim spaniel

Blennerhassett, Harman

Blennerhassett Island

Blériot, Louis

Blessed Damozel, The

Blessed Sacrament

Blessed Trinity

Blessed Virgin

Blessed Virgin Mary

Blessing-Riemon College of Nursing

Bleuler, Eugen

Bligh, William

Blinded American Veterans Foundation

Blinded Veterans Association

Blind Faith

Blind Leading the Blind, The

Blind River

Blind Service Association

Blinn College

Bliss, Sir Arthur

Bliss, Tasker Howard

Blitzen

Blitzstein, Marc

Bloch, Ernest [American composer]

Bloch, Ernst [German philosopher]

Bloch, Felix

Bloch, Konrad E.

Bloch, Ray

Blockbuster Entertainment Corporation

Block Drug Company, Inc.

Blocker, Dan

Blocker, Dirk

Block Island

Block Island Sound

Bloemfontein

Blok, Alexandr Aleksandrovich

Blomstedt, Herbert

Blondel, François

Blondel, Jacques François

Blondell, Gloria

Blondell, Joan

Blondie

Blood, Thomas

Blood Indian

Blood of Jesus, The

Bloods

Blood, Sweat and Tears [musical group]

"Blood, toil, tears and sweat" [Churchill's remark]

Blood Wedding

Bloody Maria

Bloody Mary [nickname for Mary I]

Bloody Mary, n., pl. Bloody Marys [cocktail]

Bloom, Allan

Bloom, Claire

Bloom, Hyman

Bloom County

Bloomer, Amelia Jenks

Bloomfield

Bloomfield, Leonard

Bloomfield College

Bloomfieldian

Bloomingdale

Bloomingdale's department store

Bloomingdale's, Inc.

Bloomington

Bloomsburg

Bloomsburg University of Pennsylvania

Bloomsbury

Bloomsbury Group

Bloomsbury Square

Blore, Eric

Blossom

Blount, Roy, Jr.

Blount Foundation, Inc.

Blount Inc.

Blowin' in the Wind

Blücher, Gebhard Leberecht von

Blue, Ben

Blue, Bobby

Blue, Vida

Blue Angels, The

Blue Angels Association

Blue Ash

Bluebeard

Blue Boy, The

Blue Cross

Blue Cross and Blue Shield Association

Blue Cross™ insurance

Blue Danube, The

Blue Diamond Growers

blue-eyed Mary

Bluefield

Bluefield College

Bluefield State College

Bluegrass music

Bluegrass Region or region

Blue Ice™

Blue Island

Blue Key

Blue Mesa Dam

Blue Mesa Reservoir

blue Monday

Blue Mountain

Blue Mountain College

Blue Mountain Community College

Blue Mountains

Blue Nile

Blue Ridge

Blue Ridge Community College

Blue Ridge Dam

Blue Ridge Mountains

Blue Ridge Parkway

Blue Shield

Blue Shield™ insurance

Bluestone Scenic River National Parkway

Blue Veil

Bluffton

Bluffton College

Bluhm, Neil Gary

Blum, Léon

Blume, Judy

Blume, Peter

Bly, Nellie

Bly, Robert

Blyth, Ann

Blythe

Blythe, David Gilmour

Blytheville

Blytheville Air Force Base

BMC Software Inc.

BMW of North America, Inc.

B'nai B'rith

B'nai B'rith Hillel Foundations

B'nai B'rith
  International
B'nai B'rith Women
Boabdil
Boadicea
Board of Foreign
  Scholarships
Boas, Franz
Boating Party
  Luncheon, The
Boatmen's
  Bancshares, Inc.
Boatmen's National
  Bank
Boat Owners
  Association of the
  United States
Bob and Ray Show,
  The
Bobbin and Joan
Bobbsey Twins
Bobby Blue Band
Bobby Vinton
  International Fan
  Club
Bob Considine Show,
  The
Bob Crosby's Bobcats
Bob Crosby Show,
  The
Bob Evans Farms, Inc.
Bob Hope Show, The
Bob Jones University
Bob Newhart Show,
  The
Bob Wills and the
  Texas Playboys
Boca Raton
Boccaccino,
  Boccaccio
Boccaccio, Giovanni
Boccherini, Luigi

Bocciono, Umberto
BOC Group, The
BOC Group Inc., The
Bochco, Steven
Bock, Jerry
Böcklin, Arnold
Bodanzky, Artur
Bode, Johann Elert
Bode Museum
Bodenheim, Maxwell
Bode's law
Bodhisattva
Bodleian Library
Bodley, George
  Frederick
Bodley, Sir Thomas
Bodö
Bodoni
Bodoni, Giambattista
Body Count
body English
Body of Christ
Boehm, Sydney
Boehm, Theobald
Boehmenism
Boehmenist
Boehm system
Boeing, William E.
Boeing Company, The
Boeing Company
  Charitable Trust
Boer
Boer War
Boesky, Ivan F.
Boethian
Boethius
Boethius, Anicius
  Manlius Severinus
Bofors gun

Bogalusa
Bogan, Louise
Bogarde, Dirk
Bogart, Humphrey
Bogart, Paul
Bogdanovich, Peter
Boggs, Wade
Bogguss, Suzy
Bogomil occas.
  Bogomile
Bogomilian
Bogotá [* Colombia]
Bogota [* NJ]
Bogotá El Dorado
  Airport
Bohemia
Bohemian
Bohemian Brethren
Bohemian Forest
Bohemian literature
Bohemian ruby
Bohemian waxwing
Bohlen, Charles
Böhm, Dominikus
Böhm, Jakob
Böhm, Karl
Böhme, Jakob
Bohol
Bohol Strait
Bohr, Aage Niels
Bohr, Christian
Bohr, Niels
Bohr atom
Bohr effect
Bohr magneton
Bohr theory
Boiardo, Matteo Maria
Boieldieu, François
  Adrien

Boileau-Despréaux, Nicholas

Bois de Boulogne

Boise

Boise Air Terminal

Boise Bible College

Boise Cascade Corporation

Boise City

Boise National Forest

Boise Peace Quilt Project

Boise project

Boise State University

Boise State University Broncos

Boitano, Brian

Boito, Arrigo

Bojangles

Bojer, Johan

Bok, Derek

Bok, Edward

Bokhara clover

Bokmål

Bok Singing Tower

Boland, Edward P.

Boland, Mary

Boland Amendment

Bolan Pass

Bold and Beautiful, The

Bolden, Buddy

Boldini, Giovanni

Boléro

Boles, John

Boleyn, Anne

Bolger, Ray

Bolingbroke

Bolingbroke, Henry [Shakespeare's Henry IV]

Bolingbroke, Henry Saint John [English essayist]

Bolivar

Bolívar, Simón

Bolivia

Bolivian

Böll, Heinrich

Bolland, Jean

Bollandist

Bolla Wine

Bolling Air Force Base

Bologna

Bolognese, *n.*, *pl.* Bolognese

Bolsa de Madrid

Bolshevik, *n.*, *pl.* Bolsheviks *occas.* Bolsheviki

Bolshevik Revolution

Bolshevism

Bolshevist

Bolshevistic

Bolshoi *or* Bolshoy Ballet

Bolshoi *or* Bolshoy Opera

Bolshoi *or* Bolshoy Theatre

Bolton

Bolton, Herbert Eugene

Bolton, Michael

Boltzmann, Ludwig

Boltzmann *occas.* Boltzmann's constant

Boltzmann distribution

Bolzano, Bernhard

Bolzano-Weierstrasse theorem

Bombardier Inc.

Bombay

Bombay Airport

Bombay duck

Bombay Sensitive Index

Bombeck, Erma

Bomu

Bonaire

Bonanno, Joseph

Bonanza

Bonanza Creek

Bonanza Peak

Bonaparte, Jérôme

Bonaparte, Joseph

Bonaparte, Louis

Bonaparte, Louis Napoléon

Bonaparte, Lucien

Bonaparte, Napoleon

Bonapartism

Bonapartist

Bon Appétit

Bonaventura, Saint

Bonaventure Island

Bonavista Bay

Bond, Carrie Jacobs

Bond, James

Bond, Julian

Bond, Ward

Bond Corporation Holdings Ltd.

Bondi, Beulah

Bonds, Barry

Bonds, Bobby

Bonds, Gary U. S.

Bond Street

B-1B Lancer

B-111

Bonerz, Peter

Bonet, Lisa

Bonham

Bonham-Carter, Helena

Bonheur, Rosa

Bonhomme Richard

Boniface

Boniface, Saint

Boniface I, Saint

Boniface IV, Saint

Bonington, Richard Parks

Bonin Islands

Bon Jovi

Bon Jovi, Jon

Bon Marché, The

Bonn

Bonnard, Pierre

Bonnaz *occas.* bonnaz embroidery

Bonners Ferry

Bonneville Dam

Bonneville Flats

Bonneville National Speed Trials

Bonneville Raceway

Bonneville Salt Flats

Bonneville Salt Flats International Speedway

Bonney, William H.

Bonnie and Clyde

Bonnie Prince Charlie

Bono, Sonny

Bononcini, Giovanni Battista

Bononcini, Giovanni Maria

Bononcini, Marc Antonio

Bontecu, Lee

Bontempelli, Massimo

Bonus March

Bonus Marcher

Bonwit Teller and Company

Boogie Down Productions

Book Beat

Book Bin

Book Case

Book Cellar

Book Corner, The

Book Dealers World

Booke, Sorrell

Book Emporium

Book End, The

Bookends

Booker T. and the MGs

Booker T. Washington Foundation

Booker T. Washington National Monument

Bookery, The

Book Exchange

Book Gallery, The

Bookhaven

Book House

Bookland

Booklist

Book Mark

Book Market, The

Book Nook, The

Book of Amos

Book of Books

Book of Changes

Book of Common Prayer

Book of Concord

Book of Daniel

Book of Esther

Book of Ezekiel

Book of Ezra

Book of Genesis

Book of Habakkuk

Book of Haggai

Book of Hosea

book of hours *occas.* Book of Hours

Book of Isaiah

Book of Jeremiah

Book of Job

Book of Joel

Book of Jonah

Book of Judges

Book of Judith

Book of Kells

Book of Malachi

Book of Micha

Book of Mormon

Book of Nahum

Book of Nehemiah

Book of Numbers

Book of Obadiah

Book of Odes

Book of Proverbs

Book of Psalms

Book of Revelation

Book of Ruth

Book of Samuel

Book of the Dead

Book of the Duchess

Book-of-the-Month Club, Inc.

Book of Zechariah
Book of Zephaniah
Book Rack, The
Books-a-Million
Book Seller, The
Books Etc.
Book Shelf
Bookshop, The
Books Inc.
Books In Print
Booksmith, The
Books 'N Things
Books of Chronicles
Books of Kings
Book Stall, The
Bookstar
Book Stop
Bookstore, The
Books Unlimited
Book Trader, The
Book Warehouse
Bookworld
Bookworm, The
Boole, George
Boolean algebra
Boolean ring
Boolean sum
Boole's inequality
Boomer State
Boone
Boone, Daniel
Boone, Debby
Boone, Pat
Boone, Richard
Boonesboro
Booneville
Boonton
Boop, Betty
Boorstin, Daniel J.

Boosler, Elayne
Boötes
Booth, Ballington
Booth, Edwin
Booth, Evangeline Cory
Booth, John Wilkes
Booth, Junius Brutus
Booth, Shirley
Booth, Tony
Booth, William
Boothe, Powers
Boothia Peninsula
Boot Hill
Bootlace Worm
Booz, Allen and Hamilton Inc.
Bophuthatswana
Bora-Bora or Borabora
Borah, William E.
Borah Peak
Bordeaux
Bordeaux mixture
Bordeaux [wine], n, pl. Bordeaux
Bordelais [region]
Bordelaise [sauce]
Borden, Gail
Borden, Lizzie
Borden Foundation
Borden, Inc.
Bordentown
Border collie
Borders Book Shop
Border States
Border terrier
Bordone, Paris
Bordoni, Irene

Borel, Émile
Borel-Lebesgue theorem
Borg, Bjorn
Borg, Malcolm Austin
Borge, Victor
Borger
Borges, Jorge Luis
Borghese
Borghese Gallery
Borghese Palace
Borghese Villa
Borgia, Cesare
Borgia, Lucrezia
Borglum, Gutzon
Borglum, Solon Hannibal
Borgnine, Ernest
Borg-Warner Corporation
Borg-Warner Foundation
Bori, Lucrezia
Boricua College
Boris
Boris Godunov
Borja Cevallos, Rodrigo
Borland International, Inc.
Borland™ software
Borman, Frank
Bormann, Martin
Born, Max
born-again Christian
Bornean
Borneo
Bornholm
Bornholm disease
Born Loser, The

Born on the Fourth of July

Born Yesterday

Borobudur

Borodin, Alexander *or* Alexandr

Borodino

Boron

Boros, Julius

borough English

Borromeo College of Ohio

Borromini, Francesco

Borrovian

Borrow, George

Bors, Sir

Borscht Belt, the

Borstal

Borstal Boy

Borstal Prison

Borstal system

Bosch, Hieronymus

Bosch, Juan

Bosco, Philip

Bosc pear

Bose, Sir Jadagis Chandra

Bose, Satyendra Nath

Bose, Subhas Chandra

Bose-Einstein statistics

Bösendorfer, Ignaz

Bösendorfer™ piano

Boskop skull

Bosley, Tom

Bosnia-Herzegovina [*form.* Bosnia-Hercegovina]

Bosnian

Bosom Buddies

Bosporan

Bosporian

Bosporus

Bossier City

Bossier Parish Community College

Bosson, Barbara

Bossuet, Jacques Bénigne

Bossy, Mike

Bostic, Earl

Boston

Boston Academy of Music

Boston African-American National Historic Site

Boston Architectural Center

Boston Army Base

Boston Athenaeum

Boston bag

Boston baked beans

Boston Ballet Company

Boston Bay

Boston Blackie

Boston Brahmin

Boston brown bread

Boston Bruins

Boston bull

Boston Business Journal

Boston Camerata

Boston Celtics

Boston College

Boston College Eagles

Boston Common

Boston Conservatory

Boston Conservatory of Music

Boston cream pie

Boston Edison Company

Boston Edison Foundation

Boston fern

Boston Festival Orchestra

Boston Five Cents Savings Bank

Boston Flamenco Ballet

Boston Garden

Boston General Edward Lawrence Logan International Airport

Boston Globe, The

Boston Globe Foundation

Boston Globe Magazine

Boston Harbor

Boston Herald

Boston hip

Boston hooker

Bostonia

Bostonian

Bostonians, The [novel]

Bostonian Society

Boston ivy

Boston Latin School

Boston lettuce

Boston Magazine

Boston Marathon

Boston Massacre

Boston Mountains

[Boston] Museum of Fine Arts

Boston National Historical Park

Boston Phoenix, The

Boston Pops Orchestra

Boston Red Sox

Boston Review

Boston ridge

Boston rocker

Boston Safe Deposit and Trust Company

Boston Stock Exchange, Inc.

Boston Strangler

Boston Symphony Orchestra

Boston Tea Party

Boston terrier

Boston Theological Institute

Boston University

Boston University Law Review

Boston University Observatory

Boston University Terriers

Bostwick, Barry

Boswell, James

Boswellian

Bosworth, Brian

Bosworth Field

Botanical Society of America

Botany Bay

Botany 500™

Botany wool

Botha, Louis

Botha, Pieter W.

Bothnian

Botkin, Benjamin Albert

Botstein, Leon

Botswana [*form.* Bechuanaland]

Botticelli, Sandro

Bottomley, Jim

Bottoms, Joseph

Bottoms, Sam

Bottoms, Timothy

Bottrop

Botvinik, Mikhail

Bouchard, Henri

Bouché, Louis

Boucher, François

Boucher, Hart

Boucher de Crèvecoeur de Perthes, Jacques

Bouches-du-Rhone

Bouchet, Edward

Boucicault *or* Bourcicault, Dion

Boudiaf, Mohammed

Boudreau, Lou

Bougainville

Bougainville, Louis Antoine de

Bougainville Strait

Bouguereau, Adolphe William

Boulanger, Georges Ernest

Boulanger, Nadia

Boulangism

Boulangist

Boulder

Boulder Canyon

Boulder City

Boulder Dam [*now* Hoover Dam]

Boulevard Montmartre

Boulez, Pierre

Boulogne

Boult, Sir Adrian

Boumedienne, Houari

Boundary Peak

Bound Brook

Bound East for Cardiff

Bountiful

Bourbaki, Nicolas

Bourbon, Charles

Bourbonism

Bourbonist

Bourbon royal family

Bourbon Street

Bourcicault *var. of* Boucicault, Dion

Bourdon, Eugène

Bourdon tube

Bourdon-tube gauge

Bourget, Paul

Bourguiba, Habib

Bourke-White, Margaret

Bourne

Bournemouth

Bournemouth International Airport

Bourse de Bruxelles

Bouton, Jim

Boutros-Ghali, Boutros

Bouvier des Flandres, *n., pl.* Bouviers des Flandres

Bovary, Emma

Bovet, Daniel

Bow

Bow, Clara

Bowater Inc.
Bow bells
Bowditch, Nathaniel
Bowdler, Thomas
Bowdoin, James
Bowdoin College
Bowen, Catherine
   Drinker
Bowen, Elizabeth
Bowen, John T.
Bowens disease
Bowers, Claude
   Gernard
Bowers v. Hardwick
Bowery, the
Bowery Boys, The
Bowes, Major
Bowie
Bowie, David
Bowie, James
Bowie, William
Bowie State
Bowie State
   University
Bowlers Journal
Bowles, Chester
Bowles, Paul
Bowles, Samuel
Bowling Digest
Bowling Green
Bowling Green State
   University
Bowling Green State
   University Falcons
Bowling Green State
   University Firelands
   College
Bowling Green State
   University Popular
   Press
Bowling Magazine

Bowling Proprietors'
   Association of
   America
Bowman, Christopher
Bowman, Sir William
Bowman's capsule
Bow Street
Box Car Willie
Boxer, Barbara
Boxer Rebellion
Boxer Uprising
Boxing Day
Boxleitner, Bruce
Boyd, Belle
Boyd, Louise
Boyd, Stephen
Boyd, William
Boyer, Charles
Boy George
Boyle, Kay
Boyle, Peter
Boyle, Robert
Boyle's law
Boylton, Michael
Boymans-Van
   Beunigen Museum
Boyne
Boynton, Sandra
Boynton Beach
Boys' and Girls'
   Brigades of
   America
Boys and Girls Clubs
   of America
Boys' Brigade
Boys Clubs of
   America
Boy Scout
Boy Scouts of
   America

Boys' Life
Boys State
Boys Town
Boyz N the Hood
Boyz II Men
Bozcaada Island
Bozeman
Bozeman, John M.
Bozeman Pass
Bozeman Trail
Boz Scaggs
Bozzaris, Marco
BP America
B power supply
BP Prudhoe Bay
   Royalty Trust
Brabant
Brabant Copper™
Brabantine
Bracco, Lorraine
Brachiopoda
Bracken, Eddie
Brackenridge
Brackett series
Bradbury, Ray
Braddock
Braddock, Edward
Braddock, James J.
Bradenton
Bradenton South
Bradey Center
Bradford
Bradford, Barbara
   Taylor
Bradford, Gamaliel
Bradford, Roark
Bradford, William
Bradford College

Bradford Exchange, The

Bradford spinning

Bradford system

Bradlee, Ben

Bradlees Bookstore

Bradley

Bradley, Bill

Bradley, Ed

Bradley, Francis H.

Bradley, Milton

Bradley, Omar N.

Bradley, Tom

Bradley, Truman

Bradley Beach

Bradley Center, The

Bradley University

Bradley University Braves

Bradshaw, Terry

Bradstreet, Anne

Bradstreet, Simon

Brady

Brady, Alice

Brady, Diamond Jim

Brady, Mathew B.

Brady, Nicholas

Brady, Scott

Brady, William A.

Brady Bunch, The

Brady Handgun Violence Prevention Act

Braeden, Eric

Braga, Sonia

Bragdon, Claude

Bragg, Braxton

Bragg, Sir William Henry

Bragg, Sir William Lawrence

Bragg angle

Bragg's law

Brahe, Tycho

Brahma

Brahman [cattle; see also Brahmin]

Brahman, n., pl. Brahmans [priestly Hindu; see also Brahmin]

Brahmani occas. Brahmanee

Brahmanism

Brahmanist

Brahmaputra

Brahmi

Brahmin, n., pl. Brahmin or Brahmins [aristocrat; see also Brahman]

Brahminism

Brahminist

Brahms, Johannes

Brahmsian

Brahmsite

Braille, Louis

Braille Institute

braillewriter occas. Braillewriter

Braillist

Brailowsky, Alexander

Brainerd

Brainerd Community College

Braintree

Brain Trust occas. brain trust

Bramah, Joseph

Bramante, Donato

Bramantino

Branagh, Kenneth

Branch Davidian

Brancusi, Constantin

Brand, Max

Brand, Neville

Brand, Stewart

Brandeis, Louis

Brandeis University

Brandenburg

Brandenburg Concertos

Brandenburger

Brandenburg Gate

Brandes, Georg Morris

Brandi

Brando, Jocelyn

Brando, Marlon

Brandon

Brandon University

Brandt, Willy

Brandy, n., pl. Brandys [given name]

brandy Alexander

Brandy Station

Brandywine

Brandywine College of Widener University

Brandywine Creek

Branestawm, Professor

Branford [* CT; see also Brantford]

Brangus, n., pl. Branguses

Braniff, Inc.

Brannan, Sam

Branson

Brant, Joseph

Brantford [* Ontario; see also Branford]

Branting, Karl Hjalmar

Braque, Georges

Bras d'Or Lake

Brasher's doubloon

Brasília

Brasília International Airport

Brasselle, Keefe

Brasstown Bald

Bratislava

Brattain, Walter

Brattleboro

Braudel, Ferdinand Paul

Brauhaus

Braun, Carol Mosely

Braun, Eva

Braun, Karl Ferdinand

Braun, Wernher von

Braunschweiger *often* braunschweiger

Brautigan, Richard

Brave New World

Braver, Rita

Bravo

Brawley

Braxton, Anthony

Braxton Hicks' contractions

Brazil

Brazil Current

Brazilian

Brazilian chrysolite

Brazilian emerald

Brazilian guava

Brazilian literature

Brazilian morning glory

Brazilian pepper tree

Brazilian peridot

Brazilian rhatany

Brazilian rosewood

Brazilian ruby

Brazilian sapphire

Brazil nut

Brazos

Brazosport College

Brazzaville

Brazzaville Maya-Maya Airport

Brazzi, Rossano

Brea

Bread and Chocolate

Bread for the World

Bread Loaf Writers Conference

Breakfast Club, The

Break the Bank

Bream, Julian

Breasted, James

Breathalyzer™

Breathed, Berke

Breaux Bridge

Brecht, Bertolt

Breckenridge

Breckinridge, John

Breckinridge, John Cabell

Breckinridge, Sophonisba Preston

Breckinridge Hills

Brecksville

Breda

Breeches Bible, The

Breeders' Cup

Breeders' Cup Classic

Breedlove, Craig

Breed's Hill

Breen, Bobby

Breeze, The

Bregenz

Bregman, Tracey E.

Brel, Jacques

Bremen

Bremen Art Gallery

Bremerhaven

Bremerton

Bren, Donald Leroy

Brenau College

Brenda

Brendan, Saint

Brendel, Alfred

Bren, *occas.* bren gun

Brenham

Brennan, Bernard F.

Brennan, Eileen

Brennan, Walter

Brennan, William J.

Brenner, David

Brenner Pass

Brennus

Brent

Brent, George

Brentano's Bookstore

Brentwood

Brera Picture Gallery

Brereton, Lewis H.

Brer *or* Br'er Fox

Brer *or* Br'er Rabbit

Brer Rabbit™ molasses

Brescia

Brescia College

Breshkovsky, Catherine

Breslau

Breslin, Jimmy

Bresnahan, Roger

Brest

Brest-Litovsk

Brethren Church

Brethren in Christ

Brethren in Christ Church

Brethren of the Common Life

Breton

Breton, André

Breton, Jules Adolphe

Breton lace

Breton literature

Brett

Brett, George

Brett, Jeremy

Bretton Woods

Bretton Woods Conference

Breuer, Josef

Breuer, Marcel

Breuer chair

Brevard

Brevard College

Brevard Community College

Breviary of Alaric

Brewer, Ebenezer Cobham

Brewer, Teresa

Brewer, Thomas M.

Brewers' Association of America

Brewer's blackbird

Brewer's Dictionary of Phrase and Fable

Brewer's Dictionary of 20th-Century Phrase and Fable

Brewer's mole

Brewer State Junior College

Brewster, Sir David

Brewster, Kingman, Jr.

Brewster, William

Brewster angle

Brewster chair

Brewster's law

Brewton

Brewton-Parker College

Breyers™ ice cream [*see also* Dreyer's]

Brezhnev, Leonid I.

Brezhnev Doctrine

Brian

Brian Boru

Briand, Aristide

Briar Cliff College

Briarcliffe School, Inc., The

Briarcliff Manor

Briard

Briarwood College

Brice, Fanny

Brice's Cross Roads

Brices Cross Roads National Battlefield Site

Bridalveil Fall *occas.* Falls [Yosemite attraction]

Bride's

Bridge of San Luis Rey, The

Bridge of Sighs

Bridge on the River Kwai, The

Bridge over Troubled Waters

Bridgeport

Bridgeport Dam

Bridgeport Engineering Institute

Bridger, Jim

Bridger's Pass

Bridger-Teton National Forest

Bridges, Beau

Bridges, Calvin Blackman

Bridges, Harry

Bridges, Jeff

Bridges, Lloyd

Bridges, Robert

Bridges, Todd

Bridgestone Corporation

Bridgestone/Firestone, Inc.

Bridgestone Museum of Art

Bridgestone Tire Company Ltd.

Bridget *or* Brigid *or* Birgit *or* Birgitta, Saint

Bridget of Sweden, Saint

Bridgeton [* MO; NJ]

Bridgetown [* Barbados; Nova Scotia]

Bridge View

Bridgeville

Bridgewater

Bridgewater College

Bridgewater Madonna, The

Bridgewater State College

Bridge World

Bridgman, Frederic Arthur

Bridgman, Percy Williams

Brie

Brie cheese

Brielle

Brieux, Eugène

Brigadoon

Brigantine

Briggs, Clare

Briggs, Henry

Briggs, Joe Bob

Briggs and Stratton Corporation

Briggs and Stratton Corporation Foundation

Briggsian logarithm

Brigham

Brigham City

Brigham Street Inn

Brigham Young University

Brigham Young University Cougars

Bright, John

Bright, Richard

Brighter Day, The

Brighton

Brighton Beach Memoirs

Bright's disease

Brigit

Brigit of Ireland, Saint

Brigit of Kildare, Saint

Brigitte

Brill, A. A.

Brillat-Savarin, Anthelme

Brill's disease *occas.* Brill-Zinsser disease

Brimley, Wilford

Brimmer, Andrew F.

Brindisi

Brinell, Johann A.

Brinell hardness

Brinell hardness number

Brinell machine

Brinell number

Brinell test

Brinell tester

Bringing up Baby

Brinker International, Inc. [*form.* Chili's Inc.]

Brinkley, David

Brink's armored car

Brink's Home Security

Brink's Incorporated

Brinton, Crane

Brisbane

Brisebois, Danielle

Bristol

Bristol Art Gallery

Bristol Bay

Bristol board

Bristol Channel

Bristol Community College

Bristol fashion

Bristol International Raceway

Bristol-Myers Company

Bristol-Myers Fund

Bristol-Myers Squibb Company

Bristol University

Brit

Britain

Britannia

Britannia metal

Britannic

Brith Milah

Briticism

British

British Acadaemy

British Aerospace

British Aerospace, Inc.

British Airways

British Antarctic Territory

British Broadcasting Corporation

British Coal Corporation

British Columbia

British Columbia Railway Company

British Commonwealth of Nations [*now* Commonwealth]

British East India Company

British Empire

British English

Britisher

British Expeditionary Forces

British gallon

British Gas

British Guiana [*now* Guyana]

British gum

British Honduras [*now* Belize]

British Imperial State Crown

British India

British Indian Ocean Territory

British Isles

Britishism

British Legion

British Museum, The

Britishness

British North America Act

British Open

British Petroleum Company, The

British Sky Broadcasting

British Solomon Islands

British Somaliland

British Steel

British Tele-communications

British thermal unit

British Virgin Islands

British warm

British West Indies

British Windward Islands

Briton

BritRail Pass

Britt, Mai

Brittany

Brittany, Morgan

Brittany spaniel

Britten, Benjamin

Brittingham, Jack

Brittingham, Robert

Brittney

Britton, Barbara

Brix, Alfred F.

Brix scale

Brno

Broad, Charlie

Broad, Eli

Broadcasting

Broadcast Music, Inc.

Broadcast News Service

Broad Church

Broad Churchman

Broadview

Broadview Heights

Broadway

Broadway Boogie-Woogie

Broadwayite

Broadway Melody

Broadway Melody of [year]

Broadway show

Broadway theater, a

Broadway Theater, the

Brobdingnag

Brobdingnagian

Broca, Paul P.

Broca's area

Broca's convolution

Broca's gyrus

Brock, Lou

Brock, Sir Thomas

Brocken

Brockport

Brockton

Brock University

Brocot, Achille

Brocot escapement

Brocot suspension

Broder, David

Broderbund Software

Broderick

Broderick, Helen

Broderick, John

Broderick, Matthew

Brodie, Steve

Brodsky, Joseph

Brody, Jane

Brody, Lane

Broglie, Achille Charles Léonce Victor

Broglie, Jacques Victor Albert

Broglie, Louis de

Broglie, Maurice

Brokaw, Tom

Broken Arrow

Broken Bow

Broken Commandment, The

Broken Hill

Broken Hill Proprietary Company Ltd., The

Brolin, James

Bromberg, J. Edward

Bromfield, Louis

Brompton

Brompton cocktail

Brompton mixture

Brompton stock

Bronco Billy

Bronfman, Edgar Miles, Sr.

Bronson, Charles

Brontë, Anne

Brontë, Charlotte

Brontë, Emily Jane

Bronx, the

Bronx cheer

Bronxville

Bronx Zoo

Bronze Age

Bronze Star Medal

Bronzino, Agnolo

Brook, Alexander

Brookdale Community College

Brooke

Brooke, Edward William

Brooke, Sir James

Brooke, Rupert

Brooke Army Medical Center

Brooke Group Ltd.

Brook Farm

Brookfield

Brookfield Zoo

Brookhaven

Brookhaven College

Brookhaven National Laboratory

Brookings

Brookings, Robert Somers

Brookings Institution

Brooklawn

Brookline

Brooklyn

Brooklyn Academy of Music

Brooklyn Bridge

Brooklyn Center

Brooklyn Coast Guard Air Station

Brooklyn College

Brooklyn College Kingsmen

Brooklyn Dodgers

Brooklynese

Brooklyn Heights

Brooklyn Institute of Arts and Sciences

Brooklynite

Brooklyn Law School

Brooklyn-Manhattan Transit Company

Brooklyn Park

Brooklyn Union Gas Company, The

Brook Park

Brooks, Albert

Brooks, Avery

Brooks, Foster

Brooks, Garth

Brooks, Gwendolyn

Brooks, James L.

Brooks, Mel

Brooks, Phillips

Brooks, Stephen

Brooks, Van Wyck

Brooks Air Force Base

Brooks Brothers

Brooks College

Brookshier, Tom

Brooks Institute

Brooks Range

Brooksville [* FL; KY]

Brookville [* IN; NY; OH; PA]

Broome Community College

Broom Hilda

Broonzy, Big Bill

Brosnan, Pierce

Brotherhood of Locomotive Firemen and Enginemen

Brotherhood of Maintenance of Way Employees

Brotherhood of Railroad Signalmen

Brotherhood of Railway Carmen Division/Transportation Communications Union

Brotherhood of Shoe and Allied Craftsmen

Brother Industries, Ltd.

Brother International Corporation

Brother Jonathan

Brothers

Brothers, Joyce

Brothers Grimm

Brothers Johnson

Brothers Karamazov, The

Brothers of the Christian Schools

Brothers of the Coast

Brothers of the Immaculate Conception of the

Blessed Virgin Mary

Broun, Heywood

Brouthers, Dan

Brouwer, Adriaen

Brouwer, Luitzen Egbertus Jan

Brouwer fixed-point theorem

Broward Community College

Browder, Earl

Brower, David

Brown, Blair

Brown, Bobby

Brown, Bryan

Brown, Charles Brockden

Brown, Charlie

Brown, Clifford

Brown, Dennis

Brown, Edmund G. "Pat"

Brown, Edmund G., Jr. "Jerry"

Brown, Father

Brown, Harold

Brown, Helen Gurley

Brown, Herbert Charles

Brown, H. Rap

Brown, Iona

Brown, Jack E.

Brown, James [musician]

Brown, James L. [actor]

Brown, Jim

Brown, Joe E.

Brown, John

Brown, Kathleen

Brown, Les

Brown, Mordecai

Brown, Murphy

Brown, Nacio Herb

Brown, Owsley, II

Brown, Paul

Brown, Peter

Brown, Ray

Brown, Robert

Brown, Sawyer

Brown, Sterling A.

Brown, T. Graham

Brown, Unsinkable Molly

Brown, Vanessa

Brown, William Lee Lyons, Jr.

Brown, William Wells

Brown, Willie

Brown and Williamson Tobacco Corporation

brown Betty

Brown Deer

Brown Derby, The

Browne, Charles Farrar

Browne, Dik

Browne, Jackson

Browne, Roscoe Lee

Browne, Sir Samuel

Browne, Sir Thomas

brown-eyed Susan

Brownfield Network

Brown-Forman Corporation

Brown Group Inc.

Brown Group Inc. Charitable Trust

Brownian motion

Brownian movement

Brownie, *n.*, *pl.* Brownies [Girl Scout]

Brownie Girl Scouts

Brownie *occas*, brownie point

Browning, Elizabeth Barrett

Browning, John M.

Browning, Kurt

Browning, Robert

Browning automatic rifle

Browning-Ferris Industries, Inc.

Browning machine gun

Brownlee Dam

Brownlee Park

Brownlee Reservoir

Brown Lung Association

Brown Mackie College, The

Brown Palace

Brownsburg

Brown Shirt *occas.* brown shirt

Brownsville

Brown Swiss

Brown University

Brown University Bears

Brown University Bruins

Brown v. Board of Education of Topeka

Brownwood

Broz, Josip

BRS Information
Technologies

Brubeck, Dave

Bruce

Bruce, Ed

Bruce, Lenny

Bruce, Nigel

Bruce, Robert the

Bruce, Stanley
Melbourne

Bruce, Virginia

Bruch, Max

Bruckner, Anton

Brueghel *or* Bruegel
or Breughel, Jan the
Elder

Brueghel *or* Bruegel
or Breughel, Pieter
the Elder

Brueghel *or* Bruegel
or Breughel, Pieter
the Younger

Bruges

[Bruges] Municipal
Fine Arts Museum

Brumaire

Brummell, Beau

Brundtland, Gro
Harlem

Brunehilde *var. of*
Brunhilde

Brunei Darussalam

Brunei International
Airport

Brunelleschi *or*
Brunellesco, Filippo

Brunetière, Ferdinand

Brunhild [queen in
Germanic legend]

Brunhilde *or*
Brunehilde [queen
of the Franks]

Brunhoff, Jean de

Brunner, Emil

Bruno, Giordano

Bruno I, Saint

Bruno of Cologne,
Saint

Bruno's, Inc.

Brunswick

Brunswick College

Brunswick
Community College

Brunswick
Corporation

Brunswick Foundation

Brunswick Naval Air
Station

Brunswick stew

Brush, Katherine

Brussels

[Brussels] Ancient Art
Museum

Brussels carpet

Brussels griffon

Brussels International
Airport

Brussels lace

[Brussels] Modern Art
Museum

brussels *occas.*
Brussels sprouts

Brustein, Robert

Brutus, Decimus
Junius

Brutus, Marcus Junius

Bryan

Bryan, William
Jennings

Bryan-Chamarro
Treaty

Bryant, Anita

Bryant, Paul "Bear"

Bryant, William
Cullen

Bryant and Stratton
Business Institute

Bryant College

Bryaxis

Bryce, James

Bryce Canyon
National Park

Bryggman, Larry

Bryn Mawr

Bryn Mawr College

Brynner, Yul

Bryophyta

Bryson, Peabo

Brython

Brythonic

Brzezinski, Zbigniew

B-17 Flying Fortress

B-66 Destroyer

BSN Groupe

B supply

B-36

B-25 Mitchell

B-24 Liberator

B-29 Superfortress

B-26 Invader

B-26 Marauder

B-2 stealth bomber

Bubba

Buber, Martin

Bucaramanga

Bucephalus

Buchan, John

Buchanan, Buck

Buchanan, Edgar

Buchanan, Jack

Buchanan, James

Buchanan, Pat

Bucharest

Bucharest Baneasa
Airport

Bucharest Otopani
Airport

Buchenwald

Buchholz, Horst

Buchman, Frank N. D.

Buchmanism

Buchmanite

Buchner, Eduard

Buchwald, Art

Buck, Frank

Buck, Gene

Buck, Pearl S.

Buckaroo Banzai

Bucket, Charlie

Buckeye State

Buckhanon

Buckingham, George
Villiers

Buckingham Fountain

Buckingham Palace

Buckinghamshire

Buck Island Reef
National Monument

Buckle, Henry
Thomas

Buckley

Buckley, Betty

Buckley, William F.,
Jr.

Buckminster Fuller
Institute

Bucknell University

Bucknell University
Bison [usually no
final s]

Bucknell University
Press

Buckner, Simon
Bolivar

Buck Owens and His
Buckaroos

Buck Rogers

Bucks County
Community College

Bucyk, John

Bucyrus

Budapest

Budapest Ferihegy
Airport

[Budapest] Fine Arts
Museum

Budd, Zola

Budd-Chiari syndrome

Budd Company, The

Buddenbrooks

Buddha

Buddhahood

Buddha Purnima

Buddhism

Buddhist

Buddhist Churches of
America

Buddhist iconography

Buddhist literature

Buddhology

Buddy Basch Feature
Syndicate

Buddy Holly and the
Crickets

Buddy Holly
Memorial Society

Bud 500

Budge, Don

Budget Inn

Budget Rent A Car™

Budweiser at the Glen,
The

Budweiser Cleveland
Grand Prix

Budweiser 500

Buell, Don Carlos

Buena Park

Buenaventura

Buena Vista

Buena Vista College

Buena Vista Pictures

Buena Vista
Television

Buenos Aires

Buenos Aires Ezeiza
Airport

Buenos Aires Jorge
Newberry Airpark

[Buenos Aires]
National Museum
of Fine Arts

Buerger's disease

Buffalo

Buffalo Bayou

Buffalo Bill
[pseudonym of
William Frederick
Cody]

Buffalo Bills [sports
team]

Buffalo Bob

Buffalo Grove

Buffalo Indian

Buffalo National
River Parkway

Buffalo News, The

Buffalo Philharmonic
Orchestra

Buffalo Sabres

Buffalo Spree
Magazine

Buffalo Springfield

Buffalo Zoological
Gardens

Buffet, Warren

Buffett, Jimmy

Buffett, Susan
Thompson

Buffett, Warren
Edward

Buffon, Georges Louis
Leclerc de

Buffon's needle
problem

Buford

Bugatti, Arco Isidoro

Bugatti, Ettore

Bug River

Bugs Bunny

Bugs Bunny and
Tweety Show, The

Bugs Bunny/Road
Runner Hour, The

Bugs Bunny Show,
The

Buick, David Dunbar

Buick Motor Car
Division (General
Motors
Corporation)

Builders' Hardware
Manufacturers
Association

Building and
Construction Trades
Department—
AFL-CIO

Building Design
Journal

Building Owners and
Managers
Association
International

Bujold, Genevieve

Bujumbura

Bujumbura
International
Airport

Bukavu

Bukhara

Bukharin, Nikolai

Bukovina

Bulawayo *or*
Buluwayo

Bulfinch, Charles

Bulfinch, Thomas

Bulfinch's Mythology

Bulgakov, Mikhail

Bulganin, Nikolai A.

Bulgar

Bulgaria

Bulgarian

Bulgarian Eastern
Orthodox Church

Bulgarian languages

Bulgarian literature

Bulkeley, Morgan G.

Bull, Ole Bornemann

Bull and Bear Service
Center, Inc.

Bullard's Bar Dam

Bullard's Bar
Reservoir

Bulldog Drummond

Bulletin Syndicate

Bullitt, William C.

Bull Moose

Bull Mooser

Bullock, William

Bullock's department
store

Bullock's oriole

Bullpup missile

Bull Run

Bullwinkle Show, The

Bulova Corporation

Bülow, Bernhard von

Bülow, Claus von

Bülow, Hans

Bülow, Martha
"Sunny" von

Bultmann, Rudolf

Buluwayo *var. of*
Bulawayo

Bulwer, Sir Henry

Bulwer-Lytton,
Edward George
Earle

Bulwer-Lytton,
Edward Robert

Bumbry, Grace

Bumpers, Dale

Bumppo, Natty

Bumstead, Blondie

Bumstead, Dagwood

Buna-N™ synthetic
rubber

Buna-S™ synthetic
rubber

Buna™ synthetic
rubber

Bunche, Ralph

Bundesbahn

Bundesbank

Bundesrat

Bundestag

Bundles for Britain

Bundy, Brooke

Bundy, McGeorge

Bundy, Ted

Bunin, Ivan
Alekseyevich

Bunker, Archie

Bunker Hill

Bunker Hill
Community College

Bunkie

Bunraku
Bunsen, Robert W.
Bunsen burner
Bunshaft, Gordon
Buntline, Ned
Buñuel, Luis
Bunyan, John
Bunyan, Paul
Bunyanesque
Buono, Angelo
Buono, Victor
Burbage, James
Burbage, Richard
Burbank
Burbank, Luther
Burbank-Glendale-
  Pasadena Airport
Burchfield, Charles
Burchfield, Robert
  William
Burckhardt, Jakob
Burdick, Eugene
Burdines department
  store
Burdon, Eric
Burdos, Jerry
Bureau of Alcohol,
  Tobacco and
  Firearms
Bureau of Engraving
  and Printing
Bureau of Indian
  Affairs
Bureau of Land
  Management
Bureau of Prisons
Bureau of
  Reclamation
Bureau of the Census
Buren, Abigail Van
Burford, Tom

Burger, Warren E.
Burger King
  Corporation
Burger King
  restaurant
Burgess, Anthony
Burgess, Gelett
Burgess, Guy
Burgess, Hugh
Burgess, John William
Burgess, Smokey
Burgess, Thornton
  Waldo
Burghers of Calais,
  The
Burghoff, Gary
Burgoyne, John
Burgundian
Burgundy
Burgundy mixture
Burgundy trefoil
Burgundy *or* burgundy
  [*wine*], *n.*, *pl.*
  Burgundies *or*
  burgundies
Burial at Ornans
Burial of Count
  Orgaz, The
Buridan, Jean
Buridan's ass
Burkburnett
Burke, Billie
Burke, Delta
Burke, Edmund
Burke, Johnny
Burke, Paul
Burke's Peerage
Burkett, Jesse
Burkina Faso [*form.*
  Upper Volta]
Burkitt, Denis Parsons

Burkitt's *occas.*
  Burkitt lymphoma
Burleigh, Harry
  Thacker
Burley
Burlingame
Burlingame, Anson
Burlingame Treaty
Burlington
Burlington Coat
  Factory Warehouse
  Corporation
Burlington College
Burlington County
  College
Burlington Free Press,
  The
Burlington Holdings
  Inc.
Burlington Industries
  Foundation
Burlington Industries,
  Inc.
Burlington
  International
  Airport
Burlington Northern
  Foundation
Burlington Northern
  Inc.
Burlington Northern
  Railroad Company
Burlington Resources
  Inc.
Burma [*aka*
  Myanmar]
Burman, *n.*, *pl.*
  Burmans
Burma Road
Burma Shave sign
Burmese, *n.*, *pl.*
  Burmese
Burmese glass

Burmese jade

Burne-Jones, Sir
Edward Coley

Burnett, Carol

Burnett, Frances Eliza

Burnett, Frances
Hodgson

Burnette, Smiley

Burney, Charles

Burney, Fanny

Burnham, Daniel H.

Burnham,
Frederick R.

Burning of the Houses
of Parliament, The

Burns, David

Burns, George

Burns, Kenneth

Burns, Robert

Burns, Tommy

Burns and Allen
Show, The

Burnside, Ambrose

Burnt Norton

Burpee, David

Burpee, Washington
Atlee

Burr, Aaron

Burr, Raymond

Burrillville

Burroughs, Edgar Rice

Burroughs, John

Burroughs, William S.

Burroughs
Bibliophiles, The

Burroughs
Corporation

Burroughs Wellcome
Company

Burroughs Wellcome
Fund

Burrows, Abe

Burrud, Bill

Burstyn, Ellen

Burton, Gary

Burton, LeVar

Burton, Richard
[actor]

Burton, Sir Richard
Francis [English
explorer]

Burton, Robert

Burundi

Burundian

Bury My Heart at
Wounded Knee

Bury Saint Edmunds

Buscaglia, Leo F.

Busch, Adolphus

Busch, August, IV

Busch, August, Jr.

Busch, August, III

Busch, Fritz

Busch, Mae

Busch, Niven

Busch Gardens

Busch Gardens—The
Dark Continent

Busch Gardens—The
Old Country

Busch Stadium
[facility in Saint
Louis; see also
Bush Stadium]

Busey, Gary

Busfield, Timothy

Bush, Barbara

Bush, George

Bush, Lincoln

Bush, Neil

Bush, Vannevar

Bushido

Bushman, Francis X.

Bushmiller, Ernie

Bush Negro, n., pl.
Bush Negroes

Bushnell

Bush Stadium [facility
in Indianapolis; see
also Busch
Stadium]

Bush trainshed

Business Council

Business Council for
the United Nations

business English

Business Express, Inc.

Businessland, Inc.

Business New
Hampshire
Magazine

Business-Professional
Advertising
Association

Business Prospers

Business Radio
Network

Business Roundtable

Business Video
Communications
Company

Business Week

Business Wire

Busk-Ivanhoe Tunnel

Busoni, Ferruccio

Buster Brown collar

Butare

Butchart Gardens

Bute Island

Butenandt, Adolf

Butera, Sam

Buthelezi,
Mangosuthu Gatsha

Butkus, Dick

Butler

Butler, Benjamin Franklin

Butler, John

Butler, Nicholas Murray

Butler, Rhett

Butler, Samuel

Butler County Community College

Butler Manufacturing Company

Butler Manufacturing Company Foundation

Butler's Rangers

Butler University

Butler University Bulldogs

Butt, Charles C.

Butte

Butte College

Butterfield, Billy

Butterfield, John

Butterfield, Paul

Butterfield and Butterfield

Butterfield Youth Services

Butterflies Are Free

Butterworth, Charles

Button, Dick

Buttons, Red

Buttram, Pat

Butung Island

Butyl™

Buxtehude, Diderik

Buys Ballot, Christoph

Buys-Ballot's law

Buzzards Bay

buzz bomb *often* Buzz Bomb

Buzzi, Ruth

B.V.D.™ underwear

BX cable

Byas, Don

Bye Bye, Birdie

Byelarus *var of* Belarus [*form.* Byelorussian Soviet Socialist Republic]

Byelarussian

Byelorussian

Byelorussian Soviet Socialist Republic [*now* Belarus]

Byington, Spring

by Jove

Byng, Julian

Bynner, Witter

Byrd, Harry Flood

Byrd, Richard E.

Byrd, Robert

Byrd, William

Byrds, The

Byrne, David

Byrne, Gabriel

Byrnes, Edd Kookie

Byrnes, James Francis

Byron, George Gordon Lord

Byronic

Byronism

Byron Nelson Golf Classic

Byron Society, The

Byte

Byzantine

Byzantine architecture

Byzantine art

Byzantine chant

Byzantine Church

Byzantine Empire

Byzantine iconography

Byzantine music

Byzantine rite

Byzantinism

Byzantinist

Byzantium

C

Caan, James

Cabala

Caballé, Montserrat

Cabanatuan

Cabaret

Cabell, James Branch

Cabernet

Cabet, Étienne

Cabeza de Vaca, Álvar Núñez

Cable, George Washington

Cable Act

Cable and Wireless

Cable Education Network, Inc.

Cable News Network

Cable Satellite Public Affairs Network

Cabletron Systems, Inc.

Cable Value Network, Inc.

Cable Video Store

Cablevision Systems Corporation

Cabo da Roca

Cabo San Lucas

Cabot, Bruce

Cabot, John

Cabot, Sebastian

Cabot Corporation

Cabot Corporation Foundation

Cabral, Pedro Álvars

Cabrillo, Juan

Cabrillo College

Cabrillo Music Festival

Cabrillo National Monument

Cabrini College

Cabrini-Green housing project

Caccini, Giulio

Cache la Poudre River

Cactus Flower

Cadbury Schweppes

Caddo, n., pl. Caddo or Caddos

Caddoan

Caddy

Cadence Design Systems, Inc.

Cadette Girl Scout

Cadillac, Antoine de La Mothe

Cadillac Man

Cadillac Motor Car Division (General Motors Corporation)

Cadiz [* OH]

Cádiz [* Spain]

Cadman, Charles

Cadmean

Cadmean victory

Cadmus

Cadogan teapot

Cadoria, Sherian Grace

Caedmon

Caelian Hill

Caen

Caen, Herb

Caen stone

Caeremoniale Episcoporum

Caernarvon

Caernarvonshire

Caerphilly cheese

Caesar, Gaius Julius

Caesar, Julius

Caesar, Sid

Caesar and Cleopatra

Caesarean or Caesarian

Caesarean operation

Caesarean section

Caesarism
Caesarist
Caesar salad
Caesars Atlantic City
Caesar's Head
Caesar's Hour
Caesars Palace
Caesars Tahoe
Caesars World, Inc.
Cafaro, William
  Michael
Café de la Paix
Café La Mama
Cage, John
Cage, Nicolas
Cagliostro, Alessandro
  di
Cagney, James
Cagney and Lacy
Cagoulard
Cahill, Catherine M.
Cahn, Sammy
Cahokia
Cahokia Mounds
Cahuilla
Caiaphas
Caicos Islands
Cain
Cain, James M.
Cain and Abel
Caine, Hall
Caine, Michael
Caine Mutiny, The
  [book; movie]
Caine Mutiny Court
  Martial, The [play]
Caingang, *n.*, *pl.*
  Caingang *or*
  Caingangs
Cainism

Cainite
Caird, Edward
Caird Coast
Cairene
Cairngorms
Cairngorm stone
Cairo
Cairo Conference
Cairo International
  Airport
Caissons Go Rolling
  Along
Caitlin
Caius, Saint
Caja de Ahorros y de
  Pensiones de
  Barcelona
Cajetan, Saint
Cajon Pass
Cajun *occas.* Cajan
Cajun cooking
Cajun music
Calabar
Calabar bean
Calabria
Calabrian
Calais
Calamity Jane
Calcutta
Calcutta (West
  Bengal) Airport
Calcutta pool
Caldecott, Randolph
Caldecott Medal
Calder, Alexander
Calder, Alexander
  Milne
Calder, Alexander
  Stirling
Calder Cup

Calderón Bridge
Calderón de la Barca,
  Pedro
Calder Race Course
Caldor bookstore
Caldwell
Caldwell, Erskine
Caldwell, Sarah
Caldwell, Taylor
Caldwell, Zoë
Caldwell College
Caldwell Community
  College and
  Technical Institute
Caleb
Caledonia
Caledonian
Caledonian Canal
Calender
Calexico
Cal Farley's Boys
  Ranch
CalFed, Inc.
Calgary
Calgary Flames
Calgary International
  Airport
Calgary Philharmonic
  Orchestra
Calgary Stampede
Calgon Carbon
  Corporation
Calhern, Louis
Calhoun, John C.
Calhoun, Rory
Calhoun Falls
Cali
Caliban
Cali cartel
California

California Aerospace Museum

California Angels

California Angler

California Baptist College

California barberry

California barracuda

California Biotechnology

California bluebell

California Bowl

California Business

California Channel, The

California College for Health Sciences

California College of Arts and Crafts

California College of Podiatric Medicine

California condor

California Current

California dandelion

California Family Study Center

California fan palm

California Farm Network

California Features International, Inc.

California Federal Bank

California First Bank

California fuchsia

California gold fern

California gull

California Institute of Tchnology

California Institute of the Arts

California job case

California Joe

California Journal

California laurel

California Law Review

California lilac

California live oak

California Lutheran University

California Maritime Academy

California Museum of Science and Industry

Californian

California nutmeg

California-Oregon Broadcasting Inc.

California Palace of the Legion of Honor

California pepper tree

California Polytechnic State University [school at San Luis Obispo; see also California State Polytechnic University]

California poppy

California privet

California Public Utilities Commission

California quail

California Raisins™, The

California red fir

California redwood

California rose

California rosebay

California School of Professional Psychology

California sea lion

California sound

California State College System

California State Polytechnic University [school at Pomona; see also California Polytechnic State University]

California State Prison at San Quentin

California State University, Bakersfield

California State University, Chico

California State University, Dominguez Hills

California State University, Fresno

California State University, Fresno Bulldogs

California State University, Fullerton

California State University, Fullerton Titans

California State University, Hayward

California State University, Long Beach

California State University, Long Beach 49ers

California State University, Los Angeles

California State University, Northridge

California State University Press

California State University, Sacramento

California State University, Sacramento Hornets

California State University, San Bernardino

California State University, San Marcos

California State University, Stanislaus

California Trail

California University of Pennsylvania

California Western School of Law

Californio

Caligula

Calisher, Hortense

Calistoga

Calixtine *occas.* Calixtin

Calixtus

Calixtus I, Saint

Calixtus Cemetery

Callaghan, Morley

Callas, Charlie

Callas, Maria

Callejas, Rafael L.

Calley, William L.

Callias

Callicrates *or* Kallikrates

Callimachus

Calliope

Callippic cycle

Callippus

Callisthenes

Callisto

Callistratus

Call Me Madam

Call of the Wild, The

Callot, Jacques

Calloway, Cab

Calmat Company

Calories Don't Count

Calpurnia

Calumet

Calumet City

Calumet College of Saint Joseph

Calumet Farm

Calumet Harbor

Calumet Park

Calusa

Calvados [* France]

calvados *often* Calvados [brandy]

Calvary

Calvary Bible College

Calvary cross

Calvé, Emma

Calvert, Sir George

Calvert, Leonard

Calvet, Corinne

Calvin, John

Calvin and Hobbes

Calvin College

Calvinism

Calvinist

Calvinistic

Calvinistic Methodist Church

Calvino, Italo

Calvin Theological Seminary

Calvo, Carlo

Calvo Clause

Calvo Doctrine

Calypso

Camacho, Hector

Camagüey

Camara Inn

Camarillo

Cambert, Robert

Camberwell

Camberwell beauty

Cambodia [*form.* Kampuchea]

Cambodian

Cambodian architecture

Cambodian art

Cambrai

Cambria Air Force Station

Cambrian

Cambrian Mountains

Cambrian Period

Cambridge

Cambridge, Godfrey

Cambridge City

Cambridge Club

Cambridge College/ Institute of Open Education

Cambridge Complex, The

Cambridge Law Journal, The

Cambridge Platform

Cambridge Platonism
Cambridge Platonist
Cambridge School
Cambridgeshire
Cambridgeshire and
Isle of Ely
Cambridge Singers
Cambridge University
Cambridge University
Press
Camden
Camden County
College
Camden Festival
Camelback Mountain
Camel Grand Prix of
Greater San Diego
Camel Grand Prix of
Monterey
Camel Grand Prix of
the Heartland
Camellia
Camelot
Camembert cheese
Cameo
Cameron
Cameron, James
Cameron, Kirk
Cameron, Richard
Cameronian
Cameron University
Cameroon
Cameroon Airlines
Cameroonian
Cameroon Mountain
Cameroons
Camille
Camille Claudel
Camilo, Michel
Cammaerts, Émile

Camoëns, Luis Vaz de
Camp, Hamilton
Camp, Walter
Campagna di Roma
Campagnola,
Domenico
Campanella, Joseph
Campanella, Roy
Campaneris, Bert
Campania
Campanian
Campari
Camp Beauregard
Campbell
Campbell, Alexander
Campbell, Bill
Campbell, Donald
Campbell, Earl
Campbell, Glen
Campbell, Sir John
Campbell, Joseph
Campbell, Sir
Malcolm
Campbell, Mrs.
Patrick
Campbell, Robert
Campbell, Tevin
Campbell, Thomas
Campbell-Bannerman,
Sir Henry
Campbellism
Campbellite
Campbell Mountain
Campbell Soup
Company
Campbell Soup Fund
Campbellsville
Campbellsville
College
Campbell University

Campbell University
Fighting Camels
Camp David
Camp David Accords
Campeau Corporation
Campeche
Campers and Hikers
Association, Inc.
Camp Fire Boy
Camp Fire Girl
Camp Fire, Inc.
[form. Camp Fire
Girls, Inc.]
Camp Grant
Camp Grant massacre
Camp Hill
Camp H. M. Smith
Campho-Phenique™
Campignian
Campin, Robert
Campina Grande
Campinas
Campion, Albert
Campion, Thomas
Camp Kilmer
Camp Lejeune
Campobello
Campo Formio
Campo Grande
Campos
Camp Pendleton
Campton Place
Cam Ranh Bay
Camus, Albert
Cana
Canaan
Canaanite
Canada
Canada balsam

Canada barberry
Canada bluegrass
Canada College
Canada Company
Canada crookneck
Canada Cup
Canada Day
Canada First movement
Canada goose
Canadair Ltd.
Canada jay
Canada Life Assurance Company
Canada lily
Canada lynx
Canada mayflower
Canada moonseed
Canada potato
Canada rice
Canada's Wonderland
Canada thistle
Canada Wide Feature Service Limited
Canadian
Canadian Airlines International Ltd.
Canadian architecture
Canadian art
Canadian Automobile Sports Club
Canadian bacon
Canadian Brass
Canadian Broadcasting Corporation
Canadian Business
Canadian English
Canadian football

Canadian Football League
Canadian French
Canadian hemlock
Canadian Imperial Bank of Commerce
Canadianism
Canadian literature
Canadian *or* Canada lynx
Canadian National Railway Company
Canadian Opera Company
Canadian Pacific Ltd.
Canadian Rockies
Canadian Shield
Canadian whisky, *n.*, *pl.* whiskies; *occas.* whiskey, *n.*, *pl.* whiskeys *or* whiskies
Canady, Alexa
Canajoharie
Canaletto, Antonio
Canal Zone
Canandaigua
Canandaigua Lake
Canaries, the
Canaries Current
Canary Islands
Canaveral National Seashore
Canaveral Peninsula
Canberra
Canby, E. R. S.
Canby, Henry Seidel
Canby, Vincent
Can-Can
Cancer
Cancer Care, Inc.

Cancer Fund of America
Cancer Research Council
Cancer Research Foundation of America
Cancer Research Institute, Inc.
Cancer Ward
Cancun
Candace
C + C Music Factory
Candice
Candida
Candid Camera
Candide
Candlemas
Candlemas Day
Candler, Asa
Candlestick Park
Candlewood Lake
Candoli, Pete
C and R Clothiers Inc.
Candy, John
Candyman
Caney Fork
Canfield Fisher, Dorothy
Caniff, Milton
Canine Companions for Independence
Canisius College
Canisius College Golden Griffins
Canis Major
Canis Minor
Canned Heat
Cannell, Stephen J.
Cannery Row

Cannes

Cannes Film Festival

Canning, Charles John

Canning, George

Cannon, Annie Jump

Cannon, Curt

Cannon, Dyan

Cannon, Harriet Starr

Cannon, Joseph

Cannon, Walter Bradford

Cannon Air Force Base

Cannon House Office Building

Cannon Mountain

Cannon's International Business College of Honolulu

Cano, Alonso

Canon City

Canon Inc.

Canon *occas.* canon law

Canonsburg

Canon USA, Inc.

Canopic

Canopic jar

Canopic vase

Canopus

Canova, Antonio

Canova, Judy

Canseco, José

Cantabrian Mountains

Cantabrigian

Cantata Singers

Canterburian

Canterbury

Canterbury bell

Canterbury Cathedral

Canterbury Downs

Canterbury Tales, The

Canticle for Leibowitz, A

Canticle of Canticles

Canticles

Cantinflas

Canton [* China] [*now* Guangzhou]

Canton [* GA; IL; MA; MS; MO; NY; NC; OH; PA]

Canton crepe

Cantonese, *n.*, *pl.* Cantonese

canton *often* Canton flannel

Canton Island

Canton linen

Canton ware

Cantor, Eddie

Cantor, Georg

Cantor set

Cantorternary set

Cantos

Cantrell, Lana

Canuck

Canute

Canute IV, Saint

Canute the Dane

Canute the Great

Canute the Saint

Canyon

Canyon de Chelly National Monument

Canyon Diablo

Canyonlands National Park

Can You Top This?

Caodism

Capa, Robert

Capablanca, José Raúl

Cape Actium

Cape Agulhas

Cape Ann

Cape Astrolabe

Cape Bir

Cape Bon

Cape Breton

Cape Breton Highlands National Park

Cape Breton Island

Cape Brett

Cape buffalo

Cape Canaveral [*form.* Cape Kennedy]

Cape Canaveral Air Force Station

Cape Canso

Cape Catoche

Cape Charles

Cape Chelyuskin

Cape Chidley

Cape Churchill

Cape Cod

Cape Cod Bay

Cape Cod Canal

Cape Cod Coast Guard Air Station

Cape Cod Community College

Cape Cod cottage

Cape Cod Life

Cape Cod lighter

Cape Cod National Seashore

Cape Colored

Cape Columbia

Cape Comorin
Cape cowslip
Cape Delgado
Cape Dezhnev
Cape Diamond
Cape Disappointment
Cape Dorset
Cape Espíritu Santo
Cape Fairweather
Cape Farewell
Cape Fear
Cape Fear Community College
Cape Fear River
Cape Finisterre
Cape Flattery
Cape Flyaway
Cape forget-me-not
Cape Foulweather
Cape Girardeau
Cape Glossa
Cape Guardafui
Cape Hatteras
Cape Hatteras National Seashore
Cape Helles
Cape Henry
Cape Horn
Cape Horner
Cape Horn fever
Cape Horn Mountain
Capek, Karel
Cape Kennedy [now Cape Canaveral]
Cape Krio
Cape Krusenstern National Monument
Capella
Capella, Martianus

Cape Lookout National Seashore
Cape Martello
Cape Matapan
Cape May
Cape May Coast Guard Training Center
Cape May warbler
Cape Mendocino
Cape Miseno
Cape Morris Jessup
Cape Nordkyn
Cape of Good Hope
Cape of Good Hope Colony [now Cape Province]
Cape Ortegal
Cape periwinkle
Cape pondweed
Cape Prince of Wales
Cape Province [form. Cape of Good Hope Colony]
Cape Race
Capernaum
Cape Roca
Cape ruby
Cape Sable
Cape Sable Island
Cape Saint Vincent
Cape Skagen
Cape Spartivento
Capet, Hugh
Capetian
Capetonian
Cape Town
Cape Trafalgar
Cape Verde
Cape Verde Islands

Cape Wrath
Cape York
Cape York Peninsula
Capital Centre
Capital Cities/ABC, Inc.
Capital Cities/ABC, Inc. Foundation
Capital City Junior College of Business
Capital Features Syndicate
Capital Holding Corporation
Capital University
Capitan Peak
Capitol
Capitol College
Capitol Federal Savings and Loan Association
Capitol Heights
Capitol Hill
Capitoline Hill
Capitoline Museums
Capitoline Venus
Capitol News Service
Capitol Radio Networks/Virginia
Capitol Reef National Park
Capitol Steps, The
Capiz shell
Capobianco, Tito
Capodimonte National Museum and Gallery
Capone, Al
Capote, Truman
Capp, Al
Capper's

Capra, Frank
Capra, Frank, Jr.
Capri
Capriati, Jennifer
Capriccio Espagnol
Capriccio Italien
Capricorn
Capricornus
Capriote
Capri pants, n., pl. Capris [usually pl.]
Capshaw, Kate
Captain and Tenille, The
Captain Beefheart
Captain Beefheart and the Magic Band
Captain Hook
Captain Jack
Captain Kangaroo
Captain Midnight
Captain Nemo
Captain Planet and the Planeteers
Captains Courageous
Captain's Daughter, The
Captain Video
Capuchin
Capucine
Capulet, Juliet
Capulin Volcano National Monument
Cara, Irene
Caracalla
Caracas
[Caracas] Fine Arts Museum
Caramoor Festival
Car and Driver

Caravaggio, Michelangelo Merisi da
Caravaggio, Polidor Caldara da
Caray, Harry [sports announcer; see also Carey, Harry]
Carberry, John Joseph Cardinal
Carboloy™
Carbonate Mountain
Carbondale
Carboniferous
Carborundum™
Cardamom Hills
Cardamom Mountains
Cardan joint
Cardano, Geronimo or Gerolamo or Girolamo
Cárdenas, Lázaro
Cardiff
Cardiff-by-the-Sea
Cardiff giant
Cardigan, James Thomas Brudenell
Cardigan Bay
Cardiganshire
Cardigan Welsh corgi
Cardin, Pierre
Cardinale, Claudia
Cardinal Mountain
Cardinal of the Kremlin, The
Cardinal Richelieu
Cardinal Stritch College
Cardozo, Benjamin
Card Players, The
Carducci, Bartolomeo

Carducci, Giosuè
CARE
Care Bear Family, The
CARE, Inc.
Carew, Rod
Carew, Thomas
Carey
Carey, George L.
Carey, Harry [actor; see also Caray, Harry]
Carey, Joseph M.
Carey, Macdonald
Carey, Mariah
Carey, Max
Carey, Philip
Carey, Ronald
Carey Land Act
Cargill, James R.
Cargill, Margaret
Cargill Foundation
Cargill Inc.
cargo cult occas. Cargo Cult
Carías Andino, Tiburcio
Carib, n., pl Carib or Caribs
Cariban
Caribbean
Caribbean Center for Advanced Studies
Caribbean Community and Common Market
Carribean current
Caribbean Indies [form. West Indies]
Caribbean Sea
Caribbean University College

Caribbees

Cariboo Mountains [* British Columbia; *see also* Caribou Mountains]

Caribou

Caribou Mountain

Caribou Mountains [* Alberta; *see also* Cariboo Mountains]

Caribou National Forest

Carillo, Leo

Carinus

Carioca

Cariou, Len

Carissimi, Giacomo

Carl

Carl Albert Junior College

Carle, Frankie

Carleton College

Carleton University

Carlin, George

Carlinville

Carlisle

Carlisle, Belinda

Carlisle, Kitty

Carlisle Barracks

Carlisle Companies Inc.

Carlisle Indian School

Carlism

Carlist

Carloman

Carlos

Carlos, Don

Carlos, Wendy

Carlos the Jackal

Carlota

Carlota Santana Spanish Dance Arts Company

Carlotta

Carlovingian

Carlow College

Carl Sandburg College

Carl Sandburg Home National Historic Site

Carlsbad

Carlsbad Caverns

Carlsbad Caverns National Park

Carlsbad Decrees

Carlsberg Architectural Prize

Carl's Jr.™

Carlson, Chester

Carlson, Curtis LeRoy

Carlson, Evans

Carlson Companies, Inc.

Carlson's Raiders

Carlstadt

Carlton

Carlton, Steve

Carlton Club

Carlton desk

Carlton House table

Carlton table

Carlucci, Frank

Carlyle

Carlyle, Thomas

Carman, Bliss

Carman, Harry James

Carmarthen

Carmarthenshire

Carmel

Carmel-by-the-Sea

Carmelite

Carmelite friar

Carmen

Carmen, Eric

Carmen Jones

Carmi

Carmichael

Carmichael, Hoagy

Carmichael, Ian

Carmichael, Stokely

Carmon

Carnaby Street

Carnap, Rudolph

Carnarvon arch

Carnation Company

Carne, Judy

Carneades

Carnegie

Carnegie, Andrew

Carnegie, Dale

Carnegie Corporation of New York

Carnegie Foundation for the Advancement of Teaching

Carnegie Hall

Carnegie Hero Fund Commission

Carnegie library

Carnegie Medal

Carnegie-Mellon Magazine

Carnegie-Mellon University

Carner, JoAnne

Carnera, Primo

Carnes, Kim

Carney, Art

Carney, Harry

Carnival Cruise Lines, Inc.

Carnival of the Animals, The

Carnot, Lazare Nicolas Marguerite

Carnot, Marie François Sadi

Carnot, Nicolas Léonard Sadi

Carnot cycle

Carnot engine

Carnot refrigerator

Carnot's theorem

Carnovsky, Morris

Caro, Heinrich

Carol

Carol Burnett Show, The

Carol City

Carole

Carolean

Carolina

Carolina Academic Press

Carolina allspice

Carolina bay

Carolina campaign

Carolina chickadee

Carolina jessamine

Carolina lily

Carolina moonseed

Carolina parakeet

Carolina Playmakers

Carolina Power and Light Company

Carolina Quarterly

Carolina rail

Carolina rhododendron

Carolina vanilla

Carolina wren

Caroline

Caroline Affair

Caroline Islands

Caroline of Ansbach

Caroline of Brunswick

Carolines, the

Carolingian

Carolingian architecture

Carolingian art

Carolingian miniscule

Carolinian

Caron, Leslie

Carondelet, Francisco

Caro's acid

Carothers, Wallace Hume

Carousel

Carowind

Carpaccio, Vittore

Carpathian Mountains

Carpathians, the

Carpatho-Ukraine

Carpeaux, Jean Baptiste

Carpenter, John Alden

Carpenter, Karen

Carpenter, Mary-Chapin

Carpenter, M. Scott

Carpenter, Richard

Carpenters, The

Carpentersville

Carpenter Technology Corporation

Carpeteria

Carpinteria

Carpocrates

Carr, Alan

Carr, Emily

Carr, John Dickson

Carr, Vikki

Carrà, Carlo

Carracci, Agostino

Carracci, Annibale

Carracci, Lodovico

Carradine, David

Carradine, John

Carradine, Keith

Carradine, Robert

Carrantuohill

Carranza, Venustiano

Carrara

Carrara marble

Carrascolendas

Carrel, Alexis

Carreras, José

Carrère, John Merven

Carrere, Tia

Carriage Association of America

Carrillo, Leo

Carrizo Springs

Carrol

Carroll

Carroll, Charles

Carroll, Diahann

Carroll, Earl

Carroll, Leo G.

Carroll, Lewis

Carroll, Nancy

Carroll, Pat

Carroll and Company

Carroll College

Carrollton

Carruthers, George E.

Carruthers, Peter

Carry Me Back to Old Virginny

Cars, The

Carse of Gowrie

Carson

Carson, Jack

Carson, Johnny

Carson, Kit

Carson, Rachel

Carson City

Carson Lake

Carson National Forest

Carson-Newman College

Carson Pass

Carson Peak

Carson Pirie Scott and Company

Carson River

Carson Sink

Carswell Air Force Base

Cartagena

Carte, Richard D'Oyly

Carte Blanche™ credit card

Car-Temps™ rental car

Carter, A. P.

Carter, Benny

Carter, Betty

Carter, Billy

Carter, Dixie

Carter, Don

Carter, Elliott

Carter, Gerard Emmett Cardinal

Carter, Hodding

Carter, Howard

Carter, Jack

Carter, Jimmy

Carter, John

Carter, June

Carter, Mrs. Leslie

Carter, Lynda

Carter, Maybelle

Carter, Nell

Carter, Nick

Carter, Ron

Carter, Rosalynn

Carteret

Carteret, John

Carteret, Philip

Carteret Community College

Carteret Savings Bank

Carter Family, The

Carter Hawley Hale Stores, Inc.

Carters Dam

Carter Sisters

Carter's Little Pills™

Carters Reservoir

Cartersville [* GA]

Carterville [* IL; MO]

Carter-Wallace, Inc.

Cartesian

Cartesian coordinates

Cartesian devil

Cartesian diver

Cartesian doubt

Cartesianism

Cartesian philosophy

Cartesian plane

Cartesian product

Carthage

Carthage College

Carthaginian

Carthusian

Cartier, Jacques

Cartier-Bresson, Henri

Cartier, Inc.

Cartoonists and Writers Syndicate

Cartwright, Alexander

Cartwright, Bill

Cartwright, Edmund

Cartwright, John

Caruba Organization

Carus

Caruso, Enrico

Carvel, Tom

Carver, Dana

Carver, George Washington

Carver, John

Carver, Jonathan

Carver, Lucille

Carver chair

Carver State Technical College

Cary

Cary, Alice

Cary, Henry Francis

Cary, Joyce

Cary, Phoebe

Casabianca [poem; *see also* Casablanca]

Casabianca, Louis de

Casablanca [city; movie; *see also* Casabianca]

Casablanca Conference

Casa Bonita

Casadesus, Gaby

Casadesus, Robert

Casa Grande

Casa Grande National Monument

Casals, Pablo

Casals, Rosemary

Casanova, Francesco

Casanova de Seingalt, Giovanni Jacopo *or* Giovanni Giacomo

Casaubon, Isaac

Casbah

Casca

Cascade Range

Cascades, the

Cascade Tunnel

Cascadia

Casco Bay

Casco Bay College

Casement, Sir Roger David

Case Western Reserve University

Casey

Casey at the Bat

Casey Jones

Cash, Johnny

Cash, Rosalind

Cash, Rosanne

Cash, Tommy

Casimir

Casio Computer Company, Ltd.

Caslon, William

Casnoff, Philip

Caspar [1 of the Magi; *see also* Casper]

Casparian strip

Casper [given name; * WY; *see also* Caspar]

Casper, Billy

Casper College

Casper the Friendly Ghost

Caspian

Caspian Sea

Caspian tern

Cass, Peggy

Cassa di Risparmio delle Provincie Lombarde

Cassandra

Cassatt, Mary

Cassavetes, John

Cassegraine

Cassegraine telescope

Cassegrainian telescope

Cassel brown

Cassel earth

Cassel State Art Collections

Cassel yellow

Cassidy, Butch

Cassidy, David

Cassidy, Hopalong

Cassidy, Joanna

Cassidy, Patrick

Cassidy, Shaun

Cassini, Giovanni Domenico

Cassini, Jacques

Cassini, Jean Dominique

Cassini, Oleg

Cassini *occas.* Cassini's division

Cassino

Cassiodorus, Flavius

Cassiope

Cassiopeia

Cassiopeia's Chair

Cassirer, Ernst

Cassius

Cassius Longinus, Gaius

Cassius Longinus, Quintus

Cassius Viscellinus, Spurius

Castagno, Andrea del

Castelfranco altarpiece

Castel Gandolfo

Castellanos, Julio

Castello, Giovanni Battista

Castelnuovo-Tedesco, Mario

Castelo Branco, Humberto

Castel Sant'Angelo

Castenada, Carlos

Castiglione, Baldassare

Castiglione, Giovanni Benedetto

Castiglioni, Niccolò

Castile

Castile and Aragon

Castilian

Castille soap

Castillo, Antonio

Castillo de San Marcos National Monument

Castle, Irene

Castle, Vernon

Castle Air Force Base

Castle and Cooke Residential Inc.

Castle Clinton National Monument

Castle Dracula

Castle Junior College

Castle of Otranto, The

Castle Peak

Castle Pinckney

Castlereagh, Robert

Castle Shannon

Castleton State College

Castle walk

Castor

Castor and Pollux

Castro, Fidel

Castroism

Castroite

Castrop-Rauxel

Castro Valley

Castroville

Casual Corner store

Catalan

Catalan art

Catalan language

Catalan literature

Catalina Island

Catalonia

Catalonian

Catalonian jasmine

Catamarca

Cat and the Fiddle, The

Catania

Catanzaro

Catasauqua

Catawba

Catawba College

Catawba grape

Catawba [Indian], n., pl. Catawba or Catawbas

Catawba Valley Community College

Catcher in the Rye, The

Catch-22

Caterpillar Club

Caterpillar Financial Services Corporation

Caterpillar Foundation

Caterpillar, Inc.

Cates, Phoebe

Cat Fanciers' Association, Inc.

Cathay

Cathay Pacific Airways Ltd.

Cathedral Church of Saint John the Divine

Cathedral of Notre Dame

Cathedral of Saint Bavon

Cathedral of Saint John the Divine

Cathedral of Saint Michael

Cathedral of Saints Peter and Paul

Cathedral of the Annunciation

Cather, Willa

Catherine

Catherine, Saint

Catherine of Alexandria, Saint

Catherine of Aragon

Catherine of Bologna, Saint

Catherine of Braganza

Catherine of Genoa, Saint

Catherine of Siena, Saint

Catherine of Sweden, Saint

Catherine of Valois

Catherine Tekakwitha

Catherine the Great

catherine occas. Catherine wheel

Catholic

Catholic Action

Catholic Apostolic Church

Catholic Church

Catholic Church Extension Society of the United States of America

Catholic Daughters of the Americas

Catholic Emancipation

Catholic Emancipation Act

Catholic Epistles

Catholic Hour, The

Catholicism

Catholic Library Association

Catholic Medical Center of Brooklyn and Queens, Inc.

Catholic Press Association of the United States and Canada

Catholic Reformation

Catholic Theological Union

Catholic University of America

Catholic University of America Press, The

Catholic University of Puerto Rico

Catholic War Veterans of the United States of America

Catholic Youth Organization

Cathy

Catilinarian

Catiline

Catlett, Big Sid

Catlett, Walter

Catlettsburg

Catlin, George

Catoctin Mountain Park

Cat on a Hot Tin Roof

Caton-Jones, Michael

Catonsville

Catonsville Community College

Cato of Utica

Cato Street Conspiracy

Cato the Censor

Cato the Elder

Cato the Younger

Cats

CAT scan

CAT scanner

Cat's Cradle

Catskill

Catskill Aqueduct

Catskill Mountains

Cats Magazine

Catt, Carrie Chapman

Cattegat var. of Kattegat

Cattell, James McKeen

Catton, Bruce

Catullus, Gaius Valerius

Catulus

Caucasia or Caucasus

Caucasian

Caucasian Gates

Caucasian languages

Caucasian lily

Caucasoid

Caucasus

Caucasus Mountains

Cauchy, Augustin Louis

Cauchy integral formula

Cauchy integral theorem

Cauchy-Reimann equation

Cauchy-Schwarz inequality

Cauchy sequence

Cauchy's inequality

Cauchy's integral theorem

Caudine Forks

Caulfield, Joan

Cauthen, Steve

Cauvery

Cavafy, Constantine

Cavalcade

Cavalier, Jean

Cavalieri, Francesco Bonaventura

cavalier King Charles spaniel

Cavalier poets

Cavallaro, Carmen

Cavalleria Rusticana

Cavanaugh, Hobart

Cavedone, Giacomo

Cavell, Edith

Cavendish

Cavendish, Henry

Cavendish banana

Cavendish experiment

Cavendish Laboratory

Caves of the Thousand Buddhas

Cavett, Dick

Cavour, Camillo Benso

Cawnpore

Caxias

Caxias du Sol

C-axis, *n.*, *pl.* C-axes

Caxton, William

Cayce

Cayenne

Cayley, Arthur

Cayman Islands

Cayman Trench

Cayuga County Community College

Cayuga Heights

Cayuga [Indian], *n.*, *pl.* Cayuga *or* Cayugas

Cayuga Lake

Cayuse [Indian], *n.*, *pl.* Cayuse *or* Cayuses

Cazenovia College

C battery

CBC Symphony

CBI Industries, Inc.

CBN University

CBS Broadcast Group

CBS Children's Film Festival, The

CBS Early Morning News

CBS Evening News

CBS Foundation

CBS Inc. [*form.* Columbia Broadcasting System]

CBS Morning News, The

CBS News

CBS News Nightwatch

CBS Radio Networks

CBS Reports

CBS Sports

CBS Sports Spectacular

CBS Television City

CBS Television Network

CBS This Morning

C clef

Ceausescu, Nicolas

Cebú

Cecil

Cecil, Robert

Cecil, William

Cecil Community College

Cecil Field Naval Air Station

Cecilia

Cecilia, Saint

Cecils College

Cecropia moth

Cedar Breaks National Monument

Cedarburg

Cedar City

Cedar Creek

Cedar Creek Dam

Cedar Creek Peak

Cedar Crest College

Cedar Falls

Cedar Grove

Cedar Hammock

Cedar Hill

Cedarhurst

Cedar Lake

Cedar Mountains

cedar of Lebanon

Cedar Point

Cedar Rapids

Cedars Home for Children Foundation, Inc.

Cedars-Sinai Medical Center

Cedartown

Cedar Valley College

Cedarville College

Cedd *or* Cedda, Saint

Cedric

C-8A Buffalo

Cela, Camilo José

Celan, Paul

Celanese™

Celebes

Celebesian

Celebes Sea

Celebrated Jumping Frog of Calaveras County, The

Celebrezze, Anthony

Celeste

Celeste Arena

Celestial Arts™ Books

Celestial City

Celestial Empire

Celestine

Celestine V, Saint

Celestine I, Saint

Celiac Sprue Association/United States of America

Celina

Céline, Louis Ferdinand

Cellini, Benvenuto

Cellini's halo

Cellular Communications, Inc.

Celluloid™

Celotex™

Celsius, Anders

Celsius scale

Celsius temperature scale

Celt

Celtic

Celtic art

Celtic Church

Celtic cross

Celticism

Celticist

Celtic languages

Celtic literature

Celto-Germanic

Cenci, The

Cenci, Beatrice

Cendrars, Blaise

Cenozoic

Census in Bethlehem, The

Centaurus

Centel Corporation

Centenary College

Centenary College Gentlemen

Centenary College of Louisiana

Centennial

Center

Center for Advanced Studies on Puerto Rico and the Caribbean

Center for Applied Behavioral Sciences

Center for Auto Safety

Center for Community Change

Center for Creative Studies—College of Art and Design

Center for Humanistic Studies

Center for Law and Social Policy

Center for Marine Conservation

Center for Media Studies [now Freedom Forum Media Studies Center]

Center for National Policy

Center for Population Options

Center for Public Justice

Center for Science in the Public Interest

Center for the Defense of Free Enterprise

Center for Women Policy Studies

Center for Zoroastrian Research

Centerior Energy Corporation

Center Line

Center Moriches

Center Point

Centerport

Centers for Disease Control and Prevention [form. Centers for Disease Control]

Center Stage

Centerville [* AL; DE; IA; MI; MO; OH; PA; SD; TN; TX; UT; see also Centreville]

Centerville or Centreville [* VA; see also Centreville]

Centerville-Dublin Gulch

Centex Corporation

Centoxin™

Central African Republic

Central Alabama Community College

Central America

Central American

Central American Common Market

Central and South West Corporation

Central Arizona College

Central Baptist College

Central Baptist Theological Seminary

Central Bible College

Central Carolina Community College

Central Christian College of the Bible

Central City

Central City Business Institute

Central City Opera Festival

Central College

Central Committee for Conscientious Objection

Central Community College

Central Conference of American Rabbis

Central Connecticut State University Blue Devils

Central Daylight Time

Central Educational Network

Central Falls

Central Fidelity Bank

Central Florida Community College

Central Highlands

Central Hudson Gas and Electric Corporation

Centralia

Centralia College

Central Independent Television USA Inc.

Central Intelligence Agency

Central Louisiana Electric Company, Inc.

Central Maine Medical Center School of Nursing

Central Maine Power Company

Central Maine Technical College

Central Methodist College

Central Michigan University

Central Michigan University Chippewas

Central Missouri State University

Central News Agency, Inc.

Central Newspapers, Inc.

Central Ohio Technical College

Central Oregon Community College

Central Pacific Railroad

Central Park

Central Pennsylvania Business School

Central Piedmont Community College

Central Powers

Central Service

Central Soya Company Inc.

Central Soya Foundation

Central Standard Time

Central State University

Central Texas College

Central Time

Central Treaty Organization

Central University of Iowa

Central Utah Project

Central Valley

Central Valley Project

Central Virginia Community College

Central Washington University

Central Wesleyan College

Central Wyoming College

Central Yeshiva Tomchei Tmimim Lubavitch America

Centre College

Centreville [* IL; MD; see also Centerville]

Centrex™

centrist occas. Centrist

Century of Progress Exposition

Century Plaza Hotel and Tower

Century Telephone Enterprises, Inc.

Century 21 real estate service

Cephalonia

Cepheid

Cepheid variable

Cepheus

Cephisodotus

Ceram

Ceraunian Mountains

Cerberean

Cerberic

Cerberus

Cerenkov occas. Cherenkov, Pavel A.

Cerenkov radiation

Ceres

Cerf, Bennett

Cermak, Anton

Cernan, Eugene

Cernuda, Luis

Cerritos College

Cerro Coso Community College

Cerro Gordo

Cerro Tololo

Cerro Tololo Inter-American Observatory

Certified Public Accountant

Certosa di Pavia

Cervantes Saavedra, Miguel de

Cesca chair

Cesena

Cessna Aircraft Company

Cetus

Cetus Corporation

Cévennes

Ceylon [now Sri Lanka]

Ceylon cinnamon

Ceylonese

Ceylon gooseberry

Ceylon morning-glory

Ceylon moss

Ceylon tea

Cézanne, Paul

Cézanne Self-Portrait

C-54 Skymaster

C-5 Galaxy

C-45 Expediter

C-47 Dakota

C-47 Skytrain

C-46 Commando
Chablis
Chablis [wine], *n.*, *pl.*
  Chablis
Chabot College
Chabrier, Emmanuel
Chacksfield, Frank
Chaco
Chaco Canyon
Chaco Culture
  National Historical
  Park
Chaco War
Chaculluta
  International
  Airport
Chad
Chadian
Chadron [* NE; *see
  also* Chardon]
Chadron State College
Chadwick, Florence
Chadwick, George
  Whitefield
Chadwick, Henry
Chadwick, Sir James
Chaetognatha
Chaffee, Roger B.
Chaffee, Suzy
Chaffey Community
  College
Chagall, Marc
Chagas, Carlos R.
Chagas' disease
Chagos Archipelago
Chagres
Chagrin Falls
Chain, Sir Ernst Boris
Chair and Pipe
Chairman, Federal
  Reserve System

Chair of Forgetfulness
Chair of Saint Peter
Chakiris, George
Chalcedon
Chalcedonian
Chalcidice
Chalcolithic
Chaldea *occas.*
  Chaldaea
Chaldean
Chaldean rite
Chaleur Bay
Chaliapin, Fyodor
  Ivanovich
Chalk River Nuclear
  Laboratories
Challenger
Challenger disaster
Challenger expedition
Challis National
  Forest
Chalmers, Alexander
Châlons
Chambered Nautilus
Chamberlain, Sir
  Austen
Chamberlain, George
  Agnew
Chamberlain, John
Chamberlain, Joseph
Chamberlain, Neville
Chamberlain, Richard
Chamberlain, Wilt
Chamberlin, Thomas
  Chrowder
Chamber Music
  America
Chamber Music
  Society of Lincoln
  Center

Chamber of
  Commerce of the
  United States
Chambers, Anne Cox
Chambers, Robert
Chambers, Whittaker
Chambers, Sir
  William
Chambersburg
[Chambers]
  Cyclopedia
Chambers
  Development
  Company, Inc.
Chambertin
Chambéry
Chamblee
Chaminade, Cécile
  Louise Stéphanie
Chaminade University
  of Honolulu
Chamizal National
  Memorial
Chamonix
Chamorro, *n.*, *pl.*
  Chamorro *or*
  Chamorros
Chamorro, Violeta
  Barrios de
Champagne [region in
  France; that
  region's sparkling
  wine]
Champaign [city in
  IL]
Champion, Gower
Champion, Marge
Champion Federal
  Savings and Loan
  Association
Champion
  International
  Corporation
Champion of England

Championship Auto
  Racing Teams, Inc.

Champion™ spark
  plug

Champion Spark Plug
  500

Champlain, Samuel de

Champlain Canal

Champlain College

Champollion, Jean
  François

Champs Élysées

Chan, Charlie

Chan, Dennis

Chance, Frank

Chancellor, John

Chancellor
  Broadcasting
  Network

Chancellor of the
  Exchequer

Chancellorsville

Chandernagor *occas.*
  Chandernagar

Chandigarh

Chandler

Chandler, Gene

Chandler, Happy

Chandler, Jeff

Chandler, Raymond

Chandler wobble

Chandris Fantasy/
  Celebrity Cruises

Chanel, Coco

Chanel Boutique

Chanel, Inc.

Chaney, Lon

Chaney, Lon, Jr.

Chang [*form.*
  Yangtze]

Chang, Michael

Chang, Sarah

Chang and Eng

Changchiakou [*now*
  Zhangjiakou]

Changchou [*now*
  Changzhou]

Changchun

Changhua

Changing Times

Changing Times
  Education Service

Changing Times—The
  Kiplinger
  Washington Editors,
  Inc.

Changsha

Changzhou [*form.*
  Changchou]

Chanin, Irwin

Channel Islands

Channel Islands
  National Park

Channel One

Channel Tunnel

Channing, Carol

Channing, Edward

Channing, Stockard

Channing, William
  Ellery

Channing, William
  Henry

Chantels, The

Chanticleer

Chantilly

Chantilly lace

Chanukah *var. of*
  Hanukkah

Chanute

Chanute, Octave

Chanute Air Force
  Base

Chao Phraya

Chao Tzu-yang [*now*
  Zhao Ziyang]

Chapel, Christine

Chapel Hill

Chapel Royal

Chapin, Harry

Chaplain's
  International
  Association

Chaplin, Charlie

Chaplin, Geraldine

Chaplin, Oona O'Neill

Chapman, Eric

Chapman, Frank M.

Chapman, George

Chapman, Graham

Chapman, John
  Gadsby

Chapman, John Jay

Chapman, Lonny

Chapman, Tracy

Chapman College

Chappaquiddick

Chappaquiddick
  bridge

Chappaquiddick
  Island

Chap Stick™

Chapter One
  bookstore

Chapters bookstore

Chapultepec

Char, René

Charbonneau, Jean
  Baptiste

Charbonneau,
  Toussaint

Charcot, Jean Martin

Chardin, Jean Baptiste
  Siméon

Chardon [* OH; *see also* Chadron]

Charente

Charente-Maritime

Charge of the Light Brigade, The

Charing Cross

Charing Cross Road

Charioteer of Delphi

Chariots of Fire

Charisse, Cyd

Chariton

Charlemagne

Charlene

Charleroi *occas.* Charleroy

Charles

Charles, Ezzard

Charles, Jacques

Charles, Les

Charles, Nick

Charles, Nora

Charles, Ray

Charles Borromeo, Saint

Charles City

Charles County Community College

Charles C. Thomas, Publisher

Charles I Hunting

Charles I in Hunting Dress

Charles I on Horseback

Charles in Charge

Charles' law

Charles Martel

Charles Melvin Price Support Center

Charles Mound

Charles of Bavaria

Charles of Blois

Charles of Luxembourg

Charles of Valois

Charles of Viana

Charles Pinckney National Historic Site

Charles R. Drew University

Charles River

Charles River Bridge Case

Charles Schwab Corporation

Charles Scribner's Sons

Charles S. Mott Community College

Charles Stewart Mott Foundation

Charles the Bald [French king]

Charles the Bold [Burgundian duke]

Charles the Fair

Charles the Fat

Charles the Great

Charles the Hammer

Charles the Mad

Charles the Simple

Charles the Victorious

Charles the Well-Beloved

Charles the Wise

Charleston [* AR; IL; MS; MO; SC; WV; *see also* Charlestown]

Charleston, Oscar

Charleston Air Force Base

Charleston Gazette

Charleston International Airport

Charleston Naval Shipyard

Charleston Naval Station

Charleston Naval Weapons Station

Charleston Peak

Charlestown [* IN; NH; RI; West Indies; section of Boston; *see also* Charleston]

Charles Town [* WV]

Charles University

Charlevoix

Charley

Charlie

Charlie and the Chocolate Factory

Charlie Daniels Band, The

Charlie Noble

Charlie's Angels

Charlot, Jean

Charlotte

Charlotte Amalie

Charlotte Coliseum

Charlotte Douglas International Airport

Charlotte Hornets

Charlotte Motor Speedway

Charlottenburg

Charlottenburg Palace

Charlottenburg Palace Museums

Charlotte Observer, The

Charlottesville

Charlotte's Web

Charlottetown

Charlton

Charming Shoppes, Inc.

Charo

Charolais

Charon

Charonian

Charonic

Charpentier, Gustave

Charpentier, Marc Antoine

Chartered Life Underwriter

Charterhouse

Charterhouse of Parma, The

Charteris, Leslie

Charter Oak

Charter Oak College

Chartism

Chartist

Chartres

Chartres Cathedral

Charybdian

Charybdis

Chase, Charlie

Chase, Chevy

Chase, David Theodore

Chase, Ilka

Chase, Mary Ellen

Chase, Philander

Chase, Salmon P.

Chase, Samuel

Chase, Stuart

Chase, Sylvia

Chase, William Merritt

Chase City

Chase Field Naval Air Station

Chase Lincoln First Bank

Chase Manhattan Bank

Chase Manhattan Corporation, The

Chase Manhattan Foundation

Chasid, *n.*, *pl.* Chasidim

Chassériau, Théodore

Châteaubriand, François René

Château d'If

Château d'Yquem *occas.* Yquem

Chateaugay

Chateaugay Lake

Châteauroux

Château-Thierry

Chatfield College

Chatham

Chatham, William Pitt

Chatham College

Chatham Islands

Chattahoochee

Chattahoochee National Forest

Chattahoochee Review, The

Chattahoochee River National Recreation Area

Chattahoochee Valley State Community College

Chattahoochee Technical Institute

Chattanooga

Chattanooga campaign

Chattanoogan

Chattanooga News—Free Press

Chattanooga State Technical Community College

Chattanoogian

Chatterton, Ruth

Chatterton, Thomas

Chattertonian

Chatwood

Chaucer, Geoffrey

Chaucerian

Chaumont

Chauncey

Chausson, Ernest

Chautauqua *often* chautauqua

Chautauqua Institution, The

Chautauqua Lake

Chautauqua Literary and Scientific Circle, The

Chautauqua movement

Chauvin, Nicolas

Chavez, Carlos

Chavez, Cesar

Chayefsky, Paddy

Cheapside

Cheap Trick

Chebacco boat

Cheboygan [* MI; *see also* Sheboygan]

Cheboygan River

Checker, Chubby

Checkpoint Charlie

Checotah

Cheddar *or* cheddar cheese

Cheech

Cheech and Chong

Cheektowago

Cheers

Cheeseman Dam

Cheetah and Stag with Two Indians

Cheever, John

Cheever, Susan

Chehalis

Chehalis [Indian], *n.*, *pl.* Chehalis *or* Chehalises

Chehalis River

Cheju

Cheka

Chekhov, Anton

Chekhov, Pavel

Chekhovian

Chekiang [*now* Zhejiang]

Chelmno

Chelsea

Chelsea ware

Cheltenham

Chemeketa Community College

Chemical Bank

Chemical Banking Corporation

Chemical Mace™

Chemical Manufacturers Association

Chemical Waste Management, Inc.

Chemin des Dames

Chemnitz [*form.* Karl-Marx-Stadt]

Chemotherapy Foundation

Chen, Zuohang

Chenab

Chen and Dancers

Chenenko, Konstantin

Cheney

Cheney, Richard B.

Cheng-chou [*now* Zhengzhou]

Ch'eng-tu [*now* Chengdu]

Chénier, André

chenin blanc *or* Chenin Blanc

Chennault, Claire

Chén Tu-Hsui

Cheops

Chequamegon National Forest

Cher

Cheraw

Cherbourg

Cherenkov, Pavel A.

Cherenkov radiation

Cherkassky, Shura

Chernenko, Konstantin

Chernobyl

Chernobyl nuclear accident

Chernobyl nuclear power plant

Chernomydrin, Viktor

Cherokee

Cherokee Dam

Cherokee Group, The

Cherokee [Indian], *n.*, *pl.* Cherokee *or* Cherokees

Cherokee Nation

Cherokee National Forest

Cherokee Nation v. State of Georgia

Cherokee Outlet

Cherokee rose

Cherokee Strip

Cherokee War

Cherry Blossom Festival

Cherry Heering

Cherry Hill

Cherry Hills Village

Cherry Orchard, The

Cherry Point Marine Corps Air Station

Cherryvale

Cherryville

Cherubini, Luigi

Cheryl

Chesapeake

Chesapeake and Delaware Canal

Chesapeake and Ohio Canal

Chesapeake and Ohio Canal National Historical Park

Chesapeake Bay

Chesapeake Bay Bridge-Tunnel

Chesapeake Bay Magazine

Chesapeake Bay retriever

Chesapeake College

Chesapeake Corporation

Chesbro, Jack

Chesebrough-Pond's, Inc.

Cheshire

Cheshire cat

Cheshire cheese

Chesnokov, Andrei

Chesnut, Mary

Chesnutt, Charles W.

Chessman, Caryl

Chester

Chesterfield

Chesterfield, Philip

Chesterfieldian

Chesterfield-Marlboro Technical College

Chesterton, G. K.

Chestertown

Chester White

Chestnut, Morris

Chestnut Hill

Chestnut Hill College

Chestnutt, Charles Waddell

Chesuncook Lake

Cheswick

Chet Huntley Reporting

Chetnik

Chevalier, Maurice

Cheverly

Cheviot

Cheviot Hills

Chevrolet, Louis

Chevrolet Motor Division (General Motors Corporation)

Chevron Corporation

Chevy Chase

Chevy Chase Savings Bank

Chewings fescue

Cheyenne

Cheyenne, The [sculpture]

Cheyenne Airport

Cheyenne-Arapaho War

Cheyenne Frontier Days

Cheyenne Frontier Days Rodeo

Cheyenne [Indian], *n.*, *pl.* Cheyenne *or* Cheyennes

Cheyenne Mountain Complex

Cheyenne River Sioux Tribe

Cheyne, Thomas Kelly

Cheyne-Stokes respiration

Cheyney University of Pennsylvania

CH-53E Super Stallion

CH-47 Chinook

CH-46 Sea Knight

Chiang Ch'ing [*now* Jiang Qing]

Chiang Ching-kuo

Chiang Kai-shek

Chiang Kai-Shek International Airport

Chiang Mai *or* Chiangmai

Chiang Rai *or* Chiangrai

Chaing Soong Mei-ling

Chianti

Chianti Mountains

Chian turpentine

Chiapas

Chiba Bank Ltd.

Chicago

Chicago Academy of Sciences

Chicagoan

Chicago and Northwestern Railroad

Chicago Bears

Chicago Black Hawks

Chicago blues

Chicago Board of Trade

Chicago Bulls

Chicago College of Osteopathic Medicine

Chicago Conspiracy Trial

Chicago Cubs

Chicago Defender

Chicago Heights

Chicago History

Chicago International Film Festival

Chicago jazz

ChicagoLand TV-CLTV

Chicago Magazine

Chicago Manual of Style, The

Chicago Mercantile Exchange

Chicago Midway Airport

Chicago, Milwaukee, Saint Paul and Pacific Railway

Chicago Musical College

Chicago Natural History Museum [*now* Field Museum of Natural History]

Chicago O'Hare International Airport

Chicago Pacific Corporation

Chicago Pacific Corporation Charitable Fund

Chicago Ridge

Chicago River

Chicago, Rock Island and Pacific Railroad

Chicago Sanitary and Ship Canal

Chicago school of architecture *or* Chicago School of Architecture

Chicago school of jazz *or* Chicago School of Jazz

Chicago School of Professional Psychology

Chicago Seven

Chicago Sinfonia

Chicago Stadium

Chicago State University

Chicago State University Cougars

Chicago Strike

Chicago-style jazz

Chicago Sun-Times

Chicago Sun-Times Charity Trust

Chicago Sun-Times Inc.

Chicago Symphony Orchestra

Chicago Theological Seminary

Chicago Transit Authority

Chicago Tribune

Chicago Tribune Foundation and Charities

Chicago Tribune Magazine

Chicago White Sox

Chicago Zoological Society

Chicana, *fem.*, *n.*, *pl.* Chicanas

Chicano, *masc.*, *n.*, *pl.* Chicanos

Chicano Law Review

Chichén Itzá

Chichester, Sir Francis

Chichicastenango

Chickahominy

Chickamauga

Chickamauga and Chattanooga National Military Park

Chickamauga Dam

Chickasaw [Indian], *n.*, *pl.* Chickasaw *or* Chickasaws

Chickasaw National Recreation Area

Chickasha

chicken Kiev

Chickering, Jonas

Chickering piano

Chico

Chico and the Man

Chicopee

Chicopee Center

Chicopee Falls

Chief Bender

Chief Big Foot

Chief Black Hawk

Chief Canonicus

Chief Cornplanter

Chief Crazy Horse

Chief Crowfoot

Chief Dull Knife

Chief Executive

Chief Gall

Chief Hendrick

Chief John Ross

Chief Joseph

Chief Justice of the United States

Chief Keokuk

Chief Little Turtle

Chief Lone Wolf

Chief Manuelito

Chief Massasoit

Chief Metacomet

Chief Moses

Chief Nemacolin

Chief of Naval Operations

Chief of Staff

Chief Osceola

Chief Plenty Coups

Chief Pontiac

Chief Popé

Chief Poundmaker
Chief Powhatan
Chief Red Bird
Chief Red Cloud
Chief Red Eagle
Chief Red Jacket
Chief Roman Nose
Chief Seattle
Chief Sequoyah *occas.*
  Sequoya
Chief Sitting Bull
Chief Spotted Tail
Chief Tammany
Chief Tecumseh
Chief Uncas
Chief Victorio
Chiffons, The
Chihuahua
CHI Institute
Chikamatsu
  Monzaemon
Chilcotin
Child, Francis James
Child, Julia
Child, Lydia Maria
Childbirth Education
  Foundation
Childbirth without
  Pain Education
  Association
Childe, Vere Gordon
Childebert
Childe Harold
Childe Harold's
  Pilgrimage
Childermas
Childe Roland
Childe Roland to the
  Dark Tower Came
Childersburg

Child Find of
  America, Inc.
Childhelp USA
Children, Inc.
Children International
Children of a Lesser
  God
Children's Aid
  International
Children's Aid Society
Children's Book
  Council
Children's Bureau
Children's Corner
Children's Crusade
Children's Day
Children's Defense
  Fund
Children's Digest
Children's Hour, The
Children's Legal
  Foundation
Children's Library
Children's Mercy
  Fund
Children's Radio
  Network
Children's Television
  Act
Children's Television
  Workshop
Child's Garden of
  Verses, A
Child's Play
Child Welfare League
  of America
Chile
Chilean
Chilean arborvitae
Chilean bellflower
Chilean guava

Chilean tarweed
Chile niter
Chile-Peruvian War
Chile saltpeter
Chili's Inc. [*now*
  Brinker
  International, Inc.]
Chilkat, *n., pl.* Chilkat
  or Chilkats
Chilkoot
Chilkoot Pass
Chillicothe
Chiltern Hills
Chiltern Hundreds
Chilton Book
  Company
Chilton™ manuals
Chimborazo
Chimney Rock
  National Historic
  Site
Chimu, *n., pl.* Chimu
  or Chimus
Chin, Tiffany
China
China Airlines, Ltd.
China aster
China Beach
China brown
China-Burma-India
  Veterans
  Association
China Daily (North
  American Edition)
China grass
China grass cloth
China Incident
China Lake Naval
  Weapons Center
Chinaman, *n., pl.*
  Chinamen

Chinaman's chance
China oil
China rose
China Sea
China silk
China stone
China syndrome
China Today
Chinatown
China white
Chincoteague
Chincoteague Bay
Chincoteague Island
Chindwin
Ch'in dynasty
 [221–206 BC; see
 also Ch'ing
 dynasty]
Chinese, n., pl.
 Chinese
Chinese-American
Chinese anise
Chinese architecture
Chinese art
Chinese artichoke
Chinese banana
Chinese boxes
Chinese cabbage
Chinese calendar
Chinese checkers
Chinese chestnut
Chinese Chippendale
Chinese cinammon
Chinese copy
Chinese crescent
Chinese Empire
Chinese evergreen
Chinese examination
 system

Chinese exclusion
 policy
Chinese fan palm
Chinese fleece-vine
Chinese forget-me-not
Chinese gelatin
Chinese glue
Chinese gooseberry
Chinese Gordon
Chinese hibiscus
Chinese house
Chinese ink
Chinese isinglass
Chinese-Japanese
 wars
Chinese jujube
Chinese juniper
Chinese lacquer
Chinese lantern
Chinese-lantern plant
Chinese literature
Chinese lug
Chinese music
Chinese New Year
Chinese parsley
Chinese pavilion
Chinese pistachio
Chinese potato
Chinese primrose
Chinese puzzle
Chinese quince
Chinese red
Chinese remainder
 theorem
Chinese restaurant
 syndrome
Chinese Revolution
Chinese rocks
Chinese scholar tree

Chinese snowball
Chinese tag
Chinese temple block
Chinese trumpet
 creeper
Chinese Turkestan
Chinese vermillion
Chinese Wall
Chinese watermelon
Chinese waterplant
Chinese water torture
Chinese wax
Chinese white
Chinese windlass
Chinese wisteria
Chinese wood block
Chinese wood oil
Chinese yam
Chingachgook
Ch'ing dynasty [AD
 1644–1912; see
 also Ch'in dynasty]
Chinghai [now
 Qinghai]
Chingtao [now
 Qingdao]
Chin Hills
Chino
Chinook, n., pl.
 Chinook or
 Chinooks
Chinookan
Chinook jargon
Chi Omega
Chios var. of Khíos
 Island
Chipewyan
Chi Phi
Chipley
Chipmunks, The

Chipola Junior College

Chippendale

Chippendale, Thomas

Chippewa

Chippewa Falls

Chippewa [Indian], *n.*, *pl.* Chippewa *or* Chippewas

Chippewa National Forest

Chippewa Valley Technical College

CHiPs

Chi Psi

Chiquita Brands International, Inc.

Chi-Rho, *n.*, *pl.* Chi-Rhos

Chiricahua, *n.*, *pl.* Chiricahua *or* Chiricahuas

Chiricahua Apache

Chiricahua Mountains

Chiricahua National Monument

Chirico, Giorgio de

Chiron

Chiron Corporation

Chisholm, Jesse

Chisholm, Shirley

Chisholm Trail

Chisum, John S.

Chitimacha

Chittenango

Chitty-Chitty-Bang-Bang

Ch'iu Ch'u-chi

Chloe

Choate, Joseph Hodges

Choate, Rufus

Chocano, José Santos

Chocolate Decadence™

Chocolate Grinder, No. 1

Choctaw, *n.*, *pl.* Choctaw *or* Choctaws

Choctawhatchee Bay

Choctawhatchee River

Choctaw-root

Cholon

Chomsky, Noam

Chomskyan

Chong, Rae Dawn

Chong, Tommy

Chongqing [*form.* Ch'ung-ch'ing]

Chopin, Frédéric

Chopin, Kate

Chopsticks

Choral Symphony

Chordata

C-horizon

Chorus Line, A

Chou dynasty

Chou En-lai [*now* Zhou En-lai]

Choukoutien

Chouteau, August Pierre

Chouteau, Jean Pierre

Chouteau, Pierre

Chouteau, René Auguste

Chowan College

Chowchilla

Chrétien *or* Chrestien de Troyes

Chris-Craft Industries, Inc.

Christ

Christadelphian

Christ Catholic Church

Christ Church [*aka* Old North Church]

Christchurch [* England; New Zealand]

Christchurch Grantley Adams International Airport

Christchurch International Airport

Christ College Irvine

Christe eleison

Christendom

Christendom College

Christhood

Christian

Christian, Charlie

Christian, Fletcher

Christian, Linda

Christiana

Christian and Missionary Alliance, The

Christian Appalachian Project, Inc.

Christian Blind Mission International

Christian Bookstore

Christian Brethren

Christian Broadcasting Association

Christian Broadcasting Network

Christian Brother

Christian Brothers™ brandy

Christian Brothers College

Christian Brothers University

Christian Catholic Church

Christian Children's Fund, Inc.

Christian Church (Disciples of Christ)

Christian Churches and Churches of Christ

Christian Congregation [formal organization]

Christian congregation [generic group]

Christian democracy

Christian Endeavor

Christian Era

Christian existentialism

Christian Herald

Christian Heritage College

Christian iconography

Christianism

Christianity

Christianity Today

Christianization

Christianizer

Christian Laity Counseling Board

Christian Light Bookstore

Christianlike

Christianly

Christian Methodist Episcopal Church

Christian Motorcyclists Association

Christian name

Christian Nation Church USA

Christian of Anhalt

Christian of Brunswick

Christian of Halberstadt

Christian Record Services, Inc.

Christian Reformed Church

Christian Reformed Church in North America

Christiansand

Christiansburg

Christian Science

Christian Science Monitor

Christian Science Publishing Society, The

Christian Scientist

Christian socialism occas. Socialism

Christian socialist occas. Socialist

Christiansted National Historic Site

Christian Theological Seminary

Christian Union

Christian year

Christie

Christie, Dame Agatha

Christie, Julie

Christie's International

Christina

Christine

Christ Jesus

Christless

Christlike

Christliness

Christly

Christmas

Christmasberry

Christmasberry tree

Christmas cactus

Christmas card

Christmas Carol, A

Christmas club

Christmas Day

Christmas disease

Christmas Eve

Christmas factor

Christmas fern

Christmas Island

Christmas Oratorio

Christmas pantomime

Christmas pudding

Christmas rose

Christmas seal

Christmas stocking

Christmassy or Christmasy

Christmastide

Christmastime

Christmas tree

Christo [artist]

Christo- [combining form]

Christocentric

Christ of the Andes

Christ of the Apocalypse

Christogram

Christological

Christologist

Christology

Christophany

Christophe, Henri

Christopher

Christopher, John

Christopher, Saint

Christopher, Warren

Christopher, William

Christopher Newport College

Christopher Robin

Christ's-thorn

Christ the King Seminary

Christ Washing the Disciples' Feet

Christ Within

Christy, *n.*, *pl.* Christies [skiing maneuver]

Christy, *n.*, *pl.* Christys [given name]

Christy, Howard Chandler

Christy, June

Chromel™

Chronicle Books

Chronicle Features

Chronicle of Higher Education, The

Chronicles of England, Scotland, and Ireland

Chronotron™

Chrysippus

Chrysler, Walter P.

Chrysler Building

Chrysler Capital Corporation

Chrysler Corporation

Chrysler Corporation Fund

Chrysler Financial Corporation

Chrysler Performance Parts Association

CH2M Hill Inc.

Chuang-tzu

Chubb Corporation, The

Chubb Group of Insurance Companies

Chugach Mountains

Chugach National Forest

Chu Hsi

Chukchi, *n.*, *pl.* Chukchi *or* Chukchi

Chukchi Peninsula

Chukchi Sea

Chukot Range

Chula Vista

Chumash

Chun Doo Hwan

Chung, Connie

Chungking *occas.* Ch'ung-ch'ing [*now* Chongqing]

Chun King™ foods

Chunnel

Chuo Trust and Banking Company, Ltd.

Church, Frederick

Church and Dwight Company, Inc.

Church Divinity School of the Pacific

Churches of Christ

Churches of Christ in Christian Union

Churches of God in North America

Churchill

Churchill, John

Churchill, Randolph

Churchill, Sarah

Churchill, Winston [American author]

Churchill, Sir Winston [English statesman and author]

Churchill Downs

Churchill Falls

Churchill River

Churchill Truck Lines, Inc.

Church of Christ

Church of Christ, Scientist

Church of England

Church of God [religious organizations in IN; TN]

Church of God, The [religious organization in AL]

Church of God by Faith

Church of God in Christ

Church of God in Christ, Congregational

Church of God in Christ, International

Church of God of Prophecy

Church of God School of Theology

Church of Ireland

Church of Jesus Christ, The

Church of Jesus Christ of Latter-day Saints

Church of Rome

Church of Saint Mary-le-Bow

Church of Scientology

Church of Scotland

Church of South India

Church of the Brethren

Church of the Holy Sepulcher

Church of the Lutheran Brethren of America

Church of the Lutheran Confession

Church of the Nazarene

Church of the New Jerusalem

Church of the Transfiguration

Church of the United Brethren in Christ

Church Point

Church Slavic *or* Slavonic

Church Women United

Chu Teh

Ciano, Galeazzo

Ciardi, John

Ciba Consumer Pharmaceuticals

Ciba-Geigy, Ltd.

Cibber, Colley

Cibola National Forest

Cicero

Cicero, Marcus Tullius

Cicero, Quintus Tullius

Ciceronian

Ciceronianism

Cid, The

Cienfuegos

Cigarette

Cigarette Labeling and Advertising Act

Cigar-Makers' International Union

CIGNA Corporation

CIGNA Foundation

CIGNA Property and Casualty Company

CILCORP Inc.

Cilea, Francesco

Cilicia

Cilician

Cilician Gates

Cima, Giovanni Battista

Cimabue, Giovanni

Cimarosa, Domenico

Cimarron

Cimarron Territory

Cimber

Cimino, Michael

Cincinnati

Cincinnatian

Cincinnati Art Museum

Cincinnati Bell Foundation

Cincinnati Bell, Inc.

Cincinnati Bengals

Cincinnati Bible College

Cincinnati College of Mortuary Science

Cincinnati Enquirer, The

Cincinnati Financial Corporation

Cincinnati Gas and Electric Company, The

Cincinnati Magazine

Cincinnati May Festival

Cincinnati Milacron Foundation

Cincinnati Milacron Inc.

Cincinnati/New Orleans City Ballet

Cincinnati Observatory

Cincinnati Post, The

Cincinnati Reds

Cincinnati Symphony Orchestra

Cincinnati Technical College

Cincinnatus, Lucius Quinctius

Cinco de Mayo

Cinderella

Cinderella Softball League

Cineman Syndicate

Cinema Paradiso

CinemaScope™

Cinemax

Cineplex™

Cineplex Odeon Corporation

Cinerama™

CineTellFilms

Cinna, Lucius Cornelius

Cinque Ports

Cioffi, Charles

Circassia

Circassian

Circassian walnut

Circe

Circean

Circle in the Square

Circle K Corporation, The

Circle K International

Circle K store

Circle Repertory Company

Circleville

Circleville Bible College

Circuit City Stores, Inc.

Circular Forms

Circus Circus Enterprises, Inc.

Circus Circus—Las Vegas

Circus Circus—Reno

Circus Fans Association of America

Circus Maximus

Cirque de Gavarnie

Cirque du Soleil

Cisalpine Gaul

Cisalpine Republic

Ciscaucasia

Cisco

Cisco Junior College

Cisco Kid

Cisneros, Henry

Cistercian

Cistercianism

Cistercian monk

Cistercian nun

Cistercians of the Common Observance

Cistercians of the Stricter Observance

Citadel Bulldogs

Citadel, The—The Military College of South Carolina

Citgo Petroleum Corporation

Citibank [*form.* First National City Bank]

Citibank (South Dakota)

Citicorp

Citicorp Center

Citizen Genêt

Citizen Kane

Citizens Alliance for VD Awareness

Citizens and Southern Corporation

Citizens and Southern Fund

Citizens and Southern National Bank, Atlanta

Citizens and Southern National Bank, Florida

Citizens and Southern National Bank of South Carolina

Citizens and Southern National Bank of

South Carolina Foundation

Citizens Band Radio Patrol

Citizens Federal Bank

Citizens for Decency Through Law

Citizenship Day

Citizens Savings Bank

Citizens' Scholarship Foundation of America, Inc.

Citizens Utilities Company

Citlaltepetl

Citroën, André-Gustave

Citrus Bowl

Citrus College

City Colleges of Chicago

City Lights

City National Corporation

City News Bureau of Chicago

City News Service, Inc.

City of Angels

City of Baguio

City of Brotherly Love

City of Cebu

City of Chicago

City of David

City of God [*aka* Jerusalem]

City of God, The [work by Saint Augustine]

City of Hope Medical Center

City of Light
City of Rocks
  National Preserve
City of Seven Hills
City Rises, The
City Savings
City Spire building
City University of
  New York
Ciudad Bolívar
Ciudad Juárez
Ciudad Obregon
Ciudad Victoria
Civil Aeronautics
  Administration
Civil Aeronautics
  Board
Civil Air Patrol
Civilian Conservation
  Corps
Civilian Health and
  Medical Program
  for the Uniformed
  Services
Civil Rights Act
Civil Service Reform
  Act
Civil War
Civil War Round
  Table of New York
Civil War Times
  Illustrated
Civitan International
Clackamas
  Community College
Clactonian culture
Claflin College
Claiborne, Craig
Claiborne, Liz
Claiborne's Rebellion
Clair, René

Clairault, Alexis
  Claude
Clairault's equation
Clair de Lune
Claire, Ina
Clair Engle Lake
Clairol, Inc.
Clairton
Clallam
Clampett, Elly May
Clampett, Jed
Clancy, Liam
Clancy, Paddy
Clancy, Tom
Clancy Brothers, The
Clancy Brothers and
  Tommy Makem
Clanton
Clapp, Norton
Clapton, Eric
Clara Barton National
  Historic Site
Clare, John
Clare, Saint
Clare Island
Claremont
Claremont Colleges
Claremont Graduate
  School
Claremont McKenna
  College
Claremont Men's
  College
Claremont University
  Center
Claremore
Clarence
Clarendon, Edward
  Hyde
Clarendon College

Clarendon Code
Clare of Assissi, Saint
Claretian
Clarinda
Clarion
Clarion Books™
Clarion hotel
Clarion Suites
Clarion University of
  Pennsylvania
Clarissa School of
  Fashion Design
Clark, Alfred James
Clark, Ann Nolan
Clark, Bobby
Clark, Buddy
Clark, Champ
Clark, Dane
Clark, Dick
Clark, Fred
Clark, George Rogers
Clark, Jim
Clark, John Bates
Clark, Mark Wayne
Clark, Mary Higgins
Clark, Petula
Clark, Ramsey
Clark, Roy
Clark, Susan
Clark, Tom
Clark, Walter van
  Tilburg
Clark, Will
Clark, William
Clark Air Base
Clark Atlanta
  University
Clark County
  Community College
Clarke, Arthur C.

Clarke, Bobby

Clarke, Fred

Clarke, George S.

Clarke, James Freeman

Clarke, Joe

Clarke, Kenny

Clarke beam

Clarke College

Clark Equipment Company

Clarke's gazelle

Clark Fork River [waterway in ID and MT; see also Clarks Fork River]

Clark occas. Clark's nutcracker

Clarksburg

Clark's crow

Clarksdale

Clarks Fork River [waterway in MT and WY; see also Clark Fork River]

Clarkson, John

Clarkson N. Potter™ Books

Clarkson Potter Publishers

Clarkson University

Clarks Summit

Clark State Community College

Clarkston

Clarksville

Clark University

Clary, Robert

Clashing Rocks

Classical Revival occas. classical revival

Classic Bookshops

Classic Car Club of America

Classic Car Digest

Classic Inn

Classics Club

Classics Illustrated

Clatsop

Clatsop Community College

Claude, Albert

Claude, Saint

Claudel, Paul

Claude Lorrain

Claudian

Claudius

Clausewitz, Carl von

Clausius, Rudolf

Clausius cycle

Clavell, James

Clawson

Clay, Andrew Dice

Clay, Bertha M.

Clay, Cassius [boxer; now Muhammad Ali]

Clay, Cassius Marcellus [American politician]

Clay, Henry

Clay, Lucius D.

Clayburgh, Jill

Clay Center

Clayderman, Richard

Claymation™

Clayton

Clayton, Buck

Clayton, Henry De Lamar

Clayton Antitrust Act

Clayton-Bulwer Treaty

Clayton fern

Clayton Homes, Inc.

Clayton State College

Clean Air Act

Clean Energy Research Institute

Cleanthes

Clean Water Act

Clear and Present Danger

Clearasil™

Clear Creek Baptist Bible College

Clearfield

Clearing House Interbank Payments

Clear Lake

Clearwater

Clearwater Christian College

Clearwater Mountains

Clearwater National Forest

Cleary, Beverly

Cleary College

Cleaveland, Moses

Cleaver, Beaver

Cleaver, Bill

Cleaver, Eldridge

Cleaver, Vera

Cleburn

Cleese, John

Cleland, John

Clemenceau, Georges

Clemens, Roger

Clemens, Samuel Langhorne

Clemens, Wenzel
  Metternich
Clement
Clement I, Saint
Clemente, Roberto
Clementi, Muzio
Clementine
Clement of
  Alexandria, Saint
Clement of Rome
Clementon
Clemson, Thomas
  Green
Clemson University
Clemson University
  Tigers
CLEO
  Communications
Cleomenes
Cleopatra
Cleopatra's Needles
Clergy and Laity
  Concerned
Clergy Reserves
Clermont
Clermont-Ferrand
Cleveland
Cleveland, Frances
  Folsom
Cleveland, Grover
Cleveland, James L.
Cleveland Browns
Cleveland Cavaliers
Cleveland
  Chiropractic
  College
Cleveland-Cliffs, Inc.
Cleveland College of
  Jewish Studies
Cleveland Community
  College

Cleveland Electric
  Illuminating
  Company
Cleveland Electric
  Illuminating
  Foundation
Cleveland Heights
Cleveland Hopkins
  International
  Airport
Cleveland Indians
Cleveland Institute of
  Art
Cleveland Institute of
  Electronics
Cleveland Institute of
  Music
Cleveland Magazine
Cleveland Metroparks
  Zoo
Cleveland Municipal
  Stadium
Cleveland Museum of
  Art
Cleveland Museum of
  Natural History
Cleveland National
  Air Show
Cleveland National
  Forest
Cleveland Orchestra
[Cleveland] Plain
  Dealer
Cleveland Play House
Cleveland Quartet
Cleveland/San Jose
  Ballet
Cleveland Stadium
Cleveland State
  Community College
Cleveland State
  University

Cleveland State
  University Vikings
Clew Bay
Cliff, Jimmy
Clifford, Clark
Clifford, Nathan
Clifford, William
  Kingdom
Cliffside Park
Cliffs Notes™
Clift, Montgomery
Clifton
Clifton Forge
Clifton Heights
Climax Blues Band,
  The
Clinch
Clinch Valley College
  of the University of
  Virginia
Cline, Patsy
Clingmans Dome
Clinton
Clinton, Bill
Clinton, Chelsea
Clinton, DeWitt
Clinton, George
Clinton, Sir Henry
Clinton, Hillary
  Rodham
Clinton, James
Clinton Community
  College
Clinton Junior College
Clio
Clio [award], *n.*, *pl.*
  Clios
Clipperton Island
Clive, Colin
Clive, Robert

Clockmaker, The
Cloister and the Hearth, The
Cloisters, The
Clooney, Rosemary
Cloquet
Clorox Company, The
Clorox Company Foundation, The
Close, Glenn
Close Encounters of the Third Kind
Closter
Clotaire
Clotilda, Saint
Cloud *occas.* Clodoald *or* Chlodovald, Saint
Cloud County Community College
Clouet, François
Clouet, Jean
Clough, Arthur Hugh
Clouseau, Inspector
Clover
Cloverdale
Clovers, The
Clovio, Giorgio Giulio
Clovis
Clovis culture
Clowns
Club Med, Inc. [no period after Med]
Club Med resort
Club MTV
Club of Paris
Cluniac order
Cluny
Cluny lace
Cluny Museum

Clurman, Harold
Clute City
Clyde
Clyde, Andy
Clyde McPhatter and the Drifters
Clydesdale
Clymer Publishing
Clytemnestra
CML Company
CMS Energy Corporation
CNA Financial Corporation
CNG Foundation
Cnidaria
CNN Radio Network
Cnossus *var. of* Knossos
Coachella
Coachella Valley
Coachmen Industries, Inc.
Coade stone
Coahoma Community College
Coahuila
Coahuiltec
Coal City
Coal Grove
Coalinga
Coalition for Literacy
Coanda, Henri Marie
Coase, Ronald H.
Coastal Carolina College Chanticleers
Coastal Carolina Community College
Coastal Corporation, The

Coasters, The
Coast Federal Bank
Coast Guard Medal
Coastline Community College
Coast Mountains
Coast Range
Coast Salish
Coates, Eric
Coatesville
Coatsworth, Elizabeth
Cobb, Irwin S.
Cobb, Julie
Cobb, Lee J.
Cobb, Ty
Cobbett, William
Cobble Mountain Dam
Cobble Mountain Reservoir
Cobden, Richard
Cobham, John Oldcastle
Cobleskill
Cobourg Peninsula
Coburn, Charles
Coburn, James
Coca, Imogene
Coca-Cola™
Coca-Cola Company, The
Coca-Cola Enterprises Inc.
Coca-Cola Foundation
Coca-Cola 600
Coca-Cola 600 Winston Cup
Cochabamba
Cochimi

Cochin *or* cochin chicken

Cochin China

Cochise

Cochise College

Cochran, Barbara Ann

Cochran, Eddie

Cochran, Jacqueline

Cochrane, Mickey

Cochran School of Nursing

Cockaigne

Cockburn, Bruce

Cockcroft, Sir John Douglas

Cocker, Joe

Cock Robin

Cocktail Party, The

Coco, James

Cocoa

Cocoa Beach

Cocoanuts, The

Cocoa West

Coconino National Forest

Coconino Plateau

Coconut Grove

Cocopa

Cocos Islands

Cocteau, Jean

Coddington, William

Code Napoléon

Code of Canon Law

Code of Hammurabi

Code of Manu

Cody

Cody, Iron Eyes

Cody, John Patrick Cardinal

Cody, William Frederick

Coe, Sebastian

Coe College

CO-ED-HI-Y club

Coen, Ethan

Coen, Joel

Coetzee, Gerrie

Coeur, Jacques

Coeur d'Alene

Coeur d'Alene Lake

Coeur d'Alene Mountains

Coeur d'Alene National Forest

Coeur de Lion

Coffeeville [* MO]

Coffeyville [* KS]

Coffeyville Community College

Coffin, Henry Sloane

Coffin, Levi

Coffin, Robert

Coffin, William Sloan

Cognac

Cogswell chair

Cogswell College

Cohan, George M.

Cohasset

Cohen, Arthur G.

Cohen, Leonard

Cohen, Mickey

Cohen, Morris

Cohen, Myron

Cohen, Octavus Roy

Cohn, Al

Cohn, Ferdinand Julius

Cohn, Marc

Cohn, Mindy

Cohn, Seymour

Cohoes

Coin World

Coit Tower

Coke™

Coke, Sir Edward

Coker College

Cokesbury bookstore

Colasanto, Nicholas

Colbert, Claudette

Colbert, Jean Baptiste

Colbert, Robert

Colby

Colby, Anita

Colby cheese

Colby College

Colby Community College

Colby Mountain

Colby-Sawyer College

Colden, Cadwallader

Colden Mountain

Cold Harbor

Coldstreamers

Coldstream Guards

Cold War *occas.* cold war

Coldwell Banker Real Estate Group, Inc.

Cole, Cozy

Cole, Gary

Cole, Natalie

Cole, Nat "King"

Cole, Olivia

Cole, Thomas

Cole, Timothy

Colegio Biblico Pentecostal de Puerto Rico

Coleman

Coleman, Cy

Coleman, Dabney

Coleman, Desiree

Coleman, Gary

Coleman, Ornette

Coleman College

Coleridge, Mary

Coleridge, Samuel Taylor [English poet]

Coleridge-Taylor, Samuel [English composer]

Coleridge-Taylor Choral Society

Coles the Book People

Colet, John

Colette [given name; pseudonym of Sidonie Gabrielle Colette; see also Collette]

Colfax, Schuyler

Colgate, William

Colgate Comedy Hour, The

Colgate-Palmolive Company

Colgate Rochester-Bexley Hall-Crozer Divinity School Seminary

Colgate University

Colgate University Red Raiders

Colicos, John

Colima [Mexican city; Mexican state; volcano; see also Coloma]

Colin

Colisee de Quebec

Coliseum var. of [Roman] Colosseum

Colket, Tristram C., Jr.

Collaborative Research

Collective Federal Savings Bank

College Board

College Bowl

Collège de France

College English

College English Association

College Entrance Examination Board

College Football Hall of Fame

College for Developmental Studies

College for Human Services

College Garden

College Level Examination Program

College Misericordia

College Music Society

College of Aeronautics

College of Alameda

College of Arms

College of Associated Arts

College of Boca Raton

College of Cardinals

College of Charleston

College of Du Page

College of Eastern Utah

College of Great Falls

College of Idaho

College of Lake County

College of Marin

College of Micronesia

College of Mount Saint Joseph

College of Mount Saint Vincent

College of New Rochelle

College of Notre Dame

College of Notre Dame of Maryland

College of Oceaneering

College of Osteopathic Medicine of Oklahoma State University

College of Osteopathic Medicine of the Pacific

College of Our Lady of the Elms

College of Propaganda

College of Saint Benedict

College of Saint Catherine

College of Saint Elizabeth

College of Saint Francis

College of Saint Joseph

College of Saint Mary

College of Saint Rose

College of Saint Scholastica

College of Saint Thomas

College of San Mateo

College of Santa Fe

College of Southern Idaho

College of the Atlantic

College of the Holy Cross

College of the Holy Cross Crusaders

College of the Southwest

College of William and Mary

College of William and Mary Tribe

College of Wooster

College Park

College Place

College Placement Council

College Press Service

College Station

Collegeville

Colles' fracture

Collette [given name; see also Colette]

Collier, Jeremy

Collin County Community College

Collingdale

Collingswood

Collingwood, Charles

Collins, Dorothy

Collins, Eddie

Collins, Gary

Collins, Hunt

Collins, Jackie

Collins, Jimmy

Collins, Joan

Collins, Judy

Collins, Martha

Collins, Michael

Collins, Pauline

Collins, Phil

Collins, Ray

Collins, Stephen

Collins, Wilkie

Collins, William

Collins Foods, Inc. [now Sizzler International, Inc.]

Collinsville

Collodi, Carlo

Colloquy of Poissy

Collor de Mello, Fernando

Collyer, Bud

Colman, Ronald

Colman, Saint

Cologne

Cologne-Bonn International Airport

Cologne brown

Cologne Cathedral

Cologne occas. cologne spirits

Coloma [CA gold discovery site; see also Colima]

Colombes

Colombia [nation in South America; see also Columbia]

Colombo [capital of Sri Lanka; see also Columbo]

Colombo agent

Colombo National Museum

Colombo Plan

Colón

Colón Archipelago

Colonel Blimp

Colonel Blimpism

Colonel Bogey March

Colonel Sanders

Colonial Country Club

Colonial Dames of America

Colonial Heights

Colonial Motor Freight Line, Inc.

Colonial National Historical Park

Colonial National Invitational Golf Tournament

Colonial Penn Insurance Company

Colonial Williamsburg

Colonie

Colonna, Jerry

Colophon

Colophon Books™

Colophonian

Coloradan

Colorado

Colorado Aero Tech

Coloradoan

Colorado Aqueduct

Colorado beetle

Colorado-Big Thompson Project

Colorado Christian University

Colorado City

Colorado College

Colorado Desert

Colorado Homes and Lifestyles

Colorado Institute of Art

Colorado Mountain College

Colorado National Monument

Colorado Northwestern Community College

Colorado Plateau

Colorado potato beetle

Colorado red cedar

Colorado Review

Colorado River

Colorado River Association

Colorado River Storage Project

Colorado Rockies

Colorado School of Mines

Colorado Springs

Colorado spruce

Colorado State University

Colorado State University Rams

Colorado Technical College

Color Me Badd

Color Purple, The

Colossae

Colosseum *occas.* Coliseum

Colossian

Colossus of Memnon

Colossus of Rhodes

Colt, Samuel

Colt™ firearms

Colt .45™ malt liquor

Colton

Coltrane, John

Colum, Padraic

Columba

Columba, Saint

Columban *or* Columbanus, Saint

Columbia [* MD; MO; SC; feminine personification of United States; magazine; space shuttle; *see also* Colombia]

Columbia Basin College

Columbia Basin Project

Columbia Bible College and Seminary

Columbia Broadcasting System [*now* CBS Inc.]

Columbia Center

Columbia Christian College

Columbia City

Columbia College

Columbia College of Nursing

Columbia Features, Inc.

Columbia Gas System, Inc., The

Columbia Glacier

Columbia-Greene Community College

Columbia Heights

Columbia Journalism Review

Columbia Junior College

Columbia Law Review

Columbian

Columbiana

Columbia Peak

Columbia Pictures Entertainment Inc.

Columbia Pictures Television

Columbia Plateau

Columbia-Princeton Electronic Music Center

Columbia River

Columbia River Gorge

Columbia Savings and Loan Association

Columbia sheep

Columbia space shuttle

[Columbia] State, The

Columbia State Community College

Columbia Symphony Orchestra

Columbia, the Gem of the Ocean

Columbia Theological Seminary

Columbia Union College

Columbia University

Columbia University Lions

Columbia University Press

Columbia University Teachers College

Columbine

Columbo [television series; *see also* Colombo]

Columbo, Russ
Columbus
Columbus, Chris
Columbus, Christopher
Columbus Air Force Base
Columbus College
Columbus College of Art and Design
Columbus Day
Columbus Dispatch, The
Columbus International Airport
Columbus State Community College
Columbus Technical Institute
Colusa
Colville
Colville National Forest
Colvin
Coma Berenices
Comanche
Comanchean
Comanche [Indian], n., pl. Comanche or Comanches
Comaneci, Nadia
Combat Infantryman Badge
Combe-Capelle man
Combs, Earle
Combustion Engineering
Comcast Corporation
Comden, Betty
Comdisco, Inc.

Comédie Française
Comedy Central
Comedy of Errors, The
Comedy Television
Comenius, John Amos
Comer, Gary Campbell
Comerica Bank
Comerica Inc.
Comet
Comet, Catherine
Comet Group
Comfort Inn
Comfort Suites
Comines, Phillippe de
Cominform
Cominformist
Coming to America
Comintern
Comin' Thro' the Rye
Comiskey, Charles A.
Comiskey Park
Commack
Commager, Henry Steele
Commander Cody
Commander Islands
Commendation Medal
Commerce
Commerce City
Commerce Clearing House, Inc.
Commerce Town
Commercial Federal Bank
Commercial Law League of America
Commerzbank

Commines, Philippe de
Commissioned Officers Association of the United States Public Health Service
Commissioners Standard Ordinary Table
Commission on Civil Rights
Committee for a Constructive Tomorrow, The
Committee for a National Pension Plan
Committee for a Sane Nuclear Policy
Committee for Economic Development
Committee for Food and Shelter
Committee for Humane Legislation
Committee for State Security
Committee of Public Safety
Commodity Credit Corporation
Commodity Exchange Authority
Commodity Exchange Inc.
Commodity Futures Trading Commission
Commodity News Services, Inc.
Commodity Quotations, Inc.

Commodity Research Bureau

Commodity Research Bureau's Futures Price Index

Commodore Cruise Line

Commodore International Ltd.

Commodores, The

Commodus, Lucius

Common Bible, The

Common Cause

Common Cause Magazine

Commoner, Barry

Common Era

Common Market *occas.* common market

Commons, John R.

Common Sense

Common Sense Book of Baby and Child Care, The

Commonwealth [*form.* British Commonwealth of Nations]

Commonwealth Club of California

Commonwealth College

Commonwealth College of Funeral Service

Commonwealth Day

Commonwealth Edison Company

Commonwealth Fund

Commonwealth Games

Commonwealth Life Insurance Company

Commonwealth of Independent States

Commonwealth of Nations [*form.* British Commonwealth of Nations]

Communard

Commune of Paris

Communications International/National News

Communications Satellite Corporation

Communications Workers of America

Communion Sunday

Communism

Communist

Communist Bloc *or* bloc

Communist-Bloc *or* -bloc nations

Communist China

Communist International

Communist League of Youth

Communist Manifesto

Communist Party

Community and Suburban Press Service

Community Antenna Television

Community College of Allegheny County

Community College of Aurora

Community College of Beaver County

Community College of Denver

Community College of Micronesia

Community College of Philadelphia

Community College of Rhode Island

Community College of the Air Force

Community College of the Finger Lakes

Community College of Vermont

Community College System

Community Hospital of Roanoke Valley College of Health Sciences

Community Psychiatric Centers

Comnenus, *n., pl.* Comneni

Como, Perry

Comoro Islands

Comoros

Compagnie des Machines Bull

Compañía Mexicana de Aviación

Compañía Panameña de Aviacón

Company [play]

Company, the [nickname for the CIA]

COMPAQ Computer Corporation

COMPAQ Computer Foundation

Comparative and International Education Society

Compassion International, Inc.

Compazine™

Compiègne

Compleat Angler, The

Composers String Quartet

Composite Order

Compound E

Compound W™

Comprehensive Crime Control Act

Comprehensive Employment and Training Act

Compromise of Breda

Compromise of 1850

Compton

Compton, Arthur Holly

Compton, Betty

Compton, Karl Taylor

Compton-Burnett, Dame Ivy

Compton Community College

Compton-Debye effect

Compton effect

Compton Observatory [*form.* Gamma Ray Observatory]

Compton's Encyclopedia

Compton's MultiMedia Encyclopedia

Comptroller General of the United States

Comptroller of the Currency

CompUSA

CompuServe Information Services, Inc.

COMPUTE

Computer Associates International, Inc.

Computer Features

Computer Graphics World

Computerland

Computer Sciences Corporation

Computer Shopper

Computerworld

Comsat™

Comstock, Anthony

Comstock, Henry

Comstockery *occas.* comstockery

Comstockian

Comstock Law

Comstock Lode

Comstock Silver Lode

Comte, Auguste

Comtesse d'Haussonville

Comtian *or* Comtean doctrine

Comtism

Comtist

COMTRAD INDUSTRIES

Comtrex™

Comus

ConAgra Charitable Foundation

ConAgra, Inc.

Conakry

Conakry G'bessia International Airport

Conant, James B.

Conant, Roger

Conan the Barbarian

Conan the Destroyer

Concentration

Concepción

Conception Seminary College

Concern for Dying

Concert Champêtre

Concertgebouw Orchestra [of Amsterdam]

Concert of Europe

Conchos

Concord

Concordat of 1801

Concordat of Worms

Concord coach

Concord College

Concorde

Concord grape

Concordia

Concordia College

Concordia College at Moorhead

Concordia College— Saint Paul

Concordia Lutheran College

Concordia Seminary

Concordia Teachers College

Concordia Theological Seminary

Concordia University

Concordia University, Wisconsin

Concord Naval Weapons Station

Concord River

Concord String Quartet

Condé, Louis II de Bourbon

Condé Museum

Condé Nast Traveler

Condillac, Étienne Bonnot de

Condon, Eddie

Condon, Edward U.

Condorcet, Marie Jean

Conecuh National Forest

C-118 Liftmaster

C-141 Starlifter

Conelrad

Conemaugh

C-119 Flying Boxcar

Conestoga

Conestoga Valley

Conestoga wagon

C-130 Hercules

C-133 Cargomaster

C-124 Globemaster

C-123 Provider

Coney Island

Confederacy, the

Confederacy of Dunces, A

Confederate Air Force

Confederate Memorial Day

Confederate Museum

Confederate rose

Confederate States

Confederate States of America

Confederate vine

Confederate violet

Confederation Life Insurance Company

Confederation of Arab Republics

Confederation of Bar

Confederation of the Rhine

Conference of Berlin

Conference of Genoa

Conference of San Remo

Conference on Security and Cooperation in Europe

Confessing Church

Confessions, The

Confessions of Nat Turner, The

Confiteor

Confiteor Deo

Confraternity of Christian Doctrine

Confrerie de la Chain des Rotisseurs, Baillage des United States of America

Confucian

Confucianism

Confucianist

Confucius

Congaree

Congaree Swamp National Monument

Congel, Robert J.

Congo [*now* Zaire]

Congo color

Congo dye

Congo eel

Congolese, *n.*, *pl.* Congolese

Congo red

Congo River

Congregational Holiness Church

Congregationalism

Congregationalist churches

Congregation of Jesus and Mary

Congregation of Saint Maur

Congregation of the Missionary Sons of the Immaculate Heart of Mary

Congregation of the Most Holy Redeemer

Congregation of the Oratory

Congregation of the Oratory of Saint Philip Neri

Congressional Budget Office

Congressional Digest

Congressional Directory

Congressional district

Congressional Information Service, Inc.

Congressional Medal of Honor [correctly Medal of Honor]

Congressional Quarterly Books

Congressional Quarterly, Inc.

Congressional Quarterly Service

Congressional Record

Congressional Space Medal of Honor
Congress of Berlin
Congress of Laibach
Congress of Paris
Congress of Racial Equality
Congress of the United States
Congress of Troppau
Congress of Verona
Congress of Vienna
Congreve, William [English dramatist]
Congreve, Sir William [English inventor]
Congreve rocket
Coni, Sally
Coniferophyta
Conkling, Roscoe
Conlan, Jocko
Conlee, John
Conley, Earl Thomas
Conlin, Thomas B.
Connally, John
Connaught
Connaught Tunnel
Conneault
Connecticut
Connecticut Bank and Trust Company
Connecticut chest
Connecticut College
Connecticut Compromise
Connecticut General Life Insurance Company
Connecticut Lakes
Connecticut Mutual Life Foundation

Connecticut Mutual Life Insurance Company
Connecticut National Bank
Connecticut Reserve
Connecticut River
Connecticut warbler
Connecticut Wits
Connecticut Yankee, A [movie; play]
Connecticut Yankee in King Arthur's Court, A [book]
Connell, Evan S.
Connell, Grover
Connellsville
Connelly, Jennifer
Connelly, Marc
Connemara
Conner, Dennis
Conner, Nadine
Conner Peripherals, Inc.
Connersville
Connery, Sean
Connick, Harry, Jr.
Conniff, Ray
Connolly, Cyril
Connolly, Maureen
Connolly, Tom
Connolly, Walter
Connor, Ralph
Connor, Roger
Connors, Chuck
Connors, Jimmy
Connors, Mike
Connors State College
Conn Smythe Trophy
Conn's syndrome

Conoco Inc.
Conover, Catherine Mellon
Conowingo Dam
Conowingo Lake
Conrad
Conrad, Barnaby
Conrad, Charles, Jr.
Conrad, Con
Conrad, Joseph
Conrad, Mike
Conrad, Paul
Conrad, Robert
Conrad, William
Conrad of Marburg
Conrad the Red
Conrail
Conrail train
Conreid, Hans
Conroe
Conroy, Pat
Conservation Foundation, The
Conservation International
Conservation International Foundation
Conservative Baptist
Conservative Baptist Association of America
Conservative Baptist Fellowship
Conservative Congregational Christian Conference
Conservative Jew
Conservative Judaism
Conservative Party

Conservatory of Music of Puerto Rico

Conshocken

Considine, Bob

Consolidated Edison Company of New York, Inc.

Consolidated Freightways, Inc.

Consolidated Natural Gas Company

Consolidated Papers Foundation

Consolidated Papers Inc.

Consolidated PBY Catalina

Consolidated Rail Corporation

Consortium for Graduate Study in Management

Constable, Henry

Constable, John

Constance

Constans

Constant, Benjamin

Constant de Rebecque, Henri Benjamin

Constantian Society, The

Constantine

Constantine, Michael

Constantine the Great

Constantinople [now Istanbul]

Constantinopolitan Creed

Constantinopolitan rite

Constantius

Constar International Inc.

Constitution [aka Old Ironsides]

Constitutional Convention

Constitution clock

Constitution Gardens

Constitution Island

Constitution mirror

Constitution of Athens

Constitution of the United States

Construction Industry Manufacturers Association

Construction Specifications Institute

Constructivism occas. constructivism

Consumer Discount Network

Consumer Federation of America

Consumer Guide

Consumer News and Business Channel

Consumer Price Index

Consumer Product Safety Commission

Consumer Protection Institute

Consumer Reports

Consumer Reports Books

Consumers Digest

Consumers Union of the United States

Consus

Conte, Richard

Contel Cellular Inc.

Contel Corporation

Contemporary Art Museum, Sao Paulo University

Contemporary Books, Inc.

Contemporary Chamber Ensemble

Contemporary Chamber Players

contempt of Congress

Conti, Tom

Continental Airlines Holdings, Inc.

Continental Airlines, Inc.

Continental Army

Continental Assurance Company

Continental Baking Company

Continental Bank

Continental Bank Corporation

Continental Basketball Association

Continental Celtic

Continental Congress

Continental Corporation, The

Continental Corporation Foundation

Continental Divide

Continental Grain Company

Continental Insurance Companies

Continental Medical Systems, Inc.

Continental System

Continent Ostomy Centers, The

Contra Costa Community College

Control Data Corporation

Convention of Kloster-Zeven

Conventual Mass

Converse, Frederick Shepherd

Converse College

Conversion of Saint Paul

Convex Computer Corporation

Convy, Bert

Conway

Conway, Tim

Conway Cabal

Conway School of Landscape Design

Cooder, Ry

Coogan, Jackie

Cook, Barbara

Cook, Frederick

Cook, George

Cook, James

Cook, Jane Bancroft

Cook, Peter

Cook, Robin

Cook, Thomas

Cook, William Alfred

Cooke, Alistair

Cooke, Hope

Cooke, Jack Kent

Cooke, Jay

Cooke, Phoebe Hearst

Cooke, Sam

Cooke, Terrence Cardinal

Cooke County College

Cookeville

Cookie Monster

Cooking Light

Cook Inlet

Cook Islands

Cook's tour

Cook Strait

Cooley, Charles Horton

Cooley, Spade

Cooley, Thomas B.

Cooley's anemia

Coolidge, Calvin

Coolidge, Grace

Coolidge, Rita

Coolidge, William D.

Coolidge Dam

Coolidge tube

Cooney, Gerry

Cooney, Joan Ganz

Coon Rapids

Coonts, Stephen

Cooper, Alice

Cooper, Gary

Cooper, Gladys

Cooper, Jackie

Cooper, James Fenimore

Cooper, Jeanne

Cooper, Leroy Gordon, Jr.

Cooper, Marilyn

Cooper, Melville

Cooper, Peter

Cooper, Stoney

Cooper, Susan

Cooper, William

Cooperative Extension System

Cooperative for American Relief Everywhere

Cooperative League of the United States of America

Cooper Companies, Inc., The

Cooper Industries Foundation

Cooper Industries Inc.

Coopers and Lybrand

Coopers Animal Health Inc.

Cooper's hawk

Cooperstown

Cooper Tire and Rubber Company

Cooper Union

Coordinated Universal Time

Coors, Adolph

Coosa

Coos Bay

Copacabana Beach

Copas, Cowboy

Copenhagen

Copenhagen Airport West

Copenhagen International Airport

[Copenhagen] Royal Museum of Fine Arts

Copenhagen ware

Copernican

Copernicanism

Copernican revolution

Copernican system

Copernicus, Nicolaus

Copiague

Copiah-Lincoln Community College

Copland, Aaron

Copley, Helen Kinney

Copley, John Singleton

Copley Newspapers/ The Copley Press, Inc.

Copley News Service

Coppard, A. E.

Coppée, François

Coppélia

Copper

Copper Age

Copperas Cove

Copper Bowl

Copperfield, David

Copperhead

Copperheadism

Coppermine

Coppin State College

Coppin State College Eagles

Coppola, Francis Ford

Cops

Copt

Coptic

Coptic art

Coptic Church

Coptic language

Coptic Orthodox Church

Copyright Act

Coquelin, Benoît Constant

Coquille

Coquille River

Coquille- *occas.* coquille-Saint-Jacques

Coral Gables

Coral Gables Federal Savings and Loan Association

Coral Sea

Coramine™

Coraopolis

Corbett, "Gentleman" Jim

Corbin

Corby, Ellen

Corcoran

Corcoran, William Wilson

Corcoran Gallery of Art

Corcoran School of Art

Corcovado

Cord, Alex

Cord automobile

Corday d' Armont, Charlotte

Cordele

Cordero, Angel

Cordesman, Anthony

Córdoba

Cordovan

Cordura™

Corea, Chick

Coreggio

Corelli, Arcangelo

Corelli, Franco

Corelli, Marie

CoreStates Bank

CoreStates Financial Corporation

Corey

Corey, Jeff

Corey, Wendell

Corfam™

Corfu

Corian™

Corinth

Corinth, Lovis

Corinthian

Corinthian brass

Corinthian Order

Corinthian War

Coriolanus

Coriolanus, Gaius Marcius

Coriolis, Gaspard Gustave de

Coriolis acceleration

Coriolis effect

Coriolis force

Cork

Cormack, Allan

Corn Belt

Corneille, Pierre

Cornelia

Cornelius

Cornelius, Helen

Cornelius, Peter von

Cornelius, Saint

Cornell

Cornell, Don

Cornell, Ezra

Cornell, Joseph

Cornell, Katharine

Cornell College

Cornell Law Review

Cornell University

Cornell University Big Red

Cornell University Medical Center

Cornell University Statutory Colleges

Cornerstone Christian Bookstore

Cornhuskers Ordnance Plant

Corning

Corning, Erastus

Corning Community College

Corning Inc.

Corning Inc. Foundation

Cornish

Cornish College of the Arts

Cornish cream

Cornish engine

Cornish hen

Cornish literature

Cornishman, n., pl. Cornishmen

Cornish stone

Corn Law

Cornwall

Cornwallis, Charles

Coromandel Coast

Coromandel work

Corona

Corona Australis

Corona Borealis

Coronado

Coronado, Francisco Vásquez de

Coronado National Forest

Coronado National Memorial

Coronado Naval Amphibious Base

Coronary Heart Disease Research Project

Coronation of the Virgin

Corot, Jean Baptiste Camille

Corporate Angel Network

Corporate Average Fuel Economy standard

Corporation Act

Corporation for Public Broadcasting

Corps of Engineers

Corpus Christi

Corpus Christi Bay

Corpus Christi International Airport

Corpus Christi Naval Air Station

Corpus Christi State University

Corpus Jurus Canonici

Corpus Jurus Civilis

Correggio

Corregidor

Correll, Charles

Correr Museum

Correspondence Chess League of America

Corrèze

Corriedale

Corrigan, Wrong Way

Corry

Corsica

Corsican

Corsicana

Corsican sandwort

Corso, Gregory

Cortaid™

Cortázar, Julio

Corte Madera

Corte-Real, Gaspar

Cortes [Spanish legislature; see also Cortez]

Cortés, Hernán or Hernando

Cortez [* CO; see also Cortes]

Corti, Alfonso

Cortland

Cortona, Pietro da

Corvallis

Corvus

Corwin, Norman Lewis

Cory

Coryate or Coryat, Thomas

Corydon

Coryell, John Russell

Coryell, Larry

Cosa Nostra

Cosby, Bill

Cosby Show, The

Cosell, Howard

Cosgrave, William Thomas

Coshocton

Cosi Fan Tutte

Cosmoline™

Cosmopolitan

Cosmopolitan International

Cosmos

Cossack

Costa, Lorenzo

Costa Brava

Costa Cruises

Costa del Sol

Costain, Thomas B.
Costa Mesa
Costa Rica
Costa Rican
Costa Rica nightshade
Costas, Bob
Costco Wholesale
  Corporation
Costello, Dolores
Costello, Elvis
Costello, Helene
Costello, John
  Aloysius
Costello, Lou
Costello, Maurice
Coster, Nicolas
Costner, Kevin
Cosumnes River
Cosumnes River
  College
Côte d'Azur
Côte d'Ivoire
Côte d'Or
Côtes d'Nord
Cotonu
Cotonu International
  Airport
Cotopaxi
Cotswold
Cotswold Hills
Cotswolds, the
Cottage Grove
Cottage Hills
Cotten, Joseph
Cottey College
Cottian Alps
Cotton, John
Cotton Belt *occas.*
  cotton belt
Cotton Bowl

Cotton Bowl Festival
Cotton Club
Cotton Club, The
  [movie]
Cotula
Coty, René
Coudersport
Coué, Émile
Couéism
Couette flow
Cougar, John
Cougar Dam
Cougar Reservoir
Coughlin, Father
Coulee Dam
Coulee Dam National
  Recreation Area
Coulomb, Charles
  Augustin de
Coulomb's law
Coulson, C. A.
Coulter, Ellis Morton
Coulter, John Merle
Coulter, Thomas
Coulter, Wallace
  Henry
Coulter pine
Council Bluffs
Council for
  Advancement and
  Support of
  Education
Council for Aid to
  Education
Council for Basic
  Education
Council for
  International
  Development

Council for Mutual
  Economic
  Assistance
Council for the
  Advancement and
  Support of
  Education
Council Grove
Council of Arab
  Economic Unity
Council of Basel
Council of Better
  Business Bureaus
Council of Chalcedon
Council of Clarendon
Council of Constance
Council of
  Constantinople
Council of Economic
  Advisers
Council of Ephesus
Council of Europe
Council of Florence
Council of Graduate
  Schools in the
  United States
Council of Jewish
  Federations
Council of Lyons
Council of Nicaea
Council of Pisa
Council of State
  Governments
Council of the Reich
Council of Trent
Council of Vienne
Council on Career
  Development for
  Minorities
Council on Economic
  Priorities
Council on Family
  Health

Council on Foreign Relations

Council on Hemispheric Affairs

Council on International Educational Exchange

Council on Price and Wage Stability

Council on Social Work Education

Council on Tall Buildings and Urban Habitat

Council on Undergraduate Research

Count Basie Band

Count Dracula

Count Dracula Fan Club

Count Dracula Society

Counter Reformation

Count of Monte Cristo, The

Country Almanac

Country America

Country Decorating Ideas

Country Home

Country Joe and the Fish

Country Journal

Country Living

Country Music

Country Music Association

Country Music Hall of Fame and Museum, The

Country Music Television

Country Music Wax Museum

Country of the Gillikins

Country Woman

County College of Morris

County Kerry

Couperin, François

Couperus, Louis

Couples, Fred

Courbet, Gustave

Couric, Katie

Courier, Jim

Courréges, André

Court, Margaret Smith

Courtauld Institute Galleries

Courtenay, Tom

Courtier, The

Courtney

Court of Honor

Court of Saint James's *occas.* James

Courtship of Eddie's Father, The

Courtship of Miles Standish, The

Cousin, Jean

Cousin, Philip R.

Cousin, Victor

Cousin, Cousine [movie]

Cousin Jack, *n.*, *pl.* Cousin Jacks

Cousins, Norman

Cousteau, Jacques Yves

Cousteau Society, Inc., The

Cousy, Bob

Couture, Thomas

Covarrubias, Miguel

Coveleski, Stan

Covenant, The

Covenant College

Covenanters

Covenant House

Covenant of the League of Nations

Covenant Theological Seminary

Covent Garden

Coventry

Coventry bell

Coventry Cathedral

Coventry Play

Coverdale, Miles

Coverley, Sir Roger de

Covina

Covington

Coward, Sir Noël

Cowboy Channel, The

Cowboy Hall of Fame and Western Heritage Center

Cowell, Henry Dixon

Cowie, Edward

Cowl, Jane

Cowles Media Company

Cowles Media Foundation

Cowley, Abraham

Cowley, Malcolm

Cowley County Community College

Cow Palace

Cowpens National Battlefield

Cowper, William

Cowper's gland
Cox, Bobby
Cox, David
Cox, Edwin Lochridge, Sr.
Cox, James Middleton
Cox, John Lee
Cox, Kenyon
Cox, Palmer
Cox, Ronny
Cox, Wally
Cox Enterprises, Inc.
Coxey, Jacob S.
Coxey's Army
Coxsackie
Coxsackie virus
Coxwell chair
Coyote, Peter
Coysevox, Antoine
Cozad
Cozens, Alexander
Cozens, John Robert
Cozey, Jacob
Cozumel
Cozzens, James Gould
CPA Journal, The
CPC Education Foundation
CPC International Inc.
CPI Corporation
Crabbe, Buster
Crabbe, George
Crab Nebula
Crabtree, Lotta
Cracker Jack™
Cracow
Craddock, Crash
Craft Fashion Institute
Crafton

Crafton Hills College
Crafts Magazine
Cragin Federal Bank for Savings
Craig
Craig, Edward Gordon
Craig, Jenny
Craig, Roger
Craigie, Sir William
Craik, Dinah Maria
Crain, Gertrude Ramsay
Crain, Jeanne
Crain News Service
Cram, Ralph Adams
Cramer, Floyd
Cramer, Gabriel
Cramer's rule
Cramerton
Cranach, Lucas the Elder
Cranach, Lucas the Younger
Cranbrook Academy of Art
Cranbrook Foundation
Crandall Junior College
Crane, Bob
Crane, Hart
Crane, Ichabod
Crane, Roy
Crane, Stephen
Crane Company
Crane Naval Weapons Support Center
Cranford
Cranmer, Thomas
Cranston
Cranston, Alan

Crapper, Sir Thomas
Crashaw, Richard
Crassus, Marcus Licinius
Cratchit, Bob
Cratchit, Tiny Tim
Crater Lake
Crater Lake National Park
Crater Mound
Craters of the Moon National Monument
Crates
Cratinus
Craven, Avery Odell
Craven, Wes
Craven Community College
Crawford, Broderick
Crawford, Cindy
Crawford, Francis Marion
Crawford, Joan
Crawford, Johnny
Crawford, Michael
Crawford, Ralston
Crawford, Sam
Crawford, Thomas
Crawford and Company
Crawford Notch
Crawfordsville
Cray, Robert
Crayola™ crayons
Crayon Power
Cray Research Foundation
Cray Research Inc.
Crazy Eights
Crazy Guggenheim

Crazy Horse Memorial

C. R. Bard, Inc.

CRC Radio Network (Cadena Radio Centro)

Creasey, John

Creation of Adam, The

Credit Agricole Mutuel

Creditanstalt-Bankverein

Credit Commercial de France

Crédit Lyonnais

Crédit Mobilier of America

Crédit Mobilier scandal

Credito Italiano

Crédit Suisse

Credit Union Executives Society

Credit Union National Association

Cree, *n.*, *pl.* Cree *or* Crees

Creede

Creedence Clearwater Revival

Creek Confederacy

Creek [Indian], *n.*, *pl.* Creek *or* Creeks

Creel, George

Creeley, Robert

Cregar, Laird

Creighton University

Creighton University Bluejays

Cremer, Sir William Randal

Cremnitz white

Cremona

Crenna, Richard

Creole, *n.*

creole *often* Creole, *adj.*

Creole Jazz Band

crepe de Chine

Crerar, John

Crescas, Hasdai

Crescent City

Crescent Court

Crespi, Giuseppe Maria

Crespin, Régine

Cressida

Crestar Bank

Crestar Financial Corporation

Crestar Foundation

Crest Hill

Crestline

Creston

Creston, Paul

Crestview

Cretaceous Period

Cretan

Cretan bear's tail

Cretan bull

Cretan mullein

Cretan spikenard

Crete

Creuse

Creutzfeldt-Jakob *occas.* Creutzfeldt-Jakob disease

Creve Coeur

Crèvecoeur, J. Hector Saint John

Crews, Harry

Crews, Laura Hope

Crichton, James

Crichton, Michael

Crichton College

Crick, Francis H. C.

Cricket

Crickets, The

Cries and Whispers

Crile, George Washington

Crimea

Crimean

Crime and Punishment

Crimean War

Criminal Investigation Division

Crippen, Robert L.

Cripple Creek

Cripple Creek strikes

Cripps, Sir Stafford

Crips street gang

Crisfield

Crisis Investing

Crisp, Donald

Crispin, Saint

Crispinian, Saint

Crist, Judith

Cristiani, Alfredo

Cristiansand *var. of* Kristiansand [Norwegian port on the Skaggerak; *see also* Cristiansund]

Cristiansund *var. of* Kristiansund [Norwegian port on the Atlantic; *see also* Cristiansand]

Cristóbal

Criswell College

Critical Care America, Inc.

Critics Circle Award

Critique of Practical Reason

Critique of Pure Reason

Crittenden, George

Crittenden, John

Crittenden, Thomas

Crittenden Compromise

Crivelli, Carlo

CRN International Inc.

Croat

Croatan National Forest

Croatia

Croatian

Croatoan

Croce, Benedetto

Croce, Jim

Crochet World

Crocker, Charles

Crockett, Davy

Crocodile Dundee

Crocodile Dundee II

Crocodile River

Croesus

Croft, Sandy

Crofts, Dash

Crohn's disease

Croix de Feu

Croix de Guerre

Cro-Magnon

Cro-Magnon man

Cro-Magnon race

Cromarty

Cromarty Firth

Crome, John

Cromerian

Crompton, Samuel

Crompton and Knowles Corporation

Cromwell, James

Cromwell, Oliver

Cromwell, Richard

Cromwell, Thomas

Cromwell current

Cromwellian

Cromwellian chair

Cronin, A. J.

Cronin, Joe

Cronkite, Walter

Cronyn, Hume

Cronyn, Tandy

Crook, George

Crookes, Sir William

Crookes dark space

Crookes space

Crookes tube

Crookston

Crooksville

Crop Science Society of America

Crosby, Bing

Crosby, Bob

Crosby, Cathy Lee

Crosby, David

Crosby, Denise

Crosby, Fanny

Crosby, Gary

Crosby, John

Crosby, Kathryn

Crosby, Mary

Crosby, Norm

Crosby, Stills and Nash

Crosby, Stills, Nash and Young

Crosley, Powell

Cross, Ben

Cross, Christopher

Cross, Irv

Cross, Milton

Crosse, Gordon

Crosset

Cross-Examination Debate Association

Crossfire

Cross-Florida Waterway

CrossLand Savings

Cross of Calvary

Cross of Lorraine

Crossville

Crothers, Scatman

Croton Aqueduct

Croton bug

Croton-on-Hudson

Crouch, Andrae

Crouse, Lindsay

Crouse, Russel

Crowd, The

Crowder College

Crowell, Rodney

Crow [Indian], *n.*, *pl.* Crow *or* Crows

Crowley

Crowley, John

Crowley, Patricia

Crowley's Ridge College

Crown, Lester

Crown Books

Crown Books bookstore

Crown Central Petroleum Corporation

Crown Cork and Seal Company, Inc.

Crown Cruise Line

Crown Life Insurance Company

Crown of the Andes

Crown Point

Crown Publishing Group

Crowsnest Pass

Crows Nest Peak

Crucible, The

Crucifixion

Crucifixion of Saint Peter, The

Cruikshank, George

Cruise, Tom

Cruising World

Crum and Forster Corporation

Crum and Forster Foundation

Crumb, George

Crumb, Robert

Crumbo, Woodrow

Crusader Rabbit

Crusades, the

Crusher, Dr. Beverly

Crux

Cruz, Celia

Cryovac™

Crystal

Crystal, Billy

Crystal Brands, Inc.

Crystal Cathedral

Crystal City

Crystal Lake

Crystal Palace

Crystals, The

Crystal Springs

Cry, the Beloved Country

C-7A Caribou

CS Holding

Csonka, Larry

C-SPAN

C-SPAN II

CSX Corporation

Ctenophora

CTV Television Network

C-23 Sherpa

Cuba

Cuba libre

Cuban

Cubana Airlines

Cuban heel

Cuban lily

Cuban missile crisis

Cuban pine

Cuban royal palm

Cubi XIX

Cubism *often* cubism

Cub Scout

Cucamonga

CUC International Inc.

Cudahy

Cudahy, Michael

Cudahy Packing Company

Cuernavaca

Cuero

Cuesta College

Cugat, Xavier

Cuiabá

Cuicuilco

Cukor, George

Culbertson, Ely

Culbro Corporation

Culinary Institute of America

Culkin, Macaulay

Cullen, Bill

Cullen, Countee

Cullinan diamond

Cullman

Culloden Moor

Cullum, John

Culm Measures

Culp, Robert

Culpeper, Thomas

Cult

Cult Awareness Network

Cultural Revolution

Culture Club

Culver City

Culverhouse, Hugh Franklin

Culver's root

Culver-Stockton College

Cumaná

Cumberland

Cumberland Caverns

Cumberland College

Cumberland College of Tennessee

Cumberland Compact

Cumberland County College

Cumberland Gap

Cumberland Gap National Historical Park

Cumberland Island National Seashore

Cumberland Mountains

Cumberland Plateau

Cumberland Presbyterian Church

Cumberland Road

Cumberland Sound

Cumberland University

Cumberland Valley

Cumbria

Cumbrian

Cumbrian Mountains

Cummings, Candy

Cummings, Constance

Cummings, E. E. *or* cummings, e. e.

Cummings, Robert

Cummins Engine Company, Inc.

Cummins Engine Foundation

Cunard, Sir Samuel

Cunard Line

Cunningham, Merce

Cuomo, Mario

Cupertino

Cupid

Cupid's arrow

Cupid's bow

Cupid's dart

Cuquenán Falls

Curaçao

Curb, Mike

Cure, The

Curecanti National Recreation Area

Curia Regis

Curia Romana

Curie, Marie

Curie, Pierre

Curie point

Curie's law

Curie temperature

Curie-Weiss law

Curitiba

Curless, Dick

Curley, James M.

Curragh, the

Current Affair, A

Current Affair Extra, A

Currie, Finlay

Currier, Andrea B.

Currier, Lavinia M.

Currier, Michael S.

Currier, Nathaniel

Currier and Ives

Curry, John Steuart

Curry College

Cursor Mundi

Curti, Merle

Curtin, Jane

Curtis

Curtis, Cyrus

Curtis, Edward S.

Curtis, Jamie Lee

Curtis, Keene

Curtis, Ken

Curtis, Tony

Curtis Bay Coast Guard Yard

Curtis Institute of Music

Curtiss, Glenn Hammond

Curtiss JN4 Jenny

Curtius, Ernst

Curtius, Marcus

Curwensville

Curzon, George Nathaniel

Curzon Line

Cusack, Cyril

Cusack, Joan

Cusack, John

Cushing, Caleb

Cushing, Harvey

Cushing, Peter

Cushing, Richard Cardinal

Cushing's disease

Cushing's syndrome

Cushitic

Cushman, Charlotte

Cushman Inc.

Cussler, Clive

Custer

Custer, Elizabeth Bacon

Custer, George Armstrong

Custer Battlefield National Monument [*now* Little Bighorn Battlefield National Monument]

Custer National Forest

Custer's last stand

Custis-Lee Mansion

Cut Bank

Cuthbert

Cuthbert, Saint

Cutler Naval Communication Unit

Cutler Ridge

Cutpurse, Moll
Cutty Sark
Cuvier, Georges
Cuyahoga
Cuyahoga Community College
Cuyahoga Falls
Cuyahoga Valley National Recreation Area
Cuyamaca College
Cuyler, Kiki
Cuyp or Cuijp, Albert
Cuyp or Cuijp, Jacob Gerritsz
Cuyumacas Mountains
Cuzco
Cwmbran
Cybele
Cycadophyta
Cyclades
Cycladic
Cycladic art
Cyclone™ fence
Cyclone Mountain
Cyclopean occas. cyclopean
Cyclopean occas. cyclopean concrete
Cyclops, n., pl. Cyclopes; occas. cyclops, n., pl. cyclopes

Cyclops Industries, Inc.
Cygnus
Cymbeline
Cynic
Cynthia
Cynthiana
Cypress [* CA; see also Cyprus]
Cypress College
Cypress Gardens
Cypress Minerals Company
Cypress Semiconductor Corporation
Cyprian
Cyprian, Saint
Cypriot occas. Cypriote
Cyprus [island; nation; see also Cypress]
Cyprus Airways
Cyprus Minerals Company
Cyprus Museum
Cyrano de Bergerac
Cyrano de Bergerac, Savinien de
Cyrenaic
Cyrenaica
Cyrene

Cyril, Saint
Cyrillic
Cyril of Alexandria, Saint
Cyril of Jerusalem, Saint
Cyrus
Cyrus, Billy Ray
Cyrus the Great
Cyrus the Younger
Cystic Fibrosis Foundation
Cy Young Award
Czech
Czech language
Czech Legion
Czech literature
Czechoslovak
Czechoslovakia
Czechoslovakian
Czech Philharmonic Orchestra
Czech Republic [form. Czech Socialist Republic]
Czech Socialist Republic [now Czech Republic]
Czerny, Karl
Czolgosz, Leon F.

D

Dabah, Morris
Dab Dab the duck
Dabney S. Lancaster
  Community College
Da Capo Chamber
  Players
Dacca
Dachau
Daché, Lily
Dacko, David
Dacron™
Dada
Dadaism *occas.*
  dadaism
Dadaist *occas.* dadaist
Dadaistic *occas.*
  dadaistic
Daddi, Bernardo
Daddy Long-Legs
Daddy Warbucks
Dade
Dadeville
Daedalian *or*
  Daedalean
Daedalid
Daedalus
Daemen College
Daewoo Group
Daffy-Down-Dilly
Daffy Duck

Daffy Duck Show,
  The
Dafoe, Willem
Dafydd ap Gwilym
Dagestan carpet
Dagmar
Dagobert
Dago red
Daguerre, Louis
  Jacques Mandé
Dagwood sandwich
Da Hinggan Ling
Dahl, Arlene
Dahl, Roald
Dahlak Archipelago
Dahlberg, Edward
Dahlem Museum
Dahlgren, John
Dahmer, Jeffrey
Dahomey [*now* Benin]
Dahurian larch
Daigleville
Daihatsu Motor
  Company Ltd.
Dai-Ichi Kangyo
  Bank, Ltd.
Dai-Ichi Kangyo Bank
  Nederland
Dai-Ichi Life
  Insurance Company

Dail Eireann
Dailey, Dan
Dailey, Irene
Dailey, Janet
Daily, Bill
Daily Racing Form
Daily Variety
Daimler, Gottlieb
Daimler-Benz
Daingerfield
Dairen
Dairy and Food
  Industries Supply
  Association
Dairy Belt
Dairylea Cooperative
Daisy Duck
Daisy Girl Scouts
Daisy Miller
Daiwa Bank, Ltd.
Dakar
Dakar-Yoff
  International
  Airport
Dakin, Henry
  Drysdale
Dakin's solution
Dakota, *n., pl.*
  Dakotas [states]
Dakota Giant Network

175

Dakota [Indian], n., pl.
Dakota or Dakotas

Dakotan

Dakota Outdoors

Dakota River

Dakota State
University

Dakota Territory

Dakota Wesleyan
University

Daktari

Daladier, Édouard

Dalai Lama

Dale, Sir Henry Hallet

Dale, Jim

Dale, Sir Thomas

d'Alembert, Jean le
Rond

d'Alembert's test

Daley, Richard J.

Daley, Richard M.

Dalhart

Dalhart, Vernon

Dalhousie, George
Ramsay

Dalhousie, James
Andrew Broun

Dalhousie University

Dali, Salvador

Dallapiccola, Luigi

Dallas

Dallas, George Mifflin

Dallas Baptist
University

Dallas Christian
College

Dallas Cowboys

Dallas-Fort Worth
International
Airport

Dallas Institute of
Funeral Service

Dallas Life Magazine

Dallas Love Field

Dallas Mavericks

Dallas Morning News,
The

Dallas Naval Air
Station

Dallas Opera

Dallas Peak

Dallas Symphony
Orchestra

Dallas Texans

Dallas Theater Center

Dallas Theological
Seminary

Dallas Times Herald

Dallastown

Dalles, The

Dalles Dam, The

Dallin, Cyrus

Dallis grass

Dall or Dall's sheep

Dalmane™

Dalmatia

Dalmatian, adj. [of or
pertaining to
Dalmatia]

Dalmatian occas.
dalmatian, n. [dog]

Dalrymple, Sir David

Dalrymple, Jean

Dalton

Dalton, Abby

Dalton, Emmet

Dalton, Grattan

Dalton, J. Frank

Dalton, John

Dalton, Lacy J.

Dalton, Robert

Dalton, Timothy

Dalton College

Dalton gang

Daltonian

Daltonism

Dalton plan

Dalton's law

Dalton's law of partial
pressures

Dalton System

Daltrey, Roger

Daly, Augustin

Daly, James

Daly, John

Daly, Marcus

Daly, Tyne

Daly City

Damascene

Damascus

Damascus
International
Airport

Damascus steel

Damascus ware

Damasus I, Saint

D'Amato, Alfonse

Damavand

d'Amboise,
Christopher

D'Amboise, Jacques

Dame Commander of
the Order of the
British Empire

Dame Grand Cross of
the British Empire

Dameron, Tadd

Dame Shirley

Damien, Father

Damnation of Faust, The

Damn Yankees

Damoclean

Damocles

Damon

Damon, Cathryn

Damon and Pythias

Damone, Vic

Damon Runyon-Walter Winchell Cancer Research Fund

Dampier, William

Damrosch, Frank

Damrosch, Leopold

Damrosch, Walter

Dan

Dana

Dana, Bill

Dana, Charles Anderson

Dana, James Dwight

Dana, Richard Henry, Jr.

Dana, Richard Henry, Sr.

Dana College

Dana Corporation

Dana Corporation Foundation

Danae and the Shower of Gold

Dana Farber Cancer Institute

Danaher Corporation

Danang occas. Da Nang

Danang International Airport

Danbury

Danbury Hatters' Case

Danbury Mint, The

Dance, The

Dance Alloy

Dance Fever

Dance Magazine

Dance of Death

Dance of the Hours

Dance of the Seven Veils, The

Dance of the Sylphs

Dance Party USA

Dancer

Dancer Putting on Her Stockings

Dances with Wolves

Dance Theatre of Harlem

Dancin'

D & B Reports

Dandie Dinmont terrier

Dandridge, Dorothy

Dandridge, Ray

Dandridge, Ruby

Dane

Danegeld occas. danegeld

Danelaw

Danforth, William

D'Angelo, Beverly

Dangerfield, Rodney

Daniel

Daniel, Samuel

Daniel and Florence Guggenheim Foundation

Daniel Boone National Forest

Daniell, Henry

Daniell, John F.

Daniell cell

Danielle

Daniels, Bebe

Daniels, Bill

Daniels, Charlie

Daniels, Jeff

Daniels, Jonathan

Daniels, Josephus

Daniels, William

Danielson

Daniel Webster College

Danilova, Alexandra

Danish

Danish Brotherhood in America

Danish language

Danish literature

Danish pastry

Danish West Indies [now Virgin Islands of the United States]

Dankworth, Johnny

Dannay, Frederic

Dannemora

Danner, Blythe

D'Annunzio, Gabriele

Danny and the Juniors

Danny Kaye Show, The

Danny Thomas Show, The

Dano, Royal

Dano-Norwegian

Danova, Cesare

Dan River

Danske Bank

Danson, Ted

Dansville

Dante Alighieri

Dantean

Dante chair

Dantes, Edmond

Dantesca chair

Dantesque

Dantine, Helmut

Danton, Georges Jacques

Danube

Danube rudder

Danubian

Danubian Principalities

Danvers

Danville

Danville Area Community College

Danville Community College

Dan Wagoner and Dancers

Danza, Tony

Danzig

Danzig, Glenn

Danziger, Maia

Daphne [nymph]

Daphnis [shepherd]

Daphnis and Chloe or Chloë

Darby

Darby, John N.

Darby, Ken

Darby, Kim

D'Arby, Terence Trent

Darby and Joan

Darby and Joan settee

Darbyite

D'Arcy Masius Benton and Bowles

Dardanelles

Dare, Virginia

Dar es Salaam occas. DaresSalaam

Dar es Salaam International Airport

Darien

Darien Gap

Darien Scheme

Darin, Bobby

Darío, Rubén

Darius

Darius the Great

Darius the Mede

Darjeeling or Darjiling

Darjeeling tea

Dark Ages

Dark Continent

Darkei Noam Rabbinical College

Darkman

Dark Shadows

Darktown Strutters' Ball

Darlan, Jean Louis

Darlene

Darling

Darling, Erik

Darling, Jay Norwood

Darling, Joan

Darling Downs

Darling Range

Darling River

Darlington

Darlington International Raceway

Darman, Richard

Darmstadt

Darnell, Linda

Darren, James

Darrieux, Danielle

Darrow, Clarence

D'Arsonval, Jacques A.

D'Arsonval galvanometer

Dart, William A.

d'Artagnan, Charles de Batz-Castelmore

Darth Vader

Dartington Hall

Dartington Summer School

Dartmoor

Dartmoor Prison

Dartmouth

Dartmouth College

Dartmouth College Big Green

Dartmouth College Case

Darton College

Darvon™

Darvon Compound™

Darwell, Jane

Darwin

Darwin, Charles

Darwin, Erasmus

Darwinian

Darwinian theory

Darwinism

Darwinist

Darwinite

Darwin's finches

Darwin tulip

Daryl

Das Boot
Dasher
Dasht-e-Kavir
Dasht-e-Lut
Da Silva, Howard
Das Kapital
Das Rheingold
Dassault Falcon
Dassault-Mirage IV-A
Dassault-Mirage III-R
Dassault Super Mirage
Dassin, Jules
Data, Lieutenant
  Commander
Data General
  Corporation
Datamation
Dataproducts
  Corporation
Date Line
Date with Judy, A
Dating Game, The
Datsun
Daubigny, Charles
  François
Daudet, Alphonse
Daudet, Léon
Daugherty, James
daughter of Eve
Daughter of the
  Regiment, The
Daughters of the
  American
  Revolution
Daughters of the Nile
Daughters of the
  Republic of Texas
Daughters of Union
  Veterans of the
  Civil War
Daumier, Honoré

Dauphin, Claude
Dauphiné
Dave and Sugar
Dave Clark Five, The
Davenant or
  D'Avenant, Sir
  William
Davenport
Davenport, Elizabeth
  Lupton
Davenport, Harry
Davenport, Nigel
Davenport College of
  Business
David
David, Gerard
David, Hal
David, Jacques Louis
David, Saint
David and Goliath
David Brinkley's
  Journal
David Copperfield
David D'Angiers
David Gordon/Pick
  Up Company
David Holzman's
  Diary
Davidic
David Lipscomb
  University
Davidson, Ben
Davidson, Eileen
Davidson, Jo
Davidson, John
Davidson, William
  Morse
Davidson College
Davidson College
  Wildcats

Davidson County
  Community College
David Susskind Show,
  The
Davies, Arthur Bowen
Davies, Dennis
  Russell
Davies, Joseph
  Edward
Davies, Marion
Davies, Robertson
da Vinci, Leonardo
Davis
Davis, Alexander
  Jackson
Davis, Angela
Davis, Ann B.
Davis, Benjamin O.,
  Jr.
Davis, Benjamin O.,
  Sr.
Davis, Benny
Davis, Bette
Davis, Brad
Davis, Clifton
Davis, Sir Colin
Davis, Elmer
Davis, Geena
Davis, James Elsworth
Davis, Jefferson
Davis, Jim [actor]
Davis, Jimmie [singer]
Davis, Joan
Davis, John
Davis, John William
Davis, Judy
Davis, Junior
Davis, Lockjaw
Davis, Mac
Davis, Marvin Harold

Davis, Miles

Davis, Ossie

Davis, Owen

Davis, Patti

Davis, Paul

Davis, Rebecca Harding

Davis, Richard Harding

Davis, Sammy, Jr.

Davis, Shelby Cullom

Davis, Skeeter

Davis, Stuart

Davis and Elkins College

Davis apparatus

Davis College

Davis Cup

Davis-Monthan Air Force Base

Davis Mountains

Davison

Davison, Bruce

Davison, Wild Bill

Davis' quadrant

Davisson, Clinton Joseph

Davisson-Germer experiment

Davis Strait

Davis Submerged Escape Apparatus

DAV Magazine

Davout, Louis Nicolas

Davy, Sir Humphry

Davy Crockett National Forest

Davy Jones

Davy Jones' locker

Davy lamp

Dawber, Pam

Daw Books

Dawes, Charles G.

Dawes, Henry L.

Dawes Act

Dawes Commission

Dawes Plan

Dawkins, Pete

Dawn

Dawson

Dawson, Sir John William

Dawson, Len

Dawson, Richard

Dawson, William L.

Dawson City

Dawson Community College

Dawson Consumer Products, Inc.

Dawson Creek

Dawson Springs

Dax

Dax hot springs

Day, Benjamin

Day, Clarence

Day, Dennis

Day, Doris

Day, Dorothy

Day, Laraine

Dayak, *n.*, *pl.* Dayak *or* Dayaks

Dayan, Moshe

Day at the Races, A

Day-Glo™

Day-Lewis, Cecil

Day-Lewis, Daniel

Daylight Saving Time

Day of Atonement

Day of Christ

Day of Jesus Christ

Day of Judgment

Day of the Lord

Day of Yahweh

Day One *occas.* day one

Days and Nights of Molly Dodd, The

Days Inn

Days of Our Lives

Days of Thunder

Days of Wine and Roses [movie]

Days of Wine and Roses, The [song]

Dayton

Dayton, Jonathan

Daytona Beach

Daytona Beach Community College

Daytona 500

Daytona International Speedway

Dayton Ballet Association

Dayton Contemporary Dance Company

Dayton Daily News

Dayton Hudson Corporation

Dayton Hudson Department Store Company

Dayton Hudson Foundation

Dayton International Airport

dBase™ computer equipment

D battery

DC Comics

D. C. Heath and Company

d-Con™ pest control

D-Day

DDB Needham Worldwide Inc.

Deacon, Richard

Deaconess College of Nursing

Dead Christ, The

Dead End Kid

Dead Kennedys

Dead Poets Society

Dead River

Dead Sea

Dead Sea fruit

Dead Sea Scrolls

Deadwood

Deadwood Dick

Deafness Research Foundation

Deal Island

Dean, Billy

Dean, Christopher

Dean, Daffy

Dean, Dizzy

Dean, James

Dean, Jimmy

Dean, John, III

Dean, Morton

Deane, Silas

Dean Foods Company

De Angeli, Marguerite Lofft

Dean Institute of Technology

Dean Junior College

Dean Martin Comedy Hour, The

Dean Martin Show, The

Dean Witter

Dean Witter Financial Services Group Inc.

Dean Witter Reynolds Inc.

De Anza College

Dear Abby

Dearborn

Dearborn, Henry

Dearborn Heights

Dear John letter

Death Be Not Proud

Death Comes for the Archbishop

Death in Venice

Death of Actaeon, The

Death of a President

Death of a Salesman

Death of General Wolfe, The

Death of Ivan Ilyich, The

Deathtrap

Death Valley

Death Valley Days

Death Valley National Monument

Deauville

Deaver, Michael

DeBakey, Michael

de Bardi, Beatrice

DeBartolo, Edward John

DeBeck, Billy

De Beers Consolidated Mines Ltd.

Deborah

Debra

De Broglie, Louis

De Broglie equation

De Broglie wave

Debs, Eugene V.

DeBusschere, Dave

Debussy, Claude

Deby, Idriss

Debye, Peter J. W.

Decade of the Brain

Decalogue

Decameron, The

Decameronic

DeCamp, Rosemary

DeCarlo, Yvonne

Decatur

Decatur, Stephen

Deccan

December

Decembrist

Decembrist uprising

Decius, Gaius Messius

Decker Slaney, Mary

Deck the Hall with Boughs of Holy

Declaration of Breda

Declaration of Independence

Declaration of London

Declaration of Paris

Declaration of Tashkent

Declaration of the Rights of Man and Citizen

Decline and Fall of the Roman Empire, The

Decorah

Decoration Day [now Memorial Day]

deCordova, Fred
de Cuellar, Javier Perez
Dedalus, Stephen
Dedekind, Julius
Dedekind cut
Dedham
Dedman, Robert Henry, Sr.
Dee, Frances
Dee, John
Dee, Kiki
Dee, Ruby
Dee, Sandra
Deepfreeze™
Deeping, Warwick
Deep Purple
Deep Sea Drilling Project
Deep South
Deep Springs College
Deep Throat
Deere, John
Deere and Company
Deerfield
Deerfield Beach
Deer Hunter, The
Deer Lodge
Deerlodge National Forest
Deer Park
Deerslayer, The
Defence of Poetry
Defender of the Faith
Defenders, The
Defenders of Wildlife
Defense Clothing and Textile Supply Center

Defense Commissary Agency
Defense Construction Supply Center
Defense Distinguished Service Medal
Defense Electronics
Defense Information Systems Agency
Defense Intelligence Agency
Defense Intelligence College
Defense Language Institute
Defense Mapping Agency
Defense News
Defiance
Defiance College
Def Leppard
Defoe, Daniel
Defore, Don
De Forest, John William
De Forest, Lee
DeFranco, Buddy
De Funiak Springs
Degas, Edgar
De Gasperi, Alcide
de Gaulle, Charles
DeGeneres, Ellen
de Ghelderode, Michel
Degrassi High
Degrassi Junior High
De Greiff, Monica
de Haas, Jacob
DeHartog, Jan
De Haven, Gloria
de Havilland, Olivia
Dehner, John

De Hooch, Pieter
De Horsey rig
Dehra Dun
Deighton, Len
Dei gratia
Deirdre
Deity
DeJohnette, Jack
De Jong, Meindert
De Kalb
de Kalb, Johann
Dekalb College
DeKalb Technical Institute
Dekker, Albert
Dekker, Thomas
de Klerk, Frederik W.
de Kooning, Willem
De Koven, Reginald
de Kruif, Paul
Delacorte, George T.
Delacroix, Eugène
Delagoa Bay
Delahanty, Ed
Delaine Merino
de la Madrid Hurtado, Miguel
de la Mare, Walter
De Land
Deland, Margaret
Delaney, Shelagh
Delaney amendment
Delaney clause
Delannoy, Marcel
Delano
Delany, Dana
de la Renta, Oscar
de la Roche, Mazo
Delaroche, Paul

de la Rue, Warren
De La Soul
Delaunay, Robert
De Laurentiis, Dino
Delavan
Delavigne, Jean
    François Casimir
Delaware
Delawarean
Delaware Aqueduct
Delaware Bay
Delaware County
    Community College
Delaware [Indian], *n.*,
    pl. Delaware *or*
    Delawares
Delaware National
    Scenic River
    Parkway
Delaware Prophet
Delaware River Basin
    Compact
Delaware State
    College
Delaware State
    College Hornets
Delaware Technical
    and Community
    College
Delaware Valley
    College
Delaware Water Gap
Delaware Water Gap
    National Recreation
    Area
De La Warr, Baron
Delbrück, Max
Delcassé, Théophile
Del City
Del Coronado Hotel
Delderfield, R. F.
Deledda, Grazia

Delerue, Georges
Delfonics, The
Delft
Delgado Community
    College
Delhi
Delhi (Indira Gandhi
    International)
    Airport
Delhi Sultanate
Delian
Delian League
Delian problem
Delibes, Léo
Delilah
DeLillo, Don
Delius, Frederick
Dell, Floyd
Dell, Michael
Della Chiesa,
    Vivienne
Della Crusca
Della Cruscan poets
della Francesca, Piero
della Robbia, Andrea
della Robbia, Luca
Dell Computer
    Corporation
Dello Joio, Norman
Dell Publishing
    Company, Inc.
Dells, The
Dellums, Ronald
Del Mar
Del Mar College
Del Mar
    Thoroughbred Club
Delmarva Peninsula
Delmarva Power and
    Light Company

Delmonico, Lorenzo
Delmonico's
    Restaurant
Delmonico *occas.*
    delmonico steak
Del Monte Foods
Deloitte and Touche
Deloitte Haskins and
    Sells
Deloitte Haskins and
    Sells Foundation
Delon, Alain
De Lorean, John
De Lorean car
Deloria, Vine, Jr.
Delorme *or* de
    l'Orme, Philibert
Delos
de los Angeles,
    Victoria
Delphi
Delphian
Delphic
Delphic oracle
Delphi Museum
Delphos
Delpy, Julie
Delray Beach
Del Rey™ Books
Del Rio
Del Rio, Dolores
Delsarte, François
Delsarte method
Delsarte system
Delsartian
del Sarto, Andrea
Delta
Delta Air Lines, Inc.
Delta Chi
Delta College

Delta Delta Delta

Delta Downs

Delta Gamma

Delta International
Machinery
Corporation

Delta Junior College

Delta Kappa Epsilon

Delta Kappa Gamma
Society
International

Delta National Forest

Delta Phi

Delta Phi Epsilon

Delta Psi

Delta Queen
Steamboat
Company

Delta Sigma Phi

Delta Sigma Pi

Delta Sigma Theta

Delta State University

Delta Steamship
Lines, Inc.

Delta Tau Delta

Delta Upsilon

Delta Woodside
Industries, Inc.

Delta Zeta

Deltiologists of
America

Deluge, the

De Luise, Dom

Deluxe Corporation

Deluxe Corporation
Foundation

Delvaux, Laurent

Delvaux, Paul

Delvecchio, Alex

Del Webb hotel

Demarest

Demarest, William

de Maupassant, Guy

Demavend

Demerol™

Demeter

Demetrius

Demichev, Pyotr

de Mille, Agnes

DeMille, Cecil B.

Deming

Demjanjuk, John

Demme, Jonathan

Democracy in
America

Democrat

Democratic
Governors'
Conference

Democratic
Leadership Council

Democratic National
Committee

Democratic National
Convention

Democratic Party

Democratic People's
Republic of Korea

Democratic-
Republican Party

Democratic Socialists
of America

Democritus

Democritus Junior

Demogorgon

de Moivre, Abraham

de Moivre's theorem

Demolay International

Demopolis

De Morgan, Augustus

De Morgan, William
Frend

De Morgan's laws

De Mornay, Rebecca

Demosthenes

Dempsey, Jack

Dempster, Arthur
Jeffrey

Demuth, Charles

Denali

Denali National Park
[*form.* Mount
McKinley National
Park]

Denali National
Preserve

Déné, *n., pl.* Déné *or*
Dénés

Deneb

Deneuve, Catherine

Deng Xiaoping [*form.*
Teng Hsiao-ping]

Deng Yingchao [*form.*
Teng Ying-chao]

Denham, Sir John

Denham Springs

Deniker, Joseph

Denikin, Anton

DeNiro, Robert

Denis, Saint

Denise

Denison

Denison, Anthony
John

Denison Dam

Denison University

Denmark

Denmark Strait

Denmark Technical
College

Dennehy, Brian

Dennis

Dennis, John

Dennis, Sandy

Dennis et al. v. United States

Dennison

Dennis the Menace

Denny, Reginald

Denny's restaurant

Dent Blanche

Denton

D'Entrecasteaux Channel

D'Entrecasteaux Islands

Dents du Midi

Dentsu Inc.

Denver

Denver, Bob

Denver, James William

Denver, John

Denver and Rio Grande Western Railroad Company

Denver Automotive and Diesel College

Denver boot

Denver Broncos

Denver City

Denver Conservative Baptist Seminary

Denver Dynamite

Denver Institute of Technology

Denver Nuggets

Denver Post, The

Denver Stapleton International Airport

Denver Symphony Orchestra

Denver Technical College

Deo favente

Deo gratias

Deo juvante

Deo Optimo Maximo

Deo volente

DePalma, Brian

De Palma, Ralph

Depardieu, Gerard

Department of Agriculture

Department of Commerce

Department of Defense

Department of Education

Department of Energy

Department of Health and Human Services

Department of Housing and Urban Development

Department of Justice

Department of Labor

Department of State

Department of the Air Force

Department of the Army

Department of the Interior

Department of the Navy

Department of the Treasury

Department of Transportation

Department of Veterans Affairs

[*form.* Veterans Administration]

DePaul University

DePaul University Blue Demons

De Pauw, Washington Charles

DePauw University

Depeche Mode

De Pere

Depew

Depew, Chauncey

Depo-Provera™

Deposition

Depp, Johnny

Depression glass

DePriest, James

De Profundis

Deputy Dawg

De Quincey

De Quincey, Thomas

Derain, André

Derby

Derby Lane—Saint Petersburg Kennel Club

Derbyshire

Derbyshire chair

Derby ware

Derek

Derek, Bo

Derek, John

Derek and The Dominos

De Ridder

Deringer, Henry

Dermarest™

Dermocaine™

Dermott

Dern, Bruce

Dern, Laura
Der Rosenkavalier
Derry
Dershowitz, Alan M.
Der Spiegel
Derwent
de Sade, Donaten Alphonse François
Desai, Anita
De Sales School of Theology
DeSalvo, Albert
Desargues, Gerard
Desargues' theorem
Descartes, René
Descartes' law
Descendants of the Signers of the Declaration of Independence
Descent from the Cross
Deschutes
Deschutes National Forest
Desdemona
Deseret
Deseret Book Company
Deseret bookstore
Deseret Management Corporation
Deseret News
Desert Inn
Desert Rose Band, The
Desert Song, The
De Seversky, Alexander P.
DeShannon, Jackie
De Sica, Vittorio

Desiderio, Robert
Desiderius
Designing Women
Desire under the Elms
Desktop Publisher
De Smet, Pierre Jean
Des Moines
Des Moines Area Community College
Des Moines International Airport
Des Moines Metro Summer Festival of Opera
Des Moines Register, The
Desmond, Paul
Desmoulins, Camille
De Soto, Hernando
De Soto car
De Soto National Forest
De Soto National Memorial
Desperate Hours, The
Despiau, Charles
Desplaines
Des Prés, Joaquin
de-Stalinization
de-Stalinize, v. de-Stalinized, de-Stalinizing
d'Este, Beatrice
d'Este, Isabella
de Stijl style of art
Destry Rides Again
DeSylva, Buddy
Detective Comics
Detmers, Maruschka
Detrick

Detroit
Detroit Arsenal
Detroit City Airport
Detroit College of Business
Detroit College of Law
Detroit Dam
Detroit Drive
Detroit Edison Company, The
Detroit Edison Foundation
Detroit Free Press
Detroit Free Press Magazine, The
Detroit Institute of Fine Arts
Detroit Lakes
Detroit Lions
Detroit Metropolitan (Wayne County) Airport
Detroit Monthly
Detroit News, The
Detroit Pistons
Detroit Red Wings
Detroit Reservoir
Detroit Symphony Orchestra
Detroit Tigers
Detroit Zoo
Deuel
Deukmejian, George
Deusdedit, Saint
Deus misereatur
Deus Ramos, João de
Deus vobiscum
Deus vult
Deuteronomic
Deuteronomist

Deuteronomy

Deutsch, Babette

Deutsche Bank

Deutsche blumen

Deutsche Genossen-
schaftsbank

Deutsche
Girozentrale-
Deutsche
Kommunalbank

Deutsche
Grammophon™
recording label

Deutsche Lufthansa

Deutscher, Isaac

Deutsches Reich

Deutsches Theater

Deutschland

Deutschland über
Alles

Deux-Sèvres

De Valera, Eamon

de Valois, Dame
Ninette

Devanagari

Devane, William

De Varona, Donna

Devereux, Robert

Devereux Foundation,
The

Devil

Devil and Daniel
Webster, The

Devil and Doctor
Faustus

Devil's Dictionary,
The

Devil's Disciple, The

Devil's Island

Devil's Lake

Devil's Night

Devils Postpile
National Monument

Devils Tower National
Monument

Devine, Andy

DeVito, Danny

Devo

De Vol, Frank

Devon

Devon Horse Show

Devonian

Devon Island

Devonshire

Devonshire cream

DeVos, Richard
Marvin

De Voto, Bernard

De Vries, Hugo

De Vries, Peter

DeVry Institute of
Technology

de Waart, Edo

Dewar, Sir James

Dewar *occas.* dewar
flask

Dewar *occas.* dewar
vessel

Dewey, George

Dewey, John

Dewey, Melvil

Dewey, Thomas E.

Deweyan

Dewey decimal
classification

Dewey decimal
system

Dewhurst, Colleen

De Wilde, Brandon

De Witt

DeWitt, Joyce

DEW Line

De Wolfe, Billy

Dexamil™

Dexedrine™

Dexter

Dexter, John

Dexter, Pete

Dexter Corporation,
The

Dexter Corporation
Foundation

Dey, Susan

De Young, Cliff

Dhahran

Dhaka/Zia Kurmitola
International
Airport

Dhaulagiri

Dhu'l-Hijja

Dhu'l-Qa'dah

Diabelli, Antonio

Diabetes Self-
Management

Diabetes Trust Fund,
Inc.

Diablo Dam

Diablo Reservoir

Diablo Valley College

Diaghilev, Sergei
Pavlovich

Diagnostic Products
Corporation

Dial Books for Young
Readers

Dial Corporation, The
[*form.* Greyhound
Dial Corporation]

Dial Magazine

Dialog™ information
service

Dialogue Information
Services, Inc.

Dialogue Mass

Diamond, David

Diamond, Neil

Diamond, Selma

Diamond Comic
Distributors

Diamond Head

Diamond Mountains

Diamonds, The

Diamond Shamrock,
Inc.

Diamond State

Diamond State
Telephone

Diana

Diane

Diane de France

Diane de Poitiers

Dianos, Kathryn

Diary of Anne Frank,
The

Dias, Bartolomeu

Diaspora *occas.*
diaspora

Diaz, Bo

Díaz, Porfirio

Diaz de la Peña,
Narcisco Virgilio

Díaz del Castillo,
Bernal

Díaz de Solís, Juan

Díaz Mirón, Salvador

Díaz Ordaz, Gustavo

Díaz Rodríguez,
Manuel

Diba, Farah

Dibango, Manu

Dibelius, Martin

D'Iberville

Dichta, Misha

Dick, George F.

Dick, Gladys

Dick, Philip K.

Dick Cavett Show,
The

Dickens, Charles

Dickens, Little Jimmy

Dickensian

Dickenson, Vic

Dickerson, Eric

Dickey, Bill

Dickey, James

Dickinson

Dickinson, Angie

Dickinson, Charles

Dickinson, Edwin

Dickinson, Emily

Dickinson, John

Dickinson, Preston

Dickinson College

Dickinson Multi-
Media Services,
Inc.

Dickinson School of
Law

Dickinson State
University

Dickson

Dickson, Leonard

Dickson City

Dick test

Dick Tracy

Dick Turpin

Dick Van Dyke Show,
The

Dictaphone™

Dictaphone
Corporation

Dictionary of
American
Biography

Dictionary of
American Regional
English

Dictionary of National
Biography

Dictionary of the
English
Language, A

Dictograph™

Dicumarol™

Diddley, Bo

Diderot, Denis

Didion, Joan

Didius Julianos

Dido

Dido and Aeneas

Dido's problem

Didot, François

Didot, François-
Ambroise

Didot, Pierre-François

Didot point system

Didrichsen Art
Museum

Didymus Chalcenterus

Didymus of
Alexandria

Diebenkorn, Richard

Diebold, Inc.

Die Brücke

Diefenbaker, John

Die Fledermaus

Diego Garcia

Diego-Suarez

Diegueño

Die Hard

Diehard 500

Die Hard 2

Diels, Otto

Diels-Alder reaction

Die Meistersinger

Die Meistersinger von Nürnberg

Dienbienphu

Dieppe

Dies, Martin

Diesel, Rudolf

Dies irae

Diet

Diet Coke™

Diet of Worms

Diet Pepsi™

Dietrich, Marlene

Diet 7UP™

Dietz, Howard

Die Walküre

Die Welt

Different World, A

Diffie, Joe

Diff'rent Strokes

Digby, Sir Kenelm

Digger

Digges, Dudley

Digital Equipment Corporation

Digital Underground

Dihigo, Martin

Dijon

Dijon Museum

Dijon mustard

Dilantin™

Dilaudid™

Dillard, Annie

Dillard, James Henry

Dillard Department Stores Inc.

Dillard University

Diller, Phyllis

Dillinger, John

Dillman, Bradford

Dillon, C. Douglas

Dillon, John

Dillon, Matt

Dilthey, Wilhelm

DiMaggio, Dom

DiMaggio, Joe

Dime Savings Bank of New York

DiMucci, Dion

Dinah

Dinah's Place

Dinaric Alps

d'Indy, Vincent

Dine, Jim

Diners Club™ credit card

Diners Club International

Dinesen, Isak

Ding Dong School

Dingell, John D.

Dinka, *n., pl.* Dinka *or* Dinkas

Dinkins, David N.

Dinosaur National Monument

Dinuba

Dinwiddie, Robert

Diocese of the Armenian Church of America

Diocletian

Diocletian window

Diodorus Siculus

Diogenes

Diogenes Laërtius

Diogenes of Apollonia

Diomede Islands

Dion

Dion and the Belmonts

Dion Cassius

Dion Chrysostom

Dionne, Annette

Dionne, Cécile

Dionne, Émilie

Dionne, Marcel

Dionne, Marie

Dionne, Yvonne

Dionne quintuplets

Dion of Syracuse

Dionysia

Dionysiac

Dionysian

Dionysius, Saint

Dionysius Exiguus

Dionysius of Alexandria, Saint

Dionysius of Halicarnassus

Dionysius the Areopagite

Dionysius the Elder

Dionysius the Younger

Dionysius Thrax

Dionysus *or* Dionysos

Diophantine equation

Diophantus

Dior, Christian

Dipylon vase

Dirac, Paul Adrien Maurice

Dirac delta function

Direct Communication Service, Inc.

Directions

Direct Marketing Association

Directoire

Directoire style

Director of Central Intelligence

Director, Office of Management and Budget

Directors Guild of America

Direct Relief International

Direct Selling Association

Dire Straits

Dirichlet, Peter

Dirichlet integral

Dirks, Rudolph

Dirksen, Everett M.

Disabled American Veterans

Di Salvo Trucking Company

Disasters of War

Disciples of Christ

Discourse on Method

Discover [magazine]

Discover™ credit card

Discoverer [satellite]

Discoverers' Day occas. Discovery Day

Discovery [space shuttle]

Discovery Channel, The

Discovery Inlet

Discus Thrower, The

Disko

Dismal Swamp

Disney, Lillian Bounds

Disney, Roy Edward

Disney, Walt

Disney Afternoon

Disney Channel, The

Disney Foundation

Disneyland

Disney-MGM Studios theme park

Disney's Caribbean Beach Resort

Disney's Grand Floridian Beach Resort

Disney Sunday Movie, The

Disney's Wonderful World

Disney Village

Dispatch Features

Disposable Heroes of Hiphoprisy

Disraeli, Benjamin

Distillery, Wine and Allied Workers International Union

Distinguished Conduct Medal

Distinguished Flying Cross

Distinguished Service Cross

Distinguished Service Medal

Distinguished Service Order

District Heights

District of Columbia

Distrito Federal

diSuvero, Mark

Ditka, Mike

Ditko, Steve

Ditmars, Raymond Lee

Dittersdorf, Karl Ditters von

Dives

Dividing Range

Divine Comedy, The

Divine Father

Divine Liturgy

Divine Mind

Divine Mother

Divine Office

Divine Word College

Divini Redemptoris

Divinity, the

Divisionism

Divisionist

Divorce Court

Diwali

Dix, Dorothea [American philanthropist and reformer]

Dix, Dorothy [pseudonym of Elizabeth M. Gilmer]

Dix, Otto

Dix, Richard

Dixie

Dixie College

Dixiecrat

Dixiecratic

Dixiecrat Party

Dixie™ cup

Dixie Highway

Dixie Hummingbirds, The

Dixieland

Dixielander

Dixieland jazz

Dixie National Forest
Dixmoor
Dixon
Dixon, Dean
Dixon, Fitz Eugene
Dixon, Franklin
Dixon, Ivan
Dixon, Jeane
Dixon, Jeremiah
Dixon, Sharon Pratt
Dixon, Willie
Djaja Peak
Djakarta *var. of* Jakarta
Djebel Kafzeh man
Djerba
Djibouti [*form.* French Somaliland]
Djibouti *or* Jibuti [capital of Djibouti]
Djibouti Airport
Djilas, Milovan
D. J. Jazzy Jeff and the Fresh Prince
D Layer
Dnepropetrovsk
Dnieper
Dniester
Doane College
Doan's™ pills
Dobbins Air Force Base
Dobbs, Mattiwilda
Dobbs Ferry
Dobell's solution
Doberman pinscher
Dobie, J. Frank
Dobie Gillis
Döbin, Alfred

Dobos *occas.* dobos torte, *n.*, *pl.* Dobos *occas.* dobos tortes
Dobruja
Dobrynin, Anatoly
Dobson, Austin
Dobson, Kevin
Dobyns, Lloyd
Docetism
Docetist
Dockers™ clothing
Dock Junction
Dock Street Theatre
Doctor Christian
Doctor Dolittle
Doctor Faustus
Doctor Fu Manchu
Doctor of Business Administration
Doctor of Chiropractic
Doctor of Dental Surgery
Doctor of Divinity
Doctor of Education
Doctor of Engineering
Doctor of Laws
Doctor of Letters
Doctor of Library Science
Doctor of Literature
Doctor of Medicine
Doctor of Music
Doctor of Optometry
Doctor of Philosophy
Doctor of Podiatric Medicine
Doctor of the Church
Doctor of Theology
Doctor of Veterinary Medicine
Doctorow, E. L.

Doctors, The
Doctors' Commons
Doctor's Dilemma, The
Doctor Who
Doctor Zhivago [movie; *see also* Dr. Zhivago]
Doctrine of Musical Figures
Doctrine of the Affections
Dodd, Christopher
Dodd, William Edward
Dodds, Baby
Dodds, Johnny
Dodecanese *or* Dodecanesus
Dodge, Charles
Dodge, Grenville
Dodge, Mary Elizabeth
Dodge City
Dodge City Community College
Dodgem™ car
Dodger Stadium
Dodgeville
Dodsworth
Doe, Samuel K.
Doenitz, Karl
Doerr, Bobby
Doesburg, Theo van
Doge, The
Dog Fancy
Dogger Bank
dog-Latin
Dogman and the Shepherds
Dogpatch, USA

Dogrib

Dog Star

Dog World

Doha

Doheny, Edward Laurence

Doherty, Shannon

Dohnányi, Ernő

Dokes, Michael

Doktor, Paul

Dolan, Charles Francis

Dolby, Thomas

Dolby Laboratories Licensing Corporation

Dolby™ sound system

Dole, Bob

Dole, Elizabeth

Dole Food Company, Inc.

Dolenz, Mickey

Dole Packaged Foods Company

Dolgeville

Dolin, Sir Anton

Dollar Bank

Dollar Dry Dock Savings Bank

Dollar General Corporation

Dollar Rent A Car

Dollars for Scholars

Dollfuss, Engelbert

Doll's House, A

Dolly Varden

Dolly Varden pattern

Dollywood

Dolomite Alps

Dolomites, the

Dolphin Cruise Line

Dolphin Hellas Cruise Line

Dolphy, Eric

Dolton

Domagk, Gerhard

Domenichino

Domenici, Pete

Domenico Veneziano

Domenico Zampieri

Dome of the Rock

Domesday *occas.* Doomsday Book

Domingo, Placido

Dominic, Saint

Dominica

Dominican

Dominican Airlines

Dominican College of Blauvelt

Dominican College of San Rafael

Dominican Family [*form.* Dominican order]

Dominican House of Studies

Dominican Republic

Dominican School of Philosophy and Theology

Dominion Bank

Dominion Day

Dominion Resources, Inc.

Dominique

Domino, Fats

Dominus

Dominus vobiscum

Domitian

Domremy-la-Pucelle

Don

Donahue [*form.* The Phil Donahue Show]

Donahue, Elinor

Donahue, Phil

Donahue, Troy

Donald

Donald, David

Donald Byrd/The Group

Donald Duck

Donald I. Fine, Inc.

Donaldson, Sam

Donaldson, Walter

Donaldson Company, Inc.

Donaldsonville [* LA]

Donalsonville [* GA]

Dona Nobis Pacem

Donat, Peter

Donat, Robert

Donatello [sculptor]

Donatello, The [San Francisco hotel]

Donath, Helen

Donation of Constantine

Donatism

Donatist

Donatus

Donaueschingen

Don Bosco Technical Institute

Don Carlos

Don Cossacks

Donegal

Donegal tweed

Donets

Donets Basin

Donetsk
Donets River
Dong, Pham Van
Don Giovanni
Dongola kid
Dongola leather
Dongola process
Donizetti, Gaetano
Don Juan
Don Juanism
Donleavy, J. P.
Donlevy, Brian
Donna
Donna Reed Show, The
Donn-Byrne, Brian Oswald
Donne, John
Donnell, Jeff
Donnelley, Gaylord
Donnells Dam
Donnelly College
Donner
Donner Lake
Donner Party
Donner Pass
Donner Peak
Donner Trail
Donny and Marie
Donnybrook
Donnybrook Fair
Donohue, Mark
Donovan
Donovan, King
Donovan, Wild Bill
Don Pasquale
Don Quixote
Don Quixote de la Mancha

Don Rodrigo
Don't It Make My Brown Eyes Blue
Don't Worry, Be Happy
Don Youngblood and the Hoosier Beats
Doobie Brothers, The
Doogie Howser, M.D.
Doohan, James
Dooley, Thomas A.
Doolittle, Eliza
Doolittle, H. D.
Doolittle, Jimmy
Doolittle raid
Doomsday var. of Domesday Book
Doomsday Clock
Doonesbury
Doors, The
Doppler, Christian
Doppler effect
Doppler radar
Doppler shift
Doral Resort and Country Club
Doral/Ryder Open PGA Golf Tournament
Doran, Ann
Dorati, Antal
Doraville
Dorcas
Dorcas society
Dorchester
Dorchestershire
Dordogne
Dordt College
Doré, Gustave
Doria, Andrea

Dorian
Dorian Gray
Dorian mode
Dorian Toccata and Fugue
Doric
Doric order
Doris
Doris Day Show, The
Dorking
d'Orléans, Louis Phillippe Joseph
Dorman, Isaiah
Dormont
Dorn, Michael
Dornier, Claudius
Dorobo, n., pl. Dorobo or Dorobos
Dorothea, Saint
Dorothy
Dorothy Chandler Pavilion
Dorr, Thomas Wilson
Dorrance, Bennett
Dorrance, John T., III
Dorr's Rebellion
Dors, Diana
Dorset
Dorset Horn
Dorsetshire
Dorsett, Tony
Dorsey, Jimmy
Dorsey, Lee
Dorsey, Thomas A.
Dorsey, Tommy
Dorticós, Osvaldo
Dortmund
Dortmund-Ems Canal
Dos Passos, John

Dosso Dossi
Dostoyevsky, Fyodor
Dothan
Dotrice, Roy
Dou, Gerard
Douala
Douay Bible
Douay-Rheims Bible
Douay-Rheims
   Version
Douay Version
Double, The
Double Dare
Doubleday, Abner
Doubleday, Frank
   Nelson
Doubleday Book Club
Doubleday Book Shop
Doubleday Publishing
   Company
Double Gloucester
   cheese
double Spanish burton
Doubletree hotel
Doubs
doubting Thomas
Doughty, Charles
   Montagu
Doughty, Thomas
Douglas
Douglas, Aaron
Douglas, Buster
Douglas, David
Douglas, Donald
Douglas, Donna
Douglas, James
   [American mining
   engineer]
Douglas, Sir James
   [Scottish military
   leader]

Douglas, Kirk
Douglas, Lloyd C.
Douglas, Melvyn
Douglas, Michael
Douglas, Mike
Douglas, Norman
Douglas, Paul
Douglas, Stephen A.
Douglas, Sir William
Douglas, William O.
Douglas Dam
Douglas fir
Douglas hemlock
Douglas-Home, Sir
   Alexander
Douglas MacArthur
   State Technical
   College
Douglas pine
Douglass, Frederick
Douglass, Robyn
Douglas spruce
Douglasville
Doukhobor
Doulton, John
Doulton ware
Douris or Duris
Douro
Dove, Arthur
Dove, Heinrich W.
Dove prism
Dover
Dover, Thomas
Dover Air Force Base
Dover Beach
Dover Corporation
Dover Downs
   International
   Speedway
Dover sole

Dover's powder
Dovzhenko,
   Alexander P.
Dow, Charles Henry
Dow, Herbert Henry
Dow, Neal
Dowagaic
DowBrands
Dow Chemical
   Company, The
Dow Chemical
   Company
   Foundation
Dow Corning
   Corporation
Dow Corning
   Foundation
Dowden, Edward
Dowding, Sir Hugh C.
Dow Jones and
   Company Inc.
Dow Jones average
Dow Jones
   Foundation
Dow Jones index
Dow Jones News/
   Retrieval
Dow Jones News
   Service
Dowland, John
Dowling, Father
Dowling College
Dowmetal™
Down, Lesley-Anne
Down Beat
Down by the Old Mill
   Stream
Down East
Downers Grove
Downes, Edward O. D.
Downes, Olin

Downey
Downey, Morton
Downey, Morton, Jr.
Downey, Robert, Jr.
Downey Savings and
  Loan Association
Downing, Andrew
  Jackson
Downing, Sir George
Downing Street
Downingtown
Downs, Hugh
Down's occas. Down
  syndrome
Downtowner Motor
  Inn
Down Under
Dowson, Ernest
Dow theory
Doyle, Alexander
Doyle, Sir Arthur
  Conan
Doyle, David
Doyle, Popeye
Doylestown
D'Oyly Carte, Richard
D'Oyly Carte Opera
  Company
Dozenal Society of
  America
Dozier, Lamont
DPL Inc.
DQE Inc.
D-Q University
Drabble, Margaret
Draco
Draconian occas.
  draconian
Draconic
Dracula

Dragnet
Drago, Luis Maria
Drago Doctrine
Dragon, Carmen
Dragon, Daryl
Drake, The
Drake, Alfred
Drake, Sir Francis
Drake, Francis Marion
Drake, Joseph
  Rodman
Drake, Larry
Drake, Saint Clair
Drake-Chennault
  Enterprises, Inc.
Drakensberg
  Mountains
Drake Passage
Drakes Bay
Drake Swissôtel
Drake University
Drake University
  Bulldogs
Drama Critics Circle
  Award
Drama Desk
Drama Desk Award
Dramamine™
Dramatists Guild, Inc.,
  The
Dramatists Play
  Service, Inc.
Draper, Henry
Draper, Irene
Draper, John William
Draper, Ruth
Draper World
  Population Fund/
  Population Crisis
  Committee

Draughons Junior
  College
Drava
Dravidian
Dravidian languages
Dravidic
Dravosburg
Drayton, Michael
Dream, The
Dreamgirls
Drechsler, Heike
Dred Scott case
Dred Scott decision
Dred Scott v. Sanford
D region
Dreiser, Theodore
Dreiseszun,
  Sherman W.
Dresden
Dresden Altarpiece,
  The
Dresden Amen
[Dresden] Art Gallery
  of the Old Masters
Dresden™ china
Dresden Philharmonic
  Orchestra
Dresden porcelain
Dresden Staatskapelle
Dresden ware
Dresdner Bank
Dresser, Louise
Dresser, Paul
Dresser Foundation
Dresser Industries Inc.
Dressler, Marie
Drew, Charles Richard
Drew, Elizabeth
Drew, Ellen
Drew, John

Drew, Mrs. John

Drew, Nancy

Drewrys Bluff

Drew University

Drexel, Katharine

Drexel Burnham
Lambert, Inc.

Drexel University

Drexel University
Dragons

Drexler, Clyde

Dreyer's™ ice cream
[see also Breyers]

Dreyfus, Alfred

Dreyfus affair

Dreyfusard

Dreyfus Corporation,
The

Dreyfuss, Richard

Dreyfus Service
Corporation

Dr. Feelgood

Dr. Hook

Drifters, The

Driftless Area

Driftwood, Jimmy

Drinkwater, John

Drinkwater, Terry

Driver's Independent
Race Tracks

Driving Miss Daisy

Dr. Jekyll and Mr.
Hyde

Dr. Kildare

Dr. Martin Luther
College

Drogheda

Drôme

Droste-Hülshoff,
Annette

Dr. Pangloss

Dr Pepper/Seven-Up
Companies, Inc. [no
period after Dr]

Dr. Scholl's™

Dr. Seuss

Dr. Strangelove; Or,
How I Learned to
Stop Worrying and
Love the Bomb

Dru, Joanne

Drucker, Mort

Drug, Chemical and
Allied Trades
Association

Drug Emporium

Drug Emporium, Inc.

Drug Enforcement
Administration

Drug Policy
Foundation

Druid

Druidess

Druid stone

Drummond, Henry

Drummond, Thomas

Drummond, William

Drummond, William
Henry

Drummond light

Drummondville

Drumright

Drum-Roll Symphony

Drury, James

Drury College

Drury Lane

Drury Lane Theatre

Druse or Druze

Drusean

Drusian

Drusus, Nero Claudius

Druten, John van

Druze var. of Druse

Dr. William M. Scholl
College of Podiatric
Medicine

Dryburgh Abbey

Dryden, Hugh

Dryden, John

Dryden, Ken

Dryer, Fred

Dry Ice™ or dry ice

Dry Salvages, The

Drysdale, Don

Dry Tortugas

Dr. Zhivago [book;
see also Doctor
Zhivago]

D-state

Dual Alliance

Dual Monarchy

Duarte

Duarte, José Napoleón

Duart Laboratories

Dubai

du Barry, Madame

Du Barry Was a Lady

Dubawnt

Dubawnt Lake

Dubček, Alexander

Dubin, Al

Dubinsky, David

Dublin

Dublin Airport

Dubliner

Dubliners

Du Bois

Dubois, Eugène

du Bois, Guy Pène

DuBois, Ja'net

Du Bois, W. E. B.

du Bois, William Pène
Dubos, René Jules
Dubrovnik
Dubuffet, Jean
Dubuque
Dubuque, Julien
Duccio di
  Buoninsegna
Duc de Vendôme
Du Chailu, Paul
Duchamp, Marcel
Duchamp-Villon,
  Raymond
Duchess of Gloucester
Duchess of Kent
Duchess of Malfi, The
Duchess of Windsor
Duchess of York
Duchin, Eddy
Duchin, Peter
Duchossois, Richard
  Louis
Duchy of Cornwall
Duchy of Lancaster
Duck Lake
Duck Soup
Ducks Unlimited, Inc.
Ducommun, Élie
Dudley, Robert
Dudley, Thomas
Dudley Do-Right
Duel, The
Duel in the Sun
Duesenberg
Duesenberg, Frederick
  Samuel
Dufay, Guilaume
Duff, Howard
Duffy, Hugh

Duffy, Julia
Duffy, Patrick
Duffy's Tavern
Dufour, Val
Dufy, Raoul
Dugan, Dennis
Dugway Proving
  Ground
Duhamel, Georges
Duhamel's theorem
Duisburg
Dukakis, Kitty
Dukakis, Michael
Dukakis, Olympia
Dukas, Paul
Duke, Benjamin N.
Duke, David
Duke, Doris
Duke, James B.
Duke, Jennifer
  Johnson
Duke, Patty
Duke, Vernon
Duke Endowment
Duke Kahanamoku
Duke Law Journal
Duke of Albuquerque
Duke of Argyll
Duke of Bedford
Duke of Burgundy
Duke of Cornwall
Duke of Edinburgh
Duke of Gloucester
Duke of Kent
Duke of Marlborough
Duke of Monmouth
Duke of Wellington
Duke of Westminster
Duke of Windsor

Duke of York
Duke of York Islands
Duke Power Company
Duke Power Company
  Foundation
Dukes, David
Dukes of Dixieland
Dukes of Hazzard,
  The
Duke University
Duke University Blue
  Devils
Dulcinea
Dullea, Keir
Dulles, Allen
Dulles, John Foster
Dulles International
  Airport
Dull Knife Memorial
  College
Duluth
Duluth International
  Airport
Dumas, Alexandre
Du Maurier, Daphne
Du Maurier, George
Du Maurier, Sir
  Gerald
Dumbarton
Dumbarton Oaks
Dumbarton Oaks
  Concerto
Dumbarton Oaks
  Conference
Dumbartonshire
dumb Dora
Dumbo
Dumbrille, Douglass
Dumdum
Dumdum fever
Dumfries

Dumfriesshire

Dumont

Du Mont, Allan B.

Dumont, Margaret

Dumpster™ trash container

Dun, R. G.

Dun and Bradstreet™

Dun and Bradstreet Corporation, The

Dun and Bradstreet Corporation Foundation

Dun and Bradstreet Million Dollar Directory

Dunant, Jean Henri

Dunaway, Faye

Dunbar

Dunbar, Paul Laurence

Dunbar, William

Dunbar-Nelson, Alice

Duncan

Duncan, Isadora

Duncan, Johnny

Duncan, Robert

Duncan, Sandy

Duncan Phyfe

Duncanville

Dunciad, The

Dundalk

Dundalk Community College

Dundee

Dunedin

Dunellen

Dunes Hotel and Country Club

Dungeness

Dungeness crab

Dungeons and Dragons™

Dunham, Katherine

Dunkel Sports Research Service

Dunker or Dunkard

Dunkers

Dunkirk

Dunlap, William

Dunlop, John Boyd

Dunlop cheese

Dunmore

Dunmore, John Murray

Dunmore's War

Dunn

Dunn, Holly

Dunn, James

Dunn, Michael

Dunn, Mignon

Dunn, Nora

Dunn, Thomas

Dunne, Dominick

Dunne, Finley Peter

Dunne, Griffin

Dunne, Irene

Dunne, John Gregory

Dunnock, Mildred

Dunsany, Lord

Dunsinane

Dun's Magazine

Dunsmuir

Duns Scotus, John

Dunstable, John

Dunstan, Saint

Dunwoody Industrial Institute

Dupont

du Pont, Alexis Felix, Jr.

du Pont, Éleuthère Irénée

du Pont, Irénée, Jr.

du Pont, Pierre Samuel

du Pont, Samuel Francis

du Pont, Willis Harrington

Du Pont™ chemicals

du Pont de Nemours, Pierre Samuel

Du Pont™ fibers

Dupré, Jules

Dupré, Marcel

Duquesne

Duquesne Light Company

Duquesne University

Duquesne University Dukes

Du Quoin

Duracell International Inc.

Duran Ballen, Sixto

Durand

Durand, Asher Brown

Duran Duran

Durango

Durant

Durant, Ariel

Durant, Thomas C.

Durant, Will

Durant, William Crapo

Durante, Jimmy

Duranty, Walter

Durban

Durbin, Deanna

Dürer, Albrecht

Dürer Self-Portrait

D'Urfey, Thomas
Durham
Durham, Monte
Durham rule
Durham Technical
  Community College
Duris, *var. of* Douris
Durkheim, Émile
Durning, Charles
Duroc
Durocher, Leo
Duroc-Jersey
Durrell, Lawrence
Durrell, Michael
Durst, David M.
Durst, Royal H.
Durst, Seymour B.
Durst, Will
Dury, Ian
Duryea
Duryea, Charles
Duryea, Dan
DuSable Museum of
  African-American
  History
Dusay, Marj
Duse, Eleanora
Dussault, Nancy
Düsseldorf
Dust Bowl
Dustin
Dutch
Dutch and Flemish
  literature
Dutch auction
Dutch Belted
Dutch bob
Dutch Bond
Dutch Borneo

Dutch chair
Dutch cheese
Dutch circle
Dutch clover
Dutch courage
Dutch cupboard
Dutch door
Dutch East India
  Company
Dutch East Indies
Dutch elm disease
Dutchess Community
  College
Dutch foot
Dutch gold
Dutch Guiana [*now*
  Suriname]
Dutch Harbor
Dutch hoe
Dutch Inn
Dutch Interior
Dutch language
Dutch lap
Dutch lunch
dutchman, *n., pl.*
  dutchmen; *occas.*
  Dutchman, *n., pl.*
  Dutchmen
Dutchman's-breeches,
  n., pl. Dutchman's-
  breeches
Dutchman's land
Dutchman's log
Dutchman's-pipe, *n.,*
  pl. Dutchman's-
  pipes
Dutch metal
Dutch oven
Dutch paper
Dutch Reformed

Dutch Reformed
  Church
Dutch rush
Dutch Schultz
Dutch settle
Dutch Settlers Society
  of Albany
Dutch straight
Dutch treat
Dutch 200
Dutch uncle
Dutch Wars
Dutch West India
  Company
Dutch wife
dutchwoman, *n., pl.*
  dutchwomen; *occas.*
  Dutchwoman, *n., pl.*
  Dutchwomen
Dutton, E. P.
Dutton Children's
  Books
Duty Free
  International, Inc.
Duvalier, François
Duvalier, Jean Claude
Duvall, Gabriel
Duvall, Robert
Duvall, Shelley
Duveneck, Frank
Duvoisin, Roger
Dvina
Dvina Bay
Dvořák, Antonin
Dwight
Dworshak Dam
Dworshak Reservoir
Dyer, John
Dyersburg
Dyersburg State
  Community College

Dyersville

Dyess Air Force Base

Dying Centaur, The

Dyke College

Dylan, Bob

Dynasty

Dynel™

Dyophysite

Dyothelite

D'Youville College

Dysart, Richard

Dysautonomia
   Foundation

Dyson, Charles Henry

Dyson, Freeman J.

Dzerzhinsk

Dzerzhinsky Square

Dzundza, George

E

E! [Entertainment Television]

Eadmer *or* Edmer

Eadmund the Martyr *var. of* Edmund the Martyr, Saint

Eadred *or* Edred

Eads, James Buchanan

Eadwig *or* Edwy

Eagels, Jeanne

Eagle Forum

Eagle Industries, Inc.

Eagle Pass

Eagle-Picher Industries Inc.

Eagles, The

Eagle Scout

Eagleton, Thomas

Eagleton Village

Eaker, Ira

Eaker Air Force Base

Eakins, Thomas

Eames, Charles

Eames, Emma

Eames™ chair

Eames design

E. & J. Gallo Winery

Earhart, Amelia

Earhart, Anne Catherine Getty

Earl, Ralph

Earl Carrol's Vanities

Earl Grey™ tea

Earlham College

Earlier Han dynasty

Earlimart

Earlington

Earl Klugh Trio, The

Earl Marshal, *n., pl.* Earl Marshals

Earl of Cardigan

Earl of Chesterfield

Earl of Clarendon

Earl of Essex

Earl of Gloucester

Earl of Greystoke

Earl of Leicester

Earl of Shaftesbury

Earl of Snowdon

Earl of Strafford

Earl of Surrey

Earl of Ulster

Earl of Warwick

Earl Scheib Inc.

Earl Warren Legal Training Program

Early, Jubal Anderson

Early American

Early Christian

Early English

Early Hebrew

Early Modern English

Early Renaissance

Earp, Wyatt

earth *often* Earth [planet]

Earthcare Network

Earth Day

Earth First!

Earth Island Institute

Earthling

Earthquake Engineering Research Institute

Earth Summit

Earthwatch

Earth, Wind and Fire

EA-6B Prowler

EA-6 Intruder

Easley

East African Community

East Alton

East Anglia

East Anglian

East Arkansas Community College

East Ashtabula

East Aurora

East Bengal

East Berlin

Eastbourne

East Cape

East Carolina University

East Carolina University Pirates

East Central College

East Central Community College

East Central University

East Chicago

East Chicago Heights

East China Sea

East Cleveland

East Coast Bible College

East Coast jazz

East Coker

East Conemaugh

East Detroit

Easter

Easter candle

Easter daisy

Easter egg

Easter Island

Easter lily

Easter Monday

Eastern Air Lines, Inc.

Eastern Arizona College

Eastern Baptist Theological Seminary

Eastern Chin dynasty

Eastern Christian College

Eastern Church

Eastern College

Eastern College Athletic Conference

Eastern Connecticut State University

Eastern Daylight Time

Eastern Desert

Eastern Educational Television Network

Eastern Enterprises

Easterner

Eastern European Council, Ltd.

Eastern European Mutual Assistance Treaty

Eastern Ghats

eastern hemisphere *often* Eastern Hemisphere

Eastern Hindi

Eastern Illinois University

Eastern Illinois University Panthers

Eastern Iowa Community College

Eastern Kentucky University

Eastern Kentucky University Colonels

Eastern Lobby Shops

Eastern Maine Technical College

Eastern Mennonite College

Eastern Michigan University

Eastern Michigan University Hurons

Eastern Montana College

Eastern Mountain Sports Inc.

Eastern Nazarene College

Eastern New Mexico University

Eastern Oklahoma State College

Eastern Oregon State College

Eastern Orthodox

Eastern Orthodox Church

Eastern Orthodoxy

Eastern Public Radio Network

Eastern Question *occas.* question

Eastern Review

Eastern rite

Eastern rite church

Eastern Roman Empire

Eastern Shore

Eastern Shore Community College

Eastern Slavs

Eastern Standard Time

Eastern Time

Eastern Utilities Associates

Eastern Virginia Medical School

Eastern Washington University

Eastern Washington University Eagles

Eastern Wyoming College

Easter Oratorio

Easter Parade

Easter Rebellion

Easter Rising

Easter Seal

Easter Seal Research Foundation

Easter Sunday

Eastertide

Eastfield College

East Flanders

East Gaffney

East Gary

East Georgia College

East Germany

East Goth

East Grand Forks

East Grand Rapids

East Greenland Current

East Hampton

East Hartford

East Haven

East Hills

East India Company

East Indiaman, *n., pl.* Indiamen

East Indian

East Indian lotus

East Indian rose-bay

East Indian walnut

East Indies

Eastlake

Eastlake, Sir Charles

Eastlake, William

Eastlake style

East Lansing

East Liverpool

East London

East Longmeadow

East Los Angeles

East Los Angeles College

East Lothian

East Lyme

Eastman

Eastman, George

Eastman, Max

Eastman Kodak Charitable Trust

Eastman Kodak Company

Eastman School of Music

East Massapequa

East Meadow

East Midlands International Airport

East Mississippi Community College

East Moline

East Northport

East of Eden

East of the Sun and West of the Moon

Easton

Easton, Sheena

East Orange

East Pakistan [*now* Bangladesh]

East Palestine

East Paterson

East Peoria

East Point

East Providence

East Prussia

East Prussian

East Punjab

East Ridge

East Riding

East River

East Rochester

East Rockaway

East Rutherford

East Saint Louis

East Siberian Sea

East Side *occas.* Eastside

East Sider *occas.* Eastsider

East Stroudsburg

East Stroudsburg University of Pennsylvania

East Suffolk

East Sussex

East Syracuse

East Tennessee State University

East Tennessee State University Buccaneers

East Texas Baptist University

East Texas State University

East-West Center

East West Journal

East-West University

East Wilmington

Eastwood, Clint

East York

Easy Street

Eating Right Pyramid

Eating Well

Eaton

Eaton, Cyrus S.

Eaton, Theophilus

Eaton, Timothy

Eaton Charitable Fund

Eaton Corporation

Eatontown

Eau Claire

Eau Claire River

eau de Cologne
eau de Javelle
Eban, Abba
Ebb, Fred
Ebbets Field
Eberhart, Richard
Eberle, Abastenia St. Leger
Ebersol, Dick
Ebersole, Christine
Ebert, Roger
Ebony
Ebro
Ebsen, Buddy
Eccles, Sir John Carew
Ecclesiastes
Ecclesiasticus
Echegaray, José
Echeverría, Esteban
Echeverría Álvarez, Luis
Echinodermata
Echiura
Echlin Inc.
Eck, Johann
ECKANKAR
Eckehart or Eckart or Eckhart, Johannes
Eckerd College
Eckermann, Johann Peter
Eckersburg, Christoffer Vilhelm
Eckersley, Dennis
Eckstine, Billy
Eclogues
Eco, Umberto
Ecolab Inc.
École de Paris

École des Beaux-Arts
Ecological Society of America
Ecology Action Centre
Ecology Center
Econo-Car™ auto rental
Econo-Lodge
Economic Community of West African States
Economic Cooperation Organization
Economic Development Association
Economic Policy Institute
Economic World
Economist, The
Economy
Ecorse
Ecotrin™
ECO 2000
ECPI Computer Institute
Ecstasy
Ecstasy of Saint Theresa, The
Ectoprocta
Ecuador
Ecuadoran or Ecuadorean or Ecuadorian
Ecumedia News Service
Ecumenical Church Federation
Edam
Edam cheese

Edberg, Stefan
Edda
Eddings, David
Eddington, Sir Arthur Stanley
Eddy, Mary Baker
Eddy, Nelson
Eddystone Light
Eddystone Rocks
Edelman, Herb
Edelman, Marian Wright
Eden
Eden, Sir Anthony
Eden, Barbara
Edenic
Eden Theological Seminary
Edenton
Ederle, Trudy
Edgar
Edgar Allan Poe National Historic Site
Edgecombe Community College
Edge of Night, The
Edgewater
Edgewood
Edgewood Arsenal
Edgewood College
Edgeworth, Maria
Edict of Emancipation
Edict of Milan
Edict of Nantes
Edict of Worms
Edie Adams Cut and Curl
Edina

Edinboro University of Pennsylvania

Edinburg [* TX]

Edinburgh [* Scotland]

Edinburgh Airport

Edinburgh Castle

Edinburgh Festival

Edison

Edison, Thomas Alva

Edison Brothers Stores, Inc.

Edison Community College

Edison effect

Edison Electric Institute

Edison National Historic Site

Edison State Community College

Edith

Editor & Publisher

Editorial Eye, The

Editorial Freelancers Association

Editorial Research Reports

Editorials on File™

Editor's Copy Syndicate

Editor's Press Service, Inc.

Edman, Irwin

Edmer var. of Eadmer

Edmond [given name; * OK]

Edmonds [* WA]

Edmonds, Walter Dumaux

Edmonds Community College

Edmondson Junior College of Business

Edmonton

Edmonton Journal, The

Edmonton Oilers

Edmund

Edmund, Saint

Edmund or Eadmund the Martyr, Saint

Edmund Campion, Saint

Edmund Ironside

Edna

Edom

Edomite

Edred var. of Eadred

EDS Corporation

Edsel

Edsel Ford Range

Edson, John Orin

Ed Sullivan Show, The

Educational Broadcasting Corporation

Educational Film Library Association

Educational Press Association of America

Educational Testing Service

Education Commission of the United States

Education Dynamics Institute

Education Funding Research Council

Education of Henry Adams, The

Edward

Edwardian

Edwardianism

Edward J. DeBartolo Corporation

Edward Nyanza

Edwards, Anthony

Edwards, Blake

Edwards, Cliff

Edwards, Douglas

Edwards, Gus

Edwards, Jonathan

Edwards, Ralph

Edwards, Sherman

Edwards, Tommy

Edwards, Vince

Edwards Air Force Base

Edward Scissorhands

Edward VI as Prince of Wales

Edwardsville

Edward the Black Prince

Edward the Confessor, Saint

Edward the Elder

Edward the Martyr

Edward the Peacemaker

Edward Waters College

Edwy var. of Eadwig

Eeckhout, Gerbrand van den

E-8A J-STARS

Eel River

Eeyore

Effect of Gamma Rays on Man-in-the-

Moon Marigolds, The

Effie

Effigy Mounds National Monument

Effingham

EF-111 Raven

Egan, Richard

EG & G, Inc.

Egbert

Eggar, Samantha

Egghead Discount Software

Eggleston, Edward

Eggleston, George Cary

eggs Benedict

Eglevsky, André

Eglin Air Force Base

Egmont

Egmont Overture

Egypt

EgyptAir

Egyptian

Egyptian alfalfa weevil

Egyptian architecture

Egyptian art

Egyptian calendar

Egyptian clover

Egyptian cobra

Egyptian cotton

Egyptianism

Egyptianization

Egyptianize, v. Egyptianized, Egyptianizing

Egyptian language

Egyptian lotus

Egyptian Mau

Egyptian Museum

Egyptian religion

Egyptologist

Egyptology

Ehlers-Danlos syndrome

Ehrenbreitstein

Ehrenburg, Ilya

Ehrlich, Paul

Ehrlich, Paul Ralph

Ehrlichman, John D.

Eichhorn, Lisa

Eichmann, Adolf

E. I. du Pont de Nemours and Company

Eielson Air Force Base

Eifel plateau

Eiffel, Alexandre Gustave

Eiffel Tower

Eigen, Manfred

8½

Eighteenth *occas.* 18th Amendment [to the Constitution]

1812 Festival Overture

1812 Overture

Eightfold Path

Eighth Air Force Historical Society

Eighth *occas.* 8th Amendment [to the Constitution]

Eight Is Enough

Eight-Week Cholesterol Diet

82nd Airborne Division Association

Eikenberry, Jill

Eileen

Eilshemius, Louis Michel

Eindhoven

Eine kleine Nachtmusik

Einstein, Albert

Einstein, Alfred

Einstein equation

Einsteinian

Einstein shift

Einstein's photoelectric equation

Einstein's theory of relativity

Einthoven, Willem

Eire

Eisen, Marc

Eisenhower, Dwight D.

Eisenhower, Mamie

Eisenhower, Milton

Eisenhower Doctrine

Eisenhower Exchange Fellowships, Inc.

Eisenhower jacket

Eisenhower National Historic Site

Eisenmenger complex

Eisenstaedt, Alfred

Eisenstein, Ferdinand

Eisenstein, Sergey

Eisenstein's irreducibility criterion

Eisley, Anthony

Eisner, Michael

Eiteljorg Museum of the American

Indian and Western Art

Ekberg, Anita

Ekland, Britt

Ekman, Vagn Walfrid

Ekman dredge

Ekman layer

Ekman spiral

Ektachrome™

Ektacolor™

Elaine

El Alamein *var. of* Al-Alamein

El Al Israeli Airlines Ltd.

Elam

Elam, Jack

Elamite

Elamitic

E-layer

Elba [island]

Elbe [river]

Elberta

Elberton

Elbrus

Elburz

El Cajon

El Camino College

El Camino Real

El Campo

El Capitan

Elcar, Dana

El Centro

El Centro College

El Centro Naval Air Facility

El Cerrito

El Cordobés

Elder, Mark

Elder-Beerman Stores

Elder Edda

Elderhostel

El Dorado [movie; place of great wealth; * AR; KS]

Eldorado [* IL; TX]

Eldorado National Forest

Eldorado Springs

Eldredge, Todd

Eldridge, Florence

Eldridge, Roy

Eleanor of Aquitaine

Eleanor of Castile

Eleanor of Provence

Eleanor Roosevelt National Historic Site

Eleatic school

Eleazar

Election Day

Electoral College

Electra

Electra complex

Electric Auto Association

Electric Light Orchestra, The

Electric Peak

Electric Power Research Institute

Electrochemical Society

Electronic Computer Programming Institute

Electronic Data Processing College

Electronic Industries Association

Electronic Institutes

Elegy Written in a Country Churchyard

Elektra Records

Elementary and Secondary Education Act

Elements of Style, The

Elephanta Island

Elephant Butte Dam

Elephant Butte Reservoir

Elephant Man, the [person]

Elephant Man, The [play; movie]

Eleusinia

Eleusinian

Eleusinian mysteries

Eleuthera

Eleutherius, Saint

Elevation of the Cross

Elevation of the Host

Eleventh *occas.* 11th Amendment [to the Constitution]

Elgar, Sir Edward

Elgart, Les

Elgin

Elgin Community College

Elgin Marbles

El Giza

Elgon

El Greco

Elias

Elias, Rosalind

Eli, Eli, lama sabachthani? *occas.*

Eloi, Eloi, lama sabachthani?

Elihu

Elijah

Elijah's chair

Elijah's cup

Eli Lilly and Company

Eli Lilly and Company Foundation

Eliot, Charles William

Eliot, George

Eliot, John

Eliot, T. S.

Elisha

Elisha Monte Dance Company

Elite Guard

Elizabeth

Elizabeth, Saint

Elizabethan

Elizabethan Age

Elizabethan collar

Elizabeth Ann Seton, Saint

Elizabethan sonnet

Elizabethan theater

Elizabeth Arden Company

Elizabeth Charlotte of Bavaria

Elizabeth City

Elizabeth City State University

Elizabeth Farnese

Elizabeth Islands

Elizabeth Kaye Collection

Elizabeth of Hungary, Saint

Elizabeth of Valois

Elizabeth Petrovna

Elizabeth R

Elizabethton [* TN]

Elizabethtown [* IL; KY; NC; NY; PA]

Elizabethtown College

Elizabethtown Community College

Elizondo, Hector

Elk City

Elk Grove

Elk Grove Village

Elkhart

Elk Hills

Elk Hills oil reserves

Elkhorn Tavern

Elkin, Stanley

Elk Island National Park

Elko

Elks Magazine, The

Elle

Elle Decor

Elle International

Ellensburg

Ellenville

Ellerbee, Linda

Ellery Queen's Mystery Club

Ellery Queen's Mystery Magazine

Ellesmere Island

Ellice Islands [now Tuvalu]

Ellington, Duke

Ellington, Mercer

Ellington Air Force Base

Elliott, Bob

Elliott, Denholm

Elliott, Mama Cass

Elliott, Sam

Elliott, Stephen

Elliott, Sumner Locke

Elliott eye

Ellis, Alpheus Lee

Ellis, Havelock

Ellis, Jimmy

Ellis, Perry

Ellis Island

Ellis Island Immigration Museum

Ellison, Harlan

Ellison, Lawrence J.

Ellison, Ralph

Ellroy, James

Ellsworth

Ellsworth, Lincoln

Ellsworth, Oliver

Ellsworth Air Force Base

Ellsworth Community College

Ellwood City

El Malpais National Monument

Elman, Mischa

Elman, Ziggy

El Mansura

Elmendorf Air Force Base

Elmer Gantry

Elm Grove

Elmhurst

Elmhurst College

Elmira

Elmira College

Elmira Heights

Elmira Southeast
El Misti
Elmo, Saint
Elmont [* NY]
El Monte [* CA]
El Morro National Monument
Elmwood Park
El Niño
Elohim
Elohist
Eloi, Eloi, lama sabachthani? *var. of* Eli, Eli, lama sabachthani?
Elon
Elon College
El Paso [city]
El Paso City [song]
El Paso County Community College
El Paso International Airport
El Paso LNG Company (El Paso Tanker Companies)
El Paso Natural Gas Company
El Pensador Mexicano
El Pueblo de Los Angeles Historic Park
El Reno
El Reno Junior College
El Rio
El Salvador
El Segundo
Elsevier Science Publishing Co., Inc.
Elsheimer, Adam

Elsmere
El Taco restaurant
El Torito Restaurant
El Toro Marine Corps Air Station
Elul
Elvira
Elvira Madigan
Elvis Forever TCB Fan Club
Elvis Presley Mansion
Elvis Presley Performing Arts Scholarship Foundation
Elvis Presley Plaza
Elway, John
Elwood
Ely
Ely, Ron
Elyria
Élysée
Elysian Fields
Elysium, *n.*, *pl.* Elysiums *or* Elysia
Elzevir, Louis
Emancipation Proclamation
Emanuel
Embargo Act
Embarkation for Cythera, The
Embassy Suites
Ember day
Embroiderers' Guild of America
Embroidery Trade Association
Embry-Riddle Aeronautical University

Emerald City
Emerald Isle
Emergency!
Emerson
Emerson, Faye
Emerson, Ralph Waldo
Emerson Charitable Trust
Emerson College
Emerson Electric Company
Emersonian
Emerson, Lake and Palmer
Emerson Radio Corporation
Emerson String Quartet
Emery Air Freight Corporation
Emery Aviation College
Emery Worldwide Airlines, Inc.
Emhart Corporation
Emigrant Aid Company
Emigrants, The
Emigrant Savings Bank
Emile, *French* Émile [given name]
Émile [novel by Rousseau]
Emilia-Romagna
Emily
Eminescu, Mihail
Emir of Kuwait
Emmanuel
Emmanuel, Pierre

Emmanuel College

Emmanuel College School of Christian Ministries

Emmanuel School of Religion

Emmaus

Emmaus Bible College

Emmentaler *or* Emmenthaler cheese

Emmett, Daniel

Emmy, *n.*, *pl.* Emmys [given name]

Emmy, *n.*, *pl.* Emmys *occas.* Emmies [award]

Emory and Henry College

Emory oak

Emory University

Empedocles

Emperor [Concerto]

Emperor Akihito

Emperor Jones, The

Emperor Justinian and His Court

Emperor Napoleon Bonaparte

Emperor's College of Traditional Oriental Medicine

Emperor's New Clothes, The

Empicharmus

Empire Brass Quintet

Empire Day

Empire of the Golden Horde

Empire State

Empire State Building

Empire Strikes Back, The

Empire style

Employee Retirement Income Security Act

Employers Insurance of Wausau Mutual Company

Emporia

Emporia State University

Empress Eugénie

Empress Michiko

Empress Theodora and Her Court

Empson, William

Empty Nest

Enberg, Dick

Enchanted Mesa

Encina, Juan del

Encore Books

Encyclopaedia Britannica

Encyclopaedia Britannica Educational Corporation

Encyclopaedia Britannica, Inc.

Encyclopedia Americana, The

Encyclopédie

encyclopedist *often* Encyclopedist

Endangered Species Act

Endeavor spacecraft

Endecott, John

Enderby Land

Enders, John F.

Endicott

Endicott College

Endless Vacation

Endymion

Enemy of the People, An

Energy Conservation Coalition

Energy Foundation

Enesco, Georges

Enfield

Enfield Grammar School

Enfield rifle

Engadine

Engel, Ernst

Engel, Georgia

Engel, Lehman

Engelhard, Jane B.

Engelhard Corporation

Engelmann, George

Engelmann spruce

Engels, Friedrich

Engel's law

Engineering Contractors Association

England

England Air Force Base

Englander

Engle, Paul

Englewood

Englewood Cliffs

English

English architecture

English art

English bond

English breakfast tea

English bulldog

English Channel

English Channel Tunnel

English Civil War

English cocker spaniel

English daisy

English Derby

English elm

Englisher

English foxhound

English gooseberry

English holly

English horn

English iris

Englishism

English ivy

English Journal

English language

English Language Notes

English laurel

English literature

Englishman, *n.*, *pl.* Englishmen

Englishman at the Moulin Rouge, The

English muffin

English National Opera

Englishness

English Pale

English primrose

English red

English Restoration

English Revolution

English running horse

English saddle

English setter

English shepherd

English sonnet

English sparrow

English-Speaking Union of the United States

English springer spaniel

English system

English toy spaniel

English units of measurement

English walnut

Englishwoman, *n.*, *pl.* Englishwomen

English yew

Englund, Robert

Enid

Eniwetok *occas.* Enewetak

Enlightenment, the

Ennis

Ennis, Skinnay

Ennius, Quintus

Enoch

Enoch Arden

Enola Gay

Enright, D. J.

Enright, Elizabeth

Enriquez, Rene

Enron Corporation

Enron Foundation

Enron Oil and Gas Company

Ensenada

ENSERCH Corporation

Ensor, James

ENSR Consulting and Engineering

Ent Air Force Base

Entebbe

Entente Cordiale

Entergy Corporation

Enterprise

Enterprise Rent-A-Car

Enterprise State Junior College

Enterra Corporation

Entertainment and Sports Programming Network

Entertainment Industries Council

Entertainment News Syndicate

Entertainment This Week

Entertainment Tonight

Entertainment Weekly

Enthroned Madonna and Child

Entombment, The

Entomological Society of America

Entoprocta

Entre Nous

Entrepreneurial Woman

Entrepreneur Magazine

Enumclaw

Enver Pasha

Environment

Environmental Action

Environmental Action Coalition

Environmental Action Foundation

Environmental Defense Fund

Environmental Policy Institute

Environmental Protection Agency

En Vogue

Eocene

E-1 Tracer

Eos

Eötvös, Roland

Eötvös torsion balance

Eötvös unit

Eozoic

Epaminondas

EPCOT Center

E. P. Dutton™

Ephesian

Ephesus

Ephesus Museum

Ephraem, Saint

Ephraemi Syri

Ephraim

Ephraimite

Ephrata [* PA; WA; see also Ephratah]

Ephrata Cloisters

Ephratah or Ephrath [Caleb's wife; see also Ephrata]

Ephron, Delia

Ephron, Henry

Ephron, Nora

Ephron, Phoebe

Epic of American Civilization, An

Epic of Gilgamesh, The

Epictetus

Epicurean

Epicureanism

Epicurus

Epigraphic Society, Inc., The

Epilepsy Foundation of America

Epimarchus

Epipaleolithic

Epiphany, n., pl. Epiphanies

Epiphany of Our Lord

Epiritoki Lines

Episcopal

Episcopal Church

Episcopal Church in the United States of America, The

Episcopal Divinity School

Episcopalian

Episcopalianism

Episcopal Life

Episcopal Synod of America

Episcopal Theological Seminary of the Southwest

Epistle of James

Epistle of Jude

Epistles of John

Epistles of Peter

Epistles to the Corinthians

Epistles to the Thessalonians

Epistle to Dr. Arbuthnot

Epistle to Philemon

Epistle to the Colossians

Epistle to the Ephesians

Epistle to the Galatians

Epistle to the Hebrews

Epistle to the Philippians

Epistle to the Romans

E Pluribus Unum

Epping Forest

Eppler Guerin and Turner

Epsilon Sigma Alpha

Epsilon Sigma Phi

Epsom

Epsom Derby

Epsom Downs

Epsom salts occas. salt

Epson America, Inc.

Epstein, Alvin

Epstein, Sir Jacob

Epstein, Michael Anthony

Epstein-Barr virus

Epworth League

Equal Employment Opportunity Commission

Equalizer, The

Equal Rights Amendment

Equatorial Guinea

Equatorial Islands

Equifax Inc.

Equipment Manufacturers Institute

Equipment Manufacturing Institute

Equitable, The

Equitable Foundation

Equitable Life Assurance Society of the United States

Equitable Resources, Inc.

Equitable Variable Life Insurance Company

Equus

Erasistratus of Ceos

Erasmian

Erasmus

Erasmus, Desiderius

Erasmus, Saint

Erastian

Erastianism

Erastus, Thomas

Eratosthenes of Cyrene

Ercilla, Alonso de

Erckmann-Chatrian

Erdman, Richard

Erebus

Erechtheum

Erector™ set

E region

Eretria [* ancient Greece; see also Eritrea]

Erhard, Ludwig

Erhard, Werner

Eric

Erica

ERIC Clearinghouse on Reading and Communication Skills

Erick Hawkins Dance Company

Erickson, Leif [actor]

Ericson or Eriksson, Leif [explorer]

Eric or Erik the Red

Erie

Erie Canal

Erie Community College

Erie Institute of Technology

[Erie] Times-News

Erigena, John Scotus

Erikson, Erik H.

Erin

Erin go bragh

Eritrea [Ethiopian province; see also Eretria]

Erlander, Tage

Erlanger

Erlenmeyer, Emil

Erlenmeyer flask

Ernest

Ernie Kovacs

Ernst, Max

Ernst, Richard R.

Ernst and Whinney

Ernst and Whinney Foundation

Ernst and Young Inc.

Eroica Symphony

Eros

Errol, Leon

Erskine, John

Erskine College

Erté

Ervin, Sam

Ervine, St. John Greer

Erving, Julius

Erwin

Erymanthus

Erzberg

Erz Mountains

Esau

Escanaba

Escapees, Inc.

Eschenbach, Christoph

Eschenbach, Wolfram von

Escobar, Marisol

Escobar, Roberto

Escobar Gaviria, Pablo

Escobedo v. Illinois

Escoffier, Auguste

Escondido

Escorial

Escudero, Vincente

Escuela de Artes Plasticas

Esdraelon

Eshkol, Levi

E-6 TACAMO II

Eskimo, n., pl. Eskimo or Eskimos

Eskimo-Aleut

Eskimoan

Eskimo curlew

Eskimo dog

Eskimologist

Eskimology

Española [island]

Espanola [* NM; Ontario]

Esperantism

Esperantist

Esperanto

Esperanto, Doctor

Esperanto League for North America

Espírito Santo [Brazilian state; island off coast of that state]

Espíritu Santo [island in Vanuatu; island off coast of Baja California]

Espíritu Santo Bay
Esposito, Phil
Espronceda, José de
Espy, Mike
Esquiline Hill
Esquimalt
Esquire
Essay on Criticism, An
Essay on Man, An
Essen
Essence
Essequibo
Essex
Essex, Robert Devereux
Essex Community College
Essex County College
Essex Junction
Essex Junto
Essex table
Essexville
Establishment, the
Estates General
Este
Este, Alberto
Este, Alfonso
Este, Azzo
Este, Borso
Este, Cesare
Este, Ercole
Este, Folco
Este, Francesco
Este, Ippolito
Este, Leonello
Este, Nicolò
Este, Obizzo
Este, Rinaldo

Este, Welf
Estée Lauder Inc.
Estefan, Gloria
Esterhaza castle
Esterházy, Ferenc
Esterhazy, Marie Charles
Esterházy, Miklós
Esterházy, Miklós József
Esterházy, Moritz
Esterházy, Pál
Esterházy, Pál Antal
Estes, Eleanor
Estes Park
Estevez, Emilio
est Foundation
Esther
Estherville
Estonia [form. Estonian Soviet Socialist Republic]
Estonian
Estonian Soviet Socialist Republic [now Estonia]
Estrada, Erik
Estremadura
est training
E-Systems, Inc.
Eta Kappa Nu
Eta Sigma Phi
Eteocles
Eternal City, The
Eternal Word TV Network
Étex, Antoine
Ethan
Ethan Allen Inc.
Ethan Frome

Ethel Barrymore Theater
Ethelbert
Ethelred the Unready
Etherege, Sir George
Etheridge, Melissa
Ethical Culture Movement
Ethical Culture Society
Ethics and Public Policy Center
Ethics in Government Act
Ethics Resource Center
Ethiopia
Ethiopian
Ethiopian Airlines
Ethiopian Church
Ethiopian Highlands
Ethiopic
E-3 Sentry
Ethyl Corporation
ETI Technical College
Eton
Eton collar
Eton College
Etonian
Eton jacket
Etosha Game Park
Etowah
Etowah Mounds
Etruria
Etrurian
Etruscan
Etruscan art
Etruscan civilization
Etruscan ware
Etruscology

Ettarre

E. T.: The Extra-
Terrestrial

E. T.: The Extra-
Terrestrial
Storybook

Etting, Ruth

E-2 Hawkeye

Eubanks, Bob

Eucharist

Eucharistic

Eucharistical

Eucharistic theology

Euclid

euclidean *or* euclidian
often Euclidean *or*
Euclidian

Euclidean *occas.*
Euclid's algorithm

euclidian *often*
Euclidian domain

euclidian *often*
Euclidian geometry

euclidian *often*
Euclidian group

euclidian *often*
Euclidian space

Euclid of Megara

Euclid's algorithm *var.*
of Euclidean
algorithm

Eudist

Eudora

Eudoxus of Cnidus

Eudoxus of Cyzicus

Eufaula

Eugene

Eugene I, Saint *var. of*
Eugenius, Saint

Eugene Bible College

Eugene of Savoy

Eugene O'Neill
Memorial Theater
Center

Eugene O'Neill
National Historic
Site

Eugene O'Neill
Theater

Eugenie

Eugenius *or* Eugene I,
Saint

Euhemerus

Eulenspiegel *or*
Ulenspiegel, Till

Euler, Leonhard

Euler characteristic

Euler's constant

Euler's formula

Euler's function

Eumetozoa

Eunapius

Eunice

Eupen and Malmédy

Euphratean

Euphrates

Eurailpass

Euramerican

Eurasia

Eurasian

Eurasian wigeon

Euratom

Eure-et-Loire

Eureka

Eureka College

Euripidean

Euripides

Euro-American

Eurobond

Euroclydon

Eurocommunism

Eurocommunist

Eurocrat

Eurocurrency

Euro Disneyland

Eurodollar

Eurofighter

Eurofima

Euromarket

Euromart

Europa

Europa, Europa

Europe

European

Europeans, The

European American
Bank

European Atomic
Energy Community

European Bank for
Reconstruction and
Development

European beech

European bird cherry

European
blastomycosis

European chafer

European chestnut

European Coal and
Steel Community

European Commission

European Common
Market

European Community

European corn borer

European Court of
Human Rights

European cranberry

European Currency
Unit

European Economic
Community

European elder

European fan palm

European Fighter
Aircraft

European fly
honeysuckle

European Free Trade
Association

European globeflower

European goldenrod

European Investment
Bank

Europeanism

Europeanization

Europeanize, v.
Europeanized,
Europeanizing

European larch

European linden

European mallow

European Monetary
Agreement

European Monetary
Cooperation Fund

European Monetary
System

European
Organization for
Nuclear Research

European Payments
Union

European plan

European raspberry

European Recovery
Program

European red mite

European Southern
Observatory

European Space
Agency

European Space
Research
Organization

European spruce
sawfly

European white
hellebore

Europocentric

Eurotunnel

Eurovision
International Ltd.

Eurydice

Eurythmics, The

Eusebius, Saint

Eusebius of Caesarea

Eusebius of
Nicodemia

Eusebius of Vercelli,
Saint

Eustace

eustachian often
Eustachian tube

Eustachio,
Bartolommeo

Eustathius

Eustathius, Saint

Eustis

Eutychianus or
Eutychian, Saint

Eutychides

Evan

Evangel College

Evangelical, adj. [of
or pertaining to an
Evangelical
Church]

Evangelical, n. [one
holding evangelical
principles; an
Evangelical Church
member]

evangelical often
Evangelical, adj. [of
or pertaining to

Christian
fundamentalism]

Evangelical Alliance

Evangelical and
Reformed Church

Evangelical Church

Evangelical
Congregational
Church

Evangelical Covenant
Church, The

Evangelical Free
Church of America

Evangelical Friends
Alliance

Evangelical League

Evangelical Lutheran
Church in America

Evangelical Lutheran
Synod

Evangelical
Mennonite Church

Evangelical Methodist
Church

Evangelical
Presbyterian Church

Evangelical School of
Theology

Evangelical Seminary
of Puerto Rico

Evangelical United
Brethren Church

Evangelical Wesleyan
Church

Evangeline

Evangelista, Linda

Evans, Sir Arthur John

Evans, Bill

Evans, Dale

Evans, Daniel Leroy

Evans, Dame Edith

Evans, Gene

Evans, Gil

Evans, Herbert
McLean

Evans, James Emmett

Evans, Linda

Evans, Mary

Evans, Maurice

Evans, Oliver

Evans, Robert

Evans, Rudolph

Evans, Thomas
Mellon

Evans, Walker

Evans and Novak

Evansdale

Evanston

Evansville

Evaristus, Saint

Evarts, William

Evdokimova, Eva

Eve

Eve, Trevor

Eveleth

Evelyn

Evelyn, John

Evelyn, Judith

Evelyn Wood™
speed-reading
method

Evening at Pops

Evening Prayer

Evening Shade

Eve of St. Agnes, The

Eveready Battery
Company, Inc.

Everest, Sir George

Everest syndrome

Everett

Everett, Chad

Everett, Edward

Everett Community
College

Everglades

Everglades National
Park

Evergood, Philip

Evergreen

Evergreen Park

Evergreen State

Evergreen State
College

Evergreen Valley
College

Everhart, Bob

Everly, Don

Everly, Phil

Everly Brothers

Evers, Charles

Evers, Johnny

Evers, Medgar

Evert, Chris

Every Breath You
Take

Everyman [play]

Everyman *or*
everyman
[representation of
the common
person]

Everyman in His
Humour

Everyman out of His
Humour

Everyman's Library

Everything You
Wanted to Know
about Sex but Were
Afraid to Ask

every Tom, Dick, and
Harry

Evian™ natural spring
water

Evian Waters of
France

Evigan, Greg

Evinrude, Ole

Evinrude™ outboard
motor

Evita

Evora

Ewell, Richard
Stoddert

Ewell, Tom

Ewe tribe

Ewing

Ewing, Alfred Cyril

Ewing, James

Ewing, Maurice

Ewing, Thomas

Ewok

E. W. Scripps
Company

Excalibur

Excelsior Springs

Exchangite

Exclusive Press
Syndicate

Executioner's Song,
The

Executive Female

Executive Life
Insurance Company

Executive Life
Insurance Company
of New York

Executive
Management
Services
Corporation

Executive Mansion

Executive Office of
the President

Exercycle™

Exeter
Exeter Book
Exide Corporation
Exile
Eximbank *or* Exim Bank
Exmoor
Exodus
Exorcist, The
Exorcist III, The
Exorcist II: The Heretic
Expectation Sunday
Expectation Week
Experimental Aircraft Association
Experimental Prototype Community of Tomorrow

Exploratorium, The
Explorer
Exploring
Exploring Magazine
Export-Import Bank of Japan
Export-Import Bank of the United States
Expressionism *occas.* expressionism
Expressionist *occas.* expressionist
Express Mail Next Day Service™
EXPRESS PHOTO™ photo service
Extreme
Extreme Unction

Exxon Company International
Exxon Company, U.S.A.
Exxon Corporation
Exxon Education Foundation
Exxon Pipeline Company
Exxon Valdez
Eyck, Hubert *or* Huybrecht van
Eyck, Jan van
Eyes on the Prize
Eyes on the Prize II
Eyre Peninsula
Eytinge, Rose
Ezekiel
Ezekiel, Moses Jacob
Ezra

F

Fabares, Shelley
Fabens
Faber, John Eberhard
Faber, Red
Fabergé, Carl Gustavovich
Fabergé egg
Fabian
Fabian, Saint
Fabianism
Fabianist
Fabian Society
Fabius Maximus
Fabray, Nanette
Fabre, Jean Henri
Fabriano, Gentile da
Fabri-Centers of America, Inc.
Fabricius, Johan Christian
Fabricius, Johan Wigmore
Fabritius, Carel
Fabry, Charles
Fabry-Perot interferometer
Face the Nation
F.A.C.-P.A.C., Inc.
Facts of Life, The
Facts on File™

Fadeyev, Aleksander
Fadiman, Clifton
F/A-18 Hornet
Faerie Queene, The
Faerie Tale Theater
Faeroe *occas.* Faröe Islands
Faeroese, *n.*, *pl.* Faeroese
Faggi, Alfeo
Fahey, John
Fahlstrom, Oyvind
Fahnestock clip
Fahrenheit, Gabriel Daniel
Fahrenheit 451
Fahrenheit scale
Fahrenheit temperature scale
Fain, Sammy
Fair, A. A.
Fairbanks
Fairbanks, Douglas, Jr.
Fairbanks, Douglas, Sr.
Fairbanks International Airport
Fairborn

Fairbury
Fairchild, Morgan
Fairchild Air Force Base
Fairchild Corporation, The
Fairchild Space and Defense Corporation
Fairchild Space Company
Fairchild Syndication
Fair Deal
Fair Employment Practices Commission
Fairfax
Fairfax, Thomas
Fairfield
Fairfield University
Fairfield University Stags
Fairhaven [* MA]
Fair Haven [* NJ]
Fairhope
Fair Isle
Fair Isle knitwear
Fair Labor Standards Act
Fair Lawn

219

Fairleigh Dickinson University

Fairleigh Dickinson University Knights

Fairleigh Dickinson University Press

Fairmont [* MN; NC; WV; *see also* Fairmount]

Fairmont at Illinois Center

Fairmont City

Fairmont Hotel, The

Fairmont State College

Fairmount [* IN]

Fair Oaks

Fair Plain

Fairport

Fairview

Fairview Park

Fairway

Fairy Falls

Faisal

Faith, Percy

Faith Baptist Bible College and Seminary

Faith for Today

Faithfull, Marianne

Falana, Lola

Falange

Falangist

Falasha, *n.*, *pl.* Falasha *or* Falashas

Falcon Crest

Falcon Heights

Falcon Jet Corporation

Faldo, Nick

Falernian

Falfurrias

Falk, Peter

Falkenburg, Jinx

Falkirk

Falkland Islands

Falkland Islands Dependencies

Falklands War

Fall, The [novel]

Falla, Manuel de

Fallbrook

Fallen Timbers

Falletta, JoAnn

Fall Guy, The

Fall of Man, The

Fall of the House of Usher, The

Fallon

Fallon Naval Air Station

fallopian *occas.* Fallopian tube

Fallopio, Gabriello

Fall Pippin

Fall River

Fall River Legend

Falls Church

Falls City

Falls of Gersoppa

Falmouth

False Decretals

Falstaff

Falstaff, Sir John

Falstaffian

Falster

Faludi, Susan

Falwell, Jerry

Famagusta

Famagusta Bay

Fame

Fameuse

Family, The

Family Affair

Family and Court of Ludovico Gonzaga II

family Bible

Family Channel, The

Family Circle

Family Circle Great Ideas

Family Circus

Family Compact

Family Dollar Stores, Inc.

Family Feud, The

Family Guide Network

Family Handyman, The

Family Inns of America

Family Life Insurance Company

Family Matters

Family Motor Coach Association

Familynet

Family of Charles IV

Family Service Association of America

Family Stations Inc.

Family Ties

Famous Adventures of Mr. Magoo, The

Famous Music Publishing

fancy Dan

Fancy Free

Faneuil, Peter

Faneuil Hall

Fanfare for the Common Man

Fangio, Juan Manuel

Fanning Island

Fanny

Fanny and Alexander

Fanny Hill, or the Memoirs of a Woman of Pleasure

Fan Si Pan

Fantasia

Fantasia on Greensleeves

Fantasticks, The

Fantasy Island

Fantasy Island Theme Park

Fanti

Fantin-Latour, Henri

F. A. O. Schwarz

Farabundo Marti National Liberation Front

Faraday, Michael

Faraday dark space

Faraday effect

Faraday's law

Farah Inc.

Farallon Islands

Farberman, Howard

Fard, Wallace D.

Far East

Far Eastern

Farentino, James

Farey sequence

Far from the Madding Crowd

Fargo

Fargo, Donna

Fargo, William G.

Faribault

Farina, Dennis

Farjeon, Eleanor

Farley, James

Farley Industries Inc.

Farm Aid

Farm Aid concert

Farm and Home Savings Association

Farm Credit Administration

Farm Credit System

Farmer, Art

Farmer, Fannie

Farmer, Frances

Farmer, James

Farmer, Richard T.

farmer John

Farmer-Labor Party

Farmer's Almanac, The

Farmers Branch

Farmers' Educational and Co-Operative Union of America

Farmers Group, Inc.

Farmers Home Administration

Farmer's reducer

Farmersville [* CA; TX]

Farmerville [* LA]

Farm Family America

Farm Futures

FarmHouse

Farmingdale

Farmington

Farmington Hills

Farm Journal

Farmstead

Farmville

Farnborough

Farnborough air show

Farnese, Alessandro

Farnese Bull

Farnese Palace

Farnsworth, Philo T.

Farnum, Dustin

Farnum, William

Faröe *var. of* Faeroe Islands

Farquhar, George

Farr, Jamie

Farragut, David G.

Farrakhan, Abdul Haleem

Farrar, Geraldine

Farrar, Straus & Giroux, Inc.

Farrell

Farrell, Charles

Farrell, Eileen

Farrell, Glenda

Farrell, James T.

Farrell, J. G.

Farrell, Mike

Farrow, Mia

Farsi

Far Side, The

Far West

Far Western

FarWest Savings and Loan Association

Fasching

Fascist, *n., pl.* Fascists [member of a Fascist party]

Fascista, *n., pl.* Fascisti [member of

a former Italian political party]

Fashion Institute of Design and Merchandising

Fashion Institute of Technology

Fashion 'n Figure

Fashoda Incident

Fassbänder, Brigitte

Fassbinder, Rainer Werner

Fast, Howard

Fastnet Rock

Fast of Esther

Fast of Gedaliah

Fatah, Al

Fatal Attraction

Fata Morgana

Fates

Father Brown stories

Father Christmas

Father Divine

Father Dowling Mysteries

Father Flanagan's Home for Boys

Fatherhood

Father Hugo's rose

Father's Day

Fathers of the Church

Father Time

Fátima

Fatimah occas. Fatima

Faubus, Orval

Faulkner, William

Faulkner University

Fauré, Gabriel

Faust

Faust, Johann

Faustian

Faustino, David

Faust Overture

Faust Symphony

Faustus

Faustus, Saint

Fauve

Fauvism

Fauvist

Faversham, William

Fawcett, Farrah

Fawcett, George

Fawcett™ Books

Fawkes, Guy

Fawlty Towers

Fay, Frank

Fay, W. G.

Faye, Alice

Fayette

Fayetteville

Fayetteville North

Fayetteville State University

Fayetteville Technical Community College

Fazenda, Louise

F.B.I., The [television series]

FBI Law Enforcement Bulletin

FB-111

F clef

F distribution

Fearless Fosdick

Feast of Booths

Feast of Consecration

Feast of Corpus Christi

Feast of Dedication

Feast of Fools

Feast of Lanterns

Feast of Lights

Feast of Lots

Feast of Orthodoxy

Feast of Saint Nicholas

Feast of Saint Peter's Chains

Feast of the Maccabees

Feast of the Sacred Heart of Jesus

Feast of the Tabernacles

Feast of Weeks

Feather River

Feather River Community College

Feature Enterprises

Feature News Service

February, n., pl. Februaries

February Revolution

Fechner, Gustav Theodor

Fechner's law

Fedders Corporation

Federal, adj. [of or pertaining to United States in the Civil War]

federal or Federal, adj. [of or pertaining to the United States' system of government]

Federal Aviation Administration

Federal Bar Association

Federal Bureau of Investigation

Federal Communications Commission

Federal Constitutional Convention

Federal Crop Insurance Corporation

Federal Deposit Insurance Corporation

Federal District

Federal Election Commission

Federal Emergency Management Agency

Federal Employees Veterans Association

Federal Energy Regulatory Commission

Federal Express™

Federal Express Corporation

Federal Farm Credit Board

Federal Hall

Federal Hall National Memorial

Federal Highway Administration

Federal Home Loan Bank Board

Federal Home Loan Mortgage Corporation

Federal Housing Administration

Federal Housing Finance Board

Federal Insurance Contributions Act

Federalist, The

Federalist Party

Federal Labor Relations Authority

Federal Land Bank

Federal Maritime Commission

Federal Mediation and Conciliation Service

Federal Mine Safety and Health Review Commission

Federal-Mogul Corporation

Federal-Mogul Corporation Charitable Trust Fund

Federal National Mortgage Association

Federal Open Market Committee

Federal Paper Board Company, Inc.

Federal Parliament

Federal Party

Federal Power Commission

Federal Register

Federal Reserve Act

Federal Reserve Bank

Federal Reserve Board

Federal Reserve district

Federal Reserve note

Federal Reserve System

Federal Retirement Thrift Investment Board

Federal Signal Corporation

Federal Theatre Project

Federal Trade Commission

Federated Department Stores, Inc.

Federated States of Micronesia

Federation for American Immigration Reform

Fédération Internationale de l'Automobile

Fédération Internationale de Natation Amateur

Fédération Internationale de Ski

Federation of American Scientists

Federation of Egalitarian Communities

Federation of Fly Fishers

Federation of Tax Administrators

Federation of the Handicapped

FedEx™

Fedin, Konstantin

Fenney, Charles F.

Fehling, Hermann

Fehling's solution

Feiffer, Jules

F-8 Crusader

F-18 Hornet

F-84 Thunderstreak

F-89 Scorpion

F-80 Shooting Star

F-86 Sabre
Feininger, Andreas
Feininger, Lyonel
Feinstein, Alan
Feinstein, Dianne
Feinstein, Michael
Feke, Robert
Fekkai, Frédéric
Feld, Fritz
Feld Ballet
Feldman, Corey
Feldman, Marty
Feldman, Morton
Feldon, Barbara
Feldshuh, Tovah
Felicia
Felician College
Feliciano, Jose
Felipe, León
Felix
Felix I, Saint
Felix IV, Saint
Felix the Cat
Felix III, Saint
Fell, Norman
Feller, Bob
Fellini, Federico
Fellini-Satyricon
Fellowship of
  Christian Athletes
Fellowship of Grace
  Brethren
Fellowship of Grace
  Brethren Church
Fellowship of
  Reconciliation
Fellowship of the
  Inner Light
Feltsman, Vladimir

Feminist Alliance
  Against Rape
Feminist Majority
  Foundation
Feminist Press, The
Feminists for Life of
  America
Fences
Fender, Freddy
Fenech Adami, Eddie
Fénelon, François
Fenian
Fenian cycle
Fenianism
Fenian movement
Fenneman, George
Fens, the
Fenton
Fenway Park
Fenwick, Millicent
Feodor
Ferber, Edna
Ferber, Herbert
Ferdinand
Ferdinand the Bull
Ferdinand the Catholic
Ferdinand the Great
Fergus Falls
Fergus Falls
  Community College
Ferguson
Ferguson, Elsie
Ferguson, Maynard
Ferguson, Sarah
Ferlinghetti, Lawrence
Fermat, Pierre de
Fermat's last theorem
Fermat's principle
Fermat's theorem

Fermi, Enrico
Fermi Award
Fermi-Dirac statistics
Fermi National
  Accelerator
  Laboratory
Fermi prize
Fermi surface
Fernandel
Fernandez, Gigi
Fernandez, Juan
Fernandez, Mary Joe
Fernández de Lizardi,
  José
Fernandina Beach
Fernando de Noronha
Fernando Po
Ferndale
Ferrante, Arthur
Ferrante and Teicher
Ferrari
Ferrari, Enzo
Ferrari, Gaudenzio
Ferraris, Galileo
Ferraro, Geraldine
Ferré, Gianfranco
Ferrell, Conchata
Ferrell, Rick
Ferrell, William
Ferrell's law
Ferrer, José
Ferrer, Mel
Ferrero, Guglielmo
Ferri, Alessandra
Ferriday
Ferrigno, Lou
Ferris, George
Ferris State University
Ferris wheel

Ferro Corporation

Ferrum College

Fertile Crescent

Fescinnine verses

Fessenden, Reginald Aubrey

Fessenden, Thomas G.

Fessenden, William Pitt

Festa, Costanzo

Festival of Fools

Festival of Lights

Festival of Two Worlds

Festival Singers of Canada

Festus

Fete at Rambouillet

Fetterman, William Judd

Fetterman Massacre

Fetti *or* Feti, Domenico

Feuchtwanger, Lion

Feuerbach, Anselm

Feuerbach, Ludwig A.

Feulgen, Robert

Feulgen reaction

Février, Henri

Feydeau, Georges

Feynman, Richard Phillips

Fez

FFA [*form.* Future Farmers of America]

F-15 Eagle

F-5 Freedom Fighter

F-5 Tiger

F-4 Phantom II

F-14 Tomcat

Fhimah, Lamen Khalifa

Fianna Fáil

Fibber McGee and Molly

Fiberglas™

Fibonacci, Leonardo

Fibonacci number

Fibonacci sequence

Fibranne™

Fichte, Johann G.

Fichtean

Fichteanism

Fickett, Mary

Fiddler on the Roof

Fidelio

Fidelism

Fidelist

Fidelista

Fidelity and Guaranty Life Insurance Company

Fidelity Bank

Fidelity Bankers Life Insurance Company

Fidelity Brokerage Services, Inc.

Fidelity Distributors Corporation

Fidelity Federal Bank

Fidelity Investments

Fiedler, Arthur

Fiedler, John

Fiedler, Leslie

Field, Betty

Field, Cyrus West

Field, Erastus Salisbury

Field, Eugene

Field, Frederick W.

Field, Marshall

Field, Rachel

Field, Sally

Field & Stream

Fieldcrest Cannon, Inc.

Field Foundation, Inc.

Fielding, Henry

Fielding Institute

Field Museum of Natural History [*form.* Chicago Natural History Museum]

Field of the Cloth of Gold

Field Poll

Fields, Dorothy

Fields, Gracie

Fields, Herbert

Fields, Joseph

Fields, Kim

Fields, Lew

Fields, Totie

Fields, W. C.

Fields of Mourning

Fierstein, Harvey

Fiesta Bowl

Fifteenth *occas.* 15th Amendment [to the Constitution]

Fifth *occas.* 5th Amendment [to the Constitution]

Fifth Avenue

Fifth Dimension

Fifth Lateran Council

Fifth Monarchy Men

Fifth Republic

Fifth Third Bancorp

Fifty-four forty or fight *or* Fifty-four Forty or Fight

$50,000 Pyramid, The

52 Association for the Handicapped

Figaro

Fight Back! With David Horowitz

Fight for Sight Research Division

Fighting French

Fighting Temeraire, The

Fig Newtons™

Figueres, José

Fiji

Fijian

Fiji Islands

Filipina, *fem., n., pl.* Filipina

Filipino, *masc., n., pl.* Filipinos [*see also* Pilipino]

Fillmore, Abigail Powers

Fillmore, Caroline

Fillmore, Millard

Fina, Inc.

Final Days, The

Financial Advisory Services

Financial Analysts Federation

Financial Analysts Journal

Financial Executives Institute

Financial Marketing Association

Financial Times

Financial Women International

Financial World

Finch, Peter

Findlay

Fine, Larry

Fine Arts Quartet

Fine Champagne

Fine Gael

Fine Kaye, Sylvia

Fine Young Cannibals

Fingal's Cave

Finger, Charles

Fingerhut Companies, Inc.

Finger Lakes

Finger Lakes Racetrack

Fingers, Rollie

Finian's Rainbow

Finistère

Fink, Mike

Fink truss

Finland

Finlander

Finlandia

Finlay, Carlos Juan

Finletter, Thomas

Finley, Charles

Finn

Finn, Huckleberry

Finnair

Finnegans Wake

Finney, Albert

Finnic

Finnish

Finnish language

Finnish literature

Finnish-Russian War

Finnish spitz

Finnissy, Michael

Finno-Russic War

Finno-Ugrian

Finno-Ugric

Finsteraarhorn

Fiorello!

Fiorito, Ted

Firdausi

Firebird, The

Firehouse

Fire Island

Fire Island Beach

Fire Island National Seashore

Fireman, Paul

Fireman's Fund Foundation

Fireman's Fund Insurance Company

Fire Marshals Association of North America

Firestone, Harvey S.

Firestone Tire and Rubber Company

Firestone Tournament of Champions

Firestone Trust Fund

Firing Line

Firkušny, Rudolf

First Alabama Bank

First *occas.* 1st Amendment [to the Constitution]

First American National Bank

Firstar Corporation

First Balkan War

First Bank

First Bank System Foundation

First Bank System, Inc.

First Bank Tower

First Boston Foundation Trust

First Boston Inc.

First Brands Corporation

First Capital Life Insurance Company

First Chicago Corporation

I or 1 Chronicles

First Church of Christ, Scientist

First City Bankcorporation of Texas, Inc.

First Colony Life Insurance Company

I or 1 Corinthians

First Council of Lyons

First Council of Nicaea

First Day occas. first day

First Empire

First Executive Corporation

First Family often first family

First Federal of Michigan

First Federal Savings and Loan Association

First Federal Savings Bank

First Fidelity Bancorporation

First Fidelity Bank

First Financial Bank

First Financial Management Corporation

First Florida Bank

First for Women

First Gibraltar Bank

First Hawaiian Bank

First International

First Interstate Bancorp

First Interstate Bank of Arizona

First Interstate Bank of Arizona Charitable Foundation

First Interstate Bank of California

First Interstate Bank of California Foundation

First Interstate Bank of Denver

First Interstate Bank of Denver Foundation

First Interstate Bank of Oregon

First Interstate Bank of Texas

First Interstate World Center

I or 1 John

First Kentucky National Charitable Foundation

First Kentucky National Corporation

I or 1 Kings

first lady often First Lady

First Lateran Council

First Lord

First Mississippi Corporation

First National Bank of Chicago

First National Bank of Chicago Foundation

First National Bank of Maryland

First National City Bank [now Citibank]

First Nationwide Bank

First Nationwide Financial Corporation

First Noel, The

First of America Bank Corporation

I or 1 Peter

First Punic War

First Reader

First Reich

First Republic

First RepublicBank Corporation

I or 1 Samuel

First Sunday of the Passion

First Tennessee Bank

I or 1 Thessalonians

First Time Ever I Saw Your Face, The

I or 1 Timothy

First Triumvirate

First Union Corporation

First Union Foundation

First Union 400

First Union National Bank

First Union National Bank of Florida

First Vatican Council

First Virginia Banks, Inc.

First Wachovia Corporation [*now* Wachovia Corporation]

First Wisconsin Corporation

First Wisconsin Foundation

First World War

First Zen Institute of America

Firth, Peter

Firth of Clyde

Firth of Forth

Firth of Tay

Fischer, Bobby

Fischer, Edwin

Fischer, Emil

Fischer, Hans

Fischer-Dieskau, Dietrich

Fischer-Tropsch process

Fischer von Erlach, Johann

Fish, Hamilton

Fish, Nicholas

Fishbein, Morris

Fishburne, Larry

Fisher, Amy

Fisher, Avery

Fisher, Bud

Fisher, Carrie

Fisher, Donald George

Fisher, Doris F.

Fisher, Dorothy Canfield

Fisher, Eddie

Fisher, Fred

Fisher, Ham

Fisher, Irving

Fisher, John J.

Fisher, Lawrence

Fisher, Max Martin

Fisher, M. F. K.

Fisher, Robert J.

Fisher, Vardis

Fisher, William F.

Fisher, Zachary

Fisher College

Fisher King [of Arthurian legend]

Fisher King, The [book]

Fisher-Price, Inc.

Fishers Hill

Fishlake National Forest

Fisk, Carlton

Fisk, James

Fiske, John

Fiske, Minnie Maddern

Fisk University

Fitch, Clyde

Fitch, John

Fitchburg

Fitchburg State College

Fittipaldi, Emerson

Fitzgerald, Barry

Fitzgerald, Edmund

FitzGerald, Edward

Fitzgerald, Ella

Fitzgerald, F. Scott

FitzGerald, George F.

Fitzgerald, Geraldine

Fitzgerald, J. F.

Fitzgerald, Zelda

FitzGerald contraction

FitzGerald-Lorentz contraction

Fitzsimmons, Bob

Fitzsimmons, Thomas

Fitzsimmons Army Medical Center

Fitzwater, Marlin

Fitzwilliam Museum

Fitzwilliam Virginal Book

Five Civilized Nations

Five Civilized Tribes

Five Dynasties

Five Dynasties and Ten Kingdoms

Five Elements School

Five Forks

Five Nations

Five Pennies, The

Five-Power Treaty

Five Satins, The

Five Towns College

Five-Year Plan

Fixx, Jim

Flack, Roberta

Flag Day

Flagello, Ezio

Flagg, Ernest

Flagg, Fannie

Flagg, James Montgomery

Flagler, Henry M.

Flagler Career Institute

Flagler College

Flagler Dog Track

Flag Research Center, The

Flagstad, Kirsten

Flagstaff

Flaherty, Robert

Flaming Gorge Dam

Flaming Gorge Reservoir

Flaming Rainbow University

Flaminian Way

Flamininus, Titus

Flaminius, Gaius

Flammarion, Camille

Flamsteed, John

Flanagan, Father

Flanagan, Fionnula

Flanders

Flanders, Ed

Flanders Field

Flanders poppies

Flandrin, Hippolyte Jean

Flannagan, John Bernard

Flanner, Janet

Flannery, Susan

Flash Gordon

Flat Earth Research Society International

Flatford Mill

Flathead

Flathead [Indian], n., pl. Flathead or Flatheads

Flathead Lake

Flathead National Forest

Flathead Valley Community College

Flatley, Thomas John

Flatliners

Flat River

Flat Rock

Flatt, Lester

Flatt and Scruggs

Flatwoods

Flaubert, Gustave

Flavian

Flavian, Saint

Flavian Amphitheater

Flavian of Antioch

Flavin, Dan

Flaxman, John

F layer

Fleck, Bela

Fleet Charitable Trust

Fleet National Bank

Fleet/Norstar Financial Group, Inc.

Fleet Post Office

Fleet Prison

Fleet Reserve Association

Fleet Street

Fleetwood, Mick

Fleetwood Enterprises, Inc.

Fleetwood Mac

Fleischer, Max

Fleischman, Sidney

Fleisher, Leon

Fleming, Sir Alexander

Fleming, Art

Fleming, Ian

Fleming, Sir John Ambrose

Fleming, Peggy

Fleming, Rhonda

Fleming, Walter Lynwood

Fleming Companies, Inc.

Flemish

Flemish architecture

Flemish art

Flemish bond

Flemish coil

Flemish fake

Flemish giant

Flemish horse

Flemish knot

Flemish language

Flemish school

Flemish scroll

Fletcher, Horace

Fletcher, John

Fletcher, John Gould

Fletcher, Louise

Fletcher Challenge Ltd.

Fletcherism

Fletcherize, v. Fletcherized, Fletcherizing

Flettner, Anton

Flettner control

Fleury, André Hercule de

Fleury, Claude

Flexible Flyer™

Flexner, Abraham

Flexner, Simon

Flexner, Stuart Berg

Flexography™

Flick, Elmer

Flight into Egypt, The

Flight of the Bumble Bee, The

Flight Safety Foundation

Flight Safety International, Inc.

Flinders, Matthew

Flinders bar

Flinders Island

Flinders Range

Flint

Flint, Austin

Flint, Timothy

Flint River

Flintshire

Flintstone, Fred

Flintstone, Wilma

Flintstone Kids, The

Flintstones, The

Flippen, Jay C.

Flipper, Henry O.

Flip Wilson Show, The

Flodden Field

Flora

Floral Park

Floréal

Floren, Myron

Florence

[Florence] Academy Gallery

Florence-Darlington Technical College

Florence fennel

Florence flask

Florentine

Flores

Flores Sea

Florey, Sir Howard Walter

Florham Park

Florida

Florida Agricultural and Mechanical University

Florida Agricultural and Mechanical University Ramblers

Florida Agrinet

Florida Atlantic University

Florida Baptist Theological College

Florida Bay

Florida Bible College

Florida cat's claw

Florida Christian College

Florida City

Florida College

Florida Community College at Jacksonville

Florida Current

Florida Cypress Gardens

Florida East Coast Industries, Inc.

Florida Federal Savings Bank

Florida Institute of Technology

Florida International University

Florida International University Golden Panthers

Florida Island

Florida Keys

Florida Keys Community College

Florida Marlins

Florida Memorial College

Florida moss

Floridan var. of Floridian

Florida National Jazz Festival

Florida panhandle

Florida Power and Light Company

Florida Progress Corporation

Florida Radio Network Inc.

Florida Southern College

Florida Spaceport Authority

Florida's Sunken Gardens

Florida State University

Florida State University Seminoles

Florida Strait

Florida Suncoast Dome

Florida Times-Union, The

Florida Tobacco and Candy Association

Florida velvet bean

Floridian or Floridan

Florio, James J.

Florio, John

Florissant

Florissant Fossil Beds National Monument

Florists' Transworld
Delivery
Association

Flossenburg death
camp

Flossmoor

Flotow, Friedrich von

Flower Drum Song

Flower Hill

Flower People

Flowers, Gennifer

Flowers Industries,
Inc.

Floyd, Carlisle

Floyd, Ray

Floydada

Floyd College

Fluor Corporation

Fluor Foundation

Flushing

Flushing Meadow

Flushing Meadow
Park

Flying

Flying Doctor Service

Flying Dutchman
[legendary mariner;
legendary ship]

Flying Dutchman, The
[opera]

Flying Safety

Flying Tigers

Flying Wallendas, The

Flynn, Errol

Flynn, Joe

Fly River

Fly without Fear

FMC Corporation

FMC Foundation

FMC Gold Company

Foch, Ferdinand

Foch, Nina

Fodor, Eugene

Fodor's travel guides

Fodor's Travel
Publications, Inc.

Fogarty, Anne

Fogelberg, Dan

Fogerty, John C.

Fogg Art Museum

Foggy Bottom

Foggy Mountain Boys

Foggy River Boys

Fogo Island

Fokine, Michel

Fokker, Anthony

Fokker Aircraft
U.S.A. Inc.

Folcroft

Foley, Red

Foley, Thomas S.

Foley's department
store

Folger, Emily Jordan

Folger, Henry Clay

Folger Shakespeare
Memorial Library

Folies-Bergère

Folio

Folk Medicine

Folksbiene

Folkwang Museum

Follett, Ken

Follies [Sondheim
musical]

Follies, The [London,
England, series of
shows]

Follies of 1907
[American revue]

Folsom

Folsom culture

Folsom man

Folsom point

Folsom Prison

Fomalhaut

Fonda, Bridget

Fonda, Henry

Fonda, Jane

Fonda, Peter

Fond du Lac

F-111

F, layer

F-105 Thunderchief

F-104 Starfighter

F-101 Voodoo

F-106 Delta Dart

F-102 Delta Dagger

F-117 stealth fighter

Fong, Benson

Fong, Hiram

Fonseca Bay

Fontaine, Frank

Fontaine, Joan

Fontainebleau

Fontainebleau château

Fontainebleau School

Fontana

Fontana Dam

Fontane, Theodor

Fontanne, Lynn

Fontbonne College

Fonteyn, Dame
Margot

Fonzarelli, Arthur

Foochow [now
Fuzhou]

Food and Agriculture
Organization

Food & Beverage
  Marketing
Food and Drug
  Administration
Food & Wine
Food, Drug and
  Cosmetic Act
Food for the Hungry,
  Inc.
Food Giant Inc.
Food Lion, Inc.
Food Pyramid
Food Stamp Program
Football Digest
Football News
Foote, Andrew
Foote, Arthur
Foote, Horton
Foote, Shelby
Foote, Cone and
  Belding
  Communications,
  Inc.
Foot Guards
Foothill College
Foppa, Vincenzo
Forain, Jean Louis
Forbes
Forbes, Esther
Forbes, Malcolm S.
Forbes, Malcolm S.,
  Jr.
Forbes Air Force Base
Forbes-Robertson, Sir
  Johnston
For Better or for
  Worse
Forbidden City
Ford, Betty
Ford, Edsel
Ford, Faith

Ford, Ford Madox
Ford, Frankie
Ford, Gerald R.
Ford, Glenn
Ford, Guy Stanton
Ford, Harrison
Ford, Henry
Ford, John
Ford, Josephine Clay
Ford, Lita
Ford, Mary
Ford, Paul
Ford, Tennessee Ernie
Ford, Wallace
Ford, Whitey
Ford, William Clay
Ford, Worthington
Ford City
Ford Foundation, The
Fordham University
Fordham University
  Press
Fordham University
  Rams
Ford Model A
Ford Model T
Ford Motor Company
Ford Motor Company
  Fund
Ford Motor Company
  Lincoln-Mercury
  Division
Ford Motor Company
  of Canada Ltd.
Ford Motor Credit
  Company
Ford's Theatre
Ford's Theatre
  National Historic
  Site
Ford Times

Ford Tri-motor
Fordyce
Forefathers' Day
Foreign Affairs
Foreign Agricultural
  Service
Foreign Claims
  Settlement
  Commission
Foreigner
Foreign Legion
Foreign Policy
  Association
Foreman, George
Forest Acres
Forest City [* IA; NC;
  PA; see also Forrest
  City]
Forester, Christie
Forester, C. S.
Forester, June
Forester, Kathy
Forester, Kim
Forester Sisters, The
Forest Grove
Forest Heights
Forest Hill [* TX]
Forest Hills [* NY;
  PA]
Forest History Society
Forest Industries
  Council
Forest Institute of
  Professional
  Psychology
Forest Laboratories,
  Inc.
Forest Lawn
  Memorial Park
Forest Lawn
  Memorial Park—
  Hollywood Hills

Forest Negro

Forest of Arden

Forest of Ardennes

Forest of Dean

Forest Park

Forest Products Research Society

For He's a Jolly Good Fellow

Forillon National Park

Formalin™

Forman, Michael Robert

Forman, Milos

Formica™

Formosa

Formosa Bay

Formosan

Formosa Plastics Group

Formosa Strait

Formosus

Formula One *or* 1 car

Formula One *or* 1 racing

Formula Three *or* 3 car

Formula Three *or* 3 racing

Formula Two *or* 2 car

Formula Two *or* 2 racing

Fornax

Forrest, Edwin

Forrest, Helen

Forrest, Nathan Bedford

Forrest, Steve

Forrestal, James V.

Forrest City [* AR; *see also* Forest City]

Forster, E. M.

Forstner bit

Forsyte Saga, The

Forsyth

Forsyth, Bruce

Forsythe, Henderson

Forsythe, John

Forsyth Technical Community College

Fort Abercrombie

Fort Albany

Fort Ancient

Fort Anne National Historic Park

Fort A. P. Hill

Fortas, Abe

Fort Atkinson

Fort Baker

Fort Banks

Fort Belknap College

Fort Belvoir

Fort Benjamin Harrison

Fort Benning

Fort Benton

Fort Berry

Fort Bethold Community College

Fort Bliss

Fort Boise

Fort Bowie National Historic Site

Fort Bragg

Fort Branch

Fort Bridger

Fort Bridger State Park

Fort Campbell

Fort Caroline

Fort Caroline National Memorial

Fort Carson

Fort Casper

Fort Chaffee

Fort Clatsop National Memorial

Fort Clayton

Fort Collins

Fort Cronkhite

Fort Custer

Fort-Dauphin

Fort Davis

Fort Davis National Historic Site

Fort Dearborn

Fort de Chartres

Fort-de-France

Fort Deposit

Fort DeRussy

Fort Des Moines

Fort Detrick

Fort Devens

Fort Dix

Fort Dodge

Fort Donelson

Fort Donelson National Battlefield

Fort Douglas

Fort Drum

Fort Duquesne

Forte, Chet

Fort Edward

Fortensky, Larry

Fort Erie

Fort Ethan Allen

Fort Eustis

Fort Fairfield

Fort Fisher

Fort Francis E. Warren

Fort Frederica
  National Monument

Fort Funston

Fort Gaines

Fort George C. Meade

Fort Gillem

Fort Gordon

Fort Greely

Fort Hall

Fort Hamilton

Fort Hancock

Fort Hays State
  University

Fort Henry

Fort Hood

Fort Howard
  Corporation

Fort Howard Paper
  Foundation

Fort Huachuca

Fort Hunter Liggett

Fortin, Jean Nicolas

Fortin's barometer

Fort Irwin

Fort Jackson

Fort Jay

Fort Jefferson

Fort Jefferson
  National Monument

Fort Kearney

Fort Kent

Fort Knox

Fort-Lamy [now
  N'Djamena]

Fort Laramie

Fort Laramie National
  Historic Site

Fort Larned National
  Historic Site

Fort Lauderdale

Fort Lauderdale
  College

Fort Lauderdale-
  Hollywood
  International
  Airport

[Fort Lauderdale]
  Sun-Sentinel

Fort Lawton

Fort Leavenworth

Fort LeBoeuf

Fort Lee

Fort Leonard Wood

Fort Lesley J. McNair

Fort Lewis

Fort Lewis College

Fort Locke

Fort MacArthur

Fort Madison

Fort Mason

Fort Massachusetts

Fort Matanzas
  National Monument

Fort McClellan

Fort McCoy

Fort McHenry

Fort McHenry
  National Monument

Fort McPherson

Fort Meade

Fort Meigs

Fort Michilimackinac

Fort Mill

Fort Mims

Fort Mitchell

Fort Monmouth

Fort Monroe

Fort Morgan

Fort Moultrie

Fort Myer [military
  installation]

Fort Myers [city]

Fort Nashborough

Fort Nassau

Fort Necessity

Fort Necessity
  National Battlefield

Fort Nelson

Fort Niagara

Fort Oglethorpe

Fort Omaha

Fort Orange

Fort Ord

Fort Patrick Henry
  Dam

Fort Payne

Fort Peck Community
  College

Fort Peck Dam

Fort Peck Reservoir

Fort Pickens

Fort Pickett

Fort Pierce

Fort Pierre

Fort Pillow

Fort Plain

Fort Point National
  Historic Site

Fort Polk

Fort Pulaski

Fort Pulaski National
  Monument

Fort Raleigh National
  Historic Site

Fort Randall Dam

Fortrel™

Fortress America

Fortress Europe

Fortress Monroe

Fort Riley

Fort Ritchie

Fort Rucker

Fort Sam Houston

Fort Schuyler

Fort Scott

Fort Scott Community College

Fort Scott National Historic Site

Fort Shafter

Fort Sheridan

Fort Sill

Fort Smith

Fort Smith National Historic Site

Fort Snelling

Fort Stanwix

Fort Stanwix National Monument

Fort Stewart

Fort Stockton

Fort Story

Fort Sumter

Fort Sumter National Monument

Fort Supply Dam

Fort Thomas

Fort Ticonderoga

Fort Totten

Fortuna

Fortune

Fortune Bay

Fortune 500

Fortune 1000

Fortune Savings Bank

Fortune Society, Inc.

Fort Union

Fort Union National Monument

Fort Union Trading Post National Historic Site

Fortuny, Mariano

Fort Valley

Fort Valley State College

Fort Vancouver National Historic Site

Fort Wadsworth

Fort Walton Beach

Fort Washington

Fort Wayne

[Fort Wayne] Journal-Gazette, The

Fort William

Fort William Henry

Fort Worth

Fort Worth Star-Telegram

48 Hours

Forty Hours devotion

Forty-Niner *or* 49er [member of San Francisco football team]

forty-niner *occas.* Forty-Niner [participant in California Gold rush]

42nd Parallel, The

42nd Street

Forty-Sixth Street Theater

40 Wall Tower

For Whom the Bell Tolls

Fosbury, Richard

Fosbury flop

Fosdick, Harry Emerson

Foss, Lukas

Foss, Sam

Fosse, Bob

Fossey, Dian

Fossil Butte National Monument

Foster, Hal

Foster, Jodie

Foster, Lawrence

Foster, Meg

Foster, Preston

Foster, Rube

Foster, Stephen

Foster, William Z.

Foster Farms Poultry, Inc.

Foster Grandparents Program

Foster Parents Plan, Inc. (USA)

Foster's Brewing Group Ltd.

Foster Wheeler Corporation

Fostoria

Fotomat™

Foucault, Jean Bernard Léon

Foucault, Michel

Foucault *occas.* Foucault's pendulum

Foujita, Tsugouharu

Foundation for Children with Learning Disabilities

Foundation for Economic Education

Foundation for Independent Higher Education

Foundation Health Corporation

Foundation of the Litton Industries

Foundation of the Wall and Ceiling Industry

Fountain, Pete

Fountain of Youth

Fountains Abbey

Fountains of Rome

Fountain Valley

Fouquet, Jean

Fouquet, Nicholas

Fouquier-Tinville, Antoine

Four Aces, The

Four Corners

4day Tire Store

Fourdrinier, Henry

Fourdrinier, Sealy

Fourdrinier machine

4-F

Four Forest Cantons, the

Four Freedoms

Four Freshmen, The

4-H Club

4-H'er

Four Horsemen of the Apocalypse

Four Horsemen of the Apocalypse, The [novel]

Four Hundred or 400, the

Fourier, Charles

Fourier, Jean Baptiste Joseph

Fourier analysis

Fourierism

Fourierist

Fourierite

Fourier series

Fourier's theorem

Fourier transform

Four Lads, The

Four Lakes

Fournier, Alain

Four Noble Truths

401 (k) plan

Fourposter, The

Four Preps, The

Four Quartets

Four Seasons, The

Four Seasons Hotel—Clift

Four Seasons Hotel—Houston Center

Four Seasons Hotel—Philadelphia

Four Seasons hotels and resorts

Four Seasons Olympic Hotel

Fourteen Points

Fourteenth *occas.* 14th Amendment [to the Constitution]

Four Temperaments, The

Fourth *occas.* 4th Amendment [to the Constitution]

fourth estate *often* Fourth Estate

Fourth International

Fourth Lateran Council

Fourth of July

Fourth Republic

Four Tops, The

4X Network

Fouts, Dan

Fowler, Harlan D.

Fowler, Henry H.

Fowler, H. W.

Fowler flap

Fowler's toad

Fowles, John

Fox, Charles James

Fox, Fontaine

Fox, George

Fox, James

Fox, John William, Jr.

Fox, Margaret

Fox, Michael J.

Fox, Nellie

Fox, Paula

Foxboro Stadium

Foxborough

Fox Broadcasting Company

Foxe, John

Foxe Basin

Fox Inc.

Fox Indian

Fox Islands

Fox Lake

Fox Point

Fox River

Fox Talbot, W. H.

Fox Valley Technical College

Foxworth, Robert

Foxx, Jimmy

Foxx, Redd
Foy, Eddie
Foy, Eddie, Jr.
Foyt, A. J.
FPL Foundation
FPL Group, Inc.
Frackville
Fra Diavolo
Fraggle Rock
fragile X syndrome
Fragonard, Jean
  Honoré
Frakes, Jonathan
Fraktur [German style
  of lettering]
Fraktur or fraktur
  [traditional
  Pennsylvania Dutch
  calligraphy]
Fra Lippo Lippi
Frame, Janet
Framingham
Framingham State
  College
Frampton, Peter
Françaix, Jean
France
France, Anatole
France Ancient
France Modern
Frances
Francesca, Piero della
Francesca da Rimini
Francescatti, Zino
Franceshini,
  Baldassare
Frances Xavier
  Cabrini, Saint
Franchetti, Anne
Franchetti Gallery

Franchi, Sergio
Franchise of
  Americans Needing
  Sports
Francia
Franciosa, Anthony
Francis
Francis, Anne
Francis, Arlene
Francis, Connie
Francis, Dick
Francis, Genie
Francis, Kay
Francis, Marion
Francis Borgia, Saint
Franciscan
Franciscan nightshade
Franciscan School of
  Theology
Franciscan University
  of Steubenville
Franciscan University
  Press
Franciscus, James
Francis E. Warren Air
  Force Base
Francis Ferdinand
Francis Hopp Museum
  of Eastern Asiatic
  Arts
Francis Marion
  College
Francis Marion
  National Forest
Francis of Assisi,
  Saint
Francis of Paoloa,
  Saint
Francis of Sales, Saint
Francistown
Francis Xavier, Saint

Franck, César
Franck, James
Franco, Francisco
Franco-American
Franco-Belgian
  system
Franconia
Franconia Mountains
Franconian
Franconia Notch
Francophile
Francophilia
Francophobe
Francophobia
Francophobic
Franco-Prussian War
Franc Zone, The
Franglais
Frank
Frank, Anne
Frank, Barney
Frank, Bruno
Frank, Leonhard
Frank, Robert
Frank, Waldo
Frank and Ernest
Frankel, Max
Franken, Al
Frankenheimer, John
Frankenstein
Frankenstein, Victor
Frankensteinian
Frankenstein, or the
  Modern Prometheus
Frankenstein's occas.
  Frankenstein
  monster
Frankenthaler, Helen
Frankford Arsenal

Frankfort [* KY; MI; NY]

Frankfurt [* Germany]

Frankfurter, Felix

Frankfurt Group

Frankfurt horizontal

Frankfurt-Main International Airport

Frankfurt Stock Exchange

Frankie and Johnnie

Frankie Goes to Hollywood

Frankie Lyman and the Teenagers

Frankish

Frank J. Selke Trophy

Franklin

Franklin, Aretha

Franklin, Benjamin

Franklin, Bonnie

Franklin, Joe

Franklin, Sir John

Franklin and Eleanor Roosevelt Institute

Franklin and Marshall College

Franklin College

Franklin College of Indiana

Franklin Distributors, Inc.

Franklin D. Roosevelt Lake [*form.* Grand Coulee Reservoir]

Franklin D. Roosevelt Philatelic Society

Franklin Group of Funds

Franklin Institute

Franklin Institute Science Museum and Planetarium

Franklin Lakes

Franklin Life Insurance Company, The

Franklin Mint, The

Franklin Mint Collectors Society

Franklin Mint Museum

Franklin Park

Franklin Pierce College

Franklin Pierce Law Center

Franklin Resources, Inc.

Franklin Savings Association

Franklin's gull

Franklin Square

Franklin stove

Franklin University

Franklin Watts, Inc.

Frank Lloyd Wright School of Architecture

Franko, Ivan

Frank Phillips College

Frank Zappa and the Mothers of Invention

Frann, Mary

Frans Hals Museum

Franz, Dennis

Franz Josef

Franz Josef Land

Franscati

Frasch, Herman

Frasch process

Frasconi, Antonio

Fraser

Fraser, Antonia

Fraser, Douglas

Fraser, James

Fraternal Order of Eagles

Fraternal Order of Police

Fratianne, Linda

Frau, *n.*, *pl.* Frauen, *English* Fraus

Fräulein, *n.*, *pl.* Fräulein, *English* Fräuleins

Fraunces, Samuel

Fraunces Tavern

Fraunhofer, Joseph von

Fraunhofer lines

Frawley, William

Frazer, Sir James

Frazier, Clyde

Frazier, Joe

Frazier, Owsley Brown

Frears, Stephen

Freberg, Stan

Fred Astaire Dance Studios

Freddie Hart and the Heartbeats

Freddie Mac

Frederic, Harold

Frederica

Frederick

Frederick, Pauline

Frederick and Nelson department store

Frederick Barbarossa

Frederick Community College

Frederick Douglass National Historic Site

Frederick Law Olmsted National Historic Site

Fredericksburg

Fredericksburg and Spotsylvania County Battlefields National Military Park

Frederick's of Hollywood, Inc.

Frederick the Fair

Frederick the Great

Frederick the Warlike

Frederick the Winterking

Frederick the Wise

Fredericktown [* MO]

Fredericton [* New Brunswick]

Fred Meyer, Inc.

Fredonia

Fredonian Rebellion

Free and Accepted Masons

Free Church of Scotland

Freed, Alan

Freed-Hardeman College

Freedmen's Bureau

Freedom

Freedom Bowl

Freedom Forum, The

Freedom Forum Media Studies Center [*form.*

Center for Media Studies]

Freedom from Hunger Foundation

Freedom from Religion Foundation

Freedom House, Inc.

Freedom of Information Act

Freedom of Information Center

Freedoms Foundation at Valley Forge

Free French

Freehold

Freeland

Freeman, Al, Jr.

Freeman, Douglas Southall

Freeman, Mansfield

Freeman, Mary E.

Freeman, Morgan

Freeman, Paul

Freeman, Richard

Free Mason

Free Masonry

Free Methodist Church of North America

Freeport

Freeport-McMoRan Copper and Gold Inc.

Freeport-McMoRan Inc.

Freer, Charles Lang

Freer Gallery of Art

Frees, Paul

Free-Soiler

Free-Soil Party

Free-Soil territory

Free State

Free Stater

Free Territory of Trieste

Freetown

Freetown Lungi International Airport

Free Will Baptist

Free Will Baptist Bible College

Free World

Frege, Gottlob

F region

Fréjus Tunnels

Freleng, Friz

Frelinghuysen, Frederick

Fremantle

Fremont

Frémont, Jesse Benton

Frémont, John Charles

Fremont National Forest

French

French, Alice

French, Daniel Chester

French, Marilyn

French Academy

French and Indian War [1 of French and Indian Wars]

French and Indian Wars [4 wars, 1689–1763]

French arch

French architecture

French art

French bean

French bread
French brier
French Broad River
French bulldog
French Canadian
French chalk
French Chef, The
French chop
French Community
French Connection, The
French Connection II
French cuff
french curve
French door
French drain
French dressing
French East India Company
French endive
French Equatorial Africa
French fake
French flat
French foot
French Foreign Legion
French fried potato, n., pl. potatoes
french fry often French fry, n., pl. french fries often French fries
french fry often French fry, v.
French Guiana
French Guianan
French Guianese
French harp
French heel
French honeysuckle

French horn
French ice cream
Frenchify, v. Frenchified, Frenchifying
French Indochina
French Institute
French kid
French kiss, n.
French-kiss, v.
French knot
French language
French leave
French letter
French literature
French lug
Frenchman, n., pl. Frenchmen
French marigold
French Morocco
French mulberry
Frenchness
French nettle
French Open
French overture
French pancake
French pastry
French pitch
French polish, n.
French-polish, v.
French Polynesia [form. French Settlements in Oceania]
French pox
French provincial style
French Quarter
French Revolution

French Revolutionary calendar
French Revolutionary Wars
French Riviera
French roll
French roof
French rose
French seam
French Separatists
French Settlements in Oceania [now French Polynesia]
French Somaliland [now Djibouti]
French Sudan [now Mali]
French system
French tamarisk
French telephone
French toast
French truss
French twist
French Union
Frenchweed
French West Africa
French West Indies
French window
Frenchwoman, n., pl. Frenchwomen
Freneau, Philip
Frenet formula
Freon™
Frescobaldi, Girolami
Fresh Air
Freshman, The
Fresh Prince of Bel Air, The
Fresnel, Augustin Jean
Fresnel lens

Fresnel mirrors
Fresno
Fresno Bee, The
Fresno City College
Fresno Pacific College
Freud, Anna
Freud, Sigmund
Freudian
Freudianism
Freudian slip
Freudian theory
Freund, Jules T.
Freund's adjuvant
Freytag, Gustav
Friar Preacher, *n.*, *pl.*
  Friars Preacher
Friars Club
Friars Minor
Friars Minor Capuchin
Friars Minor
  Coventual
Friar Tuck
Fribourg
Fribourg, Michel
Frick, Ford
Frick, Henry Clay
Frick, Mr.
Frick Collection
Fricke, Janie
Fricker, Brenda
Fricker, Peter Racine
Friday
Friday Night Videos
Friday the 13th
Frideswide, Saint
Fridley
Fried, Alfred
Friedan, Betty
Friedel-Crafts reaction

Fried Green Tomatoes
  [movie]
Fried Green Tomatoes
  at the Whistle Stop
  Cafe [book]
Friedkin, William
Friedlander, Leo
Friedländer's bacillus
Friedländer's
  pneumobacillus
Friedman, Milton
Friedreich, Nikolaus
Friedreich's ataxia
Friedreich's Ataxia
  Group in America
Friedrich, Caspar
  David
Friedrich Krupp
Friendly Islands
Friends General
  Conference
Friendship
Friendship Hill
  National Historic
  Site
Friendship Inn
Friendship 7
Friends Historical
  Association
Friends of Animals,
  Inc.
Friends of SOS
  Children's Villages
Friends of the Earth
Friends of the Earth
  Foundation
Friends United
  Meeting
Friends University
Friends World College
Frietschie, Barbara
Friganza, Trixie

Frigidaire™
Frigid Zone
Frimaire
Friml, Rudolf
Frisbee™
Frisch, Frank
Frisch, Max
Frisco, Joe
Frise, George
Frise aileron
Frisian
Frisian carving
Frisian Islands
Frisian language
Fritz the Cat
Frizzell, David
Frizzell, Lefty
Frizzell, Lou
Frobe, Gert
Frobisher, Sir Martin
Frobisher Bay
Froebe, Gert
Froebel *or* Fröbel,
  Friedrich
Froebel method
Frohman, Charles
Frohman, Daniel
Froissart, Jean
From a Distance
Froman, Jane
Froment, Nicolas
Fromentin, Eugène
From Here to Eternity
Fromm, Erich
Fromme, Lynette
  "Squeaky"
Fromm Music
  Foundation
From the New World

Fronde of the Parlement

Fronde of the Princes

Frondizi, Arturo

Front de Libération du Québec

Frontline

Front Range

Front Range Community College

Front Royal

Frost, David

Frost, Phillip

Frost, Robert

Frost Belt *occas.* Frostbelt

Frostburg

Frostburg State University

Frostproof

Froude, James Anthony

Fructidor

Fruehauf Trailer Corporation

Frugal Gourmet, The

Fruit of the Loom, Inc.

Frumentius, Saint

Fry, Christopher

Fry, Franklin

Frye, David

Frye, Northrop

F-scope

F-16 Fighting Falcon

F-state

FTD™ florist service

F-20 Tigershark

F-22 advanced tactical fighter

F_2 layer

Fuchs, Klaus

Fudd, Elmer

Fudgsicle™

Fuegian

Fuentes, Carlos

Fuertes, Louis

Fugard, Athol

Fugger, Anton

Fugger, Jakob

Fugitive, The

Führer *or* Fuehrer

Fuisz, Robert E.

Fuji

Fujian

Fuji Bank, Ltd.

Fuji Electric Company, Ltd.

Fuji Heavy Industries Ltd.

Fujikawa, Mayumi

Fujimori, Alberto

Fuji Photo Film Company, Ltd.

Fugisan

Fujitsu Ltd.

Fujiyama

Fukien

Fukuoka

Fula *or* Fulah, *n., pl.* Fula *or* Fulas *or* Fulah *or* Fulahs

Fulani, *n., pl.* Fulani *or* Fulanis

Fulbright, James W.

Fulbright Act

Fulbright Scholarship

Fuller, Albert

Fuller, Alfred C.

Fuller, Blind Boy

Fuller, Buckminster

Fuller, Charles

Fuller, George

Fuller, Henry

Fuller, Margaret

Fuller, Melville Weston

Fuller, Penny

Fuller, Robert

Fuller Brush man

Fuller rose beetle

Fuller Theological Seminary

Fullerton

Fullerton College

Full House

Fulton

Fulton, Eileen

Fulton, Robert

Fulton Fish Market

Fulton-Montgomery Community College

Fu Manchu mustache

Funchal

Fundamental Methodist Church

Fundamental Orders

Fund American Companies, Inc., The

Fund for Animals, Inc., The

Fund for an Open Society

Fund for Peace, The

Fund for the Feminist Majority

Fundy National Park

Funicello, Annette

Funk, Isaac K.

Funkadelic

Funk & Wagnalls™

Funky Winkerbean

Funny Face

Funny Girl

Funny Lady

Funny Thing Happened on the Way to the Forum, A

Funston, Frederick

Funt, Allen

Fuquay Springs

Furies

Furman University

Furman University Paladins

Furman v. Georgia

Furnas, J. C.

Furneaux Group

Furness, Betty

Furness, Horace Howard

Furnivall, Frederick James

Furstenberg, Diane von

Furtwängler, Wilhelm

Fury and Hecla Strait

Fusco Brothers

Fuseli, Henry

Futabatei, Shimei

Futrell, Mary Hatwood

Futuna Islands

Future Farmer

Future Farmers of America [now FFA]

Future Farmers of America Foundation, Inc.

Future Homemakers of America

Futures for Children, Inc.

Futurism occas. futurism

Futurist occas. futurist

Futurist, The [magazine]

Fuzhou [form. Foochow]

F. W. Woolworth Company

G

G., Kenny
Gabel, Martin
Gable, Clark
Gabo, Naum
Gabon
Gabonese, *n.*, *pl.*
    Gabonese
Gabor, Dennis
Gabor, Eva
Gabor, Zsa Zsa
Gaboriau, Émile
Gaborone
Gaborone Sir Seretse
    Khama
    International
    Airport
Gabriel
Gabriel, Jacques Ange
Gabriel, John
Gabriel, Peter
Gabriel, Roman
Gabriel, Saint
Gabrieli, Andrea
Gabrielino
Gabrieli Quartet
Gabriella
Gabrielle
Gabrilowitsch, Ossip
Gacy, John Wayne

Gaddi, Agnolo
Gaddi, Taddeo
Gaddis, William
Gadsden
Gadsden, James
Gadsden Purchase
Gadsden State
    Community College
Gadzooks
Gael
Gaelic
Gaelic football
Gaelic literature
Gaffney
Gág, Wanda
Gagarin, Yuri
Gage, Thomas
Gahagan Douglas,
    Helen
Gail
Gail, Max
Gaillard, David Du
    Bose
Gaillard, Slim
Gaillard Cut
Gaines, Ernest J.
Gaines, William
Gainesville
Gainesville College

Gainsborough,
    Thomas
Gaîté Parisienne
Gaithersburg
Gaitskell, Hugh
Gaius [Biblical
    personages; Roman
    jurist]
Gaius *or* Caius, Saint
Gajdusek, D. Carleton
Gala and the Angelus
    of Millet
    Immediately
    Preceding the
    Arrival of the Conic
    Anamorphoses
Galahad, Sir
Galanos, James
Galapagos finches
Galápagos Islands
Galatia
Galatian
Galavision
Galax
Galb, Servius
    Sulpicius
Galbraith, John
    Kenneth
Galbreath, Daniel
    Mauck

244

Galcha, *n.*, *pl.* Galcha or Galchas

Gale

Gale, Zona

Galen

Galena

Galena Park

Galenic pharmacy

Galenism

Galenist

Gale Research Inc.

Galerius, Caius

Galesburg

Gale's compound

Galesi, Francesco

Galibi, *n.*, *pl.* Galibi or Galibis

Galicia

Galician

Galilean, *adj.* [of or pertaining to Galileo]

Galilean, the, *n.* [name for Jesus]

Galilean satellites

Galilean telescope

Galilean transformation

Galilee

Galileo

Galion

Galla, *n.*, *pl.* Galla or Gallas

Gallagher, Helen

Gallagher, Megan

Gallagher and Shean

Gallant, Mavis

Gallatin

Gallatin, Albert

Gallatin National Forest

Gallaudet, Thomas Hopkins

Gallaudet University

Gallaudet University Press

Gallegos, Rómulo

Gallery Magazine

Gallery of Naive Art, The

Gallic

Gallican

Gallicanism

Gallican liberties

Gallican rite

Gallican tradition

Gallicism *occas.* gallicism

Gallico, Paul

Galli-Curci, Amelita

Gallic Wars

Gallienus

Gallipoli

Gallipoli campaign

Gallipoli Peninsula

Gallipolis

Gallo, Ernest

Gallo, Julio

Galloping Gourmet, The

Gallo-Romance

Galloway

Gallup

Gallup, George H.

Gallup Organization Inc.

Gallup poll

Gallup Poll Monthly

Gallus

Galois, Évariste

Galois field

Galois theory

Galsworthy, John

Galt

Galton, Sir Francis

Galtonian

Galuppi, Baldassare

Galvani, Luigi

Galveston

Galveston Bay

Galveston College

Galveston Island

Galveston plan

Galvin, Pud

Galvin, Robert William

Galway

Galway, James

Galway Bay

Gam, Rita

Gama, Vasco da

Gamaliel

Gamay *or* gamay

Gambetta, Léon

Gambia [river]

Gambia, The [nation]

Gambia Islands

Gambino, Carlo

Gambino, Joseph

Gambino, Thomas

Gambino family

Gambler, The

Gamblers Anonymous

Gambler's Book Club

Gambling Times

Gambrinus

Games People Play

Gamma-Liaison Photo Agency

Gamma Phi Beta

Gamma Ray Observatory [*now* Compton Observatory]

Gamma Sigma Sigma

Ganda, *n., pl.* Ganda *or* Gandas

Gander

Gandhi

Gandhi, Indira

Gandhi, Mohandas K.

Gandhi, Rajiv

Gandhian

Gandhi cap

Gandhism

Gandhist

Ganelin Trio

Ganges

Gann, Ernest K.

Gann, Paul

Gannett Company, Inc.

Gannett Foundation

Gannett News Service

Gannett Peak

Gannett Radio

Gannon University

Gansevoort, Peter

Ganymede

Gap, Inc., The

Garagiola, Joe

Garamond *or* Garamont, Claude

Garamycin™

Garand, John C.

Garand rifle

Garbage Magazine

Garbo, Greta

Garcia, Andy

Garcia, Jerry

García Lorca, Federico

García Marquez, Gabriel

Gard

Gardam, Jane

Gardelli, Lamberto

Garden, Mary

Gardena

Garden City

Garden City Community College

Garden Club of America

Gardendale

Garden Grove

Gardenia, Vincent

Garden of Delights

Garden of Earthly Delights, The

Garden of Eden

Garden of Gethsemane

Garden of the Finzi-Continis, The

Garden of the Gods

Gardiner, Reginald

Gardiner, Samuel Rawson

Gardiners Bay

Gardiners Island

Gardner

Gardner, Ava

Gardner, Erle Stanley

Gardner, Herb

Gardner, Isabella Stewart

Gardner, John

Gardner-Webb College

Gareth, Sir

Garfield

Garfield, James A.

Garfield, John

Garfield, Leon

Garfield, Lucretia Rudolph

Garfield Heights

Garfunkel, Art

Gargantua

Gargantua and Pantagruel

gargantuan, *occas.* Gargantuan

Garibaldi, Giuseppe

Garibaldian

Garland

Garland, Beverly

Garland, Hamlin

Garland, Judy

Garland, Red

Garland County Community College

Garlits, Don

Garment Center

Garment District

Garmisch-Partenkirchen

Garn, Jake

Garner, Alan

Garner, Erroll

Garner, James

Garner, John Nance

Garoua *or* Garua

Garoua International Airport

Garr, Teri

Garrett

Garrett, Betty
Garrett, Mike
Garrett, Pat
Garrett Community College
Garrett-Evangelical Theological Seminary
Garrick, David
Garrick Club
Garrick Theatre
Garrison, Jim
Garrison, Snapper
Garrison, William Lloyd
Garrison, Zina
Garrison Dam
Garrison finish
Garroway, Dave
Garson, Greer
Garth Fagan's Bucket Dance Theatre
Garuda Indonesia
Garvey, Marcus
Garvey, Steve
Garwood
Gary
Gary, Elbert H.
Gary Lewis and the Playboys
Gary Puckett and the Union Gap
Gas Appliance Manufacturers Association
Gas City
Gascoigne, George
Gascon
Gascony
Gaskell, Elizabeth
Gasoline Alley

Gasparilla Pirate Invasion
Gaspé Bay
Gaspé Peninsula
Gas Research Institute
Gassendi, Pierre
Gassman, Vittorio
Gaston, Cito
Gaston College
Gastonia
Gate of Poitou
Gates, Bet-a-Million
Gates, Charles Cassins, Jr.
Gates, Daryl F.
Gates, Horatio
Gates, Larry
Gates, Paul Wallace
Gates, Robert
Gates, William
Gates, William Henry, III
Gates of Paradise
Gates of the Arctic National Park
Gates of the Arctic National Preserve
Gatesville
Gateway Arch
Gateway bookstore
Gateway Community College
Gateway Electronics Institute
Gateway National Recreation Area
Gateway Technical College
Gatlin, Larry
Gatlin, Rudy
Gatlin, Steve

Gatlin Brothers Band, The
Gatling, Richard
Gatling gun
Gatorade™
Gatorade Ironman World Championships
Gator Bowl
Gator Bowl Festival
Gator Bowl Stadium
Gatsby, Jay
Gatun
Gatun Lake
GATX Corporation
Gaucher's disease
Gaudeamus igitur
Gaudete Sunday
Gaudí, Antonio
Gauguin, Paul
Gaul
Gauleiter
Gauley
Gauley River National Recreation Area
Gaulish
Gaullism
Gaullist
Gauss, Carl Friedrich
Gaussian
Gaussian curve
Gaussian distribution
Gaussian domain
Gaussian image
Gaussian integer
Gauss occas. Gauss' law
Gauss' lemma
Gauss plane
Gautama, Siddhartha

Gautier, Dick

Gautier, Théophile

Gavarnie

Gavarnie Falls

Gavilan College

Gaviria, Pablo Escobar

Gaviria Trujillo, César

Gawain, Sir

Gay, John

Gay, Noel

Gay Activists' Alliance

Gay Divorce [play]

Gay Divorcée, The [movie]

Gaye, Marvin

Gayle, Crystal

Gay Liberation Front

Gay Liberation Movement

Gaylord, Edward Lewis

Gay-Lussac, Joseph Louis

Gay-Lussac's law

Gay Nineties

Gaynor, Gloria

Gaynor, Janet

Gaynor, Mitzi

Gay Sisters

Gay Veterans Association

Gaza

Gaza Strip

Gazzara, Ben

Gdansk

G. D. Searle and Company

G. D. Searle and Company Charitable Trust

Gear Broadcasting International, Inc.

Geary, Anthony

Gebel-Williams, Gunther

Gedda, Nicolai

Geddes, Sir Patrick

Geer, Will

Geertgen tot Sint Jans

Geffen, David

Gehenna

Gehrig, Lou

Gehringer, Charley

Geiberger, Al

GEICO Corporation

GEICO Philanthropic Foundation

Geiger, Hans

Geiger, Johannes

Geiger counter

Geiger-Müller counter

Geiger-Müller threshold

Geiger-Müller tube

Geiger threshold

Geisel, Theodore

Geissler tube

Gelasius I, Saint

Gelbart, Larry

Geldof, Bob

Geller, Uri

Gellius

Gellman, Murray

Gelsenkirchen

Gemara

Gemini

Geminiani, Francesco

Gemini-Titan

GEM Publishing Group

GenCorp Foundation

GenCorp Inc.

Gene Autry Western Heritage Museum

Genentech, Inc.

General Accounting Office

General Agreement on Tariffs and Trade

General American English

General American Life Insurance Company

General American Speech

General Assembly [of the United Nations]

General Assembly of the Presbyterian Church (U.S.A.)

General Association of General Baptists

General Association of Regular Baptist Churches

General Cinema Corporation

General Conference, Mennonite Church, The

General Conference of Churches of God

General Conference of Mennonite Brethren Churches

General Contractors of America

General Council, Christian Church of North America

General Court

General Dynamics Corporation

Generale Bank

General Electric Capital Corporation

General Electric Company

General Electric Foundation

General Electric Theater

General Federation of Women's Clubs

General Foods Corporation

General Foods Fund

General Grant National Memorial

General Hospital

Generall Historie of Virginia, New England, and the Summer Isles, The

General Mills Foundation

General Mills, Inc.

General Mitchell International Airport

General Motors Acceptance Corporation

General Motors Cancer Research Foundation

General Motors Corporation

General Motors Corporation (Buick Motor Division)

General Motors Corporation (Cadillac Motor Division)

General Motors Corporation (Chevrolet Motor Division)

General Motors Corporation (Oldsmobile Motor Division)

General Motors Corporation (Pontiac Motor Division)

General Motors Foundation

General Public Utilities Corporation

General Re Corporation [no period after Re]

General Rent-A-Car

General Services Administration

General Sherman Tree

General Signal Corporation

General Social Survey

General Society of Colonial Wars

General Society of Mayflower Descendants

General Theological Seminary

General Time Corporation

General Tire Inc.

General Tom Thumb

Generation of '98

Genesco Inc.

Genesee

Genesee Community College

Geneseo

Genesis

Genesse, Bryan

Genêt

Genet, Jean

Genetics Institute

Geneva

Geneva Accords

Geneva Agreements

Geneva Arbitration

Geneva bands

Geneva Bible

Geneva College

Geneva Committee

Geneva Conference

Geneva Convention

Geneva cross

Geneva gown

Geneva International Airport

Genevan

Geneva nomenclature

Geneva Protocol

Genevese, *n., pl.* Genevese

Genevieve

Genevieve, Saint

Genghis Khan

Genie

Gennaro, Peter

Genoa

Genoese, *n., pl.* Genoese

Genovese, Vito

Genovese family

Gentile, Giovanni

Gentileschi, Artemisia

Gentileschi, Orazio

Gentleman's Agreement

Gentleman Usher of the Black Rod

Gentlemen Prefer Blondes

Gentry, Bobbie

Genuine Parts Company

Geoffrey

Geoffrey of Monmouth

Geoffrey Plantagenet

Geological Society of America

Geordie

George

George, David Lloyd

George, Gladys

George, Henry

George, Jean Craighead

George, Lynda Day

George, Phyllis

George, Saint

George, Stefan

George A. Hormel and Company

George Air Force Base

George Corley Wallace State Community College at Dothan

George Corley Wallace State Community College at Selma

George Fox College

George M!

George Mason University

George Mason University Patriots

George of Podebrad

George of Trebizond

George Rogers Clark College

George Rogers Clark National Historical Park

Georges Bank

Georgesman

George Strait Fan Club

Georgetown [* CO; DC; DE; GA; KY; MA; OH; SC; TX; Guyana; Ontario; Prince Edward Island]

George Town [* Australia, Caribbean Indies]

George Town *now usually* Penang [* Malaysia]

Georgetown College

Georgetown Law Journal

Georgetown Timehri International Airport

Georgetown University

Georgetown University Hoyas

Georgetown University Press

Georgette

George Washington Birthplace National Monument

George Washington Bridge

George Washington Carver National Monument

George Washington Memorial Parkway

George Washington National Forest

George Washington University

George Washington University Colonials

George White's Scandals

Georgia [Asian nation; *form.* Georgian Soviet Socialist Republic]

Georgia [state]

Georgia College

Georgia Dome

Georgia Federal Bank

Georgia Gulf Corporation

Georgia Institute of Technology

Georgia Institute of Technology Rambling Wrecks

Georgia Institute of Technology Yellow Jackets

Georgia Living

Georgia Military College

Georgian

Georgian Bay

Georgian Court College

Georgia Network

Georgian literature

Georgian Military Road

Georgian poets

Georgian rite

Georgian Soviet
  Socialist Republic
  [*now* Georgia]

Georgian style

Georgia on My Mind

Georgia-Pacific
  Corporation

Georgia-Pacific
  Foundation

Georgia pine

Georgia Power
  Company

Georgia Power
  Foundation

Georgia Southern
  University

Georgia Southern
  University Eagles

Georgia Southwestern
  College

Georgia Sportsman

Georgia State Museum
  of Science and
  Industry

Georgia State
  University

Georgia State
  University Crimson
  Panthers

Georgia World
  Congress Center

Georgie Porgie

Gephardt, Richard

Geraint, Sir

Geraldo

Gerard, Gil

Gerber Companies
  Foundation

Gerber Products
  Company

Gere, Richard

Géricault, Théodore

Gerlachovka

German

German-American

German architecture

German art

German Baptist
  Brethren

German camomile

German catchfly

German cockroach

German flute

Germanic

Germanic languages

Germanic laws

Germanic religion

Germanicus Caesar

Germanism

Germanist

German ivy

German knot

German language

German lapsis

German literature

German measles

Germanna Community
  College

Germanophile

Germanophobe

Germanophobia

German police dog

German Requiem

German shepherd

German shorthaired
  pointer

German siding

German silver

German sixth

Germantown

Germanus of Auxerre,
  Saint

German wirehaired
  pointer

Germany

Germer, Lester
  Halbert

Germinal

Gernreich, Rudy

Gernsback, Hugo

Gérôme, Jean Léon

Geronimo

Gerry, Elbridge

Gerry and the
  Pacemakers

Gerry Society

Gers

Gershwin, George

Gershwin, Ira

Gershwin Theatre

Gertie the Dinosaur

Gertrude

Gerulaitis, Vitas

Gervase of Canterbury

Gervase of Tilbury

Gervin, George

Gesell, Arnold

Gestalt group therapy

Gestalt psychology

Gestalt theory

Gestapo

Gesta Romanorum

Gesualdo, Carlo

Gethsemane

Gethsemane cheese

Geto Boys, The

Get Out Your
  Handkerchiefs

Get Smart

Getty, Caroline Marie

Getty, Estelle

Getty, Eugene Paul

Getty, Gordon Peter

Getty, J. Paul

Getty Petroleum
Corporation

Gettysburg

Gettysburg Address

Gettysburg campaign

Gettysburg College

Gettysburg National
Military Park

Getz, Stan

Gevaert, François
Auguste

gewürztraminer *often*
Gewürztraminer

G-force

Ghana [*form.* Gold
Coast]

Ghanaba

Ghana Empire

Ghanaian

Ghanian

Ghats

Ghazālī, al-

G. Heileman Brewing
Company, Inc.

Ghent

Ghent azalea

Ghibelline

Ghiberti, Lorenzo

Ghiordes

Ghiordes knot

Ghirardelli Square

Ghirlandajo,
Domenico

Ghose, Chimnoy

Ghostbusters

Ghostbusters II

Ghostley, Alice

Ghost of Jacob Marley

Giacometti, Alberto

Giamatti, A. Bartlett

Giambologna

Giancana, Sam

Giannini, Amadeo P.

Giannini, Giancarlo

Giant Bicycle, Inc.

Giant Food
Foundation

Giant Food Inc.

Giants' Causeway

Giant Soft Fan, Ghost
Version

Giants Stadium

Gibb, Andy

Gibb, Barry

Gibb, Cynthia

Gibb, Maurice

Gibb, Robin

Gibbon, Edward

Gibbons, Euell

Gibbons, Grinling

Gibbons, James
Cardinal

Gibbons, Leeza

Gibbons, Orlando

Gibbs, James

Gibbs, Josiah Willard

Gibbs, Marla

Gibbs, Sir Philip

Gibbs, Teri

Gibbs, Wolcott

Gibbs free energy

Gibbs function

Gibbs' phase rule

GI Bill of Rights

Gibraltar

Gibraltar Peninsula

Gibran, Kahlil

Gibson

Gibson, Althea

Gibson, Bob

Gibson, Charles Dana

Gibson, Debbie

Gibson, Don

Gibson, Henry

Gibson, Hoot

Gibson, Josh

Gibson, Kenneth

Gibson, Kirk

Gibson, Mel

Gibson, William

Gibson Desert

Gibson girl

Gibson Greetings, Inc.

Gide, André

Gideon

Gideon Bible

Gideons International

Gideon v. Wainwright

Gielgud, Sir John

Giemsa, Gustav

Giemsa *occas.*
Giemsa's stain

Gieseking, Walter

Gifford, Frank

Gifford, Kathie Lee

Gifford Pinchot
National Forest

Gifts in Kind America

Gigi

GI Joe

G. I. Joe's Camel Gran
Prix

Gila

Gila Cliff Dwellings National Monument

Gila *occas.* gila monster

Gila National Forest

Gila woodpecker

Gilbert, Billy

Gilbert, Cass

Gilbert, Sir Humphrey

Gilbert, John

Gilbert, Melissa

Gilbert, Sir William S.

Gilbert and Sullivan

Gilbert and Ellice Islands

Gilbertian

Gilbert Islands

Gilberto, Astrud

Gilbert's disease

Gil Blas

Gilcrease, Thomas

Gilda

Gildas, Saint

Gilded Age [historical period]

Gilded Age, The [novel]

Gildersleeve, Throckmorton P.

Gilead

Gileadite

Gilels, Emil G.

Giles, Herbert A.

Giles, Saint

Giles, Warren

Gilgamesh

Gilgamesh Epic

Gill, Eric Rowland

Gill, Johnny

Gill, John Wilson

Gill, Vince

Gilles

Gillespie, Dizzy

Gillette

Gillette, Anita

Gillette, King Camp

Gillette, William

Gillette Charitable and Educational Foundation

Gillette Company, The

Gilley, Mickey

Gilley's Club

Gilliam, Terry

Gilligan's Island

Gilman, Arthur

Gilman, Daniel Coit

Gilmer

Gilpin, Charles

Gilroy

Gilroy, Frank

Gilson, Étienne

Gilsonite™

Gimme a Break

Ging, Jack

Gingerbread Man, The

Gingold, Hermione

Gingrich, Newt

Ginkgophyta

Ginnie Mae, *usually pl.* Ginnie Maes

Ginsberg, Allen

Ginsburg, Ruth Bader

Ginty, Robert

Ginza, the

Giono, Jean

Giordano, John

Giordano, Luca

Giordano, Umberto

Giottino

Giotto

Giovanni, Nikki

Giovanni Arnolfini and His Bride

Giovanni de Paolo

Gipper, the

Gipson, Lawrence Henry

Gipsy Baron, The

Girard

Girard, Stephen

Girard College

Girardon, Francois

Giraudoux, Jean

Girl and Her Duenna

girl Friday

Girl Guides

Girl I Left behind Me, The

Girl in the Red Velvet Swing

Girl of the Golden West, The

Girls Association Inc.

Girl Scouts of the United States of America

Girls State

Girl with a Watering Can

Girodet-Trioson, Anne Louis

Gironde

Girondism

Girondist

Giroud, François

Girtin, Thomas

Girton College

Giscard d'Estaing, Valerie

Giselle

Gish, Dorothy

Gish, Lillian

Gissing, George

Gitano Group, Inc., The

Giulini, Carlo Maria

Giulio Romano

Giunta Pisano

Givenchy, Hubert de

Givens, Robin

Giza *var. of* Al Jizah

Glaber, Raoul

Glacier Bay National Park

Glacier Bay National Preserve

Glacier National Park

Glackens, Willam

Gladewater

Gladstone

Gladstone, William Ewart

Gladstone bag

Gladstone claret

Gladstone wine

Glad Tidings bookstore

Gladys Knight and the Pips

Glagolitic

Glamorgan

Glamorganshire

Glamour

Glan-Thompson prism

Glanville-Hicks, Peggy

Glarus

Glaser, Paul Michael

Glasgow

Glasgow, Ellen

Glasgow Air Force Base

Glasgow Airport

Glashow, Sheldon Lee

Glaspell, Susan

Glass, Carter

Glass, Philip

Glass, Ron

Glassboro

Glassboro State College

Glass Menagerie, The

Glass Molders, Pottery, Plastics, and Allied Workers International Union

Glassport

Glastonbury

Glastonbury Abbey

Glastonbury chair

Glastonbury thorn

Glaswegian

Glatzer Neisse

Glauber, Johann Rudolf

Glauber's *occas.* Glauber salt

Glaxo Holdings

Glazer, Guilford

Glazunoff, Alexander *or* Alexandr

Gleason, Jackie

Gleason, James

Gleizes, Albert

Glencairn cycle

Glen Canyon Dam

Glen Canyon National Recreation Area

Glencoe

Glen Cove

Glendale

Glendale Community College

Glendale Federal Bank

Glendive

Glendora

Glendower, Owen

Glen Ellyn

GLENFED, Inc.

Glen Lyon

Glenn, John

Glenn, Scott

Glenn Miller's Orchestra

Glennville [* GA; *see also* Glenville]

Glen Oaks Community College

Glenolden

Glen Ridge

Glen Rock

Glens Falls

Glenview

Glenview Naval Air Station

Glenville [* WV; *see also* Glennville]

Glenville State College

Glenwood

Glenwood Springs

Gless, Sharon

Glière, Reinhold

Glinka, Mikhail

Glitter, Gary

Global Exchange

Global Horizons

Global Hunger Project, The

Global Marine Inc.

Global Press Review

Global Television
Network

Global Van Lines, Inc.

Globe

Globe Syndicate

Globe Theatre

Glock™ handgun

Glock, Inc.

Gloria Dei National
Historic Site

Gloria Estefan and the
Miami Sound
Machine

Gloria in excelsis

Gloria in excelsis Deo

Gloria Marshall
Figure Salon

Gloria Patri

Glorious Revolution

Glorious Twelfth

Gloucester

Gloucester City

Gloucester County
College

Gloucestershire

Glover, Danny

Gloversville

Gluck, Alma

Gluck, Christoph W.

Glyn, Elinor

Glyndebourne Festival

Glyndebourne Festival
Opera

Glynn, Carlin

Glyptothek

GMAC™ financing

G-man, *n., pl.* G-men

GMI Engineering and
Management
Institute

Gnetophyta

Gnostic

gnosticism *often*
Gnosticism

Goa

Goa powder

Goascoran

Goat

Gobel, George

Gobelin

Gobi

Gobian

God

God Almighty

Godard, Benjamin

Godard, Jean Luc

Godavari

God Bless America

Goddard, Paulette

Goddard, Robert
Hutchings

Goddard College

Goddard Institute for
Space Studies

Goddard Space Flight
Center

Godden, Rumer

Gödel, Kurt

Gödel's theorem

Godey, Louis Antoine

Godey's Lady's Book

Godfather, The

Godfather Part III,
The

Godfather Part II, The

God-fearing

God-forsaken *occas.*
god-forsaken

Godfrey, Arthur

Godfrey of Bouillon

God-given

Godhead

God Is an Englishman

Godowsky, Leopold

God Rest Ye *or* You
Merry Gentlemen

God's acre

God save the King

God save the Queen

God's Bible School
and College

God's country

Gods Must Be Crazy,
The

Gods Must Be Crazy
2, The

Godspeed

Godspell

God's penny

God's plenty

God's Word

Godthåb *or* Godthaab

God the Father

Godunov, Alexander

Godunov, Boris

Godwin, Gail

Godwin, Mary
Wollstonecraft

Godwin, William

Godwin-Austen,
Henry Haversham

Godzilla

Goebbels, Joseph

Goedicke, Alexander

Goering, Hermann

Goes, Hugo van der

Goethals, George
Washington

Goethe, Johann
Wolfgang von

Goetz, Bernhard H.

Goff, Norris

Goffin, Gerry

Gog

Gog and Magog

Gogebic

Gogebic Community
College

Gogmagog

Gogol, Nikolai

Going My Way

Going Places

Go Kart™

Golan Heights

Golconda

Gold, Ernest

Gold, Herbert

Gold, Tracey

Goldbach conjecture

Goldberg, Arthur

Goldberg, Gary David

Goldberg, Rube

Goldberg, Whoopi

Goldbergian

Goldblum, Jeff

Gold Coast [*now*
Ghana]

Gold Coast [wealthy
residential area]

Gold Diggers, The

Golden

Golden, John

Golden Age

Golden American
Network

Golden Ass, The

Goldenberg, Billy

Golden Books™

Golden Bough

[mythologic
mistletoe]

Golden Bough, The
[study by J. Frazer]

Golden Bowl, The
[novel by H. James]

Golden Bull

Golden Delicious

Golden Eagle Pass

Golden Fleece

Golden Gate

Golden Gate Baptist
Theological
Seminary

Golden Gate Bridge

Golden Gate Fields

Golden Gate National
Recreation Area

Golden Gate Park

Golden Gate Quartet,
The

Golden Gate
University

Golden Girls, The

Golden Globe award

Golden Gloves
Tournament

Golden Goose, The

Golden Horde

Golden Horn

Golden Legend, The

Golden Nugget [*now*
Mirage Resorts,
Inc.*]

Golden Palm Award

Golden Rectangle

Golden Rule

Golden Section

Golden Spike National
Historic Site

Golden State

Golden State Warriors

Golden Triangle

Golden Valley

Golden West™ Books

Golden West College

Golden West Financial
Corporation

Golden Years
Magazine

Goldey Beacom
College

Goldfield

Goldfinger

Goldilocks

Golding, Louis

Golding, William

Goldman, Edwin
Franko

Goldman, Emma

Goldman, Lillian

Goldman, Rhoda H.

Goldman, Richard
Franko

Goldman, William
Gerald

Goldman Sachs
Group, The

Goldmark, Karl

Goldome

Goldoni, Carlo

Goldovsky, Boris

Gold Prospectors
Association of
America

Goldsboro

Goldsboro, Bobby

Goldsmith, Jerry

Goldsmith, Oliver

Gold Standard Act

Gold Star Medal

Goldthwait, Bob

Goldwater, Barry M.

Gold Wing Road
    Riders Association

Goldwyn, Samuel

Goldwyn, Samuel, Jr.

Goldwyn Girls

Goldwynism

Golf [magazine; *see
    also* Golf
    Magazine]

Golf Digest

Golf Illustrated

Golf Journal

Golf Magazine [*see
    also* Golf]

Golf Manor

Golgi, Camillo

Golgi apparatus

Golgi body

Golgotha

Goliard

Goliardic songs

Goliath

Goliath crane

Gollum

Golschmann, Vladimir

Gomer Pyle, U.S.M.C.

Gomez, Lefty

Gómez de la Serena,
    Ramón

Gomorrah

Gompers, Samuel

Gomulka, Wladyslaw

Gonçalves Dias,
    Antonio

Goncharev, Ivan

Goncourt, Edmond
    Louis Antoine Huot
    de

Goncourt, Jules Alfred
    Huot de

Gondwana

G, phase

Gone with the Wind

Góngora y Argote,
    Luis de

Gongorism

Gongorist

Gong Show, The

Gonzaga University

Gonzaga University
    Bulldogs

Gonzales, Felipe

Gonzales, Henry

Gonzales, Pancho

Gonzales, Rodolfo

Gooch, George
    Peabody

Goodall, Jane

Good Book, the

Good Conduct Medal

Good Day Sunshine
    Beatles Fan Club

Gooden, Dwight

Goodenough-Harris
    test

Goodfellas

Goodfellow, Robin

Goodfellow Air Force
    Base

Good Friday

Good Friday massacre

Good Friday music

Good Guys, The

Good Housekeeping

Good Housekeeping
    Seal of Approval

Goodhue, Bertram G.

Good Humor™ bar

Good Humor Ice
    Cream Corporation

Good Humor™ man

Gooding, Cuba, Jr.

Good-King-Henry, *n.,
    pl.* Good-King-
    Henries

Good King Wenceslas
    occas. Wenceslaus
    [Christmas carol]

Good King
    Wenceslaus [*aka*
    Saint Wenceslaus]

Goodland

Goodman, Benny

Goodman, Dody

Goodman, Ellen

Goodman, John

Goodman Theater
    Center of the Art
    Institute of Chicago

Good Morning
    America

Good Neighbor Policy

Good News Bible

Good News bookstore

Goodnight, Charles

Goodnight trail

Goodpasture's
    syndrome

Goodrich, Benjamin F.

Goodrich, Samuel
    Griswold

Good Samaritan [of
    the Biblical parable]

good samaritan *often*
    Good Samaritan
    [one ready to help
    those in distress]

Good Samaritan laws

Good Sam
    Recreational
    Vehicle Club

Good Shepherd

Goodson, Mark

Goodspeed Opera House

Good Thief, the

good-time Charlie *or* Charley

Goodwill Industries of America, Inc.

Goodwill Industries Volunteer Services

Goodwin Sands

Goodwrench 500

Goody, Sam

Goodyear, Charles

Goodyear blimp

Goodyear Tire and Rubber Company, The

Goodyear Tire and Rubber Company Fund

Goody Two-Shoes

Goolagong Cawley, Evonne

Goose Bay

Goose Island Bird and Girl Watching Society

Goossens, Sir Eugene

Gorbachev, Mikhail S.

Gorbachev, Raisa

Gorbasm

Gorbymania

Gorcey, Leo

Gordian

Gordian knot

Gordimer, Nadine

Gordium

Gordon, Chinese

Gordon, Dexter

Gordon, Gale

Gordon, Mack

Gordon, Mary

Gordon, Ruth

Gordon College

Gordon-Conwell Theological Seminary

Gordone, Charles

Gordon Institute, The

Gordon setter

Gore, Al, Jr. [Clinton's vice president]

Gore, Al, Sr.

Gore, Al, III

Gore, Bob

Gore, Karenna

Gore, Kristen

Gore, Lesley

Gore, Pauline

Gore, Sara

Gore, Tipper

Goren, Charles H.

Gore-Tex™

Gorey, Edward

Gorgas, William Crawford

Gorgon

Gorgonian

Gorgonzola

Gorki *or* Gorkiy *or* Gorky [*now* Nizhniy *or* Nizhny Novgorod]

Gorky, Arshile

Gorky, Maxim

Gorky Park

Gorman, Cliff

Gorme, Eydie

Gorshin, Frank

Gortner, Marjoe

Gosden, Freeman

Gosdin, Vern

Goshen

Goshen Biblical Seminary

Goshen College

Gosiute

Goslin, Goose

gospel *occas.* Gospel

Gospel Music Association

Gospels, the

Gosse, Sir Edmond

Gossett, Louis, Jr.

Göteborg

Go Tell It on the Mountain

Goth

Gotham

Gotham City

Gothamite

Gothenburg

Gothenburg Art Gallery

Gothic

Gothic arch

Gothic architecture

Gothic armor

Gothic art

Gothicism

Gothicist

Gothic language

Gothic novel

Gothic revival

Gothic romance

Gothic style

Gotland

Gotlander

Götterdämmerung

Gotti, John

Gotti, Peter

Gottlieb, Adolph

Gottlieb, Robert A.

Gottschalk, Ferdinand

Gottschalk, Louis Moreau

Gottschalks Inc.

Gottwald, Bruce Cobb

Gottwald, Floyd Dewey, Jr.

Gottwald, Klement

Goucher College

Gouda

Goudge, Elizabeth

Goudy, Frederic William

Gough, Michael

Goujon, Jean

Gould, Chester

Gould, Elliott

Gould, Glenn

Gould, Harold

Gould, Jay

Gould, Kingdon, Jr.

Gould, Morton

Gould, Stephen Jay

Goulding, Ray

Goulds

Goulds Pumps, Inc.

Goulet, Robert

Gounod, Charles

Gourmet

Gourmont, Rémy de

Gouverneur

Government Employees Insurance Company

Government Finance Officers Association

Government National Mortgage Association

Governor Moonbeam

Governors Island

Governors State University

Governor Winthrop desk

Gowanda

Gowdy, Curt

Gower, John

Goya Self-Portrait

Goya y Lucientes, Francisco José de

Goyen, Jan van

Gozzoli, Benozzo

GQ [magazine]

Graaf, Reinier de

Graafian follicle

Graafian vesicle

Grable, Betty

Gracchi, the

Gracchus, Gaius Sempronius

Gracchus, Tiberius Sempronius

Grace Bible College

Grace College

Grace College of the Bible

Grace Energy Corporation

Grace Foundation

Grace Gospel Fellowship

Graceland

Graceland College

Graces

Grace Theological Seminary

Graduate Management Admission Test

Graduate Record Examination

Graduate School of Political Management

Graduate Theological Union

Graeffe method

Graf, Steffi

Graf Spee

Grafton

Grafton, Sue

Graf Zeppelin

Graham

Graham, Bill [impresario]

Graham, Billy [minister]

Graham, Donald

Graham, Donald E.

Graham, John

Graham, Katharine

Graham, Martha

Graham, Otto

Graham, Sheilah

Graham, Thomas

Graham, Virginia

Grahame, Gloria

Grahame, Kenneth

Graham family

Graham Land

Graham-Paige car

Graham's law of diffusion

Graham-Tewksbury feud

Graian Alps

Grail

Grainger, David William

Grainger, Percy

Gram, Hans J. C.

Grambling

Grambling State University

Grambling State University Tigers

Gramm, Phil

Grammer, Kelsey

Gramm-Rudman-Hollings budget law

Grammy, n., pl. Grammys or Grammies

Gram-negative

Grampian, The

Grampian Hills

Grampian Mountains

Grampian region

Gram-positive

Gram-Schmidt orthogonalization

Gramsci, Antonio

Gram's method

Gram's solution

Gram's or Gram stain

Granada [* Nicaragua; Spain; see also Grenada]

Granados, Enrique

Granatelli, Andy

Gran Chaco

Grand Alliance

Grand Army of the Republic

Grand Bahama

Grand Banks

Grand Bay

Grand Bay Hotel at Equitable Center

Grand Canal

Grand Canyon

Grand Canyon Airlines, Inc.

Grand Canyon National Park

Grand Canyon of the Colorado

Grand Canyon of the Snake

Grand Canyon of the Tuolumne

Grand Canyon of the Yellowstone

Grand Canyon University

Grand Cayman

Grand Cayman Owen Roberts International Airport

Grand Combin

Grand Coulee

Grand Coulee Dam

Grand Coulee Reservoir [now Franklin D. Roosevelt Lake]

Grand Cross of the Bath

Grand Cross of the British Empire

Grand Duchy of Moscow or Muscovy

Grand Duke of Muscovy

Grand Effie Award

Grande Prairie

Grande-Terre

Grand Forks

Grand Forks Air Force Base

Grand Forks International Airport

Grand Funk Railroad

Grand Guignol

Grand Haven

Grand Hotel

Grand Island

Grand Junction

Grand Lama

Grand Ledge

Grand Manan

Grandmaster

Grandmaster Flash

Grand Mesa National Forest

Grand Metropolitan

Grandmothers for Peace

Grand Mufti

Grand National Rodeo, Horse and Stock Show

Grand National Rodeo, Horse Show and Livestock Exposition

Grand National Steeplechase

Grand Old Party

Grand Ole Opry

Grand Ole Opry Fan Club

Grand Ole Opry House

Grand Palais

Grand Portage National Monument

Grand Prairie

Grand Prix, n., pl Grand Prix or

Grands Prix *or* Grand Prixes

Grand Prix de Rome

Grand Rapids

Grand Rapids Air Force Base

Grand Rapids Baptist College and Seminary

Grand Rapids Junior College

Grand Rapids Press, The

Grand Rapids School of the Bible

Grand River

Grand Teton

Grand Teton National Park

grand tour *occas.* Grand Tour

Grand Traverse Bay

Grand Trunk Western Railroad Company

Grand United Order of Antelopes

Grand United Order of Odd Fellows

Grand Valley State College

Grandview

Grand View College

Grandview Heights

Grandville

Grange

Grange, Red

Granger

Granger, Farley

Granger, Stewart

Granger cases

Granger laws

Granger movement

Grangeville

Granite City

Granite Falls

Granjon, Robert

Granny Smith

Granolith™

Gran Paradiso

Gran Sasso d'Italia

Grant, Amy

Grant, Bud

Grant, Cary

Grant, Sir Francis

Grant, Gogi

Grant, Heber Jedediah

Grant, Lee

Grant, Ulysses S.

Grantham College of Engineering

Grant-Kohrs Ranch National Historic Site

Gran Tourismo

Grants Pass

Grant's Tomb

Granville, Bonita

Granville-Barker, Harley

Granz, Norman

Grapes of Wrath, The

Graphic Arts Monthly

Graphic Communications International Union

Graphic NEWS Bureau

Grappelli, Stephane

Grasmere

Grass, Günter

Grasse

Grassman, Hermann

Grassman's law

Grasso, Ella

grass-of-Parnassus

Grateful Dead, The

Gratian

Gra-TRI-Y club

Grattan, Henry

Grattan Massacre

Gratz College

Grau, Shirley Ann

Grauer, Ben

Graustark

Graustarkian

Gravella Roller

Gravely, Samuel L., Jr.

Gravenstein

Graves

Graves, Morris

Graves, Peter

Graves, Robert

Graves' disease

Gravettian

Gray, Asa

Gray, Coleen

Gray, Dolores

Gray, Elizabeth Janet

Gray, Erin

Gray, Harold

Gray, Henry

Gray, Linda

Gray, Spalding

Gray, Thomas

Gray, William H., III

Gra-Y club

Gray Eminence

Gray Friar

Gray Lady

Gray Line
Gray Panthers
Gray Panthers Project Fund
[Gray's] Anatomy, Descriptive and Surgical
Grays Harbor College
Gray's Inn
Grayson, David
Grayson, Kathryn
Grayson County College
Gray's Sporting Journal
Graz
Graziano, Rocky
Grease
Grease 2
Great Abaco
Great Ajax
Great America
Great American Bank, A Federal Savings Bank
Great American Desert
Great American Life Insurance Company
Great American Telecommunications Services
Great Artesian Basin
Great Atlantic and Pacific Tea Company, Inc., The
Great Australian Bight
Great Awakening
Great Barrier Reef
Great Basin
Great Basin National Park

Great Bear
Great Bear Lake
Great Bend
Great Britain
Great Chicago Fire
Great Dane
Great Depression
Great Dismal Swamp
Great Divide
Great Dividing Range
Great Dog
Great Entrance
Greater Antilles
Greater Buffalo International Airport
Greater East Asia Co-Prosperity Sphere
Greater Hartford Community College
Greater New Haven State Technical College
Greater New York Savings Bank
Greater Pittsburgh International Airport
Greater Portland Magazine
Greater Rochester International Airport
Greater Sunda Islands
Greater Washington Organization for Government Funding of Social Services
Greater Wollongong
Greater Yellowstone Coalition

Greatest Show on Earth, The
Greatest Sports Legends
Great Expectations
Great Falls
Great Gatsby, The
Great Gildersleeve, The
Great Indian Desert
great jumping Jehoshaphat
Great Khingan
Great Lakes
Great Lakes Bancorp, A Federal Savings Bank
Great Lakes Bible College
Great Lakes Chemical Corporation
Great Lakes Fisherman
Great Lakes Junior College of Business
Great Lakes Naval Training Center
Great Lakes Sailor
Great Lakes-Saint Lawrence Seaway
Great Leap Forward
Great Man-Made River
Great Mogul
Great Mosque of Samarra
Great Mother of the Gods
Great Neck
Great Neck Estates
Great Neck Plaza

Great Northern Nekoosa Corporation

Great Northern Nekoosa Foundation

Great Northern Peninsula

Great Northern Railway Company

Great Ouse

Great Pee Dee

Great Performances

Great Plague

Great Plains

Great Pyramid of Cheops

Great Pyramid of Khufu

Great Pyramids of Gîza *or* Al-Gizeh *or* Al-Jizah

Great Pyrenees

Great Rebellion

Great Revival

Great Rift Valley

Great Russian

Great Saint Bernard Pass

Great Salt Desert

Great Salt Lake

Great Salt Lake Desert

Great Salt Plains Dam

Great Sand Dunes National Monument

Great Sandy Desert

Great Sanhedrin

Great Schism

Great Seal of the United States

Great Slave Lake

Great Smoky Mountains

Great Smoky Mountains National Park

Great Society

Great South Bay

Great Space Coaster, The

Great Sphinx

Great Spirit

Great Sunday

Great Synagogue

Great Train Robbery, The

Great Victoria Desert

Great Vowel Shift

Great Wall of China

Great War, the

Great Week

Great Western Bank

Great Western Financial Corporation

Great Western Forum, The

Great West Life and Annuity

Great-West Life Assurance Company

Great Whale River Project

Great White Father

Great White Hope, The

Great White Way

Great Zab

Great Ziegfeld, The

Greaves, Captain

Grecian

Grecian bend

Grecian profile

Greco, Buddy

Greco, José

Greco-Roman

Greco-Roman art

Greco-Roman wrestling

Greece

Greed

Greek

Greek Anthology, The

Greek architecture

Greek art

Greek Catholic

Greek Church

Greek cross

Greekdom

Greek fire

Greekish

Greek juniper

Greek language

Greek-letter fraternity

Greek-letter sorority

Greek literature

Greek music

Greek Orthodox Archdiocese of North and South America

Greek Orthodox Church

Greek religion

Greek Revival *occas.* revival

Greek Revivalism *occas.* revivalism

Greek Revivalist *occas.* revivalist

Greek rite

Greek tortoise
Greek valerian
Greeley
Greeley, Andrew
Greeley, Horace
Greeley Gas
  Company, Inc.
Greely, Adolphus
  Washington
Green, Adolph
Green, Al
Green, Henry
Green, Hetty
Green, John Richard
Green, Julian
Green, Paul
Green, Pincus
Green, William
Green Acres
Greenaway, Kate
Greenbacker
Greenbackism
Greenback Party
Green Bay
Green Bay Packers
Greenbelt
Green Berets
Greenberg, Hank
Greenberg, Maurice
Greenberg, Philip B.
Greenbrier, The
Greencastle
Green Cove Springs
Greendale
Greene, Bette
Greene, Bob
Greene, Ellen
Greene, Evans
Greene, Graham

Greene, Jack
Greene, James
Greene, Joe
Greene, Lorne
Greene, Michael
Greene, Michele
Greene, Nathanael
Greene, Robert
Greene, Shecky
Greeneville [* TN; see
  also Greenville]
Greenfield
Greenfield, Meg
Greenfield
  Community College
Greenfield Village
Greenham Common
Green Hornet, The
Greenland
Greenlandair, Inc.
Greenlander
Greenland Sea
Greenland whale
Greenlawn
Green Mountain
Green Mountain Boys
Green Mountain Club,
  The
Green Mountain
  College
Green Mountain
  National Forest
Green Mountains
Green Mountain State
Greenough, Horatio
Green Party
Greenpeace
  International
Greenpeace USA
Green Peter Dam

Green Point Savings
  Bank
Green Revolution
Green River
Green River
  Community College
Green River
  Ordinance
Greens
Greensboro
Greensboro College
Greensburg
Greensleeves
Greenspan, Alan
Green's theorem
Greenstreet, Sydney
Greentree
Greenville [* AL; GA;
  IL; KY; MI; MS;
  MO; OH; PA; SC;
  TX; see also
  Greeneville]
Greenville College
Greenville News-
  Piedmont, The
Greenville Technical
  College
Greenwich
Greenwich Civil Time
Greenwich hour angle
Greenwich Mean
  Time
Greenwich Meridian
Greenwich time
Greenwich Village
Greenwood
Greenwood, Caleb
Greenwood, Lee
Greenwood Trust
  Company
Greer

Greer, Germaine
Greer, Jane
Gregg, John Robert
Gregg, William
Gregg shorthand
Gregoire, Paul
  Cardinal
Gregorian
Gregorian calendar
Gregorian chant
Gregorian mode
Gregorian telescope
Gregorian water
Gregory
Gregory I, Saint
Gregory II, Saint
Gregory III, Saint
Gregory, Lady
  Augusta
Gregory, Cynthia
Gregory, Diana
Gregory, Dick
Gregory, Horace
Gregory, James
Gregory, Lisa
Gregory of Nazianzus,
  Saint
Gregory of Nyssa,
  Saint
Gregory of Rimini
Gregory of Sinai
Gregory of Tours,
  Saint
Gregory the
  Illuminator, Saint
Gremlins
Gremlins 2: The New
  Batch
Grenada [nation in
  Caribbean Indies;
  see also Granada]

Grenadian
Grenadier Guards
Grenadines
Grendel
Grenfell, Sir Wilfrid
  Thomason
Grenoble
Grenville, Sir Richard
Gresham, Sir Thomas
Gresham's law
Gretchen
Gretna
Gretna Green
Gretna Green
  marriage
Gréty, André Ernest
  Modeste
Gretzky, Wayne
Greuze, Jean Baptiste
Greville, Fulk
Grey, Charles
Grey, Earl
Grey, Lady Jane
Grey, Joel
Grey, Zane
Grey Cup
Greyhound™ bus
Greyhound
  Corporation, The
Greyhound Dial
  Corporation [now
  Dial Corporation,
  The]
Greyhound Financial
  Corporation
Greyhound Lines, Inc.
Greyhound Lines of
  Canada Ltd.
Greyhound Park
Greyhound-Trailways
Gridley

GRiD Systems
  Corporation
Grieg, Edvard
Grien or Grün, Hans
Grier, Rosey
Griese, Bob
Griffes, Charles
  Tomlinson
Griffey, Ken, Jr.
Griffey, Ken, Sr.
Griffin
Griffin, Merv
Griffin College
Griffiss Air Force
  Base
Griffith
Griffith, Andy
Griffith, Clark
Griffith, D. W.
Griffith, Emile
Griffith, Hugh
Griffith, Melanie
Griffith Joyner,
  Florence
Griffith Observatory
  and Planetarium
Griffith Park
Grignard, Victor
Grignard reaction
Grignard reagent
Grillparzer, Franz
Grimaldi, Joseph
Grimaldian
Grimaldi man
Grimes, Burleigh
Grimes, Tammy
Grimes Golden
Grimes Grave
Grimké, Angelina

Grimké, Archibald
Grimké, Sarah
Grimm, Jacob
Grimm, Wilhelm
Grimm's Fairy Tales
Grimm's law
Grim Reaper
Grinnell
Grinnell, Josiah Bushnell
Grinnell College
Gripsholm
Gris, Juan
Griselda
Grisham, John
Grissom Air Force Base
Grit
Grizzard, George
Grizzard, Lewis
Grocery Manufacturers of America
Grodin, Charles
Groenendael
Groening, Matt
Grofé, Ferde
Groh, David
Grolier de Servières, Jean
Grolier design
Grolier, Inc.
Gromyko, Andrei
Grooms, Red
Groote, Gerhard
Gropius, Walter
Gropper, William
Gros, Antoine Jean
Grosbard, Ulu
Gross, Chaim

Gross, Mary
Gross, Michael
Gross Clinic, The
Grosse Point
Grosse Point Farms
Grosse Point Park
Grosse Point Woods
Grossinger's Hotel
Grossmont College
Grosvenor, Gerald
Grosvenor, Gilbert
Grosvenor Gallery
Grosvenor Square
Gros Ventre
Gros Ventre of the Prairie
Grosz, George
Grote, George
Grotian
Grotius, George
Groton
Groundhog Day
Group against Smokers' Pollution
Groupe des Banques Populaires
Group for Contemporary Music
Group of Seven
Group of 77
Group W. Productions
Grove, Frederick
Grove, Sir George
Grove, Lefty
Grove City
Grove City College
Grover
Groves
Groves, Leslie

Groveton
Growing Pains
Gruberova, Edita
Grub Street
Gruenberg, Louis
Gruening, Ernest
Grumman, Leroy
Grumman Corporation
Grundyism
Grundyist
Grundyite
Grünewald, Matthias
Gruyère
G. Schirmer, Inc.
GSM News Service/ Garden State Media
G spot
Gstaad
G-string
G suit
GTE Corporation
GTE Foundation
G_2 phase
Guadalajara
Guadalcanal
Guadalcanal Diary
Guadalupe [* CA, Costa Rica, and Mexico; island in Pacific Ocean; river in TX; see also Guadeloupe]
Guadalupe Day
Guadalupe Hidalgo
Guadalupe Mountains
Guadalupe Mountains National Park
Guadalupe palm
Guadalupe River

Guadeloupe [islands in Caribbean Indies; *see also* Guadalupe]

Guadiana

Guam

Guamanian

Guam Community College

Guanajuato

Guaneri String Quartet

Guangdong [*form.* Kwangtung]

Guangzhou [*form.* Canton]

Guantánamo

Guantánamo Bay

Guantánamo Bay Naval Base

Guaporé

Guarani, *n., pl.* Guarani *or* Guaranis

Guaranty Federal Savings Bank

Guard, Dave

Guardi, Francesco

Guardian [*form.* Manchester Guardian]

Guardian, The [magazine]

Guardian Angels

Guardian Life Insurance Company of America

Guardian Savings and Loan Association

Guardino, Harry

Guare, John

Guarini, Guariño

Guarneri, Andrea

Guarneri, Giuseppe Antonio

Guarneri, Pietro

Guarnerius

Guatemala

Guatemala City

Guatemala City La Aurora Airport

Guatemalan

Guayaquil

Guaymas

Gub Gub the pig

Guccione, Robert

Guderian, Heinz

Gudermannian

Gudmundson

Guedala, Philip

Guelph

Guelphs and Ghibellines

Guelph Spring Festival

Guercino

Guericke, Otto von

Guerickian

Guernica

Guernsey [cattle], *n., pl.* Guernseys

Guernsey [island]

Guernsey lily

Guerrero

Guess Who, The

Guest, Edgar A.

Guest Quarters hotel

Guevara, Ché

Guggenheim, Daniel

Guggenheim, Meyer

Guggenheim, Solomon R.

Guggenheim Fellowship

Guiana [region; *see also* Guyana]

Guiana Current

Guiana Highlands

Guianese, *n., pl.* Guianese

Guibert of Ravenna

Guicciardini, Francesco

Guide Dog Foundation for the Blind

Guide Michelin

Guideposts

Guiding Eyes for the Blind

Guiding Light

Guido d'Arezzo

Guido of Siena

Guidry, Ron

Guignol

Guildenstern

Guildhall School of Music and Drama

Guild of Carillonneurs in North America

Guilford

Guilford College

Guilford Courthouse National Military Park

Guilford Mills, Inc.

Guilford Technical Community College

Guillain-Barré syndrome

Guillaume, Robert

Guillaume de Machaut

Guillén, Jorge

Guillén, Nicolás

Guinea

Guinea-Bissau
Guinea corn
Guinea Current
Guinean
Guinea pepper
Guinea worm
Guinevere
Guinier, Ewart
Guinness, Sir Alec
Guiness Book of Records, The
Güiraldes, Ricardo
Guise, Françoise de Lorraine
Guise, Henri de Lorraine
Guisewite, Cathy
Guitry, Sacha
Guizhou [form. Kweichow]
Guijarat
Gujarati
Gujarat States
Gulag Archipelago, The
Gulager, Clu
Gulbenkian Museum
Gulf Coast
Gulf Coastal Plain
Gulf Coast Community College
Gulf Intracoastal Waterway
Gulf Islands National Seashore
Gulf, Mobile and Ohio Railroad Company
Gulf of Aden
Gulf of Aegina
Gulf of Alaska
Gulf of Almería

Gulf of Aqaba
Gulf of Boothia
Gulf of Bothnia
Gulf of California
Gulf of Carpentaria
Gulf of Corinth
Gulf of Darien
Gulf of Finland
Gulf of Fonseca
Gulf of Gabès
Gulf of Genoa
Gulf of Guarnero
Gulf of Guinea
Gulf of Iskenderu
Gulf of Izmir
Gulf of Lepanto
Gulf of Lions
Gulf of Maine
Gulf of Maracaibo
Gulf of Martaban
Gulf of Mexico
Gulf of Nicoya
Gulf of Panama
Gulf of Papagayo
Gulf of Papua
Gulf of Patras
Gulf of Riga
Gulf of Saint Lawrence
Gulf of Salerno
Gulf of Salonika
Gulf of San Blas
Gulf of Saros
Gulf of Siam
Gulf of Sidra
Gulf of Smyrna
Gulf of Suez
Gulf of Taganrog
Gulf of Taranto

Gulf of Tehuantepec
Gulf of Thailand
Gulf of the Astronauts
Gulf of the Lions
Gulf of Tonkin
Gulf of Tonkin Resolution
Gulf of Trieste
Gulf of Venezuela
Gulf of Venice
Gulfport
Gulfport Naval Construction Battalion Center
Gulf Power Company
Gulf Power Company Foundation
Gulf States
Gulf States Utilities Company
Gulf Stream
Gulf Stream, The [painting]
Gulfstream Aerospace Corporation
Gulfstream Park
Gulfstream system
Gulf War
Gulick, Luther H.
Gullah
Gulliver's Travels
Gumble, Bryant
Gumble, Greg
Gumby
Gumby Show, The
Gummi Bears
Gump's
Gun Digest
Gunga Din
Gunn, Moses

Gunnarsson, Gunnar
Gunnison
Gunnison National
  Forest
Gunpowder Plot
Guns and Ammo
Guns and Ammo
  Annual
Guns Magazine
Gunsmoke
Guns N' Roses
Gunter, Edmund
Gunter Air Force
  Base
Gunter's chain
Guntersville
Gunther, John
Gun World
Gunzenhauser,
  Stephen
Gupton Jones College
  of Funeral Service
Gurkha, *n.*, *pl.* Gurkha
  or Gurkhas
Gurney, Dan
Gurney, Joseph John
Gurneyite
Gurpurab
Gustavus

Gustavus Adolphus
  College
Guston, Philip
Gutenberg, Johann
Gutenberg Bible
Guthrie, A. B., Jr.
Guthrie, Arlo
Guthrie, Janet
Guthrie, Sir Tyrone
Guthrie, Woody
Guthrie test
Guthrie Theatre
Gutiérrez, José
  Angel
Gutiérrez Nájera,
  Manuel
Guttenberg, Steve
Guy, Buddy
Guy, Jasmine
Guy, Rosa
Guyana [*form.* British
  Guiana; *see also*
  Guiana]
Guyana Airways
  Corporation
Guyanese
Guy F. Atkinson
  Company of
  California

Guy Fawkes Day
Guymon
Guy of Lusignan
Guy of Warwick
Guyon, Madame
Guys, Constantin
Guys and Dolls
Guzman, Abimael
Guzmán, Martín Luis
Gwari, *n.*, *pl.* Gwari
  or Gwaris
Gwathmey, Robert
Gwenn, Edmund
Gwinnett, Button
Gwyn *or* Gywnne,
  Nell
Gwynedd-Mercy
  College
Gwynn, Tony
Gwynne, Fred
Gynt, Peer
Gypsy [people], *n.*, *pl.*
  Gypsies
Gypsy [play]
Gypsy Madonna, The
Gypsy music
Gypsy Woman with
  Baby
Gyro International

H

Haakon

Haarlem [* the Netherlands; *see also* Harlem]

Haas, Fritz Otto

Haas, John Charles

Haas, Josephine

Haas, Peter E., Jr.

Haas, Peter E., Sr.

Haas, Robert D.

Hába, Alois

Habakkuk

Haber, Fritz

Habermas, Jurgen

Haber process

Habima Theater

Habitat for Humanity International

Hachette

Hackensack

[Hackensack] Record, The

Hackett, Bobby

Hackett, Buddy

Hackett, Charles

Hackett, Raymond

Hackettstown

Hackman, Gene

Hadas, Moses

Hadassah, the Women's Zionist Organization of America

Haddon, Alfred Cort

Haddonfield

Haddon Heights

Hadean

Haden, Charlie

Hades

Hadhramaut *or* Hadramaut *or* Hadhramawt

Hadhramautian *or* Hadramautian *or* Hadhramawtian

Hadley, Henry Kimball

Hadley chest

Hadrian

Hadrian's Mausoleum

Hadrian's Mole

Hadrian's Wall

Haeckel, Ernest

Haeckelian

Haeckelism

Hafey, Chick

Hafez al-Assad

Haffner Serenade

Haffner Symphony

Hafiz

Hagar

Hagar the Horrible

Hagegård, Håkan

Hagen, Uta

Hagen, Walter

Hagerman Fossil Beds National Monument

Hagerstown

Hagerstown Business College

Hagerstown Junior College

Hagerty, Julie

Haggadah, *n.*, *pl.* Haggadoth

Haggard, Sir Henry Rider

Haggard, Merle

Haggin, Ben Ali

Hagia Sophia

Hagiographa

Hagler, Marvin

Hagman, Larry

Hague, The

Hague, Albert

Hague, Frank

Hague Conference

[Hague] Municipal Museum

Hague Tribunal
Hahn, Jessica
Hahn, Otto
Hahnemann, Otto
Hahnemann, Samuel
Hahnemannian
Hahnemannism
Hahnemann
  University
Haid, Charles
Haid, Sid
Haida, *n., pl.* Haida *or*
  Haidas
Haidinger, Karl von
Haidinger fringes
Haifa
Haig, Alexander M.,
  Jr.
Haig, Douglas
Haight-Ashbury
Hail *occas.* hail
  Columbia [severe
  punishment]
Hail Columbia [song]
Haile Mariam
  Mengistu
Haile Selassie
Hailey, Arthur
Hail Mary, *n., pl.* Hail
  Marys
Hail to the Chief
Hainan
Hainan Strait
Haines, Jesse
Haines, Larry
Haines City
Haiphong
Hair
Haiti
Haitian

Haitian Creole
Haje, Khrystyne
Halakah, *n., pl.*
  Halakoth
Halas, George
Halberstam, David
Halcion™
Haldane, J. B. S.
Haldane, John Scott
Haldane, Richard
  Burdon
Haldeman, H. R.
Hale, Alan, Jr.
Hale, Barbara
Hale, Edward Everett
Hale, George Ellery
Hale, Nathan
Hale, Sarah Josepha
Haleakala
Haleakala National
  Park
Haledon
Hale Observatories
Hales Corners
Halévy, Fromental
Halévy, Ludovic
Haley, Alex
Haley, Bill
Haley, Jack
Haleyville
Half Dome
Halford, Rob
Half Price Books,
  Records and
  Magazines
Halfway
Half-Way Covenant
Halicarnassus
Halifax

Halifax Community
  College
Halifax International
  Airport
Haligonian
HAL, Inc.
Hall, Aaron
Hall, Anthony
  Michael
Hall, Arsenio
Hall, Charles Francis
Hall, Charles Martin
Hall, Daryl
Hall, Deidre
Hall, Donald Joyce
Hall, Edwin H.
Hall, Fawn
Hall, Glenn
Hall, Granville
  Stanley
Hall, Huntz
Hall, James
Hall, James Norman
Hall, Monty
Hall, Tom T.
Hallam, Arthur Henry
Hallam, Henry
Hallandale
Hall and Oates
Halle
Halleck, Fitz-Greene
Halleck, Henry Wager
Hall effect
Hallel
Hallelujah *occas.*
  Alleluia
Hallelujah, Baby!
Hallelujah Chorus
Hallé Orchestra

Hallett Motor Racing Circuit

Halley, Edmund

Halley's comet

Halliburton, Richard

Halliburton Company

Halliburton Foundation

Hallmark Cards, Inc.

Hallmark Hall of Fame

Hallmark Institute of Technology

Hall of Fame Bowl

Hall of Fame for Great Americans

Hall of Fame Game

Hall of Famer

Halloween

Hallowell

Hallowmas [now All Saints' Day]

Hallstrom, Lasse

Hallwachs, Wilhelm

Hallwachs effect

Hallyday, Johnny

Halmahera

Halpern, Steven

Hals, Frans

Halsey, Brett

Halsey, William F.

HALT, Inc.

Haltom City

Hamblen, Stuart

Hambletonian

Hambletonian Association

Hamburg

Hamburg Art Gallery

Hamden

Hamel, Veronica

Hamelin

Hamhung

Hamilcar Barca

Hamill, Dorothy

Hamill, Mark

Hamilton

Hamilton, Alexander

Hamilton, Alice

Hamilton, Bernie

Hamilton, Billy

Hamilton, Charles

Hamilton, Chico

Hamilton, Dorrance Hill

Hamilton, Edith

Hamilton, Lady Emma

Hamilton, George [actor]

Hamilton, George, IV [musician]

Hamilton, Sir Ian

Hamilton, Linda

Hamilton, Margaret

Hamilton, Murray

Hamilton, Scott

Hamilton, Virginia

Hamilton Air Force Base

Hamilton Collection, The

Hamilton College

Hamilton Grange National Memorial

Hamiltonian

Hamiltonianism

Hamilton Inlet

Hamilton Oil Company Inc.

Hamilton Oil Corporation

Hamilton Philharmonic Orchestra

Hamite

Hamitic

Hamito-Semitic

Hamlet [protagonist in a play of the same name]

Hamlet, The [novel]

Hamlin, Hannibal

Hamlin, Harry

Hamline University

Hamlisch, Marvin

Hammacher Schlemmer, Inc.

Hammarskjöld, Dag

Hammer

Hammer, Armand

Hammer, Mike

Hammermill Foundation

Hammermill Paper Company

Hammerstein, Arthur

Hammerstein, Oscar

Hammerstein, Oscar, 2d

Hammett, Dashiell

Hammett's Learning World

Hammon, Jupiter

Hammond

Hammond, Laurens

Hammond Organ Company

Hammons, John Quentin

Hammonton

Hammurabi

Hamner, Earl, Jr.

Hampden, Walter

Hampden boat

Hampden-Sydney
    College

Hampshire

Hampshire, Susan

Hampshire College

Hampshire Down

Hampshire sheep

Hampshire swine

Hampstead

Hampsten, Andy

Hampton

Hampton, Lionel

Hampton, Slide

Hampton, Wade

Hampton boat

Hampton Court
    Conference

Hampton Court Palace

Hampton National
    Historic Site

Hampton Roads

Hampton Roads
    Conference

Hampton University

Hamsun, Knut

Hamtramck

Hancock, Herbie

Hancock, John

Hancock, Winfield
    Scott

Hancock Fabrics, Inc.

Hand, Learned

Handel, George
    Frideric

Handel and Haydn
    Society

Handelian

Handel Opera

Handleman Company

Handlin, Oscar

H & R Block, Inc.

H & R Block™ tax
    service

Handsome Lake

Hand-Weavers Guild
    of America

Handy, W. C.

Handy Man [*aka
    Homo habilis*]

Han dynasty

Hanes 500

Hanes Hosiery, Inc.

Han Fei Tzu

Hanford

Hanford Works

Hang-chou [*now*
    Hangzhou]

Hangen, Bruce B.

Hanging Gardens of
    Babylon

Hangzhou [*form.*
    Hang-chou]

Hanks, Tom

Hanley, William

Hanley Hills

Hanlon, Lorraine

Hanna, Bill

Hanna, Mark

Hanna-Barbera
    Productions, Inc.

Hannaford Brothers
    Company

Hannah

Hannah, Daryl

Hannah, John

Hannibal

Hannibal-LaGrange
    College

Hanno

Hanoi

Hanoi Gia Lam
    Airport

Hanoi Hilton

Hanotaux, Gabriel

Hanover

Hanover College

Hanoverian

Hanover Insurance
    Company

Hanover International
    Airport

Hansard

Hansard, Luke

Hansa yellow

Hansberry, Lorraine

Hans Brinker

Hans Christian
    Andersen Medal

Hanscom Air Force
    Base

Hanseatic

Hanseatic League

Hänsel *often* Hansel
    and Gretel

Hansen, Armauer

Hansen, Duane

Hansen, Peter

Hansen's disease

Hansom, J. A.

Hanson, Howard

Hanson, John

Hanukkah *occas.*
    Chanukah

Happiness Is a Warm
    Puppy

Happy Birthday to
    You

Happy Days

Happy Days Are Here Again

Happy Land Social Club

Happy Land Social Club fire

Harahan

Harare

Harbert, John Murdoch, III

Harbin

Harburg, E. Y.

Harcourt Brace Jovanovich, Inc.

Harcum Junior College

Hardcastle and McCormick

Hard Copy

Hardecanute

Hardee's 500

Harden, Marcia Gay

Hardenberg, Friedrich von

Hardie, Mary Jane Hoiles

Hardin

Hardin, John Wesley

Hardin, Ty

Harding, Florence

Harding, Tonya

Harding, Warren G.

Harding University

Harding University Graduate School of Religion

Hardin-Simmons University

Hardin-Simmons University Cowboys

Hardison, Kadeem

Hard Rock Cafe

Hard Times

Hard to Kill

Hardwicke, Sir Cedric

Hardy, Andy

Hardy, Godfrey Harold

Hardy, Joseph Alexander, III

Hardy, Oliver

Hardy, Thomas

Hardy Boys

Hardy-Weinberg Law

Hare, Augustus

Hare and the Tortoise, The

Hare Indian

Hare Krishna

Harewood, Dorian

Hargis, Billy James

Hargitay, Mariska

Hargitay, Mickey

Hargreaves, James

Harkin, Tom

Harkness, Edward

Hark! The Herald Angels Sing

Harlan, John Marshall

Harlan County, USA

Harleian Library

Harleian Manuscripts, The

Harleian Society, The

Harlem [district in New York City; see also Haarlem]

Harlem Globetrotters

Harlemite

Harlem Renaissance

Harlem River

Harlequin

Harlequin Books

Harley, Robert

Harley-Davidson, Inc.

Harley Lyrics

Harley Street

Harlingen

Harlow, Jean

Harman International Industries, Inc.

Harmon, Mark

Harmon, Tom

Harmonicats, The

Harmonist

Harmony

Harmony Society

Harmsworth, Alfred Charles William

Harmsworth, Harold Sidney

Harnack, Adolf von

Harnett, William

Harney Peak

Harnischfegger Industries, Inc.

Harold

Harold Bluetooth

Harold Fairhair

Harold Hardhada

Harold Harefoot

Harold in Italy

Harold Simmons Foundation

Harper, Jessica

Harper, Tess

Harper, Valerie

Harper Brothers, The

HarperCollins Publishers, Inc.

Harper's Bazaar

Harper's Bazaar en
Español

Harpers Bizarre
[musical group]

Harpers Ferry

Harpers Ferry
National Historical
Park

Harper's Index

Harper's Magazine

Harper Woods

Harp Quartet

Harpy, n., pl. Harpies

Harrelson, Woody

Harridge, Will

Harrier II

Harriman, Edward
Henry

Harriman, W. Averell

Harrington, Michael

Harrington, Pat, Jr.

Harrington Institute of
Interior Design

Harrington Park

Harris, Sir Arthur
Travers

Harris, Barbara

Harris, Bucky

Harris, Ed

Harris, Emmylou

Harris, Franco

Harris, Frank

Harris, Joel Chandler

Harris, Julie

Harris, Mark

Harris, Mel

Harris, Neil Patrick

Harris, Patricia
Roberts

Harris, Phil

Harris, Richard

Harris, Rosemary

Harris, Roy

Harris, Thaddeus
William

Harris, Thomas Lake

Harris, Wynonie

Harris Bankcorp, Inc.

Harris Bank
Foundation

Harrisburg

Harrisburg Area
Community College

[Harrisburg] Patriot-
News, The

Harris Corporation

Harris Foundation

Harris Hill

Harrison

Harrison, Benjamin

Harrison, Caroline
Scott

Harrison, George

Harrison, Gregory

Harrison, Peter

Harrison, Rex

Harrison, Wallace K.

Harrison, William
Henry

Harrisonburg

Harrison red

Harrisonville

Harris-Stowe State
College

Harris Survey

Harris Trust and
Savings Bank

Harrods

Harrodsburg

Harrovian

Harrow

Harrowing of Hell

Harry, Debbie

Harry M. Ayers State
Technical College

Harry S Truman
Home and National
Historic Site

Harry S Truman
Library and
Museum

Harry S Truman
Sports Complex

Harsco Corporation

Hart, Albert Bushnell

Hart, Freddie

Hart, Gary

Hart, Johnny

Hart, Lorenz

Hart, Marvin

Hart, Mary

Hart, Moss

Hart, William S.

Hartack, Bill

Harte, Bret

Hartford

Hartford,
Huntington, II

Hartford, John

Hartford City

Hartford Civic Center
Coliseum

Hartford College for
Women

Hartford Convention

Hartford Courant, The

Hartford fern

Hartford Foundation

Hartford Graduate
Center

Hartford Insurance Group

Hartford Insurance Group Foundation

Hartford Life Insurance Company

Hartford Monthly

Hartford Seminary

Hartford/Springfield Bradley International Airport

Hartford State Technical College

Hartford Steam Boiler Inspection and Insurance Company

Hartford Symphony Orchestra

Hartford Whalers

Hartford Wits

Hartigan, Grace

Hartley, Mariette

Hartley, Marsden

Hartman, David

Hartman, Lisa

Hartman, Paul

Hartman, Phil

Hartmann, Eduard von

Hartmann, Nicolai

Hartmarx Charitable Foundation

Hartmarx Corporation

Hart Memorial Trophy

Hartnell College

Hartnett, Gabby

Hartselle

Hartsfield International Airport

Hartsville

Hart to Hart

Hartt School of Music

Hartung, Hans

Hartwell

Hartwick College

Harun al-Rashid

Harunobu

Harvard

Harvard, John

Harvard beets

Harvard Business Review

Harvard Business School Press

Harvard chair

Harvard College Observatory

Harvard Dramatic Club

Harvardian

Harvard Law Review

Harvard Magazine

Harvard Medical School

Harvard Musical Association

Harvard University

Harvard University Crimson

Harvard University Press

Harvesters, The

Harvey

Harvey, Laurence

Harvey, Paul

Harvey, Raymond C.

Harvey, William

Harvey Mudd College

Harvey Wallbanger

Harwood, Vanessa

Harwood Heights

Harz Mountains

Hasbro Children's Foundation

Hasbro Inc.

Hasbrouck Heights

Hasdrubal

Hašek, Jaroslav

Hashemite

Hashimoto's thyroiditis

Hasid, *n.*, *pl.* Hasidim

Hasidism

Haskalah

Haskell

Haskell, Jimmie

Haskell, Peter

Haskell Indian Junior College

Hassam, Childe

Hassel, Odd

Hasselhoff, David

Hasso, Signe

Hastie, William H.

Hastings

Hastings, Bob

Hastings, Don

Hastings, Thomas

Hastings, Warren

Hastings Books, Music and Video

Hastings College

Hastings Law Journal

Hastings-on-Hudson

Hasty Pudding Club

Hasty Pudding show

Hatboro

Hatch, Carl A.

Hatch, Orrin

Hatch Act
Hatchet, Molly
Hatch Political
  Activities Act
Hatfield, Hurd
Hatfield, Mark
Hatfields and McCoys
Hathaway, Anne
HA! The TV Comedy
  Network
Hathor
Hathor column
Hathor-headed
Hathoric
Hatif, Abdul Rahim
Hatlo, Jimmy
Hatta, Mohammed
Hatteras Island
Hattiesburg
Hauer, Rutger
Hauptmann, Bruno
Hauptmann, Gerhart
Hauraki Gulf
Hausa, *n.*, *pl.* Hausa
  or Hausas
Hausa language
Hausa States
Hausdorff space
Haussmann, Georges
Haute-Garonne
Haute-Loire
Haute-Marne
Hautes-Alpes
Haute-Saône
Haute-Savoie
Hautes-Pyrénées
Haute-Vienne
Haut-Rhin
Hauts-de-Seine

Havana
Havana brown
Havana cigar
Hava Nagilah
Havarti cheese
Havasupai
Have Gun Will Travel
Havel
Havel, Václav
Havens, Richie
Haver, June
Haverford College
Haverhill
Havers, Clopton
Haversian canal
Haverstraw
Haviland, John
Havlicek, John
Havoc, June
Havre
Hawaii
Hawaii-Aleutian
  Standard Time
Hawaii-Aleutian Time
Hawaiian
Hawaiian Airlines,
  Inc.
Hawaiian Christmas
  Song
Hawaiian Electric
  Industries, Inc.
Hawaiian Eye
Hawaiian goose
Hawaiian guitar
Hawaiian
  honeycreeper
Hawaiian Islands
Hawaiian shirt
Hawaii Five-O
Hawaii Loa College

Hawaii Pacific
  College
Hawaii Volcanoes
  National Park
Hawke, Ethan
Hawke, Robert
Hawker Siddeley
  Group
Hawkes, John
Hawkeye Institute of
  Technology
Hawkeye State
Hawking, Stephen
Hawkins, Sir Anthony
  Hope
Hawkins, Coleman
Hawkins, Erskine
Hawkins, Jack
Hawkins, Ronnie
Hawkins,
  "Screamin' " Jay
Hawkinsville
Hawks, Howard
Hawksmoor, Nicholas
Hawley, Joseph
Hawley, Willis C.
Hawley-Smoot Tariff
  Act
Hawn, Goldie
Hawthorne
Hawthorne, Nathaniel
Hawthorne effect
Hawthorne Naval
  Ammunition Depot
Hawthorne Race
  Course
Hawthornesque
Hay, John
Haya
Hay-Adams hotel
Hayakawa, Sessue

Hayakawa, S. I.
Hayden
Hayden, Carl
Hayden, Melissa
Hayden, Sophie
Hayden, Sterling
Hayden Planetarium
Haydn, Franz Joseph
Haydn, Michael
Haydn Quartets
Hayek, Fredrich August von
Hayes, Bob
Hayes, Elvin
Hayes, Gabby
Hayes, Helen
Hayes, Isaac
Hayes, Lucy Webb
Hayes, Peter Lind
Hayes, Roland
Hayes, Rutherford B.
Hay-Herrán Treaty
Haymarket
Haymarket Square
Haymarket Square Riot
Haymes, Dick
Haynes, Elwood
Haynes, Henry
Haynes, Roy
Hay-Pauncefort Treaty
Hays
Hays, Arthur Garfield
Hays, Robert
Hays, Will
Haysville
Hay Wain, The
Hayward
Hayward, Leland

Hayward, Susan
Haywood, Big Bill
Haywood, Spencer
Haywood Community College
Hayworth, Rita
Hazard
Hazard Community College
Hazel
Hazel Crest
Hazel Park
Hazelwood
Hazelwood, Joseph
Hazlehurst
Hazleton
Hazlitt, William
H-beam
H. B. Fuller Company
H. B. Fuller Company Foundation
H-bomb
HCA Foundation
Head, Edith
Headline News
Headly, Glenne
Head of the Class
Headroom, Max
Head Start program
Heald Business College
Heald Colleges
Heald 4C's College
Heald Institute of Technology
Healdsburg
Healdton
Health
Health Care Financing Administration

Health Care Property Investors, Inc.
Health Industry Manufacturers Association
Health Promotion Features and Training Consultants
Health Show, The
HEALTHSOUTH Rehabilitation Corporation
HealthWatch
Healy, George
Healy, Mary
Healy, Ted
Heard, John
Hearn, George
Hearn, Lafcadio
Hearne
Hearns, Thomas
Hearst, David Whitmore, Jr.
Hearst, George Randolph, Jr.
Hearst, Patricia
Hearst, Phoebe Apperson
Hearst, Randolph Apperson, Jr.
Hearst, William Randolph
Hearst, William Randolph, Jr.
Hearst Castle
Hearst Corporation, The
Hearst Newspapers
Heart
Heartbreak Ridge

Heart Is a Lonely Hunter, The

Heart of Darkness

Heart of Dixie

Heart of the Matter, The

Heath, Sir Edward

Heath, Percy

Heath, Ted

Heathcliff

Heather

Heatherton, Joey

Heathman

Heathrow Airport

Heavenly City

Heaviside, Oliver

Heaviside-Kennelly layer

Heaviside layer

Heaviside unit function

Hebbel, Friedrich

Hebbronville

Hébert, Jacques René

Hebraic

Hebraism

Hebraist

Hebraistic

Hebrew

Hebrew-Aramaic

Hebrew calendar

Hebrew College

Hebrew Immigrant Aid Society

Hebrew language

Hebrew literature

Hebrew National™ meats

Hebrew Theological College

Hebrew Union College

Hebrew Union College Press

Hebrew University

Hebrides

Hebron

Hecate

Hecatean

Hecht, Ben

Heckart, Eileen

Heckle and Jeckle

Hector

Hector International Airport

Hecuba

Hedda Gabler

Hedgerow Theatre

Hedin, Sven Anders

Hedison, David

Hedren, Tippi

Hee Haw

Heem, Cornelius

Heem, Jan

Heemskerck, Maarten

Heflin, Howell

Heflin, Van

Hefner, Christie Ann

Hefner, Hugh

Hefner, Kimberley

Hefner-Alteneck, Friedrich von

Hefner candle

Hefner lamp

Hefti, Neal

Hegel, Georg Wilhelm Friedrich

Hegelian

Hegelian dialectic

Hegelianism

Hegira *occas.* hegira

Heian

Heidegger, Martin

Heidelberg

Heidelberg Catechism

Heidelberg College

Heidelberg jaw

Heidelberg man

Heiden, Eric

Heidenstam, Verner von

Heidi

Heidi Chronicles, The

Heidt, Horace

Heifer Project International

Heifetz, Jascha

Heilmann, Harry

Heimlich, Henry J.

Heimlich maneuver

Heimlich Maneuver™ educational program

Heine, Heinrich

Heine-Borel theorem

Heinlein, Robert A.

Heinz, Henry J.

Heinz, Teresa F.

Heinz Southern 500

Heisenberg, Werner

Heisenberg's indeterminacy principle

Heisenberg's uncertainty principle

Heisman, John

Heisman Memorial Trophy

Heiss, Carol

Hekla

HeLa cell
Held, Anna
Held, John, Jr.
Held, Julius
Helen
Helena
Helena, Saint
Helena National
  Forest
Helene Curtis
  Industries, Inc.
Helene Fuld School of
  Nursing
Helen Hayes Theater
Helen Keller
  International, Inc.
Helen Keller Services
  for the Blind
Helen of Troy
Helgoland
Helicon
Helio
Heliopolis
Helix
Helldorado Festival
  and Rodeo
Hellenic
Hellenic College—
  Holy Cross Greek
  Orthodox School of
  Theology
Hellenism
Hellenist
Hellenistic
Hellenistic civilization
Heller, Joseph
Heller, Walter
Hellertown
Hellespont
Helleu, Paul César
Hellfire missile

Hell Gate
Hell Gate Bridge
Hellman, Lillian
Hello, Dolly [song]
Hello, Dolly! [play]
Hell's *often* Hells
  Angels
Hells Canyon
Hell's Kitchen
Hellzapoppin
Helmand
Helmerich and Payne,
  Inc.
Helme Tobacco
  Company
Helmholtz, Hermann
  von
Helmholtz free energy
Helmholtz function
Helmholtzian
Helmond, Katherine
Helms, Jesse
Helms, Richard
Helmsley, Harry B.
Helmsley, Leona M.
Helmsley Enterprises
  Inc.
Helmsley Hotels
Helmsley Palace
Heloise [given name]
Heloise *occas.* Héloïse
  [of Abelard and
  Heloise]
Help Abolish Legal
  Tyranny
Help Hospitalized
  Veterans
Helprin, Mark
Helsinki
Helsinki Accords

Helsinki-Vantao
  International
  Airport
Helsinki Watch
Helvetia
Helvetian
Helvetic
Helvetic Republic
Helvétius, Claude
  Adrien
Hemans, Felicia
Hemet
Hemichordata
Hemingway, Ernest
Hemingway, Margot
  [*form.* Margaux]
Hemingway, Mariel
Hemion, Dwight
Hemisfair Arena
Hemmings, David
Hemmings Motor
  News
Hémon, Louis
Hempstead
Hemsley, Sherman
Henderson
Henderson, Brice
Henderson, Fletcher
Henderson, Florence
Henderson, Ray
Henderson, Rickey
Henderson, Skitch
Henderson
  Community College
Henderson State
  University
Hendersonville
Hendrix, Jimi
Hendrix College
Henie, Sonja

Henley, William
Ernest

Henley Group, Inc.,
The

Henley-on-Thames

Hennepin, Louis

Henner, Marilu

Henning, Doug

Henny-Penny

Henreid, Paul

Henri, Robert

Henrietta

Henry

Henry, Buck

Henry, John

Henry, O.

Henry, Patrick

Henry, Will

Henry Beauclerc

Henry E. Huntington
Library and Art
Gallery

Henryetta

Henry Ford
Community College

Henry Ford Museum
and Greenfield
Village

Henry Holt and
Company, Inc.

Henry J. Kaiser
Family Foundation,
The

Henry of Burgundy

Henry of Flanders

Henry of Huntingdon

Henry of Lancaster

Henry of Navarre

Henry of Portugal

Henry Pu Yi *var. of*
Pu Yi

Henry's law

Henry Street
Settlement

Henry the Fowler

Henry the Great

Henry the Lion

Henry the Minstrel

Henry the Navigator

Henry the Proud

Henson, Jim

Henson, Matthew A.

Henty, George Alfred

Henze, Hans Werner

hepatitis A

hepatitis B

hepatitis C

Hepburn, Audrey

Hepburn, Katharine

Hephaestus

Hephzibah

Heppenheimer, T.

Hepplewhite

Hepplewhite, George

Heptateuch

Hepworth, Dame
Barbara

Hera

Heraclitean

Heracliteanism

Heraclitus [Greek
philosopher]

Heraclius [Byzantine
emperor]

Heralds' College

Heralds' Office

Hérault

Herb, Marvin

Herb Alpert and the
Tijuana Brass

Herbart, Johann
Friedrich

Herbartarian

Herbert, A. P.

Herbert, Frank

Herbert, George

Herbert, Henry

Herbert, Hugh

Herbert, Victor

Herbert Hoover
National Historic
Site

Herbert of Cherbury

Herblock

herb Paris, *n., pl.*
herbs Paris

herb Robert, *n., pl.*
herbs Robert

Herculean

Hercules

Hercules and Antaeus

Hercules at the
Crossroads

Hercules beetle

Hercules'-club

Hercules cluster

Hercules Computer
Technology, Inc.

Hercules Inc.

Hercules' Pillars

Herculon™

Herder, Johann
Gottfried von

Hereford

Hereford cattle

Herefordshire

Herero, *n., pl.* Herero
or Hereros

Here's Lucy

Hergesheimer, Joseph

Her Imperial Majesty

Herington
Heritage College
Heritage Features
  Syndicate
Heritage Foundation,
  The
Heritage USA
Herkimer
Herkimer, Nicholas
Herkimer County
  Community College
Herlihy, Ed
Herlihy, James Leo
Her Majesty
Her Majesty's Service
Her Majesty's Ship
Her Majesty's
  Stationery Office
Herman, Babe
Herman, Billy
Herman, Jerry
Herman, Pee-Wee
Herman, Woody
Herman Miller, Inc.
Hermann-Mauguin
  symbol
Herman's Hermits
Hermes
Hermetic books
Hermione
Hermiston
Hermitage
Hermitage Museum
Hermite, Charles
Hermite equation
Hermitian conjugation
Hermitian matrix
Hermit Kingdom
Hermit of Saint
  Augustine

Hermosa Beach
Hermosillo
Hernández, José
Hernández, Miguel
Herndon, William
  Henry
Herne, James A.
Hero
Hero and Leander
Herod
Herod Agrippa
Herod Antipas
Herodian
Herodias
Herodotus
Heroic Age
Heroic Captive, The
Hérold, Louis Joseph
Hero of Alexandria
Herophilus
Hero's formula
Herr, *n., pl.* Herren,
  English Herrs
Herrera, Francisco de
Herrick, Robert
Herriman, George
Herrin
Herriot, Edouard
Herriot, James
Herrmann, Bernard
Herrmann, Edward
Her Royal Highness
Herschel, Sir John
  Frederick William
Herschel, Sir William
Herschensohn, Bruce
Hersey, John
Hershey
Hershey, Barbara

Hershey Bar™
Hershey Foods
  Corporation
Hershey Foods
  Corporation Fund
Hershey's™ chocolate
Hershfield, Harry
Hershiser, Orel
Hersholt, Jean
Hertford
Hertfordshire
Hertz, Gustav
Hertz, Heinrich
  Rudolph
Hertz Corporation,
  The
Hertz effect
Hertzian
Hertzian wave
Hertzsprung, Ejnar
Hertzsprung-Russell
  diagram
Hertz Systems Inc.
Herzberg, Gerhard
Herzing Institute
Herzl, Theodor
Herzog, Chaim
Herzog, Werner
Herzog, Whitey
Herzog Anton Ulrich
  Museum
Heshvan
Hesiod
Hesiodic
Hesperia
Hesperian
Hesperides
Hesperus
Hess, Leon
Hess, Dame Myra

Hess, Rudolf

Hess, Troy

Hesse, Eva

Hesse, Hermann

Hesse-Kassel

Hesselman engine

Hesseman, Howard

Hesser College

Hessian

Hessian boot

Hessian fly

Hessische Landesbank-Girozentrale

Hess's Department Stores, Inc.

Hesston College

Hestia

Heston, Charlton

Hesychius of Alexandria

Hetch Hetchy Valley

Heteroousian

Heublein Foundation

Heublein, Inc.

Heusler, Conrad

Heusler alloy

Hevel, Johannes

Hevelian halo

Hewanorra International Airport

Hewett, Christopher

Hewlett, Maurice Henry

Hewlett, William Redington

Hewlett-Packard Company

Hewlett-Packard Company Foundation

Hexateuch

Heydrich, Reinhard

Heyerdahl, Thor

Heyman, Samuel J.

Heyrovsky, Jaroslav

Heyse, Paul

Heyward, DuBose

(Hey Won't You Play) Another Somebody Done Somebody Wrong Song

Heywood, Eddie

Heywood, John

Heywood, Thomas

Hezbollah

Hezekiah

H. F. Ahmanson and Company

HH-53B Super Jolly Green Giant

H-hinge

H-hour

HH-60 Blackhawk

HH-60J Jayhawk

Hialeah

Hialeah Park Race Track

Hi and Lois

Hiawatha

Hiawatha National Forest

Hibbing

Hibernia

Hibernian

Hibernia National Bank

Hibernianism

Hibernicism

Hiberno-Saxon

Hichens, Robert Smythe

Hickam Air Force Base

Hickel, Walter J.

Hickey, James Aloysius Cardinal

Hickman, Darryl

Hickman, Dwayne

Hickok, Wild Bill

Hickory

Hickory Hills

Hicks, Edward

Hicks, Elias

Hicks, Granville

Hicks, Thomas

Hicksite

Hickson, Joan

Hicksville

Hicks yew

Hidalgo

Hidalgo, Juan

Hidalgo y Costilla, Miguel

Hidatsa, *n.*, *pl.* Hidatsa or Hidatsas

Hide-A-Bed™

Hideki Tojo

Hideyoshi

Higginbotham, J.

Higgins, Andrew J.

Higgins, Joel

Higgins, William R.

Higginson, Thomas Wentworth

Higginsville

High Chaparral, The

High Church

High Churchman, *n.*, *pl.* High Churchmen

Highet, Gilbert

High German

High Holiday

High Holy Day

Highland

Highland Community College

Highlander

Highland Falls

Highland fling

Highland Heights

Highland Park

Highland Park Community College

Highlands, the

Highlights for Children

Highline Community College

High Mass

High Noon

High Point

High Point College

High Renaissance

High School

High Self-Esteem Toys Corporation

High Tatra

High-Tech Institute

High Times

Hightstown

High Twelve International

Highway 101

Highway Patrol

Highway to Heaven

Highwood

High Wycombe

Hilarius *or* Hilarus, Saint

Hilary of Arles, Saint

Hilary of Poitiers, Saint

Hilbert, David

Hilbert College

Hilbert cube

Hilbert space

Hilda, Saint

Hildegarde

Hill, Ambrose Powell

Hill, Anita

Hill, Arthur

Hill, Benny

Hill, Calvin

Hill, George Roy

Hill, Graham

Hill, James Jerome

Hill, Joe

Hill, Margaret Hunt

Hill, Pamela

Hill, Phil

Hill, Robin

Hill, Sandy

Hill, Steven

Hill Air Force Base

Hillary

Hillary, Sir Edmund P.

Hillbilly Jim

Hillbilly Joe

Hill College

Hillcrest Heights

Hillel

Hillel Foundation

Hillel the Elder

Hillenbrand, Daniel A.

Hillenbrand, W. August

Hillenbrand Industries, Inc.

Hiller, Dame Wendy

Hillerman, John

Hillerman, Tony

Hilliard

Hillis, Margaret

Hillman, Henry Lea

Hillman, Howard Butcher

Hillman, Sidney

Hillman, Tatnall Lea

Hill of Tara

Hill reaction

Hills, Carla

Hillsboro [* IL; KS; MO; ND; OH; OR; TX]

Hillsborough [* CA; NC; NH]

Hillsborough Community College

Hillsdale

Hillsdale College

Hillsdale Free Will Baptist College

Hillside

Hillside Strangler

Hill Street Blues

Hillyer, Robert

Hilo '

Hilo International Airport

Hilton, Conrad N.

Hilton, James

Hilton and Towers

Hilton Hotel

Hilton Hotels Corporation

Hilton Inn

Hilton International Nile Cruises

Hilton on Hilton Square

Himalaya

Himalaya berry

Himalaya Mountains

Himalayan

Himalayan fleabane

Himalayan musk rose

Himalayan tahr

Himalayas, the

Himes, Chester

Himmler, Heinrich

Hinckley, John, Jr.

Hindemith, Paul

Hindenburg

Hindenburg, Paul von

Hindenburg disaster

Hindenburg Line

Hindi

Hinds Community College

Hindu occas. Hindoo

Hindu calendar

Hindu iconography

Hinduism

Hindu Kush

Hindu Kush Mountains

Hindu music

Hindus, Maurice Gerschon

Hindustan

Hindustani occas. Hindostani

Hines, Earl Fatha

Hines, Gregory

Hines, Jerome

Hingle, Pat

Hinsdale

Hinshelwood, Sir Cyril Norman

Hinton

Hinton, S. E.

Hinton, William A.

Hipparchus

Hippocrates

Hippocratic

Hippocratic oath

Hippodrome Theatre

Hippolyta occas. Hippolyte

Hippolytus

Hippolytus, Saint

Hiram

Hiram College

Hiram Walker-Gooderham and Worts Ltd.

Hiranuma, Kiichiro

Hirchsprung's disease

Hirohito

Hiroshige, Ando

Hiroshima

Hirsch, Elroy "Crazylegs"

Hirsch, Judd

Hirschfeld, Al

Hirschhorn, Joel

Hirshhorn, Joseph H.

Hirshhorn Museum and Sculpture Garden

Hirt, Al

His Imperial Majesty

His Majesty

His Majesty's Service

His Majesty's Ship

His Majesty's Stationery Office

Hispanic

Hispanic-American

Hispanicism

Hispanicist

Hispanic Link News Service

Hispanic USA

Hispaniola

Hispanist

Hispano

His Royal Highness

Hiss, Alger

Histadrut

Hitachi Foundation

Hitachi, Ltd

Hitchcock, Alfred

Hitchcock, Lambert

Hitchcock chair

Hitchhiker's Guide to the Galaxy, The

Hitler, Adolf

Hitlerism

Hitlerite

Hit Parade, The

Hittite

Hittite art

Hittitology

Hittorf dark space

Hittorf method

Hit Video USA

Hiwassee College

HI-Y club

H. J. Heinz Company

H. J. Heinz Company Foundation

H. M. Gousha™ travel books and maps

HMS Beagle

HMS Bounty

HMS Pinafore

HMS Titanic

Ho, Don

Hoban, James

Hoban, Lillian

Hoban, Russell

Hobart

Hobart and William Smith Colleges

Hobbema, Meindert

Hobbes, Thomas

Hobbesian

Hobbism

Hobbist

Hobbit, The

Hobbs

Hobbs Act

Hobby, Oveta Culp

Hobe Sound

Hobe Sound Bible College

Hobey Baker Award

Hoboken

Hobson, John Atkinson

Hobson, Laura Zametkin

Hobson, Thomas

Hobson's Choice [play]

Hobson's choice [the thing offered, or nothing]

Hobson State Technical College

Hoccleve, Thomas

Hochhuth, Rolf

Ho Chi Minh

Ho Chi Minh City [*form.* Saigon]

Ho Chi Minh City Airport

Ho Chi Minh Trail

Hockey Digest

Hockey Hall of Fame and Museum

Hockey News

Hocking, William Ernest

Hocking Technical College

Hockney, David

Hodge, Stephanie

Hodges, Gil

Hodges, Johnny

Hodges, Russ

Hodgkin, Sir Allan Lloyd

Hodgkin, Dorothy Crowfoot

Hodgkin, Thomas

Hodgkin's disease

Hodiak, John

Hodler, Ferdinand

Hoe, Richard

Hoechst

Hoechst Celanese Corporation

Hofburg Palace

Hofer, Karl

Hoffa, Jimmy

Hoffa, Portland

Hoffer, Eric

Hoffman, Abbie

Hoffman, Dustin

Hoffman, Gaby

Hoffman, Malvina

Hoffmann, E. T. A.

Hoffmann, Roald

Hoffmann-La Roche Foundation

Hoffmann-La Roche Inc.

Hofmann, Hans

Hofmansthal, Hugo von

Hofstadter, Richard

Hofstra University

Hofstra University Flying Dutchmen

Hogan, Ben

Hogan, Paul

Hogan Family, The

Hogan's Heroes

Hogansville

Hogarth, Burne

Hogarth, William

Hogarth chair

Hogarthian

HO gauge

Hogg, James

Hogrogian, Nonny

Hogwood, Christopher

Hohokam Pima National Monument

Hohokus

Hoiles, Harry Howard

Hoisington

Hokan-Siouan

Hokinson, Helen

Hokkaido

Hokkaido Takushoku Bank, Ltd.

Hokuriku Bank Ltd.

Hokusai

Holarctic

Holbein, Hans the Elder

Holbein, Hans the
  Younger
Holbrook
Holbrook, Hal
Holbrook, Stewart H.
Holden
Holden, Fay
Holden, William
Holder, Geoffrey
Hölder condition
Hölderlin, Johann
Holdredge
Holdridge, Lee
Holger Nielsen
  method
Holiday, Billie
Holiday Bowl
Holiday Corporation
Holiday Inn
Holiday Inn Trav-L-
  Park
Holinshed, Raphael
[Holinshed's]
  Chronicles of
  England, Scotland,
  and Ireland
Holladay, Ben
Holland
Holland, Brian
Holland, Eddie
Holland-America Line
Holland-America Line
  Westours, Inc.
Holland, Dozier and
  Holland
Hollander
Hollander, John
Holland finish
Holland House
Holland Land
  Company

Hollands *occas.*
  Holland gin
Holland Tunnel
Hollerith, Herman
Hollerith card
Hollerith code
Holliday, Doc
Holliday, Jennifer
Holliday, Judy
Holliday, Polly
Hollidaysburg
Hollies, The
Holliman, Earl
Hollings, Ernest
Hollings, Fritz
Hollingsworth,
  John D.
Hollins College
Hollister
Holliston
Hollofil™
Holloman Air Force
  Base
Holloway, Sterling
Hollow Men, The
Holly
Holly, Buddy
Holly, Doyle
Holly Hill
Holly Springs
Holly Springs
  National Forest
Hollywood
Hollywood Argyles,
  The
Hollywood bed
Hollywood Bowl
Hollywooder
Hollywood Foreign
  Press Association

Hollywood Hills
Hollywoodian
Hollywood Inside
  Syndicate
Hollywoodish
Hollywood Park
Hollywood Reporter
Hollywood Squares,
  The
Hollywood Star
  Sidewalk
Hollywood Television
  Theatre
Hollywood Wax
  Museum
Holm, Celeste
Holm, Hanya
Holmes, Jennifer
Holmes, John Haynes
Holmes, Larry
Holmes, Oliver
  Wendell
Holmes, Oliver
  Wendell, Jr.
Holmes, Sherlock
Holmes Brothers, The
Holmes Community
  College
Holmesian
Holmes light
Holnam Inc.
Holocaine™
Holocaust
Holocaust Day
Holocaust Oral
  History Project
Holocene
Holofernes
Holophane™
Holst, Gustav
Holstein

Holstein-Friesian

Holt, Henry

Holt, Jack

Holt, John

Holt, Tim

Holt, Rinehart and Winston, Inc.

Holtz, Lou

Holy Alliance

Holy Apostles College and Seminary

Holy Ark

Holy Bible

Holy City

Holy Communion

Holy Cross College

Holy Eucharist

Holy Family

Holy Family College

Holy Father

Holyfield, Evander

Holy Ghost

Holy Grail

Holy Innocents

Holy Innocents' Day

Holy Island

Holy Joe

Holy Lamb

Holy Land

Holy Land Christian Mission

Holy League

holy Moses

Holy Mysteries

Holy Names College

Holy Office

Holyoke

Holyoke Community College

Holy One

Holy Orders

Holy Roller

Holy Rollerism

Holy Roman Empire

Holy Rood

Holyrood Palace

Holy Sacrament

Holy Saturday

Holy Scripture *often* Holy Scriptures

Holy See

Holy Sepulcher

Holy Spirit

Holy Synod

Holy Thursday

Holy Trinity

Holy Trinity Orthodox Seminary

Holy War *occas.* holy war

Holy Week

Holy Writ

Holy Year

Home

Home Again with Bob Vila

Home Alone

Home & Away

Home Box Office Inc.

Homecoming, The

Home Depot, Inc., The

Homefed Bank

Homeier, Skippy

Home Life Insurance Company

Home Mechanix

Home Office

Home of Franklin D. Roosevelt National Historic Site

Home on the Range

HomeOwner

Homeownership and Opportunity for People Everywhere

Homer

Homer, Winslow

Homer and Jethro

Homeric

Homeric hymns

Homeric laughter

Homeric legend

Homeric simile

Home Rule

Home Savings Association of Kansas City

Home Savings of America

Home Secretary

Home Shopping Network, Inc.

Home Show, The

Homestake Mining Company

Homestead

Homestead Act

Homestead Air Force Base

Homestead National Monument

Homestead Savings

Homestead strike

Home, Sweet Home

Hometown

Homewood

Homochitto National Forest

Homo erectus

Homoiousian

Homoiousianism

Homolka, Oscar

Homoousian

Homoousianism

Homo sapiens

Honda, Soichiro

Honda Motor Company, Ltd.

Hondo

Hondo Air Force Base

Honduran

Honduras

Honea Path

Honecker, Erich

Honegger, Arthur

Honesdale

Honest John

Honey, I Shrunk the Kids

Honeysuckle Bower, The

Honeywell Foundation

Honeywell Inc.

HonFed Bank

Hong Kong

Hong Kong and Shanghai Banking Corporation

Hong Kong International Airport

Hong Kong Stock Exchange

Hon Industries Inc.

Honolulu

Honolulu International Airport

Honolulu Star-Bulletin

Honolulu Symphony Orchestra

Honorius

Honorius, Flavius

Honshu

Honthorst, Gerrit van

Hooch *or* Hoogh, Pieter de

Hood, John Bell

Hood, Raymond

Hood, Thomas

Hood College

Hood River

Hoogh *var. of* Hooch, Pieter de

Hooghly

Hoogstraten, Samuel van

Hooke, Robert

Hooker, John Lee

Hooker, Joseph

Hooker, Richard

Hooker, Thomas

Hooker's green

Hooke's law

Hook of Holland

Hooks, Benjamin L.

Hooks, Jan

Hooks, Robert

Hoopa

Hooper, Harry

Hoopeston

Hoosac Range

Hoosick Falls

Hoosier

Hoosierdom

Hoosier Dome

Hoosier National Forest

Hoosier State

Hoover, Herbert

Hoover, J. Edgar

Hoover Dam [*form.* Boulder Dam]

Hoover Institution on War, Revolution and Peace

Hoover Institution Press

Hooverville

Hope

Hope, Anthony

Hope, Bob

Hope, Laura Lee

Hope College

Hope School

Hopewell

Hopewell Village National Historic Site

Hopi, *n.*, *pl.* Hopi *occas.* Hopis

Hopkin, Mary

Hopkins

Hopkins, Anthony

Hopkins, Bo

Hopkins, Sir Frederick Gowland

Hopkins, Gerard Manley

Hopkins, Harry

Hopkins, Johns

Hopkins, Lightnin'

Hopkins, Mark

Hopkins, Miriam

Hopkinsian

Hopkinsianism

Hopkinson, Francis

Hopkins Syndicate, Inc.

Hopkinsville

Hopkinsville Community College
Hoppe, Willie
Hopper, Dennis
Hopper, DeWolf
Hopper, Edward
Hopper, Edna Wallace
Hopper, Hedda
Hopper, William
hopping John
Hoqiuam
Horace
Horace Heidt and His Musical Knights
Horatian
Horatian ode
Horatio
Horatio Alger Award
Horatio Alger Society
Horatius
Horatius at the Bridge
Horchow catalog
Horchow Mail Order, Inc.
Horgan, Paul
Horizon Cruises
Horizon Healthcare Corporation
Hormisdas, Saint
Horn, Tom
Hornblower, Horatio
Horn Book Magazine, The
Horne, Lena
Horne, Marilyn
Horner, Jack
Horner, William G.
Horner's method
Horner's syndrome
Horn Island

Hornsby, Rogers
Horn Signal Symphony
Hornung, Paul
Horowitz, David
Horowitz, Vladimir
Horry-Georgetown Technical College
Horse Guards
Horse Guards Parade
Horsehead Nebula
Horseheads
Hörselberge Mountains
Horseshoe Bend
Horseshoe Bend National Military Park
Horseshoe Falls
Horsford, Anna Marie
Horsley, Lee
Horst Wessel song
Horszowski, Mieczyslaw
Horta, Victor
Horton, Edward Everett
Horton, Robert
Horton, Willie
Horus
Hosanna
HO scale
Hosea
Hoskins, Bob
Hospital Corporation of America
Hospitaler
Host
Hostetter, Amos Barr, Jr.
Host hotel

Host International
Hotchner, A. E.
Hot Club of France
Hot Club of Paris
Hotel del Coronado
Hôtel des Invalides
Hotel Employees and Restaurant Employees International Union
Hotel Nikko Chicago
Hotels of the World
Hotel 21 East
Hot 1 Baltimore
Hot Rod Magazine
Hot Springs
Hot Springs National Park
Hotspur
Hottentot
Hottentot or Hottentot's bread
Hottentot fig
Houdin, Jean Eugène
Houdini, Harry
Houdon, Jean Antoine
Hough, Emerson
Houghton
Houghton, Amory, Jr.
Houghton, Katharine
Houghton College
Houghton Mifflin Company
Houlton
Houma
Hounsfield, Godfrey Newbold
Houphouët-Boigny, Félix
Hour Magazine

Hour of Power
Housatonic
Housatonic
  Community College
House, Edward M.
House & Garden
House Beautiful
Household Bank
Household
  International Inc.
Houselander, Caryll
Houseman, John
House of Angevin
House of Anjou
House of Aragon
House of Blois
House of Bourbon
House of Bourbon-
  Orléans
House of Burgesses
House of Burgundy
House of Capet
House of Commons
House of Conti
House of Councilors
House of David
House of Delegates
house of God
House of Grimaldi
House of Hanover
House of Hapsburg
House of
  Hohenstaufen
House of
  Hohenzollern
House of Keys
House of Lancaster
House of Lanvin
House of Lords
House of Normandy

House of Orange-
  Nassau
House of Parliament
House of Plantagenet
House of
  Representatives
House of Savoy
House of Saxe-Coburg
  and Gotha
House of Stuart
House of the Seven
  Gables, The
House of Tudor
House of Valois
House of Windsor
House of York
House Party
House That Jack
  Built, The
House Un-American
  Activities
  Committee
Housman, A. E.
Housman, Laurence
Houston
Houston, David
Houston, Sam
Houston, Whitney
[Houston] Astrodome
Houston Astros
Houston Baptist
  University
Houston Baptist
  University Huskies
Houston Chronicle
Houston Community
  College
Houston Graduate
  School of Theology
Houston Grand Opera

Houston Industries
  Inc.
Houston
  Intercontinental
  Airport
Houston Metropolitan
  Magazine
[Houston] Museum of
  Fine Arts
Houston Oilers
Houston Post, The
Houston Rockets
Houston Symphony
  Orchestra
Houyhnhnm
Hovenweep National
  Monument
Hovercraft™
Hovey, Richard
Hovhaness, Alan
Howard
Howard, Bronson
Howard, Catherine
Howard, Cathy
Howard, Chuck
Howard, Clint
Howard, Curly
Howard, Elizabeth
  Jane
Howard, Elston
Howard, Eugene
Howard, Jan
Howard, Jerry
Howard, Joe
Howard, Ken
Howard, Leslie
Howard, Moe
Howard, Robert
  Staples
Howard, Ron
Howard, Roy Wilson

Howard, Shemp
Howard, Sidney
Howard, Tom
Howard, Trevor
Howard, Willie
Howard College
Howard Community
  College
Howard Johnson hotel
Howard Johnson
  restaurant
Howard Law Journal
Howard Payne
  University
Howard Savings Bank
Howard University
Howard University
  Bison
Howard University
  Press
How Are Things in
  Glocca Morra?
Howdy Doody
Howe, Elias
Howe, Gordie
Howe, Irving
Howe, Julia Ward
Howe, Richard
Howe, Samuel G.
Howe, Steve
Howe, Sir William
Howell
Howell, C. Thomas
Howells, William
  Dean
Howes, Sally Ann
Howe truss
How Green Was My
  Valley
Howland Island

Howlin' Wolf
How to Avoid Probate
How to Be a Jewish
  Mother
How to Succeed in
  Business without
  Really Trying
How to Win Friends
  and Influence
  People
Hoxha, Enver
Hoyle, Edmond
Hoyle™ games and
  playing cards
Hoyt, Charles
Hoyt, Henry, Jr.
Hoyt, Monty
Hoyt, Waite
Hrawi, Elias
Hrdlička, Aleš
Hrosvitha *occas.*
  Hrotsvitha
HSBC Holdings
Hsia dynasty
Hsia Kuei
Hsiaokang
  International
  Airport
H-steel
Hua Guofeng
Huang [*form.* Hwang]
Huang Ti
Huascaran
Huastec, *n., pl.*
  Huastec *or*
  Huastecs
Huautla Plateau
Huautla Plateau caves
Hubbard
Hubbard, Cal
Hubbard, Elbert

Hubbard, Freddie
Hubbard, L. Ron
Hubbard, Stanley Stub
Hubbard squash
Hubbard Street Dance
  Company
Hubbell, Carl
Hubbell Inc.
Hubbell Trading Post
  National Historic
  Site
Hubble, Edwin P.
Hubble effect
Hubble's constant
Hubble's law
Hubble Space
  Telescope
Hubble time
Hubel, David Hunter
Hubert H. Humphrey
  Metrodome
Hubertusburg
Hubli-Dharwar
Huckleberry Hound
Huddersfield
Huddersfield Choral
  Society
Huddleston, David
Hudson
Hudson, Henry
Hudson, Keith
Hudson, Rock
Hudson, William H.
Hudson Bay
Hudson City Savings
  Bank
Hudson County
  Community College
Hudson-Essex
  Terraplane
Hudson Falls

Hudson Foods, Inc

Hudsonian curlew

Hudson Institute

Hudson River school

Hudson's Bay blanket

Hudson's Bay Company

Hudson seal

Hudson Strait

Hudson Valley Community College

Hudsonville

Hué

Huerta, Victoriano

Huertas Junior College

Huey Lewis and the News

Hueytown

Huffington, Roy Michael

Huffy Corporation

Huggett Family

Huggins, Miller

Huggins, Nathan I.

Huggins, Sir William

Hughes, Barnard

Hughes, Charles Evans

Hughes, Howard

Hughes, John

Hughes, Langston

Hughes, Richard

Hughes, Rupert

Hughes, Ted

Hughes, Thomas

Hughes, William Morris

Hughes Aircraft Company

Hughes Airwest

Hughes Markets Inc.

Hughes Television Network

Hugh O'Brian Youth Foundation

Hugh of Lincoln, Saint

Hugh of Saint Victor

Hugh the Great

Hugo, Victor

Hugo rose

Huguenot

Huguenotism

Huguenot Wars

Huidobro, Vicente

Hui Tsung

Huizenga, H. Wayne

Huizinga, Johan

Hula Hoop™

Hulce, Tom

Hulk Hogan

Hull

Hull, Bobby

Hull, Cordell

Hull, Henry

Hull, Isaac

Hull, Josephine

Hull House

Humana Foundation

Humana Inc.

Humane Society of the United States

Human Fly

Human Relations Area Files

Humber

Humberside

Humberside International Airport

Humbert

[Humbleback, Denmark] Louisiana Museum

Humboldt

Humboldt, Alexander von

Humboldt, Wilhem von

Humboldt Bay

Humboldt Current

Humboldt Glacier

Humboldt National Forest

Humboldt State University

Hume, David

Humism

Hummel, Johann

Hummel figurine

Hummelstown

Humperdinck, Engelbert

Humphrey, Doris

Humphrey, Hubert H.

Humphreys College

Humphreys Peak

Humpty Dumpty

Humpty Dumpty's Magazine

Hun

Hunan

Hunchback of Notre Dame, The

Hund, Friedrich

Hundred Days

Hundred Years' occas. Hundred Years War

Huneker, James

Hung, Richard Morris
Hungarian
Hungarian brome grass
Hungarian Dances
Hungarian goulash
Hungarian language
Hungarian lilac
Hungarian literature
Hungarian National Museum
Hungarian pointer
Hungarian Reformed Church in America
Hungarian Rhapsodies
Hungary
Hunger Project, The
Hungry Horse Dam
Hungry Horse Reservoir
Hunkers
Hunlike
Hunnicutt, Gayle
Hunnish
Hunnishness
Hunt, Caroline Rose
Hunt, Helen
Hunt, H. L.
Hunt, Holman
Hunt, Johnnie Bryan
Hunt, Leigh
Hunt, Linda
Hunt, Pee Wee
Hunt, Ray Lee
Hunt, Richard M.
Hunt, William Holman
Hunt, William Morris
Hunt Cantata
Hunter, Catfish

Hunter, Evan
Hunter, Holly
Hunter, Ivory Joe
Hunter, Jeffrey
Hunter, Kim
Hunter, Rita
Hunter, Ross
Hunter, Tab
Hunter Army Air Field
Hunter College
Hunter-Gault, Charlayne
Hunt for Red October, The
Huntingburg
Huntingdon [* PA; TN; Quebec; * see also Huntington]
Huntingdon College
Huntingdonshire
Huntington [* IN; NY; WV; see also Huntingdon]
Huntington, Collis Porter
Huntington, George
Huntington, Henry E.
Huntington, Samuel
Huntington Bancshares Inc.
Huntington Beach
Huntington Botanical Garden
Huntington College
Huntington Junior College of Business
Huntington National Bank
Huntington Park
Huntington's chorea

Huntington's disease
Huntington's Disease Society of America, Inc.
Huntington Station
Huntington Woods
Huntley, Chet
Hunt Quartet
Huntsman, Jon Meade
Huntsville
Hunt Symphony
Hunyadi, János
Hunza
Huon pine
Hupeh [now Hupei]
Hupmobile
Hurd, Peter
Hurlburt Field
Hurok, Sol
Huron, n., pl. Huron or Hurons
Huron-Manistee National Forest
Huron University
Hurst
Hurst, Fannie
Hurst, Rick
Hurston, Zora Neale
Hurt, John
Hurt, Mary Beth
Hurt, Mississippi John
Hurt, William
Husak, Gustav
Hu Shih
Husing, Ted
Husky, Ferlin
Husky Oil Ltd.
Huss, John
Hussein, Saddam

Husserl, Edmund
Hussey, Olivia
Hussey, Ruth
Hussian School of Art
Hussite
Hussite Wars
Hussitism
Husson College
Hustler
Huston, Anjelica
Huston, John
Huston, Walter
Huston-Tillotson
College
Hutchins, Robert
Maynard
Hutchinson
Hutchinson, Anne
Hutchinson, John
Hutchinson, Thomas
Hutchinson
Community College
Hutchinsonian
Hutchinson Naval Air
Base
Hutchison Whampoa
Ltd.
Hüther, Julius

Hutter, Jakob
Hutterian Brethren
Hutterite
Hutton, Betty
Hutton, Lauren
Hutton, Tim
Huxleian
Huxley, Aldous
Huxley, Andrew
Fielding
Huxley, Sir Julian
Huxley, T. H.
Hu Yaobang [*form.*
Hu Yao-Pang]
Huygens, Christiaan
Huygens eyepiece
Huygens principle
Huysmans, Cornelis
Huysmans, Jacob
Huysmans, Joris
Huysum, Jan van
Hwang [*now* Huang]
Hyacinthus
Hyannis
Hyannis Port
Hyatt, Joel
Hyatt Corporation

Hyatt Hotel
Hyatt Hotels and
Resorts
Hyatt Legal Services
Hyatt Regency Grand
Cypress
Hyatt Regency Hotel
Hyatt Regency
Westshore
Hyattsville
Hyde, Douglas
Hyde, Edward
Hyde Park
Hyderabad
Hyde-White, Wilfrid
Hydra
Hydrus
Hyginus, Saint
Hyland, Brian
Hyland, Diana
Hyman, Earle
Hymen
Hyperion
Hypermnestra
Hypnos
Hypsicles of
Alexandria
Hyundai Group

I

Iacocca, Lee

Iago

I Am a Fugitive from a Chain Gang

I Am Curious (Yellow)

IAM Presence

IAM Religious Activity

Ian

Ian, Janis

Ibadan

Ibarbourou, Juana de

I beam

Iberia

Iberia Airlines of Spain

Iberian

Iberian Gates

Iberian Mountains

Iberian Peninsula

Ibert, Jacques

Iberville, Sieur d'

Ibizan hound

IBM Credit Corporation

IBM Systems Journal

Ibn Saud

Ibo, *n.*, *pl.* Ibo *or* Ibos

Ibolium privet

Ibota privet

IBP, Inc.

Ibsen, Henrik

Ibsenian

Ibsenism

Ibsenite

Icahn, Carl

I Can't Stop Loving You

Icaria

Icarian

Icarian Sea

Icarus

Ice Age

Ice Cube

Iceland

Icelandair

Icelander

Icelandic

Icelandic language

Icelandic literature

Iceland moss

Iceland poppy

Iceland spar

Icelus

Iceman Cometh, The

Ice Observation Service

Ice-T

Ichabod

I Ching

Ickes, Harold

I, Claudius

ICS Center for Degree Studies

Ida

Idabel

Idaho

Idahoan

Idaho Cities

Idaho Falls

Idaho National Engineering Laboratory

Idaho panhandle

Idaho potato

Idaho Potato Commission

Idaho Power Company

Idaho State University

Idaho State University Bengals

IDB Communications Group Inc.

ID card

Ideas for Better Living

IDEA: The Association for

Fitness Professionals
Ides of March
Idiot, The
Iditarod Trail
Iditarod Trail Sled Dog Race
Idle, Eric
Idlewild Airport [*now* John F. Kennedy International Airport]
Ido
Idoism
Idoist
Idol, Billy
I Dream of Jeannie
Idris
IDS Financial Corporation
IDS Life Insurance Company
Idylls of the King, The
IEEE Press
If Life Is a Bowl of Cherries—What Am I Doing in the Pits?
Ifuago, *n., pl.* Ifuago *or* Ifuagos
I G A, Inc.
Iglesias, Julio
Ignatius, Saint
Ignatius of Constantinople
Ignatius of Loyola, Saint
Igor
Igorot, *n., pl.* Igorot *or* Igorots
Iguassú

Iguassú Falls
Iguvine Tables
I Have a Dream Foundation
Ijssel *or* Issel *or* Yssel
Ijssel *or* Issel *or* Yssel Lake
Ike and Tina Turner
Ike jacket
Ikhnaton *var. of* Akhenaton
Il Duce
Ile-de-France
Il Giorgione
Iliad, The
Iliadic
Iliff School of Theology
Ilitch, Michael
Ille-et-Vilaine
Illilouette Falls
Illimani
Illini Books™
Illinoian
Illinois
Illinoisan
Illinois Bell Telephone Company
Illinois Benedictine College
Illinois Central College
Illinois Central Corporation
Illinois Central Railroad Company
Illinois College
Illinois College of Optometry

Illinois Eastern Community Colleges
Illinoisian
Illinois [Indian], *n., pl.* Illinois
Illinois Institute of Technology
Illinois Magazine
Illinois News Network
Illinois Power Company
Illinois State University
Illinois State University Redbirds
Illinois Technical College
Illinois Tool Works Foundation
Illinois Tool Works Inc.
Illinois Valley Community College
Illinois Waterway
Illinois Wesleyan University
Illuminating Engineering Society of North America
Illustrated London News, The
Illyria
Illyrian
Il Moretto
Ilocano, *n., pl.* Ilocano *or* Ilocanos
I Love Lucy
Il Penseroso
Il Perugino
Il Pesellino
Il Rosso
IL-78 Midas

IL-76 Mainstay
Il Sodoma
IL-38 May
Il Trovatore
IL-20 Coot-A
IL-28 Beagle
IL-22 Coot-B
Ilyichev, Leonid F.
Ilyushin, Sergëi Vladimoroic
Ilyushin Il62
Imagination Stations Network, The
I. Magnin
Imamite
Iman
Imasco Ltd.
IMCERA Group Inc.
IMC Fertilizer Group, Inc.
IMC Foundation
Imhotep
Imitation of Christ, The
Immaculata College
Immaculate Conception [event]
Immaculate Conception, The [painting]
Immaculate Conception Seminary of Seton Hall University
Immaculate Heart
Immaculate Mary
Immanuel
Immelmann
Immelmann, Max
Immigration and Nationality Act

Immigration and Naturalization Service
IMN/Eastman
I'm Not Rappaport
Imo Industries Inc.
Impact of Science on Society
Imperial
Imperial Beach
Imperial bushel
Imperial Chemical Industries
Imperial Council of the Ancient Arabic Order of the Nobles of the Mystic Shrine for North America
Imperial eagle
Imperial Federal Savings Association
Imperial 400™ motel
Imperial *occas.* imperial gallon
Imperial Holiday
Imperial Holly Corporation
Imperial House™ motel
Imperial Life Assurance Company of Canada
Imperial Oil Ltd.
Imperial Valley
Imperial Valley College
Implement Workers of America
Importance of Being Earnest, The
Impressions, The

Improved Benevolent Protective Order of Elks of the World
Improved Order of Red Men
Inauguration Day
In Business
Inca
Incan
Incarnate Word College
Inchcape Rock
Inchon
inCider/A+
Inc. Magazine
In Cold Blood
Inco Ltd.
Income Opportunities
In Court Television
Incredible Hulk, The
In Defense of Animals
Independence
Independence Bowl
Independence Community College
Independence Day
Independence Hall
Independence National Historical Park
Independent Association of Questioned Documents Examiners
Independent Bankers Association of America
Independent College Funds of America
Independent Federation of Flight Attendants

Independent Florida Agrinet

Independent Fundamental Churches of America

Independent Living

Independent Order of Foresters

Independent Order of Odd Fellows

Independent Order of Vikings

Independent Subway

Index Expurgatorius, *n.*, *pl.* Indices Expurgatorius

Index Librorum Prohibitorum, *n.*, *pl.* Indices Librorum Prohibitorum

Index of Leading Economic Indicators

Index on Censorship

India

India chintz

India drugget

India ink

Indiaman, *n.*, *pl.* Indiamen

Indian

Indiana

Indiana, Robert

Indiana Army Ammunition Plant

Indiana ballot

Indiana Bell Telephone Company

Indiana Central University

Indian Dunes National Lakeshore

Indian agency

Indian agent

Indiana Harbor

Indiana Institute of Technology

Indiana Jones and the Last Crusade

Indiana Jones and the Temple of Doom

Indiana Pacers

Indianapolis

Indianapolis Colts

Indianapolis 500

Indianapolis 500 Festival

Indianapolis International Airport

Indianapolis Monthly

Indianapolis Motor Speedway

Indianapolis Motor Speedway Hall of Fame

Indianapolis Motor Speedway Museum

Indianapolis News, The

Indianapolis Raceway Park

Indianapolis Speedrome

Indianapolis Star, The

Indian apple

Indian architecture

Indiana Review

Indian art

Indiana State University

Indiana State University Sycamores

Indian Territory

Indiana University

Indiana University East

Indiana University Hoosiers

Indiana University Northwest

Indiana University of Pennsylvania

Indiana University Press

Indiana University— Purdue University

Indiana University Southeast

Indiana Vocational Technical College

Indiana Wesleyan University

Indian balsam

Indian bison

Indian bread

Indian breadroot

Indian cherry

Indian club

Indian cobra

Indian corn

Indian cress

Indian cup

Indian currant

Indian Desert

Indian elephant

Indian Empire

Indian fig

Indian file

Indian giver

Indian giving

Indian hawthorn

Indian header

Indian hemp

Indian Hill

Indian Hills
  Community College

Indian hippo

Indianian

Indianism

Indian jujube

Indian Law Resource
  Center

Indian lettuce

Indian licorice

Indian literature

Indian lotus

Indian madder

Indian mallow

Indian meal

Indian millet

Indian mulberry

Indian Mutiny

Indian National
  Congress

Indian nut

Indian Ocean

Indianola

Indian paintbrush

Indian philosophy

Indian pink

Indian pipe

Indian pitcher

Indian potato

Indian pudding

Indian red

Indian Removal Act

Indian Reorganization

Indian rice

Indian River

Indian River
  Community College

Indian Runner

Indian salad

Indian sanicle

Indian shot

Indian sign

Indian silk

Indian Space Research
  Organization

Indian Springs Air
  Force Base

Indian States

Indian subcontinent

Indian summer

Indian tea

Indian Territory

Indian tobacco

Indian turnip

Indian wars

Indian wolf

Indian wrestling

Indian yellow

India-Pakistan wars

India paper

India print

India *or* india rubber

India- *or* india-rubber
  tree

India silk

India wheat

Indic

Indienne

Indies

Indio

Indo-Aryan

Indo-British

Indochina *occas.*
  Indo-China *or* Indo
  China

Indo-Chinese, *n., pl.*
  Indo-Chinese

Indo-European

Indo-Germanic

Indo-Hittite

Indo-Iranian

Indo-Malayan

Indonesia

Indonesian

Indoor Sports Club

Indo-Pacific

Indre

Indre-et-Loire

In Dubious Battle

Indurain, Miguel

Indus

Indus civilization

Industrial Bank of
  Japan, Ltd.

Industrial Designers
  Society of America

Industrial Health
  Foundation

Industrial Revolution

Industrial Union of
  Marine and
  Shipbuilding
  Workers of America

Industrial Workers of
  the World

Industrial World

Industry Week

Indus Valley

Indus Valley
  civilization

in Dutch

IndyCar *or* Indy Car

INFORM

Information Computer
  Systems Institute

Information Exchange, The

Information Industry Association

Information Week

InfoWorld

Ing C. Olivetti and Company

Inge, William

Inge, William Ralph

Ingelow, Jean

Ingels, Marty

Ingersoll, Robert

Ingersoll-Rand Company

Ingleside

Inglewood

In God We Trust

Ingram, Erskine Bronson

Ingram, James

Ingram, Luther

Ingram, Rex

Ingres, Jean Auguste Dominique

Initial Defense Satellite Communications System

Initial Teaching Alphabet

Inkatha Freedom Party

Ink Spots, The

Inkster

Inland Container Corporation Foundation

Inland Marine Underwriters Association

Inland Sea

Inland Steel Industries, Inc.

Inland Steel-Ryerson Foundation

in like Flynn

In Living Color

Inn

Inner Hebrides

Inner Light

Inner Light Foundation

Inner Mongolia

Inner Peace Movement

Inner Temple

Inner Word

Inness, George

I.N.N. News

Innocent

Innocent, The

Innocent I, Saint

Innocents' Day

Inn on the Park

Innsbruck

Inns of Court

Inouye, Daniel

In Performance at Wolf Trap

In Praise of Folly

Inquisition

INSA, The International Service Association for Health

In Search of

In Search of Excellence

Inside Chicago

Inside Detective

Inside Edition

Inside Hollywood

Inside Passage

Inside Sports

Inside Washington

Insilco Corporation

Inspiration Resources Corporation

Institut de France

Institute for a Drug-Free Workplace

Institute for Advanced Study

Institute for American Values

Institute for Christian Education

Institute for Defense Analyses

Institute for Humane Studies

Institute for Scientific Information

Institute of American Indian Arts Museum

Institute of Cultural Affairs, The

Institute of Design and Construction

Institute of Electrical and Electronics Engineers

Institute of Electronic Technology

Institute of Environmental Sciences

Institute of France

Institute of Funeral Service

Institute of Gas Technology

Institute of General Semantics

Institute of Industrial Engineers

Institute of International Education

Institute of Management Consultants

Institute of Mathematical Statistics

Institute of Nautical Archaeology

Institute of Navigation

Institute of Paper Science and Technology

Institute of Space and Astronautical Science

Institute of Textile Technology

Institute of Transportation Engineers

Instituto Comercial de Puerto Rico Junior College

Instituto Tecnico Comercial Junior College

Instructor Magazine

Insular Celtic

Insull, Samuel

Insurance Institute for Highway Safety

Insurance Institute of America

Integrated Missile Early Warning Satellite

Integrated Resources Life Insurance Company

Intel Corporation

Intel Foundation

Intelsat

Interaction: American Council for Voluntary International Action

Interactive Network

Interaid Inc./Interaid International

Inter-American

Inter-American Development Bank

Inter-American Highway

Inter-American University of Puerto Rico

Interavia

Interboro Institute

Interborough Rapid Transit

INTERCO Inc.

INTERCO Inc. Charitable Trust

Intercollegiate Association of Amateur Athletes of America

Intercollegiate Ice Hockey Association

Intercontinental Media Services, Ltd.

Interdenominational Theological Center

Interfaith Medical Center School of Nursing

Interfinance Credit

Interfirst Plaza Tower

Interflora British Unit

Interflora, Inc.

Intergraph Corporation

Interior Designers Institute

Interior Salish

Interlake Corporation, The

Interlake Foundation

Interlaken

Interlingua

Interlochen

Interlochen Arts Academy

Intermedia News and Feature Service

Intermed-USA, Inc.

Internal Revenue Service

International Academy of Merchandising and Design

International Aerospace Museum Hall of Fame

International Affairs

International Air Line Employees Association

International Airline Passengers Association

International Air Line Pilots Association

International Air Transport Association

International Al Jolson Society

International Alliance of Theatrical Stage Employees and Moving Picture Machine Operators of the United States and Canada

International Amateur Athletic Foundation

International Amateur Radio Union

International Association for Hydrogen Energy

International Association for Identification

International Association for Pollution Control

International Association of Bridge, Structural and Ornamental Iron Workers

International Association of Business Communicators

International Association of Chiefs of Police

International Association of Correctional Officers

International Association of Educators for World Peace

International Association of Fairs and Expositions

International Association of Fire Chiefs

International Association of Fire Fighters

International Association of Lions Clubs, The

International Association of Machinists and Aerospace Workers

International Association of Poets, Playwrights, Editors, Essayists, and Novelists

International Association of Professional Bureaucrats

International Association of Rebekah Assemblies, IOOF

International Association of Registered Financial Planners

International Association of the Wall and Ceiling Industries

International Association of Torch Clubs

International Atomic Energy Agency

International Atomic Time

International Bank for Reconstruction and Development

International Basketball Federation

International Bible College

International Board on Books for Young People

International Boxing Federation

International Boxing Hall of Fame

International Bridge, Tunnel and Turnpike Association

International Broadcast Systems, Ltd.

International Brotherhood of Boilermakers, Iron Shipbuilders, Blacksmiths, Forgers and Helpers

International Brotherhood of Electrical Workers

International Brotherhood of Firemen and Oilers

International Brotherhood of Locomotive Engineers

International Brotherhood of Magicians

International Brotherhood of Painters and Allied Trades Workers

International Brotherhood of Teamsters, Chauffeurs, Warehousemen and Helpers of America

International Bureau of Weights and Measures

International Business College

International Business Information Service

International Business Machines Corporation

International Business Man News Bureau

International Cat Association, The

International Chamber of Commerce

International Channel, The

International Cheerleading Foundation

International Chemical Workers Union

International Chili Society

International Chiropractors Association

International Church of the Foursquare Gospel

International Circulation Managers Association

International City Management Association

International Civil Aviation Organization

International Code

International Code of Signals

International College of Broadcasting

International College of Surgeons

International Committee of the Red Cross

International Confederation of Free Trade Unions

International Consumer Credit Association

International Controls Corporation

International Council of Community Churches

International Council of Scientific Unions

International Council of Shopping Centers

International Country Music Fan Fair

International Court of Justice

International Credit Association

International Criminal Investigators Association

International Criminal Police Organization

International Dairy Queen, Inc.

International Date Line *occas.* international date line

International Development Association

Internationale, The

International Energy Agency

International Evangelism Crusades

International Executive Service Corps

International Eye Foundation

International Falls

International Fan Club Organization

International Features, Inc.

International Federation for Human Rights

International Federation of Football Associations

International Finals Rodeo

International Finance Corporation

International Fine Arts College

International Flavors and Fragrances Inc.

International Flying Farmers

International Frisbee Association

International Fund for Agricultural Development

International Fund for Animal Welfare

International Game Fish Association

International Game Technology

International Geophysical Year

International Gothic

International Grenfell Association

International Harvester [*now* Navistar International Transportation Corporation]

International Helicopter Association

International Hobby Corporation

International Hot Rod Association

International Hydrological Decade

International Ice Hockey Federation

International Ice Patrol

International Information Management Congress

International Institute of Rural Reconstruction

International Institute of Technology

International Insurance Society

International Interculture Programs, AFS

International Investment Bank

International Jazz Federation

International Joseph Diseases Foundation

International Juggler's Association

International Kennel Club of Chicago

International Labor Organization

International Ladies' Garment Workers' Union

International Lawn Tennis Championship

International League of Professional Baseball Clubs

International Leather Goods, Plastic and Novelty Workers' Union

International Longshoremen's and Warehousemen's Union

International Longshoremen's Association

International Maritime Organization

International Medical Tribune Syndicate

International Minerals and Chemical Corporation

International Monetary Fund

International Morse Code

International Motor Sports Association

International Multifoods Charitable Foundation

International Multifoods Corporation

International Museum of Photography

International Newspaper Marketing Association

International Numismatic Society Authentication Bureau

International Olympic Committee

International Orange

International Order of Job's Daughters

International Order of Job's Daughters, Supreme Guardian Council

International Organization for Migration

International Organization of Good Templars

International Organization of Professionals in Parliamentary Law

International Over the Hill Gang

International Ozone Association

International Paintball Players Association

International Paper Company

International Paper Company Foundation

International Peace Academy

International Peace Garden

International Pen Friends

International Phonetic Alphabet

International Photography Hall of Fame and Museum

International Photo News

International Planetarium Society

International Plastic Modelers Society

International Platform Association

International Radio and Television Society

International Reading Association

International Real Estate Institute

International Red Cross

International Red Cross and Red Crescent Movement

International Relief Organization

International Rescue Committee

International Screen Printing Association

International Show Car Association

International Sinatra Society

International Society for Krishna Consciousness

International Society for Philosophical Enquiry

International Society for Traumatic Stress Studies, The

International Society for Arboriculture

International Society of Certified Electronics Technicians

International Society of Christian Endeavor

International Society of Financiers

International Society of Friendship and Good Will

International Society of Wang Users

International Space Hall of Fame

International Standard Book Number

International Standard Serial Number

International style

International System of Units

International Table Tennis Foundation

International Technical Institute

International Technology Corporation

International Telecommunications Satellite Organization

International Telecommunication Union

International Telephone and Telegraph Corporation

International Television Network, The

International Tennis Federation

International Trade Commission

International Trademark Association [form. United States Trademark Association]

International Trade Organization

International Traditional Karate Federation

International Training in Communication

International Travelall

International Union for Quarternary Research

International Union of Allied Novelty and Production Workers

International Union of Bricklayers and Allied Craftsmen

International Union of Electronic, Electrical, Salaried, Machine, and Furniture Workers

International Union of Operating Engineers

International Union of United Mine Workers of America

International Union, United Automobile, Aerospace and Agricultural Workers

International United Pentecostal Church

International University Foundation

International Volleyball Federation

International Watch Company

International Weightlifting Federation

International Whaling Commission

International Wizard of Oz Club

International Woodworkers of America—U.S. AFL-CIO

International Workingmen's Association

International Yacht Racing Union

International Year of the Quiet Sun

International Youth Council

International Zen Association

Inter-Parliamentary Union

Interpol

Interpress of London and New York

Interpublic Group of Companies, Inc., The

Interracial Council for Business Opportunity

Interstate Bakeries Corporation

Interstate Commerce Commission

Intertel, Inc.

Interview

Inthanon

In the Heat of the Night

In the Salon at the Rue des Moulins

Intimations of Immortality

Intimism occas. intimism

Intolerable Acts

Intolerance

Into the Woods

Intourist

Intracoastal Waterway

Intron™

Intruder in the Dust

Inuit

Inuvik

Invar™

Inventors Association of America

Inventors Clubs of America

Inveraray Castle

Invercargill

Inver Grove Heights

Inver Hills Community College

Inverness

Inverness cape

Invernesshire

Invincible Armada

Invisible Empire Knights of the Ku Klux Klan

INXS

Inyo Mountains

Inyo National Forest

Io

Iolani Palace

Iolanthe

Iomega Corporation

Iomoth

Iona College

Iona College Gaels

Ionesco, Eugène

Ionia

Ionian

Ionian Islands

Ionian mode

Ionian school

Ionian Sea

Ionic

Ionic order

Iota Beta Sigma

Iota Lambda Sigma

Iota Phi Lambda

Iota Sigma Pi

Iowa

Iowa Army Ammunition Plant

Iowa Central Community College

Iowa City

Iowa Falls

Iowa-Illinois Gas and Electric Company

Iowa [Indian], n., pl. Iowa or Iowas

Iowa Lakes Community College

Iowa Law Review

Iowan, The

Iowa Park

Iowa Radio Network

Iowa Resources, Inc.
Iowa Review, The
Iowa State University
Iowa State University
  Cyclones
Iowa State University
  of Science and
  Technology
Iowa State University
  Press
Iowa Valley
  Community College
Iowa Wesleyan
  College
Iowa Western
  Community College
I Pagliacci
IPALCO Enterprises,
  Inc.
Ippolitov-Ivanov,
  Mikhail
  Mikhailovic
I-proposition
Ipswich
Iqbal, Muhammed
Iran
Iran Air
Iran-contra scandal
Irangate
Irani
Iranian
Iranian languages
Iranian Plateau
Iran-Iraq war
Iraq
Iraqgate
Iraqi, n., pl. Iraqis
Iraqi Air Force
Iraqi Airways
Iraq Museum
Ireland

Ireland, Jill
Ireland, John
Irenaeus, Saint
Irene
Irian Jaya
IRI Holding
Irish
Irish-American
Irish-American
  Cultural Institute
Irish apple
Irish apricot
Irish boat
Irish bridge
Irish bull
Irish Christian Brother
Irish coffee
Irish confetti
Irish daisy
Irish elk
Irish English
Irish Free State
Irish Gaelic
Irish International
  Airlines
Irishism
Irish Land Question
Irish language
Irish literary
  renaissance
Irish lord
Irish mail
Irishman, n., pl.
  Irishmen
Irish moss [plant]
Irish Moss™ liqueur
Irishness
Irish pale
Irish pennant

Irish plum
Irish potato, n., pl.
  Irish potatoes
Irish Republican
  Army
Irishry, n., pl. Irishries
Irish Sea
Irish setter
Irish stew
Irish terrier
Irish tweed
Irish water spaniel
Irish whiskey
Irish wolfhound
Irishwoman, n., pl.
  Irishwomen
Irish yew
Irkutsk
Irma La Douce
Irminger Current
Iron, Ralph
Iron Age
Iron Butterfly
Iron Castings Society
Iron Chancellor
Iron Cross
Iron Crown of
  Lombardy
Iron Curtain
Iron Duke
Iron Gate occas. Gates
Iron Guard
Iron Maiden
Iron Mountain
Iron River
Irons, Jeremy
Ironside
Ironton
Ironweed

Iroquoian

Iroquois, *n., pl.*
Iroquois

Iroquois Confederacy

Iroquois League

Irrawaddy

Irtish

Irvin, Monte

Irvine

Irvine Valley College

Irving

Irving, Amy

Irving, George S.

Irving, Sir Henry

Irving, Isabel

Irving, John

Irving, Laurence

Irving, Washington

Irving Bank
Corporation

Irving G. Thalberg
Award

Irving One Wall Street
Foundation

Irvington

Irwin

Irwin, Bill

Irwin, Hale

Irwin, James B.

Irwin, Wallace

Irwin, Will

Irwin, Wynn

Isaac

Isaac Asimov's
Science Fiction
Magazine

Isaacs, Gregory

Isaacs, Jorge

Isaacs, Susan

Isaak, Chris

Isabel

Isabella

Isabella of Castile

Isabella Stewart
Gardner Museum

Isabella the Catholic

Isabel of Bavaria

Isaiah

Isaian

Isar

Iscariotism

Ischia

Isenheim Altarpiece

Isère

Iseult *occas.* Isolde,
Isond, Isode,
Ysonde the Fair

Iseult of the White
Hands

Isherwood, Benjamin

Isherwood,
Christopher

Isherwood framing

Isherwood system

Ishi

Ishihara *or* Ishihara's
test

Ishkabibble

Ishmael

Ishmaelite

Ishmaelitism

Ishpeming

Ishtar

Isidore of Seville,
Saint

Isidorus of Mieltus

Isis

Isis International

Isis-Women's
International Cross-
Cultural Exchange

Islam

Islamabad

Islamic

Islamic architecture

Islamic art

Islamic calendar

Islamic Development
Bank

Islamic era

Islamic Jihad

Islamic Resistance
Movement

Islamic Revolutionary
Guards Corps

Islamism

Islamist

Islamization

Islamize, *v.* Islamized,
Islamizing

Island No. 10

island of Reil

Island of the Sun

Island Park

islands *or* islets of
Langerhans

Islands of the Blessed

Isle of Athelney

Isle of Capri

Isle of Ely

Isle of Guernsey

Isle of Man

Isle of Pines [*now* Isle
of Youth]

Isle of Purbeck

Isle of Sheppey

Isle of Shoals boat

Isle of Skye

Isle of Thanet

Isle of Wight

Isle of Youth [*form.* Isle of Pines]
Isle Royale
Isle Royale National Park
Isles of Scilly
islets *var. of* islands of Langerhans
Isley, Ervin
Isley, Marvin
Isley, O'Kelly
Isley, Ronald
Isley, Rudolph
Isley Brothers, The
Ismail
Isocrates
Isonzo
Isothermal Community College
Ispahan
Israel
Israel Discount Bank
Israeli, *n., pl.* Israelis *occas.* Israeli
Israelite
Israel Museum
Israel Philharmonic Orchestra
Issa, *n., pl.* Issa *or* Issas
Issei, *n., pl.* Issei
Issues and Answers
Issyk-Kul
Istanbul
Istanbul Ataturk International Airport
Isthmian games
Isthmus of Corfu
Isthmus of Corinth
Isthmus of Darien

Isthmus of Kra
Isthmus of Panama
Isthmus of Perekop
Isthmus of San Blas
Isthmus of Suez
Isthmus of Tehuantepec
Istituto Bancario San Paolo di Torino
Istria *occas.* Istrian Peninsula
Isuzu, Joe
Isuzu Motors Ltd.
It
Italian
Italian, The [movie]
Italian-American
Italian-American Cultural Society
Italian architecture
Italian art
Italian aster
Italianate
Italian clover
Italian corn salad
Italian cypress
Italian dressing
Italian East Africa
Italianesque
Italian greyhound
Italian hand
Italian Historical Society of America
Italian honeysuckle
Italianism
Italianist
Italian jasmine
Italian language
Italian literature
Italian pointer

Italian provincial style
Italian reed
Italian rye grass
Italian sandwich
Italian Somaliland
Italian sonnet
Italian Wars
Italicism
Italic languages
Italo-Ethiopian War
Italo-phile
Italy
Italy-America Chamber of Commerce
Itawamba Community College
It Came Upon a Midnight Clear
Itel Corporation
Ithaca
Ithaca College
Ithacan
It Happened One Night
Ito, Midori
Ito, Robert
Ito-Yokado Company, Ltd.
It's a Long Way to Tipperary
It's a Mad Mad Mad Mad World
It's a Wonderful Life
It's Garry Shandling's Show
Itsy Bitsy Teenie Weenie Yellow Polka Dot Bikini
ITT Corporation

ITT Financial
  Corporation
ITT Rayonier
  Foundation
ITT Rayonier Inc.
ITT Technical
  Institute
Iturbi, Amparo
Iturbi, José
Ivan
Ivanhoe
Ivanov, Vsevolod
Ivan the Great
Ivan the Terrible
IVAX Corporation

I've Got a Secret
Ives, Burl
Ives, Charles
Ives, Frederich
  Eugene
Ives, James M.
Ivey, Dana
Ivey, Judith
Ivey's
Ivo, Tommy
Ivo of Chartres, Saint
Ivor
Ivory Coast
Ivry-sur-Seine
Ivy League

Ivy Leaguer
Iwo Jima
I Write the Songs
Ixtacihuatl
Ixtapa
Iyar
Izaak Walton League
  of America
Izetbegovic, Alija
Izmir
Izmir Adnan
  Menderes
  International
  Airport
Izvestia

J

Jabalpur

Jabara, Paul

Jabbar, Kareem Abdul

Jabberwock [fictitious monster]

jabberwocky *occas.* Jabberwocky [meaningless language]

Jabberwocky [poem]

Jacinto City

Jack

Jack and Jill

Jack and the Beanstalk

Jack Benny Program, The

Jack Daniel Distillery

Jack Eckerd Corporation

Jack Eckerd Corporation Foundation

Jackee

Jack Frost

Jack Horner

Jackie Gleason Show, The

Jackie Robinson Foundation

Jack Ketch

jack *occas.* Jack Mormon

Jack Rose

Jack Russell terrier

Jackson

Jackson, Alan

Jackson, Alexander

Jackson, Andrew

Jackson, Anne

Jackson, Barbara

Jackson, Bo

Jackson, Glenda

Jackson, Helen Hunt

Jackson, Isaiah

Jackson, Janet

Jackson, Jermaine

Jackson, Jesse

Jackson, Joe

Jackson, Kate

Jackson, Keith

Jackson, La Toya

Jackson, Mahalia

Jackson, Mary

Jackson, Maynard

Jackson, Michael

Jackson, Mick

Jackson, Milt

Jackson, Reggie

Jackson, Robert H.

Jackson, Sherry

Jackson, Shirley

Jackson, Stonewall

Jackson, Travis

Jackson, Victoria

Jackson, Wanda

Jackson, William

Jackson Air Force Base

Jackson Community College

Jackson Day

Jackson Five

Jackson Hole

Jacksonian

Jackson International Airport

Jacksonism

Jackson National Life Insurance Company

Jacksons, The

Jackson State Community College

Jackson State University

Jackson State University Tigers

Jacksonville

Jacksonville College

312

Jacksonville International Airport

Jacksonville Kennel Club

Jacksonville Naval Air Station

Jacksonville State University

Jacksonville University

Jacksonville University Dolphins

Jackson Whites

Jack Sprat

Jack the Giant Killer

Jack the Ripper

Jacob

Jacob, John Edward

Jacob, Max

Jacob ben Asher

Jacob Blessing the Sons of Joseph

Jacobean, *adj.* [of or pertaining to the period 1603–1625 in England; *see also* Jacobian]

Jacobean style

Jacobethan architecture

Jacobi, Derek

Jacobi, Lou

Jacobian [mathematical determinant; *see also* Jacobean]

Jacobin

Jacobinism

Jacobite

Jacobite Church

Jacobite glass

Jacobitism

Jacob K. Javits Convention Center

Jacobs, Jeremy Maurice

Jacobs, Richard E.

Jacobs, Walter L.

Jacobsen, Jens Peter

Jacobs Engineering Group Inc.

Jacob's ladder

Jacobson's organ

Jacobson Stores Inc.

Jacob's staff, *n., pl.* Jacob's staves

Jacoby, Jim

Jacquard, Joseph

jacquard *often* Jacquard card

jacquard *often* Jacquard harness

jacquard *often* Jacquard head motion

jacquard *often* Jacquard loom

jacquard *often* Jacquard weave

Jacqueline

Jacquerie

Jacques

Jacques Bonhomme

Jacquet, Illinois

Jacuzzi, Candido

Jacuzzi™ bath

Jae, Jana

Jaeckel, Richard

Jaffa

Jaffe, Sam

Jagger, Dean

Jagger, Mick

Jaguar Ltd.

Jahn, Hans

Jahn, Helmut

Jain

Jainism

Jaipur

Jakarta *occas.* Djakarta

Jakarta Halim Perdanakusuma International Airport

Jakarta Kemaypran Airport

Jakes, John

Jakobsen, Roman

Jalapa

Jalisco

Jam, The

Jamaica

Jamaica Bay

Jamaica ginger

Jamaica gold fern

Jamaica honeysuckle

Jamaican

Jamaica rum

Jamaica shorts

Jamail, Joseph Dahr, Jr.

Jamal, Ahmad

JAMA: The Journal of the American Medical Association

James

James, Daniel, Jr.

James, Dennis

James, Frank

James, Harry

James, Henry

James, Jesse

James, John

James, P. D.

James, Rick

James, Saint

James, Sonny

James, Tommy

James, William

James A. Garfield National Historic Site

James Bay

James Bond 007 Fan Club

James Dean Foundation

James H. Faulkner State Junior College

Jamesian

James Madison University

James Madison University Dukes

James Norris Memorial Trophy

Jameson, Sir Leander Starr

Jameson, Storm

Jameson Raid

James Range

James River

James River Corporation of Virginia

James S. Copley Foundation

James Sprunt Community College

James the Great, Saint

James the Less, Saint

Jamestown

Jamestown Business College

Jamestown College

Jamestown Community College

Jamestowne Society

Jamestown Festival Park

Jamestown weed

Jamie

Jamie Green

Jamieson, Bob

Janáček, Leoš

Jan and Dean

Jane

Jane Addams' Hull House

Jane Addams Peace Association

Jane Austen Society of North America

Jane Avril

Jane Doe

Jane Eyre

Jane Fonda's Workout Book

Jane Q. Citizen

Jane Q. Public

Jane Seymour

Jane's Information Group Ltd.

Janesville

Janet

Janet, Pierre

Janice

Janis

Janis, Conrad

Janis, Elsie

Janissarian

Janissary *occas.* Janizary, *n., pl.* Janissaries *occas.* Janizaries

Janissary music

Jan Mayen

Jannings, Emil

Jansen, Cornelis

Jansenism

Jansenist

Jansenistic

Jansky, K. G.

Jansky noise

Janssen, David

Januarius, Saint

January, *n., pl.* Januaries

Janus

Janus cloth

Janus-faced

Janus green

Japan

Japan Air Lines Company, Ltd.

Japan cedar

Japan clover

Japan Current

Japan Development Bank

Japanese, *n., pl.* Japanese

Japanese-American

Japanese American Citizens League

Japanese andromeda

Japanese arborvitae

Japanese architecture

Japanese art

Japanese artichoke

Japanese barberry

Japanese barnyard millet

Japanese beetle

Japanese black pine

Japanese bobtail

Japanese burnet
Japanese cedar
Japanese cherry
Japanese chestnut
Japanese chin [*form.*
 Japanese spaniel]
Japanese clematis
Japanese flowering
 cherry
Japanese gelatin
Japanese holly
Japanese honeysuckle
Japanese iris
Japanese isinglass
Japanese ivy
Japanese lacquer
Japanese language
Japanese lantern
Japanese larch
Japanese laurel
Japanese lawn grass
Japanese leaf
Japanese lily
Japanese literature
Japanese maple
Japanese millet
Japanese morning-
 glory
Japanese music
Japanese oyster
Japanese pagoda tree
Japanese paper
Japanese pear
Japanese persimmon
Japanese plum
Japanese quail
Japanese quince
Japanese river fever
Japanese silk

Japanese spaniel [*now*
 Japanese chin]
Japanese spurge
Japanese tree peony
Japanese wisteria
Japanese wolf
Japanese yew
Japanesque
Japanism
Japan Society, Inc.
Japan Stream
Japan tea
Japan wax
Japurá River
Jaques-Dalcroze,
 Emile
Jardine Matheson
 Holdings Ltd.
Jared
Jargon Society
Jarre, Maurice
Jarreau, Al
Jarrell, Randall
Jarrett, Keith
Jarriel, Tom
Jarry, Alfred
Jaruzelski, Wojciech
Jarvi, Neeme
Jarvik-7™ artificial
 heart
Jarvis, Anna
Jarvis Christian
 College
Jarvis Island
Jasmine
Jason
Jason-Leigh, Jennifer
Jason of Cyrene
Jasper
Jasper dip

Jasper National Park
Jaspers, Karl
Jasper's Dilemma
Jaurès, Jean Léon
Java
Java black rot
Java cotton
Java fig
Java man
Javanese, *n.*, *pl.*
 Javanese
Javanese music
Javary River
Java Sea
Java sparrow
Java willow
Javelle *occas.* Javel
 water
Javits, Jacob
Jawlensky, Alexey
 von
Jaworski, Leon
Jaws
Jaws of Life™
Jaws 3-D
Jaws 2
Jay, John
Jay and the Americans
Jaycee
Jaycees International
 [*form.* Junior
 Chamber of
 Commerce]
Jaycees Magazine
jayhawker *often*
 Jayhawker
Jay's Treaty
Jazz Age
Jazz at the
 Philharmonic

Jazz Composer's Orchestra Association

Jazzercise™

Jazz Messengers

Jazz Singer, The

Jazz Tap Ensemble

Jazz World Society

Jazzy Jeff and the Fresh Prince

J-bar lift

J. B. Hunt Transportation Services, Inc

J. B. Lippincott Company

J. B. Speed Art Museum

J. C. Penney Company, Inc.

J-curve

J. D. Power and Associates

Jean

Jean, Kenneth

Jean Baptiste de la Salle, Saint

Jean-Baptiste Vianney, Saint

Jean de Florette

Jeanette

Jean Hersholt Humanitarian Award

Jeanie with the Light Brown Hair

Jean LaFitte National Historical Park

Jeans, Sir James

Jebb, Sir Richard Claverhouse

Jebel ed Druze *or* Jebel Druze

Jebel Musa

Jedda *var. of* Jidda

Jeep™ [civilian brand name]

jeep [military designation]

Jeeves, Reginald

Jeeves the butler

Jeffers, Robinson

Jefferson

Jefferson, Blind Lemon

Jefferson, Joseph

Jefferson, Thomas

Jefferson Airplane

Jefferson Barracks

Jefferson City

Jefferson College

Jefferson Community College

Jefferson Davis' Birthday

Jefferson Davis State Junior College

Jefferson Day

Jefferson Downs Race Track

Jefferson Educational Foundation

Jefferson Foundation

Jefferson Heights

Jeffersonian

Jeffersonianism

Jefferson Memorial

Jefferson National Expansion Memorial National Historic Site

Jefferson National Forest

Jefferson-Pilot Corporation

Jefferson-Pilot Life Insurance Company

Jefferson Proving Ground

Jeffersons, The

Jefferson Starship

Jefferson State Community College

Jefferson Technical College

Jeffersonville

Jeffery

Jeffrey

Jeffrey pine

Jeffreys, Anne

Jeffries, James J.

Jehoshaphat

Jehovah

Jehovah God

Jehovahism

Jehovahist

Jehovahistic

Jehovah's Witnesses

Jehu

Jekyll, Gertrude

Jekyll-and-Hyde personality

Jemima

Jemima Puddleduck

J. E. Morgan

Jeni, Richard

Jenkins, Allen

Jenkins, Dave

Jenkins, Ferguson

Jenkins, Gordon

Jenkins, Hayes

Jenkins, Snuffy

Jenkinson, Robert Banks

Jenna

Jenner, Bruce

Jenner, Edward

Jenney, William Le Baron

Jennifer

Jennifer Muller—The Works

Jennings

Jennings, Hugh

Jennings, Peter

Jennings, Waylon

Jenny Craig, Inc.

Jenrette, Rita

Jens, Salome

Jensen

Jensen, Arthur R.

Jensenism

Jensen Motors Ltd.

Jeopardy

Jeremiah

Jeremy

Jeremy P. Tarcher, Inc.

Jericho

Jeroboam

Jerome

Jerome, Jerome K.

Jerome, Saint

Jerome Robbins' Broadway

Jerry [*British*: German soldier], *n.*, *pl.* Jerries

Jerry [given name], *n.*, *pl.* Jerrys

Jerry Garcia Band

Jerry Jeff Walker Fan Club

Jerry Springer Show, The

Jersey [cattle], *n.*, *pl.* Jerseys

Jersey [island]

Jerseyan

Jersey City

Jersey City State College

Jerseyite

Jersey pine

Jersey Shore

Jerseyville

Jerusalem

Jerusalem artichoke

Jerusalem Bible

Jerusalem cherry

Jerusalem cricket

Jerusalem cross

Jerusalem date

Jerusalemite

Jerusalem oak

Jerusalem sage

Jerusalem thorn

Jervis Bay

Jespersen, Otto

Jess

Jessamyn

Jesse

Jesse H. Jones Hall for the Performing Arts and Wortham Theatre Center

Jessel, George

Jesse tree

Jesse window

Jessica

Jesu

Jesuit

Jesuitic

Jesuitism

Jesuitist

Jesuit Relations

Jesuit School of Theology at Berkeley

Jesuits' resin

Jesuit ware

Jesus

Jesus boots

Jesus Christ

Jesus Christ Superstar

Jesus freak

Jesus Island

Jesus movement

Jesus of Nazareth

Jesus People

Jesus sandals

Jet

Jethro

Jethro Tull

Jet Propulsion Laboratory

Jett, Joan

Jeu de Paume Museum

Jevons, William Stanley

Jew

Jew-baiting

Jewel Cave National Monument

Jewel Food Stores

Jewelry Industry Council

Jewett, Sarah Orne

Jewish

Jewish-American
Princess *often*
Jewish American
Princess

Jewish Book Council

Jewish calendar

Jewish Community
Centers of North
America

Jewish Defense
Organization

Jewish lightning

Jewish liturgical
marriage

Jewishness

Jewish piano

Jewish Telegraphic
Agency

Jewish Television
Network

Jewish Theological
Seminary of
America

Jewish typewriter

Jewish War Veterans
of the United States
of America

Jewish Wedding in
Morocco

Jewison, Norman

Jew of Malta, The

Jezebel

Jezebelian

Jezebelish

J. F. Drake State
Technical College

J. F. Ingram State
Technical College

J. Geils Band

Jhansi

Jhelum River

Jiang Qing [*form.*
Chiang Ch'ing]

Jiangsu [*form.*
Kiangsu]

Jiangxi [*form.*
Kiangsi]

Jiang Zemin

Jibuti *var. of* Djibouti
[capital of Djibouti]

Jidda *occas.* Jedda

Jiddu Krishnamurti

Jillian

Jillian, Ann

Jim and Jesse and the
Virginia Boys

Jim Crow

Jim Crowism

Jim Crow law

Jim Dandy

Jimenez, José

Jiménez, Juan Ramón

Jimi Hendrix
Experience

Jim Kobak's Kirkus
Reviews [*form.*
Kirkus Reviews]

Jimmy Carter National
Historic Site

Jimmy Green

Jimmy Swaggart Bible
College and
Seminary

Jim Thorpe Award

Jinan [*now* Tsinan]

Jingle Bells

Jinnah, Mohammed
Ali

Jívaro, *n., pl.* Jívaro *or*
Jívaros

J. K. Gill Company

J. K. Gill store

J. K. Lasser™ books

J. K. Lasser's Your
Money Manager™
software

J. M. Smucker
Company

Joachim, Saint

Joanna

Joan of Arc, Saint

Joan of Kent

Joanou, Phil

João, Pessoa

Job Corps

Jobim, Antonio Carlos

Jobs, Steve

Job's comforter

Jobs for Progress/SER

Job's tears

Jocassee Dam

Jocasta

Jockey Club, The

Jockeys before a Race

Jockeys' Guild

Jock Scot

Jodhpur

Jodl, Alfred

Jodrell Bank
Observatory

Joe Blow

Joe College

Joe Cool

Joe Doakes, *n., pl.* Joe
Doakes

Joe Goode
Performance Group

Joel

Joel, Billy

Joe Louis Arena

Joe Miller's Jestbook

Joe Public

Joe Robbie Stadium

Joe Shmo

Joe versus the Volcano

Joffre, Joseph

Joffrey, Robert

Joffrey Ballet

Joffrey II ballet

Jogbra™

Johannesburg

Johannesburg Art Gallery

Johannesburg Jan Smuts International Airport

Johannisberger wine

Johanos, Donald

Johansson, Ingemar

John

John I, Saint

John, Augustus

John, Elton

John A. Gupton College

John Alden Life Insurance Company

John A. Logan College

John Ascuaga's Nugget

John Baptist de la Salle, Saint

John Barleycorn

John Bastyr College

John Berchmans, Saint

John Bircher or Bircher

John Birches or Birches

John Birchism or Birchism

John Birchite or Birchite

John Birch Society

John Bosco, Saint

John Brown's Body

John Brown University

John B. Stetson University

John Bull

John Bullish

John Bullishness

John Bullism

John Carroll University

John Carter Brown Library

John C. Calhoun State Community College

John C. Harland Company

John Chrysostom, Saint

John Climax, Saint

Johncock, Gordon

John Crerar Library

John Damascene, Saint

John D. and Catherine T. MacArthur Foundation

John Day

John Day Dam

John Day Fossil Beds National Monument

John Deere Foundation

John Doe

John Dory, *n., pl.* John Dories

John D. Rockefeller, Jr. Memorial Parkway

Johne, Heinrich A.

Johne's disease

John Fisher, Saint

John F. Kennedy International Airport [*form.* Idlewild Airport]

John F. Kennedy National Historic Site

John F. Kennedy Space Center

John F. Kennedy University

John G. Shedd Aquarium

John Hancock

John Hancock Bowl [*form.* Sun Bowl]

John Hancock Building

John Hancock Center

John Hancock Mutual Life Insurance Company

John Hancock Tower

John Henry [legendary person]

John Henry [one's signature] *n., pl.* John Henries

John Howard Association

John Jay College of Criminal Justice

John Labatt Ltd.

John Lalande, Saint

John Law

John Marshall Law School

John M. Patterson State Technical College

John Muir National Historic Site

John Nepomucene Neumann, Saint

Johnny, *n.*, *pl.* Johnnys

Johnny Appleseed

Johnny Belinda

Johnny collar

Johnny-come-lately, *n.*, *pl.* Johnny-come-latelies *or* Johnnies-come-lately

Johnny-jump-up

Johnny-on-the-spot

Johnny Reb

Johnny smokers

Johnny Tremain

John of Austria

John of Brienne

John of Damascus, Saint

John of Ephesus

John of Gaunt

John of God, Saint

John of Lancaster

John of Leyden

John of Luxemburg

John of Procida

John of Salisbury

John of the Cross, Saint

John o'Groat's

John o'Groat's House

John Paul Mitchell Systems

John Pelham Historical Association

John Q. Citizen

John Q. Public

John R. Wooden Award

Johns, Glynis

Johns, Jasper

Johns Hopkins Hospital

Johns Hopkins University

Johns Hopkins University Press, The

John Simon Guggenheim Memorial Foundation

Johnson, Andrew

Johnson, Anne-Marie

Johnson, Arte

Johnson, Ban

Johnson, Barbara Piasecka

Johnson, Ben [actor; athlete; *see also* Jonson, Ben]

Johnson, Bunk

Johnson, Charles Spurgeon

Johnson, Chic

Johnson, Clarence Kelly

Johnson, Don

Johnson, Earvin "Magic"

Johnson, Eastman

Johnson, Edward Crosby, III

Johnson, Gary

Johnson, Gerald White

Johnson, Henry

Johnson, Hiram

Johnson, Howard

Johnson, Jack

Johnson, James Loring

Johnson, James P.

Johnson, James Weldon

Johnson, Jean

Johnson, J. J.

Johnson, John Harold

Johnson, Judy

Johnson, Lady Bird

Johnson, Lyndon Baines

Johnson, Pamela Hansford

Johnson, Pauline

Johnson, Philip Cortelyou

Johnson, Roy

Johnson, Samuel [American clergyman; English lexicographer; *see also* Johnston, Samuel]

Johnson, Uwe

Johnson, Van

Johnson, Virginia E.

Johnson, Walter

Johnson and Johnson Consumer Products, Inc.

Johnson and Johnson Family of Companies Contribution Fund

Johnson and Wales University

Johnson Bible College

Johnson City

Johnson Controls Foundation

Johnson Controls Inc.

Johnson County Cattle War

Johnson County Community College

Johnson C. Smith University

Johnsonese

Johnson grass

Johnsonian

Johnsonianism

Johnson noise

Johnson Publishing Company, Inc.

Johnsons, The

Johnson State College

Johnson Technical Institute

Johnston [* RI; SC; see also Johnstown]

Johnston, Albert Sidney

Johnston, Christopher

Johnston, Joseph Eggleston

Johnston, Mary

Johnston, Samuel [political leader in American Revolution; see also Johnson, Samuel]

Johnston Community College

Johnston Island

Johnston's organ

Johnstown [* NY; OH; PA; see also Johnston]

Johnstown flood

Johnstown Flood National Memorial

John the Baptist, Saint

John the Divine, Saint

John the Fearless

John Tyler Community College

John Vianney, Saint

John Wanamaker Department Store

John Wayne Airport

John Wesley College

John Wiley and Sons, Inc.

John Wood Community College

Johore or Johor

Johore Strait

Joint Center for Political and Economic Studies

Joint Chiefs of Staff

Joint Council on Economic Education

Joinville, Jean de

Joliet

Joliet or Jolliet, Louis

Joliet Junior College

Joliot-Curie, Frédéric

Joliot-Curie, Irène

Jolliet var. of Joliet, Louis

Jolly, Phillip von

Jolly balance

Jolly Old Saint Nicholas

Jolly Roger

Jolo

Jolson, Al

Jonah

Jonah and the whale

Jonah crab

Jonahesque

Jonathan

Jonathan Livingstone Seagull

Jonathan spot

Jonathon

Jones, Allan

Jones, Bobby

Jones, Booker T.

Jones, Brian

Jones, Buck

Jones, Carolyn

Jones, Casey

Jones, Charlie

Jones, Chuck

Jones, Davy

Jones, Deacon

Jones, Dean

Jones, Ed "Too Tall"

Jones, Elvin

Jones, George

Jones, Glenn

Jones, Grace

Jones, Grandpa

Jones, Henry

Jones, Howard Mumford

Jones, Indiana

Jones, Inigo

Jones, Jack

Jones, James

Jones, James Earl

Jones, Jennifer

Jones, Jenny

Jones, Jesse

Jones, Jo

Jones, John Paul

Jones, LeRoi

Jones, L. Q.

Jones, Mother

Jones, Philly Joe

Jones, Quincy
Jones, Rufus Matthew
Jones, Shirley
Jones, Spike
Jones, Stan
Jones, Terry
Jones, Thad
Jones, Thomas ap
  Catesby
Jones, Tom
Jones, Tommy Lee
Jones Beach
Jonesboro
Jones College
Jones County Junior
  College
Joneses
Jonestown
Jonestown massacre
Jong, Erica
Jonker diamond
Jonquière
Jonson, Ben
  [dramatist; see also
  Johnson, Ben]
Jonsonian
Jooss, Kurt
Joplin
Joplin, Janis
Joplin, Scott
Jordaens, Jacob
Jordan [given name]
Jordan [form.
  Transjordan]
Jordan, Barbara
Jordan, Camille
Jordan, David Starr
Jordan, Michael
Jordan, Richard
Jordan, Verdon

Jordan, Vernon E.
Jordan almond
Jordan arc
Jordan College
Jordan curve
Jordan curve theorem
Jordan engine
Jordan-Hölder
  theorem
Jordania, Vakhtang
Jordanian
Jordan Valley
Jorgensen, Christine
Jory, Victor
José often Jose
José Limón Dance
  Company
Joselito
José Marti Rancho
  Boyeros
  International
  Airport
Joseph
Joseph, Father
Joseph, Saint
Joseph Barsabas, Saint
Joseph Holmes Dance
  Theater
Josephine
Josephine's-lily
Josephite
Joseph of Arimathea,
  Saint
Joseph of Cupertino,
  Saint
Joseph of Exeter
Joseph's-coat
Josephson, Brian D.
Josephson effects
Josephson junction

Josephus, Flavius
Joshua
Joshua's Christian
  Stores
Joshua tree
Joshua Tree National
  Monument
Josiah
Joslyn, Allyn
Joslyn Art Museum
Jos Museum
Jos Plateau
Josquin des Prez
Joss, Addie
Jossey-Bass Inc.,
  Publishers
Jostens Foundation
Jostens, Inc.
Joubert, Joseph
Jouett, Matthew
Jouhaux, Léon
Joule, James P.
Joule's law
Joule-Thomson effect
Jourdan, Charles
Jourdan, Louis
Jourgensen, Al
Journal of the Plague
  Year, A
Journal Press
  Syndicate
Journey
Jouve, Pierre Jean
Jouvenet, Jean
  Baptiste
Jove
Jove Publications, Inc.
Jovian, Flavius
Jovian planets
Jowett, Benjamin

Joyce, James
Joycean
Joyce Trisler
  Danscompany
Joyner, Al
Joyner-Kersee, Jackie
Joy of Cooking
Joy of Life, The
Joy Technologies Inc.
Joy to the World
J. Paul Getty Museum
J. Paul Getty Trust
J. P. Morgan and
  Company Inc.
J. P. Stevens and
  Company Inc.
J. P. Stevens and
  Company Inc.
  Foundation
J. Sargeant Reynolds
  Community College
Juan B. Castagnino
  Municipal Museum
  of Fine Arts
Juan de Fuca Strait
Juan de Pareja
Juan Fernández
Juan Santa Maria
  International
  Airport
Juárez
Juárez, Benito
Juba
Jubilate Sunday
Jubilee rig
Judah
Judah, Theodore
Judah ha-Levi
Judahite
Judaic
Judaica

Judaism
Judaist
Judaistic
Judas
Judas Iscariot
Judas of Galilee
Judas Priest
Judas tree
Judd, Donald
Judd, James
Judd, Naomi
Judd, Wynonna
Judds, The
Jude, Saint
Judea
Judean
Judeo-Christian
Jude the Obscure
Judge Advocate
  General School
Judge Lynch
Judgment Book
Judgment Day
Judgment of Paris
Judith
Judson College
Judy
Juggernaut [Hindu
  god]
Juggernaut *often*
  juggernaut
  [massive, crushing
  force]
Jugoslavia *var. of*
  Yugoslavia
Juilliard, Augustus
Juilliard Musical
  Foundation
Juilliard Quartet
Juilliard School, The

Juilliard School
  Theater
Jujamycin Theatres
Jukes Family
Julia
Julia, Raul
Julian, Saint
Juliana
Julian Alps
Juliana of Norwich
Julian calendar
Julian Day
Julian the Apostate
Julie
Julie Andrews Hour,
  The
Juliet
Juliet cap
Julius
Julius I, Saint
Julius Caesar
July, *n., pl.* Julies
July Fourth
July Revolution
Jumada I
Jumada II
Jumel Mansion
Jumna
Jump, Gordon
jumping Jehoshaphat
Junction City
June
Juneau
Juneau International
  Airport
June beetle
Juneberry, *n., pl.*
  Juneberries
June bug

June Days
June grass
Juneteenth
Jung, Carl Gustav
Jünger, Ernst
Jungfrau
Jungfraujoch
Jungian
Jungle, The
Jungle Books, The
Juniata College
Junior Achievement
Junior Chamber of
  Commerce [*now*
  Jaycees
  International]
Junior Girl Scouts
Junior League
Junior Leaguer
Junior Optimist Clubs
Junior Scholastic
Junius
Junker
Junkerdom
Junkerism

Junkers, Hugo
Junkers JU.87 Stuka
Junkyard Dog
Juno
Junoesque
Junot, Philippe
Jupiter
Jupiter's beard
Jupiter Symphony
Jura
Jurado, Katy
Jurassic
Jurassic Park
Jurgens, Curt
Jurgensen, Sonny
Juris Doctor
Juruá River
Jusserand, Jean
Just, Ernest Everett
Justin
Justine
Justinian
Justinian Code
Justin the Martyr,
  Saint

Just So Stories for
  Little Children
Just the Way You
  Are
Justus of Ghent
Justus of Tiberia
Jute
Jutish
Jutland
Juvarra, Filippo
Juvenal
Juvenalian
Juvenile Diabetes
  Foundation
  International
JVC Company of
  America
JVC Jazz Festival
  [*form.* Newport
  Jazz Festival]
J. Walter Thompson
  Company
J. W. Marriott at
  Century City
JWP Inc.
Jyväskylä

K

Kaaba

Kabalevsky, Dmitri

Kabuki drama

Kabul

Kabul International
Airport

Kabul Museum

Kádár, János

Kadavy, Caryn

kaddish *often*
Kaddish, *n., pl.*
kaddishim *often*
Kaddishim

Kael, Pauline

Kaempfert, Bert

Kaes College

Kaesong

Kaffir *or* Kafir
[African people] *n.,
pl.* Kaffir *or* Kaffirs
or Kafir *or* Kafirs
[*see also* Kafir]

Kaffir bean tree

Kaffraria

Kaffrarian

Kafir [Afghan
people], *n., pl.* Kafir
or Kafirs [*see also*
Kaffir]

Kafka, Franz

Kafkaesque

Kafue

Kafue National Park

Kaganovich, Lazar

Kagawa, Toyohiko

Kagemusha

Kagera

Kahane, Meir

Kahn, Albert

Kahn, Gus

Kahn, Herman

Kahn, Louis

Kahn, Madeline

Kahng, Gemma

Kahn test

Kahoolawe Island

Kaibab National
Forest

Kaido crab apple

Kaieteur Falls

Kaifu, Toshiki

Kaigetsudo

Kailas

Kailasanatha Temple

Kailua

Kailua Bay

Kain, Karen

Kaiser, Georg

Kaiser, Henry J.

Kaiser Aluminum
Corporation

Kaiser Foundation
Health Plan, Inc.

Kaiser Permanente

Kaiser Permanente
Medical Group

Kaiserslauten

Kaiser Wilhelm

Kalahari

Kalahari Gemsbok
National Park

Kalakaua Avenue

Kalamazoo

Kalamazoo College

Kalamazoo Valley
Community College

Kalashnikov assault
rifle

Kalaupapa leper
colony

Kalaupapa National
Historical Park

Kalb, Johann

Kalemi [*form.*
Albertville]

Kalgoorlie

Kalikow, Peter
Stephen

Kaline, Al

Kalinin, Michael

Kaliningrad

Kaliningrad Flight Control Center

Kalispel [Indian language]

Kalispell [city]

Kallikak

Kallikak family

Kallikrates *var. of* Callicrates

Kalmar Sound

Kaloko-Honokahau National Historical Park

Kama

Kamakura

Kaman Sciences Corporation

Kamasutra *occas.* Kama Sutra

Kamchatka

Kamchatkan

Kamehameha

Kamehameha Day

Kamehameha dynasty

Kamehameha the Great

Kamerlingh Onnes, Heike

kamikaze *occas.* Kamikaze

Kamloops

Kampala

Kampgrounds of America™

Kampuchea [*now* Cambodia]

Kamuzu International Airport

Kanaka

Kanaly, Steve

Kanarese, *n.*, *pl.* Kanarese

Kanawha

Kanchenjunga *occas.* Kanchanjanga *or* Kinchinjunga

Kander, John

Kandinsky, Wassily

Kane, Carol

Kane, Charles Foster

Kane, Elisha K.

Kane, Helen

Kane, John

Kane, Paul

Kane Basin

Kanehoe Bay Marine Corps Air Station

Kanellopoulos, Panayotis

Kanem

Kaneohe

Kaneohe Bay

Kanga

Kangaroo Island

Kaniksu National Forest

Kanin, Garson

Kankakee

Kankakee Community College

Kannopolis

Kano

Kanpur

Kansa

Kansai Gaidai Hawaii College

Kansan

Kansas *occas.* Kaw [river]

Kansas

Kansas! [magazine]

Kansas Agriculture Network

Kansas City, *n.*, *pl.* Kansas Citys

Kansas City Art Institute

Kansas City Business College

Kansas City Chiefs

Kansas City College and Bible School

Kansas City Downtown Airport

Kansas City International Airport

Kansas City International Raceway

Kansas City jazz

Kansas City Jazz Festival

Kansas City Kansas Community College

Kansas City Live!

Kansas City Royals

Kansas City Southern Industries, Inc.

Kansas City Star, The

Kansas City style

Kansas City Times, The

Kansas College of Technology

Kansas Gas and Electric Company

Kansas gay feather

Kansas Information Network

Kansas-Nebraska Act

Kansas Newman College

Kansas Power and Light Company, The

Kansas State University

Kansas State University Wildcats

Kansas Television Network

Kansas Wesleyan

Kant, Immanuel

Kanter, Hal

Kantian

Kantianism

Kantist

Kantner, Paul

Kantor, MacKinlay

kapellmeister *often* Kapellmeister

Kapitza, Pëtr

Kaplan, Gabe

Kaplan, Hyman

Kaplan, Justin

Kaplan, Mordecai

Kaposi, Moritz

Kaposi's sarcoma

Kapp, Richard P.

Kappa Alpha

Kappa Alpha Order

Kappa Alpha Psi

Kappa Alpha Society

Kappa Alpha Theta

Kappa Delta

Kappa Delta Epsilon

Kappa Delta Phi

Kappa Delta Pi

Kappa Delta Rho

Kappa Epsilon

Kappa Eta Kappa

Kappa Gamma Pi

Kappa Kappa Gamma

Kappa Kappa Iota

Kappa Kappa Psi

Kappa Mu Epsilon

Kappa Omicron Nu

Kappa Phi Kappa

Kappa Pi International

Kappa Psi

Kappa Psi Kappa

Kappa Sigma

Kappa Tau Alpha

Kapustin Yar Launch Center

Karachi

Karaganda

Karaism

Karaite

Karaitism

Karajan, Herbert von

Karakoram Mountains

Karakoram Pass

Karakorum

Karakul sheep

Kara Kum *occas.* Qara Qum

Karamanlis, Constantine

Karami, Rashid

Karan, Donna

Karankawa

Kara Sea

Karelia

Karelian

Karelian Isthmus

Karen [given name]

Karen [people] *n.*, *pl.* Karen *or* Karens

Karfiol, Bernard

Kariba Dam

Kariba Lake

Karlen, John

Karl-Marx-Stadt *occas.* Karl Marx Stadt [*now* Chemnitz]

Karloff, Boris

Karlovy Vary

Karlsruhe

Kármán, Theodor von

Karman trail

Karnatka [*form.* Mysore]

Karnes, Kim

Karns, Roscoe

Karok

Karpis, Alvin

Karpov, Anatoly

Karras, Alex

Karrer, Paul

Karroo *occas.* Karoo

Karsavina, Tamara

Karst

Karun

Kasdan, Lawrence

Kasem, Casey

Kasha, Al

Kashmir

Kashmiri [language]

Kashmiri [people] *n.*, *pl.* Kashmiri *or* Kashmiris

Kashmirian

Kashmir rug

Kaska

Kaskaskia

Kaskaskia College

Kaskaskia Island

Kaskel, Howard

Kasparov, Garry

Kassebaum, Nancy

Kasserine Pass

Kastler, Alfred

Kästner, Erich

Kasznar, Kurt

Katanga, *n., pl.*
  Katangese

Kate and Allie

Katharine

Katharine Gibbs
  School

Katharine of Aragón

Katherine

Kathleen

Kathmandu *var. of*
  Katmandu

Kathryn

Katie

Katmai National Park

Katmai National
  Preserve

Katmandu *occas.*
  Kathmandu

Katmandu Tribhuvan
  International
  Airport

Katowice

Katrina

Katt, William

Kattegat *occas.*
  Cattegat

Katyn Massacre

Katzenbach, Nicholas

Katzenjammer Kids,
  The

Kauai

Kauffman, Angelica

Kauffman, Ewing
  Marion

Kaufman, George S.

Kaufman and Broad
  Home Corporation

Kaukauna

Kaunda, Kenneth

Kavafian, Ida

Kaverin, Veniamin

Kavir Desert

Kavner, Julie

Kaw

Kawabata, Yasunari

Kawasaki

Kawasaki disease

Kawasaki Heavy
  Industries Ltd.

Kawasaki Steel
  Corporation

Kawasaki syndrome

Kay, Sir

Kay, Ulysses

Kaye, Danny

Kaye, Dena

Kaye, M. M.

Kaye, Nora

Kaye, Sammy

Kaye, Stubby

Kayibanda, Grégoire

Kay Kyser's Kollege
  of Musical
  Knowledge

Kayla

Kazakh *or* Kazak

Kazakh Soviet
  Socialist Republic
  [*now* Kazakhstan]

Kazakhstan [*form.*
  Kazakh Soviet
  Socialist Republic]

Kazan, Elia

Kazan, Lainie

Kazantzakis, Nikos

Kazin, Alfred

KBS Inc.

KC and the Sunshine
  Band

KC-135 Stratotanker

KC-10

Keach, Stacy

Kealakekua

Kealakekua Bay

Kean, Charles

Kean, Mrs. Charles

Kean, Edmund

Kean College of New
  Jersey

Keane, Bil

Kearney [* NE; *see
  also* Kearny]

Kearney State College

Kearns

Kearny [* NJ; *see also*
  Kearney]

Kearny, Philip

Kearny, Stephen

Keating, Charles H.

Keating, Paul

Keaton, Buster

Keaton, Diane

Keaton, Michael

Keats, John

Keble, John

Keck, Howard
  Brighton

Keck, William Myron

Kedar

Kedarite

Kedrova, Lila

Keefe, Tim

Keego Harbor

Keel, Howard

Keeler, Christine

Keeler, Ruby

Keeler, Wee Willie

Keeling Islands

Keen, Geoffrey

Keene

Keene, Carolyn

Keene State College

Keep America Beautiful Association

Keeshan, Bob

Keesler Air Force Base

Kefauver, Estes

Keflavík

Keflavík Airport

Kehillath Yakov Rabbinical Seminary

Keillor, Garrison

Keinath, Pauline MacMillan

Keino, Kip

Keiser College of Technology

Keister-Williams Newspaper Services, Inc.

Keitel, Harvey

Keitel, Wilhelm

Keith

Keith, Brian

Keith, David

Keith, Ian

Keith, Minor C.

Keith, William

Kejimkujik National Park

Kekkonen, Urho

Kekulés formula

Kekulé von Stradonitz, Friedrich

Kell, George

Kellaway, Cecil

Keller, Gottfried

Keller, Helen

Keller Graduate School of Management

Kellerman, Sally

Kelley, DeForest

Kelley, Edgar

Kelley, Joe

Kelley, Kitty

Kellin, Mike

Kellner eyepiece

Kellogg

Kellogg, Frank B.

Kellogg, Will K.

Kellogg-Briand Pact

Kellogg Community College

Kellogg Company

Kellogg Foundation

Kellwood Company

Kelly

Kelly, Ellsworth

Kelly, Emmett

Kelly, Gene

Kelly, George

Kelly, Grace

Kelly, Jack

Kelly, Jim

Kelly, King

Kelly, Leontine T. C.

Kelly, Nancy

Kelly, Patsy

Kelly, Walt

Kelly, William Russell

Kelly Air Force Base

Kelly *occas.* kelly green

Kelly Services, Inc.

Keloland TV

Kelsey-Jenney College

Kelso

Kelthane™

Kelton, Pert

Kelvin, William Thomson

Kelvin effect

Kelvin scale

Kemal Atatürk

Kemalism

Kemal Pasha

Kemble, Agnes

Kemble, Charles

Kemble, Fanny

Kemerovo

Kemp, Jack

Kemper Corporation

Kemper Investors Life Insurance Company

Kemper Military School and College

Kempff, Wilhelm

Kenai Fjords National Park

Kenai Peninsula

Kendall, Kay

Kendall College

Kendall College of Art and Design

Kendall green

Kendalls, The

Kendall sneck bent

Kendra

Kendrew, Sir John Cowdery

Kendricks, Eddie
Kenilworth
Kenilworth ivy
Kenmore
Kennametal Inc.
Kennan, George F.
Kennebec
Kennebec Valley
  Technical College
Kennebunk
Kennebunkport
Kennedy, Anthony M.
Kennedy, Arthur
Kennedy, Bobby, Jr.
Kennedy, Edgar
Kennedy, Ethel
Kennedy, George
Kennedy, Jayne
Kennedy, Joan
Kennedy, John F.
Kennedy, Joseph P.
Kennedy, Joseph P., Jr.
Kennedy, Patrick
Kennedy, Robert F.
Kennedy, Rose
Kennedy, Ted
Kennedy Center for
  the Performing Arts
  National Memorial
Kennelly-Heaviside
  layer
Kenner
Kenner Products
  Company
Kennesaw Mountain
Kennesaw Mountain
  National Battlefield
  Park
Kennesaw State
  College

Kenneth
Kennewick
Kenny, Sister
  Elizabeth
Kenny method
Kenny treatment
Kenosha
Kenrick-Glennon
  Seminary
Kensett, John
Kensico Dam
Kensico Reservoir
Kensington
Kensington Palace
Kensington Rune
  Stone
Kent
Kent, Allegra
Kent, Clark
Kent, James
Kent, Rockwell
Kent, William
Kent International
  Airport
Kentish
Kentish fire
Kentish man, n., pl.
  Kentish men
Kentish tracery
Kentish woman, n., pl.
  Kentish women
Kenton, Stan
Kent State University
Kent State University
  Golden Flashes
Kent State University
  Press
Kentuckian
Kentucky
Kentucky and Virginia
  Resolutions

Kentucky bluegrass
Kentucky Christian
  College
Kentucky coffee tree
Kentucky College of
  Business
Kentucky colonel *or*
  Colonel
Kentucky Dam
Kentucky Derby
Kentucky Derby
  Festival
Kentucky Horse Park
Kentucky Lake
Kentucky Living
Kentucky Mountain
  Bible College
Kentucky Network
Kentucky rifle
Kentucky River
Kentucky saddler
Kentucky State
  University
Kentucky Utilities
  [*now* KU Energy
  Corporation]
Kentucky warbler
Kentucky Wesleyan
  College
Kentucky windage
Kenya
Kenyan
Kenyatta, Jomo
Kenyon, John Samuel
Kenyon College
Kenyon Review, The
Keogh, Eugene James
Keogh plan
Keokuk
Kepler, Johannes
Keplerian

Kepler's laws
Kepler telescope
Kercheval, Ken
Kerch Strait
Kerensky, Aleksandr
Kerguelen Islands
Kerkorian, Kirk
Kermit the Frog
Kern
Kern, Jerome
Kern Community
    College
Kerns, Joanna
Kerouac, Jack
Kerr, Clark
Kerr, Deborah
Kerr, Graham
Kerr, Jean
Kerr, John
Kerr, Michael
Kerr, Walter
Kerr cell
Kerr effect
Kerrey, Bob
Kerr-McGee
    Corporation
Kerrville
Kerry
Kerry blue terrier
Kerst, Donald
Kert, Larry
Kesey, Ken
Kessel, Barney
Kesselring, Albert
Ketch, Jack
Ketcham, Hank
Ketchikan
Ketchum, Hal
Ketèlby, Albert

Kettering
Kettering, Charles
Kettering College of
    Medical Arts
Keuka College
Keuka Lake
Kevin
Kevin, Saint
Kevlar™
Kevorkian, Jack
Kewanee [city in NY]
Keweenaw [peninsula
    in Lake Superior]
Kew Gardens
Kewpie™ doll
Key, Francis Scott
Key, Ted
Key Biscayne
Key Club
    International
KeyCorp
Keyes, Evelyn
Key Largo
Key lime *occas.* key
    lime pie
Keynes, John
    Maynard
Keynesian
Keynesianism
Keyser, Thomas de
Keyserling, Hermann
Keystone International
    Inc.
Keystone Junior
    College
Keystone Kops *or*
    Cops
Keystone Provident
    Life Insurance
    Company
Keystoner

Keystone State
Key West
Key West
    International
    Airport
Key West Naval Air
    Station
Khabarovsk
Khabur
Khachaturian, Aram
KHADRA
    International Folk
    Ballet
Khamenei, Ali
    Hoseini
Khan, Chaka
Khanh, Nguyen
Kharijite
Kharkov
Khartoum
Khartoum
    International
    Airport
Khartoum North
Khashoggi, Adnan
Khatanga
Khíos *occas.* Chios
    Island
Khirbat Qumran
Khmer, *n., pl.* Khmer
    or Khmers
Khmer Empire
Khmer Rouge
Khoikhoi
Khomeini, Ayatollah
    Ruhollah
Khrushchev, Nikita
    Sergeyevich
Khyber knife
Khyber Pass
Kiangsi [*now* Jiangxi]

Kiangsu [*now* Jiangsu]
Kiaochow
Kibbee, Guy
Kickapoo, *n.*, *pl.* Kickapoo *or* Kickapoos
Kicking Horse
Kicking Horse Pass
Kidd, Captain
Kidder, Margot
Kidderminster carpet
Kidder, Peabody and Company, Inc.
Kidder Peabody Foundation
Kidman, Nicole
Kid Ory
Kids "R" Us™ [company logo shows "R" reversed]
Kidwaves Radio Network, Inc.
Kiel
Kiel Canal
Kientpoos
Kiepura, Jan
Kierkegaard, Søren
Kierkegaardian
Kierkegaardianism
Kiev
Kievan
Kievan Russia
Kigali
Kiker, Douglas
Kikuyu, *n.*, *pl.* Kikuyu *or* Kikuyus
Kilauea
Kilauea Military Camp
Kilbride, Percy

Kildare
Kildare, Dr.
Kiley, Richard
Kilgallen, Dorothy
Kilgore
Kilgore College
Kilian Community College
Kilimanjaro
Kilkenny
Kilkenny tails
Killarney
Kill Devil Hill
Killebrew, Harmon
Killeen
Killingly
Killing Me Softly with His Song
Killingworth
Kill Van Kull
Killy, Jean-Claude
Kilmarnock
Kilmer, Joyce
Kilpatrick, Hugh
Kilroy
Kimball, Fiske
Kimball International, Inc.
Kimberly
Kimberly-Clark Corporation
Kimberly-Clark Foundation
Kimberly diamond mines
Kim Il Sung
Kim Young Sam
Kinabalu
Kincaid, Jamaica
Kincaid, Thomas

Kincardine
Kincardineshire
Kincheloe Air Force Base
Kinchinjunga *var. of* Kanchenjunga
Kindergarten Cop
Kinderhook
Kiner, Ralph
King, Alan
King, B. B.
King, Billie Jean
King, Carole
King, Coretta Scott
King, Ernest J.
King, Frank
King, Karl
King, Larry [talk-show host]
King, Larry L. [writer]
King, Mackenzie
King, Martin Luther, Jr.
King, Pee Wee
King, Peggy
King, Perry
King, Richard
King, Rodney
King, Rufus
King, Stephen
King, William Lyon Mackenzie
King Abd al-Aziz International Airport
King and I, The
King Arthur
King Baudouin
King Carl XVI Gustaf
King Charles' head

King Charles spaniel
King Cole Trio
King College
King Cotton
Kingdom Hall
Kingdom of Heaven
Kingdom of Sardinia
Kingdom of the Two
  Sicilies
King Fahd ibn Abdul
  Aziz Al Saud
King Fahd
  International
  Airport
King Faisal
King Farouk
King Features
  Syndicate, Inc.
King Ferdinand II
King George
King George VI Falls
King George's War
King Harald V
King Hassan
King Hussein
King Hussein ibn
  Talal *occas.*
  Hussain ibn Talal
King James Bible
King James Version
King James Version of
  the Bible
King John
King Khalid
  International
  Airport
King Kong
Kinglake, Alexander
King Lear
Kingman
Kingman Reef

King Mark
King Menelaus
King Midget
King of England
King of Hearts
King of Kings *occas.*
  kings
King of the Jews
King Oliver
King Peak
King Pelles
King Philip
King Philip's War
King Ranch
King Ranch, Inc.
Kings Bay Naval
  Submarine Base
King's Bench
King's Birthday
king's bounty *occas.*
  King's Bounty
Kings Canyon
  National Park
King's Champion
King's College
king's colour *occas.*
  King's colour *or*
  King's Colour
King's Counsel
Kings Dominion
king's *or* King's
  English
Kings Island
Kingsley, Ben
Kingsley, Charles
Kingsley, Sidney
Kingsley Field
King's mark
Kings Mountain

Kings Mountain
  National Military
  Park
King Solomon's
  Mines
Kings Peak
Kings Point
Kingsport
King's Proctor
King's Remembrancer
Kings River
  Community College
King's Singers, The
Kingston [* MA; MO;
  NH; NY; PA; RI;
  TN; Jamaica;
  Ontario; *see also*
  Kingstown;
  Kinston]
Kingston, Maxine
  Hong
Kingston Trio, The
Kingstown [* Saint
  Vincent and the
  Grenadines; *see
  also* Kingston]
Kingsville
Kingsville Naval Air
  Station
King Tut
King William
King William Island
King William's War
King World Company
King World
  Productions, Inc.
Kinison, Sam
Kinks, The
Kinney Shoe Store
Kinsey, Alfred
Kinsey report
Kinshasa [*form.*
  Léopoldville]

Kinski, Klaus

Kinski, Nastassja

Kinsley, Michael

Kinston [* NC; *see also* Kingston]

Kiowa, *n., pl.* Kiowa *or* Kiowas

Kipling, Rudyard

Kiplinger's Personal Finance Magazine

Kiplinger Washington Letter

Kipnis, Alexander

Kipnis, Igor

Kirby, Bruno

Kirby, Durward

Kirby, Jack

Kirby, Rollin

Kirby-Smith, Edmund

Kirchhoff, Gustav Robert

Kirchhoff's law

Kirchner, Ernst Ludwig

Kirchner, Leon

Kirghiz *or* Kirgyz, *n., pl.* Kirghiz *or* Kirghizes *or* Kirghyz *or* Kirghyzes

Kirghizia *var. of* Kirghiz Soviet Socialist Republic [*now* Kyrgyzstan]

Kirghizian

Kirghiz Soviet Socialist Republic *or* Kirgizia [*now* Kyrgyzstan]

Kirghiz Steppe

Kiribati

Kirilenko, Andrei

Kirin

Kirin Brewery Company, Ltd.

Kiritimati Island

Kirk, Captain James

Kirk, Grayson

Kirk, Lisa

Kirkland

Kirkland, Gelsey

Kirkland, Jack

Kirkland, Kenny

Kirkland, Lane

Kirkland, Sally

Kirkpatrick, Jeane

Kirksville

Kirksville College of Osteopathic Medicine

Kirkus Reviews [*now* Jim Kobak's Kirkus Reviews]

Kirkwood

Kirkwood Community College

Kirkwood's gaps

Kirlian, Semyon D.

Kirlian, Valentina K.

Kirlian photography

Kirman carpet

Kirov

Kirov Ballet

Kirov Opera

Kirstein, Lincoln

Kirsten, Dorothy

Kirtland

Kirtland, Jared P.

Kirtland Air Force Base

Kirtland Community College

Kirtland's warbler

Kisangani [*form.* Stanleyville]

Kisatchie National Forest

K. I. Sawyer Air Force Base

Kishi, Nobosuke

Kishwaukee College

Kislev

Kismet

Kiss

Kissimmee

Kissinger, Henry A.

Kiss Me, Kate

Kitakyushu

Kit-Cat Club

Kitchen Cabinet

Kitchener

Kitchener, Horatio Herbert

Kitchener's army

Kite, Tom

Kitredge, George Lyman

Kitt, Eartha

Kittakachorn, Thanom

Kittatinny Mountain

Kittery

Kitt Peak

Kitt Peak National Observatory

Kittredge, George

Kitty Hawk

Kivu

Kiwanian

Kiwanis

Kiwanis club

Kiwanis International

Ki-Wives International

Kizil Irmak

Klamath

Klamath Falls

Klamath [Indian], *n.*, *pl.* Klamath *or* Klamaths

Klamath Lake

Klamath National Forest

Klamath weed

Klan

Klanism

Klansman, *n.*, *pl.* Klansmen

Klanwatch

Klanwatch Intelligence Report

Klaxon™

Klebs, Edwin

Klebs-Löffler bacillus

Klee, Paul

Kleenex™

Kleiber, Erich

Klein, A. M.

Klein, Anne

Klein, Calvin

Klein, Chuck

Klein, Felix

Klein, Kelly

Klein, Melanie

Klein, Robert

Klein bottle

Kleinian

Kleist, Heinrich von

Kleistian

Klem, Bill

Klemperer, Otto

Klemperer, Werner

Kliban, B.

Klikitat

Klimt, Gustav

K-line

Kline, Benjamin S.

Kline, Franz

Kline, Kevin

Klinefelter, Harry F.

Klinefelter's syndrome

Klinefelter's Syndrome Association of Canada

Kline test

Klinger, Max

Klingon

KLM Royal Dutch Airlines

Klondike

Klondike gold rush

Klondike Gold Rush National Historical Park

Klopstock, Friedrich Gottlieb

Kluane National Park

Kluge, John Werner

Klugman, Jack

Kluwer Academic Publishers

Kmart Corporation

Kmart store

K-meson

Knef, Hildegarde

Knesset

Knickerbocker

Knickerbocker, Diedrich

Knickerbocker Arena

Knickerbocker Group

Knies, Karl Gustav Adolf

Knievel, Evel

Knievel, Robbie

Knife and Fork Club International

Knife River Indian Villages National Historic Site

Knight, Bobby

Knight, Charles

Knight, Eric

Knight, Frank Hyneman

Knight, Gladys

Knight, Jonathan

Knight, Jordan

Knight, Philip Hampson

Knight, Sarah Kemble

Knight, Shirley

Knight, Ted

Knight Commander of the Order of the British Empire

Knight Commission on Intercollegiate Athletics

Knight, Death, and the Devil

Knight Grand Cross of the British Empire

Knightly Association of Saint George the Martyr

Knight News Wire

Knight-Ridder Financial News

Knight-Ridder Inc.

Knights Hospitalers

Knights of Aquarius Order

Knights of Columbus

Knights of Jerusalem

Knights of Labor

Knights of Malta

Knights of Pythias

Knights of Rhodes

Knights of Saint Crispin

Knights of Saint John of Jerusalem

Knights of the Bath

Knights of the Golden Circle

Knights of the Ku Klux Klan

Knights of the Maccabees

Knights of the Round Table

Knights of the Sword

Knights of the White Camellia

Knights Templar, Grand Encampment, U.S.A.

Knight Templar, *n.*, *pl.* Knights Templar [member of a Masonic order]

Knight Templar, *n.*, *pl.* Knights Templars [member of military and religious order of the Crusades]

K-9

K-9 corps

Knitted Textile Association

Knitting Guild of America, The

Knoop scale

Knopf, Alfred A.

Knopfler, Mark

Knossos *occas.* Cnossus

Knots Landing

Knotts, Don

Knotts Berry Farm

Knowledge Systems Institute

KnowledgeWare, Inc.

Knowles, John

Know-Nothing movement

Knox, Frank

Knox, Henry

Knox, John

Knox, Philander Chase

Knox College

Knoxville

Knoxville Business College

Knoxville College

Knudsen, Martin

Knudsen, William S.

Knudsen effect

Kobe

Kobuk Valley National Park

Koch, Charles de Ganahl

Koch, David Hamilton

Koch, Edward I.

Koch, Frederick Robinson

Koch, Kenneth

Koch, William Ingraham

Kochanowski, Jan

Köchel, Ludwig Ritter von

Köchel number

Koch Industries, Inc.

Kodak™

Kodály, Zoltán

Kodel™

Kodiak bear

Kodiak Coast Guard Support Center

Kodiak Island

Kodiak Naval Air Station

Koenig, Walter

Koestler, Arthur

Koffka, Kurt

Kohan, Buz

Kohinoor *or* Koh-i-noor diamond

Kohl, Helmut

Kohlberg, Jerome Spiegel, Jr.

Kohlberg Kravis Roberts and Company

Köhler, Wolfgang

Kohler family

Kohl's Department Stores

Kohoutek comet

Koh's Food Stores

Kojak

Kokomo

Kokoschka, Oskar

Kola Peninsula

Kolbe, Georg

Kollwitz, Käthe

Kol Nidre

Kol Yaakov Torah Center

Kolyma

Kolyma forced-labor camp

Kolyma Gold Fields

Kolyma Range

Komodo dragon ‑

Komsomol

Kona

Kondratieff, N. D.

Kondratieff waves

Koner, Pauline

Kongo, *n.*, *pl.* Kongos or Kongo

Konica Business Machines U.S.A., Inc.

Konica Corporation

Konigsberg, Elaine

Konitz, Lee

Kon-Tiki

Kon-Tiki expedition

Kool-Aid™

Kool and the Gang

Koolau Range

Kool Moe Dee

Koontz, Dean R.

Koop, C. Everett

Koopmans, Tjaling Charles

Koor Industries Ltd.

Kootenai

Kootenai National Forest

Kootenai National Park

Kootenay *var. of* Kutenai Indian

Kootenay Lake

Kopechne, Mary Jo

Kopell, Bernie

Koplik, Henry

Koplik's spots

Koppel, Ted

Koppers Company, Inc.

Koran *occas.* Quran

Koranic

Korat

Koratron™

Korbut, Olga

Korea

Korea Bay

Korean

Korean Air

Korean azalea

Korean conflict

Korean lawn grass

Korean Peninsula

Korean War

Korean War Veterans Association

Korean War Veterans Memorial

Korea Strait

Korematsu v. United States

Koren, Arthur

Koren, Edward

Koresh, David

Korman, Harvey

Kornberg, Arthur

Korngold, Erich Wolfgang

Kornilov, Lavrenti

Kors, Michael

Korsakoff's psychosis

Korsakoff's syndrome

Kort nozzle

Korzybski, Alfred

Kosciusko, Thaddeus

Kosinski, Jerzy

Kossuth, Ferenc

Kossuth, Lajos

Kostelanetz, André

Kosygin, Aleksei Nikolaevich

Kotex™

Kotto, Yaphet

Kotzebue

Kotzebue, August von

Kotzebue, Otto von

Kotzebue Sound

Kouchibouguac National Park

Koufax, Sandy

Kouric, Katherine

Koussevitzky, Serge

Kovacs, Ernie

Kovalevsky, Sonia

Kowloon

Kowloon City

Kowloon Peninsula

Koyaanisqatsi

Koyukon

Kozlowski, Linda

KPMG Peat Marwick

Krafft-Ebing, Richard von

Kraft *or* Krafft, Adam

Kraft General Foods Foundation

Kraft General Foods, Inc.

Kraft Music Hall, The

Kraft Television Theatre

Krakatau *occas.* Krakatoa

Kraków

Kramer, Jack

Kramer, Joseph

Kramer, Stanley

Kramer, Stepfanie

Kramer vs. Kramer
Krantz, Judith
Krapp, George
K ration
Kraus, Karl
Krauss, Clemens
Kravis, Henry R.
Kravitz, Lenny
Krebs, Sir Hans Adolf
Krebs cycle
Kredietbank
Krehbiel, John
  Hammond, Sr.
Kreisler, Fritz
Kremlin
Kremlinologist
Kremlinology
Křenek, Ernst
Kresge, Sebastian S.
Kresge Foundation
Kreskin
Kress, Samuel H.
Kretschmer, Ernst
Kretschmer's types
Kreutzer, Rodolphe
Kreutzer Sonata
  [musical piece]
Kreutzer Sonata, The
  [novel]
Kreymborg, Alfred
Krieghoff, Cornelius
Krips, Josef
Krishna
Krishnaism
Krishna Menon,
  Vengalil Krishnan
Krishnamurti, Jiddu
Kris Kross
Kriss Kringle

Krista
Kristallnacht
Kristen
Kristiansand or
  Cristiansand
  [Norwegian port on
  the Skaggerak; see
  also Kristiansund]
Kristianstad
Kristiansund or
  Cristiansund
  [Norwegian port on
  the Atlantic; see
  also Kristiansand]
Kristin
Kristina
Kristofferson, Kris
Kroc, Joan Beverly
Kroc, Ray A.
Kroch's & Brentano's
Krokodil
Kroeber, Alfred L.
Krofft, Marty
Krofft, Sid
Kroft, Steve
Kroger Company, The
Kroger Company
  Foundation
Kroger Nascar 200
Krogh, Auguste
Krogh, Christian
Krol, John Joseph
  Cardinal
Kroll, Leon
Kronberger, Louis
Kronborg castle
Kronecker, Leopold
Kronecker delta
Kronos Quartet
Kropotkin, Pyotr
  Alekseyevich

KRS-One
KRTN News Wire
Kruger, Otto
Kruger, Paul
Kruger National Park
Krugerrand
Krugersdorp
Krumgold, Joseph
Krupa, Gene
Krupp, Alfred
Krupp, Friedrich
Krupp, Friedrich
  Alfred
Krupp Stahl
Krupp Steel of
  America Inc.
Krupp Steel Products
  Inc.
Krupp von Bohlen
  und Halbach, Alfred
Krupp von Bohlen
  und Halbach,
  Gustav
Krupskaya, Nadezhda
Krusenstern, Adam
Krutch, Joseph Wood
Krypton
Kryptonian
Kryptonite™ lock
Krystal
K-shell
KSN Television
  Group
KTLA/United Video
K-truss
KTVT/United Video
Kuala Lumpur
Kubelík, Jan
Kubelík, Rafael
Kubicka, Terry

Kubitschek, Juscelino

Kublai Khan *occas.* Kubla Khan

Kübler-Ross, Elisabeth

Kubota Corporation

Kubrick, Stanley

KU Energy Corporation [*form.* Kentucky Utilities]

Kuhlman, Kathryn

Kuhn, Bowie

Kuhn, Maggie

Kuhn, Richard

Kuhn, Thomas Samuel

Kuhn, Walt

Kuhnau, Johann

Ku K'ai-chih

Kukla, Fran and Ollie

Ku Klux

Ku Kluxer

Ku Kluxism

Ku Klux Klan

Ku Klux Klanner

Kulp, Nancy

Kultur

Kulturkampf

Kulturkreis, *n., pl.* Kulturkreise

Kumgang San

Kun, Béla

Kung, *n., pl.* Kung *or* Kungs

Küng, Hans

Kunigunde, Saint

Kunitz, Stanley

Kuniyoshi, Yasuo

Kunlun

K'un-ming [*now* Kunming]

Kunsthistorisches Museum

Kunstler, William

Kunstlied, *n., pl.* Kunstlieder

Kuomintang

Kupcinet, Irv

Kupka, František

Kuprin, Alexander Ivanovich

Kup's Show

Kura

Kuralt, Charles

Kurd

Kurdish

Kurdistan

Kurfürstendamm

Kuril *or* Kurile Islands

Kurokawa, Noriaki

Kurosawa, Akira

Kurt Jooss Ballet

Kurtz, Swoosie

Kushan Empire

Kuskokwim

Kutcher Quartet

Kutchin Indian

Kutenai *occas.* Kootenay Indian

Kutuzov, Mikhail Illaronovich

Kutztown

Kutztown University of Pennsylvania

Kuwait

Kuwaiti

Kuznets, Simon

Kuznetsk Ala-Tau

Kuznetsk Basin

Kwajalein

Kwak, Sung

Kwakiutl

Kwan, Nancy

Kwangju

Kwangtung [*now* Guangdong]

Kwanzaa

Kweichow [*now* Guizhou]

Kyd, Thomas

Kyle

Kyoto

Kyowa Bank, Ltd.

Kyrgyz

Kyrgyzstan [*form.* Kirghiz Soviet Socialist Republic]

Kyrie

Kyrie eleison

Kyser, Kay

Kyushu

Kyzyl Kum

L

Laar *var. of* Laer, Pieter van

La Bamba

LaBelle, Patti

La Belle Dame sans Merci

La Belle Époque

Labette Community College

Labiche, Eugène Marin

La Bohème

Labor and Socialist International

Laboratory Institute of Merchandising

Labor Day

Laborers' International Union of North America

Laborite, *British* Labourite

Labor-Management Reporting and Disclosure Act

Labor, *British* Labour, Party

Labor Relations Act

labors of Hercules

Laboure College

Labrador

Labrador Current

Labrador duck

Labradorean

Labrador retriever

labrador *occas.* Labrador tea

Labrador-Ungava

La Brea

La Brea tar pits

La Bruyère, Jean de

Labuan

La Cage aux Folles

La Cage aux Folles II

Lacalle, Luis Alberto

Laccadive Islands

Lac Courte Oreilles Ojibwa Community College

Lachaise, Gaston

Lachine

Lachine Canal

Lackawanna

Lackawanna Junior College

Lackland Air Force Base

Laclède, Pierre

Laclede Gas Charitable Trust

Laclede Gas Company

La Comédie-Française

Laconia

Laconian

La Coruña

Lacoste, René

Lacretelle, Jacques de

Lacroix, Christian

La Crosse

Lacrosse Foundation

Lacrosse Hall of Fame

LACSA [airline]

Ladd, Alan

Ladd, Cheryl

Ladd, Diane

Ladewig, Marion

Ladies Auxiliary to Veterans of Foreign Wars of the United States

Ladies' Day

Ladies' Home Journal

Ladies' Peace

Ladies Pro Bowlers Tour

Ladies Professional Golf Association

Ladino

Ladino clover

Ladislaus

Ladislaus, Saint

La Dolce Vita
Ladue
Lady Abracadabra
Lady Baltimore cake
Lady Banks' rose
Lady Bountiful
Lady Bracknell
Lady Byng Memorial Trophy
Lady chapel
Lady Chatterley's Lover
Lady Day
Lady Godiva
Lady Hamilton in a Straw Hat
Lady Lever Art Gallery
Lady Macbeth
Lady Macduff
Lady Maxine
Lady of Shalott
Lady of the Lake, The
Lady of the Lamp
Lady's Circle
Ladysmith
Ladysmith Black Mambazo
Lady's Not for Burning, The
Lady Washington geranium
Laer or Laar, Pieter van
Laertes
Laetare Medal
Laetare Sunday
Laettner, Christian
La Farge, Christopher
La Farge, John

La Farge, Oliver
Lafarge Corporation
LaFaro, Scott
Lafayette [* AL; CA; CO; IN; LA; TN]
La Fayette [* GA; see also Lafayette]
La Fayette, Marie de
La Fayette or Lafayette, Marquis de
Lafayette College
Lafayette College Leopards
Lafayette Escadrille
Lafayette Southwest
Lafayette squadron
L.A. Features Syndicate
Laffer, Arthur
Laffer Curve occas. curve
Laffite, Jean
Lafleur, Guy
La Follette, Belle Case
La Follette, Robert Marion, Jr.
La Follette, Robert Marion, Sr.
La Fontaine, Jean de
Laforet, Carmen
LaForge, Lieutenant Commander Geordi
La Forza del Destino
Lafosse, Charles de
La Fournarina
La Fresnaye, Roger de
Lag b'Omer
L.A. Gear Inc.
Lagerfield, Karl

Lagerkvist, Pär
Lagerlöf, Selma
La Gioconda
Lago Maggiore
Lagoon Islands
Lagoon Nebula
Lagoon of Venice
Lagos
La Goulue
La Grande
La Grande Chartreuse
Lagrange [* IN]
La Grange [* GA; IL; KY; NC; TX]
Lagrange, Joseph Louis
LaGrange College
Lagrange multipliers
La Grange Park
Lagrange's method
Lagrange theorem
Lagrangian
Lagrangian function
La Guardia, Fiorello H.
La Guardia International Airport
Laguerre, Edmond Nicholas
Laguerre equation
Laguna
Laguna Beach
Laguna Seca Raceway
La Habra
Lahore
Lahore Museum
Lahore party
Lahr, Bert
Lahti, Christine

Laine, Cleo

Laine, Frankie

Laing, R. D.

Laingian

Laird, Melvin

Lajoie, Napoleon

La Jolla

La Jolla Academy of Advertising Arts

La Junta

Lake, Simon

Lake, Veronica

Lake Agassiz

Lake Albano

Lake Albert

Lake Area Vocational-Technical Institute

Lake Argentino

Lake Arthur

Lake Athabasca

Lake Baikal *occas.* Baykal

Lake Balkhash

Lake Bangweulu *or* Bangweolo

Lake Baykal *var. of* Baikal

Lake Bistineau

Lake Bluff

Lake Bomoseen

Lake Bonneville

Lake Bridgeport

Lake Calumet

Lake Carmel

Lake Chad

Lake Champlain

Lake Chany

Lake Chargog-gagoggman-chaugagogg-chaubun-agungamaug

Lake Charles

Lake Chelan

Lake Chelan National Recreation Area

Lake Chinook

Lake Chudskoye

Lake City

Lake City Community College

Lake Clark National Park

Lake Clark National Preserve

Lake Como

Lake Constance

Lake Country

Lake District

Lake Edward

Lake Erie

Lake Erie College

Lake Eyre

Lake Forest

Lake Forest College

Lake Forest Graduate School of Management

Lake Garda

Lake Geneva

Lake George

Lake George Opera Festival

Lake Havasu

Lake Havasu City

Lakehead University

Lake Hula *or* Huleh

Lake Huron

Lakehurst

Lakehurst Naval Air Station

Lakehurst Naval Engineering Center

Lake Ijssel *or* Issel *or* Yssel

Lake Ilmen

Lake Itasca

Lake Jackson

Lake Karun

Lake Kemp

Lake Kissimee

Lake Kivu

Lake Koocanusa

Lake Kyoga

Lake Ladoga

Lake Lahontan

Lakeland

Lakeland College

Lakeland Community College

Lakeland terrier

Lake Louise

Lake Lugano

Lake Magadi

Lake Maggiore

Lake Malawi

Lake Managua

Lake Manitoba

Lake Maracaibo

Lake McClure

Lake Mead

Lake Mead National Recreation Area

Lake Melville

Lake Memphremagog

Lake Meredith

Lake Meredith National Recreation Area

Lake Michigan

Lake Michigan College

Lake Mills

Lake Minnetonka

Lake Mistassini

Lake Mohawk

Lakemore

Lake Murray

Lake Mweru

Lake Nasser

Lake Natron

Lake Nemi

Lake Neusiedler

Lake Nicaraugua

Lake Nipigon

Lake Nipissing *occas.* Nepissing

Lake Nyasa

Lake of Bienne

Lake of Constance

Lake of Death

Lake of Dreams

Lake of Lucerne

Lake of Neuchâtel

Lake of the Cherokees

Lake of the Ozarks

Lake of the Woods

Lake of Thun

Lake of Wallenstadt

Lake of Zurich

Lake Ohrid

Lake Okeechobee

Lake Onega

Lake Onondaga

Lake Ontario

Lake Orion

Lake Ouachita

Lake Park

Lake Peipus

Lake Pend Oreille

Lake Pepin

Lake Placid

Lake Plescheyevo

Lake Poets

Lake Ponchartrain

Lake Poopó

Lake Powell

Lake Powell Reservoir

Lake Prespa

Lake Providence

Lake Quinalt

Lake Ronkonkoma

Lake Rudolf

Lake Saint Clair

Lake Saint Francis

Lake Saint John

Lake Sakajewea

Lake School

Lake Scutari

Lake Sevan

Lakeshore Technical College

Lakeside Speedway

Lake Simcoe

Lakes of Killarney

Lake Success

Lake Sumner

Lake-Sumter Community College

Lake Superior

Lake Superior State University

Lake Taal

Lake Tahoe

Lake Tahoe Community College

Lake Tana

Lake Tanganyika

Lake Taupo

Lake Texcoco

Lake Texoma

Lake Titicaca

Lake Torrens

Lake Traverse

Lake Turkana

Lake Urmia

Lake Victoria

Lakeview

Lakeview College of Nursing

Lake Village

Lakeville

Lake Volta

Lake Wales

Lake Washington

Lake Washington Canal

Lake Washington Floating Bridge

Lake Windermere

Lake Winnebago

Lake Winnibigoshish

Lake Winnipeg

Lake Winnipegosis

Lake Winnipesaukee

Lake Wobegon

Lakewood

Lakewood Community College

Lake Worth

Lake Worth Village

Lake Xochimilco

Lake Zurich

Lakmé

La Lanne, Jack

L.A. Law

La Leche League
  International
Lalo, Édouard
La Loge
Lamaism
Lamaist
La Mama
  Experimental
  Theatre Club
La Manch
Lamar
Lamar, Mirabeau
  Buonaparte
Lamarck, Jean Baptist
  de
Lamarckian
Lamarckism
Lamarck's theory of
  evolution
Lamar Community
  College
La Marque
Lamarr, Hedy
La Marseillaise
Lamartine, Alphonse
  Marie Louis de
Lamar University
Lamar University
  Cardinals
Lamas, Fernando
Lamas, Lorenzo
La Maurice National
  Park
Lamaze, Fernand
Lamaze method
Lamaze technique
Lamb, Charles
Lamb, Gil
Lamb, Harold
Lamb, Mary Ann
Lamb, Willis Eugene

Lambaréné
Lambda Chi Alpha
Lambeau Field
Lambert, Jack
Lambert, Johann
  Heinrich
Lambert, Hendricks
  and Ross
Lambert conformal
  projection
Lambert projection
Lambert-Saint Louis
  International
  Airport
Lambertville
Lambeth
Lambeth Conference
Lambeth degree
Lambeth Palace
Lambeth walk
Lamb of God
Lambs, The
Lambuth College
Lame Duck
  Amendment
Lamentation of Christ,
  The
Lamentations
La Mesa [* CA]
Lamesa [* TX]
La Mirada
Lammas
Lammas Day
Lammastide
Lamont
La Mothe, Antoine de
La Motta, Jake
Lamour, Dorothy
L'Amour, Louis
Lampasas

Lampedusa
Lampedusa, Giuseppe
  di
Lampert, Zohra
Lampley, Jim
Lamp unto My Feet
Lamson Junior
  College
Lamy, John Baptiste
Lamy's theorem
Lanacane Laboratories
Lanai
Lancashire
Lancashire chair
Lancashire cheese
Lancashire hearth
Lancaster
Lancaster, Burt
Lancaster Bible
  College
Lancaster Mills
Lancaster New Era
Lancaster Sound
Lancaster Theological
  Seminary
Lancastrian
Lance, Inc.
Lancelot var. of
  Launcelot, Sir
Lance missile
Lancet
Lanchester, Elsa
LanChile Airlines
Lanchow [now
  Lanzhou]
Lancret, Nicolas
Land, Edwin Herbert
Landau, Lev
Landau, Martin

Landegger, Carl Clement

Landegger, George Francis

Lander

Lander College

Landers, Ann

Landers, Audrey

Landers, Judy

Landes

Landesberg, Steve

Land Grant Act

Landini, Francesco

Landini cadence

Landis, Carole

Landis, Jessie Royce

Landis, John

Landis, Kenesaw Mountain

Land League

Landmark College

Landmark Communications, Inc.

Landmark Tower

Land of Beulah

Land *occas.* land of Nod

Land of Opportunity

Land of Oz

Land of Promise

Land of Steady Habits

Land of the Lost

Land of the Midnight Sun

Land of the Rising Sun

Land O'Lakes, Inc.

Landon, Alfred M.

Landon, Michael

Landor, Walter Savage

Landowska, Wanda

Landrace swine

Landrum-Griffin Act

Landry, Greg

Landry, Tom

Landsat

Landscape at Collioure

Landseer, Sir Edwin Henry

Land's *occas.* Lands End

Lands' End, Inc.

Landsteiner, Karl

Landsturm

Landwehr

Lane, Abbe

Lane, Burton

Lane, Charles

Lane, Diane

Lane, FitzHugh

Lane, Priscilla

Lane Bryant

Lane College

Lane Community College

Laneuville

Laney College

Lanfranco, Giovanni

Lang, Andrew

Lang, Eddie

Lang, Fritz

Lang, k. d. *occas.* Lang, K. D.

Lang, Pearl

Lang, Stephen

Langdon, Harry

Langdon, Sue Ane

Lange, Dorothea

Lange, Hope

Lange, Jessica

Langella, Frank

Langer, Susanne

Langer, William Leonard

Langerhans, Paul

Langford, Frances

Langford, Gordon

Langhans, Theodor

Langhans' layer

Langland *occas.* Langley, William

Langley, Samuel Pierpont

Langley *var. of* Langland, William

Langley Air Force Base

Langley Park

Langley Research Center

Langmuir, Irving

Langston University

Langton, Stephen Cardinal

Langtry, Lillie

Languedoc

Languedocian

Languedoc-Rousillon

Lanier, Bob

Lanier, Sydney

Lankester, Michael

Lansbury, Angela

Lansdale School of Business

Lansdowne

Lansing

Lansing, Robert

Lansing, Sherry Lee

Lansing Community
   College
Lanson, Snooky
Lantana
Lantz, Walter
Lanza, Mario
Lanzhou [*form.*
   Lanchow]
Lao, *n., pl.* Lao *or*
   Laos
Laocoön
La Opinion
Laos
Laotian
Lao-tzu *occas.* Lao-tse
   or Lao-tsze
La Paz
La Paz El Alto
   International
   Airport
Lapeer
La Pérouse, Jean
La Pérouse Strait
Laplace, Pierre Simon
Laplace equation
Laplace operator
Laplace transform
Laplacian
Lapland
Laplander
La Plata
La Porte
Lapotaire, Jane
Lapp
Lappish
Lapsang souchong tea
Laptev Sea
La Puente
Laputa
Laputan

La Quinta Motor Inn
Laramie
Laramie County
   Community College
Laramie Range
La Raza
La Raza Newspaper
Larbaud, Valéry
Larchmont
Lardner, Ring
Lardner, Ring W., Jr.
Laredo
Laredo, Ruth
Laredo International
   Airport
Laredo Junior College
Laredo State
   University
Large White
Largo
Largo Entertainment
Larkin, Philip
Larkspur
Larksville
L'Arlésienne Suites
Lar Lubovitch Dance
   Company
Larmor, Sir Joseph
Larmor precession
Larmor theorem
Larnaca
Larnaca International
   Airport
Larned
La Roche College
La Rochefoucauld,
   François de
La Rosa, Julius
LaRouche, Lyndon H.
Larousse, Pierre

Larrigan
Larrocha, Alicia de
Larroquette, John
Larry
Larry Gatlin and the
   Gatlin Brothers
   Band
Larry King Live!
Larry King Show, The
Larson, Gary
LaRue, Lash
La Salle
La Salle, Sieur de
LaSalle Quartet
La Salle University
La Salle University
   Explorers
Las Animas
La Scala
Lascaux Cave
Las Cruces
Las Cruces
   International
   Airport
Lasell College
Lasker, Albert
Laski, Harold J.
Las Meninas
Lasorda, Tommy
Lassa fever
Lassalle, Ferdinand
Lassen College
Lassen National
   Forest
Lassen Peak
Lassen Volcanic
   National Park
Lasser, Louise
Lassie
Lassie Come Home

Last Days of Pompeii,
The

Last Emperor, The

Lastex™

Last Judgement, The
[painting]

Last Judgment [event]

Last Métro, The

Last of the Mohicans,
The

Last Supper

Last Whole Earth
Catalog, The

Las Vegas

Las Vegas Invitational
PGA Golf
Tournament

Las Vegas Review-
Journal

Las Vegas Sun

Late George Apley,
The

Late Greek

Lateiner, Jacob

Late Latin

Late Night with David
Letterman

Lateran

Lateran Church

Lateran Council

Lateran Palace

Lateran Treaty

Later Chin dynasty

Later Han dynasty

Later T'ang dynasty

Later with Bob Costas

Latimer, Hugh

Latimer, Lewis H.

Latin

Latina, *fem.* [*see also*
Latino]

Latin alphabet

Latin America

Latin-American *occas.*
Latin American,
adj.

Latin American Free
Trade Association

Latin American
Integration
Association

Latinate

Latin Church

Latin cross

Latin Empire of
Constantinople

Latinian

Latinic

Latinism

Latinist

Latin Kingdom of
Jerusalem

Latin language

Latin literature

Latino, *fem.*, *masc.*
[*see also* Latina]

Latin Quarter

Latin Rite

Latin school

Latin square

Latinus

La Tour, Georges de

La Traviata

Latrobe

Latrobe, Benjamin
Henry

Latter-day Saint
[member of original
Church]

Latter Day Saint
[member of
Reorganized
Church]

Latter-Day Saints
Business College

Lattimore, Owen

Lattimore, Richmond

Latvia [*form.* Latvian
Soviet Socialist
Republic]

Latvian

Latvian Evangelical
Lutheran Church of
America

Latvian Soviet
Socialist Republic
[*now* Latvia]

Laubach Literacy
International

Lauck, Chester

Laud, William

Lauda, Nikki

Lauder, Estée

Lauder, Sir Harry

Lauder, Leonard Alan

Lauder, Ronald Steven

Laudian

Laudianism

Laugh-In

Laughing Cavalier,
The

Laughlin

Laughlin, James L.

Laughlin Air Force
Base

Laughton, Charles

Launcelot *or* Lancelot,
Sir

Laundromat™

Launfal, Sir

Lauper, Cyndi

Laura

Laura Dean Dancers
and Musicians

Laura Ingalls Wilder
  Award
Laurasia
Laurel
Laurel, Stan
Laurel and Hardy
Lauren
Lauren, Ralph
Laurence, John
Laurence, Margaret
Laurence Olivier
  Award
Laurencin, Marie
Laurens
Laurent, Herman
Laurent, Robert
Laurentian
Laurentian Highlands
Laurentian Library,
  The
Laurentian Mountains
Laurentian Plateau
Laurentian Shield
Laurentian University
Laurentides, the
Laurentides Park
Laurent series
Laurent's theorem
Lauriat's bookstore
Laurie, Piper
Laurier, Sir Wilfrid
Laurinburg
Laurium
Lausanne
Lausanne Pact
Lausiter Neisse
Lauter, Ed
Lava Beds National
  Monument

Laval, Pierre
Laval University
Lavelle, Terri
Lavender, David
Laver, Rod
La Verne
Laverne and Shirley
Lavin, Cheryl
Lavin, Linda
Lavinia
Lavoisier, Antoine
  Laurent
Law, Andrew Bonar
Law, Bernard Cardinal
Law, John
Law and Order
Law Day USA
L.A. Weekly
Law Enforcement
  Assistance
  Administration
Lawford, Peter
law French
law Latin
Lawndale
law of Malus
Law of Moses
Law of the Medes and
  the Persians
Lawrence
Lawrence, Carol
Lawrence, D. H.
Lawrence, Elliot
Lawrence, Ernest O.
Lawrence, Gertrude
Lawrence, Jack
Lawrence, Jacob
Lawrence, John H.
Lawrence, Marc

Lawrence, M. Larry
Lawrence, Saint
Lawrence, Steve
Lawrence, T. E.
Lawrence, Sir Thomas
Lawrence, Tracy
Lawrence, Vicki
Lawrence Berkeley
  Laboratory
Lawrenceburg
Lawrence frame
Lawrence Livermore
  Laboratory
Lawrence of Arabia
Lawrence Park
Lawrence
  Technological
  University
Lawrence University
Lawrenceville
Lawrence Welk Show,
  The
Lawrencian
Lawrie, Lee
Law School
  Admission Test
Lawson, Ernest
Lawson, Robert
Lawson sofa
Lawson State
  Community College
Lawter International,
  Inc.
Lawton
Laxalt, Paul
Laxness, Halldór
Layamon
Layton
Layton, Irving
Layton, Joe

Lazar, Irving
Lazarist
Lazarus
Lazarus, Emma
Lazarus, Mell
La-Z-Boy™ chair
Lazy Mary
lazy Susan
Lazzeri, Tony
L bar
L beam
L- *occas.* l-dopa
Leach, Robin
Leachman, Cloris
Leacock, Stephen Butler
Lead
Leadbelly
Leadville
Leaf, Munro
League City
League for Industrial Democracy
League for Yiddish
League of American Theatres and Producers, The
League of American Wheelmen/Bicycle U.S.A.
League of Arab States
League of Augsburg
League of Cambrai
League of Conservation Voters
League of Historic American Theatres, The
League of Lefthanders
League of Nations

League of Red Cross and Red Crescent Societies
League of Resident Theatres
League of United Latin American Citizens
League of Women Voters of the United States
League to Save Lake Tahoe
League to Save Sierra Lakes
Leah
Leahy, Frank
Leahy, Patrick
Leahy, William
Leakey, L. S. B.
Leakey, Mary
Leakey, Richard
Leaksville
Lean, Sir David
Leander
Leaning Tower of Pisa
Lear, Edward
Lear, Evelyn
Lear, Frances
Lear, Norman
Learfield Communications Inc.
Learjet Inc.
Learned, Michael
Learning Channel, The
Learning Tree, The
Leary, Timothy
Lease Plan Group, The
Leatherette™

Leatherneck *occas.* leatherneck
Leatherstocking
Leather-Stocking Tales
Leave It to Beaver
Leavenworth
Leavenworth Prison
Leaves of Grass
Leavis, F. R.
Leawood
Lebanese
Lebanon
Lebanon Mountains
Lebanon Valley College
LeBeauf, Sabrina
Lebensfeld, Harry
Lebensraum
Lebesgue, Henri Léon
Lebesgue integral
LeBon, Simon
Le Bourget
Lebrun, Albert
Lebrun *occas.* Le Brun, Charles
Le Carré, John
Le Chapeau de Paille
Le Châtelier, Henry Louis
La Châtelier *or* Le Châtelier's principle
Le Châtelier's law
Lechmere
Lecky, William Edward Hartpole
Lecompton
Leconte de Lisle, Charles Marie
Le Coq D'or

Le Corbusier

Leda

Leda with Swan

Le Dejeuner sur l'herbe

Lederberg, Joshua

Ledoux, Chris

Ledoux, Claude Nicolas

Le Duc Tho

Ledyard

Led Zeppelin

Lee

Lee, Ann

Lee, Brenda

Lee, Bruce

Lee, Canada

Lee, Cecilia

Lee, Charles

Lee, Christopher

Lee, Doris Emrick

Lee, Fitzhugh

Lee, Francis Lightfoot

Lee, George Washington Custis

Lee, Gypsy Rose

Lee, Harper

Lee, Johnny

Lee, Light-Horse Harry

Lee, Michele

Lee, Peggy

Lee, Pinky

Lee, Richard Henry

Lee, Robert E.

Lee, Ruta

Lee, Sir Sidney

Lee, Spike

Lee, Stan

Lee, Tsung-Dao

Lee, William Henry Fitzhugh

Lee, Wilma

Leechburg

Lee College

Leeds

Leeds Festival

Leeds Piano Competition

Lee Enterprises, Inc.

Lee Evans Bowling Tournament

Lee Kuan Yew

Lees, Benjamin

Lee's Birthday

Leesburg

Lees College

Lees-McRae College

Lees Summit

Leesville

Lee Teng-hui

Leetonia

Leeuwenhoek, Anton van

Leeward Islands

LeFanu, Nicola

Lefebvre, Marcel

Le Figaro

LeFrak, Samuel Jayson

Left Bank

Lefthanders International

Le Gallienne, Eva

Le Gallienne, Richard

Legal Tender Act

Legal Tender case

Legend of Sleepy Hollow, The

Legend of the True Cross

Legendre, Adrien Marie

Legendre equation

Legendre polynomial

Léger, Alexis

Léger, Fernand

Leggett and Platt, Inc.

Leghorn

Leghorn chicken

Legionnaires' disease

Legion of Honor

Legion of Merit

Legion of Valor of the United States of America

Legrand, Michel

Le Grand Guignol

Legros, Alphonse

Le Guin, Ursula K.

Lehár, Franz

Le Havre

Lehigh

Lehigh County Community College

Lehigh Data Processing Institute

Lehighton

Lehigh University

Lehigh University Engineers

Lehigh University Press

Lehman College

Lehmann, Lilli

Lehmann, Lotte

Lehmbruck, Wilhelm

Lehrer, Jim

Lehrer, Tom

Leiber, Jerry
Leibl, Wilhelm
Leibman, Ron
Leibniz, Gottfried
  Wilhelm von
Leibovitz, Annie
Leicester
Leicester cheese
Leicester sheep
Leicestershire
Leiden
Leifer, Carol
Leif Ericson Society
Leigh, Janet
Leigh, Jennifer Jason
Leigh, Mitch
Leigh, Vivien
Leighton, Frederick
Leighton, Kenneth
Leighton, Margaret
Leinsdorf, Erich
Leipzig
[Leipzig] Gewandhaus
  Orchestra
Leisure, David
Leitmotiv *or* leitmotiv
  often Leitmotif *or*
  leitmotif
Leizhou Peninsula
Lejeune, John Archer
Le Journal de
  Montreal
Le Journal de Quebec
Leland
Leland, Mickey
Lelong, Lucièn
Lely, Sir Peter
Lem, Stanislaw
Le Mans
Le Mars

LeMay, Alan
LeMay, Curtis E.
Lembeck, Michael
Lemieux, Mario
Le Misanthrope
Lemmon, Chris
Lemmon, Jack
Lemnitzer, Lyman
Lemnos
Lemon, Bob
Lemon, Meadowlark
LeMond, Greg
Le Monde
Lemon Grove
Lemont
Lemoore Naval Air
  Station
Le Morte d'Arthur
  occas. Darthur
Lemoyne
Le Moyne College
LeMoyne-Owen
  College
Lempert, Julius
Lempert *or* Lempert's
  operation
Lemstone Books
Lena
Le Nain, Antoine
Le Nain, Louis
Le Nain, Mathieu
Lenape, *n., pl.* Lenape
  or Lenapes
Lenard, Philipp
Lenard rays
Lenard tube
Lenca, *n., pl.* Lencas
Lendl, Ivan
Lend-Lease
Lend-Lease Act

L'Enfant, Pierre
  Charles
L'Engle, Madeleine
Lenglen, Suzanne
Lenin
Leningrad [*now* Saint
  Petersburg]
Leninism
Leninist
Lenin Peak
Lenni-Lenape Indian
Lennix, Harry J.
Lennon, Dianne
Lennon, Fred A.
Lennon, Janet
Lennon, John
Lennon, Julian
Lennon, Kathy
Lennon, Peggy
Lennon Sisters, The
Lennox [* CA; SD;
  see also Lenox]
Lennox, Annie
Lennox Foundation
Lennox Industries Inc.
Leno, Jay
Lenoir
Lenoir Community
  College
Lenoir-Rhyne College
Lenore [ballet;
  symphony; see also
  Leonora]
Lenox [* MA]
Lenox Collections
Lenox Quartet
Lenox School of Jazz
Lent
Lenten *occas.* lenten
Lenten rose

Lentz, Daniel K.

Lenya, Lotte

Lenz, Heinrich

Lenz, Kay

Lenz's law

Leo

Leo I, Saint

Leo IV, Saint

Leo IX, Saint

Leo II, Saint

Leo III, Saint

Leochares

Leo Minor

Leominster

Leonard, Buck

Leonard, Eddie

Leonard, Elmore

Leonard, Jack E.

Leonard, Sheldon

Leonard, "Sugar" Ray

Leonard, William
Ellery

Leonardesque

Leonard Wood
Memorial

Leoncavallo, Ruggiero

Leone, Sergio

Leoni, Leone

Leonia

Leonid, n., pl. Leonids
or Leonides

Leonidas

Leonora often Leonore
Overture [see also
Lenore]

Leonov, Leonid

Leontief, Wassily

Leontovich, Eugenie

Leopardi, Giacomo

Leopold

Leopold, Aldo

Leopold, Nathan

Leopold, Saint

Leopold and Loeb
case

Léopoldville [now
Kinshasa]

Leo the Great

Lepanto

Lepcha, n., pl. Lepcha
or Lepchas

Le Petit Theatre du
Vieux Carre

Lepidus, Marcus
Aemilius

Lepontine Alps

Leppard, Vacant

Lepus

L'Ermitage

Lermontov, Mikhail
Yureivich

Lerner, Alan Jay

Lerner, Alfred

Lerner, Max

Lerner, Theodore
Nathan

Lerner and Loewe

Le Roy [* NY]

Leroy [given name]

LeRoy, Mervyn

Lesage, Alain René

Les Amis du Vin

Lesbian cymatium

Lesbian leaf

Lesbian ode

Lesbos

Lescaze, William

Lesch-Nyhan
syndrome

Lescoulie, Jack

Les Enfants Terribles

Les Fauves

Les Gueux

Les Halles

Lesher, Dean Stanley

Lesley

Lesley College

Leslie

Leslie, Frank

Leslie, Joan

Leslie, Miriam

Leslie Fay Companies,
Inc., The

Les Misérables

Lesotho [form.
Basutoland]

Lesotho Airways
Corporation

Les Paul and Mary
Ford

Les Préludes

Lesseps, Ferdinand
Marie de

Lesser Antilles

Lesser Sanhedrin

Lesser Slave Lake

Lesser Sunda Islands

Lessing, Doris

Lessing, Gotthold
Ephraim

Lessness Abbey

Le Sueur

Le Tartuffe

Lethal Weapon

Lethal Weapon 3

Lethal Weapon 2

Lethbridge

LeTourneau
University

Let's Make a Deal

Lett
Letterkenny
Letterkenny Army
  Depot
Letterman, David
Lettermen, The
Lettish
Leucippus
Leukemia Society of
  America
Leutze, Emanuel
Levant
Levant, Oscar
Levantine
Levant morocco
Levant red
Levant storax
Levant thaler
Levant wormseed
Le Vau, Louis
Leven, Boris
Levene, Sam
Levenson, Sam
Lever Brothers
  Company
Levert, Gerald
Levertov, Denise
Levesque, Rene
Levi
Levi, Carlo
Levi, Yoel
Leviathan, The
Levine, Ira
Levine, Irving R.
Levine, Jack
Levine, James
Levine, Joel A.
Levine, Robert
Levinson, Barry

Levi's™
Lévi-Strauss, Claude
Levi Strauss Company
Levi Strauss
  Foundation
Levite
Levitical
Levitical law
Leviticus
Levitt, William J.
Levittown
Lévy-Bruhl, Lucien
Lewin, Dennis
Lewin, Kurt
Lewis
Lewis, Anthony
Lewis, Carl
Lewis, C. Day
Lewis, C. S.
Lewis, David
Lewis, Dawnn
Lewis, Emmanuel
Lewis, Gary
Lewis, Geoffrey
Lewis, Huey
Lewis, Jerry
Lewis, Jerry Lee
Lewis, Joe E.
Lewis, John Aaron
Lewis, John L.
Lewis, Matthew
  Gregory
Lewis, Mel
Lewis, Meriwether
Lewis, Oscar
Lewis, Ramsey
Lewis, Reginald F.
Lewis, Richard
Lewis, Robert Q.

Lewis, Shari
Lewis, Sinclair
Lewis, Ted
Lewis, Wyndham
Lewis acid
Lewis and Clark
Lewis and Clark
  College
Lewis and Clark
  Community College
Lewis and Clark
  expedition
Lewis and Clark
  National Forest
Lewis and Clark Trail
Lewis and Clark Trail
  Heritage
  Foundation, Inc.
Lewis base
Lewisburg
Lewis-Clark State
  College
Lewis College of
  Business
Lewis Family
Lewis gun
Lewis Mountains
Lewisohn, Ludwig
Lewis Research
  Center
Lewiston [* ID; see
  also Lewistown]
Lewiston Orchards
Lewistown [* PA; see
  also Lewiston]
Lewis University
Lewisville
Lewis with Harris
Lewitt, Sol
Lewitzky Dance
  Foundation

Lexan™

Lexington

Lexington Blue Grass Army depot

Lexington Community College

Lexington-Fayette

Lexington Herald-Leader

Lexington Institute of Hospitality Careers

Lexington Park

Lexington Theological Seminary

Lexmark International, Inc.

Leyden

Leyden, Lucas van

Leyden jar

Leydig, Franz

Leydig cell

Leyster, Judith

Leyte

Leyte Gulf

LG & E Energy Corporation

Lhasa

Lhasa apso, *n., pl.* Lhasa apsos

L-head engine

L'Hospital, Guillaume de

L'Hospital's rule

Liakoura

Liao

Liaodong

Liao dynasty

Liaoning

Liard River

Libby, W. F.

Libby Dam

Libby Prison

Liberace

Liberace Museum

Liberace Show, The

Liberal

Liberale da Verona

Liberal Party

Liberal Republican Party

Liberia

Liberian

Liberius, Saint

Libertarian Party

Libertini, Richard

Liberty

Liberty Bell

Liberty Bible College

Liberty Bond

Liberty Bowl

Liberty Bowl Football Classic

Liberty Bowl Memorial Stadium

Liberty Broadcast Network

Liberty Island [*form.* Bedloe's Island]

Libertyland Theme Park

Liberty League

Liberty Loan

Liberty Lobby

Liberty Mutual Fire Insurance Company

Liberty Mutual Insurance Company

Liberty Party

Liberty ship

Liberty University

Libertyville

Li Bo *or* Li Po

Libra

Librarian of Congress

Library Administration and Management Association

Library of Congress

Library of Congress Classification

Library of Parliament

Libreville

Libreville Leon M'ba Airport

Librium™

Libya

Libyan

Libyan Arab Airlines

Libyan Desert

Lichtenstein, Roy

Licinius

Licking

Lick Observatory

Liddel Hart, Basil Henry

Liddy, G. Gordon

Lidice

Lido

Lido di Venezia

Lie, Jonas

Lie, Trygve

Lieberman, Nancy

Liebermann, Max

Liebert, Ottmar

Liebesträume

Liebfraumilch *occas.* liebfraumilch

Liebig, Justus von

Liechtenstein

Lied, *n., pl.* Lieder

Liederkranz™

Liège

Lie group

Life and Death of King John, The

L.I.F.E. Bible College

Life Chiropractic College—West

Life College

Life Guards

Life Insurance Company of Virginia

Life Magazine

Life of Samuel Johnson, The

Life of Emile Zola, The

Life Office Management Association

life of Riley [carefree, comfortable life]

Life of Riley, The [radio and television series]

Life of the Virgin

Life on the Mississippi

Life on the Road, A

Lifestyles of the Rich and Famous

Lifetime Television

Life with Father

Light, Judith

Lighter-Than-Air Society, The

Light-Fingered Louie

Lightfoot, Gordon

Lightfoot, Terry

Lighthouse bookstore

Lighthouse Christian bookstore

Lighthouse of Alexandria

Light in August

Liguasan March

Liguria

Ligurian

Ligurian bellflower

Ligurian Sea

Lihue

Li'l Abner

Lila Wallace-Reader's Digest Arts Stabilization Initiative

Lilienthal, David

Lilienthal, Otto

Lili Marlene

Lilith

Liliuokalani

Lille

Lillehammer

Lillie, Beatrice

Lilliput

Lilliputian often lilliputian, n.

lilliputian often Lilliputian, adj.

Lillo, George

Lilly, Bob

Lilly Endowment, Inc.

Lilongwe

Lily, William

Lily's Grammar

Lima

Lima Technical College

Limbaugh, Rush

Limbo

Limburger cheese

Lime, Harry

Limehouse

Limelight

Limeliters, The

Limerick

Limestone College

Limited, Inc., The

Limoges

Limoges porcelain

Limón, José

Limon Dance Company

Limousin

Limousine Liberal

Limpopo

Lin Biao [form. Lin Piao]

LIN Broadcasting Corporation

Lincoln

Lincoln, Abbey

Lincoln, Abraham

Lincoln, Mary Todd

Lincoln, Nancy Hanks

Lincoln, Robert Todd

Lincoln Boyhood National Memorial

Lincoln Center for the Performing Arts

Lincoln Christian College

Lincoln College

Lincoln County War

Lincoln-Douglas debates

Lincoln Electric Company

Lincoln Electric Foundation

Lincolnesque

Lincoln green
Lincoln Heights
Lincoln Highway
Lincoln Home
  National Historic
  Site
Lincolnian
Lincolniana
Lincoln Land
  Community College
Lincoln Logs™
Lincoln Memorial
Lincoln Memorial
  University
Lincoln National
  Corporation
Lincoln National
  Forest
Lincoln National Life
  Foundation
Lincoln National Life
  Insurance Company
Lincoln Park
Lincoln Park
  Zoological Gardens
Lincoln Savings and
  Loan Association
Lincoln Savings Bank
Lincoln's Birthday
Lincoln School of
  Commerce
Lincoln sheep
Lincolnshire
Lincoln's Inn
Lincoln's sparrow
Lincoln Technical
  Institute
Lincolnton
Lincoln Tunnel
Lincoln University
Lincolnwood

Lind, Jenny
Linda
Lindbergh, Anne
  Morrow
Lindbergh, Charles A.
Lindbergh kidnapping
Lindbergh law
Lindelöf, Ernst
Lindeman, George L.
Linden
Linden, Hal
Lindenhurst
Lindenwold
Lindenwood College
Lindfors, Viveca
Lindgren, Astrid
Lindisfarne
Lindisfarne Gospels
Lindley, Audra
Lindner, Carl Henry,
  Jr.
Lindsay
Lindsay, Howard
Lindsay, John V.
Lindsay, Ted
Lindsay, Vachel
Lindsborg
Lindsey
Lindsey, Mort
Lindsey Wilson
  College
Lindstrom, Fred
Lindy Hop occas.
  lindy hop
Línea Aérea Nacional
  de Chile
Linear A
Linear B
Líneas Aéreas
  Paraguayas

Line Islands
Linfield College
Ling, Jahja
Lingelbank, Johannes
Link, Edwin
Link, William
Link flight simulator
Linkletter, Art
Linkletter, Jack
Link trainer
Linnaean or Linnean
Linnaeus, Carolus
Linn-Baker, Mark
Linn-Benton
  Community College
Linné, Carl von
Linotype™
Lin Piao [now Lin
  Biao]
Lintas: Campbell-
  Ewald
Lintas: Worldwide
Linton
Linus
Linus, Saint
Linus Pauling Institute
  of Science and
  Medicine
Linus song
Linwood
Lin Yutang
Linz
Linzer torte, n., pl.
  Linzer tortes
Linz Symphony
Lionel™ electric train
Lionel Railroader
  Club
Lion in Winter, The
Lion of Janina

Lions Club
Liotta, Ray
Liouville, Joseph
Liouville's theorem
Lipari Islands [*form.* Aeolian Islands]
Lipchitz, Jacques
Li Peng
Lipizzaner *occas.* Lippizzaner
Lipkin, Seymour
Lipmann, Fritz Albert
Li Po *var. of* Li Bo
Li Po *or* Li T'ai-po
Lipper Mutual Fund Performance Averages
Lippes, Jack
Lippes loop
Lippi, Filippino
Lippi, Fra Filippo *or* Fra Lippo
Lippmann, Walter
Lippold, Richard
Lipschitz, Rudolf
Lipschitz condition
Lipscomb, William Nunn, Jr.
Lipton, Seymour
Lipton, Sir Thomas J.
Lisa
Lisa, Manuel
Lisbon
Lisbon Airport
Lisbon Falls
Lisi, Virna
Lisle
Lissajou, Jules A.
Lissajou figure
Listening, Inc.

Lister, Joseph
Listerism
Liston, Sonny
Liszt, Franz
Li T'ai-po *var. of* Li Po
Li T'ang
Litchfield
Litchfield Institute, The
Literacy Volunteers of America
Literary Guild, The
Literary Magazine Review
Lithgow, John
Lithuania [*form.* Lithuanian Soviet Socialist Republic]
Lithuanian
Lithuanian Airlines
Lithuanian Soviet Socialist Republic [*now* Lithuania]
Lititz
Little, Cleavon
Little, Floyd
Little, Lou
Little, Rich
Little, Stuart
Little Abaco Island
Little Alliance
Little America
Little Anthony
Little Anthony and the Imperials
Little Belt Mountains
Little Bighorn
Little Bighorn Battlefield National Monument [*form.*

Custer Battlefield National Monument]
Little Big Horn College
Little Black Sambo
Little Bo-Peep
Little Boy Blue
Little, Brown and Company
Little Church around the Corner
Little Chute
Little Corporal, the
Little Creek Amphibious Base
Little Daedala
Little Diomede
Little Dipper
Little Dorrit
Little Engine That Could, The
Little Englander
Little Englandism
Little Entente
Little Entrance
Little Falls
Little Feat
Little Ferry
Littlefield
Littlefield, Edmund Wattis
Little Flower of Jesus
Little Gidding
Little Golden Books™
Little Green Apples
Little Hoop Community College
Little Hours
Little House on the Prairie

Little Jack Horner
little Joe
Little John
Little League Baseball
Little League Foundation
Little Leaguer
Little League World Series
Little Levi's™
Little Lord Fauntleroy
Little Match Girl, The
Little Men
Little Mermaid, The
Little Miss Muffet
Little Missouri
Little Office
Little Orphan Annie [comic strip]
Little Orphant Annie [poem]
Little People of America
Little Pleasures, No. 174
Little Prince, The
Little Professor Book Center
Little Quemoy
Little Red Ridinghood
Little Red River
Little Richard
Little River Band, The
Little Robin Redbreast
Little Rock
Little Rock Air Force Base
Little Rock Regional Airport
Little Russia
Little Russian

Little Saint Bernard Pass
Little Silver
Little Sioux
Little Sisters of the Poor
Little Street, The
Little Tennessee
Little Tommy Tucker
Littleton
Little Walter
Little Women
Little Zab
Litton Industries, Inc.
liturgical Latin
Liturgy of the Hours
Litvinov, Maxim
Litwin, Leonard
Litz, Tommy
Liu Pang
Liu Shaoqi
Lively, Penelope
Live Oak
Livermore
Livermore Falls
Liverpool
Liverpool house
Liverpool Poets
Liverpudlian
Lives of the Poets, The
Live with Regis and Kathie Lee
Living Bible, The
Livingston
Livingston, Jay
Livingston, Jerry
Livingston, Robert R.
Livingstone, David

Livingstone, Mary
Livingstone College
Livingston University
Living Theatre Company, The
Living Word bookstore
Livonia
Livonian
Livonian Brothers of the Sword
Livonian Knights
Livy
Li Xiannin
Li Yuan
Lizard, The
Lizard Head
Lizard Point
Liz Claiborne Foundation
Liz Claiborne, Inc.
Ljubljana
[Ljubljana] National Gallery
Llano Estacado
L. L. Bean, Inc.
L. L. Cool J
Llewellyn, Richard
L-line
Lloyd
Lloyd, Bob
Lloyd, Christopher
Lloyd, David
Lloyd, Emily
Lloyd, Harold
Lloyd, Henry
Lloyd, Marie
Lloyd George, David
Lloyd's Bank International Ltd.

Lloyd's List and Shipping Gazette

Lloyd's of London

Lloyd's Register of Shipping

Lloyd Webber, Sir Andrew

LM Ericsson Telephone Company

Loafer™ shoe

Lobachevski, Nikolai Ivanovich

Lobel, Arnold

LoBianco, Tony

lobster Newburg or Newburgh

Loc, Tone

Local Initiatives Support Corporation

Locarno

Locarno Conference

Locarno Pact

Lochinvar

Loch Katrine

Loch Leven

Loch Lomond

Loch Long

Loch Maree

Lochner, Stephen

Loch Ness

Loch Ness monster

Loch of Stenness

Loch Rannoch

Loch Raven

Loch Ryan

Loch Shiel

Lockbourne Air Force Base

Locke, John

Locke, Sondra

Lockean

Lockerbie

Lockerbie disaster

Locker-Lampson, Frederick

Lockhart

Lockhart, Gene

Lockhart, June

Lock Haven

Lock Haven University of Pennsylvania

Lockheed Corporation

Lockheed Leadership Fund

Locklear, Heather

Lockport

Lockwood, Gary

Lockwood, Margaret

Lockyear College

Locofoco

Loctite Corporation

Locus, n., pl. Locuses

Locust Grove

Lodge, Henry Cabot

Lodge, Henry Cabot, Jr.

Lodge, Sir Oliver

Lodge, Thomas

Lodi

Loeb, Jacques

Loeb, Richard

Loesser, Frank

Loewe, Frederick

Loewenguth Quartet

Loews Corporation

Loews Foundation

Leows Giorgio

Loewy, Raymond

Löffler, Friedrich

Lofoten Islands

Lofting, Hugh

Logan

Logan, Ella

Logan, James

Logan, Joshua

Logan Act

Logan Airport

Logan College of Chiropractic

Logansport

Loggia, Robert

Loggins, Kenny

Loggins and Messina

Logos, n., pl. Logoi

Lohengrin

Loir [river in France]

Loire [department and longest river in France]

Loire-Atlantique

Loiret

Loir-et-Cher

Lolita

Lolland Island

Lollard

Lollardism

Lollardy

Lollobrigida, Gina

Lolo National Forest

Lom, Herbert

Loma Linda University

Loman, Willy

Lomax, Alan

Lomax, John

Lombard

Lombard, Carole

Lombard, Peter
Lombardi, Ernie
Lombardi, Vince
Lombardian
Lombardic
Lombard League
Lombardo, Carmen
Lombardo, Guy
Lombard Street
Lombardy
Lombardy poplar
Lombrosian school
Lombroso, Cesare
Lomé
London
London, Jack
London, Julie
London blitz
London Bridge
London broil
London brown
London Club
London College of
  Music
London Company
London Conference
Londonderry
Londonderry Air
Londoner
Londonesque
London Financial
  Times-Stock
  Exchange Index
London forces
London Gatwick
  Airport
London Heathrow
  Airport
Londonish
London Library, The

London Mozart
  Players
London Naval
  Conference
London Philharmonic
  Orchestra
London plane
London pride
London Review of
  Books
London School of
  Economics and
  Political Science
London Sinfonietta
London Stansted
  Airport
London Stock
  Exchange
London Symphony
  Orchestra
[London] Times, The
[London] Times
  Educational
  Supplement, The
[London] Times
  Literary
  Supplement, The
Londony
London Zoo
Lone Ranger [person]
Lone Ranger, The
  [radio; television
  series]
Lonesome Dove
Lone Star Industries,
  Inc.
Lone Star State
Long, Earl
Long, George
Long, Huey P.
Long, Richard
Long, Russell

Long, Shelley
Longacres Racecourse
Long Beach
Long Beach City
  College
Long Beach Naval
  Station
[Long Beach] Press-
  Telegram
Long Branch
Long Day's Journey
  into Night
Longet, Claudine
Longfellow, Henry
  Wadsworth
Longfellow National
  Historic Site
Longhorn Cavern
Longhorn Radio
  Network
Longinus
Long Island
Long Island City
Long Island College
  Hospital School of
  Nursing
Long Island
  Expressway
Long Island Journal,
  The
Long Island Lighting
  Company
Long Island Lolita
Long Island Savings
  Bank
Long Island Sound
Long Island
  University
Long Island
  University
  Blackbeards
Long John Silver

Long Lake
Longman Publishing Group
Long March
Longmeadow
Longmont
Long Parliament
Long Sault Rapids
Longs Drug Stores Corporation
Longs Drug Stores of California, Inc.
Longs Peak
Longstreet, James
Long-Term Credit Bank of Japan, Ltd.
Long Tom
Longueuil
Longview
Longview Community College
Longview Fibre Company
Long Voyage Home, The
Longwave Club of America
Long Wharf Theatre
Longwood
Longwood College
Longy School of Music
Lon Morris College
Lon Nol
Lookout Mountain
Look Who's Talking
Look Who's Talking Too
Looney Tunes
Loop, the
Loos, Adolf

Loos, Anita
Loose Tubes
Lopat, Eddie
Lopatnikov, Nicolai
Lope de Vega Carpio, Félix
Lopez, Al
Lopez, Nancy
Lopez, Priscilla
Lopez, Tony
Lopez, Trini
Lopez, Vincent
Lopez-Cobos, Jesus
López de Cárdenas, García
López Mateos, Adolfo
López-Portillo, José
López y Fuentes, Gregorio
Lop Nor
Lorain [* OH; see also Lorraine]
Lorain County Community College
Loral Corporation
Loras College
Lord, Bradley
Lord, Jack
Lord, Marjorie
Lord and Taylor
Lord Baltimore cake
Lord Chamberlain
Lord Chancellor
Lord Chief Justice
Lord Fairfax Community College
Lord Greystoke
Lord Haw-Haw
Lord High Chancellor
Lord Howe Island

Lord Jim
Lord Mayor
Lord of hosts *occas.* Hosts
Lord of Misrule
Lord of the Flies
Lord of the Rings, The
Lord Protector of the Commonwealth
Lord Provost
Lords, Traci
Lordsburg
Lord's Day *occas.* day
Lord's Prayer, the
Lord's Supper, the
Lord's table, the
Lordy
Lorelei
Loren, Sophia
Lorentz, Hendrik Anton
Lorentz contraction
Lorentz-FitzGerald contraction
Lorentz transformation
Lorenz, Konrad
Lorenzetti, Ambrogio
Lorenzetti, Pietro
Lorenzo, Frank
Lorenzo di Credi
Lorenzo di Pietro
Lorenzo Monaco
Loretta Livingston and Dancers
Lori
Loria, Gloria
Lorimar
Lorimar Syndication
Lorimar Television

Loring, Gloria

Loring Air Force Base

Lorna Doone

Lorne, Marion

Lorrain, Claude

Lorraine [given name; * France; see also Lorain]

Lorre, Peter

Los Alamitos

Los Alamitos Armed Forces Reserve Center

Los Alamitos Race Course

Los Alamos

Los Alamos National Laboratory

Los Altos

Los Altos Hills

Los Angeleno

Los Angeles

Los Angeles Air Force Base

Los Angeles Basin

Los Angeles Chamber Ballet

Los Angeles Chamber Symphony

Los Angeles City College

Los Angeles Clippers

Los Angeles College of Chiropractic

Los Angeles Community College

Los Angeles County Museum

[Los Angeles] Daily News

Los Angeles Dodgers

[Los Angeles] Forum, The

Los Angeles Harbor College

Los Angeles International Airport

Los Angeles Kings

Los Angeles Lakers

Los Angeles Memorial Coliseum

Los Angeles Memorial Coliseum and Sports Arena

Los Angeles Memorial Sports Arena

Los Angeles Mission College

Los Angeles Museum of Contemporary Art

Los Angeles Philharmonic Orchestra

Los Angeles Pierce College

Los Angeles Raiders

Los Angeles Rams

Los Angeles riots

Los Angeles Southwest College

Los Angeles Times

Los Angeles Times Book Review, The

Los Angeles Times Magazine

Los Angeles Times Syndicate

Los Angeles Times Syndicate International

Los Angeles Times/ Washington Post News Service

Los Angeles Trade-Technical College

Los Angeles Valley College

Los Angeles Zoo, The

Los Banos

Los Gatos

Los Hermanos Penitente

Los Lobos

Los Medanos College

Los Padres National Forest

Los Rios Community College

L'Osservatore Romano

Lost Battalion

Lost Colony

Lost Dauphin

Lost Dutchman's Mine

Lost Generation

Lost in Yonkers

Lost Weekend, The

Lot

Lot-et-Garonne

Lothair

Lothario, n., pl. Lotharios

Loti, Pierre

Lotophagi occas. lotophagi

Lotos Club

Lotos-Eaters, The

LOT Polish Airlines

Lötschberg Tunnel

Lott, Trent

Lotto, Lorenzo

Lotus Development Corporation

Lotusland

Lotus 1-2-3™ software

Lotze, Rudolf H.

Louangphrabang

Loudermilk, John D.

Loudon

Loudon, Dorothy

Loudonville

Louganis, Greg

Lou Gehrig's *or* Lou Gehrig disease

Lough Neagh

Lou Grant

Louis

Louis IX, Saint

Louis, Joe

Louis, John Jeffery

Louis, Morris

Louis, Saint

Louisburg

Louisburg College

Louis-Dreyfuss, Julia

Louise

Louise, Anita

Louise, Tina

Louise M. Davies Symphony Hall

Louise Salinger Academy of Fashion

Louis Harris and Associates

Louis heel

Louisiade Archipelago

Louisiana

Louisiana Agri-News Network

Louisiana College

Louisiana French

Louisiana heron

Louisiana Land and Exploration Company, The

Louisiana Life

Louisianan *occas.* Louisianian

Louisiana Network

Louisiana-Pacific Corporation

Louisiana Purchase

Louisiana State University

Louisiana State University and Agricultural and Mechanical College

Louisiana State University Fighting Tigers

Louisiana State University Press

Louisiana Superdome

Louisiana tanager

Louisiana Tech University

Louisiana Tech University Bulldogs

Louisiana Territory

Louisianian *var. of* Louisianan

Louis Kemp Seafood Company

Louis of Baden

Louis Philippe

Louis Quatorze

Louis Quinze

Louis Seize

Louis the Bavarian

Louis the Child

Louis the German

Louis the Great

Louis the Pious

Louis the Stammerer

Louis the Younger

Louis Treize

Louisville

Louisville and Nashville Railroad

Louisville Bluegrass Music Festival

[Louisville] Courier-Journal, The

Louisville Downs

Louisville Orchestra

Louisville Presbyterian Theological Seminary

Louisville Technical Institute

Lounsbury, Thomas R.

Lourdes

Lourdes College

Lourenço Marques

Louvre

Louvre Museum

Louÿs, Pierre

Love

Love, Nat

Love Boat, The

Love Canal

Love Connection

Lovejoy, Frank

Lovelace, Richard

Loveland

Loveless, Patty

Lovell, Sir Bernard

Lovell, James A.

Love of Life

Love's Labour's Lost

Love Song of J. Alfred Prufrock, The

Loves Park

Love Story

Lovett, Lyle

Loving

Lovington

Lovins, Amory

Lovin' Spoonful, The

Lovitz, Jon

Low, Sir David

Low, Juliette Gordon

Low Archipelago

Low Church

Low Countries

Lowe, Edmund

Lowe, Rob

Lowell

Lowell, Abbott Lawrence

Lowell, Amy

Lowell, Francis C.

Lowell, James Russell

Lowell, Percival

Lowell, Robert

Lowell National Historical Park

Lowell Observatory

Lower Carboniferous

Lower Columbia College

Lower Depths, The

Lower East Side

Lower Hell Hole Dam

Lower Klamath Lake

Lower Merion

Lower Michigan

Lower Saint Croix National Scenic River

Lower Saxony

Lowes, John Livingston

Lowe's Companies, Inc.

Lowestoft

Lowestoft china

Low German

Low Latin

Low Mass

Lowndes, William Thomas

Lowry, Malcolm

Lowry Air Force Base

Low Sunday

Loy, Myrna

Loyalist

Loyal Order of Moose

Loyalty Islands

Loyola College in Maryland

Loyola Marymount University

Loyola Marymount University Lions

Loyola University

Loyola University of Chicago

Loyola University of Chicago Runnin' Ramblers

Loyola University Press

Lozenge Composition in a Square

LPGA Hall of Fame

L-radiation

L-series

L-shell

LSI Logic Corporation

LSS Holdings Corporation

LTV Corporation, The

Luanda

Luang Prabang

Luann

Luba, *n.*, *pl.* Luba *or* Lubas

Lubang Islands

Lubavitcher

Lubbock

Lubbock, Sir John

Lubbock Christian University

Lübeck

Lubitsch, Ernst

Luboff, Norman

Lubrizol Corporation, The

Lubrizol Foundation, The

Lubyanka prison

Luby's Cafeterias, Inc.

Lucan

Lucania

Lucas, George

Lucas Industries Inc.

Lucas van Leyden

Lucci, Susan

Luce, Clare Booth

Luce, Henry R.

Lucerne

Luchese family

Lucia di Lammermoor

Lucian

Luciano, Ron

Lucifer

Lucilius, Gaius

Lucinda Childs Dance Company

Lucius I, Saint

Luckinbill, Laurence

Luckman, Sid

Lucknow

Lucky-Goldstar International Corporation

Lucretia *or* Lucrece

Lucretius

Lucrezia Borgia

Lucullan

Lucullus, Lucius Lucinius

Lucy, Saint

Lucy-Desi Comedy Hour, The

Lucy Locket

Lucy Show, The

Lucy Stoner

Ludden, Allen

Luddism

Luddite

Ludington

Ludlow

Ludlum, Robert

Ludwig, Christa

Ludwig, Daniel Keith

Ludwig, Emil

Ludwig's angina

Luening, Otto

Lufkin

Luft, Lorna

Lufthansa

Lufthansa German Airlines

Luftwaffe

Luganda

Lugar, Richard G.

Lüger, George

Lüger™ handgun

Lugosi, Bela

Luini, Bernardino

Luiseno

Luisetti, Hank

Luis Munoz Marin International Airport

Lujack, John

Lujan, Manuel, Jr.

Lukács, György

Lukas, J. Anthony

Lukas, Paul

Luke

Luke, Keye

Luke, Saint

Luke Air Force Base

Lukeman, Augustus

Lukens Inc.

Luks, George Benjamin

Luling

Lully, Jean Baptiste

Lulu

Lum and Abner

Lumbee

Lumberton

Lumet, Sidney

Lumière, Auguste

Lumière, Louis

Lumumba, Patrice

Luna

Lunar Geodetic Scout

Lunar Orbiter

Lunar Prospector

Lunar Resources Mapper

Lunar Rover

Lunceford, Jimmie

Luncheon on the Grass

Lunda

Lundberg, George A.

Lunden, Joan

Lundgren, Dolph

Lundy Isle

Lundy's Lane

Lunik

Lunt, Alfred

Lupercal

Lupercalia

Lupercalian

Lupercus

Lupica, Mike

Lupino, George

Lupino, Ida

Lupino, Stanley

LuPone, Patti

Lupton, John

Lupus

Lupus Foundation of America, Inc.

Luray

Luray Caverns

Lurçat, Jean

Lurie, Alison

Lurleen B. Wallace State Junior College

Lusaka

Lusatia

Lusatian

Lusatian Neisse

Lüshun [*form.* Port Arthur, China]

Lusitania

Lusitanian

Lust Killer, the

Lutcher

Lut Desert

Luther

Luther, Martin

Lutheran

Lutheran Bible Institute of Seattle

Lutheran Brotherhood

Lutheran Church

Lutheran Church in America

Lutheran Church— Missouri Synod

Lutheran College of Health Professions

Lutheran Education Association

Lutheranism

Lutheran School of Theology

Lutheran Theological Seminary at Gettysburg

Lutheran Theological Seminary at Philadelphia

Lutheran Theological Southern Seminary

Luther College

Lutherism

Luther Northwestern Theological Seminary

Luthuli or Lutuli, Albert

Lutine bell

Lutyens, Sir Edwin

Lützow-Holm Bay

Luvern

Luxair

Luxembourg occas. Luxemburg

Luxembourg Airport

Luxembourger or Luxemburger

Luxembourg Palace

Luxemburg, Rosa

Luxor

Luzerne County Community College

Luzon

L wave

Lyakhov Islands

Lyceum

Lyceum Theatre

Lyceum Theatre School of Acting

Lycidas

Lycophyta

Lycopodiophyta

Lycoming College

Lycra™

Lycurgus

Lycus

Lydgate, John

Lydia

Lydian

Lydian mode

Lyell, Sir Charles

Lyly, John

Lyme disease

Lymon, Frankie

Lynbrook

Lynch, David

Lynchburg

Lynchburg College

Lynde, Paul

Lyndhurst

Lyndon Baines Johnson Memorial

Grove on the Potomac

Lyndon B. Johnson National Historical Park

Lyndon B. Johnson Space Center

Lyndon State College

Lynn

Lynn, Barbara

Lynn, Diana

Lynn, Janet

Lynn, Jeffrey

Lynn, Judy

Lynn, Loretta

Lynn, Michele

Lynn, Vera

Lynn Canal

Lynnfield

Lynn Gardens

Lynn Haven

Lynnwood [* WA; see also Lynwood]

Lynryd Skynryd

Lynwood [* CA; see also Lynnwood]

Lyon, Mary

Lyon, Sue

Lyon, William

Lyon bean

Lyondell Petrochemical Company

Lyonnais [region in France]

Lyonnesse [legendary Arthurian region]

Lyon Office

Lyon Office of Arms

Lyons

Lyons, Ted
Lyra
Lyric Opera of
  Chicago

Lysander
Lysenko, Trofim
  Denisovich
Lysenkoism

Lysimachus
Lysippus
Lysistrata
Lytell, Bert

M

Ma, Yo-Yo
Maag, Peter
Ma and Pa Kettle
Maastricht
Maastricht Treaty
Maazel, Lorin
Ma Bell
Mabinogion
Mableton
Mabley, Moms
Mab the Fairy Queen
Mabuse, Jan
Mácal, Zdeněk
Macalester College
MacAndrews and
  Forbes Holdings
  Inc.
Macao
MacArthur, Arthur
MacArthur, Douglas
MacArthur, James
MacArthur Fellowship
Macartney rose
Macassar
Macassar oil
Macaulay, Dame Rose
Macaulay, Thomas
  Babington
Macaulayan

Macaulayism
Macavity
Macbeth
Maccabaeus *or*
  Maccabeus, Judas
Maccabean
Maccabees
Macchio, Ralph
MacCorkindale,
  Simon
MacCormac Junior
  College
MacDiarmid, Hugh
MacDill Air Force
  Base
Macdonald, Betty
Macdonald, Dwight
Macdonald, George
MacDonald, Jeanette
MacDonald, Jeffrey R.
Macdonald, Sir John
  Alexander
MacDonald, John D.
MacDonald, Ramsay
Macdonald, Ross
MacDowell, Andie
MacDowell, Edward
  Alexander
Mace™
Macedon

Macedonia
Macedonian
Macgillicuddy's Reeks
MacGraw, Ali
MacGyver
Mach, Ernst
Machiavelli, Niccolò
Machiavellian
Machmeter
Mach number
Macho Man
Mach's principle
Macht, Stephen
Machu Picchu
Machzikei Hadath
  Rabbinical College
MacInnes, Colin
MacInnes, Helen
Macintosh, Charles
Macintosh™
  computer
MacIver, Loren
Mack, Connie
Mack, Jillie
Mack, Ted
Mackay, John William
Macke, August
Mackenzie

Mackenzie, Sir
  Alexander

MacKenzie, Gisele

MacKenzie, Spuds

Mackenzie, William
  Lyon

Mackenzie District

Mackie, Bob

Mackinac

Mackinac Island

mackinaw *occas.*
  Mackinaw blanket

mackinaw *occas.*
  Mackinaw boat

Mackinaw City

mackinaw *occas.*
  Mackinaw coat

Mackinaw trout

Mackintosh, Charles
  Rennie

MacLachlan, Kyle

MacLaine, Shirley

MacLane, Barton

MacLean, Donald

Maclean's

MacLeish, Archibald

MacLennan, Hugh

MacLeod, Gavin

Macleod, John James
  Rickard

Maclise, Daniel

MacMahon, Aline

MacMahon, Marie
  Maurice de

MacManus, Seamus

MacMillan

MacMillan, Cargill

MacMillan, Donald
  Baxter

Macmillan, Harold

MacMillan, John
  Hugh, III

MacMillan, W.
  Duncan

MacMillan, Whitney

MacMillan Bloedel
  Ltd.

Macmillan Publishing
  Company

MacMonnies,
  Frederick William

MacMurray, Fred

MacMurray College

Macnee, Patrick

MacNeice, Louis

MacNeil, Cornell

MacNeil, Hermon
  Atkins

MacNeil, Robert

MacNeil-Lehrer News
  Hour

MacNeil-Lehrer
  Report

MacNelly, Jeff

Macomb

Macomb Community
  College

Macon

Macon, Uncle Dave

Macon College

Macon Telegraph and
  News

MacPhail, Larry

Macpherson, James

Macquarie Island

MacRae, Gordon

MacRae, Meredith

MacRae, Sheila

Macready, George

Macready, William
  Charles

Macrinus

Macrobius

MacUser

Macworld

Macy, Anne Sullivan

Macy, Bill

Macy's

Mad

Madagascan

Madagascar

Madagascar jasmine

Madagascar
  periwinkle

Madam, *n.*, *pl.*
  Madams [when
  used as a title]

Madama Butterfly

Madame, *n.*, *pl.*
  Mesdames
  [equivalent to *Mrs.*]

Madame Bovary

Madame de
  Pompadour
  [painting]

Madame Pompadour
  [person]

Madame Rosa

Madame Tussaud's
  Exhibition

Madariaga, Salvador
  de

Madawaska

Madden, John

Maddox, Lester

Madeira [river in
  Brazil; * OH; *see
  also* Madera]

Madeira Island

Madeira Islands

Madeira topaz

Madeira-vine

Madeira *occas.*
  madeira wine

Madeleine

Mademoiselle
  [magazine], *n., pl.*
  Mademoiselles

Mademoiselle, *n., pl.*
  Mademoiselles *or*
  Mesdemoiselles

Mademoiselle from
  Armentieres,
  Parlez-vous

Madera [* CA; *see
  also* Madeira]

Maderna, Bruno

Maderna *or* Maderno
  or Maderni, Carlo

Madero, Francisco
  Indalecio

Mad Hatter

Madhya Pradesh

Madigan, Amy

Madison

Madison, Dolley
  occas. Dolly

Madison, James

Madison Area
  Technical College

Madison Avenue

Madison Business
  College

Madison Heights

Madison Square
  Garden

Madison Square
  Garden Network

Madisonville

Madisonville
  Community College

Madlock, Bill

Madonna

Madonna and Child,
  The

Madonna and Child
  Jesus

Madonna and Child
  with Chancellor
  Rolin, The

Madonna and Child
  with Four Saints

Madonna College

Madonna Enthroned
  with Saints

Madonna lily

Madonna of Humility

Madonna of the
  Burgomeister
  Meyer

Madonna of the
  Goldfinch

Madonna of the Long
  Neck

Madonna of the Rocks

Madonna of the
  Rosaries

Madonna of the Stars

Madras

[Madras] Government
  Museum

Madras States

Madras thorn

Madre de Dios

Madrid

Madrid Barajas
  Airport

Madrilenian

Madrileño

Mad Tea Party

Madura

Madwoman of
  Chaillot, The

Maecenas, Gaius
  Cilnius

Maeght Foundation

Maelstrom

Maeterlinck, Maurice

Maeterlinckian

Mae West

Maffei galaxies

Maffei 1

Maffei 2

Mafia

Mafia don

Mafia princess

Mafioso

Magarac, Joe

Magazine of Fantasy
  and Science Fiction,
  The

Magazine Publishers
  Association

Magdalena

Magdalena Bay

Magdalen College [at
  Oxford University]

Magdalene, Mary

Magdalene College [at
  Cambridge
  University]

Magdalenian

Magdalen Islands

Magdeburg

Magdeburg
  hemisphere

Magee, Patrick

Magellan

Magellan, Ferdinand

Magellan barberry

Magellanic

Magellanic Cloud

Magen David *occas.*
  Mogen David

Maggie

Maggie and Jiggs

Maggie L. Walker
National Historic
Site

Magi, n., pl.; sing.
Magus

Magical World of
Disney, The

Magic Flute, The

Magic Mountain, The

Magic Show, The

Magilla Gorilla

Magilla Gorilla Show,
The

Magindanao, n., pl.
Magindanao or
Magindanaos

Maginot Line

Maginot mentality

Maglemosean

Magma Copper
Company

Magna

Magna Charta or
Carta

Magna Graecia

Magna Mater

Magnani, Anna

Magness, Bob John

MagneTek, Inc.

Magnificat

Magnificent
Ambersons, The

Magnolia

Magnolia Bible
College

Magnolia State

Magnoliophyta

Magnum, P.I.

Magnus

Magnus, Edie

Magnus, Heinrich G.

Magnus effect

Magnus hitch

Magog

Magritte, René

Magruder, Jeb Stuart

Magsaysay, Ramón

Magus, n., pl. Magi

Magus, Simon

Magyar

Mahabharatra

Mahan, Alfred

Mahan, Larry

M. A. Hanna
Company

Mahanoy City

Maharis, George

Maharishi
International
University

Maharishi Mahesh
Yogi

Mahayana Buddhism

Mahayanist

Mahayanistic

Mahdi

Mahdism

Mahdist

Mahé Island

Mahican, n., pl.
Mahican or
Mahicans

Mah-Jongg™ occas.
mah-jongg

Mahler, Gustav

Mahlerian

Mahmud

Mahmud of Ghazni

Mahomet var. of
Mohammed

Mahometan

Mahometanism

Mahoney, Jock

Mahoney, Roger
Cardinal

Mahoney, Will

Mahoning

Mahre, Phil

Maidanek

Maiden Castle

Maid Marian

Maid of Kent

Maid of Orléans

Maids of Honor, The

Maidu

Maigret, Inspector
Jules

Mailer, Norman

Mailgram™

Maillol, Aristide

Maimonidean

Maimonides

Main, Marjorie

Mainbocher

Maine

Maine coon

Maine-et-Loire

Maine Maritime
Academy

Mainer

Maine Sportsman, The

Maine Sunday
Telegram

Maine wherry

mainland China

Main Line, the

Mainstream, Inc.

Maintenon, Marquise
de

Main-Travelled Roads

Mainz
Mainz Psalter
Mairzy Doats
Mai Tai
Maitland, Frederic
  William
Majas on a Balcony
Majestic Theater
Ma Jolie
Major, John
Major Barbara
Major Bowes'
  Original Amateur
  Hour
Majorca
Major Dad
Major Indoor Lacrosse
  League
Major League
  Baseball™
Major League
  Umpires
  Association
Major Prophets
Majors, Lee
Major Taylor
  Velodrome
Makah
Makalu
Makarios III
Makarova, Natalia
Makeba, Miriam
Make Room for
  Daddy
Mako
Maksutov telescope
Malabar Coast
Malabar gourd
Malabar nightshade
Malabo
Malacca

Malacca cane
Malachi
Malachy, Saint
Maladetta Mountains
Malaga [grape]
Málaga [Spanish
  seaport and
  province]
Malagasy, n., pl.
  Malagasy or
  Malagasies
Malagasy Republic
Malaga wine
Malagueña
Malamud, Bernard
Malaprop, Mrs.
Mälaren
Malaspin
Malatesta
Malathion™
Malawi [form.
  Nyasaland]
Malawian
Malay
Malayan
Malayan camphor
Malay Archipelago
Malayo-Indonesian
  language
Malayo-Polynesian
  language
Malay Peninsula
Malaysia
Malaysian
Malaysian Airlines
  System
Malbin, Elaine
Malbone, Edward
  Greene
Malcolm

Malcolm X [no period
  after X]
Malden
Malden, Karl
Maldives [form.
  Maldive Islands]
Maldivian
Male
Malebranche, Nicolas
Malecite
Malenkov, Georgi
Malev Hungarian
  Airlines
Malevich, Kasimir
Malfitano, Catherine
Malherbe, François de
Malheur
Malheur Lake
Malheur National
  Forest
Mali [form. French
  Sudan]
Malibran, Maria
  Felicita
Malibu
Malibu Beach
Mali Empire
Malina, Judith
Malinke, n., pl.
  Malinke or
  Malinkes
Malinois
Malinovsky, Rodion
Malinowski,
  Bronislaw
Malipiero, Gian
  Francesco
Malkin, Judd David
Malkovich, John
Mallarmé, Stéphane
Malle, Louis

Mallet-Joris,
Françoise

Mallinckrodt College
of the North Shore

Mall of America

Mallon, Mary

Mallory

Mallory-Weiss
syndrome

Malmö

Malmstrom Air Force
Base

Malone

Malone, Dorothy

Malone, Dumas

Malone, Edmund *or*
Edmond

Malone, Karl

Malone, Mary Alice
Dorrance

Malone, Moses

Malone College

Malory, Sir Thomas

Malpighi, Marcello

Malpighian

Malpighian body

Malpighian corpuscle

Malpighian layer

Malpighian tube

Malpighian tubule

Malpighian tuft

Malpighian vessel

Malraux, André

Malsem, Tommy

Malta

Malta fever

Maltese, *n., pl.*
Maltese

Maltese cat

Maltese cross

Maltese Falcon, The

Malthus, Thomas R.

Malthusian

Malthusianism

Malus, Étienne Louis

Malus cosine-squared
law

Malus' law

Malvern [* AR; PA]

Malverne [* NY]

Malvern Hill

Malvern Hills

Ma Maison Sofitel

Mamaroneck

Mamas and the Papas,
The

Mame

Mameluke *var. of*
Mamluk

Mamet, David

Mamluk *or* Mameluke

Mammoth Cave

Mammoth Cave
National Park

Mammoth Hunters,
The

Mammoth Lakes

Mamoré

Managua

Manahan, George

Man and a Woman, A

Man and Superman

Manasquan

Manassas

Manassas National
Battlefield Park

Manassas Park

Manasseh

Manassite

Manatee Community
College

Manche

Manchester

Manchester, Melissa

Manchester Camerata

Manchester City Art
Gallery

Manchester College

Manchester
Community College

Manchester Guardian
[*now* Guardian]

Manchester
International
Airport

Manchester school

Manchester Ship
Canal

Manchester terrier

Manchu, *n., pl.*
Manchu *or*
Manchus

Manchu dynasty

Manchukuo

Manchuria

Manchurian

Manchurian
Candidate, The

Manchurian Incident

Mancini, Henry

Mancini, Ray "Boom
Boom"

Mandalay

Mandan, *n., pl.*
Mandan *or*
Mandans

Mandarin

Mandarin Chinese

Mandarin Oriental

Mandel, Howie

Mandel, Jack N.
Mandel, Johnny
Mandel, Joseph C.
Mandel, Morton L.
Mandela, Nelson
Mandela, Winnie
Mandelbaum Gate
Mandell, Howie
Mandelstam, Osip
Mandeville, Bernard
Mandeville, Sir John
Mandingo, n., pl.
Mandingo or
Mandingoes or
Mandingos
Mandolin and Guitar
Mandrell, Barbara
Manet, Édouard
Manetho
Man for All Seasons,
A [play, movie]
man Friday
Man from U.N.C.L.E.,
The
Mangano, Silvana
Mangas Coloradus
Mangione, Chuck
Mangravite, Peppino
Mangrum, Lloyd
Mangyshlak Peninsula
Manhattan
manhattan often
Manhattan
[cocktail]
Manhattan Beach
Manhattan Christian
College
Manhattan clam
chowder

Manhattan College
Manhattan College
Jaspers
Manhattan District
Manhattan Institute
Manhattan Island
Manhattanite
Manhattan Project
Manhattans
Manhattan Savings
Bank
Manhattan School of
Music
Manhattan Theatre
Club
Manhattan Transfer
Manhattanville
College
Manheim
Manichaean or
Manichean or
Manichee, n.
Manichaean or
Manichean or
Manicheen, adj.
Manichaeism or
Manichaeanism, n.
Manifest Destiny
Manila
Manila Bay
Manila hemp
Manila International
Airport
Manila occas. manila
paper
Manila rope
Manila tamarind
Manilow, Barry
Man in the Moon
Manistee
Manitoba

Manitoban
Manitoulin Island
Manitoulin Islands
Manitou Springs
Manitowoc
Mankato
Mankato State
University
Mankiewicz, Frank
Mankiewicz,
Joseph L.
Man Mountain Dean
Mann, Barry
Mann, Heinrich
Mann, Herbie
Mann, Horace
Mann, James Robert
Mann, Johnny
Mann, Thomas
Manna Bible Institute
Mann Act
Manne, Shelly
Mannerheim, Carl
Gustaf Emil von
Mannerheim Line
Mannes, David
Mannes, Leopold
Damrosch
Mannes College of
Music
Mannheim
Mannheim, Karl
Mannheim gold
Mannheim School
Manning
Manning, Timothy
Cardinal
Mannix
Mann's Chinese
Theatre

Man of Destiny

Manoff, Dinah

Man of Galilee

Man of God

Man of La Mancha

Man of Sorrows

Manolete

Manon

Manon of the Spring

Manoogian, Richard
Alexander

Manor Care, Inc.

Manorhaven

Manor Junior College

Man Pointing

Mansard roof

Mansart *occas.*
Mansard, François

Mansell, Nigel

Mansfield

Mansfield, Jayne

Mansfield, Katherine

Mansfield, Mike

Mansfield, Richard

Mansfield University
of Pennsylvania

Manship, Paul

Manson, Charles

Manson family

Manta Bay

Mantae America, Inc.

Manteca

Mantegna, Andrea

Mantegna, Joe

Man That Corrupted
Hadleyburg, The

Manti-LaSal National
Forest

Mantle, Burns

Mantle, Mickey

Mantoux, Charles

Mantoux test

Mantovani

Mantua

Mantuan

Manu

Manua

Manuel

Manufacture
Nationale des
Gobelins

Manufacturers'
Agents National
Association

Manufacturers and
Traders Trust
Company

Manufacturer's Bank

Manufacturers
Hanover
Corporation

Manufacturers
Hanover Trust
Company

Manufacturers Life
Insurance Company

Manufacturers
National Bank of
Detroit

Manus, *n., pl.* Manus

Manush, Heinie

Manu Smitri

Manutius, Aldo

Manville

Manville Corporation

Man with a
Magnifying Glass

Man with Gilt Helmet

Man without a
Country, The

Man with the Hoe,
The

Manx

Manx cat

Manxman, *n., pl.*
Manxmen

Manzanilla sherry

Manzoni, Alessandro

Manzù, Giacomo

Maoism

Maoist

Maori, *n., pl.* Maori *or*
Maoris

Mao Tse-tung [*now*
Mao Zedong]

Map, Walter

MAPCO Inc.

MAP International

Maple Heights

Maple Leaf Gardens

Maples, Marla

Maplewood

Maple Woods
Community College

Mapp v. Ohio

Maps on File™

Maputo

Maquoketa

Marable, Fate

Maracaibo

Marais des Cygnes

Marajó

Maranatha Baptist
Bible College

Marañon

Maranville, Rabbit

Marat, Jean Paul

Marathon

Marathonian

Marathonian bull

Marathon Oil
Company

Marathon Oil
  Foundation
Marat/Sade
Maratti *or* Maratta,
  Carlo
Maravich, "Pistol"
  Pete
Marble, Alice
Marble Arch
Marble Faun, The
Marblehead
Marburg disease
Marbury v. Madison
Marc, Franz
Marceau, Marcel
Marcel, Gabriel
Marcellinus, Saint
Marcellus
Marcellus I, Saint
Marcels, The
March
March, Fredric
March, Hal
March, William
March Air Force Base
Marchand, Nancy
Marches, the
March fly
March Hare
Marching through
  Georgia
March of Dimes Birth
  Defects Foundation
March of the Ten
  Thousand
Marcian
Marciano, Georges
Marciano, Rocky
Marcion
Marcionism

Marcionist
Marcionite
Marconi, Guglielmo
Marconi mast
Marconi Radio Award
Marconi rig
Marcos, Ferdinand
  Edralin
Marcos, Imelda
Marcus
Marcus, Saint
Marcus Aurelius
Marcuse, Herbert
Marcus Hook
Marcus Welby, M.D.
Mardi Gras
Mare and Foals
Mare Island
Mare Island Naval
  Shipyard
Marek, J.
Marek's disease
Marengo
Marfan syndrome
Margaret
Margaret Clitherow,
  Saint
Margaret Jenkins
  Dance Company
Margaret Maid of
  Norway
Margaret Mary, Saint
Margaret Maultasch
Margaret of
  Angoulême
Margaret of Anjou
Margaret of Austria
Margaret of France
Margaret of Navarre
Margaret of Parma

Margaret of Scotland,
  Saint
Margaret of Valois
Margaret Rose
Margaret Tudor
Margate
Margate City
Margolin, Janet
Margolin, Stuart
Marguerite
Maria
Maria Christina
Maria College
Maria de Molina
Maria Feodorovna
María Luisa
Marian
Mariana *or* Marianas
  Islands
Mariana Trench
Marian College
Marian College of
  Fond du Lac
Marian Court Junior
  College
Marianist
Marianna
Marianus Scotus
Maria Theresa
Maria Theresa thaler
Maria tree
Marichal, Juan
Maricopa
Maricopa County
  Community College
Marie
Marie Antoinette
Marie Byrd Land
Marie Caroline
Marie de France

Marie de L'Incarnation
Marie dé Médicis
Marie Galante
Marie Louise
Mariemont
Marienbad
Marietta
Marietta College
Marietta East
Marietta Naval Air Station
Marilyn
Marilyn Monroe International Fan Club
Marin, Cheech
Marin, John
Marina
Marinaro, Ed
Marine City
Marine Corps Base at Twenty-Nine Palms
Marine Corps League
Marine Corps Reserve Officers Association
Marine Corps War Memorial
Marine Engineer Beneficial Association/National Maritime Union
Marineland of Florida
Marine Midland Bank
Marine Midland Banks, Inc.
Mariner
Marines' Hymn, The
Marine Technology Society

Marinette
Marinetti, Filippo Tommaso
Marine World Africa USA
Marini *or* Marino, Giambattista
Marini, Marino
Marino, Dan
Mariolater
Mariolatrous
Mariolatry
Mariologist
Mariology
Marion
Marion, Anne Burnett Sowell
Marion, Francis
Marion Merrell Dow Inc.
Marion Military Institute
Marion Technical College
Marion Zimmer Bradley's Fantasy Magazine
Mariotte, Edme
Mariotte's law
Mariposa
Mariposa lily
Maris, Jacob
Maris, Mattijs
Maris, Roger
Maris, Willem
Marisat
Marisol
Marist
Marist College
Marist College Red Foxes

Maritain, Jacques
Maritime Administration
Maritime Alps
Maritime Provinces
Maritz, William Edward
Marius, Gaius
Marivaux, Pierre
Mark
Mark, Jan
Mark, Peter
Mark, Saint
Marked Tree
Mark Eisen fashions
Market Square Arena
Markevich, Igor
Mark IV Industries, Inc.
Mark Goodson Productions
Markham
Markham, Edwin
Markham, Monte
Markham, Mrs.
Mark Hopkins Hotel
Mark Hopkins Intercontinental
Mark Inn
Markkula, Armas Clifford, Jr.
Markoff *var. of* Markov chain
Markoff *var. of* Markov process
Mark of Zorro, The
Markov, Andrey
Markova, Dame Alicia
Markov *occas.* Markoff chain
Markovian

Markov *occas.*
Markoff process

Mark Russell Special

Marks and Spencer

Marksville

Mark Taper Forum,
The

Mark Trail

Mark Twain National
Forest

Marlboro *var. of*
Marlborough
[* MA; *see also*
Marlborough]

Marlboro [* VT]

Marlboro College

Marlboro 500

Marlboro Grand Prix

Marlboro Man

Marlboro Music
Festival

Marlborough [* CT;
see also Marlboro]

Marlborough *occas.*
Marlboro [* MA;
see also Marlboro]

Marlborough leg

Marley, Bob

Marlin

Marlovian

Marlowe, Christopher

Marlowe, Hugh

Marlowe, Julia

Marlowe, Philip

Marmaduke

Marmon

Marmotton Museum

Marne

Marona, Danny

Marple, Jane

Marprelate
controversy

Marquand, J. P.

Marquard, Rube

Marquesan

Marquesas Islands

Marquet, Albert

Marquette

Marquette, Jacques

Marquette University

Marquette University
Warriors

Marquis, Don

Marquis de Condorcet

Marquis de Sade

Marquise de Sévigné

Marquis of
Queensberry

Marquis of
Queensberry Rules

Marrakesh *or*
Marrakech

Marriage Feast at
Cana, The

Marriage—Italian
Style

Marriage of Figaro,
The

Married . . . with
Children

Marriner, Sir Neville

Marriott Corporation

Marriott hotel

Marriott Hotel and
Marina

Marriott-Overland
Park

Marriott's Essex
House

Marryat, Frederick

Mars

Mars, Forrest Edward,
Jr.

Mars, Forrest Edward,
Sr.

Mars, John Franklyn

Marsala [Italian
seaport]

Marsala *occas.*
marsala [wine]

Marsalis, Branford

Marsalis, Wynton

Mars brown

Marsden, Gerry

Marseilles

Marseilles cotton

Marsh, Jean

Marsh, Dame Ngaio

Marsh, Reginald

Marshall

Marshall, Barbara
Hall

Marshall, E. G.

Marshall, Garry

Marshall, George C.

Marshall, Herbert

Marshall, James

Marshall, James
Howard, II

Marshall, John

Marshall, Penny

Marshall, Peter

Marshall, Thurgood

Marshallese, *n., pl.*
Marshallese

Marshall Field and
Company

Marshall Field's store

Marshall Islands

Marshall Plan

Marshalls clothing
store

Marshalls Inc.

Marshall Space Flight Center

Marshalltown

Marshalltown Community College

Marshall University

Marshall University Thundering Herd

Marsh and McLennan Companies, Inc.

Marshfield

Mars Hill College

Marsh of Decay

Marsh test

Marsilius of Padua

Mars, Inc.

Mars Observer

Mars red

Marsten, Richard

Marston, John

Marston Moor

Mars violet

Mars yellow

Martagon lily

Martel, Charles

Martello tower

Martha

Martha, Saint

Martha and the Vandellas

Martha Graham Dance Company

Martha's Vineyard

Martha Washington chair

Martha Washington mirror

Martha Washington table

Martí, José

Martial

Martian

Martin

Martin I, Saint

Martin, Agnes

Martin, Archer John Porter

Martin, Billy

Martin, Dean

Martin, Dick

Martin, Don

Martin, Freddy

Martin, Glenn

Martin, Homer Dodge

Martin, Hugh

Martin, Judith

Martin, Kiel

Martin, Lynn

Martin, Mary

Martin, Pamela Sue

Martin, Rick

Martin, Ross

Martin, Saint

Martin, Steve

Martin, Tony

Martin Beck Theater

Martin Center College

Martin Chuzzlewit

Martin Community College

Martindale, Wink

Martin de Porres, Saint

Martin du Gard, Roger

Martineau, Harriet

Martinelli, Giovanni

Martinez

Martinez, A.

Martinez, Bob

Martinez, Carlos

Martinez East

Martinez Zuviría, Gustavo

Martini, Simone

Martinique

Martin Luther King Day

Martin Luther King, Jr. Center for Nonviolent Social Change

Martin Luther King, Jr. National Historic Site

Martin Marietta Corporation

Martin Marietta Corporation Foundation

Martinmas

Martin Methodist College

Martino, Al

Martin of Tours, Saint

Martinon, Jean

Martins, Peter

Martinsburg

Martins Ferry

Martinsville

Martinsville Speedway

Martinu, Bohuslav

Martin Van Buren National Historic Site

Marty

Marvel Comics

Marvelettes, The

Marvell, Andrew

Marvin

Marvin, Lee

Marx, Chico
Marx, Groucho
Marx, Gummo
Marx, Harpo
Marx, Johnny
Marx, Karl
Marx, Richard
Marx, Zeppo
Marx brothers
Marxian
Marxianism
Marxism
Marxism-Leninism
Marxist
Marxist-Leninist
Marxist-Leninist
  ideology
Marxist literary
  criticism
Mary
Mary, Saint
Mary Baldwin College
Mary Chesnut's Civil
  War
Marycrest College
Marygrove College
Mary Had a Little
  Lamb
Mary Holmes College
Mary Immaculate
  Seminary
Mary Jane
Mary Jane Warner
Maryknoll
Maryknoller
Maryknoll Father
Maryknoll School of
  Theology
Maryknoll Sister
Maryland

Maryland College of
  Art and Design
Maryland Day
Marylander
Maryland Institute,
  College of Art
Maryland Magazine
Maryland National
  Bank
Maryland National
  Foundation Inc.
Maryland yellowthroat
Marylhurst College
  for Lifelong
  Learning
Mary Magdalene
Mary, Mary
Marymount College
Marymount
  Manhattan College
Marymount University
Mary of Burgundy
Mary of England
Mary of Guise
Mary of Modena
Mary Poppins
Mary Queen of Scots
Marysville [* CA; KS;
  MI; OH; PA; WA;
  see also Maryville]
Mary Tudor
Mary Tyler Moore
  Show, The
Maryville [* MO; TN;
  see also Marysville]
Maryville College
Mary Warner
Mary Washington
  College
Marywood College
Mary Worth

Masaccio
Masada
Masada of the Zionist
  Organization of
  America
Masai, n., pl. Masai or
  Masais
Masaryk, Jan
Masaryk, Tomáš
  Garrigue
Masbate
Mascagni, Pietro
Mascarene Islands
Masco Corporation
Masco Industries, Inc.
Masefield, John
Maseru
M*A*S*H*
Masharbrum
Maslow, Abraham
Mason
Mason, Charles
Mason, Jackie
Mason, James
Mason, Lowell
Mason, Marsha
Mason, Perry
Mason and Dixon
  Lines, Inc.
Mason City
Mason-Dixon occas.
  Mason and Dixon's
  Line
Masonic
Masonic Relief
  Association of the
  United States and
  Canada
Masonic Service
  Association of the
  United States

Masonite™

Mason™ jar

Masonry

Masons, Ancient and Accepted Scottish Rite, Southern Jurisdiction, Supreme Council

Masons, Royal Arch, General Grand Chapter

Masons, Supreme Council 33°, Ancient and Accepted Scottish Rite, Northern Masonic Jurisdiction

Masontown

Masora or Masorah

Masorete or Massorete

Masoretic or Massoretic

Maspero, Gaston

Masque of the Red Death, The

Mass

Massachuset [Indian], n., pl. Massachuset or Massachusets

Massachusetts

Massachusetts ballot

Massachusetts Bay

Massachusetts Bay Colony

Massachusetts Bay Community College

Massachusetts Bay Company

Massachusetts College of Art

Massachusetts College of Pharmacy and

Allied Health Sciences

Massachusetts Institute of Technology

Massachusetts Maritime Academy

Massachusetts Mutual Life Insurance Company

Massachusetts School of Professional Psychology

Massacre of Chios, The

Massacre of Saint Bartholomew's Day

Massacre of the Innocents, The

Massapequa

Massapequa Park

Massasoit Community College

Mass book

Mass card

Massena

Masséna, André

Massenet, Jules

Massey, Andrew

Massey, Anna

Massey, Daniel

Massey, Raymond

Massey, Vincent

Massey-Ferguson Inc.

Massif Central

Massillon

Massine, Léonide

Massinger, Philip

MassMutual™ life insurance

Masson, André

Masson disk

Massoud, Ahmed Shah

Massys or Matsys or Messys or Metsys, Quentin

Master Builder, The

MasterCard™

Master Honoré

Master of Arts

Master of Ballantrae, The

Master of Business Administration

Master of Fine Arts

Master of Library Science

Master of Public Administration

Master of Public Health

Master of Science

Master of Social Welfare

Master of Social Work

Master of the Housebook

Master of the King's Music

Master of the Queen's Music

Masterpiece Theatre

Masters, Edgar Lee

Masters, William H.

Masters and Johnson

Master's College, The

Masterson, Bat

Masterson, Mary Stuart

Masterson, Valerie

Master spoon

Mastic Beach
Mastic Shirley
Mastrantonio, Mary Elizabeth
Mastroianni, Marcello
Mastroianni, Umberto
Masur, Kurt
Masur, Richard
Mata, Eduardo
Matabele, *n.*, *pl.* Matabele *or* Matabeles
Matagorda Bay
Matagorda Peninsula
Mata Hari
Matamoros
Matanuska
Matanuska Valley
Matawan
Mater Dei College
Material Service Corporation
Material Service Foundation
Mathematical Association of America
Mather, Cotton
Mather, Increase
Mather, John
Mather, Richard
Mather, Samuel
Mather Air Force Base
Mathers, Jerry
Matheson, Tim
Mathew
Mathews, Eddie
Mathewson, Christy
Mathias, Bob

Mathile, Clayton Lee
Mathis, Johnny
Mathis, Samantha
Mathis, Sherry
Matilda
Matilda, Saint
Matilija poppy
Matinicus boat
Matisse, Henri
Matlin, Marlee
Matlock
Mato Grosso
Mato Grosso do Sul
Matsu
Matsuoka, Yosuke
Matsushima
Matsushita Electric Corporation of America
Matsushita Electric Industrial Company Ltd.
Matsushita Foundation
Matsuyama
Mattatuck Community College
Mattea, Kathy
Mattel Foundation
Mattel, Inc.
Matterhorn
Matthau, Walter
Matthew
Matthew, Saint
Matthew of Paris
Matthew of Westminster
Matthews, Brander
Matthews, Ian
Matthew Walker
Matthias

Matthias, Saint
Matthiessen, F. O.
Matthiessen, Peter
Mattingly, Don
Mattoon
Mature, Victor
Mature Living
Mature Outlook
Matuszak, John
Matute, Ana Maria
Matzeliger, Jan
Maude
Maugham, Somerset
Maui
Mauldin, Bill
Mau Mau, *n.*, *pl.* Mau Mau *or* Mau Maus
Maumee
Mauna Kea
Mauna Kea Observatory
Mauna Loa
Maundy Thursday
Maupassant, Guy de
Maurer, Alfred Henry
Mauretania [ancient country in Africa; *see also* Mauritania]
Mauriac, François
Mauriat, Paul
Maurice
Maurice of Nassau
Maurice of Saxony
Maurist
Mauritania [modern-day nation; *see also* Mauretania]
Mauritius
Mauritius hemp

Mauritshuis Royal Picture Gallery

Maurois, André

Maury, Matthew Fontaine

Maury Povich Show, The

Mauser, Peter Paul

Mauser, Wilhelm

Mausoleum at Halicarnassus

Mauve Decade

Maverick

Maverick, Samuel Augustus

Mawson, Sir Douglas

Max, Buddy

Max, Gabriel

Max, Peter

Maxentius

Max Factor Museum of Beauty

Maxim, Hiram Percy

Maxim, Sir Hiram Stevens

Maxim, Hudson

Maxim gun

Maximian

Maximilian

Maximilian armor

Maximin

Maxim's

Maximus, Saint

Max Planck Society for the Advancement of Science

Max Schmitt in a Single Scull

Maxus Energy Corporation

Maxwell, Elsa

Maxwell, James Clerk

Maxwell, Robert

Maxwell Air Force Base

Maxwell-Boltzmann statistics

Maxwell Communication Corporation

Maxwell Davies, Peter

Maxwell demon

MAXXAM Inc.

May

May, Edna

May, Elaine

May, Peter

May, Rollo

Maya Clothed

Maya [Indian], n., pl. Maya or Mayas

Mayakovsky, Vladimir

Mayan

Maya Nude

May apple

Maybeck, Bernard R.

May beetle

Maybelline, Inc.

Mayberry R.F.D.

May blob

Mayday [distress message]

May Day [holiday]

May Department Stores Company, The

Mayenne

Mayer, Louis B.

Mayer, Maria Goeppert

Mayfair

Mayfair House

Mayfair Regent

Mayfield

Mayfield, Curtis

Mayfield Heights

Mayflower

Mayflower Compact

Mayflower Group, Inc.

Mayflower Transit Inc.

Mayfly

May Fourth Movement

Mayland Community College

Maynard

Maynard, Don

Maynard, Ken

Mayne, William

Maynor, Dorothy

Mayo, Charles Horace

Mayo, Virginia

Mayo, William James

Mayo, William Worrall

Mayo Clinic

Mayo Clinic Health Letter

Mayo Foundation for Medical Education and Research

Mayo Graduate School of Medicine

Mayo Medical School

Mayon

Mayor of Casterbridge, The

Mayo School of Health-Related Sciences

Maypole

Mayport Coast Guard Station

Mayport Naval Air Station

May queen

Mayron, Melanie

Mays, Benjamin

Mays, Willie

Mays Mission for the Handicapped

May Stores Foundation

Maysville [* KY; MO; *see also* Mayville]

Maysville Community College

Maytag Company Foundation

Maytag Corporation

Maytals, The

Maytime *occas.* Maytide

Ma Yüan

Mayuzumi, Toshirō

Mayville [* NY; ND; WI; *see also* Maysville]

Mayville State University

May wine

Maywood

Maywood Park Race Track

Mazarin, Jules

Mazarin Bible

Mazateca, *n., pl.* Mazateca *or* Mazatecas

Mazatlán

Mazda Motor Corporation

Mazo, Juan Bautista

Mazowiecki, Tadeusz

Mazursky, Paul

Mazzini, Giuseppe

Mazzinian

Mbabane

MBIA Inc.

Mboya, Thomas

Mbundu

M. Butterfly

McAdoo, Bob

MCA Foundation Ltd.

MCA Inc.

McAlester

McAlester Ammunition Plant

McAllen

McAnally, Ray

McArdle, Andrea

MCA Television International

MCA TV

McAuliffe, Christa

McBain, Ed

McBride, Patricia

McBride, Robert

McBride and the Ride

McCabe, John

McCall's

McCall's Needlework and Crafts

McCallum, David

McCambridge, Mercedes

McCann, Specs

McCann-Erickson USA, Inc.

McCarran International Airport

McCarran-Walter Act

McCarrie Schools of Health Sciences and Technology

McCarthy, Andrew

McCarthy, Charlie

McCarthy, Eugene

McCarthy, Joseph

McCarthy, Kevin

McCarthy, Mary

McCarthy, Tommy

McCarthyism

McCarthyite

McCartney, Paul

McCarver, Tim

McCaw, Bruce R.

McCaw, Craig O.

McCaw, John Elroy, Jr.

McCaw, Keith W.

McCaw Cellular Communications, Inc.

McCay, Winsor

Macero, Teo

McChord Air Force Base

McClain, Charly

McClanahan, Rue

McClatchy, James

McClatchy Newspapers, Inc.

McClatchy News Service

McClellan, George

McClellan Air Force Base

McClellan-Kerr
   Arkansas River
   Navigation System
McClendon, Sarah
McClinton, Delbert
McClory, Sean
McCloskey, John
   Cardinal
McCloud
McClung, Nellie
McClure, Doug
McClure, Sir Robert
   John Le Mesurier
McClure, Samuel
   Sidney
McClure Strait
McClure Syndicate
McClurg, Edie
McCluskey, Roger
McComb
McCone, John A.
McConnell Air Force
   Base
McCoo, Marilyn
McCook
McCord, David
McCord, Kent
McCormack, John
McCormack, John
   William
McCormack, Patty
McCormick, Cyrus
   Hall
McCormick, Robert
   Rutherford
McCormick and
   Company
McCormick reaper
McCormick
   Theological
   Seminary
McCovey, Willie

McCoy, Dr. Leonard
   Bones
McCoys, The
McCrea, Joel
McCree, Wade H., Jr.
McCullers, Carson
McCulloch, A.
   Donald, Jr.
McCullock v.
   Maryland
McCullough, Colleen
McCullough, David
McCutcheon, John T.
McDaniel, Hattie
McDaniels, Gene
McDermott
   International, Inc.
McDonald, Country
   Joe
McDonald, David
McDonald, Michael
McDonald
   Observatory
McDonald's
   Corporation
McDonald's restaurant
McDonnell, Mary
McDonnell Douglas
   Corporation
McDonnell Douglas
   Foundation
McDowall, Roddy
McDowell, Malcolm
McDowell, Ronnie
McDowell Technical
   Community College
McElhenny, Hugh
McEnroe, John
McEntire, Reba
McEvoy, Nan Tucker
McFadden, Cyra

McFadden, Gates
McFarland, Spanky
McFee, William
McFerrin, Bobby
McGarrigle, Anna
McGarrigle, Kate
McGavin, Darren
McGee, Frank
McGee, Willie
McGehee
McGill, James
McGillis, Kelly
McGillivray,
   Alexander
McGill University
McGinley, Phyllis
McGinnity, Joe
McGlaughlin, William
McGlothlin, James
McGoohan, Patrick
McGovern, Elizabeth
McGovern, George S.
McGovern, Maureen
McGovern, Patrick
   Joseph
McGraw, John J.
McGraw, Muggsy
McGraw-Hill
   Continuing
   Education Center
McGraw-Hill
   Foundation
McGraw-Hill, Inc.
McGraw-Hill
   Publications Online
McGregor
McGuane, Thomas
McGuffey, William
   Holmes

McGuffey's Eclectic Readers

McGuinn, Roger

McGuire, Al

McGuire, Dorothy

McGuire Air Force Base

McGuire Sisters, The

McGwire, Mark

McHale's Navy

McHenry, Donald E.

McHenry County College

McHugh, Frank

McHugh, Jimmy

MCI Communications Corporation

McInerney, Jay

McIntire, John

McIntire, Samuel

McIntosh, John

McIntosh, William

McIntosh apple [*see also* Apple Macintosh]

McIntosh College

McIntyre, Joe

McKay, Claude

McKay, David Oman

McKay, Jim

McKechnie, Bill

McKechnie, Donna

McKee, Lonette

McKeesport

McKees Rocks

McKellen, Gordon, Jr.

McKellen, Ian

McKendree College

McKenna, Siobhan

McKenzie

McKenzie, Robert Tait

McKenzie College

McKeon, Nancy

McKesson Corporation

McKesson Foundation

McKim, Charles F.

McKim, Charles M.

McKinley, Ida

McKinley, Ray

McKinley, William

McKinney

McKinsey and Company

McKissick, Floyd B.

McKuen, Rod

McLachlan, Sarah

McLaglen, Victor

McLane, Robert Drayton, Jr.

McLaughlin, Emily

McLaughlin, Maurice

McLaughlin Group, The

McLean, Don

McLennan Community College

McLeod, Herbert

McLeod gauge

McLerie, Allyn

McLoughlin, John

McLuhan, Marshall

McLuhanism

McMahon, Ed

McMahon, Horace

McManus, George

McMartin Pre-School case

McMaster, John Bach

McMaster University

McMillan, Edwin Mattison

McMillan, Kenneth

McMillan and Wife

McMinnville

McMurdo Sound

McMurry College

McMurtry, Larry

McNair, Barbara

McNair, Ronald

McNamara, Robert Strange

McNary Dam

McNaught Syndicate, Inc.

MCN Corporation

McNeese State University

McNeese State University Cowboys

McNeill, Don

McNichol, Kristy

McNichols Arena

McPartland, Jimmy

McPartland, Marian

McPhatter, Clyde

McPhee, John

McPherson

McPherson, Aimee Semple

McPherson College

McQueen, Butterfly

McQueen, Steve

McRae, Carmen

McRaney, Gerald

McReynolds, Jesse

McReynolds, Jim

McShane, Ian

McWethy, John F.

M-day
MD Magazine
MDU Resources Group, Inc.
Mead, George H.
Mead, Margaret
Mead Corporation, The
Mead Corporation Foundation
Meade, George Gordon
Meade, James Edward
Meader, Vaughn
Mead Johnson and Company
Mead Johnson and Company Foundation
Meadowlands Stadium
Meadows, Audrey
Meadows, Jayne
Meadows College of Business
Meadville
Meadville/Lombard Theological School
Me and My Girl
Means grass
Meany, George
Meara, Anne
Mears, Rick
Mears, Roger
Measure for Measure
Measurex Corporation
Mecca
Mecca balsam
Meccan
Mecham, Evan
Mechanicsburg
Mechanicsville [* VA]

Mechanicville [* NY]
Mechanix Illustrated
Mechlin
Mechlin lace
Meciar, Vladimir
Mecklenburg
Mecklenburg Declaration of Independence
Mecklenburg lace
Medaille College
Medal for Merit
Medal of Freedom [now Presidential Medal of Freedom]
Medal of Honor
Medawar, Peter Brian
Medcenter One College of Nursing
Medea
Me Decade
Medellín
Medellín drug cartel
Medford
Medford, Kay
Medford Lakes
Media
Media General, Inc.
Medicaid
Medi-Cal
Medical Center
Medical College Admission Test
Medical College of Georgia
Medical College of Ohio at Toledo
Medical College of Pennsylvania
Medical College of Wisconsin

Medical Device Register
Medical Education for South African Blacks, Inc.
Medic Alert™ bracelet
Medic Alert Foundation International
Medical Lake
Medical Library Association
Medical University of South Carolina
Medicare
Medici, Cosimo de'
Medici, Cosimo I
Medici, Lorenzo de'
Medici Chapel
Medici Madonna
Medicine Bow National Forest
Medicine Bow Range
Medicine Hat
Medicine Lodge
Médicis, Catherine de
Medici Venus
Medico
Medieval Academy of America
Medieval Greek
Medieval Latin
Medieval Latin literature
Medieval period
Medigap
Medill, Joseph
Medina
Mediterranean
Mediterranean climate

Mediterranean fever

Mediterranean flour moth

Mediterranean fruit fly

Mediterranean Sea

Médoc

Medtronic Foundation

Medtronic Inc.

Medusa

Medvedev, Vadim

Medwick, Joe

Meek, Donald

Meeker, Ezra

Meese, Edwin

Meet Corliss Archer

Meeting of Minds

Meet the Press

Megadeth

Megalopolis

Megan

Megarian school

Me Generation

Meghan

Meharry Medical College

Mehta, Mehli

Mehta, Zubin

Meier, Gustave

Meigs, Cornelia

Meiji

Meiji Restoration

Meiklejohn, Alexander

Mein Kampf

Meir, Golda

Meissen

Meissen porcelain

Meissonier, Jean Louis Ernest

Meistersinger, *n., pl.* Meistersinger *or* Meistersingers

Meitner, Lise

Meker, George

Meker burner

Mekong

Mekong Delta

Melachrino, George

Melachrino Strings

Melanchthon, Philipp

Melanesia

Melanesian

Melanie

Melba, Dame Nellie

Melba sauce

Melba *occas.* melba toast

Melbourne

Melbourne Airport

Melburnian

Melcher, Frederic Gershom

Melchers, Gari

Melchiades *var. of* Miltiades, Saint

Melchior

Melchior, Lauritz

Melchizedek

Meleager

Meletius, Saint

Melissa

Mellencamp, John

Mellers, Wilfrid Howard

Mellon, Andrew

Mellon, Paul

Mellon, Richard B.

Mellon, Richard King

Mellon, Richard Prosser

Mellon, Seward Prosser

Mellon, Timothy

Mellon Bank

Mellon Bank Building

Mellon Bank Corporation

Mellon Bank (East)

Mellon Bank Foundation

Mellotron™

Mello Yello 500

Melos Ensemble

Melos Quartet of Stuttgart

Melozzo da Forti

Melpomene

Melrose

Melrose Park

Melton, James

Melton, Sid

Melville, Herman

Melville Bay

Melville Corporation

Melville Island

Melville Peninsula

Melville Sound

Melvindale

Memel Territory

Memling, Hans

Memnon

Memorial Day [*form.* Decoration Day]

Memorial Sloan-Kettering Cancer Center

Memorial University of Newfoundland

Memphian

Memphis
Memphis Army Depot
Memphis Belle
Memphis Blues, The
Memphis Business Journal
Memphis College of Art
[Memphis] Commercial Appeal, The
Memphis International Airport
Memphis International Motorsports Park
Memphis Naval Air Station
Memphis Slim
Memphis State University
Memphis State University Tigers
Memphis Theological Seminary
Menai Strait
Menander
Menasha
Men at Work
Menchu, Rigoberta
Mencius
Mencken, H. L.
Menckenian
Mendel, Gregor Johann
Mendeleev, Dmitri Ivanovich
Mendeleev's law
Mendelian
Mendelian factor
Mendelian inheritance
Mendelism

Mendel's laws
Mendelson, Lee
Mendelssohn, Erich
Mendelssohn, Felix
Mendelssohn, Moses
Mendelssohnian
Menderes
Menderes, Adnan
Mendes, Sergio
Mendés-France, Pierre
Mendocino
Mendocino College
Mendocino National Forest
Mendota
Mendota Heights
Mendoza, Pedro de
Menelaus
Menelik
Menem, Carlos Saul
Menéndez de Avilés, Pedro
Menes
Mengele, Josef
Mengs, Anton
Ménière, Prosper
Ménière's disease
Ménière's syndrome
Menjou, Adolphe
Menken, Adah Isaacs
Menken, Alan
Menken, Helen
Menlo College
Menlo Park
Menninger, Karl Augustus
Menninger, William Claire
Menninger Clinic

Menninger Clinic Department of Research
Menninger Foundation
Mennonite
Mennonite Biblical Seminary
Mennonite Brethren Biblical Seminary
Mennonite Church
Mennonite College of Nursing
Mennonitism
Menominee [* NY; see also Menominie]
Menominee Falls
Menominee whitefish
Menominie [* WI; see also Menominee]
Menomini [Indian] occas. Menominee, n., pl. Menominis or Menomini occas. Menominees or Menominee
Menotti, Gian-Carlo
Mensa
Men's Fitness
Men's Garden Clubs of America
Men's Health
Men's Health Newsletter
Menshevik, n., pl. Mensheviks or Menshiviki
Menshevism
Menshevist
Mentor
Mentor™ Books
Mentor-on-the-Lake-Village

Menuhin, Sir Yehudi
Menzies, Sir Robert Gordon
Mephisto
Mephistopheles
Mephistophelian *or* Mephistophelean
Mephisto Waltz
Meramec Caverns
Mercalli scale
Mercantile Stores Company Inc.
Mercator, Gerardus
Mercator *occas.* Mercator's projection
Mercator sailing
Mercator track
Merced
Merced College
Mercedes
Mercer, Johnny
Mercer, Marian
Mercer County Community College
Mercer University
Mercer University Bears
Mercer University Graduate and Professional Center
Mercer University Press
Mercer University Southern School of Pharmacy
Merchandise Mart
Merchant Adventurers
Merchant of Venice, The
Merchants of the Staple

Merchantville
Mercia
Mercian
Merck and Company, Inc.
Merck Company Foundation, The
Merckx, Eddy
Mercouri, Melina
Mercurochrome™
Mercury
Mercury, Freddie
Mercury-Atlas
Mercury Finance Company
Mercury-Redstone
Mercy College
Mercy College of Detroit
Mercy Fund, The
Mercyhurst College
Mer de Glace
Meredith, Burgess
Meredith, Don
Meredith, George
Meredith, James Howard
Meredith, Owen
Meredith College
Meredith Corporation
Meredith Monk Vocal Ensemble
Mergenthaler, Ottmar
Merici, Saint Angela
Meriden
Meridian
Meridian Bank
Meridian™ Books
Meridian Community College

Meridian Naval Air Station
Mérimée, Prosper
Merino sheep
Merino Village
Meritor Financial Group
Meritor Savings Bank
Merit Systems Protection Board
Meriwether, Lee
Merkel, Una
Merleau-Ponty, Maurice
Merlin
Mermaid Tavern
Merman, Ethel
Mérode Altarpiece, The
Merovingian
Merovingian architecture
Merovingian art
Merovingian dynasty
Merriam
Merriam-Webster, Inc.
Merriam-Webster™ reference works
Merriam-Webster's Collegiate Dictionary—Tenth Edition
Merrick
Merrick, David
Merrick, John
Merrie Olde England
Merrill
Merrill, Bob
Merrill, Charles E.
Merrill, Dina
Merrill, Robert

Merrill Lynch and Company Foundation

Merrill Lynch and Company, Inc.

Merrill's Marauders

Merrill's Marauders Association

Merrill's Raiders

Merrimack

Merrimack College

Merriman Dam

Merritt College

Merritt Island

Merry-Go-Round Enterprises, Inc.

Merry Widow, The

Merry Wives of Windsor, The

Mersenne, Marin

Mersenne number

Mersey

Mersey beat

Mersey Tunnel

Merthiolate™

Merton, Robert King

Merton, Thomas

Merton thesis

Merv

Merv Griffin Show, The

Mervyn's department store

Merwin, W. S.

Mesa

Mesabi Range

Mesa Community College

Mesa Limited Partnership

Mesa State College

Mesa Verde National Park

Mescalero, *n., pl.* Mescalero *or* Mescaleros

Meshach

Mesha Stele

Mesilla

Mesivta of Eastern Parkway Rabbinical Seminary

Mesivta Tifereth Jerusalem of America

Mesivta Torah Vodaath Seminary

Mesmer, Franz A.

Mesolithic

Mesopotamia

Mesopotamian

Mesozoa

Mesozoic

Mesquite

Message to Garcia, A

Messalina

Messenia

Messerschmitt

Messeturm

Messiaen, Olivier

Messiah

Messiah College

Messianic

Messick, Dale

Messidor

Messier, Charles

Messier, Mark

Messier catalog

Messina

Messina, Jim

Messys *or* Metsys *var. of* Massys *or* Matsys, Quentin

Mesta, Pearl

Meštrović, Ivan

Metalious, Grace

Metallica

Metal Lumber™

Metal Powder Industries Federation

Metamorphoses

Metamorphosis, The

Metcalf, Laurie

Metcalfe bean

Met Center

Metchnikoff, Élie

Metellus

Methedrine™

Metheny, Pat

Methodism

Methodist

Methodist Church

Methodist College

Methodist Theological School in Ohio

Methodius, Saint

Methuen

Methuselah

Meton

Metonic cycle

Metro Airlines, Inc.

Metromedia Company

Metro Nashville Airport

Metropolis

Metropolitan

Metropolitan Atlanta Rapid Transit Authority

Metropolitan
  Community College

Metropolitan Federal
  Bank

Metropolitan Home

Metropolitan
  Insurance and
  Annuity Company

Metropolitan Life
  Foundation

Metropolitan Life
  Insurance Company

Metropolitan Museum
  of Art

Metropolitan Opera
  Association

Metropolitan Opera
  Company

Metropolitan Opera
  House

Metropolitan Press
  Syndicate

Metropolitan State
  College

Metropolitan State
  University

Metro Toronto
  Business Journal

Metsys *var. of* Messys
  or Massys *or*
  Matsys, Quentin

Metternich, Klemens
  Wenzel von

Metternichian

Metuchen

Metz

Metzenbaum, Howard

Metzger, Tom

Meunier, Constantin

Meursault

Meurthe-et-Moselle

Meuse

Mexia

Mexicali

Mexican

Méxicana

Mexican American
  Legal Defense and
  Educational Fund,
  Inc.

Mexican apple

Mexican architecture

Mexican art

Mexican bamboo

Mexican bean beetle

Mexican blue palm

Mexican bush sage

Mexican fire-plant

Mexican fire-vine

Mexican ground
  cherry

Mexican hairless

Mexican hat dance

Mexican ivy

Mexican jade

Mexican jumping
  bean

Mexican literature

Mexicano

Mexican onyx

Mexican orange

Mexican poppy

Mexican Riviera

Mexican Spanish

Mexican standoff

Mexican tea

Mexican War

Mexican wave

México [Mexican
  state]

Mexico [nation]

Mexico City

Mexico, Distrito
  Federal

Meyer, Adolf

Meyer, August
  Christopher

Meyer, Debbie

Meyer, Joseph

Meyerbeer, Giacomo

Meyers, Ari

Meyersdale

Meynell, Alice

M-14 rifle

MGH Institute of
  Health Professions

MGM Grand Air, Inc.

MGM Grand Inc.

MGM-Pathe
  Communications
  Company

MGM/UA
  Communications
  Company

MGM/UA films

M. H. de Young
  Memorial Museum

MH-53E Sea Dragon

MH-53J Pave Low

MH-60G Pave Hawk

Miami

Miamian

Miami Arena

Miami Beach

Miami/Budweiser
  Unlimited
  Hydroplane Regatta

Miami Christian
  College

Miami City Ballet

Miami-Dade
  Community College

Miami Dance Theatre

Miami Dolphins
Miami Fronton
Miami Grand Prix
Miami Heat
Miami Herald, The
Miami [Indian], *n., pl.*
Miami *or* Miamis
Miami International
Airport
Miami-Jacobs Junior
College of Business
Miami Jai Alai
Fronton
Miami Lakes Inn,
Athletic Club and
Golf Resort
Miamisburg
Miami Shores
Miami Sound
Machine
Miami Springs
Miami Stadium
Miami University
Miami University
Redskins
Miami Vice
Micah
Micawber, Wilkins
Micawberish
Micawberism
Michael
Michael, George
Michael, Saint
Michaelis, Leonor
Michaelis constant
Michaelmas
Michaelmas daisy
Michaelmas Day
Michaels, Al
Michaels, Lorne

Michael VII
Palaeologus
Michael the Brave
Michaux, Henri
Michel, Robert H.
Michelangelo
Michelangelo virus
Michelet, Jules
Michelin
Michelle
Michelson, Albert
Abraham
Michelson-Morley
experiment
Michener, James A.
Michigan
Michigan bankroll
Michigan Bell
Telephone
Company
Michigan Center
Michigan Christian
College
Michigan City
Michigander
Michigan Farm Radio
Network
Michiganian
Michigan
International
Raceway
Michigan
International
Speedway
Michigan Law Review
Michigan Living
Michigan National
Bank
Michigan Out-of-
Doors
Michigan roll

Michigan rummy
Michigan State
University
Michigan State
University Press
Michigan State
University Spartans
Michigan
Technological
University
Michoacán
Michurin, I. V.
Mickey Finn
Mickey Mouse
Mickey Mouse Club
Mickey Mouse
Magazine
Mickiewicz, Adam
Micmac, *n., pl.*
Micmac *or*
Micmacs
Microcomputer
Technology
Institute
Micronesia
Micronesian
Micronesian
Occupational
College
Micron Technology,
Inc.
Microsoft™
Microsoft Corporation
Microsoft Word™
Microsoft Works™
Mid-America Ag
Network
Mid-America Baptist
Theological
Seminary
Mid-America Bible
College

Mid-America College
of Funeral Service

Mid-America
Nazarene College

Midas

mid-Atlantic *occas.*
Mid-

Mid-Atlantic Ridge

Mid-Continent Baptist
Bible College

Mid-Continent Oil and
Gas Association

Mid-Continent
Railway Historical
Society

Middle Ages

Middle America

Middle American

Middle Atlantic States

Middleborough *occas.*
Middleboro [* MA;
see also
Middlesborough]

Middleburg Heights

Middlebury

Middlebury College

Middlecoff, Cary

Middle Country

Middle East

Middle East Airlines/
Air Liban

Middle Eastern

Middle Empire

Middle English

Middle English
literature

Middle Flemish

Middle French

Middle Georgia
College

Middle Greek

Middle High German

Middle Irish

Middle Kingdom

Middle Latin

Middle Low German

Middle Path

Middle Persian

Middleport

Middle River

Middlesborough
occas. Middlesboro
[* KY; *see also*
Middleborough]

Middle Scots

Middlesex

Middlesex
Community College

Middlesex County
College

Middle States

Middle Stone Age

Middle Temple

Middle Tennessee
State University

Middle Tennessee
State University
Blue Raiders

Middleton [* MA;
WI; *see also*
Middletown]

Middleton, Thomas

Middletown [* CT;
DE; IN; NY; OH;
PA; RI]

Middle Welsh

Middle West

Middlewestern

Middle White

Midfield

Midgetman missile

Midianite

Midi-Pyrénées

Midland [* MI; PA;
TX; Ontario; *see
also* Midlands]

Midland Bank

Midland Canal

Midland College

Midland Enterprises
Inc.

Midland Lutheran
College

Midland Park

Midlands [* England;
see also Midland]

Midlands Technical
College

Midlantic National
Bank

Mid-Lent Sunday

Midler, Bette

Midlothian

Mid-Michigan
Community College

Midnight Cowboy

Mid-Ohio Sports Car
Course

Midori

Mid-Plains Technical
Community College

Mid-South Coliseum

Midstate College

Mid-State Technical
College

Midsummer Day

Midsummer Eve

Midsummer Night

Midsummer Night's
Dream, A

Midvale

mid-Victorian

Midway

Midway Airlines, Inc.
Midway College
Midway Park
Midwest
Midwest City
Midwestern
Midwestern Baptist Theological Seminary
Midwesterner
Midwestern States
Midwestern State University
Midwest Express Airlines, Inc.
Midwest Resources Inc.
Midwest Stock Exchange
Mielziner, Jo
Miës van der Rohe, Ludwig
Mifune, Toshiro
MiG aircraft
Mighty Clouds of Joy
Mighty Mouse
MiG-31 Foxhound
MiG-25 Foxbat
MiG-29 Fulcrum
MiG-21 Fishbed
MiG-27 Flogger
Mikado, n., pl. Mikados
Mikado, The
Mikan, George
Mike Douglas Show, The
Mikita Stan
Mikon
Mikoyan, Anastas
Mikulski, Barbara

Milan
Milan, Victor
Milan Cathedral
Milan Decree
Milanese, n., pl. Milanese
Milanese chant
Milano, Alyssa
Milanov, Zinka
Milbury, Cassandra Mellon
Mile High Kennel Club
Mile High Stadium
Milenkovic, Stefan
Miles, Nelson Appleton
Miles, Sarah
Miles, Sylvia
Miles, Vera
Miles City
Miles College
Miles Community College
Milesian
Miles Kimball
Miletus
Milford
Milford Haven
Milford Sound
Milhaud, Darius
Milhous, Katherine
Military Chaplains Association of the United States of America, The
Military Order of Foreign Wars of the United States
Military Order of the Loyal Legion of the

United States of America
Military Order of the World Wars
Military Sea Transportation Service
Milk
Milk, Harvey
Milk, Sir John
Milk, Juliet
Milken, Lowell J.
Milken, Michael
Milking Shorthorn
Milky Way
Mill, Harriet Taylor
Mill, James
Mill, John Stuart
Millais, Sir John Everett
Milland, Ray
Millay, Edna Saint Vincent
Millbrae
Millburn
Millbury
Millcreek
Milledgeville
Mille Lacs Lake
Millennial Church
Miller, Ann
Miller, Arthur
Miller, Barry
Miller, Dennis
Miller, Dorie
Miller, Glenn
Miller, Henry
Miller, Joaquin
Miller, Joe
Miller, Johnny

Miller, Jonathan
Miller, Marilyn
Miller, Mitch
Miller, Penelope Ann
Miller, Perry G.
Miller, Roger
Miller, Steve
Miller, Walter C.
Miller, William
Millerand, Alexandre
Miller Brewing
  Company
Miller Features
  Syndicated
Miller Genuine Draft
  400
Miller index
Millerite
Millersburg
Miller's Outpost
Millersville
Millersville University
  of Pennsylvania
Milles, Carl
Millet, Francis
Millet, Jean François
Millet, Kate
Milligan College
Millikan, Robert A.
Milliken, Gerrish
Milliken, Minot
Milliken, Roger
Milliken and
  Company
Milliken Foundation
Millikin University
Millington
Millinocket
Million Dollar Man
Millipore Corporation

Milli Vanilli
Millöcker, Karl
Mills, Bunnie
Mills, Clark
Mills, Donna
Mills, Hayley
Mills, John
Mills, Juliet
Mills, Robert
Mills, Wilbur
Mills, Sir William
Millsaps College
Mills bomb
Mills Brothers, The
Mills College
Mills hand grenade
Mill Springs
Milltown
Millvale
Mill Valley
Millville
Milne, A. A.
Milne, Christopher
  Robin
Milne, David
Milne, Edward Arthur
Milne-Edwards, Henri
Milne method
Milner, Martin
Milnes, Sherrill
Milo
Milos
Milosevic, Slobodan
Milpitas
Milquetoast, Caspar
Milsap, Ronnie
Milstein, Nathan
Milstein, Paul
Milstein, Seymour

Miltiades *occas.*
  Melchiades, Saint
Milton
Milton, John
Milton Berle Show,
  The
Milton Bradley
  Company
Miltonic
Milvian Bridge
Milwaukee [* WI; *see
  also* Milwaukie]
Milwaukeean
Milwaukee Area
  Technical College
Milwaukee Brewers
Milwaukee Bucks
Milwaukee County
  Stadium
Milwaukee County
  Zoological Park
Milwaukee Institute of
  Art and Design
Milwaukee Journal,
  The
Milwaukee Magazine
Milwaukee River
Milwaukee School of
  Engineering
Milwaukee Sentinel
Milwaukee Symphony
  Orchestra
Milwaukie [* OR; *see
  also* Milwaukee]
Mimeograph™
Mimieux, Yvette
Minamata disease
Minas Basin
Mindanao
Mindanao Deep
Minden

Mind Extension
  University

Mindoro

Mindszenty, Joseph
  Cardinal

Mineo, Sal

Mineola

Mineral Area College

Mineral Wells

Minersville

Minerva

Mingan Islands

Ming dynasty

Mingo, Norman

Mingo Junction

Mingus, Charlie

Minicoy Islands

Minidoka Project

Minié, Claude Étienne

Minié ball

Mining and
  Metallurgical
  Society of America

Minke, Rachel

Minkowski, Hermann

Minkowski universe

Minkowski world

Minneapolis

Minneapolis College
  of Art and Design

Minneapolis
  Community College

Minneapolis
  Metropolitan Sports
  Center

Minneapolis-Saint
  Paul International
  Airport

Minneapolis Star and
  Tribune

Minneapolis
  Symphony
  Orchestra [now
  Minnesota
  Orchestra]

Minneapolitan

Minnehaha

Minnehaha Falls

Minnelli, Liza

Minnelli, Vincente

Minnesota

Minnesota Bible
  College

Minnesota
  Community College

Minnesota
  Independent
  Network Inc.

Minnesota Law
  Review

Minnesota Mining and
  Manufacturing
  Company

Minnesota Mining and
  Manufacturing
  Company
  Foundation

Minnesota
  Multiphasic
  Personality
  Inventory

Minnesota Mutual
  Life Foundation

Minnesota Mutual
  Life Insurance
  Company

Minnesotan

Minnesota North Stars

Minnesota Opera

Minnesota Orchestra
  [form. Minneapolis
  Symphony
  Orchestra]

Minnesota Power and
  Light Company

Minnesota Public
  Radio

Minnesota Public
  Television
  Association

Minnesota State
  University System

Minnesota Twins

Minnesota Vikings

Minnetonka

Minnevitch, Borrah

Minnie Mouse

Minoan

Minoan civilization

Minolta Camera
  Company, Ltd.

Minorca

Minorcan

Minority Features
  Syndicate

Minor Prophets

Minos

Minot

Minot Air Force Base

Minotaur

Minot International
  Airport

Minot State University

Minow, Newton

Minseito

Minsk

Minskoff Theatre

Minsky, Abraham

Minsky, Billy

Minsky, Herbert

Minsky, Morton

Minsky's burlesque
  theatre

Mint 400 Off-Road
  Desert Race

Minton, Yvonne

Minton's Playhouse
Minucius Felix,
 Marcus
Minuit, Peter
Minute Man, *n., pl.*
 Minute Men
Minuteman missile
Minute Man National
 Historical Park
Minuteman II
Miocene
Miquelon
Mir
Mirabeau, Honoré
 Gabriel de
Mirabella
Miracle of Fátima
Miracle of Lourdes
Miracle of Saint Mark,
 The
Miracle on 34th Street
Miracles, The
Miracle Worker, The
Mira Costa College
Miraflores
Mirage Resorts, Inc.
 [*form.* Golden
 Nugget]
Mira Loma
Miramar
Miramar Naval Air
 Station
Miramax Films
Miramichi River
Miranda
Miranda, Carmen
Miranda decision
Miranda v. Arizona
Miranda warning
Miriam

Mirinda
Mirisch, Walter
Miró, Gabriel
Miró, Joan
Mirrer Yeshiva
 Central Institute
Mischakoff, Mischa
Mischer, Don
Miserere
Mishawaka
Mishima, Yukio
Mishna *or* Mishnah,
 n., pl. Mishnayot
Mishnaic *or*
 Mishnahic
Miskito, *n., pl.*
 Miskito *or* Miskitos
Miss, *n., pl.* Misses
Miss America
Missa Solemnis
Miss Black America
Missing Link
Mission
Missionary Church
Missionary Ridge
Mission Basilica San
 Diego de Alcala
Mission College
Mission Dolores
Mission Hills
Mission: Impossible
Mission Indian
Mission San Antonio
 de Pala
Mission San Fernando
 Rey de España
Mission San Gabriel
 Arcángel
Mission San Luis Rey
 de Francia
Mission Viejo

Mississippi
Mississippian
Mississippi Bubble
Mississippi City
Mississippi College
Mississippi County
 Community College
Mississippi Delta
 Community College
Mississippi Gulf Coast
 Community College
Mississippi National
 River and
 Recreation Area
Mississippi Scheme
Mississippi Sound
Mississippi State
 University
Mississippi State
 University Bulldogs
Mississippi Territory
Mississippi University
 for Women
Mississippi Valley
 State University
Mississippi Valley
 State University
 Delta Devils
Miss Lonelyhearts
Miss Manners
Miss Muffet
Missoula
Missoula Southwest
Missouri
Missouri Alliance for
 Historic
 Preservation
Missourian
Missouri Baptist
 College
Missouri Compromise
Missouri gourd

Missouri [Indian], *n.*, *pl.* Missouri *or* Missouris

Missouri, Kansas and Texas Railway Company

Missouri Magazine

Missouri meerschaum

Missouri National Recreational River

Missouri Pacific Railroad Company

Missouri River Basin Project

Missouri Southern State College

Missouri Technical School

Missouri Valley

Missouri Valley College

Missouri Western State College

Miss Piggy

Miss Saigon

Miss Wades Fashion Merchandising College

Mistassini

Mister Ed

Mister Nice-Guy

Mister Roberts

Mister Rogers

Mister Rogers' Neighborhood

Mistinguett

Mistral, Frédéric

Mistral, Gabriela

Misty Fiords National Monument

Mita Copystar America, Inc.

Mitchell

Mitchell, Arthur

Mitchell, Billy

Mitchell, Cameron

Mitchell, George D.

Mitchell, George Phydias

Mitchell, Guy

Mitchell, James

Mitchell, John

Mitchell, Joni

Mitchell, Margaret

Mitchell, Maria

Mitchell, Peter Dennis

Mitchell, Roscoe

Mitchell, Sasha

Mitchell, Silas

Mitchell, Thomas

Mitchell College

Mitchell Community College

Mitchell Energy and Development Corporation

Mitchell Vocational-Technical School

Mitchelson, Marvin

Mitchum, Chris

Mitchum, Robert

Mitford, Mary

Mitford, Nancy

MIT Press, The

Mitropoulos, Dmitri

Mitsotakis, Constantine

Mitsubishi Bank Ltd.

Mitsubishi Chemical Industries Ltd. [*now* Mitsubishi Kasei Corporation]

Mitsubishi Corporation

Mitsubishi Electric Corporation

Mitsubishi Group

Mitsubishi Heavy Industries Ltd.

Mitsubishi Kasei Corporation [*form.* Mitsubishi Chemical Industries Ltd.]

Mitsubishi Motors Corporation

Mitsubishi Trust and Banking Corporation

Mitsui Group

Mitsui Taiyo Kobe Bank Ltd.

Mitsui Trust and Banking Company, Ltd.

Mittelschmerz

Mitterrand, François

Mitty, Walter

Mix, Tom

Mixtec, *n.*, *pl.* Mixtec *or* Mixtecs

Mixtón War

Miyazawa, Kiichi

Miyoshi Umeki

Mize, Johnny

Mizlou Communications Company

Mizlou Sports News Network

Mizner, Wilson

Mizrachi

M. L. Annenberg Foundation

M.L.C. Centre

M-line
MNC Financial, Inc.
Moab
Moabite
Moabite stone
Moberly
Moberly Area
  Community College
Mobil Corporation
Mobile
Mobile Bay
Mobile Coast Guard
  Aviation Training
  Center
Mobile College
Mobile Municipal
  Airport
Mobile Press-Register,
  The
Mobil Foundation
Mobil Travel Guides
Möbius, August F.
Möbius band
Möbius strip
Möbius transformation
Mobley, Mary Ann
Mobridge
Mobuto Sese Seko
Moby-Dick
Moby Grape
Mocha ware
Mochi, Francesco
Moctezuma var. of
  Montezuma
Model Parliament
Model Railroader
Model T Ford Club
  International
Model "T" Ford Club
  of America

Modernaires, The
Modern Art Museum
Modern Bride
Modern Electronics
Modern English
Modern French
Modern Greek
Modern Hebrew
Modern Icelandic
Modern Jazz Quartet
Modern Language
  Association of
  America
Modern Latin
Modern Library
Modern Maturity
Modern Persian
Modern Romances
Modern Times
Modern Woodmen of
  America
Modesto
Modesto Junior
  College
Modigliani, Amedeo
Modine, Matthew
Modjeska, Helena
Modoc, n., pl. Modoc
  or Modocs
Modoc National
  Forest
Modoc War
Modred occas.
  Mordred
Mod Squad, The
Modugno, Domenico
Moffat, Donald
Moffat Tunnel
Moffett Field
Moffo, Anna

Mogadishu
Mogadishu
  International
  Airport
Mogen David var. of
  Magen David [aka
  Star of David]
Mogen David™ food;
  wine
Mogollon Mesa
Mogollon Plateau
Mogul
Mogul architecture
Mogul art
Mogul occas. Mughal
  Empire
Mohammad Reza
  Pahlavi
Mohammed occas.
  Mahomet or
  Muhammad
Mohammed, Ali
  Mahdi
Mohammedan
Mohammedanism
Mohave var. of
  Mojave
Mohave Community
  College
Mohave var. of
  Mojave Desert
Mohawk
Mohawk [Indian], n.,
  pl. Mohawk or
  Mohawks
Mohawk Trail
Mohawk Valley
  Community College
Mohegan or Mohican,
  n., pl. Mohegan or
  Mohegans or
  Mohican or
  Mohicans

Mohegan Community College

Mohenjo-Daro

Mohican rig

Mohican sail

Mohole

Mohole Project

Moholy-Nagy, László

Mohorovičić, Andrija

Mohorovičić discontinuity

Mohs, Friedrich

Mohs' scale

Moi, Daniel T. arap

Moisant International Airport

Moiseivich, Benno

Moiseyev, Igor Alexsandrovich

Moiseyev Dance Company

Mojave *occas.* Mohave

Mojave *occas.* Mohave Desert

Mokae, Zakes

Molasses Act

Moldau

Moldavia

Moldavian

Moldavian Soviet Socialist Republic *or* Soviet Socialist Republic of Moldova [*now* Moldova]

Moldova [*form.* Moldavian Soviet Socialist Republic]

Moldovan

Molière

Molina, Luis

Molinaro, Al

Moline

Moline Acres

Molinism

Molinist

Moll, Kurt

Moll, Richard

Mollenhoff, Clark

Mollet, Guy

Moll Flanders

Mollier, Richard

Mollier diagram

Molloy College

Mollusca

Mollweide, Karl B.

Mollweide projection

Molly Hatchet

Molly Maguire

Molly Miller

Molnár, Ferenc

Moloch

Molokai

Molokan

Molotov, V. M.

Molotov cocktail

Molson Companies Ltd., The

Moltke, Helmuth Johannes von

Moltke, Helmuth Karl von

Molucca balm

Moluccan

Moluccas

Momaday, N. Scott

Mombasa

Momentum Place Building

Momma

Mommsen, Theodor

Mompou, Federico

Monaca

Monacacy National Battlefield

Monacan

Monaco

Monaco Grand Prix

Monadnock

Monagesgue

Monaghan, Thomas Stephen

Monahans

Mona Island

Mona Lisa

Mona Lisa smile

Mona Lisa theft

Mona Passage

Monarchian

Monarchianism

Monarchianist

Monarch Life Insurance Company

Monastir

Monastir Habib Bourguiba International Airport

Moncrief, William Alvin, Jr.

Moncton

Mondale, Walter F.

Monday

Monday-morning quarterback

Monday-morning quarterbacking

Mondrian, Piet

M-1A1 Abrams main battle tank

Monégasque

Monel™

M-1 rifle

Monessen

Monet, Claude

Moneta, Ernesto

Monett

Money

Money, Eddie

Money Radio Network

Moneysworth

Mongol

Mongol Empire

Mongolia

Mongolian

Mongolian fold

Mongolian gerbil

mongolianism occas. Mongolianism [now Down's occas. Down syndrome]

Mongolian languages

Mongolian People's Republic [form. Outer Mongolia]

mongolism occas. Mongolism [now Down's occas. Down syndrome]

Mongoloid

Monhegan

Monica

Monica, Saint

Monitor

Monitor and Merrimack

Monitor Channel, The

Monk, George

Monk, Meredith

Monk, Thelonious

Monkees, The

Monkey Trial

Monmouth

Monmouth, James Scott

Monmouth Beach

Monmouth College

Monmouth College Hawks

Monmouthshire

Monnaie Dance Group/Mark Morris

Monnet, Jean

Monocacy

Mono Lake

Monona

Monongahela

Monongahela National Forest

Monophysite

Monophysitic

Monophysitism

Monopoly™

Monothelite

Monothelitic

Monothelitism

Monotype™

Monroe

Monroe, Bill

Monroe, Elizabeth Kortright

Monroe, Harriet

Monroe, James

Monroe, Marilyn

Monroe, Vaughn

Monroe College

Monroe Community College

Monroe County Community College

Monroe Doctrine

Monroeville

Monrovia

Monrovia Roberts International Airport

Monsanto Company

Monsanto Fund

Monsarrat, Nicholas

Monseigneur, n., pl. Messeigneurs

Monsieur, n., pl. Messieurs

Monsignor

Montagna, Bartolomeo

Montagnais, n., pl. Montagnais or Montagnaises

Montagnard, n., pl. Montagnard or Montagnards

Montagu, Elizabeth

Montagu, Lady Mary Wortley

Montague, Romeo

Montaigne, Michel Eyquem de

Montalban, Carlos

Montalban, Ricardo

Montale, Eugenio

Montalvo, Garcia Ordóñez de

Montalvo, Juan

Montana

Montana, Bob

Montana, Claude

Montana, Joe

Montana, Patsy

Montana College of Mineral Science and Technology

Montana Magazine

Montanan

Montana Outdoors

Montana Power Company, The

Montana Radio Network

Montana State University

Montana State University Bobcats

Montand, Yves

Montauk Point

Montay College

Mont Blanc

Montcalm, Louis Joseph de

Montcalm Community College

Mont Cenis

Mont Cenis Pass

Mont Cenis Tunnel

Montclair

Montclair State College

Montebello

Monte Carlo

Monte Carlo method

Monte Cassino

Monte Cinto

Monte Corno

Montecristo *occas.* Monte Cristo [island]

Monte dei Paschi di Siena

Montego Bay

Montenegrin

Montenegro

Monte Perdido

Monterey [* CA; *see also* Monterrey]

Monterey Bay

Monterey Bay Aquarium

Monterey Bay National Marine Sanctuary

Monterey cypress

Monterey Institute of International Studies

Monterey Jack

Monterey Jazz Festival

Monterey Naval Postgraduate School

Monterey Park

Monterey Peninsula College

Monte Rosa

Monterrey [* Mexico; *see also* Monterey]

Montesquieu

Montessori, Maria

Montessori method

Montessori system

Monteux, Claude

Monteux, Pierre

Monteverdi, Claudio

Montevideo

Monte Vista

Montez, Lola

Montez, Maria

Montezuma *or* Moctezuma

Montezuma Castle National Monument

Montezuma cypress

Montezuma's revenge

Montfort, Simon de

Montgolfier, Étienne

Montgolfier, Joseph Michel

Montgomery

Montgomery, Bernard Law

Montgomery, Elizabeth

Montgomery, Lucy Laud

Montgomery, Robert

Montgomery, Ruth

Montgomery, Wes

Montgomery bus boycott

Montgomery College

Montgomery Community College

Montgomery County Community College

Montgomery Municipal Airport

Montgomeryshire

Montgomery Ward and Company

Montgomery Ward Foundation

Montgomery Ward Holding Corporation

Montherlant, Henri de

Monthly Labor Review

Months of the Year, The

Monticelli, Adolhpe

Monticello

Montmartre

Montmorency

Montmorency cherry

Montoursville

Montoya, Carlos

Montparnasse

Montpelier

Mont Pourri

Montrachet

Montreal

Montreal Canadiens

Montrealer

Montreal Expos

Montreal Forum

[Montreal] Olympic Stadium

Montreal Symphony Orchestra

Montreat-Anderson College

Montreux

Montreux Convention

Montreux-Detroit Jazz Festival

Montrose

Mont Royal

Mont-Saint-Michel

Montserrat

Montserrat College of Art

Montville

Monty, Gloria

Monty Python and the Holy Grail

Monty Python's Flying Circus

Monty Python's the Meaning of Life

MONY Financial Services

MONY Financial Services Foundation

Moody, Dwight Lyman

Moody, Helen Wills

Moody, Raymond

Moody, Robert Lee

Moody, Ron

Moody, William Vaughn

Moody Air Force Base

Moody Bible Institute

Moody Blues, The

Moody Broadcasting Network

Moody's Investors Service, Inc.

Moog, Robert

Moog™ synthesizer

Moon, Sun Myung

Moonachie

Moonie, *n.*, *pl.* Moonies

Moonlighting

Moonlight Sonata

Moon of the Caribbees, The

Moon River

Moor

Moore

Moore, Archie

Moore, Brian

Moore, Clayton

Moore, Clement C.

Moore, Constance

Moore, Demi

Moore, Douglas

Moore, Dudley

Moore, Garry

Moore, George

Moore, Gordon Earle

Moore, Grace

Moore, Henry

Moore, Jerry J.

Moore, Marianne

Moore, Mary Tyler

Moore, Melba

Moore, Roger

Moore, Sam

Moore, Terry

Moore, Thomas

Moore, Victor

Moore College of Art and Design

Moore Corporation Ltd.

Moorehead, Agnes

Moores, Dick

Moores, John Jay

Moores Creek National Battlefield

Moore-Smith convergence

Moorestown

Mooresville

Moorhead

Moorhead State University

Moorish

Moorish arch

Moorish architecture

Moorish art

Moorish idol

Moorman Company Fund

Moorpark

Moorpark College

Moorsom system

Moose

Moosehead Lake

Mooseheart

Moose Jaw

Moosic

Moraine

Moraine Park Technical College

Moraine Valley Community College

Morales, Luis de

Morality in Media

Moral Majority

Moral Re-Armament

Moran, Bugs

Moran, Edward

Moran, James Martin

Moran, Thomas

Morandi, Giorgio

Moranis, Rick

Morath, Max

Moravia

Moravia, Alberto

Moravian

Moravian Brethren

Moravian Church

Moravian Church in America

Moravian Church in America Southern Province

Moravian Church (Unitas Fratum) Northern Province

Moravian College

Moravian Gate

Moray Firth

Morbihan

Mordecai

Mordine and Company

More, Hannah

More, Paul Elmer

More, Sir Thomas

Moreau, Gustave

Moreau, Jeanne

Morehead

Morehead City

Morehead State University

Morehead State University Eagles

Morehouse College

Morehouse School of Medicine

Morel, Jean

Morel, Paul

Morelos

Moreno, Rita

Morera's theorem

Moreton Bay

Moreton Bay pine

Morey, Walt

Morgan

Morgan, Charles Langbridge

Morgan, Daniel

Morgan, Dennis

Morgan, Frank

Morgan, Frank Sherman

Morgan, Harry

Morgan, Helen

Morgan, Sir Henry

Morgan, Jaye P.

Morgan, Joe

Morgan, John Hunt

Morgan, John Pierpont, Jr.

Morgan, J. P.

Morgan, Junius Spencer

Morgan, Justin

Morgan, Lewis Henry

Morgan, Lorrie

Morgan, Misty

Morgan, Russ

Morgan, Thomas Hunt

Morgan City

Morgan Community College

Morgan Guaranty Trust Company of New York

Morgan Guaranty Trust Company of New York Charitable Trust

Morgan Hill

Morgan horse

Morgan le Fay

Morgan's Raiders

Morgan Stanley Foundation

Morgan Stanley Group Inc.

Morgan State University

Morgan State University Bears

Morganton [* NC]

Morgantown [* KY; WV]

Morgenthau, Henry

Morgenthau, Henry, Jr.

Morgernstern, Sheldon

Mori, Taikichiro

Morial, Ernest N.

Moriarty, Michael

Moriarty, Professor

Mörike, Edouard

Morini, Erika

Morison, Samuel Eliot

Morisot, Berthe

Morita, Pat

Moriyama, Mayumi

Mork and Mindy

Morland, George
Morley, Christopher
Morley, Edward
Morley, Robert
Morley, Thomas
Morman
  Manufacturing
  Company
Mormon
Mormon Battalion
Mormon campaign
Mormon Church
Mormon cricket
Mormondom
Mormonism
Mormon Tabernacle
  Choir
Mormon Trail
Mornay sauce
Morning Edition™
  public radio show
Morning Prayer
Morningside College
Moro, *n.*, *pl.* Moro *or*
  Moros
Moro, Aldo
Moro, Antonio
Moroccan
Morocco
Moroni
Moroni, Giovanni
  Battista
Moronobu Hishikawa
Morpheus
Morrice, James
  Wilson
Morricone, Ennio
Morrill Act
Morrilton
Morris

Morris, Chester
Morris, Desmond
Morris, Esther
Morris, Gary
Morris, Gouverneur
Morris, Greg
Morris, Howard
Morris, Mercury
Morris, Robert
Morris, Shellee
Morris, Wayne
Morris, William
  Shivers
Morris, Wright
Morris Brown College
morris *occas.* Morris
  chair
Morris College
Morris Dam
Morrison
Morrison, Hobe
Morrison, Jim
Morrison, Toni
Morrison, Van
Morrison College
Morrison Institute of
  Technology
Morrison Knudsen
  Corporation
Morris Plains
Morris Plan
Morris Plan bank
Morris the cat
Morristown
Morristown National
  Historical Park
Morrisville
Morro Bay
Morro Castle

Morrow, Honoré
  Willsie
Morrow, Vic
Morrow Junior Books
Morrow Point Dam
Morse, Carlton E.
Morse, Robert
Morse, Samuel F. B.
Morse, Wayne
Morse alphabet
Morse code
Mortgage Bankers
  Association of
  America
Morton
Morton, Bruce
Morton, Gary
Morton, Jelly Roll
Morton, Joe
Morton, William
  Thomas Green
Morton B. Weiss
  Museum of Judaica
Morton College
Morton Grove
Morton International,
  Inc.
Morton Thiokol
  Foundation
Morton Thiokol Inc.
Mosaic law
Mosbacher, Robert
Mosby, John S.
Mosby's Confederacy
Mosby's Rangers
Moscone Center
Mosconi, Willie
Moscow
Moscow Art Theatre
Moscow Basin

Moscow Chamber
  Orchestra
Moscow Circus
Moscow Conference
Moscow Mafia
Moscow Mule
Moscow Philharmonic
  Orchestra
Moscow University
Moseley, Henry
Moseley's law
Moselle
Moses
Moses, Edwin
Moses, Grandma
Moses, William
Moses basket
Moses boat
Moses Lake
Moskva
Moslem *var. of*
  Muslim
Mosquito Coast
Moss, Howard
Moss, Stirling
Mossad
Mossadegh,
  Mohammad
Mössbauer, Rudolph
  Ludwig
Mössbauer effect
Mossi
Moss Point
Mossyrock Dam
Mostel, Zero
Most Happy Fella,
  The
Mostovoy, Marc S.
Most Venerable Order
  of the Hospital of

Saint John of
  Jerusalem, The
Most Worshipful
  National Grand
  Lodge Free and
  Accepted Ancient
  York Masons
Mosul
Mosul Museum
Motel 6™
Moten, Bennie
Mother and Child
Mother Cabrini
Mother Carey's
  chicken
Mother Church, The
Mother Earth
Mother Earth News
Mother Goose
Mother Goose and
  Grimm
Mother Goose rhyme
Mother Goose Suite
Mother Goose tale
Mother Hubbard
Mothering Sunday
Mother Jones
Motherland, The
Mother Lode
Mother Nature
Mother of God
Mothers Against
  Drunk Driving
Mother's Day
Mothers-in-Law Club
  International
Mothers of Invention
Mothers Today
Mother Teresa
Motherwell, Robert
Motley, John Lothrop

Motley, Willard
Mötley Crüe
Motlow State
  Community College
Motorcraft Quality
  Parts 500
Motorcyclist
Motorhead
Motorland
Motorola Foundation
Motorola, Inc.
Motor Trend
Motor Vehicle
  Manufacturers
  Association of the
  United States
Motown Record
  Company
Motown sound
Mott, Charles S.
Mott, Frank Luther
Mott, Lucretia
Mott Foundation
Mo Tzu
Moulin Rouge
Moulin Rouge, "La
  Goulue"
Moulmein
Moultrie
Moultrie, William
Mound
Mound Builder
Mound City
Mound City Group
  National Monument
Moundsview
Moundsville
Mount, William
  Sydney
Mount Abu
Mount Ada

Mount Adams

Mount Aegaleous

Mountain Brook

Mountain Daylight Time

Mountain Empire Community College

Mountain Grove

Mountain Home

Mountain Home Air Force Base

Mountain Lakes

Mountain Meadows

Mountain Meadows Massacre

Mountain of the Holy Cross

Mountainside

Mountains of the Moon

Mountain Standard Time

Mountain State

Mountain States

Mountain States Technical Institute

Mountain Time

Mountain View

Mountain View College

Mount Airy

Mount Alfred

Mount Alice

Mount Allen

Mount Allison University

Mount Aloysius Junior College

Mount Anderson

Mount Angel Seminary

Mount Anne

Mount Antisana

Mount Apo

Mount Aragats

Mount Ararat

Mount Asama

Mount Assiniboine

Mount Astor

Mount Athabasca

Mount Athos

Mount Baker

Mount Baker-Snoqualmie National Forest

Mount Baldy

Mountbatten, Louis

Mount Blackburn

Mount Blackmore

Mount Bolton Brown

Mount Borah

Mount Bradley

Mount Brewer

Mount Brown

Mount Buckley

Mount Cameron

Mount Cameroon

Mount Carmel

Mount Carmel man

Mount Carstenz

Mount Churchill

Mount Clark

Mount Clay

Mount Clemens

Mount Cleveland

Mount Conness

Mount Cook

Mount Coolidge

Mount Cowen

Mount Custer

Mount Darwin

Mount Davis

Mount Democrat

Mount Desert Island

Mount Diablo

Mount Dora

Mount Dunraven

Mount Ebal

Mount Edith Cavell

Mount Egmont

Mount Elbert

Mount Elbrus

Mount Elgon

Mount Ephraim

Mount Erebus

Mount Erymanthus

Mount Etna

Mount Evans

Mount Everest

Mount Fairweather

Mount Foraker

Mount Frissell

Mount Fuji

Mount Gay

Mount Gilead

Mount Godwin Austen

Mount Greylock

Mount Hamilton

Mount Healthy

Mount Hermon

Mount Holly

Mount Holyoke College

Mount Hood

Mount Hood Community College

Mount Hood Festival of Jazz

Mount Hood National Forest

Mount Hopkins

Mount Hopkins Observatory

Mount Hudson

Mount Huila

Mount Humphreys

Mount Ida

Mount Ida College

Mountie

Mount Jefferson

Mount Joy

Mount Kanchenjunga

Mount Katahdin

Mount Kazbek

Mount Kennedy

Mount Kenya

Mount Kisko

Mount Kosciusko

Mountlake Terrace

Mount Lebanon

Mount Logan

Mount Lucania

Mount Lydia

Mount Makalu

Mount Mansfield

Mount Marcy

Mount Markham

Mount Marty College

Mount Mary College

Mount Massive

Mount Mayon

Mount McKinley

Mount McKinley National Park [now Denali National Park]

Mount Mercy College

Mount Meru

Mount Mitchell

Mount Morris

Mount Nebo

Mount of Olives

Mount of the Holy Cross

Mount Olive

Mount Olive College

Mount Oliver

Mount Olivet

Mount Olympus

Mount Orizaba

Mount Palomar

Mount Palomar Observatory

Mount Pelée

Mount Pelion

Mount Pend Oreille

Mount Penn

Mount Pinatubo

Mount Pisgah

Mount Pleasant

Mount Prospect

Mount Psiloriti

Mount Pulog

Mount Rainier

Mount Rainier National Park

Mount Revelstoke

Mount Revelstoke National Park

Mount Robson

Mount Robson Provincial Park

Mount Rushmore

Mount Rushmore National Memorial

Mount Saint Clare College

Mount Saint Elias

Mount Saint Helens

Mount Saint Helens National Monument

Mount Saint Mary College

Mount Saint Mary's College

Mount Saint Mary's College and Seminary

Mount Saint Mary's College Mountaineers

Mount San Antonio College

Mount Sanford

Mount San Jacinto College

Mount Scopus

Mount Senario College

Mount Shasta

Mount Sinai

Mount Sinai Medical Center

Mount Sinai School of Medicine

Mount Siple

Mount Sorata

Mount Sparr

Mount Stanley

Mount Steele

Mount Sterling

Mount Stromlo

Mount Stromlo Observatory

Mount Suribachi

Mount Tabor

Mount Tamalpais

Mount Townsend

Mount Union

Mount Union College

Mount Unzen

Mount Vancouver

Mount Vernon

Mount Vernon College

Mount Vernon
  Nazarene College

Mount Vesuvius

Mount Wachusett
  Community College

Mount Wade

Mount Wakely

Mount Washburn

Mount Washington

Mount Washington
  Observatory

Mountweazel, Lilian

Mount Whitney

Mount Wilhelmina

Mount Wilson

Mount Wilson
  Observatory

Mount Wood

Mount Wrangell

Mount Yale

Mount Zion

Mourne Mountains

Mourning Becomes
  Electra

Mouskouri, Nana

Moussorgsky *var. of*
  Mussorgsky,
  Modest

Movie Channel, The
  (TMC)

Movieland Wax
  Museum

Movies USA

Mowat, Farley

Mowbray, Alan

Mowgli

Moyers, Bill

Moyer's—The
  Teachers' Store

Moyle, Allan

Moynihan, Daniel
  Patrick

Mozambique

Mozambique Channel

Mozambique Current

Mozart, Leopold

Mozart, Wolfgang
  Amadeus

Mozartean *or*
  Mozartian

Mozarteum

Mr., *n., pl.* Messrs.

M-radiation

Mr. and Mrs. Robert
  Andrews

Mr. Big

Mr. Bill

Mr. Blackwell

Mr. Bones

Mr. Charlie

Mr. Clean

Mr. Dooley

Mr. Fixit

Mr. Goodwrench™

Mr. Green Jeans

Mr. Magoo

Mr. Moto

Mrs., *n., pl.* Mesdames

Mrs. America

Mrs. Frisby and the
  Rats of NIMH

Mrs. Grundy

Mrs. Malaprop

Mrs. Miniver

Mr. Smith Goes to
  Washington

Mr. Spock

Mr. Sulu

Mr. T.

Mr. Tambo

Ms.

M-series

M-shell

M-16 rifle

MTI College

MTM Entertainment,
  Inc.

MTV: Music
  Television

MTV Networks

MTV Video Music
  Award

Mubarak, Hosni

Much Ado about
  Nothing

Mudd, Roger

Mud Mountain Dam

Mueller-Stahl, Armin

Muenster

Mugabe, Robert
  Gabriel

Mugar, David Graves

Muggeridge, Malcolm

Muggs, J. Fred

Mughal *var. of* Mogul
  Empire

Muhammad *var. of*
  Mohammed

Muhammad, Elijah

Muhammad Ahmed

Muhammad Ali
  [Turkish officer;
  shah of Persia; *see
  also* Ali,
  Muhammad]

Muhammadan

Muhammad of Ghor

Muharram

Muhlenberg, Frederick

Muhlenberg, Heinrich

Muhlenberg, John Peter

Muhlenberg College

Muir, Edwin

Muir, John

Muir, Malcolm

Muir Glacier

Muir Woods National Monument

Mukden [*now* Shenyang]

Mukden Incident

Muldaur, Diana

Muldaur, Maria

Muldoon, Robert D.

Muldowney, Shirley

Mulgrew, Kate

Mulhare, Edward

Mulholland Drive

Mull, Martin

Mullavey, Greg

Müller, Friedrich

Müller, Fritz

Muller, H. J.

Müller, Wenzel

Müller, Wilhelm

Müllerian mimicry

Muller v. Oregon

Mullican, Moon

Mulligan, Gerry

Mulligan, Moon

Mulligan, Richard

Mulliken, Robert Sanderson

Mullin, Chris

Mullin, Willard

Mullins

Mulready, William

Mulroney, Brian

Multigraph™

Multilith™

Multimedia Entertainment

Multimedia, Inc.

Multnomah Falls

Multnomah Kennel Club

Multnomah School of Bible

Multscher, Hans

Mulvian Bridge

Mumford, Lewis

Mummenschanz

Mummers' Parade

Munch, Edvard

Munchausen, Baron

Münchausen, Karl Friedrich Hieronymous von

Munchausenism

Munchausen's syndrome

Munchkin

Munch Museum

Muncie

Munda

Mundelein

Mundelein College

Munhall

Muni, Paul

Munich

Munich Agreement

Munich Bach Choir and Orchestra

[Munich] Modern Art Gallery

[Munich] New Art Gallery

[Munich] Old Art Gallery

Munich Pact

Munich Philharmonic Orchestra

Munich putsch

Municipal Bond Investors Assurance Corporation

Munising

Munkácsy, Mihály von

Munn v. Illinois

Muñoz Marin, Luis

Munro, Alice

Munro, H. H.

Munro, Wilfred Harold

Munroe, Charles Edward

Munroe effect

Munsee

Munsel, Patrice

Munsey, Frank

Munsey Park

Munshin, Jules

Munson, Thurman

Münster [* Germany]

Munster [* IN]

Munsters, The

Muntu Dance Theater

Muntz metal

Muppet

Muppet Show, The

Murad

Murasaki Shikibu

Murat, Joachim

Murder, Inc.

Murder on the Orient Express

Murder, She Wrote

Murdoch, Iris

Murdoch, Rupert

Murdock, David Howard

Mures River

Murfreesboro [* AK; NC; TN; see also Murphysboro]

Murieta or Murrieta, Joaquin

Murillo, Bartolemé Estéban

Murjite

Murman Coast

Murmansk

Murnau, F. W.

Murphy

Murphy, Audie

Murphy, Ben

Murphy, Bridey

Murphy, Dale

Murphy, Eddie

Murphy, George

Murphy, Michael

Murphy, Turk

Murphy bed

Murphy Brown

Murphy game

Murphy man

Murphy Oil Corporation

Murphysboro [* IL; see also Murfreesboro]

Murphy's Law

Murray

Murray, Ann [opera singer]

Murray, Anne [pop singer]

Murray, Arthur

Murray, Bill

Murray, Don

Murray, Sir Gilbert

Murray, Sir James Augustus Henry

Murray, Jan

Murray, Kathryn

Murray, Ken

Murray, Lindley

Murray, Mae

Murray, Philip

Murray, Ty

Murray Bay

Murray Hill Association, The

Murray State College

Murray State University

Murray State University Racers

Murrieta var. of Murieta, Joaquin

Murrow, Edward R.

Murrumbidgee

Musante, Tony

Musburger, Brent

muscadet often Muscadet

Muscat

Muscat and Oman [now Oman]

Muscatine

Muscatine Community College

Muscle Shoals

Muscongus Bay

Muscongus Bay boat

Muscongus Bay sloop

Muscovite

Muscovitic

Muscovy Company

Muscovy duck

Muscular Dystrophy Association, Inc.

Muse

Musée Conti—Wax Museum of Louisiana Legends

Musée des Beaux Arts

Museum Island

Museum of Broadcasting

Museum of Modern Art

Museum of Neon Art

Museum of Primitive Art

Museum of Queen Mathilda

Museum of Science and Industry

Museum of Science and Industry and Crown Space Center

Museum of the American Indian, Heye Foundation

Musial, Stan

Music Educators National Conference

Musicland Stores Corporation

Music Library Association

Music Man, The

Music of Your Life/ Fairwest

Music Row

Music Teachers National Association

Music Television (MTV)

Muskegon

Muskegon College

Muskegon Community College

Muskegon Heights

Muskie, Edmund

Muskingum

Muskingum Area Technical College

Muskingum College

Muskogean

Muskogee

Muskogee [Indian], *n.*, *pl.* Muskogee *or* Muskogees

Muskoka Lakes

Muslim *occas.* Moslem

Muslim Brotherhood

Muslim era

Muslim League

Mussadegh, Muhammad

Musset, Alfred de

Mussolini, Benito

Mussorgsky *occas.* Moussorgsky, Modest

Mustafa

Mustafa Kemal

Mustard Seed, The

Muti, Riccardo

Mutiny on the Bounty

Mutt and Jeff

Mutual Benefit Life Charitable Trust

Mutual Benefit Life Insurance Company

Mutual Bond Investors Assurance Corporation

Mutual Broadcasting System Inc.

Mutual Life Assurance Company of Canada

Mutual Life Insurance Company of New York

Mutual of America Life Insurance Company

Mutual of Omaha Insurance Company

Muybridge, Eadweard

Muzak™

Muziano, Girolamo

MX missile

Myanmar [*aka* Burma]

Myasthenia Gravis Foundation

Mycenae

Mycenaean

Mycerinus

Mycitracin™

My Darling Clementine

Myers, Russell

Myerson, Bess

Myerstown

My Fair Lady

My Friend Flicka

My Friend Irma

Mykonos

My Lai incident

Mylan Laboratories Inc.

My Life as a Dog

My Old Kentucky Home

Myrdal, Gunnar

Myron

Myrtle Beach

Myrtle Beach Air Force Base

Myrtle Point

My Sister Eileen

Mysore [*now* Karnatka]

Mysterious Press

Mysterious Stranger, The

Mystery!

Mystery of Edwin Drood, The

Mystic

Mystic Seaport

Mystic Seaport Museum

My Three Sons

Myth-Science Arkestra

N

NAACP Legal Defense and Educational Fund, Inc.

NAACP Special Contribution Fund

Na'amat U.S.A.

Nabis

Nabisco Brands, Inc.

Nabisco Foods, Inc.

Nabiyev, Rakhmon

Nabokov, Vladimir

Nabors, Jim

NACCO Industries, Inc.

Nacogdoches [* TX; see also Nachitoches]

Nadelman, Elie

Na-Dene

Nader, Ralph

Naderite

NAES College

Nafud Desert

Nagasaki

Nagel, Conrad

Nagoya

Naguib, Mohammed

Nagurski, Bronko

Nagy, Imre

Nagy, Ivan

Nahanni National Park

Nahuatl, n., pl. Nahuatl or Nahuatls

Nahuatlan

Nahum

Naify, Robert Allen

Naipaul, V. S.

Nairn

Nairnshire

Nairobi

Naish, J. Carrol

Naismith, James

Naismith, Laurence

Naismith Memorial Basketball Hall of Fame

Nakasone, Yasuhiro

Naked and the Dead, The

Naked City

Naked Lunch

Nakian, Reuben

NAL Books™

Nalco Chemical Company

Nalco Foundation

Naldi, Nita

Nama, n., pl. Nama or Namas

Namaqualand

Namath, Joe

Nam Co Lake

Name That Tune

Namib Desert

Namibia [form. South West Africa]

Namier, Sir Lewis Bernstein

Nampa

Nanaimo

Nanchang

Nancy

Nancy Drew mysteries

Nanda Devi

Nanga Parbat

Nanking [now Nanjing]

Nankin or Nanking porcelain

Nanook of the North

Nansen, Fridtjof

Nansen bottle

Nansen cast

Nan Shan

Nantahala National Forest

Nantes

Nanticoke

Nantua sauce

Nantucket
Nanty-Glo
Naomi
Napa
Napa Valley
Napa Valley College
Naperville
Napier, John
Napier diagram
Napierian
Napierian logarithm
Napier's bones
Naples
[Naples] National
  Museum
Naples yellow
Napoleon
Napoleon Bonaparte
Napoleon brandy
Napoleonic
Napoleonic Code
Napoleonic Wars
Nappanee
Naqvi, Swaleh
Narayan, R. K.
Narbada
Narberth
Narcissa
Narcissus
Narcolepsy and
  Cataplexy
  Foundation of
  America
Narcotics Anonymous
Narew
Narnia
Naropa Institute
Narragansett
Narragansett Bay

Narragansett [Indian],
  n., pl. Narragansett
  or Narragansetts
Narrows, the
Naryn
Nasby, Petroleum V.
NASCAR Newsletter
NASCAR Winston
  500 Race
Nasco Products
  Company
NASDAQ Composite
  Index
NASDAQ National
  Market System
Nash, Beau
Nash, Charles William
Nash, Graham
Nash, Johnny
Nash, Ogden
Nash Community
  College
Nashe, Thomas
Nashoba
Nashotah House
Nashua
Nashville
Nashville Auto Diesel
  College
Nashville
  International
  Airport
Nashville Motor
  Raceway
Nashville Network,
  The
Nashville sound
Nashville State
  Technical Institute
Nashville Symphony
  Orchestra

[Nashville]
  Tennessean, The
Nashville warbler
Naskapi
Nassau
Nassau Community
  College
Nassau grouper
Nassau International
  Airport
Nassau Mountains
Nassau Veterans
  Memorial Coliseum
Nasser, Gamal Abdel
Nast, Thomas
Nastase, Ilie
Natal
Natalie
Natal orange
Natal plum
Natasha
Natchez
Natchez [Indian], *n.,
  pl.* Natchez
Natchez National
  Historical Park
Natchez Trace
Natchez Trace
  Parkway
Natchitoches [* LA;
  see also
  Nacogdoches]
Nathan
Nathan, George Jean
Nathan, Robert
Nathanael
Nathaniel
Natick
Nation, The
Nation, Carry

National Abortion Federation

National Abortion Rights Action League

National Academy of Counselors and Family Therapists

National Academy of Education

National Academy of Engineering

National Academy of Recording Arts and Sciences

National Academy of Sciences

National Academy of Sports

National Academy of Television Arts and Sciences

National Academy Press

National Accelerator Laboratory

National Accreditation Council for Agencies Serving the Blind and Visually Handicapped

National Action Council for Minorities in Engineering

National Aeronautic Association

National Aeronautics and Space Administration

National Aerospace Plane

National Agricultural Chemicals Association

National Air and Space Museum

National Airport

National Alliance for Family Life, Inc.

National Alliance for the Mentally Ill

National Alliance of Business

National Alliance to End Homelessness

National Amputation Foundation

National Anti-Vivisection Society

National Aquarium, The

National Archery Association

National Archives

National Archives and Records Administration

National Arts Centre

National Arts Centre Orchestra

National Asbestos Council

National Assembly of National Voluntary Health and Social Welfare Organizations

National Assessment of Educational Progress

National Assistance League

National Association for Creative Children and Adults

National Association for Foreign Student Affairs

National Association for Gifted Children

National Association for Hearing and Speech Action

National Association for Stock Car Auto Racing

National Association for the Advancement of Colored People

National Association for the Education of Young Children

National Association for the Visually Handicapped

National Association for Uniformed Services

National Association for Year-Round Education

National Association for Young Women's Hebrew Associations

National Association of Accountants

National Association of American Business Clubs

National Association of Arab Americans

National Association of Atomic Veterans

National Association of Bank Women

National Association of Broadcasters

National Association of Business and Educational Radio

National Association of Church Business Administration

National Association of Composers/USA

National Association of Congregational Christian Churches

National Association of Credit Management

National Association of Dealers in Antiques

National Association of Education and Training Contractors

National Association of Elementary School Principals

National Association of Emergency Medical Technicians

National Association of Engine and Boat Manufacturers

National Association of Enrolled Federal Tax Accountants

National Association of Free Will Baptists

National Association of Government Employees (Ind.)

National Association of Grocers

National Association of Hispanic Journalists

National Association of Home Builders

National Association of Intercollegiate Athletics

National Association of Investors Corporation

National Association of Junior Auxiliaries

National Association of Legal Secretaries

National Association of Letter Carriers of the United States of America

National Association of Life Underwriters

National Association of Manufacturers

National Association of Metal Finishers

National Association of Negro Musicians

National Association of Parliamentarians

National Association of Police Officers

National Association of Postmasters of the United States

National Association of Professional Educators

National Association of Professional Salespersons

National Association of Purchasing Management Index

National Association of Quality

Assurance Professionals

National Association of Quick Printers

National Association of Railroad Passengers

National Association of Real Estate Appraisers

National Association of Real Estate Brokers

National Association of Real Estate Companies

National Association of Realtors

National Association of Registered Nurses

National Association of Regulatory Utility Commissioners

National Association of Retired Federal Employees

National Association of Rocketry

National Association of Schools of Art and Design

National Association of Science Writers

National Association of Secondary School Principals

National Association of Securities Dealers

National Association of Securities Dealers Automated Quotations

National Association of Social Workers

National Association of State Mental Health Program Directors

National Association of Student Councils

National Association of Teachers of Singing

National Association of the Deaf

National Association of the Partners of the Americas

National Association of the Physically Handicapped

National Association of the Remodeling Industry

National Association of Women Artists

National Association Taunting Safety and Fairness Everywhere

National Association to Advance Fat Acceptance

National Ataxia Foundation

National Atomic Museum

National Auctioneers Association

National Audubon Society

National Australia Bank, Ltd.

National Automobile Club

National Automobile Dealers Association

National Autonomous University of Mexico

National Ballet of Canada

National Band and Choral Directors Hall of Fame

National Bank of Canada

National Bank of Detroit

National Bank of Detroit Charitable Trust

National Baptist Convention of America

National Baptist Convention, United States of America

National Barn Dance

National Baseball Congress

National Baseball Fan Association

National Baseball Hall of Fame and Museum

National Baseball League

National Basketball Association

National Bed-and-Breakfast Association

National Beer Wholesalers' Association of America

National Best Cat award

National Best Kitten award

National Bicycle Dealers Association

National Black Law Journal

National Black Network

National Blues Music Award

National Board of Review of Motion Pictures

National Board of the Young Women's Christian Association of the United States of America

National Book Award

National Book Committee of America

National Book Critics Circle

National Bowling Hall of Fame and Museum

National Boxing Association

National Braille Association

National Brith Sholom

National Broadcasting Company

National Broadcasting Network

National Bureau of Economic Research

National Bureau of Standards

National Business College

National Business Education Association

National Business Employment Weekly

National Business Woman

National Businesswomen's Leadership Association

National Cable Television Association

National Campers and Hikers Association

National Cancer Care Foundation, Inc.

National Cancer Center

National Capital Parks

National Car Rental System, Inc.

National Cartoonists Society

National Cathedral

National Catholic Educational Association

National Catholic Reporter

National Catholic Rural Life Conference

National Center for Health Statistics

National Center for Public Policy Research

National Championship Air Races

National Charter

National Children's Cancer Society, Inc.

National Cholesterol Education Program

National Christian Network

National City

National City Bank

National City Corporation

National Civic League

National Civil Rights Museum

National Classic Jazz and Ragtime Festival

National Clearinghouse for Smoking and Health

National Climatic Data Center

National Coal Association

National Coalition against Domestic Violence

National College

National College Football Hall of Fame

National College of Chiropractic

National College of Education

National College of Naturopathic Medicine

National College of Physical Education Association for Men

National College TV

National Collegiate Athletic Association

National Collegiate Body-Building Association

National Collegiate Water Ski Association

National Commission on AIDS

National Commission on Libraries and Information Science

National Committee for Adoption

National Committee for Citizens in Education

National Committee for Prevention of Child Abuse

National Committee for Responsible Patriotism

National Committee for Responsive Philanthropy

National Conference of Catholic Bishops

National Conference of Christians and Jews

National Conference of Editorial Writers

National Conference of Weights and Measures

National Congress of American Indians

National Congress of Parents and Teachers

National Consumers League

National Contract Management Association

National Convention

National Cooperative Business Association

National Corporate Fund for Dance

National Cosmetology Association

National Cotton Council of America

National Council for Geographic Education

National Council of Jewish Women

National Council of La Raza

National Council of Negro Women

National Council of Savings Institutions

National Council of Senior Citizens

National Council of State Garden Clubs

National Council of Teachers of English

National Council of Teachers of Mathematics

National Council of the Churches of Christ in the United States of America

National Council of the United States Society of Saint Vincent de Paul

National Council of Women of the United States

National Council of Young Men's Christian Associations of the United States of America

National Council on Alcoholism and Drug Dependence

National Council on Child Abuse and Family Violence

National Council on Crime and Delinquency

National Council on Death and Dying

National Council on Family Relations

National Council on the Aging

National Covenant

National Cowboy Hall of Fame and Western Heritage Center

National Credit Union Administration

National Crime Information Center

National Crime Prevention Council

National Criminal Justice Association

National Critics Institute

National Customs Brokers and Forwarders Association of America

National Dairy Board

National Dairy Council

National Day of Prayer

National Defense Education Act

National Down Syndrome Society

National Easter Seal Society

National Educational Television

National Education Association of the United States

National Education Center

National Education Center—Arizona Automotive Institute

National Education Center—Arkansas College of Technology

National Education Center—Bauder College Campus

National Education Center—Brown Institute Campus

National Education Center—Bryman Campus

National Education Center—Kentucky College of Technology Campus

National Education Center—National Institute of Technology Campus

National Education Center—Spartan School of Aeronautics Campus

National Education Center—Tampa Technical Institute Campus

National Education Center—Vale Technical Institute Campus

National Electrical Manufacturers Association

National Electronics Sales and Service Dealers Association

National Emergency Medicine Association

National Endowment for the Arts

National Endowment for the Humanities

National Enquirer

National Environmental Health Association

National Ethnic Coalition of Organizations

National Examiner

National Exchange Club

National Executive Service Corps

National Extension Homemakers Council

National Farmers Organization

National Farmers Union

National Federation for Decency

National Federation of Business and Professional Women's Clubs

National Federation of Federal Employees

National Federation of Independent Businesses

National Federation of Modern Language Teachers Associations

National Federation of Music Clubs

National Federation of Music Societies

National Federation of Press Women

National Federation of State High School Associations

National Federation of State High School Athletic Associations

National Federation of the Blind

National FFA Foundation

National Finals Rodeo

National Firearms Act

National Fire Protection Association

National Fisheries Institute

National Food Bank Network

National Food Brokers Association

National Football Conference

National Football League

National Football League Players Association

National Foreign Trade Council, Inc.

National Forest Products Association

National Forest System

National Foundation for Cancer Research, Inc.

National Foundation for Ileitis and Colitis

National Foundation on the Arts and the Humanities

National 4-H Council

National Freedom Day

National Fuel Gas Company

National Fund for Medical Education

National Future Farmers of America Organization

National Gallery Concerts

National Gallery of Art

National Gallery of Canada

National Gallery of Ireland

National Gallery of Scotland

National Gallery of Victoria

National Gardening Association

National Gay and Lesbian Task Force

National Gay Pentecostal Alliance

National Genealogical Society

National Geographic Magazine

National Geographic Society

National Geographic Traveler

National Geographic World

National Gifted and Talented Club

National Glaucoma Research Program

National Governors' Association

National Grandparents Day

National Grange

National Guard

National Guard Association of the United States

National Guard of the United States

National Guild of Saint Paul

National Hairdressers and Cosmetologists Association

National Head Injury Foundation

National Health Council

National Health Laboratories Inc.

National Hearing Aid Society

National Heart, Lung, and Blood Institute

National Heart Research

National Hemophilia Foundation

National Hispanic Scholarship Fund

National Hispanic University, The

National Hockey League

National Home Life Assurance Company

National Home Study Council

National Honor Society

National Horse Racing Hall of Fame

National Horse Show Association of America Ltd.

National Hospice Organization

National Hot Rod Association

National Humane Education Society

National Hurricane Center

National Industrial Recovery Act

National Institute for Music Theater

National Institute for Occupational Safety and Health

National Institute of Arts and Letters

National Institute of Environmental Health Sciences

National Institute of Social Sciences

National Institute of Standards and Technology

National Institutes of Health

National Interfaith Cable Coalition

National Intergroup, Inc.

National Investigations Committee on Unidentified Flying Objects

Nationalist China

Nationality Broadcasting Network

National Jewish Book Award

National Jewish Center for Immunology and Respiratory Medicine

National Jewish Welfare Board

National Junior College Athletic Association

National Junior Honor Society

National Kidney Foundation

National Knights of the Ku Klux Klan

National Labor Relations Act

National Labor Relations Board

National Lampoon

National Lampoon's Animal House

National Lampoon's European Vacation

National Lampoon's Vacation

National Law Journal, The

National League for Nursing

National League of American PEN Women

National League of Cities

National League of Families of American Prisoners Missing in Southeast Asia

National League of Postmasters of the United States

National League of POW-MIA Families

National League of Professional Baseball Clubs

National Legal Aid and Defender Association

National Lesbian and Gay Law Association

National Leukemia Association, Inc.

National Liberation Front

National Life Insurance Company

National-Louis University

National Mall

National Marine Fisheries Service

National Marine Manufacturers Association

National Medal of Science

National Mediation Board

National Medical Association

National Medical Enterprises, Inc.

National Medical Fellowships

National Mental Health Association

National Merit Scholarship Corporation

National Merit Scholarships Qualifying Test

National Model Railroad Association

National Multiple Sclerosis Society

National Museum at Poznan

National Museum at Warsaw

National Museum of African Art

National Museum of American Art

National Museum of American History

National Museum of Anthropology

National Museum of Athens

National Museum of Bardo

National Museum of Finland

National Museum of Modern Art

National Museum of Natural History

National Museum of Nepal

National Museum of Rome

National Museum of Tokyo

National Museum of Wales

National Music Camp

National Music Council

National Music Publishers' Association

National Naval Medical Center

National Naval Officers Association

National Neurofibromatosis Foundation

National News Bureau

National Oceanic and Atmospheric Administration

National Opera Association

National Opera Studio

National Opinion Research Center

National Optometric Association

National Orchestral Association

National Organization for Outlaw and Lawman History

National Organization for the Reform of Marijuana Laws

National Organization for Victim Assistance

National Organization for Women

National Organization for Women Legal

Defense and Education Fund

National Organization of Mall Walkers

National Organization of Mothers of Twins Clubs

National Osteoporosis Foundation

National Park of American Samoa

National Parks and Conservation Association

National Park Service

National Park System

National Pasta Association

National Playwrights Conference

National Poetry Day Committee

National Police Officers Association

National Police Reserve Officers Association

National Pork Producers Council

National Portrait Gallery

National Press Club

National Press Syndicate

National Press Writers Group

National Primitive Baptist Convention in the United States of America

National Professional Soccer League

National Psoriasis Foundation

National Psychological Association for Psychoanalysis

National Quilting Association

National Public Radio

National Radio Astronomy Observatory

National Railroad Adjustment Board

National Railroad Passenger Corporation

National Railway Historical Society

National Rainbow Coalition

National Recovery Administration

National Recreation and Park Association

National Recycling Coalition

National Register of Historic Places

National Rehabilitation Association

National Religious Broadcasters

National Republican Club

National Resources Defense Council

National Restaurant Association

National Retail Merchants Association

National Retinitis Pigmentosa Foundation

National Retired Teachers Association

National Review

National Reye's Syndrome Foundation

National Rifle Association of America

National Right to Life Committee

National Right to Work Legal Foundation

National Road

National Safety Council

National Safe Workplace Institute

National Savings and Loan League

National Scholastic Athletic Association

National School Boards Association

National School of Technology

National Schools Committee for Economic Education

National Science Foundation

National Science Teachers Association

National Scrabble Association

National Sculpture Society

National Security Agency/Central Security Service

National Security Council

National Semiconductor Corporation

National Service Industries, Inc.

National Ski Hall of Fame

National Small Business United

National Soccer Hall of Fame

National Socialism

National Socialist

National Socialist German Workers' Party

National Society, Colonial Dames of the XVII Century

National Society, Daughters of the American Revolution

National Society for Children and Adults with Autism

National Society for Shut-Ins

National Society for the Study of Education

National Society of Accountants for Cooperatives

National Society of Andersonville

National Society of Architectural Engineers

National Society of Arts and Letters

National Society of Colonial Dames of America

National Society of Film Critics

National Society of Professional Engineers

National Society of Public Accountants

National Society of Sons of the American Revolution

National Society of the Children of the American Revolution

National Society to Prevent Blindness

National Society, United States Daughters of 1812

National Softball Hall of Fame and Museum

National Soft Drink Association

National Solid Wastes Management Association

National Speleological Society

National Spiritualist Association of Churches

National Starch and Chemical Corporation

National Starch and Chemical Foundation Inc.

National Street Rod Association

National Stuttering Project

National Sudden Infant Death Syndrome Foundation

National Sugar Brokers Association

National Symphony Orchestra

National Symphony Orchestra Association

National Taxpayers Union

National Technical Information Service

National Technological University

National Theatre

National Theatre Conference

National Theatre Conservatory

National Theatre of England

National Theatre of the Deaf

National Track and Field Hall of Fame

National Tractor Pullers Association

National Transportation Safety Board

National Treasury Employees Union

National Trust for Historic Preservation

National University

National University Continuing Education Association

National University Extension Association

National University of Ireland

National University of Mexico

National Urban Coalition

National Urban Fellows

National Urban League

National Van Lines, Inc.

National Velvet

National Venture Capital Association

National Veterans Association

National Victim Center

National Volunteer Center

National Water Well Association

National Weather Service

National Wellness Association

National Wellness Institute

National Western Livestock Show, Horse Show and Rodeo

National Westminster Bank

National Wetlands Coalition, The

National Wheelchair Athletic Association

National Wildlife Federation

National Wildlife Refuge System

National Woman's Christian Temperance Union

National Woman's Relief Corps

National Women's Hall of Fame

National Writers Club

National Writers Union

National Youth Orchestra of Canada

National Youth Orchestra of Great Britain

National Zoological Park

Nation of Islam, The

Nation of Yahweh

NationsBank Corporation [form. NCNB Corporation]

Nation's Business

Nationwide Foundation

Nationwide Insurance

Nationwide Life Insurance Company

Native American

Native American Church

Native American Rights Fund

Native Daughters of the Golden West

Native Son

Native Sons of the Golden West

Native States

Nattier, Jean Marc

Nat Turner's Rebellion

Natural Bridge

Natural Bridges

Natural Bridges National Monument

Natural History Museum of Los Angeles County

Naturalist Society, The

Natural Resources Defense Council, Inc.

Natural Science Book Club, The

Natural Wonders bookstore

Nature

Nature Bookstore, The

Nature Boy

Nature Conservancy

Nature Conservancy Magazine, The

Naturist Society, The

Naturopathy Institute, The

Natwest Australia Bank Ltd.

Natwick, Mildred

Naugahyde™

Naugatuck

Naughton, James

Naughty by Nature

Naughty Marietta

Naumburg, Walter

Naumburg Foundation

Nauru
Nautical Almanac
Nauvoo
Navajo *or* Navaho, *n.*, *pl.* Navajo *or* Navajos *or* Navaho *or* Navahos
Navajo Code Talkers Association
Navajo Community College
Navajo Dam
Navajo National Monument
Navajo rug
Naval Air Station North Island
Naval Institute Press
Naval Jelly™
Naval Postgraduate School
Naval Reserve Association
Naval War College
Navarre
Navarrete, Juan Fernández
Navarro, Theodore Fats
Navarro College
Navasota
Navigation Act
Navistar International Transportation Corporation [*form.* International Harvester]
Navratilova, Martina
Navy and Marine Corps Medal
Navy Club of the United States of America Auxiliary

Navy Cross
Navy Island
Navy Jack
Navy League of the United States
Navy Yard City
Naxos
Nayarit
Nayhan, Zayed al-
Nazarene
Nazarene Bible College
Nazarene Theological Seminary
Nazareth
Nazareth College
Nazareth College of Rochester
Nazarite
Nazi
Nazification
Nazify, *v.* Nazified, Nazifying
Nazimova, Alla
Nazi party
Nazism *or* Naziism
NBC News
NBC News at Sunrise
NBC Radio Network
NBC Sports
NBC Symphony Orchestra
NBC Television Opera
NBC TV Network
NBD Bancorp, Inc.
NBD Bank
NCAA College Baseball World Series
NCH Corporation

NCNB Corporate Center
NCNB Corporation [*now* NationsBank Corporation]
NCNB National Bank of Florida
NCNB National Bank of North Carolina
NCNB Texas National Bank
NCR Corporation
NCR Foundation
NCTV Inc.
N'Djamena [*form.* Fort-Lamy]
N'Djamena International Airport
Neagle, John
Neal, Patricia
Neale, Alasdair P.
Nealon, Kevin
Neanderthal
Neanderthal man
Neanderthaloid
Neapolis
Neapolitan
Neapolitan ice cream
Neapolitan sixth chord
Near, Holly
Nearctic
Near East
Near Eastern
Near East Foundation
Nearer Tibet
NEA Today
Nebraska
Nebraska Christian College
Nebraska City

Nebraska Indian Community College

Nebraska Methodist College of Nursing and Allied Health

Nebraskan

Nebraska National Forest

Nebraska Wesleyan University

Nebuchadnezzar

NEC Corporation

Neches River

Necho

Necker, Jacques

Necker, Suzanne

NEC Technologies, Inc.

Nederland

Ned Kelly at Glenowran

Needham

Needles

Needlework Guild of America

Neenah

Neer, Aert van der

Neer, Eglon Hendrik van der

Nefertiti

Neff, Hildegarde

Nefud Desert

Negaunee

Negev

Negress

Negri, Pola

Negri body

Negrillo, n., pl. Negrillos or Negrilloes

Negritic

Negrito, n., pl. Negritos or Negritoes

Negro, n., pl. Negroes

Negro Ensemble Company, Inc., The

Negroid

Negroism

Negroni cocktail

Negrophile

Negrophilism

Negrophilist

Negrophobe

Negrophobia

Negro-Quiagara River

Negro River

Negros [island]

Negro spiritual

Nehru, Jawaharlal

Nehru, Motilal

Nehru jacket

Neighborhood Playhouse School of Theatre

Neighborhood Schools Improvements Act

Neighborhood Watch

Neighborhood Youth Corps

Neihardt, John

Neill, Sam

Neil Simon Theatre

Neilson, William Allan

Neiman, LeRoy

Neiman Marcus Group, Inc.

Neiman Marcus store

Neisse

Nejd

Nel Blu Dipinto di Blu

Nelligan, Kate

Nellis Air Force Base

Nelson

Nelson, Barry

Nelson, Byron

Nelson, Craig T.

Nelson, Ed

Nelson, Gene

Nelson, Harriet

Nelson, Horatio

Nelson, John

Nelson, Judd

Nelson, Ozzie

Nelson, Rick

Nelson, Sandy

Nelson, Tracy

Nelson, Willie

Nelson Mass

Nelson Riddle Orchestra

Nelsonville

Nemacolin's Path

Neman

Nematoda

Nematomorpha

Nembutal™

Nemea

Nemean

Nemean games

Nemean lion

Nemerov, Howard

Nemertina

Nemesis

Nemeth, Miklos

neo-Catholic

neo-Catholicism

Neocene

neo-Christian
neo-Christianity
neo-Confucian
neo-Confucianism
neo-Confucianist
neo-Darwinian
neo-Darwinism
neo-Darwinist
Neodesha
neo-Freudian
neo-Freudianist
neo-Gallican chant
neo-Hebraic
neo-Hegelian
neo-Hegelianism
neo-Kantian
neo-Kantianism
neo-Lamarckian
neo-Lamarckism
neo-Lamarckist
neo-Latin
Neolithic
neo-Lutheran
neo-Lutheranism
neo-Malthusian
neo-Marxism
neo-Marxist
neo-Melanesian
neo-Nazi
neo-Nazism
Neoplatonic
Neoplatonism
Neoplatonist
neo-Romanticism
Neosalvarsan™
Neosho
Neosho County
   Community College
Neosporin™

NeoSynephrine™
neo-Thomism
neo-Thomist
Neotropical *occas.*
   Neotropic
Nepal
Nepalese, *n., pl.*
   Nepalese
Nepali, *n., pl.* Nepali
   occas. Nepalis
Nepos, Cornelius
Nepos, Julius
Neptune
Neptune Beach
Neptune City
Neptunian
NERCO, Inc.
Nereid
Nereus
Ner Israel Rabbinical
   College
Nero
Nero, Caius Claudius
Nero, Franco
Nero, Peter
Nero's crown
Neruda, Jan
Neruda, Pablo
Nerva, Marcus
Nerval, Gérard de
Nervi, Pier Luigi
nervous Nellie *or*
   nervous Nelly, *n.,*
   pl. nervous Nellies
Nesbit, Evelyn
Nesbitt, Cathleen
Nesmith, Mike
Ness, Eliot
Ness, Evaline
Nesselrode

Nesselrode, Karl R.
Nessler, Julius
Nessler's reagent
Nestlé Invitational,
   The
Nestlé USA, Inc.
Nestor
Nestorian
Nestorian Church
Nestorianism
Netherlander
Netherlands
Netherlands Antilles
Netherlands Wind
   Ensemble
Netscher, Caspar
Nettiling Lake
Nettleton, Lois
Netzahualcóyotl
Neuchâtel
Neufchâtel cheese
Neuman, Alfred E.
Neumann College
Neutra, Richard
   Joseph
Neuwirth, Bebe
Nevada
Nevada Falls
Nevada Magazine
Nevadan
Nevada Power
   Company
Nevada Proving
   Ground
Nevelson, Louise
Nevers, Ernie
Neville, Aaron
Neville, Emily
Neville Brothers, The
Nevin, Ethelbert

Nevins, Allan

Nevis

New Age

New Age Journal

New Age Walkers

New Albany

New American Bible

New American
Library

New Amsterdam

New Amsterdam
Theatre

New Apostolic
Church of North
America

Newark

Newark Bay

Newark International
Airport

[Newark] Star-Ledger

New Baltimore

New Bedford

Newberg

New Berlin

New Bern

Newberry

Newberry, Walter
Loomis

Newberry College

Newberry Library

Newbery, John

Newbery Medal

Newbolt, Sir Henry
John

New Braunfels

New Brighton

New Britain

New Brunswick

New Brunswick
Theological
Seminary

New Bullards Bar
Dam

Newburg or
Newburgh [sauce]

Newburgh [* NY]

Newburgh Heights

Newbury

Newbury College

Newburyport

New Caledonia

New Canaan

New Candid Camera,
The

New Carlisle

New Castle [* DE;
IN; KY; PA; VA]

Newcastle [* New
Brunswick; WY]

Newcastle disease

Newcastle
International
Airport

New Castle School of
Trades

Newcastle-under-
Lyme

Newcastle-upon-Tyne

New Christy Minstrels

New City

New College for
Advanced Christian
Studies

New College of
California

New Columbia
Encyclopedia, The

Newcomb, Simon

Newcombe, John

New Community
College of
Baltimore

New Criticism

New Cumberland

New Cumberland
Army Depot

New Cumberland
Army Munitions
Depot

New Dance Ensemble

New Dating Game,
The

New Deal

New Dealer

New Delhi

[New Delhi] National
Gallery of Modern
Art

New Directions™
Books

New Don Pedro Dam

New Electronic
Encyclopedia, The

Newell Company

New England

New England Banking
Institute, The

New England boiled
dinner

New England clam
chowder

New England College

New England College
of Optometry

New England
Company

New England
Confederation

New England
Conservatory of
Music

New England
Culinary Institute

New England Electric
System

New Englander

New England Holidays

New England Institute of Technology

New England Journal of Medicine

New England Mutual Life Insurance Company

New England Patriots

New England Primer, The

New England School

New England School of Law

New England Telephone Company

New England theology

New English

New English Bible, The

New Exchequer Dam

New Eyes for the Needy, Inc.

Newfoundland

Newfoundlander

Newfoundland Standard Time

New Frontier

New Frontiersman

Newgate Prison

New General Catalog

New Georgia

New Georgia Islands

New Glasgow

New Granada

New Greek

New Grove Dictionary of Music and Musicians, The

New Guinea

Newhall

New Hampshire

New Hampshire chicken

New Hampshire College

New Hampshire Grants

New Hampshire Technical College

New Hampshire Technical Institute

New Hampshirite

New Hampton

New Hanover International Airport

New Harmony

Newhart

Newhart, Bob

New Haven

New Haven stem

New Haven theology

New Hebrew

New Hebrides [now Vanuatu]

New High German

New Holland

Newhouse, Donald Edward

Newhouse, Samuel I.

Newhouse News Service

Newhouser, Hal

New Hyde Park

New Iberia

Newington

New Ireland

New Jersey

New Jersey Bell Telephone Company

New Jersey Devils

New Jersey Institute of Technology

New Jerseyite

New Jersey Monthly

New Jersey Nets

New Jersey Plan

New Jersey tea

New Jerusalem

New Jerusalem Church

New Journalism

New Kensington

New Kids on the Block

New Kingdom

New Kowloon

Newlands Project

New Latin

New Learning

New Left

New Lexington

Newley, Anthony

New London

New London Naval Submarine Base

New Lost City Ramblers, The

Newlywed Game, The

New Madrid

Newman, Alfred

Newman, Barnett

Newman, Barry

Newman, Edwin

Newman, Jimmy C.

Newman, John Henry Cardinal

Newman, Laraine

Newman, Lionel

Newman, Paul

Newman, Randy

Newmanism

Newmanite

Newmar, Julie

Newmarket

Newmarket coat

New Martinsville

New Melones Lake

New Mexican

New Mexico

New Mexico Highlands University

New Mexico Institute of Mining and Technology

New Mexico Junior College

New Mexico Magazine

New Mexico Military Institute

New Mexico Museum of Natural History

New Mexico State University

New Mexico State University Aggies

New Mexico Symphony Orchestra

New Milford

Newmont Gold Company

Newmont Mining Corporation

Newnan

New Opera Company

New Orleans

New Orleans Baptist Theological Seminary

New Orleans International Airport

New Orleans Jazz and Heritage Festival

New Orleans lugger

New Orleans Naval Air Station

New Orleans Naval Support Activity

New Orleans Night

New Orleans Philharmonic Symphony Orchestra

New Orleans Rhythm Kings

New Orleans Saints

New Orleans-style jazz

[New Orleans] Times-Picayune, The

New Paltz

New Philadelphia

New Plan Realty Trust

New Plymouth

Newport

Newport Beach

Newport boat

Newport College of Salve Regina, The

Newport East

Newport Jazz Festival [now JVC Jazz Festival]

Newport Naval Education and Training Center

Newport News

Newport News Shipbuilding Company

New Port Richey

New Prague

New Providence

New Realism

New Realist

New Republic, The

New Richmond

New River

New River Community College

New River Gorge National River

New River Marine Corps Air Station

New Roads

New Rochelle

NewsBank Electronic Index

New School for Social Research

News Corporation Ltd., The

New Scotland Yard

Newsday

New Shrewsbury

New Siberian Islands

New Smyrna Beach

New South

New South Wales

New Spain

Newspaper Enterprise Association, Inc.

Newspaper Features Inc.

Newspaper Guild, The

NewsTalk Radio Network

Newstead Abbey

New Stone Age

News USA

Newsvertising—
Congressional
Monitoring
Retrieval Services

Newsweek

Newswomen's Club of
New York

New Testament

New Thought

New Thoughter

New Thoughtist

New Tic Tac Dough,
The

New Tokyo
International
Airport/Narita

Newton

Newton, Gilbert Stuart

Newton, Huey P.

Newton, Sir Isaac

Newton, Juice

Newton, Wayne

Newton Falls

Newtonian

Newtonian fluid

Newtonian focus

Newtonian mechanics

Newtonian telescope

Newton-John, Olivia

Newton's law of
gravitation

Newton's law of
universal
gravitation

Newton's laws of
motion

Newton's method

Newton's rings

New Toronto

Newtown

Newtownabbey

Newtown Pippin

New Ulm

New Valley
Corporation [form.
Western Union
Corporation]

New Wave

New Westminster

New Windsor

New Woman

New World

New World
Entertainment

New World monkey

New World Symphony

New Year's

New Year's Day

New Year's Eve

New York

New York Academy
of Sciences

New York aster

New York Bay

New York
Chiropractic
College

New York City

New York City Ballet

New York City Center

New York City
Marathon

New York City Opera

New York City Transit
Authority

New York Coast
Guard Support
Center

New York College of
Music

New York College of
Podiatric Medicine

New York cut

New York Daily News

New York Dolls

New York Drama
Critics Circle

New Yorker [person]

New Yorker, The
[magazine]

New Yorkese

New York fern

New York Giants

[New York] Giants
Stadium

New York Institute of
Technology

New York Islanders

New York Jets

New York
Knickerbockers

New York Law School

New York Life
Foundation

New York Life
Insurance and
Annuity
Corporation

New York Life
Insurance Company

New York Magazine

New York Medical
College

New York Mercantile
Exchange

New York Mets

New York Mills

New York Newsday

New York Outdoors

New York
Philharmonic
Orchestra

[New York] Post
New York Pro Musica
New York Public Library, The
New York Rangers
New York Review of Books, The
New York sailing barge
New York School of Interior Design
New York Shakespeare Festival
New York State
New York State Barge Canal
New York State College of Ceramics at Alfred University
New York State Electric and Gas Corporation
New York State Theater
New York steak
New York Stock Exchange Composite List
New York Stock Exchange, Inc.
New York-style jazz
New York, Susquehanna and Western Railroad Company
New York Telephone
New York Theological Seminary
New York Times, The
New York Times Book Review, The

New York Times Company, The
New York Times Company Foundation
New York Times Magazine
New York Times News Service
New York Times Syndication Sales Corporation
New York Today
New York University
New York University Law Review
New York University Press
New York Woodwind Quintet
[New York] Yankee pinstripes
New York Yankees
[New York] Yankee Stadium
New Zealand
New Zealander
New Zealand flax
New Zealand spinach
New Zealand wineberry
Nexö, Martin Andersen
NeXt Inc.
Next Whole Earth Catalog
Ney, Michel
Nez Percé [Indian], n., pl. Nez Percé or Nez Percés
Nez Percé National Forest

Nez Percé National Historical Park
Nez Percé War
NFL Monday Night Football
Ngo Dinh Diem
Ngo Dinh Nhu
Ngor, Haing S.
Nguyen Cao Ky
Nguyen Thi Binh
Nguyen Van Thieu
Nha Trang
Niagara
Niagara County Community College
Niagara Falls
Niagara Falls International Airport
Niagara Mohawk Power Corporation
Niagara Movement
Niagara University
Niagara University Purple Eagles
Niamey
Niarchos, Stavros
Nibelung, n., pl. Nibelung occas. Nibelungen
Nibelungenlied
Nicaea
Nicaean
Nicaragua
Nicaragua Canal
Nice
Nice, Carter
Nicene Council
Nicene Creed

nice Nelly *occas.*
  Nellie, *n.*, *pl.* nice
  Nellies
Niceno-
  Constantinopolitan
  Creed
Nicephorus
Nicephorus, Saint
Niceville
Nicholas
Nicholas I, Saint
Nicholas, Denise
Nicholas, Fayard
Nicholas, Harold
Nicholas, Saint
Nicholas Nickleby
Nicholas of Cusa
Nicholas of Myra,
  Saint
Nicholas the Great
Nicholasville
Nicholls State
  University
Nicholls State
  University Colonels
Nichols, Jeanette
  Paddock
Nichols, Kid
Nichols, Michelle
Nichols, Mike
Nichols, Red
Nichols College
Nichols Hills
Nicholson, Ben
Nicholson, Jack
Nicholson Museum
Nichrome™
Nick at Nite
Nicklaus, Jack
Nicklelodeon
Nicks, Stevie

Nicobar Islands
Nicodemus
Nicol, William
Nicolai, Otto
Nicolay, John George
Nicole
Nicolet, Jean
Nicolet Area
  Technical College
Nicolet National
  Forest
Nicol prism
Nicolson, Sir Harold
Nicolson,
  Marjorie Hope
NICOR Inc.
Nicosia
Nidetch, Jean
Niebuhr, Reinhold
Niehbur, Barthold
  Georg
Niehbur, H. Richard
Nieh Jung-chen [*now*
  Nie Rongzhen]
Niekro, Phil
Nielsen, Arthur C.
Nielsen, Brigitte
Nielsen, Carl August
Nielsen, Holger
Nielsen, Leslie
Nielsen Electronics
  Institute
Nielsen method
Nielsen rating
Niemeyer, Oscar
Niemöller, Martin
Nien Rebellion
Nierenberg, Roger
Nie Rongzhen [*form.*
  Nieh Jung-chen]

Nierstein
Niersteiner
Nietzsche, Friedrich
Nietzschean
Nietzschism
Nièvre
Niger
Niger-Congo
Nigeria
Nigeria Airways Ltd.
Nigerian
Nigerian Museum
Niger seed
Night at the Opera, A
Night before
  Christmas, The
Night Café, The
Night Court
Nighthawks
Night Heat
Nighthorse Campbell,
  Ben
Nightingale, Florence
Nightly Business
  Report, The
Nightmare on Elm
  Street, A
Nightmare on Elm
  Street 4: The Dream
  Master, A
Nightmare on Elm
  Street, Part 2:
  Freddy's
  Revenge, A
Nightmare on Elm
  Street 3: Dream
  Warriors
Night of the Long
  Knives
Night on Bald
  Mountain, A

Nights in the Gardens of Spain

Night Stalker, The

Night Watch, The

Nijinsky, Vaslav

Nike

NIKE, Inc.

Nike missile

Nike of Samothrace

Nikkei Index

Nikkei Stock Average

Nikolais, Alwin

Nikolais—Louis Foundation for Dance

Nikola Tesla Walkers

Nikolayevna, Anastasia

Nikon Inc.

Nile

Nile blue

Nile crocodile

Nile Delta

Nile green

Niles

Nilgiri Hills

Nilometer

Nilo-Saharan

Nilote, n., pl. Nilote or Nilotes

Nilsson, Anna Q.

Nilsson, Birgit

Nilsson, Bo

Nilsson, Harry

Nimitz, Chester W.

Nimoy, Leonard

Nimrod

Nimrodian

Nimrodic

Nimsgern, Siegmund

Nin, Anaïs

Niña

Niña, Pinta, and Santa Maria

Nina Wiener and Dancers

900 N. Michigan

9-1-1 or 911 [emergency phone number]

9-1-1 Magazine

1919 [novel]

Nineteenth occas. 19th Amendment [to the Constitution]

9 to 5

98¢ Clearance Center

1984 [1956 movie]

Ninety Eighty-Four [1984 movie]

Ninety Eighty-Four occas. 1984 [book]

Ninety-Five Theses

Ninety-Nines

Ninety-Six National Historic Site

Nineveh

Nine Worthies

Ninja™

Nino, Pedro Alonzo

Ninotchka

Nintendo™

Nintendo Company, Ltd.

Nintendo of America, Inc.

Ninth occas. 9th Amendment [to the Constitution]

Niobrara

Nipmuck, n., pl. Nipmuck or Nipmucks

Nipon, Albert

Nippon

Nippon chrysanthemum

Nippon Credit Bank, Ltd.

Nippon daisy

Nipponese, n., pl. Nipponese

Nippon Steel Corporation

Nippon Telegraph and Telephone Corporation

nirvana often Nirvana

Nisan [Jewish month; see also Nissan]

Nisei, n., pl. Nisei

Nisqualli

Nissan™ cars and trucks [see also Nisan]

Nissan Grand Prix of Atlanta

Nissan Grand Prix of Miami

Nissan Grand Prix of Ohio

Nissan Grand Prix of Road America

Nissan Motor Acceptance Corporation

Nissan Motor Company Ltd.

Nissan Motor Corporation U.S.A.

Nissan North America Inc.

Nissen hut

Nitralloy™

Nitty Gritty Dirt Band, The
Niue
Niven, David
Nivôse
Nixon, Agnes
Nixon, Marni
Nixon, Pat
Nixon, Richard M.
Nixonian
Niza, Marcos de
Nizam
Nizhniy or Nizhny Novgorod [form. Gorki]
Nizny Tagil
Nkrumah, Kwame
NMB Postbank Group
Noah
Noah's ark
Noah's Dove
Noank boat
Noatak
Noatak National Preserve
Nobel, Alfred Bernhard
Nobel Industries Sweden
Nobelist
Nobel Memorial Prize in Economic Science
Nobel Prize
Nob Hill
Nobile, Umberto
Noble, James
Noble, Ray
Noble Affiliates, Inc.
Noble Drew Ali

Noble House
Noble Order of the Knights of Labor
Noblesville
Nod
node of Ranvier
Nō or Noh drama
Noël
No Exit
Nofziger, Lyn
Nogales
Noguchi, Hideyo
Noguchi, Isamu
Noh var. of No drama
Nolan, Bob
Nolan, Jeanette
Nolan, Kathleen
Nolan, Lloyd
Nolde, Emil
Nolichucky
Noli Me Tangere
Noll, Chuck
Nolte, Nick
Nome
Nomura, Kichisaburo
Nomura Securities Company, Ltd., The
non-African
non-American
non-Anglican
non-Arab
non-Arabic
non-Asian
non-Asiatic
non-Attic
non-Baptist
non-Bolshevik
non-Bolshevism
non-Bolshevist

non-Bolshevistic
non-Buddhist
non-Buddhistic
non-Calvinist
non-Calvinistic
non-Catholic
non-Caucasian
non-Celtic
non-Chinese, n., pl. non-Chinese
non-Christian
Non-Commissioned Officers Association of the United States of America
non-Communist
non-Congressional
non-Darwinian
non-English
Nonesuch Press
non-Euclidean
non-European
non-French
non-Gaelic
non-Gentile
non-German
non-Gothic
non-Greek
non-Gypsy, n., pl. non-Gypsies
non-Hebraic
non-Hellenic
non-Hindu
non-Hispanic
non-Hodgkin's lymphoma
non-Homeric
non-Indian
non-Indo-European

non-Islamic
non-Israelite
non-Israelitic
non-Italian
non-Japanese
non-Jew
non-Jewish
non-Malthusian
non-Marxist
non-Mediterranean
non-Methodist
non-Mongol
non-Mongolian
non-Mormon
non-Muslim
non-Negro, *n., pl.*
non-Negros
non-Newtonian
non-Nordic
non-Norman
non-Norse
No, No, Nanette
non-Oriental
Nonpartisan League
non-Protestant
non-Roman
non-Russian
non-Scandinavian
non-Slavic
non-Spartan
non-Teuton
non-Trinitarian
non-Turk
non-Turkish
Non-U *occas.* non-U
non-Welsh
non-Western
non-Zionist
noodles Romanoff

Nootka cypress
Nootka fir
Nootka [Indian], *n.,*
pl. Nootka *or*
Nootkas
Nootka Sound
Norco
Nord
Nordau, Max Simon
Nordbanken
Norddeutsche
Landesbank
Girozentrale
Nordenskjöld, Nils
Adolf Erik
Nordenskjöld Sea
Nordhoff, Charles
Nordic
Nordic Council
NordicTrack, Inc.
Nordoff, Charles
Nordoff, Paul
Nordstrom, Bruce A.
Nordstrom, James F.
Nordstrom, John N.
Nordstrom, Inc.
Nordstrom store
Norfolk
Norfolk and Western
Railway Company
Norfolk International
Airport
Norfolk Island
Norfolk Island pine
Norfolk jacket
Norfolk Naval Base
Norfolk Naval
Shipyard
Norfolk Southern
Corporation

Norfolk Southern
Railway Company
Norfolk State
University
Norfolk terrier
[Norfolk] Virginian-
Pilot, The
Norgay, Tenzing
Noriega, Manuel
Norinchukin Bank
Normal
Norman
Norman, Greg
Norman, Jessye
Norman, Merle
Norman architecture
Norman Conquest
Normand, Mabel
Normandale
Community College
Normandy
Normandy campaign
Normandy invasion
Normanesque
Norman-French
Norman Luboff Choir
Norman Rockwell
Gallery, The
Norodom Sihanouk
Norplant™
Norrel, Norman
Norridge
Norris, Charles G.
Norris, Chuck
Norris, Diana
Strawbridge
Norris, Frank
Norris, George
William
Norris, John, Jr.

Norris, Kathleen

Norris Dam

Norrish, Ronald George

Norris-La Guardia Act

Norristown

Norse

Norseman, *n.*, *pl.* Norsemen

Norsk Hydro

Norstad, Lauris

Nortek, Inc.

North, Alex

North, Christopher

North, Frederick

North, Jay

North, Oliver

North, Sheree

North Adams

North Adams State College

North Africa

North African

North America

North American

North American Aerospace Defense Command

North American Association of Ventriloquists

North American Association of Wardens and Superintendents

North American Baptist Association [*now* Baptist Missionary Association of America]

North American Baptist Conference

North American Baptist Seminary

North American Blueberry Council

North American Bluebird Society

North American Free Trade Agreement

North American General Baptist Conference

North American Indian

North American Indian art

North American Indian music

North American Life Assurance Company

North American Nebula

North American Old Roman Catholic Church

North American Philips Corporation

North American Review, The

North American Rockwell

North American Van Lines, Inc.

North American Wildlife Foundation

North America One

North America Syndicate

Northampton

Northampton County Area Community College

Northamptonshire

North Andover

North Arkansas Community College

North Arlington

North Atlantic Cooperation Council

North Atlantic Council

North Atlantic Current

North Atlantic Drift

North Atlantic Marine Mammal Commission

North Atlantic Treaty

North Atlantic Treaty Organization

North Attleboro

North Augusta

North Baltimore

North Battleford

North Bay

North Bellmore

North Belmont

North Bend

North Bergen

North Braddock

North Branford

Northbridge

Northbrook

North Caldwell

North Canadian River

North Canton

North Cape

North Carolina

North Carolina Agricultural and Technical State University

North Carolina Agricultural and Technical State University Aggies

North Carolina Central University

North Carolina Dance Theater

North Carolina Motor Speedway

North Carolina News Network

North Carolina School of the Arts

North Carolina State University

North Carolina State University Wolfpack

North Carolina Wesleyan College

North Cascades National Park

North Catasauqua

North Caucasian

North Caucausus

North Central Bible College

North Central College

North Central Michigan College

North Central Missouri College

North Central region

North Central States

North Central Technical College

North Channel

North Chicago

Northcliffe, Alfred Harmsworth

North College Hill

Northcote, James

North Country

North Country Community College

North Country Trail Association

North Dakota

North Dakotan

North Dakota State College of Science

North Dakota State University

Northeast Alabama State Junior College

Northeast Boundary Dispute

Northeast Community College

Northeastern Bible College

Northeastern Christian Junior College

Northeasterner

Northeastern Illinois University

Northeastern Junior College

Northeastern Ohio Universities College of Medicine

Northeastern Oklahoma Agricultural and Mechanical College

Northeastern States

Northeastern State University

Northeastern University

Northeastern University Huskies

Northeastern University Press

Northeast Iowa Community College

Northeast Louisiana University

Northeast Louisiana University Indians

Northeast Magazine

Northeast Mississippi Community College

Northeast Missouri State University

Northeast Outdoors

Northeast Passage

Northeast region

Northeast Savings

Northeast State Technical Community College

Northeast Texas Community College

Northeast Utilities

Northeast Wisconsin Technical College

North Equatorial Current

Northern Arizona University

Northern Arizona University Lumberjacks

Northern Baptist Theological Seminary

Northern Chinese

Northern Cross

Northern Cross Society

Northern Crown

Northerner *occas.* northerner

Northern Essex Community College

Northern Expedition

Northern Exposure

Northern Hemisphere
occas. northern
hemisphere

Northern Illinois
University

Northern Illinois
University Huskies

Northern Illinois
University Press

Northern Indiana
Public Service
Company

Northern Ireland

Northern Kentucky
University

Northern Maine
Technical College

Northern Mariana
Islands

Northern Marianas
College

Northern Michigan

Northern Michigan
University

Northern Montana
College

Northern Nevada
Community College

Northern New Mexico
Community College

Northern Oklahoma
College

Northern Pacific
Railway Company

Northern Rhodesia
[*now* Zambia]

Northern Securities
Company v. United
States

Northern Sinfonia of
England

Northern Sporades

Northern Spy

Northern States

Northern States Power
Company

Northern State
University

Northern Telecom Inc.

Northern Telecom Ltd.

Northern Territory

Northern Textile
Association

Northern Trust
Company

Northern Trust
Company
Charitable Trust

Northern Trust
Corporation

Northern Virginia
Community College

Northern War

Northfield

Northfield Harness

North Florida Junior
College

North Frigid Zone

Northgate Computer
Systems, Inc.

North Georgia College

North Germanic

North Greenville
College

North Haledon

North Harris County
College

North Haven

North Hennepin
Community College

North Highlands

North Idaho College

North Iowa Area
Community College

North Island

North Kansas City

North Kingstown

North Korea

Northlake

North Lake College

Northland College

Northland Community
College

Northland Pioneer
College

Northlands Coliseum

North Las Vegas

North Little Rock

North Manchester

North Mankato

North Merrick

North Miami

North Miami Beach

North Muskegon

North New Hyde Park

North Olmsted

North Orange County
Community College

North Pacific

North Pacific Current

North Palm Beach

North Park College
and Theological
Seminary

North Pelham

North Plainfield

North Platte

North Platte Project

North Plymouth

North Pole

Northport

North Princeton

North Providence

North Reading

North Rhine-Westphalia

North Richland Hills

North River

North Riverside

Northrop Corporation

Northrop University

North Royalton

North Saint Paul

North Saskatchewan

North Scituate

North Sea

North Sea oil

North Seattle Community College

North Shore Animal League, Inc.

North Shore Community College

North Shreveport

North Slope

North Slope oil

North Star

North Syracuse

North Tarrytown

North Temperate Zone

North Texas State University

North Tonawanda

Northumberland

Northumberland Strait

Northumbria

Northumbrian

North Valley Stream

North Vancouver

North Vernon

North Vietnam [now part of Vietnam]

Northville

North Warning System

Northwest Airlines, Inc.

Northwest Alabama Community College

Northwest Christian College

Northwest College

Northwest College of Art

Northwest College of the Assemblies of God

North West Company

Northwest Cycle

Northwestern College

Northwestern College of Chiropractic

Northwestern Connecticut Community College

Northwestern Electronics Institute

Northwestern Michigan College

Northwestern Mutual Life Insurance Company, The

Northwestern National Life Insurance Company

Northwestern State University

Northwestern State University Demons

Northwestern University

Northwestern University Press

Northwestern University School of Music

Northwestern University Wildcats

Northwest Indian College

Northwest Institute of Acupuncture and Oriental Medicine

Northwest Iowa Technical College

Northwest Living!

Northwest Mississippi Community College

Northwest Missouri State University

North-West Mounted Police

Northwest Nazarene College

Northwest News Network

Northwest Ordinance

Northwest Passage

North West Rebellion

Northwest State University

Northwest Technical College

Northwest Technical Institute

Northwest Territories [Canadian region]

Northwest Territory [former American region]

Northwest Travel

North Wildwood

North Wilkesboro

North Wilkesboro Speedway

Northwood Institute

Northwoods

North Yemen [*now part of Republic of Yemen*]

Norton

Norton, Andre

Norton, Eleanor Holmes

Norton, Ken

Norton, Thomas

Norton Air Force Base

Norton Company

Norton Company Foundation

Norton Editor™, The

Norton Simon Museum of Art

Norton Sound

Norton Utilities™, The

Norville, Deborah

Norvo, Red

Norwalk

Norwalk Community College

Norwalk State Technical College

Norway

Norway maple

Norway pine

Norway rat

Norway saltpeter

Norway spruce

Norwegian

Norwegian Coastal Current

Norwegian Cruise Line

Norwegian Current

Norwegian elkhound

Norwegian language

Norwegian literature

Norwegian saltpeter

Norwegian Sea

Norwest Bank Minnesota

Norwest Corporation

Norwest Foundation

Norwich

Norwich terrier

Norwich University

Norwood

Norworth, Jack

Nosey *or* Nosy Parker

Nostalgia Channel, The

Nostradamic

Nostradamus

Notable Names in the American Theatre

Notes from the Underground

No Time for Sergeants

Notorious Jumping Frog of Calaveras County, The

Notre Dame

Notre Dame Bay

Notre Dame College

Notre Dame de Paris

Notre Dame Magazine

Notre Dame Mountains

Notre Dame Seminary

NOT-SAFE

Nottingham

Nottinghamshire

Nouakchott

Nouméa

Nova

NovaCare, Inc.

Novachord™

Novak, Kim

Novak, Robert

Novarro, Ramon

Nova Scotia

Nova Scotia College of Art and Design

Nova Scotian

Novato

Nova University

Novaya Zemlya

Novell, Inc.

Novello, Antonia

Novello, Don

Novello, Ivor

November

Novgorod

Novocaine™

Novosibirsk

Nowata

NOW Legal Defense and Education Fund, Inc.

Noxell Corporation

Noxell Foundation

Noyce, Robert N.

Noyes, Alfred

Noyes, John Humphrey

NSF International

N-shell

NTC Publishing Group

NTV Network

Nubia

Nubian

Nubian Desert

Nuclear Regulatory Commission

Nucor Corporation

Nude Descending a Staircase

Nueces

Nuer, *n.*, *pl.* Nuer *or* Nuers

Nuevo Laredo

Nuevo León

Nuffield Radio Astronomy Observatory, Jodrell Bank

Nugent, Elliott

Nugent, Ted

Nukualofa

Nukualofa Fua'Amotu International Airport

Nuku Hiva

Numidian crane

Numismatic Informational Service

Núñez de Balboa, Vasco

Nunivak

Nunn, Sam

Nunn, Trevor

Nun of Kent

Nunsense

Nuns of Saint Ursula

Nupercaine™

Nuremberg

Nuremberg egg

Nuremberg Laws

Nuremberg Trials

Nuremberg violet

Nureyev, Rudolf

Nuristan

Nurmi, Paavo

Nurses, The

Nutcracker, The

Nutcracker Suite

Nutley

Nutmeg State

NutraSweet Charitable Trust, The

NutraSweet Company, The

Nutri/System, Inc.

Nutrition Labeling and Education Act

Nutting, Wallace

Nuuana Pali

Nuyen, France

NWA Inc.

Nyack

Nyack College

Nyad, Diana

Nyasa

Nyasaland [*now* Malawi]

Ny Carlsberg Glyptothek

Nye, Bill

Nye, Louis

Nye, Robert

Nyerere, Julius K.

Nygaard, Jens

NYNEX Corporation

NYNEX Foundation

Nyro, Laura

NYT Pictures

NYU Press

O

Oahe Dam

Oahu

Oak Creek

Oakdale

Oak Forest

Oak Harbor

Oak Hill

Oak Hills Bible College

Oakhurst

Oakie, Jack

Oakland

Oakland, Simon

Oakland-Alameda County Coliseum

Oakland Army Base

Oakland Army Terminal

Oakland Athletics

Oakland Ballet Company

Oakland City

Oakland City College

Oakland Coliseum Arena

Oakland Community College

Oakland Festival Ballet

Oakland International Airport

Oakland Naval Supply Center

Oakland Park

Oakland Tribune, The

Oakland University

Oak Lawn

Oakley, Annie

Oakmont

Oak Park

Oak Ridge

Oak Ridge Boys, The

Oak Ridge National Laboratory

Oakton Community College

Oak Tree Savings Bank

Oakwood

Oakwood College

Oarsmen at Chatou

Oates, John

Oates, Joyce Carol

Oates, Titus

Oates, Warren

Oath of Strasbourg

Oath of the Horatii, The

Oaxaca

Ob

Obadiah

Obata, Gyo

Obed Wild and Scenic River

Oberammergau

Oberammergau Passion Play

Oberammergau Passion Players

Oberholtzer, Ellis Paxson

Oberlin

Oberlin College

Oberlin College Conservatory of Music

Oberlin College Press

Oberon

Oberon, Merle

Obesity Foundation, The

Obie Award

Oblate College

Oblate School of Theology

Oblates of Mary Immaculate

Oboler, Arch

Obote, Apollo Milton

Obrecht, Jacob

Obregón, Alvaro
O'Brian, Hugh
O'Brien, Connor
O'Brien, David
O'Brien, Edmond
O'Brien, Margaret
O'Brien, Pat
O'Brien, Robert C.
Observer
Obsessive-Compulsive Anonymous
Obsessive Compulsive Foundation
Ocala
Ocala National Forest
O Canada!
Ocasek, Ric
O'Casey, Sean
Occam's *or* Ockham's razor
Occident
Occidental
Occidental Chemical Corporation
Occidental College
Occidentalism
Occidentalist
Occidental Oil and Gas Charitable Foundation
Occidental Oil and Gas Corporation
Occidental Petroleum Charitable Foundation
Occidental Petroleum Corporation
Occupational Outlook Quarterly
Occupational Safety and Health Act

Occupational Safety and Health Administration
Occupational Safety and Health Review Commission
Occupational-Urgent Care Health Systems, Inc.
Occupation Day
Ocean, Billy
Ocean Alliance
Oceana Publications, Inc.
Ocean City
Ocean County College
Ocean Drilling Program
Oceania
Oceanian
Oceanian languages
Oceanic art
Oceanic Press Service
Oceanic Society
Oceanic Society Expeditions
Oceanport
Oceanside
Ocean Spray Cranberries, Inc.
Ocean Springs
Oceanus
Ochoa, Severo
Ochoco National Forest
O Christmas Tree
Ochs, Adolph S.
Ochs, Phil
Ocilla
O.C. International

Ockham's *var. of* Occam's razor
Ocmulgee
Ocmulgee National Monument
O Come All Ye Faithful
O Come, O Come Immanuel
Oconee
Oconee National Forest
O'Connell, Arthur
O'Connell, Daniel
O'Connell, Helen
O'Connor, Carroll
O'Connor, Donald
O'Connor, Flannery
O'Connor, Frank
O'Connor, John Joseph Cardinal
O'Connor, Sandra Day
O'Connor, Sinéad
O'Connor, Thomas Power
O'Connor, Una
Oconomowoc
Oconto
Octagon Books
Octavia
October
October Manifesto
October Revolution
Octobrist
Octopus, The
O'Day, Anita
O'Day, Molly
Odd Couple, The
Oddfellow
Oddjob

O'Dell, Scott
Odéon
Ode on a Grecian Urn
Ode on Indolence
Ode on Melancholy
Oder
Oder-Neiss Line
Odessa
Odessa College
Ode to a Nightingale
Ode to Autumn
Ode to Duty
Ode to Joy
Ode to Psyche
Ode to the West Wind
Odets, Clifford
Odetta
Odin
Odinga, Jaramogi
  Oginga
Odio, Rodrigo Carazo
Odsbodkins
Odyssean
Odysseus
Odyssey, The
Odyssey Institute
  Corporation
Odzooks
Oedipal
Oedipus
Oedipus at Colonus
Oedipus complex
Oedipus Rex
OEF International
Oelwein
Oersted, Hans
  Christian
Oerter, Al
O'Fallon

O'Faoláin, Seán
Offa's Dyke
off Broadway, n.
  phrase
off-Broadway occas.
  Off-Broadway, adj.
Offenbach, Jacques
Office, The
Office and
  Professional
  Employees
  International Union
Office Automation
  Society
  International
Office Club Inc.
Office Depot Inc.
Office of Economic
  Opportunity
Office of Management
  and Budget
Office of Naval
  Research
Office of Personnel
  Management
Office of Readings
Office of Strategic
  Services
Office of Technology
  Assessment
Office of the
  Americas
Office of the
  Comptroller of
  Currency
Office of the Federal
  Register
Office Products
  Manufacturers
  Association
Official Boy Scout
  Handbook
Official Story, The

off-off Broadway
  occas. Off-Off
  Broadway
Off Stington
Offutt Air Force Base
Of Human Bondage
O'Flaherty, Liam
Of Mice and Men
Of Time and the River
Ogallala
Ogata Kōrin
O gauge
Ogden
Ogden, C. K.
Ogden, Peter Skene
Ogden Corporation
Ogden Projects, Inc.
Ogdensburg
Ogier the Dane
Ogilvie, John
Ogilvy, David
Ogilvy and Mather
  Worldwide
Ogilvy Group Inc.
Oglala, n., pl. Oglala
  or Oglalas
Oglala Lakota College
Oglala Sioux
Oglesby
Oglethorpe,
  James Edward
Oglethorpe University
O'Hair, Madalyn
  Murray
O'Hara, John
O'Hara, John Francis
  Cardinal
O'Hara, Mary
O'Hara, Maureen
O'Hara, Paige

O'Hara, Scarlett

Oh! Calcutta!

O. Henry Award

O'Herlihy, Dan

OH-58D Kiowa

OH-58D Kiowa Warrior

Oh! Idaho

Ohio

Ohioan

Ohio and Erie Canal

Ohio Bell Foundation

Ohio Bell Telephone Company

Ohio buckeye

Ohio College of Podiatric Medicine

Ohio Company, The

Ohio Company of Associates

Ohio Dominican College

Ohio Edison Company

Ohio Educational Broadcasting Network Commission

Ohio Farmer, The

Ohio Fisherman

Ohio Institute of Photography

Ohio Magazine

Ohio National Life Insurance Company

Ohio Northern University

Ohio Players, The

Ohio State University

Ohio State University Buckeyes

Ohio State University Press

Ohio University

Ohio University Bobcats

Ohio University Press

Ohio Valley College

Ohio Washington News Service

Ohio Wesleyan University

Ohira Masayoshi

Ohlone College

Ohm, Georg Simon

Ohm's law

O Holy Night

Ohr Hameir Theological Seminary

Ohr Somayach Tanenbaum Educational Center

Oh! Susanna

Oil, Chemical and Atomic Workers International Union

Oil City

Oil Rivers

Oingo Boingo

Oise

Oistrakh, David

Ojai

Ojai Festival

O'Jays, The

Ojeda, Alonso de

Ojibwa or Ojibway, n., pl. Ojibwa or Ojibwas or Ojibway or Ojibways

Ojos del Salado

OK or O.K. or Okay or okay

Oka

Okaloosa-Walton Community College

Okanogan

Okanagan Lake

Okanogan National Forest

O.K. Corral

Okeechobee

Okeechobee Waterway

O'Keefe, Dennis

O'Keefe, Michael

O'Keeffe, Georgia

Okefenokee Swamp

O'Kelly, Seán

Okhotsk Current

Oki America Inc.

Okie

Oki Electric Industry Company, Ltd.

Okinawa

Okinawan

Oklahoma

Oklahoma! [movie; play]

Oklahoma Agrinet

Oklahoma Baptist University

Oklahoma Christian University of Science and Arts

Oklahoma City

Oklahoma City Community College

[Oklahoma City] Oklahoman

Oklahoma City University

Oklahoma City University Press

Oklahoma Gas and
  Electric Company

Oklahoma Gas and
  Electric Company
  Foundation

Oklahoma Junior
  College of Business
  and Technology

Oklahoman

Oklahoma News
  Network

Oklahoma panhandle

Oklahoma Panhandle
  State University

Oklahoma State
  University

Oklahoma State
  University
  Cowboys

Oklahoma State
  University Press

Oklahoma Today

Okmulgee

Okolono

Okovanggo

Okovanggo Basin

Oktoberfest

Olaf

Olaf, Saint

Olaf Guthfrithson

Olajuwon, Akeem

Öland

Oland, Warner

Olathe

Olcott, Chauncey

old Adam

Old Bailey

Old Believer

Old British

Old Bulgarian

Old Catholic

Old Catholic Church

Old Church Slavic

Old Church Slavonic

Old City of Jerusalem

Old Curiosity Shop,
  The

Old Dominion

Old Dominion
  University

Old Dominion
  University
  Monarchs

Old Dutch

Oldenberg, Claes

Oldenburg, Charles

Old English

Old English cut

Old English pattern

Old *occas.* old English
  sheepdog

Older Americans Act

Older Workers Benefit
  Protection Act

Old Faithful

Old Farmer's
  Almanac, The

Old Fashioned
  [cocktail]

Old Fashioned glass
  [cocktail glass]

Oldfield, Barney

Oldfield, Todd

Old Flemish

Old Forge

Old French

Old Frisian

Old Glory

Old Guard

Oldham, John

Old Harry

Old Hickory

Old High German

Old-House Journal,
  The

Old Icelandic

Old Indic

Old Ionic

Old Iranian

Old Irish

Old Ironsides

Old Italian

Old King Cole

Old Kingdom

Old Latin

Old Low Franconian

Old Low Frankish

Old Low German

Old Lyme

Old MacDonald's
  Farm

Oldman, Gary

Old Man and the Sea,
  The [book; *see also*
  Old Man of the Sea]

Old Man of the
  Mountain

Old Man of the Sea
  [character in
  Arabian Nights; *see
  also* Old Man and
  the Sea]

Old National Bancorp

Old Nick

Old Norman French

Old Norse

Old Norse literature

Old North Church

Old North French

Old Northwest

Old Oaken Bucket,
  The

Old Orchard Beach

Old Order Amish

Old Order Mennonite Church [Wisler]

Old Persian

Old Possum's Book of Practical Cats

Old Pretender

Old Prussian

Old Republic International Corporation

Old Russian

Olds, Ransom Eli

Old Saint Lazare Station

Old Saxon

Old Scratch

Old Slavic

Old Slavonic

Oldsmobile Division (General Motors Corporation)

Old South

Old Southwest

Old Spanish

Old Spanish Trail

Old Stone Age

Old Stone Bank

Old Testament

Old Town

Olduvai Gorge

Old Vic

Old Welsh

Old West

Old World

Old World monkey

Olean

Olean Business Institute

O'Leary, James Rebel

O'Leary, Jammie Ann

O'Leary, Michael

Olekma

Oligocene

Olin, Ken

Olin, Lena

Olin Corporation

Olin Corporation Charitable Trust

Oliphant, Laurence

Oliphant, Margaret

Oliphant, Patrick Bruce

O Little Town of Bethlehem

Olive Bridge Dam

Olivehurst

Oliver

Oliver, Edna May

Oliver, King

Oliver, Sy

Oliver Twist

Olivet [* MI; SD; *see also* Olivette]

Olivet [ridge near Jerusalem]

Olivet College

Oliver Nazarene University

Olivette [* MO; *see also* Olivet]

Olivetti Office USA Inc.

Olivier, Sir Laurence

Olmec, *n.*, *pl.* Olmec *or* Olmecs

Olmos, Edward James

Olmsted, Frederick Law

Olney

O'Loughlin, Gerald S.

Olsen, Merlin

Olsen, Ole

Olsen and Johnson

Olson, Charles

Olson, Nancy

Olsten Corporation

Oltman, C. Dwight

Olvera Street

Olympia

olympiad *often* Olympiad

Olympian

Olympian Games

Olympia oyster

Olympic

Olympic Airways

Olympic College

Olympic Games

Olympic Mountains

Olympic National Forest

Olympic National Park

Olympic Peninsula

Olympics, the

Olympic Saddledome

Olympic Stadium

Olympus

Olyphant

Om

Omaha

Omaha Beach

Omaha College of Health Careers

Omaha Eppley Airfield

Omaha Home for Boys

Omaha [Indian], *n.*, *pl.* Omaha *or* Omahas

Omaha World-Herald
Omak
O'Malley, J. Pat
O'Malley, Walter
Oman [*form.* Muscat and Oman]
Omar Khayyam
Omarr, Sydney
Omdurman
Omega Psi Phi
Omicron Delta Epsilon
Omicron Delta Kappa
Omni [magazine]
Omni, The [Atlanta sports facility]
Omnibus
Omnibus Budget Reconciliation Act
Omnibus Society of America
Omnibus Trade and Competitiveness Act
Omnicom Group Inc.
Omni Hotel
Omni Learning Institute
Omni Royal Orleans
Omni Theater
O'More College of Design
Omron Corporation
OMS International
Omsk
Ona, *n., pl.* Ona *or* Onas
Onalaska
Onassis, Aristotle
Onassis, Christina

Onassis, Jacqueline Bouvier Kennedy
Oñate, Juan de
Ondine
Ondrejka, Ronald
O'Neal, Patrick
O'Neal, Ron
O'Neal, Ryan
O'Neal, Shaquille
O'Neal, Tatum
One Chase Manhattan Plaza
One Day at a Time
One Flew over the Cuckoo's Nest
Onega
Onega Bay
Onega Canal
101st Airborne Division Association
$100,000 Pyramid, The
Oneida
Oneida Community
Oneida [Indian], *n., pl.* Oneida *or* Oneidas
Oneida Lake
Oneida Ltd. Silversmiths
O'Neil, Kitty
O'Neill, Dick
O'Neill, Ed
O'Neill, Eugene
O'Neill, James
O'Neill, Jennifer
O'Neill, Richard Jerome
O'Neill, Ryan
O'Neill, Thomas Philip "Tip"

One Liberty Place
One Life to Live
One Man's Family
ONEOK Inc.
Oneonta
1 Palac Kultury L. Nauki
One Shoe Crew, The
1,001 Home Ideas
One Times Square
On First Looking into Chapman's Homer
Ongais, Danny
On Golden Pond
Onions, Charles Talbut
On Liberty
Online Access Guide
Ono, Yoko
Onondaga Community College
Onondaga [Indian], *n., pl.* Onondaga *or* Onondagas
Onondaga Lake
Onsagher, Lars
Ontarian
Ontario
Ontario Hydro
Ontario International Airport
Ontario Out of Doors
On the Morning of Christ's Nativity
On the Waterfront
Ontkean, Michael
Onward, Christian Soldiers
OO gauge
Oompa-Loompas
Oom Paul

Oort, Jan H.

Oort cloud

Oost, Jacob van

Opal

Opa-Locka

Opatoshu, David

Op-Ed page

Opel

Opelika

Opelika State
Technical College

Opelousas

Open Bible Standard
Churches

Open Door Student
Exchange

Openglopish

Opening of the West

Open Space Institute

Opéra [Paris opera
house]

Opera Théatre of Saint
Louis

Operation Big Vote

Operation Crossroads
Africa

Operation Desert
Shield

Operation Desert
Storm

Operation Identity

Operation PUSH

Operation Rescue

Operation Restore
Hope

Operative Plasterers'
and Cement
Masons'
International
Association of the
United States and
Canada

Ophelia

Ophir

Opium War

Oppenheim, Phillips

Oppenheimer,
J. Robert

Opper, Frederick Burr

Opportunities
Industrialization
Centers of America,
Inc.

Opportunity

Oprah Winfrey Show,
The

Opryland USA

Optic, Oliver

Optical Manufacturers
Association

Optical Society of
America

Opticians Association
of America

Optimist International

Opus Dei

Oracle of Delphi

Oracle Systems
Corporation

Oradell

Oraibi pueblo

Oral History
Association

Oral Roberts
University

Oral Roberts
University
Educational
Fellowship

Oral Roberts
University Titans

Oran

Orange

Orange and Rockland
Utilities, Inc.

Orange Bowl

Orange Bowl Stadium

Orangeburg

Orangeburg-Calhoun
Technical College

Orange City

Orange Coast College

Orange Coast
Magazine

Orange County
Community College

Orange County
Register, The

Orange Cove

Orange Free State

Orangeism

Orangeman, n., pl.
Orangemen

Orangeman's Day

Orange Order

Orange Park

Orange Park Kennel
Club

Orange Pekoe occas.
orange pekoe

Orange River

Orbach, Jerry

Orbison, Roy

Orbiting Satellite
Carrying Amateur
Radio

ORBIT Search
Service

Orcagna

Orchard Park

Orchestre de Paris

Orczy, Emmuska

Ordeal of Richard
Feverel, The

Order of American Knights

Order of Daedalians

Order of DeMolay

Order of Friars Minor Capuchin

Order of Lenin

Order of Our Lady of Mount Carmel

Order of Preachers

Order of Saint Augustine

Order of Saint Benedict

Order of Saint John

Order of Saint Luke, Physician of America

Order of Saint Michael and Saint George

Order of Saint Victor

Order of Servants of Mary

Order of Sons of Italy in America, The

Order of the Bath

Order of the British Empire

Order of the Cistercians of the Strict Observance

Order of the Eastern Star

Order of the Eastern Star, General Grand Chapter

Order of the Elephant

Order of the Founders and Patriots of America, The

Order of the Garter

Order of the Holy Cross of Jerusalem

Order of the Indian Empire

Order of the Star of India

Order of the Thistle

Order of United Commercial Travelers of America

Order of Victoria and Albert

Ordinance of 1787

Ordinary People

Ordovician

Oregon

Oregon Business

Oregon Caves National Monument

Oregon cedar

Oregon City

Oregon Coast

Oregon Coast Aquarium

Oregon Coast Community College Press

Oregon Coast Getaway Guide

Oregon College of Oriental Medicine

Oregon crab apple

Oregon fir

Oregon Graduate Center

Oregon grape

Oregon Health Sciences University

Oregonian

Oregon Institute of Technology

Oregon myrtle

Oregon pine

Oregon Polytechnic Institute

Oregon Shakespeare Festival

Oregon Shakespearian Festival Association

Oregon State University

Oregon State University Beavers

Oregon State University Press

Oregon Steel Mills, Inc.

Oregon Symphony Orchestra

Oregon Trail

O'Reilly, Bill

Orem

Orestes

Orestes complex

Orff, Carl

Orford Quartet

Organic Gardening

Organization for Economic Cooperation and Development

Organization of African Unity

Organization of American Historians

Organization of American States

Organization of Arab Petroleum Exporting Countries

Organization of the Islamic Conference

Organization of the
Petroleum
Exporting Countries
organ of Corti
Organ Pipe Cactus
National Monument
Orient
Oriental
Oriental alabaster
Oriental beetle
Oriental carpet
Oriental cat's-eye
Oriental drama
Oriental exclusion acts
Oriental exclusion
policy
Oriental fruit moth
Orientalia
orientalism *often*
Orientalism
Oriental music
Oriental poppy
Oriental rug
Orient Express
Origin, The
Original Dixieland
Jazz Band
Origin of Species, The
Orinda
Orinda Village
O-ring
Orinoco
Oriole Park at
Camden Yards
Orion
Orion Nebula
Orion Pictures
Corporation
Oriskany
Orizaba
Orkin Pest Control

Orkney Islands
Orlando
Orlando, Tony
Orlando, Vittorio
Emanuele
Orlando Arena
Orlando College
Orlando Furioso
Orlando International
Airport
Orlando Magazine
Orlando Magic
Orlando Naval
Training Center
Orlando Predators
Orlando-Seminole Jai
Alai Fronton
Orlando Sentinel, The
Orland Park
Orleanism
Orleanist
Orléans [* France]
Orleans [* MA]
Orléans, Charles
Orléans, Ferdinand
Philippe
Orléans, Gaston
Orléans, Henri
Philippe
Orléans, Louis
Orléans, Louis
Philippe Albert
Orléans, Louis
Philippe Joseph
Orléans, Louis
Phillipe Robert
Orléans, Philippe
Orléans, Robert
Philippe Louis
Orleans Technical
Institute

Orlich, Francisco J.
Orlon™
Ormandy, Eugene
Ormond Beach
Oromo, *n.*, *pl.* Oromo
or Oromos
Orontes
Orosius, Paulus
O'Rourke, Jim
Oroville [* CA; WA;
see also Orrville]
Oroville Dam
Oroville Reservoir
Orozco, José
Clemente
Orpen, Sir William
Orphan Foundation of
America
Orphean
Orpheus
Orpheus in the
Underworld
Orphic
Orphic Mysteries
Orphism
Orphist
Orpington
Orr, Bobby
Orrville [* OH; *see
also* Oroville]
Orser, Brian
Ortega, Daniel
Ortega y Gasset, José
Orthodox Christian
Reformed Churches
Orthodox Church
Orthodox Church in
America [*form.*
Russian Orthodox
Greek Catholic

Church of North America]

Orthodox Eastern Church

Orthodox Jew

Orthodox Judaism

Orthodox Presbyterian Church

Orthodoxy Sunday

Ortler

Orvieto

Orwell, George

Orwellian

Ory, Kid

Oryx Energy Company

Oryx Press, The

Osage

Osage [Indian], *n., pl.* Osage *or* Osages

Osage orange

Osaka

[Osaka] Municipal Museum of Fine Arts

Osawatomie

Osborn, Henry Fairfield

Osborne, John

Osborne, Thomas Mott

Osborne Brothers, The

Osborne House

Osborne/McGraw-Hill

Osbourne, Ozzy

Oscar

Oscar Mayer Foods Corporation

Oscar the Grouch

Osceola

Osceola National Forest

Osco Drug, Inc.

Osco-Umbrian

Osgood, Charles

Osgood-Schlatter disease

O'Shaughnessy Dam

O'Shea, Milo

Oshkosh

Oshkosh B' Gosh, Inc.

Oshman's Sporting Goods, Inc.

Osirian

Osiris

Oskaloosa

Oskar Reinhart Foundation

Osler, Sir William

Oslin, K. T.

Oslo

Oslo Fjord *or* Fiord

[Oslo] National Gallery

Osman

Osmond, Donny

Osmond, Jimmy

Osmond, Ken

Osmond, Marie

Osmond Brothers, The

Osmonds, The

O Sole Mio

Ossa Mountain

Ossetia

Ossetia Military Road

Ossian

Ossianic

Ossietzky, Carl von

Ossining

Ossining Correctional Facility [*now* Sing Sing State Prison]

Ostade, Adriaen van

Ostend

Ostend Manifesto

Ostrogoth

Ostrogothic

Ostwald, Wilhelm

Ostyak

O'Sullivan, Gilbert

O'Sullivan, Maureen

O'Sullivan Dam

Oswald, Lee Harvey

Oswald, Saint

Oswego

Oswego tea

Otaheite apple

O Tannenbaum

Otello [opera by Verdi; *see also* Othello]

Otero, Miguel A.

Otero Junior College

Othello [play by Shakespeare; *see also* Otello]

Otis, Elisha Graves

Otis, James

Otis, Johnny

Otis Air Force Base

Otis Art Institute of Parsons School of Design

Otis Day and the Knights

Otis Elevator, Inc.

Oto [Indian] *occas.* Otoe, *n., pl* Oto *or* Otos *occas.* Otoe *or* Otoes

O'Toole, Annette

O'Toole, Peter
Otsego Lake
Ott, Mel
Ottawa
Ottawa Citizen, The
Ottawa Hills
Ottawa [Indian], *n.*, *pl.* Ottawa *or* Ottawas
Ottawa Magazine
Ottawa National Forest
Ottawa Senators
Ottawa University
Ottaway News Service
Otterbein, Philip William
Otterbein College
Otto
Otto, Frei
Ottoman Empire
Ottonian
Ottonian art
Otto of Freising
Otto the Great
Ottumwa
Otway, Thomas
Ötztal Alps
Ouachita Baptist University
Ouachita [Indian], *n.*, *pl.* Ouachita *or* Ouchitas
Ouachita Mountains
Ouachita National Forest
Ouachita *or* Washita River
Ouagadougou
Oud, Pieter
Ouija™

Our Bodies, Ourselves
Our Father
Our Lady
Our Lady of Fátima
Our Lady of Guadalupe
Our Lady of Holy Cross College
Our Lady of the Lake University
Our Little Brothers and Sisters, Inc.
Our Lively Language
Our Miss Brooks
Our Mutual Friend
Our Sunday Visitor Magazine
Ouse
Ouspenskaya, Maria
Ouspensky, Peter
Outboard Marine Corporation
Outcault, Richard
Outdoor Advertising Association of America
Outdoor Life
Outdoor Writers Association of America
Outer Banks
Outer Barrier
Outer Critics Circle
Outer Hebrides
Outer Mongolia [*now* Mongolian People's Republic]
Out of Africa
Out of the Past
Outside
Outward Bound

Outward Bound Trust
Oval Office
Overachievers Anonymous
Overbeck, Johann
Over Easy
Overeaters Anonymous
Overland
Overland Park
Overland Trail
Overlea
Overseas Development Council
Overseas Highway
Overseas Shipholding Group, Inc.
Overseas Union Bank
Overstreet, Paul
Overture 1812
Ovid
Ovidian
OV-1 Mohawk
Ovonics
Ovshinsky, Stanford R.
OV-10 Bronco
OV-10D Plus Bronco
Owatona
Owen, John
Owen, Laurence
Owen, Reginald
Owen, Robert
Owen, Wilfred
Owen Falls
Owen Glendower
Owenism
Owenist
Owenite
Owens, Buck

Owens, Gary
Owens, Jesse
Owens, Steve
Owensboro
Owensboro
  Community College
Owensboro Junior
  College of Business
Owens-Corning
  Fiberglas
  Corporation
Owens-Illinois, Inc.
Owen Stanley Range
Owens Technical
  College
Owings Mills
Owl and the
  Nightingale, The
Owl and the Pussy-
  cat, The
Owosso
Owsley acid
Owyhee
Owyhee Dam
Owyhee Reservoir
Ox-Bow Incident, The
Oxbridge
Oxenberg, Catherine
Oxfam
Oxfam America

Oxford
Oxford American
  Dictionary
Oxford Committee for
  Famine Relief
Oxford corners
Oxford down
Oxford English
  Dictionary, The
Oxford gray
Oxford Group
Oxford Industries, Inc.
Oxford movement
Oxford rule
Oxford sheep
Oxfordshire
Oxford shoe
Oxford theory
Oxford University
Oxford University
  Press, Inc.
Oxnard
Oxnard Air Force
  Base
Oxnard College
Oxonian
Oxy Oil and Gas USA
  Inc.
Oxy Petrochemical
  Inc.

Oyama, Iwao
Oyashio Current
Oyl, Olive
Oyster Bay
oysters Rockefeller
Oz
Oz, Frank
Ozal, Turgut
Ozalid™
Ozark
Ozark Christian
  College
Ozark Jubilee
Ozark Mountains
Ozark National Forest
Ozark National Scenic
  Waterways
Ozark Plateau
Ozarks, the
Ozawa, Seiji
Ozenfant, Amédée
Ozick, Cynthia
Ozona
Ozone Protection
  Campaign
Ozymandias of
  Egypt
Ozzie and Harriet

P

Paar, Jack

Pablo, Augustus

Paccar Foundation

Paccar Inc.

Pacem in Terris

Pace University

Pacheco Automotive News Service

Pachelbel, Johann

Pachelbel's canon

Pachomius, Saint

Pacific

Pacifica

Pacification of Ghent

Pacific barracuda

Pacific Bell

Pacific Christian College

Pacific Coast College

Pacific Coast States

Pacific Coliseum

Pacific Crest Trail

Pacific Daylight Time

Pacific dogwood

Pacific Enterprises

Pacific Far East Line, Inc.

Pacific Financial Companies

Pacific First Bank

Pacific Gas and Electric Company

Pacific Graduate School of Psychology

Pacific Grove

Pacific Heights

Pacific high

Pacific Islands

Pacific Legal Foundation

Pacific Lutheran Theological Seminary

Pacific Lutheran University

Pacific madrone

Pacific Margin

Pacific Missile Test Center

Pacific Mountain Network

Pacific Mutual Foundation

Pacific Mutual Life Insurance Company

Pacific News Service

Pacific Northwest

Pacific Northwest College of Art

Pacific Oaks College

Pacific Ocean

PacifiCorp

PacifiCorp Foundation

Pacific Research Institute for Public Policy

Pacific Resources, Inc.

Pacific Rim

Pacific Rim National Park

Pacific Rim nations

Pacific scandal

Pacific School of Religion

Pacific Standard Time

Pacific Stock Exchange, Inc.

Pacific sturgeon

Pacific Telesis Foundation

Pacific Telesis Group

Pacific-Ten Conference

Pacific Time

Pacific tree frog

Pacific Union College

Pacific University

Pacific West Cancer Fund

Pacini, Filippo

pan- *occas*. Pan-Arabism

Panasonic Communications and Systems Company

Panay

Pancake Tuesday

Panchen Lama

Pandit, Vijaya Lakshmi

Pandora

Pandora's box

Pan-European

Pangborn, Franklin

Pange lingua

pan- *occas* Pan-Germanism

Pangloss

Panglossian

Panhandle Eastern Corporation

Panhandle State

Panhellenic

Panhellenism

Panhellenist

Panic, Milan

Panic of 1873

Panic of 1837

Panini *var. of* Pannini, Giovanni Paolo

pan-Islam

pan-Islamic

Pankhurst, Christabel

Pankhurst, Emmeline

Pankhurst, Sylvia

Panmunjom

Panmunjom truce talks

Pannini *or* Panini, Giovanni Paolo

Panola College

pan- *occas*. Pan-Slavic

pan- *occas*. Pan-Slavism

pan- *occas*. Pan-Slavist

Pantages Theatre

Pantagruel

Pantaloon

Pantelleria

Panthéon [monument in Paris]

Pantheon [temple in Rome]

Pantheon™ Books

Panza, Sancho

Panzer Division

Paola [* KS]

Paoli [* IN]

Papadopoulos, George

Papagayo

Papago, *n.*, *pl.* Papago *or* Papagos

Papal Infallibility *occas*. papal infallibility

Papal States

Papandreou, Andreas

Papandreou, George

Papanicolaou, George

Papanicolaou smear

Papanicolaou test

Papas, Irene

Papeete

Papen, Franz von

Paperback Exchange Bookstore

Paper Chase, The

Paphian

Paphian Goddess

Paphos

Paphos International Airport

Papinian

Papp, Joseph

Pap smear

Pap test

Papuan

Papua New Guinea

Pará

Paracel Islands

Paracelsian

Paracelsianism

Paracelsist

Paracelsus

Paracelsus, Philippus Aureolus

Paraclete

Parade

Paradis, Vanessa

Paradise

Paradise Lost

Paradise Regained

Paradise Valley

Paradise Valley Community College

Paragould

Paraguay

Paraguayan

Paraguay tea

Paraíba

Paraíba do Norte

Paraíba do Sul

Paralympics

Paralyzed Veterans of America

Paramaribo

Paramor, Norrie

Paramount

Paramount Communications Foundation

Paramount Communications Inc.

Paramount Pictures Corporation

Paramount Television Group

Paramus

Paraná

Paranaíba

Pará rhatany

Pará rubber

Pará rubber tree

Parazoa

Parcheesi™

Pardee Dam

Pardee Reservoir

Paré, Ambroise

Parenting Magazine

Parents for Quality Education

Parents Magazine

Parents' Music Resource Center

Parents without Partners

Parent-Teacher Association

Parent-Teacher-Student Association

Pareto, Vilfredo

Pareto optimum

Parian

Parian ware

Parícutin

Paris

Paris Air Show

Paris Bourse

Paris Charles de Gaulle International Airport

Paris Commune

Paris Conference

Paris Conservatoire de Music

Paris daisy

Paris green

Parish, Mitchell

Parisian

Paris Junior College

Paris Le Bourget International Airport

Paris-Match

Paris Opéra

Paris Orly Airport

Paris Pacts

Paris Peace Conference

Paris Review, The

Park, Mungo

Park, Roy Hampton

Park Avenue

Park Chung Hee

Park City

Park College

Parker, Alan

Parker, Bonnie

Parker, Charlie Bird

Parker, Dorothy

Parker, Eleanor

Parker, Ely

Parker, Fess

Parker, Sir Gilbert

Parker, Isaac

Parker, Jack

Parker, Jameson

Parker, Jean

Parker, Jessica

Parker, Maceo

Parker, Mary-Louise

Parker, Quanah

Parker, Sarah Jessica

Parker, Suzy

Parker, Theodore

Parker College of Chiropractic

Parker Dam

Parker Drilling Company

Parker Hannifin Corporation

Parker Hannifin Foundation

Parker House

Parker House roll

Parker Pen USA Ltd.

Parkersburg [* WV]

Parkesburg [* PA]

Park Falls

Park Forest

Park Hills

Park Hyatt

Park Hyatt on Water Tower Square

Parkinson, C. Northcote

Parkinson, James

Parkinsonism

Parkinson's disease

Parkinson's Disease Foundation

Parkinson's law

Parkland

Parkland College

Parkman, Francis

Parkman prize

Park Range

Park Rapids
Park Ridge
Parks, Bert
Parks, Hildy
Parks, Larry
Parks, Michael
Parks, Rosa
Parks, Van Dyke
Parks College, Inc.
Parks College of Saint Louis University
Parks Junior College
Parkville
Parkyakarkus
Parley, Peter
Parliament
Parliament hinge
Parma
Parma Heights
Parmenidean
Parmenides
Parmesan cheese
Parmigianino *or* Parmigiano
Parnaíba
Parnassian
Parnassus *or* Parnassós
Parnell, Charles Stewart
Parochial Church Council
Paro International Airport
Paropamisus
Paros
Parque Central Torres de Oficinas
Parr, Catherine
Parra, Nicanor

Parrington, Vernon Louis
Parrish, Anne
Parrish, Maxfield
Parris Island
Parris Island Marine Corps Recruit Depot
Parrot's Beak
Parry, Sir Hubert
Parry, Sir William Edward
Parry Sound
Parsee *or* Parsi
Parseeism *or* Parsism
Parsifal
Parsons
Parsons, Alan
Parsons, Estelle
Parsons, Gram
Parsons, Louella
Parsons, Talcott
Parsons Ballet Company
Parsons table
Partch, Harry
Parthenon
Parthia
Parthian
Parthian shot
Partisan Review
Partitions of Poland
Partners of the Americas, Inc.
Parton, Dolly
Partridge, Eric
Partridge Family, The
Party of God
Pasadena
Pasadena City College

Pasadena Community Playhouse
Pasadena Tournament of Roses
Pascagoula
Pascal, Blaise
Pascal, Francine
Pascal celery
Pascal's law
Pascal's theorem
Pascal's triangle
Pascal's wager
Paschal
Paschal I, Saint
Paschal Lamb
Paschen, Friedrich
Paschen-Back effect
Paschen series
Pascin, Jules
Pasco
Pasco-Hernando Community College
Pasco West
Pasdar, Adrian
Pas-de-Calais
Pashto
Pasolini, Pier Paolo
Pasó por Aquí
Paso Robles
Pass, Joe
Passaic
Passaic County Community College
Passamaquoddy Bay
Pass Christian
Passion cross
Passion cycle
Passionist
Passion of Jesus

Passion play

Passion Sunday

Passiontide

Passion Week

Passive Space Surveillance System

Pass of Killiecrankie

Passos, John Dos

Passover

Passport Inn

Password

Passy, Frédéric

Passy, Paul Edouard

Pasternak, Boris

Pasternak, Joe

Pasteur, Louis

Pasteur effect

Pasteur Institute

Pasteur treatment

Pastor, Tony

Pastoral Epistle

Pastoral Symphony

Patagonia

Patagonian

Pat Boone Show, The

Patchen, Kenneth

Patchogue

Pater, Walter

Paterno, Joe

Paterson [* NJ; one *t*]

Paterson, Katherine

Pathé, Charles

Pathé, Emile

Pathe Communications Corporation

Pathé Gazette

Pathé News Reel

Pathétique Sonata

Pathet Lao

Pathfinder Fund, The

Patient Self-Determination Act

Patinir *or* Patinier *or* Patenier, Joachim de

Patinkin, Mandy

Patmore, Coventry

Patmos

Paton, Alan

Patri, Angelo

Patriarchal Parishes of the Russian Orthodox Church in the United States of America

Patriarch of the West

Patricia

Patrick

Patrick, Butch

Patrick, Robert

Patrick, Saint

Patrick Air Force Base

Patrick Henry Community College

Patrick Henry State Junior College

Patrimony of Saint Peter

Patriot missile

Patriots' Day

Patrons of Husbandry

Patroon painters

Patten College

Patterson, Eleanor Medill

Patterson, Floyd

Patterson, Frederick D.

Patterson, Joseph Medill

Patterson, Lee

Patti, Adelina

Patti, Carlotta

Patti Labelle and the Blue Belles

Patton

Patton, George S.

Patuxent

Patuxent Naval Air Station

Paul

Paul I, Saint

Paul, Alice

Paul, David

Paul, Les

Paul, Rodman Wilson

Paul, Saint

Paul and Paula

Paul D. Camp Community College

Paulding, James Kirke

Pauley, Jane

Pauli, Wolfgang

Pauli exclusion principle

Paulin, Scott

Pauline

Pauline Letters

Pauling, Linus

Paulinism

Paulinist

Paulinus of Nola, Saint

Paulist

Paulist Fathers

Paul Newman's Hole in the Wall Gang Camp

Paul of Aegina

Paul of Samosato

Paul of the Cross, Saint

Paul Pry

Paul Quinn College

Paul Revere and the Raiders

Paul Revere's Ride

Paulsboro

Paulsen, Pat

Paul Smith's College of Arts and Sciences

Paulson, Allen Eugene

Pauls Valley

Paul Taylor Dance Company

Paul the Deacon

Paulucci, Luigino Francesco

Paul Whiteman Band

Paul Winchell and Jerry Mahoney

Paul Winter Consort

Paunceforte, Julian

Pausias

Pavarotti, Luciano

Pavlov, Ivan Petrovich

Pavlova, Anna

Pavlovian

Pavlovian conditioning

Pavlovian reflex

Pavlov's dog

Pawcatuck

Pawhuska

Pawnee, *n.*, *pl.* Pawnee *or* Pawnees

Paw Paw

Paw Paw Lake

Pawtucket

Pax

Pax Britannica

Paxinou, Katina

Paxos

Pax Romana

Paxson, Frederick Logan

Paxson, John

Paxton

Paxton, Tom

Paycheck, Johnny

Payette

Payette National Forest

Payless Car Rental System Inc.

Payless rental car

Payless Shoe Source

Payne-Aldrich Tariff Act

Pay N Pak Stores, Inc.

Pay N Save Drug Stores Inc.

Pay N Save Inc.

Pays, Amanda

Payson

Payton, Walter

Paz, Juan Carlos

Paz, Octavio

PBA National Championship

PC Computing

P-Celtic

PC Magazine

PC Today

PC World [American-based magazine; *see also* Personal Computer World]

P. D. Q. Bach

Peabody

Peabody, Elizabeth P.

Peabody, George

Peabody Conservatory

Peabody Institute of Johns Hopkins University

Peabody Museum of Archaeology and Ethnology

Peace Bridge

Peace College

Peace Corps

Peacemaker missile

Peace of Amiens

Peace of Augsburg

Peace of Cambrai

Peace of Hubertusburg

Peace of Olivia

Peace of the Pyrenees

Peace of Utrecht

Peace of Westphalia

Peach Bowl

Peaches and Herb

Peach Tree Creek

Peachtree Street

Peacock, Thomas Love

Peaks of Otter

Peale, Charles Willson

Peale, James

Peale, Norman Vincent

Peale, Raphaelle

Peale, Rembrandt

Peano, Giuseppe

Peano curve

Peano's axioms

Peano's postulates

Peanuts

Pearce, Colman
Pea Ridge
Pea Ridge National Military Park
Pearl [river; see also Pearl, The; Pearl River]
Pearl, The [poem; see also Pearl]
Pearl, Minnie
Pearl Harbor
Pearl Harbor History Associates
Pearl Harbor Naval Station
Pearl Harbor Survivors Association
Pearl Jam
Pearl River [* NY; see also Pearl]
Pearl River Community College
Pearl S. Buck Foundation, Inc., The
Pearly Gates
Pear Ridge
Pearsall
Pearson
Pearson, David
Pearson, Drew
Pearson, Lester Bowles
Pearson International Airport
Peary, Harold
Peary, Robert Edwin
Peary Land
Peasants' Dance, The
Peasants' Revolt
Peasants' War

Pease, Howard
Pease Air Force Base
Peavy, Queenie
Pebble Beach Golf Links
Pebbles
Pebbles and Bamm Bamm
Pechora
Pechstein, Max
Peck, Gregory
Peckinpah, Sam
Peck's Bad Boy
Pecksniff, Seth
Pecksniffian
Pecos
Pecos Bill
Pecos National Monument
Pediamycin™
Pedro
Pedro Jiminez
Peebles, Ann
Pee Dee
Peekskill
Peel, Emma
Peel, Sir Robert
Peele, George
Peenemünde
Peeping Tom
Peeping Tomism
Peeples, Nia
Peerce, Jan
Peer Gynt
Peer Gynt Suite
Peery, Richard Taylor
Pee-Wee's Big Adventure
Pee-Wee's Playhouse

Pegasus
Peg-Board™
Pegler, Westbrook
Pei, I. M.
Pei, Mario
Peirce, Charles Sanders
Peirce Junior College
Pekin [live duck; * IL; see also Peking duck]
Peking [* China] [now Beijing]
Peking Circus, The
Peking duck [cooked duck; see also Pekin]
Pekingese or Pekinese [dog], n., pl. Pekingese or Pekinese
Peking man [form. Sinanthropus]
Peking University
Pelagian
Pelagianism
Pelagius
Pele [Hawaiian goddess; see also Pelé]
Pelé [soccer player; see also Pele]
Pelée [volcano]
Pelee Island
Peleliu
Pele's hair
Pele's tears
Pelew Islands
Pelham
Pelham Manor
Pelican State

Pelikan, Lisa
Pellan, Alfred
Pella Rolscreen
Foundation
Pell City
Pelleas, Sir
Pellissippi State
Technical
Community College
Pelly
Pelopidas
Peloponnesian League
Peloponnesian War
Peloponnesus
Peltie, Jean
Peltier effect
Peltier heat
Pelton, Lester
Pelton water wheel
Peltz, Nelson
Pemberton, Brock
Pembroke
Pembroke College
Pembroke Pines
Pembrokeshire
Pembroke State
University
Pembroke table
Pembroke Welsh corgi
Pemex
PEN American Center
Penang
Pen Argyl
Penbrook
Pencz, Georg
Pend d'Oreille
[Indian], n., pl.
Pend d'Oreilles or
Pend d'Oreille [see
also Pend Oreille]

Penderecki, Krzysztof
Pendergast, Thomas
Pendergrass, Teddy
Pendleton
Pendleton, Nat
Pendleton Round-Up
Rodeo
Pend Oreille [river;
see also Pend
d'Oreille]
Pend Oreille Lake [see
also Pend d'Oreille]
Pendragon
Pendragon, Uther
Penelope
Penguin Books
Penguin USA
Peninsula College
Peninsular campaign
Peninsular Malaysia
Peninsular State
Peninsular War
Penitentes
Penitent Thief, the
Penn, Arthur
Penn, Sean
Penn, William
Penn and Teller
Penn Central
Corporation, The
Pennco Tech
Pennell, Joseph
Penner, Joe
Penney, James C.
Penn Hills
Pennine Alps
Pennine Chain
Pennington, Claude
Pennington, William
Norman

Penn Mutual Life
Insurance Company
Pennock, Herb
Penn Relays
Pennsauken
Penns Grove
Pennsylvania
Pennsylvania
Academy of the
Fine Arts
Pennsylvania Avenue
Pennsylvania Avenue
National Historic
Site
Pennsylvania Ballet
Pennsylvania College
of Optometry
Pennsylvania College
of Podiatric
Medicine
Pennsylvania College
of Straight
Chiropractic
Pennsylvania College
of Technology
Pennsylvania Dutch
Pennsylvania German
Pennsylvania Institute
of Technology
Pennsylvania
Magazine
Pennsylvanian
Pennsylvania Power
and Light Company
Pennsylvania Public
Television Network
Pennsylvania rifle
Pennsylvania Society
of New York
Pennsylvania State
University

Pennsylvania State University Nittany Lions

Pennsylvania State University Press

Pennsylvania Turnpike

Penn Technical Institute

Penn Valley Community College

Pennwalt Corporation

Pennwalt Foundation

Penny, Hank

Penny, Joe

Penn Yan

Penny Dreadful

Pennywhistle Press

Pennzoil Company

Penobscot

Penobscot Bay

Penobscot [Indian], *n.*, *pl.* Penobscot *or* Penobscots

Penrod

Pensacola

Pensacola Bay

Pensacola Dam

Pensacola Junior College

Pensacola Naval Air Station

Pensacola pilot boat

Pensacola Reservoir

Pension Benefit Guarantee Corporation

Penske, Roger

Pentagon, the

Pentagon Papers

Pentateuch

Pentateuchal

Pentecost

Pentecostal

Pentecostal Assemblies of the World

Pentecostal Church of God

Pentecostal Free-Will Baptist Church

Pentecostalism

Pentecostalist

Penthouse

Penticton

Pentland Firth

Pentothal™

Penutian

Penzance

People Are Funny

People for the American Way, Inc.

People for the Ethical Treatment of Animals

People for the West!

People's Bank

People's Charter

People's Commissar

People's Court, The

People's Democratic Republic of Yemen

Peoples Energy Corporation

Peoples Heritage Savings Bank

People's Party

People's Republic of China

Peoples Security Life Insurance Company

People's Temple

People-to-People Health Foundation

People to People International

People Weekly

Peoria

Peoria Heights

[Peoria] Journal Star

P.E.O. Sisterhood

Pep, Willie

Pep Boys—Manny, Moe & Jack, The

Pepe's Mexican Restaurant

Pepin

Pepin of Heristal

Pepin of Landen

Pepin the Short

Peppard, George

Pepper, Art

Pepper, Claude

Pepperdine University

Pepperdine University Waves

PepsiCo Foundation

PepsiCo Inc.

Pepsi-Cola™

Pepsi 400

Pepusch, Johann Christoph

Pepys, Samuel

Pepys' Diary

Pepysian

Pequot [Indian], *n.*, *pl.* Pequot *or* Pequots

Pequot War

Perahia, Murray

Peralta Community College

Percé Rock

Percheron
Percival
Percivale, Sir
Percodan™
Percy
Percy, Sir Henry
Percy, Thomas
Percy, Walker
Perdue, Franklin Parsons
Père David's deer
Peregrine Laziosi, Saint
Pereira, I. Rice
Pereira, William
Perelman, Ronald Owen
Perelman, S. J.
Perelman Antique Toy Museum
Perenchio, Andrew Jerrold
Peres, Shimon
Peretz, I. L.
Peretz, Martin
Perez, Carlos
Perez, Jose
Pérez de Cuéllar, Javier
Perfect Strangers
Performing Animal Welfare Society
Performing Arts Magazine
Pergamon Museum
Pergamum
Pergolese, Giovanni Battista
Peri, Jacopo
Periander
Periclean

Pericles
Pericles, Prince of Tyre
Perils of Pauline, The
Peripatetics
Perkasie
Perkin-Elmer Corporation, The
Perkins, Anthony
Perkins, Carl
Perkins, Elizabeth
Perkins, Frances
Perkins, Jack
Perkins, Maxwell
Perkins, Osgood
Perkins School for the Blind
Perlman, Itzhak
Perlman, Rhea
Perlman, Ron
Permalloy™
Permanent Court of Arbitration
Permanent Court of International Justice
Permian
Perón, Eva Duarte de
Perón, Isabel Martinez de
Perón, Juan Domingo
Perón, María de
Peronism
Peronist
Perot, H. Ross
Perpetual Savings Bank
Perrault, Charles
Perrault, Gil
Perret, Auguste
Perret, Peter J.

Perrier™
Perrin, Jean Baptiste
Perrine
Perrine, Valerie
Perris
Perry
Perry, Antoinette
Perry, Bliss
Perry, Gaylord
Perry, Lee
Perry, Matthew Calbraith
Perry, Oliver Hazard
Perry, Ralph Barton
Perry Como Show, The
Perry Drug Stores Inc.
Perrysburg
Perry's Victory and International Peace Memorial
Perryton
Perryville
Persantine™
Perse, Saint-John
Perseid
Persephone
Persepolis
Perseus
Perseus with the Head of Medusa
Pershing, John J.
Pershing missile
Persia
Persian
Persian architecture
Persian art
Persian blinds
Persian carpet
Persian cat

Persian Empire
Persian Gulf
Persian Gulf States
Persian Gulf War
Persian knot
Persian lamb
Persian language
Persian lilac
Persian literature
Persian lynx
Persian melon
Persian rug
Persian walnut
Persian Wars
Persian wild ass
Persichetti, Vincent
Persistence of
    Memory
Persius
Persoff, Nehemiah
Personal Computer
    World [London-
    based magazine; see
    also PC World]
Personal Computing
Perspex™
Perth
Perth Amboy
Perthes' disease
Perthshire
Peru
Peru balsam
Peru Current
Perugino
Peru State College
Perutz, Max
    Ferdinand
Peruvian
Peruvian balsam
Peruvian bark

Peruvian flake
Peruvian marching
    powder
Peruvian mastic tree
Peruvian rhatany
Peruzzi, Baldassare
Pescadores
Pesci, Joe
Pescow, Donna
Peshawar
Peshtigo
Peshtigo fire
Pestalozzi, Johann
    Heinrich
Pétain, Henri Philippe
Petal
Petaluma
Peter
Peter, Laurence J.
Peter, Saint
Peter and the Wolf
Peterborough
Peter Canisius, Saint
Peter Claver, Saint
Peter Damian, Saint
Peter Gonzalez, Saint
Peter Kiewit Sons'
    Inc.
Peter Kiewit Sons'
    Inc. Foundation
Peterloo Massacre
Petermann Peak
Peter of Alcántara,
    Saint
Peter of Amiens
Peter of Blois
Peter of Bruys
Peter of Castelnau
Peter of Courtenay
Peter of Dreux

Peter of Savoy
Peter of Verona, Saint
Peter Pan
Peter Pan collar
Peter, Paul and Mary
Peter Piper
Peter Piper's Practical
    Principles of Plain
    and Perfect
    Pronunciation
Peter Principle
Peter Rabbit
Peters, Arno
Peters, Bernadette
Peters, Brock
Peters, Jean
Peters, Mike
Peters, Roberta
Petersburg
Petersburg National
    Battlefield
Petersen, Robert Einar
Peterson, Oscar
Peterson, Roger Tory
Peterson Air Force
    Base
Peterson Field Guides
Peter's pence
Peters' projection
Peter the Cruel
Peter the Great
Peter the Hermit
Peter the Venerable
Pet Inc.
Petipa, Marius
Petit, Roland
Petit Champagne
Petition of Right
Petkevich, John Misha
Peto, John F.

Petöfi, Sándor
Petosky
Petrarch
Petrarchan
Petrarchan sonnet
Petrarchism
Petrarchist
Petri *occas* petri dish
Petrie, Sir Flinders
Petrie, Milton
Petrie Stores
  Corporation
Petrified Forest, The
  [play]
Petrified Forest
  National Park
Petrillo, James C.
Petrine
Petrinism
Petrofina
Petrograd
Petróleo Brasileiro
Petróleos de
  Venezuela
Petróleos Mexicanos
Petroleum Equipment
  Institute
Petronius
Petroplavosk
Petroplavosk-
  Kamchatski
Petrouchka *var. of*
  Petrushka
Petrova, Olga
Petruchio
Petrushka *occas.*
  Petrouchka [ballet]
Petrushka chord
Pet Sematary
Pet Sematary Two

Pettet, Joanna
Petticoat Junction
Pettiford, Oscar
Pettit, Bob
Pettit, Tom
Petty, Richard
Petty, Tom
Pevsner, Antoine
Pevsner, Sir Nikolaus
Pew Charitable Trusts
Peyton Place
Pfeiffer, Michelle
Pfeiffer College
P-59 Airacomet
P-51 Mustang
Pfitzner, Hans
Pfizer Foundation
Pfizer Inc.
Pflug, Jo Ann
P-47 Thunderbolt
Pfund series
PGA Championship
PGA tour
PGA World Golf Hall
  of Fame
Phaedo *or* Phaedon
Phaedra
Phaëthon
Phantom of the Opera,
  The
Pharaoh
Pharaoh ant
Pharaoh hound
Pharaon, Ghaith
Pharisaic
Pharisaism
Pharisaist
Pharisee
Phar-Mor Inc.

Pharos of Alexandria
Pharos Peninsula
Pharr
Phelps, William Lyon
Phelps Dodge
  Corporation
Phelps Dodge
  Foundation
Phenix City [* AL;
  see also Phoenix]
P. H. Glatfelter
  Company
PHH Corporation
Phi Alpha Delta
Phi Beta Kappa
Phi Beta Kappa key
Phi Beta Sigma
Phi Delta Kappa
Phi Delta Kappan
Phi Delta Phi
Phi Delta Theta
Phidian
Phidias
Phi Epsilon Phi
Phi Eta Sigma
Phi Gamma Delta
Phi Kappa Phi
Phi Kappa Psi
Phi Kappa Sigma
Phi Kappa Tau
Phi Kappa Theta
Philadelphia
Philadelphia College
  of Bible
Philadelphia College
  of Osteopathic
  Medicine
Philadelphia College
  of Pharmacy and
  Science

Philadelphia College of Textiles and Science

Philadelphia Daily News

Philadelphia Eagles

Philadelphia Electric Company

Philadelphia Flyers

Philadelphia Inquirer

Philadelphia International Airport

Philadelphia lawyer

Philadelphia Magazine

Philadelphia Museum of Art

Philadelphian

Philadelphia National Bank

Philadelphia Naval Base

Philadelphia Naval Yard

Philadelphia Northeast Airport

Philadelphia Orchestra

Philadelphia pepper pot

Philadelphia Phillies

Philadelphia 76ers

[Philadelphia] Spectrum, The

Philadelphia Stock Exchange, Inc.

Philadelphia Zoological Gardens

Phi Lambda Chi

Philander Smith College

Philatelic Foundation

Philbin, Regis

Philby, Kim

Phil Donahue Show, The [*now* Donahue]

Philemon

Philharmonia Orchestra

Philip

Philip, Saint

Philip Augustus

Philip IV of Spain

Philip Morris Companies, Inc.

Philip Morris Inc.

Philip Neri, Saint

Philip of Bethsaida, Saint

Philip of Hess

Philip of Macedon

Philip of Swabia

Philippe de Croy

Philippi

Philippian Islands

Philippic

Philippine

Philippine Airlines, Inc.

Philippine fowl disease

Philippine Independent Church

Philippine mahogany

Philippines

Philippine Sea

Philips, Ambrose

Philipsburg [* MT; PA; *see also* Phillipsburg]

Philipsburg Manor

Philipse, Frederick

Philip II of Spain

Philips Electronics

Philipse Manor

Philip S. Golden International Airport

Philip the Arabian

Philip the Bold

Philip the Evangelist

Philip the Fair

Philip the Good

Philip the Tall

Philistine

Phillip

Phillip Beth Israel School of Nursing

Phillips

Phillips, David Graham

Phillips, Kevin

Phillips, Lou Diamond

Phillips, MacKenzie

Phillips, Mark

Phillips, Michelle

Phillips, Wendell

Phillips, Wilson

Phillips Academy

Phillipsburg [* KS; NJ; *see also* Philipsburg]

Phillips Collection

Phillips College

Phillips College of Atlanta

Phillips County Community College

Phillips curve

Phillips Exeter Academy

Phillips Graduate Seminary

Phillips Junior College

Phillips Petroleum
Company
Phillips Petroleum
Foundation
Phillips™ screwdriver
Phillips University
Phillips-Van Heusen
Corporation
Philo
Philochorus
Philoctetes
Philo Judeas
Philopoemen
Phil Spitalny and His
All-Girl Orchestra
Phi Mu
Phi Mu Delta
Phi Sigma Kappa
Phi Sigma Sigma
Phnom Penh
Phobos
Phoebe
Phoenicia
Phoenician
Phoenician art
Phoenix [* AZ; see
also Phenix City]
Pheonix, John
Phoenix, River
Phoenix Cardinals
Phoenix College
Phoenix Gazette, The
Phoenix Institute of
Technology
Pheonix International
Raceway
Phoenix Islands
Phoenix Mutual Life
Insurance Company
Phoenix Park murders

Phoenix Sky Harbor
International
Airport
Phoenix Suns
Phoenix Symphony
Orchestra
Phoenixville
Photo
Communications
Company, Inc.
Photographic Society
of America
Photostat™
Phou Bia
Phrygia
Phrygian
Phrygian cap
Phrygian mode
Phyfe, Duncan
Physicians' Desk
Reference to
Pharmaceutical
Specialties and
Biologicals
Physician's Weight
Loss Center
Piaf, Edith
Piaget, Jean
Piarco International
Airways
Piarist
Piatigorsky, Gregor
Piazza Colonna
Piazza del Popolo
Piazza di San Pietro
Piazza di Sienna
Piazza di Venezia
Piazza San Marco
Piazzetta, Giovanni
Batista
Pi Beta Phi

Picabia, Francis
Picard, Captain Jean
Luc
Picard, Jean
Picardy
Picardy third
Picasso, Pablo
Picasso Museum
Picatinney Arsenal
Picayune
Piccadilly
Piccadilly Circus
Piccard, Auguste
Piccard, Jacques
Piccard, Jean
Piccinni, Nicolò
Piccirilli, Attilio
Piccirilli, Furio
Piccone, Robin
Pic de Néthou
Pic du Midi d'Ossau
Pichincha
Pickens, Slim
Pickens, T. Boone
Pickering, Edward
Charles
Pickering, Thomas
Pickering, William
Henry
Pickett, Cindy
Pickett, George
Edward
Pickett, Joseph
Pickett, Wilson
Pickett's charge
Pickfair
Pickford, Mary
Pickle Family Circus
Pickles, Christina

Pick's disease

Pickwick, Mr. Samuel

Pickwick Club

Pickwickian

Pickwick Papers, The

Pico della Mirandola, Giovanni

Pico de Teide

Pico de Tenerife

Picon, Molly

Pico Rivera

Picotte, Susan La Flesche

Pict

Pictet, Marion MacMillan

Pictionary™

Pictish

Pictured Rocks National Lakeshore

Picture of Dorian Gray, The

Picturephone™

Pictures at an Exhibition

Pidgeon, Walter

Pidgin or pidgin English

Piedmont

Piedmont Bible College

Piedmont College

Piedmont Community College

Piedmontese, n., pl. Piedmontese

Piedmont Technical College

Piedmont Triad International Airport

Piedmont Virginia Community College

Pied Piper [legendary figure; see also Pied Pipers, The]

Pied Piper of Hamelin, The

Pied Pipers, The [musical group; see also Pied Piper]

Piedras Negras

Piegan, n., pl. Piegan or Piegans

Pierce

Pierce, Charles Sanders

Pierce, Franklin

Pierce, Webb

Pierce-Arrow

Pierce College

Pierce's disease

Piercy, Marge

Pieria

Pierian

Pierian Sodality

Pierian Spring

Piero della Francesca

Piero di Cosimo

Pier 1 Imports, Inc.

Pierpont Morgan Library, The

Pierre [capital of SD]

Pierre, The [New York City hotel]

Pierrot

Piersall, Jim

Piers Plowman

Pietà

Pietermaritzburg

Pietism

Pietist

Pi Gamma Mu

Piggly Wiggly Corporation

Piggly Wiggly Southern, Inc.

pig occas. Pig Latin

Piglet

Pigling Bland

Pi Kappa Alpha

Pi Kappa Phi

Pike, James A.

Pike, Zebulon Montgomery

Pike National Forest

Pike Place Market

Pikes Peak

Pikes Peak Community College

Pikesville [* MD]

Pikeville [* KY; TN]

Pikeville College

Pi Lambda Phi

Pilaro, Anthony Martin

Pilate, Pontius

Pilcomayo

Pilgrim

Pilgrimage of Grace

Pilgrim Fathers

Pilgrim Society

Pilgrims of the United States

Pilgrim's Pride Corporation

Pilgrim's Progress

Pilgrims' Way

Pilipino [language; see also Filipino]

Pillars of Hercules

Pillars of Islam

Pillars of the Faith
Pillsbury Baptist Bible College
Pillsbury Company, The
Pillsbury Company Foundation
Pilobolus Dance Theatre
Pilon, Germain
Pilot Club International
Pilsudski, Józef Klemens
Piltdown man
Pima cotton
Pima County Community College
Pima [Indian], *n., pl.* Pima *or* Pimas
Piman
Pimería Alta
Pimlico
Pinchot, Bronson
Pinchot, Gifford
Pinckney, Charles Cotesworth
Pinckney, Thomas
Pinckney's Treaty
Pinckneyville
Pindar
Pindar, Peter
Pindaric
Pindaric ode
Pindus
Pine Barrens
Pine Bluff
Pine Bluff Arsenal
Pine Bluff Southeast
Pinebrook Junior College

Pine Flat Dam
Pine Hill
Pinehurst
Pinel, Phillippe
Pine Lawn
Pinellas Park
Pine Manor College
Pinero, Sir Arthur Wing
Pine Tree State
Pineville
P'ing-hsiang [*now* Pingxiang]
Ping-Pong™
Pingxiang [*form.* P'ing-hsiang]
Piniella, Lou
Pinkerton, Allan
Pinkerton man
Pinkerton's Security and Investigation Services
Pink Floyd
Pinkham, Daniel
Pinkham, Lydia
Pinkie
Pink Lady
Pinkney, Pauline
Pink Panther, The
Pink Panther Show, The
Pink Panther Strikes Again, The
Pinnacles National Monument
Pinnacle West Capital Corporation
Pinocchio
Pinochet Ugarte, Augusto
Pinole

pinot blanc *occas.* Pinot Blanc
pinot noir *occas.* Pinot Noir
Pinska
Pinsk Marshes
Pinta
Pintauro, Danny
Pinter, Harold
Pintsch, Richard
Pintsch gas
Pinturicchio
pinyin *often* Pinyin
Pinza, Ezio
Pinzón, Martin Alonso
Pinzón, Vincente Yáñez
Pio, Padre
Pi Omicron
Pioneer
Pioneer Clubs
Pioneer Electric Corporation
Pioneer Electronic Corporation
Pioneer Hi-Bred International, Inc.
Piper, Rowdy Roddy
Piper and Drummer
Piper Cub
Pipe Spring National Monument
Pipestone
Pipestone National Monument
Pippi Longstocking
Pippin
Pippin, Horace
Piqua
Pirandello, Luigi

Piranesi, Giambattista
Pirate Coast
Pirates of Penzance, The
Pisa
Pisan
Pisanello, Antonio
Pisano, Andrea
Pisano, Giovanni
Pisano, Nicola
Piscataqua
Piscataway
Piscataway Park
Piscator, Erwin
Piscean
Pisces
Piscopo, Joe
Pisgah National Forest
Pisistratus
Pismo Beach
Pissarro, Camille
Piston, Walter
Pit and the Pendulum, The
Pitcairn
Pitcairn Island
Pitcairn Islands Group
Pitcher, Molly
Pithecanthropus
Pithecanthropus erectus
Pitkin, Walter
Pitman
Pitman, Sir Isaac
Pitman-Moore, Inc.
Pitman shorthand
Pitney, Gene
Pitney Bowes Inc.
Pitot, Henri

Pitot- *occas.* pitot-static tube
Pitot *occas.* pitot tube
Pit River Indian
Pitstop, Penelope
Pitt, William the Elder
Pitt, William the Younger
Pitt Community College
Pitti Gallery
Pitts, Zasu
Pittsburg [* CA]
Pittsburgh [* PA]
Pittsburgh Ballet Theatre
Pittsburgh Civic Arena
Pittsburgh Dance Alloy
Pittsburgh Institute of Aeronautics
Pittsburgh Institute of Mortuary Science
Pittsburgh Landing
Pittsburgh Magazine
Pittsburgh National Bank
Pittsburgh Penguins
Pittsburgh Pirates
Pittsburgh Playhouse
[Pittsburgh] Post-Gazette
Pittsburgh Press
Pittsburgh Steelers
Pittsburgh Symphony Orchestra
Pittsburgh Technical Institute
Pittsburgh Theological Seminary

Pittsburg State University
Pittsfield
Pittston
Pittston Company, The
Pittway Corporation
Pittway Corporation Charitable Foundation
Pitzer College
Pius
Pius I, Saint
Pius V, Saint
Pius X, Saint
Pizarro, Francisco
Pizarro, Gonzalo
Pizarro, Hernando
Pizarro, Juan
Pizza Hut
Pizza Inn
Pizzarelli, John
Pizzetti, Ildebrando
Place, Mary Kay
Place Charles de Gaulle
Place de la Concorde
Place in the Sun, A
Placentia
Placentia Bay
Place Pigalle
Placerville
Placido's disk
Placidyl™
Placozoa
Plague, The
plagues of Egypt
Plainedge
Plainfield
Plain Jane

Plain of Adana
Plain of Esdraelon
Plain of Jars
Plain of Jazreel
Plain of Sharon
Plain People
Plains Indian
Plains of Abraham
Plains of Passage, The
Plainview
Plainville
Plainwell
Planck, Max
Planck's constant
Planck's radiation law
Planetary Society
Plan International (USA)
Plank, Ed
Planned Parenthood[SM]
Planned Parenthood Federation of America
Planning and Conservation League
Planning and Conservation League Foundation
Plano
Plant, Robert
Plantagenet
Plantation
Plantation walking horse *occas.* Walking Horse
Plant City
Plante, Jacques
Plantin, Christophe
Plaquemine
plaster of Paris

Plastic and Metal Products Manufacturers Association
Plateau Indian
Plateau of Iran
Plateau of the Chotts
Plateau's problem
Plath, Sylvia
Plato
Platonic
Platonic love
Platonic solid
Platonic year
Platonism
Platonist
Platonistic
Platoon
Plato's cave
Plato's Republic
Platt, Orville Hitchcock
Platt Amendment
Platte
Platters, The
Platteville
Platt Junior College
Plattsburg [* MO]
Plattsburgh [* NY]
Plattsburgh Air Force Base
Plattsmouth
Platyminthes
Plautus, Titus
Playbill
Playboy
Playboy at Night
Playboy Channel, The
Playboy Enterprises, Inc.

Playboy Foundation
Playboy Mansion
Playboy of the Western World, The
Playboy Video Enterprises
Player, Gary
Playgirl
Playhouse 90
Playmates Toys Inc.
Play of Daniel, The
Playtex Family Products Corporation
Plaza Athénée
Plaza Business Institute
Plaza Hotel, The
Plaza San Antonio
Plaza Suite
Pleasant Grove
Pleasant Hill [* CA; IA; LA; MO]
Pleasant Hills [* PA]
Pleasanton
Pleasant Ridge
Pleasantville
Please Don't Eat the Daisies
Pleasence, Angela
Pleasence, Donald
Pleasure Ridge Park
Pledge of Allegiance
Pleiades
Pleiku
Pleistocene
Plekhanov, Georgi
Pleshette, John
Pleshette, Suzanne
Plessy v. Ferguson

Pleven, René
Plexers, Inc.
Plexiglas™
Pliesetskaya, Maya
Plimpton, George
Plimpton, Martha
Plimsoll, Samuel
Plimsoll line
Plimsoll mark
Pliny the Elder
Pliny the Younger
Pliocene
Plishka, Paul
Ploesti
Plotinian
Plotinism
Plotinus
Plott hound
Plowright, Joan
Plum
Plumas National
   Forest
Plumb, Eve
Plummer, Amanda
Plummer, Christopher
Plunkett, Jim
Plutarch
Plutarchian
Plutarch's Lives
Pluto
Plutonian
Plutonic
Pluviôse
Plymouth
Plymouth Brethren,
   The
Plymouth Colony
Plymouth porcelain
Plymouth Rock

Plymouth Sound
Plymouth State
   College
P.M. Dawn
P.M. Magazine
PNC Financial
   Corporation
PNM Foundation
Po
Pocahontas
Pocatello
Po Chü-i
Pocket Books™
Poco
Pocomoke City
Pocono International
   Raceway
Pocono Mountains
Podesta, Rossana
Podgorny, Nikolai
Podhoretz, Norman
Podunk
Poe, Edgar Allan
Poet and Peasant
   [Overture]
Poetic Edda
Poet Laureate
Poetry Society of
   America
Poets' Corner
Pogány, Willy
Pogo
Pogonophora
Pohl, Frederik
Pohlad, Carl Ray
Poincaré, Jules Henri
Poincaré, Raymond
Poindexter, Buster
Poindexter, John
Point Arguello

Point Barrow
point d'Alençon
point d'Angleterre
point de Hongrie
Pointe-à-Pitre
Pointe aux Trembles
Pointe Claire
Pointe-Noire
Pointe on South
   Mountain, The
Pointer Sisters, The
Point Four Program
pointillism occas.
   Pointillism
pointillist occas.
   Pointillist
Point Judith
Point Loma Nazarene
   College
Point Mugu Pacific
   Missile Test Center
Point Park College
Point Pelee
Point Pelee National
   Park
Point Pleasant
Point Pleasant Beach
Point Reyes
Point Reyes lilac
Point Reyes National
   Seashore
Point Salines
   International
   Airport
Poiret, Jean
Poiret, Paul
Poirot, Hercule
Poison
Poison Affair
Poisson, Siméon
   Dennis

Poisson distribution

Poisson's *occas.*
　Poisson ratio

Poitier, Sidney

Poitiers

Polack

Poland

Poland China

Polanski, Roman

Polaris

Polaroid Corporation

Polaroid Foundation

Polar Region

Poldi Pezzoli Museum

Pole

Pole, Reginald

Pole Star

Police [magazine]

Police, The [musical
　group]

Police Story

Police Times

Policy Management
　Systems
　Corporation

Polish

Polish Army Veterans
　Association of
　America

Polish Corridor

Polish Cultural
　Society of America

Polish Genealogical
　Society of
　Connecticut

Polish language

Polish Legion of
　American Veterans

Polish literature

Polish National
　Catholic Church of
　America

Polish *occas.* polish
　sausage

Polish wheat

Politburo

Politian

Political Bureau of the
　Communist Party

Polk, James Knox

Polk, Sarah Childress

Polk Community
　College

Pollack, Ben

Pollack, Sydney

Pollaiuolo, Antonio

Pollaiuolo, Piero

Pollard, Michael J.

Pollini, Maurizio

Pollio, Caius

Pollock, Channing

Pollock, Sir Frederick

Pollock, Jackson

Pollux

Pollyanna

Pollyannaish

Polly Wolly Doodle

Polo, Marco

Polonia

Polonius

Polovtsian Dances

Poltergeist

Poltergeist II

Polvinick, Paul

Polybius

Polycarp, Saint

Polyclitus

Polycrates

Polydorus

Polyglot Bible

Polygnotus

Polygram/Polydor
　Records Inc.

Polynesia

Polynesian

Polyphemus

Polyphemus moth

Polytechnic
　University

Pomerania

Pomeranian

Pomeroy

Pommard

Pomo, *n., pl.* Pomo *or*
　Pomos

Pomona

Pomona College

Pomona glass

Pompano Beach

Pompeia

Pompeian

Pompeii [city]

Pompey [Roman
　general]

Pompidou, Georges

Pompton Lakes

Pomus, Jerome Doc

Ponape

Ponca City

Ponca [Indian], *n., pl.*
　Ponca *or* Poncas

Ponce

Ponce College of
　Technology

Ponce de León, Juan

Ponce School of
　Medicine

Poncha Pass

Ponchatoula

Ponchielli, Amilcare
Ponderosa Ranch
Pond Inlet
Pons, Lily
Ponselle, Carmela
Ponselle, Rosa
pons Varolii, *n.*, *pl.*
 pontes Varolii
Ponta Delgada
Pont du Gard
Ponti, Carlo
Pontiac
Pontiac Motor
 Division (General
 Motors
 Corporation)
Pontiac's Conspiracy
Pontiac Silverdome
Pontiac's Rebellion
Pontiac's War
Pontian, Saint
Pontifical College
Pontifical College
 Josephinum
Pontifical Mass
Pontine
Pontine Marshes
Pont l'Evêque
Pont Neuf bridge
Pontocaine™
Pontoppidan, Henrik
Pontormo, Jacopo da
Pony Baseball
Pony Express
Pony League
Pony Leaguer
Ponzi scheme
Pooh Bah
Poor Clare
Poor Little Rich Girl

Poor People's March
Poor Richard's
 Almanack *often*
 Almanac
Poor Robin's plantain
Pop, Iggy
pop art *occas.* Pop Art
Pope [Catholic
 primate]
Popé [Pueblo
 medicine man]
Pope, Alexander
Pope, John Russell
Pope Air Force Base
Pope John Paul II
Pope John XXIII
 National Seminary
Popeye the sailor-man
Pop Goes the Weasel
Popish Plot
Poplar Bluff
Popocatépetl
Popp, Lucia
Popper, Sir Karl
 Raimund
Popperian
Poppins, Mary
Poppy Hill Golf
 Course
Poppy Week
Popsicle™
Popular Electronics
Popular Hot Rodding
Popular Mechanics
Popular Photography
Popular Science
Popular Woodworking
Population
 Association of
 America
Population Bomb, The

Population Council
Population Crisis
 Committee
Population Institute,
 The
Population Reference
 Bureau, Inc.
Populism
Populist
Populistic
Populist Party
Poquelin, Jean
 Baptiste
Poquoson
Porcupine
Porcupine, Peter
Porgy and Bess
Porifera
Porizkova, Paulina
Porky Pig
Porphyrean
Porphyry
Porro, Ignazio
Porro prism
Porsche Cars North
 America, Inc.
Porsena, Lars
Port Adelaide
Portage
Portage Lake
Portage la Prairie
Portageville
Portales
Port Allegany
Port Allen
Port Angeles
Port Arthur [* China]
 [*now* Lüshun]
Port Arthur
 [* Ontario; TX]

Port-au-Prince

Port-au-Prince
International
Airport

Port Authority of New
York and New
Jersey

Port Carbon

Port Charlotte

Port Chester

Port Clinton

Port du Salut

Port Elizabeth

Porter, Cole

Porter, David

Porter, David Dixon

Porter, Fairfield

Porter, Sir George

Porter, Katherine
Anne

Porter, Quincy

Porter, Rodney Robert

Porter, Sylvia

Porterville

Porterville College

Porter Wagoner Show,
The

Port Ewen

Port Gibson

Port Hudson

Port Hueneme

Port Hueneme Naval
Construction
Battalion Center

Port Huron

Portia

Portinari, Beatrice

Portinari, Candido

Port Isabel

Port Jackson

Port Jervis

Portland

portland occas.
Portland cement

Portland Community
College

Portland General
Corporation

Portland Head Light

Portland International
Airport

Portland International
Jetport

Portland International
Raceway

Portland Marathon

Portland Meadows

[Portland] Memorial
Coliseum

[Portland] Oregonian,
The

Portland Rose Festival

Portland School of Art

Portland Speedway

Portland State
University

Portland stone

Portland Trail Blazers

Portland vase

Port Lavaca

Port Louis

Portman

Portman, John

Port Moresby

Port Moresby
International
Airport

Port Neches

Portnoy's Complaint

Pôrto Alegre

Portobello

Portofino

Port-of-Spain

Portolá, Gaspar de

Porto-Novo

Port Orchard

Port Orford

Port Orford cedar

Port Phillip Bay

Portrait of a Lady, The

Portrait of Charles I
Hunting

Portrait of Stephen
and Kathie

Portrait of the Artist
as a Young Man, A

Port Royal Sound

Port Said

Port Saint Joe

Port Salut

Portsmouth

Portsmouth Naval
Shipyard

Port Sudan

Port Sulphur

Port Townsend

Portugal

Portuguese, n., pl.
Portuguese

Portuguese cherry
laurel

Portuguese
Continental Union
of the United States
of America

Portuguese cypress

Portuguese Guinea

Portuguese India

Portuguese language

Portuguese literature

Portuguese man-of-
war

Portuguese Timor

Portuguese water dog

Portuguese West
Africa [*now*
Angola]

Port Vue

Port Washington

Port Wentworth

Poseidon

Poseidon missile

Poseuille, Jean Louis
Marie

Poseuille's law

Posner, Victor

Post

Post, Emily

Post, George Browne

Post, Markie

Post, Wiley

Postal Rate
Commission

Postcards from the
Edge

Post College

Post Exchange

Postimpressionism
often
postimpressionism

Postimpressionist
often
postimpressionist

Postimpressionistic
often
postimpressionistic

Post-It™ note pad

post-Kantian

Postman Roulin, The

post-Marxian

Poston, Tom

post-Reformation

post-Renaissance

Pot, Pol

Potato Famine

Potawatomi, *n., pl.*
Potawatomi *or*
Potawatomis

Potemkin, Grigori

Potemkin village

Potlatch Corporation

Potlatch Foundation
for Higher
Education

Potok, Chaim

Potomac

Potomac Electric
Power Company

Potomac long boat

Potomac State College
of West Virginia
University

Potsdam

Potsdam Conference

Pott, Percival

Potter, Beatrix

Potter, Paul

Potteries, the

Potts, Annie

Pott's disease

Pott's fracture

Pottstown

Pottsville

Poughkeepsie

Pouilly Fuissé

Pouilly-Fumé

Poulenc, Francis

Poultry Science
Association

Pound, Ezra

Pound, Louise

Pound, Roscoe

Poundstone, Paula

Pourbus, Frans

Pourbus, Pieter

Poussaint, Alvin F.

Poussin, Gaspard

Poussin, Nicolas

Poverty Point National
Monument

Povich, Maury

Powder Puff Derby

Powder River

Powell

Powell, Adam Clayton

Powell, Anthony

Powell, Boog

Powell, Bud

Powell, Cecil Frank

Powell, Colin

Powell, Dick

Powell, Eleanor

Powell, Jane

Powell, John

Powell, John Wesley

Powell, Lewis
Franklin, Jr.

Powell, Mel

Powell, William

Power, Tyrone

Powers, Francis Gary

Powers, Hiram

Powers, J. F.

Powers, Mala

Powers, Stefanie

Powhatan

Powhatan
Confederacy

Powys, John Cowper

Powys, Llewelyn

Powys, T. F.

Poznan

PPG Industries Foundation

PPG Industries Inc.

Prado

Prado, Perez

Praeger Publishers

Praemium Imperiale

Praetorian Guard

Pragmatic Sanction of Bourges

Prague

[Prague] National Gallery

Prague Ruzne Airport

Prague School

Prague Symphony

Prairial

Prairie du Chien

Prairie Home Companion, A

Prairie Provinces

Prairie State College

Prairie View Agricultural and Mechanical University

Prairie View Agricultural and Mechanical University Panthers

Prairie Village

Prakrit

Prakrit literature

Prancer

Prandtl, Ludwig

Prandtl number

Prang, Louis

Pratt

Pratt, Matthew

Pratt Community College

Pratt Institute

Pratt truss

Prattville

Pravda

Praxiteles

Prayer of Manasses

Praying Hands

Preakness

Preakness Celebration

Precambrian

pre-Christian

Precision Castparts Corporation

pre-Columbian

pre-Columbian architecture

pre-Columbian art

Predator

Predator 2

Pre-Dawn

pre-Elizabethan

Preemption Act

Preemption-Distribution Act

Preliminary Scholastic Aptitude Test

Prelog, Vladimir

Préludes

Prelude to "The Afternoon of a Faun"

Premark International, Inc.

Premier Cruise Lines

Premiere Radio Networks

Premier Industrial Corporation

Preminger, Otto

Premont

Prendergast, Maurice Brazil

Prentice

Prentice Hall

Prentiss, Paula

Pre-Raphaelite

Pre-Raphaelite Brotherhood

Pre-Raphaelitism

Presbyterian

Presbyterian Church in America

Presbyterian Church (U.S.A.)

Presbyterian College

Presbyterianism

Presbyterian School of Christian Education

Presbyter *var. of* Prester John

Prescott

Prescott, William Hickling

Prescott College

Prescott National Forest

Presentation College

Preservation Hall Jazz Band

Presidential Medal of Freedom [*form.* Medal of Freedom]

Presidential Medal of Honor [civilian award; *not* Medal of Honor]

Presidential Range

President of the United States, The

Presidents' Day

Presidio of Monterey

Presidio of San Diego

Presidio of San Francisco

Presidio Press

Presley, Elvis

Presley, Priscilla

Presnell, Harve

pre-Socratic *or* Presocratic

Presque Isle

Press and Radio Club

Press Features International

Pressman, Lawrence

Prester *occas.* Presbyter John

Preston

Preston, Billy

Preston, Robert

Prestonsburg

Prestonsburg Community College

Prestwich [* England]

Prestwick [* Scotland]

Prestwick International Airport

Presumed Innocent

Pretenders, The

Pretoria

Pretoria Art Museum

Pretorius, Andries

Pretorius, Marthinus

Pretty Woman

Prevention

Prévert, Jacques

Previn, André

Previn, Dory

Prévost d'Exiles, Antoine François

Prevue Guide

Prevue Networks Inc.

Prey, Hermann

Priam

Priapulida

Pribilof Islands

Price

Price, Bruce

Price, George

Price, Leontyne

Price, Lloyd

Price, Margaret

Price, Nick

Price, Ray

Price, Reynolds

Price, Roger

Price, Solomon

Price, Vincent

Price Club

Price Company, The

Price Is Right, The

Price Stern Sloan, Inc.

Price Waterhouse

Price Waterhouse Foundation

Prichard

Pride, Charley

Pride, Thomas

Pride and Prejudice

pride-of-California

pride of China

pride-of-India

Pride's Purge

Priest, Ivy Baker

Priestley, J. B.

Priestley, Joseph

Priests of Saint Paul the Apostle

PRI Foundation

Prigogine, Ilya

Prima, Louis

Prima Ballerina, The

Primate of All England

Primate of Italy

Primavera

Prime Computer, Inc.

Prime Network

Primerica Corporation

Prime Sports Network

Primetime Live

Primitive Advent Christian Church

Primitive Baptist

Primitive Friends

Primitive Methodist

Primitive Methodist Church

Primo de Rivera, Miguel

Primrose, William

Prince

Prince, The

Prince, Hal

Prince, Harold S.

Prince, William

Prince Albert

Prince Albert coat

Prince Albert National Park

Prince Albert Sound

Prince Andrew

Prince and the New Power Generation

Prince Buster

Prince Charles

Prince Charming

Prince de Condé

Prince Edward Island

Prince Edward Island National Park

Prince George

Prince George's Community College

Prince Igor

Prince Juan Carlos

Prince Louis Ferdinand

Prince of Darkness

Prince of Kent

Prince of Monaco

Prince of Peace

Prince of the Apostles

Prince of Wales

Prince of Wales Island

Prince of Wales Museum

Prince Otto von Bismarck

Prince Philip

Prince Rainier III

Prince Rupert

Prince Rupert's Land

Prince Rupert's metal

Prince Saud al-Faisal Al Saud

Prince Souphanovoung

Prince Souvana Phouma

Princess Anne

Princess Caroline

Princess Cruises

Princess Diana

Princess Grace

Princess Kitty

Princess Margaret

Princess of Kent

Princess of Wales

Princess Royal, The

Princess Stephanie

Princeton

Princeton Theological Seminary

Princeton University

Princeton University Press

Princeton University Tigers

Prince William Forest Park

Prince William Sound

Prince William Sound Community College

Principal, Victoria

Principal Financial Group, The

Principal Foundation Group, The

Principal Foundation Inc., The

Principal Mutual Life Insurance Company

Príncipe

Principia College

Prine, Andrew

Prineville

Printing Industries of America

Prinze, Freddie

Prior, Matthew

Pripet

Pripet Marshes

Priscian

Priscilla

Prism

Prisoner of Zenda, The

Pritikin diet

Pritzker, Jay Arthur

Pritzker, Robert Alan

Pritzker Architecture Prize

Privacy Act

Privy Council

Priz Goncourt

Prizzi's Honor

PR Newswire

Pro-Am Sports System

Pro Arte Quartet

Pro-Bowlers' Tour

Proclus

Procopius

Procopius the Great

Procrastinators' Club of America

Procrustean

Procrustes

Procrustes' bed

Procter, William C.

Procter and Gamble Company, The

Procter and Gamble Fund

Proctor

Procul Harum

Procyon

Professional Bowlers Association of America

Professional Golfers' Association of America

Professional Photographers of America

Professional Rodeo Cowboys Association

Professional Secretaries International

Professor Branestawm

Professor Higgins

Professor Longhair

Professor Moriarty

Profiles Publishing, Inc.

Pro Football Hall of Fame

Profumo, John

Profumo affair

Program Evaluation and Review Technique

Progressive, The

Progressive Corporation, The

Progressive National Baptist Convention

Progressive Party

Prohibition Party

Project Concern International

Project Cure

Project Hope

Project Mercury

Project Orbis

Project Plowshare

Prokofiev, Sergey

Promethea moth

Promethean

Prometheus

Prometheus Bound

Prometheus Unbound

Promised Land

Promises, Promises

Promus Companies Inc., The

Propeller Club of the United States

Proper [of the Mass]

Propertius, Sextus

Prophet, The

Prophet, Ronnie

Prophet Drew Ali

Prose Edda

Proserpine

Prosky, Robert

Prospect Park

Prospero

Prosser

Protagoras

Proterozoic

Protestant

Protestant Conference (Lutheran)

Protestant Episcopal Church

Protestant Episcopal Church in the United States of America

Protestant Episcopal Theological Seminary in Virginia

Protestant ethic

Protestantism

Protestant Reformation

Protestant Reformed Churches in North America

Protestant Reformed Churches of America

Protestant Union

Protestant work ethic

Proteus

Protocols of the Elders of Zion

Protogenes

Proto-Germanic

Protopopov, Alexandr

Proudhon, Pierre Joseph

Proust, Marcel

Proustian

Provençal [language; region]

Provençale [cookery]

Provençal literature

Provençale sauce

Provence

Provence-Côte d'Azur

Provence rose

Providence

Providence boat

Providence College

Providence College Friars

Providence Journal-Bulletin, The

Providence Plantations

Providence river boat

Providence Theodore Francis Green State Airport

Provident Charitable Trust

Provident Life and Accident Insurance Company

Provident Mutual Life Insurance Company of Philadelphia

Provident National Assurance Company

Provident National Bank

Provincetown

Provincetown Players

Provisions of Oxford

Provo

Prowse, Juliet

Proxmire, William

Pruco Life Insurance Company

Prudential Foundation

Prudential Insurance Company of America

Prudential Securities Inc.

Prudentius

Prudhoe Bay

Prudhomme, Don

Prudhomme, Paul

Prud'hon, Pierre Paul

Pruett, Jeanne

Prufrock, J. Alfred

Prussia

Prussian

Prussian blue

Prussianism

Prut

Pryce, Jonathan

Prynne, Hester

Prynne, William

Pryor, Richard

Pryor Creek

Przewalski's horse

Psalms

Psalter

Psi Chi

Psilophyta

Psi Psi Psi

PSI Resources, Inc.

Psi Upsilon

P-61 Black Widow

P-63 Kingcobra

P-state

Psyche

Psyche knot

Psycho

Psychology Today

PT boat

Pterophyta

P-38 Lightning

P-39 Airacobra

P-3 Orion

P.T.L. Club, The

Ptolemaic

Ptolemaic system

Ptolemaic tables

Ptolemaist

Ptolemy

Ptolemy Philadelphus

Ptolemy Soter

P-2 Neptune

Public Broadcasting Service

Public Citizen

Public Citizen Health Research Group

Public Employees Roundtable

Public Enemy

Public Enemy No. 1

Public Health Cigarette Smoking Act

Public Health Service

Public Health Service Act

Public Relations Society of America

Public Service Alliance of Canada

Public Service Company of Colorado

Public Service Company of New Mexico

Public Service Enterprise Group Inc.

Public Works Administration

Publishers Weekly

Publix Super Markets, Inc.

Pucci, Emilio

Puccini, Giacomo

Puck

Puck, Wolfgang

Puckett, Gary

Puckett, Kirby

Puebla [Mexican city; Mexican state]

Pueblo [city in Colorado]

Pueblo Community College

Pueblo Indian

Pueblo Ordnance Depot

Puente, Tito

Puerto Montt

Puerto Montt El Tepual International Airport

Puerto Rican

Puerto Rican Legal Defense and Education Fund, Inc.

Puerto Rican royal palm

Puerto Rico

Puerto Rico Junior College

Puerto Vallarta

Pufendorf, Samuel

Puff, the Magic Dragon

Puget, Peter

Puget, Pierre

Puget Sound

Puget Sound Christian College

Puget Sound Naval Shipyard

Puget Sound Naval Station

Puget Sound Power and Light Company

Pugin, Augustus Charles

Pugin, Augustus Welby Northmore

Pukaskwa National Park

Pulaski

Pulaski, Casimir

Pulaski, Edward C.

Pulaski, Dr. Kate

Pulaski ax

Pulcinella

Puli

Pulitzer, Joseph

Pulitzer Prize

Pulliam, Keshia Knight

Pullman

Pullman, George M.

Pullman car

Pullman kitchen

Pullman Strike

Pulmotor™

Punch and Judy

Punch-and-Judy show

Punchbowl

Punic

Punic Wars

Punjab

Punjabi

Punjab States

Punky Brewster

Punta Arenas [* Chile; see also Puntarenas]

Punta Arenas International Airport

Punta del Este

Punta Gallinas

Punta Gorda

Puntarenas [* Costa Rica; see also Punta Arenas]

Punxsutawney

Punxsutawney Phil

Pupin, Michael Idvorsky

Puppeteers of America

Puppis

Purcell

Purcell, Henry

Purcell, Lee

Purcell, Sarah

Purcell Mountains

Purchas, Samuel

Purdom, Edmund

Purdue University

Purdue University Boilermakers

Purdue University Press

Pure Land

Pure Land Buddhism

Pure Land sect

Purim

Puritan

Puritan ethic

Puritanism

Puritan Revolution

Puritan spoon

Puritan work ethic

Purkinje, Johannes E.

Purkinje cell

Purkinje fiber

Purl, Linda

Purloined Letter, The

Purple Heart

Pursley, Barbara Roles

Purus

Pusan

Pusey, Edward Bouverie

Pusey, Nathan Marsh

Puseyism

Puseyite

PUSH for Excellence

Pushkin, Aleksander occas. Aleksandr Sergeyevich

Pushkin Museum of Fine Arts

Puss in Boots

Putnam

Putnam, George Haven

Putnam, George Palmer

Putnam, Israel

Putnam, Rufus

Putnam Publishing Group, The

Putumayo

Pu'uhonua o Honaunau National Historical Park

Puukohola Heiau National Historic Site

Puvis de Chavannes,
  Pierre Cécile
Puyallup
Puy-de-Dôme
  [department of
  France]
Puy de Dôme [extinct
  volcano]
Puyé Cliff Dwellings
Pu Yi *often* Henry Pu
  Yi
Puzo, Mario
P wave
Pygmalion
Pygmy, *n.*, *pl.*
  Pygmies
Pyle, Denver
Pyle, Ernie
Pyle, Gomer

Pyle, Howard
Pym, John
Pynchon, Thomas
Pyongyang
Pyramid Lake
Pyramid of Khafre
Pyramid of Khufu
Pyramids of Giza
Pyramus and Thisbe
Pyrenees
Pyrénées-Atlantique
Pyrénées-Orientales
Pyrex™
Pyrrhic
Pyrrhic victory
Pyrrhonism
Pyrrhonist
Pyrrho of Elis

Pyrrhus
Pyrrophyta
Pythagoras
Pythagoras of
  Rhegium
Pythagorean
Pythagoreanism
Pythagorean scale
Pythagorean theorem
Pythagorean tuning
Pytheas [Greek
  explorer; *see also*
  Pythias]
Pythian Games
Pythias [of Damon
  and Pythias; *see
  also* Pytheas]
Pyxis

Q

Qaddafi, Mu'ammar al- or el-
Qandahar
Qantas airliner
Qantas Airways Ltd.
Qara Qum *var. of* Kara Kum
Qatar
Qattara Depression
Q.E.D. Information Sciences, Inc.
Q fever
Qingdao [*form.* Tsingtao]
Qinghai [*form.* Chinghai]
Qinling Shan [*form.* Tsinling Shan]
Qiqihar [*form.* Tsitsihar]
Qishm
QMS, Inc.
QST
Q-Tips™
Quaalude™
Quabbin Dike
Quabbin Reservoir
Quadragesima
Quadragesimal
Quadragesima Sunday

Quadruple Alliance
Quaid, Dennis
Quaid, Randy
Quaid-E-Azam International Airport
Quai d'Orsay
Quaker
Quaker Chemical Corporation
Quakeress
Quaker gun
Quaker Industries Ltd.
Quakerish
Quakerism
Quaker- *or* quaker- ladies
Quaker Life
Quakerlike
Quakerly
Quaker meeting
Quaker Oats Company, The
Quaker Oats Foundation
Quaker State Corporation
Quaker State Oil Refining Corporation
Quaker State Open

Qualitative Research Consultants Association
Quality Control Council of America
Quality Control Supervisor's Bulletin
Quality Education for Minorities Network
Quality Paperback Book Club
Quamran
Quanex Corporation
Quant, Mary
Quantico
Quantico Marine Corps Development Command
Quantrill, William Clarke
Quantrill's raiders
Quantum Chemical Corporation
Quantum—Science Fiction and Fantasy Review
Quapaw
Qu'Apelle
Quarles, Benjamin
Quarles, Francis

Quartenary

Quarterdeck Office Systems, Inc.

Quartering Act

Quarter to Three

Quasar Company

Quasimodo

Quasimodo, Salvatore

Quasimodo Sunday

Quatre Bras

Quatro, Suzi

Quayle, Anthony

Quayle, Dan

Quayle, Marilyn

Quebec

Quebec Act

Quebec campaign

Quebec Conference

Quebecer *or* Quebecker

Quebec Nordiques

Quebecois *or* Québecois, *n.*, *pl.* Quebecois *or* Québecois

Quebec separatist movement

Quechua, *n.*, *pl.* Quechua *or* Quechuas

Queeg, Captain

Queen

Queen, Ellery

Queen Anne

Queen Anne's lace

Queen Anne style

Queen Anne's War

Queen Beatrix

Queen Carpet Corporation

Queen Charlotte Islands

Queen Charlotte Sound

Queen Elizabeth Hall

Queen Elizabeth Islands

Queen Elizabeth I

Queen Elizabeth II [monarch]

Queen Elizabeth 2 [ocean liner]

Queen Fabiola

Queen Hatshepsut

Queen Ida

Queen Juliana

Queen Latifah

Queen Mab

Queen Margrethe II

Queen Mary

Queen Mary Coast

Queen Maud Land

Queen Maud Range

Queen Mother, The

Queen Mother Elizabeth

Queen Nour

Queen of England

Queen of Hearts, The

Queen of Heaven

Queen of Sheba

Queen of Spades, The

Queen of the Holy Rosary College

Queens

Queen's Bench

Queensberry Rules

Queen's Birthday

Queen's Birthday Honours

Queensboro Bridge

queen's bounty *occas.* Queen's Bounty

Queen's Champion

Queens College

queen's colour *occas.* Queen's colour *or* Queen's Colour

Queen's Counsel

queen's *or* Queen's English

Queen's-flower

Queensland

Queensland nut

Queens-Midtown Tunnel

Queen's Official Birthday

Queen's pattern

Queen's Proctor

Queen's Remembrancer

Queensrych

Queenston [* Ontario]

Queenstown [* South Africa]

Queens Tribune

Queen's University

Queensway Tunnel

Queen Tiy

Queen Victoria

Queen Wilhelmina

Queer Street

Quemoy

Quemoy Islands

Quercia, Jacopo della

Querétaro

Quesnay, François

Quesnel, Francois

Questar Corporation

Quest International

? [Question Mark] and the Mysterians

Quetta

Quetzalcoatl

Queue Inc.

Quezon

Quezon City

Quezon y Molina, Manuel

Quiberon

Quiberon Bay

Quiché Indian

quiche lorraine *often* Lorraine

Quickdraw McGraw

Quicksilver Messenger Service

Quidde, Ludwig

Quidor, John

Quigmans, The

Quik Print Inc.

Quik Stop market

Quik Stop Markets Inc.

Quileute

Quill, Michael Joseph

Quill and Scroll [magazine]

Quill and Scroll Foundation

Quill and Scroll Society

Quill Company Inc., The

Quiller-Couch, Sir Arthur

Quimby, Phineas Parkhurst

Quimby Center

Quinault

Quincy

Quincy, Josiah

Quincy College

Quincy Junior College

[Quincy] Patriot Ledger, The

Quindlen, Anna

Quinebaug Valley Community College

Quinlan, Kathleen

Quinn, Aidan

Quinn, Anthony

Quinn, Jane Bryant

Quinn, Martha

Quinnipiac College

Quinquagesima

Quinquagesimal

Quinquagesima Sunday

Quinsigamond Community College

Quintana Roo

Quintanilla, Luis

Quintero, Joaquin Álvarez

Quintessence Inc.

Quintilian

Quintilius, Marcus Aurelius

Quintuple Alliance

Quirinal Hill

Quirinal Palace

Quirino, Elpidio

Quirinus

Quisenberry, Dan

Quisling, Vidkun

Quito

Quivira

Quixote, Don

Quixote Center

Qumran

Qumran manuscripts

Quonset™ hut

Quonset Point

Quonset Point Naval Air Station

Quota International

Quotations of Chairman Mao Tse Tung

Quotron™ electronic stock quote

Quotron Systems Inc.

Quo Vadis

Quran *var. of* Koran

QVC Network, Inc.

R

Ra *var. of* Re

Rabat

Rabaul

Rabb, Ellis

Rabbi Isaac Elchanan
Theological
Seminary

Rabbinic

Rabbinical Academy
Mesivta Rabbi
Chaim Berlin

Rabbinical Alliance of
America

Rabbinical Assembly

Rabbinical College

Rabbinical Council of
America

Rabbinical Seminary

Rabbinite

Rabbit at Rest

Rabbit Is Rich

Rabbit Redux

Rabbit, Run

Rabbitt, Eddie

Rabe, David

Rabelais, François

Rabelaisian

Rabelaisianism

Rabi

Rabi, I. I.

Rabin, Yitzhak

Rabobank Nederland

Rachel

Rachins, Alan

Rachmaninoff, Sergei

Racine

Racine, Jean

Racketeer Influenced
and Corrupt
Organization Act

Rackham, Arthur

Racquetball
Manufacturers
Association

Radbourn, Charlie

Radcliffe College

Radetzky, Joseph

Radetzky March

Radford

Radford, Arthur
William

Radford University

Radford University
Highlanders

Radical Chic and
Mau-Mauing the
Flak Catchers

Radio Advertising
Bureau

Radio Amateur
Satellite
Corporation

Radio Canada
International

Radio City

Radio City Music Hall

Radio Flyer™

Radio Free Europe

Radio Iowa

Radio Liberty

Radiomutuel Inc.

Radio Pennsylvania
Inc.

Radio Shack™

Radio-Television
News Directors
Association

Radisson, Pierre
Esprit

Radisson Inn

Radner, Gilda

Radnor

Radziwill, Lee

Rae, Charlotte

Raeburn, Sir Henry

Ra Expeditions, The

Rafferty, Gerry

Raffin, Deborah

Raffles, Sir Thomas

Raffles Hotel

Rafsanjani, Ali Akbar Hashemi

Raft, George

Raft of the Medusa, The

Ragavoy, Gerry

Raggedy Ann and Andy

Raging Bull

Raglan, Lord

Ragnarok

Ragtime

Rahal, Bobby

RAH-66 Comanche

Rahway

Raiders of the Lost Ark

Railroad Club of Chicago, The

Railroad Model Craftsman

Railroad Retirement Board

Rails-to-Trails Conservancy

Railway Labor Act

Railway Progress Institute

Raimondi, Marcantonio

Rainbow Bridge

Rainbow Bridge National Monument

Rainbow Division

Rainbow Family of Living Light

Rainbow Landscape, The

Rainbow Walkers

Rainbow Warrior

Rainer, Luise

Raines, Ella

Rainey, Joseph H.

Rainey, Ma

Rainforest Action Network

Rainforest Alliance

Rain Man

Rains, Claude

Rainwater, Marvin

Rainwater, Richard

Rainy Day Books

Rainy Lake

Raisa, Rosa

Raisin

Raisin in the Sun, A

Raisin River Massacre

Raitt, Bonnie

Raitt, John

Rajab

Rajneesh, Bhagwan Shree

Rajneesh Foundation International

Rake's Progress, The

Rákóczy, Francis

Rákóczy, George

Rákóczy, Sigismund

Rákóczy March

Ralegh var. of Raleigh, Sir Walter

Raleigh

Raleigh or Ralegh, Sir Walter

Raleigh-Durham

Raleigh-Durham International Airport

Raleigh News & Observer, The

Raley's store

Ralston, Esther

Ralston, Vera Hruba

Ralston Purina Company

Ralston Purina Trust Fund

Ramada Hotel

Ramada Inn

Ramadan

Ramada Renaissance Hotel

Ramakrishna, Sri

Raman, Sir Chandrasekhara Venkata

Ramana Maharshi

Raman effect

Raman spectrum

Ramapo College of New Jersey

Ramapo Mountains

Rama's Bridge

Ramayana

Rambeau, Marjorie

Rambo

Rambo, Dack

Ramboesque

Rambo First Blood Part II

Ramboism

Rambo III

Rambouillet

Rambouillet sheep

Ram Dass

Rameau, Jean Philippe

Ramée, Louis de la

Ramey, Samuel

Ramirez, Richard

Ramirez College of Business and Technology

Ramis, Harold

Ramone, Johnny

Ramones, The

Rampal, Jean-Pierre

Ramsauer, Carl

Ramsauer-Townsend effect

Ramsay, Allan

Ramsay, George

Ramsay, Sir William

Ramsden, Jesse

Ramsden eyepiece

Ramses

Ramsey

Ramsey, Arthur Michael

Ramsey Lewis Trio

Ran

Rancho Bernardo Inn

Rancho Cordova

Rancho Cucamonga

Rancho Santiago Community College

Rand, The

Rand, Ayn

Rand, Sally

Rand, Yeoman Janice

Randall, Tony

Rand Corporation

Rand Graduate School of Policy Studies

Rand McNally and Company

Rand McNally—The Map and Travel Store

Randolph

Randolph, A. Philip

Randolph, Edmund

Randolph, George Wythe

Randolph, John

Randolph, Joyce

Randolph, William

Randolph Air Force Base

Randolph Community College

Randolph-Macon College

Randolph-Macon Woman's College

Randolph of Roanoke, John

Random House™ Books

Random House Dictionary of the English Language, The

Random House, Inc.

Randy

Rangel, Charles

Rangeley Lakes

Ranger

Ranger Junior College

Ranger Rick

Ranger Rick's Nature Club

Rangoon [aka Yangon]

Rangos, John G., Sr.

Ranikhet disease

Rank, J. Arthur

Rank, Otto

Ranke, Leopold von

Ranken Technical College

Rankin

Rankin, Jeanette

Rankine, William J. M.

Rankine cycle

Rankine-cycle engine

Rankine scale

Rankine temperature scale

Rank Organisation, The

Ranks, Shabba

Ransom, John Crowe

Ransome, Arthur

Rantekombola

Rantoul

Ranvier, Louis A.

Rao, P. V. Narasimha

Rao, Raja

Raoul

Raoult, François

Raoult's law

Raoul Wallenberg Committee of the United States

Rapallo

Rape of Europa, The

Rape of Lucrece, The

Rape of the Daughters of Leucippus

Rape of the Lock, The

Rape of the Sabine Women, The

Raphael

Raphael, Saint

Raphael, Sally Jesse

Rapidan

Rapid City

Rapid Deployment Force

Rapp, George

Rappahannock

Rappahannock Community College
Rappaport, David
Rappist
Rappite
Rapson's slide
Rapunzel
Raritan
Raritan Valley Community College
Rarotonga
Ras al Khaymah
Rascals, The
Ras Dashan
Rashad, Ahmad
Rashad, Phylicia
Rashōmon
Rask, Rasmus Christian
Raskin, Ellen
Rasmussen, Knud
Raspberries, The
Rasputin, Grigori
Ras Shamra
Ras Tafari
Rastafarian
Rastafarianism
Ratelle, Jean
Rathaus, Karol
Rathbone, Basil
Rathenau, Walther
Rather, Dan
Rathke, Martin Heinrich
Rathke's pocket
Rathke's pouch
Rathlin Island
Rat Islands
Ratoff, Gregory

Raton
Rattigan, Sir Terence
Rattner, Abraham
Ratzenberger, John
Rauschenberg, Robert
Ravel, Maurice
Ravello cathedral
Raven, Eddy
Ravenna
Ravensbrück
Ravenswood
Ravinia Festival
Ravinia Park
Rawalpindi
Rawhide
Rawlings, Marjorie Kinnan
Rawlins
Rawlins, Lester
Rawlinson, George
Rawlinson, Sir Henry Creswicke
Rawls, Lou
Ray, Aldo
Ray, Charles
Ray, Dixy Lee
Ray, James Earl
Ray, Johnnie
Ray, Man
Ray, Satyajit
Rayburn, Gene
Rayburn, Sam
Raychem Corporation
Raychem Foundation
Ray College of Design
Ray Conniff Orchestra
Raye, Martha
Rayleigh, John William Strutt

Rayleigh disk
Rayleigh scattering
Rayleigh wave
Raymond
Raymond, Alex
Raymond, Gene
Raymond, Henry Jarvis
Raymondville
Raynaud's disease
Raynaud's phenomenon
Rayne
Rayonnant style
Ray Sports Radio Network
Raytheon Company
Raytown
Rayville
Razaf, Andy
RBC Dominion Securities Inc.
RBC Dominion Securities Ltd.
RCA Corporation
RCA Credit Corporation
RCA Rockefeller Center
RC-130 Hercules
Re *occas.* Ra
React International
Read, George
Read, Sir Herbert
Reade, Charles
Reader's Digest, The
Reader's Digest Association, Inc., The
Reader's Digest Foundation

Reader's Digest Press

Reader's Market bookstore

Reading [* MA; OH; PA; *see also* Redding]

Reading Area Community College

Reading Is Fundamental

Readmore bookstore

Reagan, Nancy

Reagan, Ron [son of Ronald Reagan]

Reagan, Ronald

Reaganomics

Real Estate Brokerage Council

Real Estate Mortgage Advisory, Ltd.

real McCoy, the

Real McCoys, The [television series]

Real People

Realpolitik *occas.* realpolitik

Real Presence

Real Thing, The

Realtor™

Realtors National Marketing Institute

Reaney, James

Reasoner, Harry

Reason Foundation

Reaumur *or* Réaumur, René Antoine Ferchault de

Reaumur *or* Réaumur scale

Rebecca

Rebecca Kelly Dance Company

Rebecca of Sunnybrook Farm

Rebekah

Rebel without a Cause

Reblochon cheese

Récamier, Madame

Récamier bed

Received Pronunciation

Received Standard English

Recife

Recklinghausen

Reconstruction

Reconstruction Acts

Reconstruction Finance Corporation

Reconstructionism

Reconstructionist

Reconstructionist Rabbinical College

Recording for the Blind

Recording Industry Association of America

Recreational Equipment, Inc.

Recreation Vehicle Industry Association

Red

Red Angus

Red Army

Red Badge of Courage, The

Red Balloon

Red Bank

Red Bluff

Redbook Magazine

Red Branch

Red Brigades

Red Carpet Real Estate Service, Inc.

Red China

Red Cloud

Red Cloud Indian School

Red Crescent

Red Cross, The

Red Cross Knight

Red Deer

Red Desert

Redding [* CA; CT; *see also* Reading]

Redding, Otis

Reddy, Helen

Redemptorist

Red Feather

Redfield, Robert

Redford, Robert

Redgrave, Lynn

Redgrave, Sir Michael

Redgrave, Vanessa

Red Guards

Red Hats

Redhead

Red Hot Chili Peppers

Red Indian

Redlands

Red Lion

Red Lion Inn

Red Lobster restaurant

Redman, Don

Redmond

Redmond Products, Inc.

Red Oak

Redon, Odilon

Redondo Beach

Red Petals

Red Poll *occas.* Red
Polled cattle

Red River

Red River of the
North

Red River Rebellion

Red River Settlement

Red River War

Red Rock chicken

Red Rocks
Community College

Red Ryder

red Sally

Red Sea

Red Skelton Show,
The

Red Square

Red Star Army
Chorus and Dance
Ensemble

Redstone, Sumner
Murray

Redstone Arsenal

Redstone missile

Red Wing

Redwood City

Redwood Falls

Redwood National
Park

Reebok Foundation

Reebok International
Ltd.

Reed, Sir Carol

Reed, Donna

Reed, Ishmael

Reed, Jerry

Reed, John

Reed, Lou

Reed, Oliver

Reed, Rex

Reed, Robert

Reed, Walter C.

Reed, Willis

Reed College

Reed International

Reed Organ Society,
Inc.

Reedsburg

Reedsport

Reelfoot Lake

Reese, Della

Reese, Pee Wee

Reese Air Force Base

Reeve, Christopher

Reeve Aleutian
Airways, Inc.

Reeves, Del

Reeves, George

Reeves, Jim

Reeves, Keanu

Reeves, Steve

Reformation

Reform Bill

Reformed Bible
College

Reformed Church in
America

Reformed Church in
the United States

Reformed Episcopal
Church

Reformed Methodist
Union Episcopal
Church

Reformed
Presbyterian Church
in North America

Reformed Theological
Seminary

Reform flask

Reform Jew

Reform Judaism

Refrigerating
Engineers and
Technicians
Association

Refugee Policy Group

Refugio

Regalbuto, Joe

Regal 8 Inn

Regan, Ronald

Régence

Regency

Regency Cruises Inc.

Regency style

Regent's Park

Regent University

Reger, Max

Regina

Reginald of Châtillon

Regional Airline
Association

Regional Plan
Association

Regional Seminary of
Saint Vincent de
Paul

Regis and Kathie Lee

Regis College

Registered Financial
Planners Institute

Registry of
Interpreters for the
Deaf

Regular Army

Regulation T

Regulation U

Regulator movement

Regulus

Regulus, Marcus
Atilius

Rehnquist, William H.
Rehoboam
Rehoboth
Rehoboth Beach
Reich
Reich, Wilhelm
Reichenbach Falls
Reichsführer
Reichsregiment
Reichstag
Reichswehr
Reid, Daphne Maxwell
Reid, Elizabeth Ann
Reid, Frances
Reid, Kate
Reid, Mike
Reid, Tim
Reid, Wallace
Reid, Whitelaw
Reid State Technical College
Reidsville
Reign of Terror
Reik, Theodor
Reil, Johann Christian
Reilly, Charles Nelson
Reimann, Georg Friedrich Bernhard
Reims *var. of* Rheims
Reims *var. of* Rheims cathedral
Reindeer Lake
Reinecke, Carl
Reiner, Carl
Reiner, Fritz
Reiner, Rob
Reinhardt, Ad
Reinhardt, Django

Reinhardt, Max
Reinhardt College
Reinhart, DeWayne B.
Reinhold, Judge
Reinking, Ann
Reiter, Hans
Reiter's disease
Reiter's syndrome
Reitman, Ivan
Reivers, The
Reliance Electric Company
Reliance Electric Company Charitable Scientific and Educational Foundation
Reliance Group Holdings, Inc.
Reliance Insurance Company
Religion in American Life
Religious Booksellers Association
Religious Education Association
Religious News Service
Religious of the Cenacle
Religious of the Sacred Heart
Religious Society of Friends
Religious Society of Friends (Conservative)
Remagen
Remarque, Erich Maria
Rembrandt

Remembrance Day
Remembrance of Things Past
Remembrance Sunday
Remick, Lee
Remington, Eliphalet
Remington, Frederic
Remington, Philo
Remington Steele
Remus
Renaissance
Renaissance architecture
Renaissance art
Renaissance Bookstore
Renaissance man
Renaissance Society of America
Renascence
Renault
Renault, Mary
Rend Lake College
Renée
Renewable Natural Resources Foundation
Renfrew
Renfrewshire
Reni, Guido
Rennie, Michael
Reno
Reno, Janet
Reno, Jesse Lee
Reno Cannon International Airport
Reno Gazette-Journal
Renoir, Jean
Renoir, Pierre Auguste

Renovo

Rensselaer

Rensselaer, Kiliaen *or* Killian van

Rensselaer, Stephen Van

Rensselaer Polytechnic Institute

Renton

Renwick, James, Jr.

Renwick Gallery

Reo

Reorganized Church of Jesus Christ of Latter Day Saints

REO Speedwagon

Repertory Dance Theatre

Repertory Theatre of Lincoln Center

Repin, Ilya

Replogle™ globe

Repplier, Agnes

Republican

Republican Governors Association

Republican National Committee

Republican National Convention

Republican Party

Republic National Bank of New York

Republic New York Corporation

Republic of China

Republic of Korea

Republic of South Africa

Republic of Togo

Republic Pictures Corporation

Requiem Mass

Resaca de la Palma

Rescue 911

Research College of Nursing

Research to Prevent Blindness Association

Research Triangle

Research Triangle Park

Reserve

Reserve Officers Association of the United States

Reserve Officer Training Corps

Reshevsky, Samuel

Resnick, Burton Paul

Resnik, Regina

Resolution Island

Resolution Trust Corporation

Resource Center for the Handicapped

Resources for the Future, Inc.

Respighi, Ottorino

Restigouche

Restless Heart

Reston, James

Restoration

Retail News Bureau

Retail, Wholesale and Department Store Union

Rethel, Alfred

Retired Enlisted Association

Retired Officer Magazine, The

Retired Officers Association

Retired Senior Volunteer Program

RETS Education Center

RETS Electronic Institute

RETS Institute of Technology

RETS Technical Center

RETS Training Center

Retton, Mary Lou

Return of Martin Guerre, The

Return of the Jedi

Return of the Jedi Storybook

Return of the Native, The

Reuben

Reuben Award

Reubenite

Reunion Arena

Reunion in Vienna

Réunion Island

Reuter, Paul Julius von

Reuters Holdings

Reuters Information Services

Reuters Ltd.

Reuther, Walter

Revelation of Saint John the Divine, The

Revelations

Revels, Hiram R.

Revelstoke

Revere

Revere, Anne

Revere, Paul

Reverend Ike

Reversing Falls of Saint John

Review and Herald Publishing Association

Revillagigedo Islands

Revised Standard Version [of the Bible]

Revised Version of the Bible

Revival of Learning

Revival of Letters

Revival of Literature

Revlon-Realistic Professional Products, Inc.

Revolutionary calendar

Revolutionary War

Revolutionary War in America

Revolution of 1848

Rex

Rexburg

Rexnord Foundation

Rexnord Inc.

Rexroth, Kenneth

Rey, Alejandro

Rey, Fernando

Reye, R. D. K.

Reye's *occas.* Reye syndrome

Reykjavik

Reykjavik Airport

Reymont, Władysław

Reynard the Fox

Reynaud, Paul

Reynolds, Burt

Reynolds, Debbie

Reynolds, Donald Worthington

Reynolds, Gene

Reynolds, Frank

Reynolds, Sir Joshua

Reynolds, Kevin

Reynolds Aluminum Recycling Center

Reynolds and Reynolds Company

Reynoldsburg

Reynolds Metals Company

Reynolds Metals Company Foundation

Reynolds number

Reynolds Self-Portrait

Reynoldsville

Reynolds Wrap™

Reynosa

Reza Shah Pahlavi

R factor

RFD-TV

RF-4 Phantom II

Rhaetian Alps

Rhanikhet disease

Rhapsody in Blue

Rhapsody on a Theme of Paganini

Rhea

Rhee, Syngman

Rheims *or* Reims

Rheims *or* Reims Cathedral

Rheims-Douay Bible

Rheims-Douay Version [of the Bible]

Rheingold

RHEMA International

Rhenish State Mountains

Rhesus factor

Rh factor

Rhine

Rhinebeck

Rhine canals

Rhinegrave breeches

Rhine-Herne Canal

Rhineland

Rhinelander

Rhineland-Palatinate

Rhine-Main-Danube Canal

Rhine-Marne Canal

Rhine Palatinate

Rhinestone Cowboy

Rhine wine

R. H. Macy and Company, Inc.

Rh negative

Rhoads, D. Dean

Rhoda

Rhode Island

Rhode Island bent

Rhode Island College

Rhode Islander

Rhode Island Monthly

Rhode Island Red

Rhode Island School of Design

Rhode Island White

Rhodes

Rhodes, Cecil John

Rhodes, Eugene Manlove

Rhodes, James Ford
Rhodes College
Rhodes grass
Rhodesia [*now* Zimbabwe]
Rhodesian
Rhodesian man
Rhodesian ridgeback
Rhodes scholar
Rhodes Scholarship
Rhodian
Rhône
Rhône-Alpes
Rhone-Poulenc
Rhone-Poulenc Rorer Inc.
Rhone wine
Rho Psi
Rh positive
Rhue, Madlyn
Rhynchocoela
Rhys, Jean
Rhys-Davies, John
Rhythm and Blues Rock and Roll Society, Inc.
Rialto
Rialto Bridge
Rialto Center
Riau Archipelago
Ribbentrop, Joachim von
Ribbon Falls
Ribera, José *or* Jusepe
Ribicoff, Abraham
Ricardo, David
Riccati, Jacopo Francesco
Riccati equation
Ricci, Sebastiano

Rice, Donna
Rice, Elmer
Rice, Grantland
Rice, Jerry
Rice, Jim
Rice, Sam
Rice Council for Market Development
Rice Growers Association
Rice Millers' Association
Rice University
Rice University Press
Rich, Adrienne
Rich, Buddy
Rich, Charlie
Rich, Frank
Rich, Marc
Rich, Robert Edward, Sr.
Richard
Richard, Cliff
Richard, Maurice
Richard Bland College of the College of William and Mary
Richard de Bury
Richard Diamond, Private Detective
Richard J. Daley Center
Richard J. Daley Plaza
Richard Nixon Presidential Museum and Birthplace
Richard of Devizes
Richard of Saint Victor

Richard Roe
Richards, Ann
Richards, I. A.
Richards, Keith
Richards, Kim
Richards, Laura
Richards, Lloyd
Richards, Theodore William
Richards, Thomas Addison
Richards, William Trost
Richards-Gebaur Air Force Base
Richardson
Richardson, Elliot
Richardson, Henry Handel
Richardson, Henry Hobson
Richardson, Sir John
Richardson, Sir Owen Williams
Richardson, Sir Ralph David
Richardson, Samuel
Richardson, Tony
Richardson ground squirrel
Richardson-Vicks Inc.
Richard the Lion-Hearted
Richard III Society
Richelieu
Richelieu, Cardinal
Richfield
Richfield Coliseum
Richie, Lionel
Richier, Germaine
Richier, Ligier

Richie Rich

Richland [* CA; WA; see also Richlands]

Richland Center

Richland College

Richland Community College

Richland Hills

Richlands [* VA]

Richler, Mordecai

Richman, Peter Mark

Rich Man, Poor Man

Richmond

Richmond College

Richmond Community College

Richmond Heights

Richmond International Airport (Byrd Field)

Richmond International Raceway

Richmond National Battlefield Park

Richmond-San Rafael Bridge

Richmond Times-Dispatch

Rich Mountain Community College

Rich Stadium

Richter, Charles F.

Richter, Conrad

Richter, Hans

Richter, Ludwig

Richter, Sviatoslav

Richter magnitude

Richter scale

Richthofen, Baron

Richthofen's Flying Circus

Richwood

Rickenbacker, Eddie

Rickey, Branch

Rickles, Don

Rickman, Alan

Rickover, Hyman

Ricks College

Ricoh Company, Ltd.

Riddle, Nelson

Ride, Sally

Rideau Canal

Rider College

Rider College Broncs

Riders of the Purple Sage

Ridgecrest

Ridgefield

Ridgefield Park

Ridgewood

Ridgway, Matthew B.

Riding Mountain National Park

Ridley

Ridley, Nicholas

Ridley Park

Riegert, Peter

Riegger, Wallingford

Riel, Louis

Riel's Rebellion

Riemann, Bernhard

Riemann, Georg

Riemannian geometry

Riemannian integral

Riemann integral

Riemann sphere

Riemann-Stieltjes integral

Riemann surface

Riemann zeta function

Riemenschneider, Tilman

Rienzi, Cola di

Riesling

Riesz space

Rietti, Vittorio

Rietveld, Gerrit Thomas

Riff, *n.*, *pl.* Riff *or* Riffi *or* Riffs

Riffe Lake

Rifleman, The

Rif Mountains

Riga

Rigby, Cathy

Rigel

Rigg, Diana

Riggs, Bobby

Riggs, John M.

Riggs' disease

Riggs-Hall, Carla

Riggs National Bank

Right Bank

Righteous Brothers, The

Righteous Harmony Fists

Right Reverend

Right Said Fred

Rigoletto

Rig-Veda

Riis, Jacob

Rijksmuseum *or* Rijks Museum *or* Ryks Museum

Rika Breuer Teachers Seminary

Riker, Commander William

Rikki-Tikki-Tavi

Riklis, Meshulam

Riklis Family
Corporation

Riles, Wilson C.

Riley, Bridget

Riley, James
Whitcomb

Riley, Jeannie C.

Rilke, Rainer Maria

Rillieux, Norbert

Rimbaud, Arthur

Rime of the Ancient
Mariner

Rimini

Rimmer, William

Rimsky-Korsakov,
Nikolai

Rinehart, Mary
Roberts

Rinehart, William
Henry

Ring Cycle

Ringer, Sydney

Ringer's *occas.* Ringer
solution

Ringling Brothers and
Barnum & Bailey
Circus

Ringling Museums

Ringling School of
Art and Design

Ring nebula

Ring of the Nibelung
[a magic ring]

Ring of the Nibelung,
The [Wagner's Ring
Cycle]

Ringwald, Molly

Ringwood

Rinker, Marshall
Edison

Rinker Companies
Foundation

Rinker Materials
Corporation

Rin Tin Tin

Río Balsas

Rio Bravo

Rio de Janeiro

Rio de Janeiro
International
Airport

[Rio de Janeiro]
Modern Art
Museum

[Rio de Janeiro]
National Museum
of Fine Arts

Río de la Plata

Rio Grande

Rio Grande City

Río Grande de
Santiago

Rio Grande Industries,
Inc.

Rio Grande National
Forest

Rio Grande Project

Rio Grande Valley
International
Airport

Rio Grande Wild and
Scenic River
National Parkway

Rio Hondo College

Río Negro

Riopelle, Jean Paul

Río Salado

Rio Salado College

Riot Act

Rio Treaty

Rio Vista

Ripken, Cal, Jr.

Ripley, George

Ripley, Robert

Ripley's Believe It or
Not

Ripon

Ripon College

Ripon Society

Rip Van Winkle

Ririe-Woodbury
Dance Company

Rise of Silas Lapham,
The

Risorgimento

Ritalin™

Ritchard, Cyril

Ritchie, Jean

Rite Aid Corporation

Rite of Spring, The

Ritschl, Albert

Ritschlian

Ritschlianism

Ritt, Martin

Rittenhouse, David

Ritter, John

Ritter, Joseph Cardinal

Ritter, Tex

Ritter, Thelma

Rittman

Ritz, Al

Ritz, Harry

Ritz, Jim

Ritz Brothers

Ritz-Carlton

Ritz *occas.* Ritz's
combination
principle

Rivera, Chita

Rivera, Diego

Rivera, Geraldo

Rivera, José de

River Avon
River Bank America
River Brethren
River Clyde
Riverdale
River Downs
River Edge
River Forest
Riverfront Coliseum
Riverfront Stadium
River Grove
Riverhead
River Jordan
River Niger, The
River Oaks
River Rouge
Rivers, Joan
Rivers, Johnny
Rivers, Larry
Rivers, Melissa
River São Francisco
River Severn
River Shannon
Riverside
Riverside Community
College
[Riverside] Press-
Enterprise, The
River Styx
River Thames
Riverton
Riverview
Riviera
Riviera Beach
Rivier College
Rixey, Eppa
Riyadh
Rizal, José
Rizal Day

Rizzio, David
Rizzo, Frank L.
Rizzoli Bookstore
Rizzuto, Phil
R. J. Reynolds
Tobacco Company
RJR Nabisco
Foundation
RJR Nabisco Holdings
Corporation
RJR Nabisco, Inc.
R. L. Polk and
Company
Roach, Hal
Roach, Max
Roach Motel™
Road & Track
Road Atlanta
Road near L'Estaque
Road Not Taken, The
Road Runner Show,
The
Roadway Express,
Inc.
Roadway Package
System, Inc.
Roadway Services,
Inc.
Roane State
Community College
Roanoke
Roanoke bells
Roanoke Bible
College
Roanoke-Chowan
Community College
Roanoke College
Roanoke colony
Roanoke Island
Roanoke Rapids

Roanoke Times and
World-News
Roaring Spring
Roaring '20s *occas.*
Roaring Twenties
Robards, Jason, Jr.
Robards, Jason, Sr.
Robbe-Grillet, Alain
Robbia, Andrea della
Robbia, Luca della
Robbins, Harold
Robbins, Jerome
Robbins, Marty
Robbins, Tim
Robbins, Tom
Robbinsdale
Robb Report
Robert
Robert Bellarmine,
Saint
Robert Campeau
Family Foundation
(United States)
Robert E. Lee
Memorial, The
Robert F. Kennedy
Memorial Stadium
Robert-Houdin, Jean
Eugènie
Robert I. Wishnick
Foundation
Robert Joffrey Ballet
Robert Montgomery
Presents
Robert Morris College
Robert Morris College
Colonials
Robert Moses Dam
Robert of Courtenay
Robert of Geneva
Robert of Gloucester

Robert of Jumièges

Robert of Molesme, Saint

Robert Q. Lewis Show, The

Roberts, Sir Charles George

Roberts, Doris

Roberts, Elizabeth Madox

Roberts, Eric

Roberts, George R.

Roberts, Julia

Roberts, Kenneth L.

Roberts, Marcus

Roberts, Oral

Roberts, Pernell

Roberts, Robin

Roberts, Tanya

Roberts, Tony

Robert Shaw Chorale

Robertson, Cliff

Robertson, Dale

Robertson, Oscar

Robertson, Pat

Robertson-Ceco Corporation

Robert's Rules of Order

Roberts Wesleyan College

Robert the Bruce

Robert the Devil

Robert the Strong

Robert Wood Johnson Foundation

Robeson, Paul

Robeson Community College

Robespierre, Maximilien

Robin

Robin, Christopher

Robin, Leo

Robin Goodfellow

Robin Hood

Robin Hood: Prince of Thieves

Robin Hood's Merry Men

Robins Air Force Base

Robinson

Robinson, Bill Bojangles

Robinson, Boardman

Robinson, Brooks

Robinson, Charles

Robinson, Eddie

Robinson, Edward G.

Robinson, Edwin Arlington

Robinson, Frank

Robinson, Holly

Robinson, Jackie

Robinson, James H.

Robinson, Jesse Mack

Robinson, Larry

Robinson, Max

Robinson, Sir Robert

Robinson, Smokey

Robinson, Sugar Ray

Robinson, Theodore

Robinson, Wilbert

Robinson Crusoe

Robinson-Patman Act

Robin's *occas.* robin's plantain

Robin the Boy Wonder

Robitussin™

RoboCop

RoboCop 2

Robotic Industries Association

Robot Man

Rob Roy

Robson, May

Robstown

Robus, Hugh

Rochambeau, Jean Baptiste de

Rochambeau International Airport

Roche, Eugene

Roche, Kevin

Roche Group

Roche Laboratories

Roche limit

Rochelle

Rochelle Park

Rochelle powders

Rochelle salt

Rochester

Rochester Business Institute

Rochester Community College

Rochester Community Savings Bank

Rochester Democrat and Chronicle

Rochester Gas and Electric Corporation

Rochester Institute of Technology

Rochester Philharmonic Orchestra

Rochester Telephone Corporation

Rochester Times-Union

Rock and Roll Hall of Fame

Rock and Roll Hall of Fame Foundation

Rock around the Clock

Rockaway

Rock Cornish

Rock Creek Park

Rockdale

Rockefeller, David

Rockefeller, Jay

Rockefeller, John D.

Rockefeller, John D., Jr.

Rockefeller, John D., III

Rockefeller, Laurance S.

Rockefeller, Nelson

Rockefeller, William

Rockefeller, Winthrop

Rockefeller Center

Rockefeller Foundation, The

Rockefeller Plaza

Rockefeller University

Rockettes, The

Rock Falls

Rockford

Rockford College

Rockford Files, The

Rock Hill

Rockhurst College

Rockies, the

Rockingham Community College

Rock Island

Rock Island Line

Rockland

Rockland Community College

Rockledge

Rockne, Knute

Rock of Gibraltar

Rockport

Rock River

Rock Springs

Rock Valley College

Rockville

Rockville Centre

Rockwell, Norman

Rockwell, Robert

Rockwell, Stanley P.

Rockwell International Corporation

Rockwell International Corporation Trust

Rockwell number

Rockwell test

Rockwood

Rocky

Rocky and Bullwinkle

Rocky V

Rocky Ford

Rocky IV

Rocky Grove

Rocky Hill

Rocky Horror Picture Show, The

Rocky Mount

Rocky Mountain Arsenal

Rocky Mountain bee plant

Rocky Mountain bighorn

Rocky Mountain Coal Mining Institute

Rocky Mountain College

Rocky Mountain College of Art and Design

Rocky Mountain elk

Rocky Mountain flowering raspberry

Rocky Mountain goat

Rocky Mountain juniper

Rocky Mountain National Park

Rocky Mountain News

Rocky Mountain oyster

Rocky Mountain red cedar

Rocky Mountains

Rocky Mountain sheep

Rocky Mountain spotted fever

Rocky Mountain States

Rocky Mountain whitefish

Rocky Mountain white pine

Rocky River

Rocky III

Rocky II

Rodale Institute

Rodale International

Rodale Press, Inc.

Rod & Custom

Roddenberry, Gene

Rodeo Drive

Roderick

Rodeway Inn

Rodgers, Jimmie

Rodgers, Richard

Rodgers and
Hammerstein

Rodgers and Hart

Rodia, Simon

Rodin, Auguste

Rodrigo, Joaquin

Rodrigues, Percy

Rodriguez, Chi Chi

Rodriguez, Johnny

Rodriguez, Richard

Rodzinski, Artur

Roe, Richard

Roebling, John A.

Roehm, Carolyne

Roeland Park

Roelas, Juan de las

Roemer, Charles E.

Roemer, Olaus

Roentgen, Wilhelm

Roentgen ray

Roerich, Nicholas

Roethke, Theodore

Roe v. Wade

Rogaine™

Rogation Day

Roger

Roger of Hoveden

Roger of Wendover

Roger Rabbit

Rogers

Rogers, Bernard

Rogers, Bruce

Rogers, Buck

Rogers, Carl

Rogers, Charles

Rogers, Fred

Rogers, Ginger

Rogers, James Gamble

Rogers, John

Rogers, Kenny

Rogers, Mimi

Rogers, Robert

Rogers, Roy

Rogers, Shorty

Rogers, Wayne

Rogers, Will

Rogers, Will, Jr.

Rogers City

Rogers Dry Lake

Rogers' Rangers

Rogers State College

Rogersville

Roger Wagner Chorale

Roger Williams
College

Roger Williams
National Memorial

Roget, Peter Mark

[Roget's] Thesaurus of
English Words and
Phrases

Rogue

Rogue Community
College

Rogue River National
Forest

Rogun Dam

Rohm and Haas
Company

Rohr Inc.

Roh Tae Woo

Rojas, Fernando de

Rokeby Venus, The

Roland

Roland, Gilbert

Rolf, Ida

Rolfe, John

Rolfing™

Rolla

Rolland, Romain

Roll Call Report
Syndicate Service

Rolle, Esther

Rolle, Michael

Rollerblade, Inc.

Rollerblade™ in-line
skates

Roller Derby™
entertainment

Roller Derby™ in-line
skates

Roller Skating Rink
Operators
Association

Rolle's theorem

Rolling Hills Estates

Rolling Meadows

Rolling Stone

Rolling Stones, The

Rollins, Howard

Rollins, Orville
Wayne

Rollins, Sonny

Rollins College

Rollins, Inc.

Rollms Environmental
Services, Inc.

Rolls-Royce Motors
Inc.

Rolscreen Company

Romagna

Romains, Jules

Roman

Roman, Ruth

Roman alphabet

Roman arch

Roman architecture

Roman art

Roman brick

Roman calendar
Roman candle
Roman Catholic
Roman Catholic
  Church
Roman Catholicism
Romance language
Roman Circus
Roman collar
Roman Curia
Roman Empire
Romanesque
Romanesque
  architecture
Romanesque art
Roman Forum
Roman holiday
Romania *occas.*
  Rumania
Romanian *occas.*
  Rumanian
Romanian language
Romanian literature
Romanian Orthodox
  Church in America
Romanian Orthodox
  Episcopate of
  America
Romanic
Romanism
Romanist
Romanistic
Roman law
Roman liturgy
Roman mile
Roman nettle
Roman nose
Roman notation clock
Roman numeral
Romano

Romanov, Mikhail
  Feodorovich
Romanov dynasty
Roman pace
Roman peace
Roman punch
Roman religion
Roman Republic
Roman ride
Roman rite
Roman roads
Romans at the
  Decadence
Roman senate
Romansh *or*
  Romansch
Roman strike
Romantic Classicism
Romantic Movement
roman *occas.* Roman
  type
Romanus
Roman walls
Roman wormwood
Romany, *n., pl.*
  Romanies
Romany rye
Romayne work
Romberg, Sigmund
Rome
Rome, Harold
Rome Airport
Rome Beauty
Rome Ciampino
  Airport
Romeo
Romeo and Juliet
Romeoville
Romero, Cesar
Romish

Romishness
Rommel, Erwin
Romney
Romney, George
Romney Marsh
Romper Room
Romulo, Carlos
Romulus
Romulus and Remus
Romulus Augustulus
Ronald
Ronald McDonald's
  Children's Charities
Ronda
Ronettes, The
Ronkokoma
Ronsard, Pierre de
Ronstadt, Linda
Rooker, Michael
Rookies, The
Rookwood pottery
Room 222
Rooney, Andy
Rooney, Mickey
Rooney, Pat
Roosevelt
Roosevelt, Eleanor
Roosevelt, Franklin
  Delano
Roosevelt, James
Roosevelt, Theodore
Roosevelt-Campobello
  International Park
Roosevelt Corollary
Roosevelt Dam
Rooseveltian
Roosevelt National
  Forest
Roosevelt Park

Roosevelt University
Root, Elihu
Root, John Wellborn
Roots
Roots blower
Roper Organization
Roper Poll
Roper Report
Rops, Félicien
Roquefort
Roquefort cheese
Rorem, Ned
Rorer Group, Inc.
Rorschach, Hermann
Rorschach test
Rosa, Salvator
Rosalind Newman and Dancers
Rosamond
Rosary College
Rose, Axl
Rose, Billy
Rose, Charlie
Rose, David
Rose, Mauri
Rose, Pete
Rose, Vincent
Roseanne
Rose Bowl
Rosebud Educational Society
Roseburg
Rosecrans, William Starke
Rosecroft Raceway
Rosedale
rose d'Anvers
Rose family

Rose-Hulman Institute of Technology
Roseland
Roselle
Roselle Park
Roselli, Cosimo
Rosellino, Antonio
Rose Marie [entertainer; operetta]
Rosemarie [given name]
Rosemary
Rosemead
Rosemont College
Rosenberg
Rosenberg, Alfred
Rosenberg, Ethel
Rosenberg, Julius
Rosenberg, Ruth Blaustein
Rosenberg case
Rosenborg Castle Collections
Rosencrantz and Guildenstern
Rosencrantz and Guildenstern Are Dead
Rosenquist, James
Rosenwald, Julius
rose of China
rose of Heaven
rose of Jericho
Rose of Lima, Saint
rose of Sharon
Rose Parade
Rose State College
Rose Tattoo, The
Rosetta stone

Roseville [* CA; MI; MN; see also Rossville]
Rosewall, Ken
Rosewood Heights
Rosh Hashanah
Rosicrucian
Rosicrucian Digest
Rosicrucianism
Rosicrucian Order
Rosie the Riveter
Roslyn
Roslyn rig
Roslyn yawl
Rosollino, Frank
Ross
Ross, Barnaby
Ross, Betsy
Ross, Diana
Ross, Harold
Ross, Sir James Clark
Ross, Sir John
Ross, Katharine
Ross, Marion
Ross, Nellie Taylor
Ross, Sir Ronald
Ross Dam
Ross Dependency
Rossellini, Isabella
Rossellini, Roberto
Rossetti, Christina
Rossetti, Dante Gabriel
Rossford
Rossford Ordnance Depot
Ross Ice Shelf
Rossini, Gioacchino
Ross Island

Ross Lake National Recreation Area

Ross Sea

Ross Stores, Inc.

Rossville [* GA; *see also* Roseville]

Rostand, Edmond

Rostand, Jean

Rosten, Leo

Rostenkowski, Dan

Rostov

Rostovtzeff, M. I.

Rostow, Eugene

Rostow, Walt Whitman

Rostropovich, Mstislav

Roswell

Roswitha

Roszak, Theodore

Rotarian [member of a Rotary Club]

Rotarian, The [magazine]

Rotarianism

Rotary Club

Rotary International

Rote, Kyle, Jr.

Roth, Cheryl

Roth, Christian Francis

Roth, David Lee

Roth, Henry

Roth, Lillian

Roth, Mark

Roth, Philip

Rothenstein, Sir William

Rothko, Mark

Rothschild, Amschel Mayer

Rothschild, Guy de

Rothschild, James *or* Jakob

Rothschild, Karl Mayer

Rothschild, Baron Lionel de

Rothschild, Lionel Nathan

Rothschild, Lionel Walter

Rothschild, Mayer Amschel

Rothschild, Nathan Mayer

Rothschild, Sir Nathan Mayer

Rothschild, Salomon Mayer

Rothstein, Arnold

Roth v. United States

Rotifera

Rotterdam

Rottweiler

Rouault, Georges

Rouen

Rouen Cathedral

Rouen lilac

Rouge

Rouget de Lisle, Claude Joseph

Rough Rider

Round Butte Dam

Roundhead

Round Lake Beach

Round Lake Park

Roundout Reservoir

Round Table

Round Table International

Roundup

Rourke, Mickey

Rous, Francis Peyton

Roush, Edd

Rous sarcoma

Rousseau, Henri

Rousseau, Jean Jacques

Rousseau, Théodore

Rousseauism

Roussel, Albert

Route 66

Route 66 Association

Routledge, Chapman and Hall, Inc.

Routt National Forest

Rover

Rover Boys

Rove Tunnel

Rovuma

Rowan, Carl

Rowan, Dan

Rowan and Martin's Laugh-In

Rowan-Cabarrus Community College

Rowan Companies, Inc.

Rowe, Nicholas

Rowlands, Gena

Rowlandson, Thomas

Rowling, Reese McIntosh

Roxas y Acuña, Manuel

Roxboro

Roxbury

Roxbury Community College

Roy

Roy, Gabrielle

Roy, Rammohun

Royal Academy

Royal Academy of Dancing, United States Branch

Royal Academy of Music

Royal Aerospace Establishment

Royal Air Force

Royal Air Maroc

Royal Albert Hall

Royal and Ancient Golf Club

Royal Australian Air Force

Royal Ballet

Royal Bank of Canada

Royal Bank of Scotland, The

Royal Botanic Gardens

Royal Canadian College of Organists

Royal Canadian Mounted Police

Royal Canadians

Royal Caribbean Cruise Line

Royal Choral Society

Royal College of Music

Royal College of Organists

Royal Cruise Line

Royal Danish Ballet

Royal Dutch-Shell Group of Companies

Royal Festival Hall

Royal Flying Doctor Service of Australia

Royal Geographical Society

Royal Gorge

Royal Greenwich Observatory

Royal Hawaiian Band

Royal Highlander

Royal Highland Regiment

Royal Highness

Royal Household of Great Britain

Royal Institute of British Architects

Royal Jordanian Airline

Royal Manchester College of Music

Royal National Theatre

Royal National Theatre Company

Royal New Zealand Air Force

Royal Oak

Royal Ontario Museum

Royal Philharmonic Orchestra

Royal Philharmonic Society

Royal Shakespeare Company, The

Royal Society of London for the Advancement of Science, The

Royal Stadium

Royal Thai Air Force

Royal Tongan Airlines

Royal Victoria Hall

Royal Viking Line

Royal Zoological Society

Royce, Josiah

Royersford

Royko, Mike

Roy Rogers Show, The

Rozelle, Pete

Rózsa, Miklós

R. R. Bowker Company

R. R. Donnelly and Sons Company

RR Lyrae variables

RTZ Corporation, The

Ruanda [now Rwanda]

Ruanda [people], *n.*, *pl.* Ruanda *or* Ruandas

Rubáiyát of Omar Khayyam, The

Rubaiyat stanza

Rub'al Khali

Rubbergate

Rubbermaid Inc.

Rubber Manufacturers Association

Rubble, Barney

Rubble, Betty

Rubbra, Edmund

Rube Goldberg contraption

Rube Goldberg device

Rube Goldbergian

Ruben, Joseph

Rubens, Peter Paul

Rubenstein, Bernard

Rubicon

Rubicon, Inc.

Rubik, Erno

Rubik's Cube™
Rubinstein, Anton
Rubinstein, Artur
Rubinstein, John
Rubinstein, Nicholas
Ruby, Harry
Ruby, Jack
Ruby Mountains
Rudd, Hughes
Rude, François
Rudin, Jack
Rudin, Lewis
Rudner, Rita
Rudolf
Rudolph
Rudolph, Alan
Rudolph, Paul
Rudolph, Wilma
Rudolph the Red-
  Nosed Reindeer
Rue de la Paix
Ruef, Abraham
Ruehl, Mercedes
Ruetgerswerke
Ruffing, Red
Ruffo, Titta
RU-486 abortion pill
Rufus, William
Rugby [* England]
rugby *occas.* Rugby
  football
Rugby School
Ruggles, Carl
Ruggles, Charlie
Ruhmkorff, Heinrich
Ruhmkorff coil
Ruhr
Ruhr Basin
Ruisdael, Jacob van

Ruisdael, Salomon
  van
Ruiz Cortines, Adolfo
Rukeyser, Louis
Rukeyser, Muriel
Rule, Janice
Rule Brittania
Rule of Saint
  Augustine
Rule of Saint Basil the
  Great
Rumania *var. of*
  Romania
Rumanian *var. of*
  Romanian
Ruml, Beardsley
Rumpelstiltskin
Rump Parliament
Rumsey, James
Rumson
Runaway Hotline
Runaway with the
  Rich and Famous
Rundgren, Todd
Rundi, *n., pl.* Rundi *or*
  Rundis
Run-D.M.C.
Rundstedt, Karl von
Runge, Carl
Runge-Kutta method
Runnemede [* NJ; *see*
  also Runnymede]
Runner's World
Running Times
Runnymede
  [* England; *see also*
  Runnemede]
Runyon, Damon
Rupert
Rupert's Land
Rupp, Adolph

Rural Advancement
  Fund of the
  National
  Sharecroppers Fund
Rural Coalition
Rural Electrification
  Administration
Ruritania
Ruritanian
Ruritan National
Rush
Rush, Barbara
Rush, Benjamin
Rush, Richard
Rush, William
Rush-Bagot
  Convention
Rushdie, Salman
Rushing, Jimmy
Rush Limbaugh Show,
  The
Rush University
Rushville
Rusie, Amos
Rusk, Dean
Ruskin, John
Ruskin Gothic
Ruskinian
Russ Berrie and
  Company, Inc.
Russell
Russell, Andy
Russell, Bertrand
Russell, Bill
Russell, Charles
  Edward
Russell, Charles
  Marion
Russell, Charles Taze
Russell, Elizabeth
Russell, Gail

Russell, George
Russell, Harold
Russell, Henry Norris
Russell, Jane
Russell, John
Russell, Ken
Russell, Kurt
Russell, Leon
Russell, Lillian
Russell, Mark
Russell, Morgan
Russell, Nipsey
Russell, Pee Wee
Russell, Richard
Russell, Rosalind
Russell, Theresa
Russell Cave National Monument
Russell Corporation
Russellite
Russell Sage College
Russell Sage Foundation
Russell's viper
Russellville
Russia [*form.* Russian Soviet Federated Socialist Republic]
Russia Company
Russia leather
Russian
Russian American Company
Russian architecture
Russian art
Russian blue
Russian Church
Russian dandelion
Russian dressing
Russian Empire

Russian language
Russian literature
Russian olive
Russian Orthodox Church
Russian Orthodox Church outside of Russia
Russian Orthodox Greek Catholic Church of North America [*now* Orthodox Church in America]
Russian Platform
Russian Revolution
Russian roulette
Russian Soviet Federated Socialist Republic [*now* Russia]
Russian State Museum
Russian steppes
Russian thistle
Russian wolfhound
Russian wormwood
Russo, Rene
Russo-Finnish War
Russo-Japanese War
Russophile
Russophobe
Russophobia
Russo-Turkish War
Russwurm, John B.
Rust Belt
Rust College
Rustin, Bayard
Rusty Nail
Rutan, Dick

Rutgers, The State University of New Jersey
Rutgers University Press
Rutgers University Scarlet Knights
Ruth
Ruth, Babe
Ruthenia
Ruthenian
Rutherford
Rutherford, Ann
Rutherford, Ernest
Rutherford, Johnny
Rutherford, Joseph Franklin
Rutherford, Margaret
Rutherford atom
Rutherford scattering
Rutland
Rutledge, Ann
Rutledge, John
Ruttan, Susan
Rutter, John
Ruwenzori
Ruyter, Michiel Adriaanszoon de
Ruzicka, Leopold
Rwanda [*form.* Ruanda]
Rwandan
Ryan
Ryan, Irene
Ryan, Meg
Ryan, Mitchell
Ryan, Nolan
Ryan, Patrick George
Ryan, Peggy
Ryan, Robert
Ryan, Roz

Ryan, Thomas
Fortune

Ryan's Hope

Rybinsk Reservoir

Rydberg, Johannes

Rydberg constant

Rydell, Bobby

Ryder, Albert
Pinkham

Ryder, Winona

Ryder Cup

Ryder System
Charitable
Foundation

Ryder System,
Inc.

Ryder Truck Rental,
Inc.

Rye

Rye House Plot

Ryeland

Ryerson, Ann

Ryken, Theodore J.

Ryks Museum *var. of*
Rijksmuseum

Ryle, Gilbert

Ryle, Sir Martin

Ryman Auditorium

Rypien, Mark

Rysanek, Leonie

Ryskind, Morrie

Ryukyu Islands

Ryun, Jim

Ryzhkov, Nikolai I.

S

Saab Automobile

Saab-Scania

Saar

Saar Basin

Saarbrücken

Saarinen, Eero

Saarinen, Eliel

Saarland

Saatchi and Saatchi Company

Saba

Sabah, Jabir al-Ahmad al-Jabir Al-

Sabata, Victor de

Sabatier, Auguste

Sabatier, Paul

Sabatini, Gabriela

Sabatini, Rafael

Sabbat

Sabbatarian

Sabbatarianism

Sabbath

Sabbath School

Sabena Belgian World Airlines

Saberhagen, Bret

Sabin, Albert B.

Sabine

Sabine Crossroads

Sabine Lake

Sabine National Forest

Sabine-Neches Waterway

Sabin vaccine

Sable Island

Sabrina

Sabu

Sac, *n.*, *pl.* Sac or Sacs

Sacagawea *occas.* Sacajawea

Sac and Fox Indians

Sacchi, Andrea

Sac City

Sacco, Nicola

Sacco-Vanzetti case

Sacher-Masoch, Leopold von

Sacher torte

Sachs, Bernard P.

Sachs, Hans

Sachs, Nelly

Sackville, Thomas

Sackville-West, Lionel

Sackville-West, Victoria "Vita"

Saco

Sacra, Kathy Lynn

Sacramentarian

Sacramentarianism

Sacramento

Sacramento Army Depot

Sacramento Bee, The

Sacramento City College

Sacramento Kings

Sacramento Magazine

Sacramento Metro Airport

Sacramento Mountains

Sacramento-San Joaquin Delta

Sacramento Savings Bank

Sacramento sturgeon

Sacramento Union, The

Sacré-Coeur basilica

Sacred Allegory

Sacred and Profane Love

Sacred College of Cardinals

Sacred Harp Singers

Sacred Heart

Sacred Heart Major Seminary/College and Theologate

Sacred Heart of Jesus

Sacred Heart School of Theology

Sacred Heart University

Sacred Nine

Sacred Roman Rota

Sacred Writ

Sadat, Anwar *occas.* Anwar el- *or* Anwar al-

Saddleback College

Saddleback Community College

Saddlebrook

Sadducean

Sadducee

Sadduceeism

Sade

Sadie Hawkins Day

Sadler's Wells Theatre

Sad Sack

SAE, International

Safar

Safdie, Moshe

SAFECO Corporation

SAFECO Insurance Company of America

SAFECO Life Insurance Company

Safer, Morley

Safety Islands

Safety-Kleen Corporation

Safeway, Inc.

Safeway Stores, Inc.

Safid Rud

Safire, William

Sagamore Hill National Historic Site

Sagan, Carl

Sagan, Françoise

Sage, Russell

Sagebrush Rebellion

Sage Junior College of Albany

Saget, Bob

Sag Harbor

Saginaw

Saginaw Bay

Saginaw Valley State University

Sagittarian

Sagittarius

Saguaro National Monument

Saguenay

Sahaptin, *n., pl.* Sahaptin *or* Sahaptins

Sahara

Saharan

Sahara Resorts

Sahel

Sahl, Mort

Sahm, Doug

Saigon [*now* Ho Chi Minh City]

Saigon cinnamon

Sailing [song]

Sailing Magazine

Sailing World

Sailor King

Saint, The

Saint, Eva Marie

Saint Agnes' Eve

Saint Albans [* England; WV]

Saint Alphonsus College

Saint Ambrose University

Saint Andrews [* Scotland]

Saint Andrew's Church

Saint Andrew's Cross

Saint Andrew's Presbyterian College

Saint Ann [* MO]

Saint Anselm College

Saint Anthony Messenger

Saint Anthony's Cross

Saint Anthony's Fire

Saint Augustine [* FL; *see also* San Augustine]

Saint Augustine's College

Saint Bartholomew's Day Massacre

Saint Basil's Cathedral

Note: Individual saints are alphabetized by first name, as in *Peter, Saint.* The abbreviation *St.* is alphabetized under *St.* The bracketed editorial comments accompanying *Saint* are meant to help sort out the differences between *Saint* as applied to persons or to places and things.

Saint Basil's College

Saint Bernard [dog; mountain pass]

Saint Bernard Parish Community College

Saint Bernard's Institute

Saint Bernard's lily

Saint Bonaventure University

Saint Bonaventure University Brown Indians

Saint Boniface [* Manitoba]

Saint Catharine College

Saint Catharines [* Ontario]

Saint Charles [* IL; MO]

Saint Charles Borromeo Seminary

Saint Charles County Community College

Saint Christopher [* British West Indies]

Saint Christopher and Nevis

Saint Christopher medal

Saint Clair [* MI; MO; PA]

Saint Clair, Arthur

Saint Clair County Community College

Saint Clair Shores

Saint Cloud

Saint Cloud State University

Saint Croix

Saint Croix Island International Historic Site

Saint Croix National Scenic River

Saint Denis, Ruth

Saint Dunstan's Church

Sainte-Anne-de-Beaupré [* Quebec]

Sainte Anne de Bellevue [* Quebec]

Saint-Beuve, Charles Augustin

Sainte-Chapelle

Saint Edward's Crown

Saint Edward's University

Saint Elias Mountains

Saint Elizabeth Hospital School of Nursing

Saint Elmo's fire

Saint Elmo's light

Sainte-Mariè, Buffy

Saint Emilion [wine]

Sainte Thérèse [* Quebec]

Saint-Exupéry, Antoine de

Saint Francis [* WI; Indian; midwest river]

Saint Francis College

Saint Francis College [NY] Terriers

Saint Francis College [PA] Red Flash

Saint Francis Indian Mission

Saint Francis in Ecstasy

Saint Francis Medical Center College of Nursing

Saint Francis National Forest

Saint Francis Seminary

Saint Francis Xavier University

Saint-Gaudens, Augustus

Saint-Gaudens National Historic Site

Saint George [* Bermuda]

Saint George and the Dragon

Saint George Island

Saint George Killing the Dragon

Saint George's [* Grenada]

Saint George's Channel

Saint George's Day

Saint George's Island

Saint-Germain-des-Prés

Saint-Germain-en-Laye

Saint Gotthard or Gothard [mountains]

Saint Gotthard Pass

Saint Gotthard tunnels

Saint Gregory's College

Saint Helena [island]

Saint Hubert [* Quebec]

Saint Hyacinth College-Seminary

Saint Hyacinthe
[* Quebec]

Saint James [* NY]

Saint James, Susan

Saint-James's-flower

Saint-James's Palace

Saint-James's-pea

Saint Jerome in the
Wilderness

Saint Joan [play]

Saint Joe National
Forest

Saint John [* New
Brunswick; IN; KS;
MO; river in
northeast United
States and southeast
Canada; see also
Saint Johns]

Saint John Fisher
College

Saint John Island

Saint John of
Damascus
Association of
Orthodox
Iconographers,
Iconologists and
Architects

Saint John on Patmos

Saint Johns
[* Antigua; AZ; MI;
Quebec; river in
FL]

Saint John's
[* Newfoundland]

Saint John's bread

Saint Johnsbury

Saint John's College

Saint John's Day

Saint John's Eve

Saint John's Night

Saint Johns River
Community College

Saint John's Seminary

Saint John's Seminary
College

Saint John's
University

Saint John's
University Redmen

Saint-John's-wort

Saint John Vianney
College Seminary

Saint Joseph [* MO]

Saint Joseph College

Saint Joseph College
of Nursing

Saint Joseph's College

Saint Joseph Seminary
College

Saint Joseph's
Hospital Health
Center School of
Nursing

Saint Joseph's Indian
School

Saint Joseph's
Seminary

Saint Joseph's Society
of the Sacred Heart

Saint Joseph's
University

Saint Joseph's
University Hawks

Saint Joseph's
University Press

Saint-Joseph's-wand

Saint Jude Children's
Research
Hospital—ALSAC

Saint Julian Cross

Saint-Just, Louis de

Saint Kitts [island]

Saint Kitts and Nevis

Saint Labre Indian
School Educational
Association

Saint-Laurent, Yves

Saint Lawrence [river]

Saint Lawrence Island

Saint Lawrence
Islands National
Park

Saint Lawrence
Seaway

Saint Lawrence
Seaway Authority
of Canada

Saint Lawrence
Seaway
Development
Corporation

Saint Lawrence skiff

Saint Lawrence
University

Saint Leo College

Saint Louis [* MO]

Saint Louis Arena

Saint Louis Blues

Saint Louis Cardinals

Saint Louis Christian
College

Saint Louis College of
Pharmacy

Saint Louis
Community College

Saint Louis
Conservatory of
Music

Saint Louis
encephalitis

Saint Louis-Lambert
International
Airport

Saint Louis Magazine

Saint Louis Movement

Saint Louis Municipal Outdoor Theatre

Saint Louis Park

[Saint Louis] Post-Dispatch

Saint Louis School

Saint Louis Symphony Orchestra

Saint Louis University

Saint Louis University Billikens

Saint Louis Zoological Park

Saint Lucia [island]

Saint Lucie cherry

Saint-Malo [* France]

Saint Mark Rescuing a Slave

Saint Mark's Church

Saint Mark's-in-the-Bouwery

Saint Martin [island]

Saint Martin's College

Saint Martin's-in-the-Fields

Saint Martin's summer

Saint Martinville

Saint Mary College

Saint Mary of the Plains College

Saint Mary-of-the-Woods College

Saint Marys [river]

Saint Mary's Church

Saint Mary's College

Saint Mary's College Gaels

Saint Mary's College of California

Saint Mary's College of Maryland

Saint Mary Seminary

Saint Marys Falls Canals and Locks

Saint Mary's Seminary and University

Saint Mary's University

Saint Matthews [* KY]

Saint Meinrad College

Saint Meinrad School of Theology

Saint Michael Altarpiece, The

Saint Michael's College

Saint-Mihiel

Saint Moritz [* Switzerland]

Saint-Nazaire [* France]

Saint Nick

Saint Norbert College

Saint Olaf College

Saint Patrick's cabbage

Saint Patrick's Cathedral

Saint Patrick's Cross

Saint Patrick's Day

Saint Patrick's Day parade

Saint Patrick's Purgatory

Saint Patrick's Seminary

Saint Paul [* MN]

Saint Paul Bible College

Saint Paul Book and Media Center

Saint Paul Chamber Orchestra

Saint Paul Civic Center and Roy Wilkins Auditorium

Saint Paul Park

Saint Paul Pioneer Press Dispatch

Saint Paul's Cathedral

Saint Paul School of Theology

Saint Paul's Church National Historic Site

Saint Paul's College

Saint Paul Sunday Morning

Saint Paul Technical College

Saint Paul Winter Carnival

Saint Peter [* MN]

Saint Peter's Basilica

Saint Petersburg [* FL]

Saint Petersburg [* Russia; *form.* Leningrad]

Saint Petersburg Beach

Saint Petersburg Junior College

Saint Petersburg Times

Saint Peter's Church

Saint Peter's College

Saint Peter's College Peacocks

Saint Philip's College

Saint Pierre and Miquelon

Saint-Saëns, Camille

Saintsbury, George

Saint-Simon, Claude Henri de

Saint-Simon, Louis de

Saint-Simonianism

Saint Sophia [*aka* Hagia Sophia]

Saint Swithin's Day

Saint Thomas [island]

Saint Thomas Aquinas College

Saint Thomas Seminary

Saint Thomas tree

Saint Thomas University

Saint-Tropez

Saint Valentine's Day

Saint Valentine's Day Massacre

Saint Vincent and the Grenadines

Saint Vincent College and Seminary

Saint Vincent Island

Saint Vitus' *occas.* Vitus dance [*now* Sydenham's chorea]

Saint Vladimir's Orthodox Theological Seminary

Saint Xavier College

Saipan

Saitama Bank Ltd.

Sajak, Pat

Sakai, *n., pl.* Sakai *or* Sakais

Sakall, S. Z.

Sakhalin

Sakharov, Andrei

Saki

Sakioka, Roy

Saks, Gene

Saladin

Salamanca

Salamis

Salazar, António de Oliveira

Salazar Bridge

Salem

Salem, Peter

Salem College

Salem Community College

Salem Depot

Salem Maritime National Historic Site

Salem secretary

Salem State College

Salem-Teikyo University

Salem witchcraft trials

Salerno

Sales, Soupy

Salesian

Salian

Salian Franks

Salic law

Salida

Salieri, Antonio

Salina [* KS]

Salinas [* CA]

Salinas de Gortari, Carlos

Salinas National Monument

Salinas River

Salinger, J. D.

Salinger, Pierre

Salisbury

Salisbury, Harrison E.

Salisbury Plain

Salisbury School

Salisbury State University

Salisbury steak

Salish

Salishan

Salish Kootenai Community College

Salk, Jonas E.

Salk, Lee

Salk vaccine

Sallai, Abdullah

Sallisaw

Sallust

Sally Forth

Sally Jesse Raphael

Sally Lunn *occas.* sally lunn

Salmagundi

Salmanazar

Salminen, Sally

Salmon

Salmon National Forest

Salmon River Mountains

Salome

Salomon, Haym

Salomon Brothers Mortgage Security Inc.

Salomon Foundation

Salomon Inc.

Salonen, Esa-Pekka

Salonika

Salonika campaigns

Salten, Felix

Salter, Lionel

Salt Institute

Salt Lake City

Salt Lake City International Airport

[Salt Lake City] Tribune

Salt Lake Community College

Salt Lake Valley

Salt-N-Pepa

Salton Sea

Salton Sink

Salt Palace

Salt River

Salt River Project

Salt River Valley

Saluda

Saluda Dam

Saluki *occas.* saluki

Salvador

Salvadoran *occas.* Salvadorian

Salvation Army, The

Salvation Army School for Officer Training

Salvationist *often* salvationist [evangelist]

Salvationist [member of Salvation Army]

Salvemini, Gaetano

Salve Regina

Salviati, Francesco

Salvini, Tommaso

Salween

Salyut

Salzburg

Salzburg Festival

Salzburg Mozarteum

Sam and Dave

Samantha

Samaras, Lucas

Samaria

Samaritan *often* samaritan [generous helper]

Samaritan [native of Samaria]

Samarkand

Samarra

Sambora, Richie

Sam Browne belt

Sam Butera and the Wildest

Sam Butera and the Witnesses

Same Time, Next Year

Sam Ford Fjord

Samford University

Samford University Bulldogs

Sam Hill

Sam Houston National Forest

Sam Houston State University

Sam Houston State University Bearkats

Sam Levenson Show, The

Sammartini, Giovanni Battista

Samms, Emma

Sammy Kaye Show, The

Samoa

Samoan

Samoa Standard Time

Samoa time

Sámos

Samoset

Samothrace

Samothracian

Samoyed [dog]

Samoyed *occas.* Samoyede [people]

Samoyedic

Sample, Joe

Sampras, Pete

Sampson Community College

SAMRA University of Oriental Medicine

Samson

Samson Agonistes

Samson and Delilah

Samsonian

Samsonov, Aleksandr

Samson post

Samsung Group

Samuel

Samuel Goldwyn Company

Samuel Merritt College

Samuelson, Paul A.

San'a *occas.* Sanaa

San Andreas Fault

San Angelo

San Anselmo

San Antonian

San Antonio

San Antonio Art Institute

San Antonio College

[San Antonio] Express-News

San Antonio International Airport

San Antonio Light

San Antonio Missions National Historical Park

San Antonio Spurs

San Antonio Symphony

San Antonio Zoo

San Augustine [* TX; see also Saint Augustine]

San Benito

San Bernardino

San Bernardino Mountains

San Bernardino National Forest

San Bernardino Valley College

San Blas

Sanborn, David

San Bruno

San Buenaventura

San Carlos

Sanchez, Oscar Arias

Sancho

Sancho Panza

Sancho the Great

San Clemente

San Cristóbal

Sanctus

Sanctus bell

Sand, George

Sandalwood Island

Sandberg, Ryne

Sandburg, Carl

Sandby, Paul

Sand Creek

Sand Creek Massacre

Sanders, Deion

Sanders, George

Sanders, Jay O.

Sanders, Lawrence

Sanders, Marlene

Sanders, Summer

Sanderson, William

Sandersville

Sandhills Community College

S & H™ trading stamps

Sandhurst

Sandia National Laboratories

San Diego

San Diego Aerospace Museum

San Diego Chargers

San Diego City College

San Diego Community College

San Diego Gas and Electric Company

San Diego Home/Garden

San Diego International Airport (Lindbergh Field)

San Diego Jack Murphy Stadium

San Diego Mesa College

San Diego Miramar College

San Diego Naval Station

San Diego Naval Training Center

San Diego Padres

San Diego State University

San Diego State University Aztecs

San Diego State University Press

San Diego Tribune

San Diego Union, The

San Diego Wild Animal Park

San Diego Zoo

Sandinista National Liberation Front

Sandor, György

Sandoz, Mari

Sandoz Ltd.

S & P 500 index

Sandpoint

Sandra

Sandrich, Jay

Sandringham House

Sand Springs

Sandusky

Sandusky South

Sandwich

Sandwich Islands [old name of Hawaiian Islands]

Sandy, Gary

Sandy City

Sandy Hook

SANE/FREEZE

San Felipe pueblo

San Fernando

San Fernando Valley

Sanford

Sanford, Isabel

Sanford and Son

Sanford-Orlando Kennel Club

Sanforized™

San Franciscan

San Francisco

San Francisco Art Institute

San Francisco Ballet Association

San Francisco Bay

San Francisco Chronicle

San Francisco College of Acupuncture

San Francisco College of Mortuary Science

San Francisco Community College

San Francisco Conservatory of Music

San Francisco Examiner

San Francisco Examiner and Chronicle

San Francisco Federal Savings and Loan Association

San Francisco 49ers

San Francisco Giants

San Francisco International Airport

San Francisco Maritime National Historical Park

San Francisco-Oakland Bay Bridge

San Francisco Opera Company

San Francisco Peaks

San Francisco State University

San Francisco Style International

San Francisco Symphony Orchestra

San Francisco Theological Seminary

San Francisco Zoo

San Gabriel

San Gabriel Dam No. 1

San Gabriel Mountains

San Gabriel Reservoir

Sangallensis

Sangallo, Antonio da

Sangallo, Giuliano da

Sangamon State University

Sanger

Sanger, Frederick

Sanger, Margaret

San Giacomo, Laura

Sangre de Cristo

Sangre de Cristo Mountains

Sanhedrin

Sanibel Island

San Ildefonso

San Isabel National Forest

San Jacinto

San Jacinto College

San Jacinto Day

San Jacinto Savings Association

San Joaquin

San Joaquin College of Law

San Joaquin Delta College

San Joaquin Valley

San Jose [* CA]

San José [* Costa Rica]

San Jose Christian College

San Jose City College

San Jose/Evergreen Community College

San Jose International Airport

San Jose Mercury News

San Jose scale

San Jose Sharks

San Jose State University

San Jose State University Spartans

San Juan

San Juan Bautista

San Juan Boundary Dispute

San Juan Capistrano

San Juan College

San Juan Hill

San Juan Island National Historical Park

San Juan Islands

San Juan Mountains

San Juan National Forest

San Juan National Historic Site

San Juan Teotihuacán

San Leandro

San Lorenzo

San Luis Dam

San Luis Obispo

San Luis Potosí

San Manuel

San Marcos

San Marino
San Martin, José de
San Mateo
San Mateo County
  Community College
San Miguel
San Pablo
San Pablo Bay
San Pedro
San Quentin
San Rafael
San Remo
San Salvador
San Sebastian
Sansei, *n.*, *pl.* Sansei
Sanskrit
Sanskritic
Sanskritist
Sanskrit literature
Sansom, Art
Sansom Park Village
Sansovino, Andrea
Sansovino, Jacopo
Sans Souci palace
Santa
Santa Ana
Santa Ana pueblo
Santa Anita Park
Santa Anna, Antonio
  López de
Santa Barbara
Santa Barbara City
  College
Santa Barbara Islands
Santa Catalina
Santa Clara
Santa Clara pueblo
Santa Clara University

Santa Clara University
  Broncos
Santa Clara Valley
Santa Clarita
Santa Claus
Santa Claus Is Comin'
  to Town
Santa Cruz
Santa Cruz de
  Tenerife
Santa Cruz Island
Santa Cruz Viru-Viru
  International
  Airport
Santa Cruz water lily
Santa Fe
Santa Fean
Santa Fe and
  Chihuahua Trail
Santa Fe Community
  College
Santa Fe Energy
  Resources, Inc.
Santa Fe Industries
Santa Fe National
  Forest
Santa Fe Opera House
Santa Fe Pacific
  Corporation
Santa Fe Pacific
  Foundation
Santa Fe Springs
Santa Fe Trail
Santa Gertrudis
Santa Isabel
Santa Maria
Santa Maria tree
Santa Marta
Santa Monica
Santa Monica College

Santa Monica
  Mountains
Santa Monica
  Mountains National
  Recreation Area
Santana
Santana, Carlos
Santander
Sant'Angelo, Giorgio
Santa Paula
Santa Rosa
Santa Rosa de Copán
Santa Rosa Island
Santa Rosa Junior
  College
Santa's reindeer
Santayana, George
Santee
Sant'Elia, Antonio
Santiago
Santiago de Cuba
Santmyer, Helen
  Hooven
Santo Domingo
Santo Domingo Las
  Americas
  International
  Airport
Santos-Dumont,
  Alberto
Sanusi, *n.*, *pl.* Sanusi
  or Sanusis
Sanwa Bank
  California
Sanwa Bank Ltd.
San Xavier del Bac
  Mission
Sanyo Electric
  Company Ltd.
Sanzio, Raphael
São Francisco River

São Miguel
Saône
Saône-et-Loire
São Paulo
São Paulo University
São Tomé and Príncipe
Sapir, Edward
Sapper
Sapphic ode
Sappho
Sapporo
Sapulpa
Saqqara
Sara [given name], n., pl. Saras
Sara [people] n., pl. Sara or Saras
Saracen
Saracenism
Saracenlike
Saragossa or Zaragoza [city in Spain; see also Zaragoza]
Sarah
Sarah Lawrence College
Sarajevo
Sara Lee Corporation
Sara Lee Foundation
Saralegui, Cristina
Saranac Lake
Saranac Lakes
Saranap
Sarandon, Chris
Sarandon, Susan
Saran Wrap™
Sarasota
Sarasota Herald-Tribune

Saratoga
Saratoga campaign
Saratoga chip
Saratoga National Historical Park
Saratoga Springs
Saratoga Trunk [book; movie]
Saratoga trunk [luggage]
Sarawak
Sarazen, Gene
Sardinia
Sardinian
Sardis
Sardis Dam
Sardi's restaurant
Sardou, Victorien
Sarducci, Father Guido
Sarg, Tony
Sargasso Sea
Sargent, Dick
Sargent, Henry
Sargent, John Singer
Sargent, Sir Malcolm
Sarnath
Sarnoff, David
Sarnoff, Dorothy
Sarofim, Fayez Shalaby
Saronic Gulf
Sarouk
Saroyan, William
Sarrazin, Michael
Sarsi
Sarthe
Sarto, Andrea del
Sarton, May
Sartor Resartus

Sartre, Jean-Paul
SAS Institute Inc.
SA-16 Albatross
Saskatchewan
Saskatchewan Plain
Saskatoon
Sasquatch
Sassafras Mountain
Sasseta, Stefano
Sassoon, Siegfried
Sassoon, Vidal
Satan
Satan Devouring His Children
Satanic Verses, The
Satanism
Satanist
SATCO Marketing
Satellite Music Network
Satie, Eric
Sato, Eisaku
Saturday
Saturday Evening Post, The
Saturday Night Fever
Saturday Night Live
Saturday-night special
Saturn
Saturnalia, n., pl. Saturnalia or Saturnalias
Saturnalian
Saturn Corporation
Saturnian
Satyricon
Saudi
Saudi Arabia
Saudi Arabian

Saudi Arabian Airlines Corporation

Saugerties

Saugus

Saugus Iron Works National Historic Site

Sauk Centre

Sauk [Indian] *n.*, *pl.* Sauk *or* Sauks

Sauk Rapids

Sauk Valley Community College

Saul

Saul, B. Francis, II

Saul of Tarsus

Sault Sainte Marie

Sault Sainte Marie Canals

Sausalito

Saussure, Ferdinand de

sauterne *occas.* Sauterne

Sava

Savage, Edward

Savage, Fred

Savage, John

Savage Island

Savage's Station

Savaii

Savalas, George

Savalas, Telly

Savanna [* IL]

Savannah [* GA; river]

Savannah Area Vocational-Technical School

Savannah College of Art and Design

Savannah sparrow

Savannah State College

Savant, Marilyn vos

Save the Children Federation, Inc.

Save the Children Fund

Save-the-Redwoods League

Savile Row

Savitch, Jessica

Savo, Jimmy

Savoie [Alpine region; *English* Savoy]

Savonarola, Girolamo

Savonarola chair

Sav-On-Drugs, Inc.

Savoy [Alpine region; *French* Savoie]

Savoyard

Savoy Ballroom

Savoy chapel, the

Savoy Conference

Savoy Theatre

Sawallisch, Wolfgang

Sawatch

Sawchuk, Terry

Sawtooth National Forest

Sawyer, Diane

Sawyer, Ruth

Sawyer, Tom

Sawyer Brown

Sax, Adolphe

Sax, Antoine Joseph

Saxe-Altenburg

Saxe-Coburg

Saxe-Coburg-Gotha

Saxe-Gotha

Saxe-Meiningen

Saxe-Weimar

Saxe-Weimar-Eisenach

Saxo Grammaticus

Saxon

Saxon, John

Saxonian

Saxonism

Saxonite

Saxony

Saxony-Anhalt

Say, Jean Baptiste

Sayan Mountains

Saybrook Institute

Sayers, Dorothy

Sayers, Gale

Sayles, John

Sayre

Sayreville

Say's law

Scaasi, Arnold

Scabbard and Blade

Scafell Pike

Scaggs, Boz

Scaife, Richard Mellon

Scali, John

Scalia, Antonin

Scalia, Jack

SCANA Corporation

Scandinavia

Scandinavian

Scandinavian Airlines System

Scandinavian architecture

Scandinavian art

Scandinavian Peninsula

Scapa Flow

Scapegoat, The

Scaramouch *occas.*
Scaramouche

Scarborough

Scarborough, Charles

Scarborough lily

Scarecrow and Mrs.
King

Scarecrow Press, Inc.

Scarlatti, Alessandro

Scarlatti, Domenico

Scarlatti, Giuseppe

Scarlet Letter, The

Scarlet Pimpernel

Scarron, Paul

Scarsdale

SCEcorp

Schaap, Dick

Schacht, Hjalmar

Schaefer, George

Schaefer, Jack

Schaeffer, Boguslaw

Schalk, Ray

Schallert, William

Schapiro, Meyer

Scharbauer, Clarence,
Jr.

Scharwenka, Franz
Xaver

Scharwenka, Ludwig
Philipp

Schary, Dore

Schecter, Solomon

Schecter v. United
States

Scheduled Castes

Scheele, Karl Wilhelm

Scheele's green

Scheherazade

Scheidemann, Philipp

Scheider, Roy

Scheidt, Samuel

Schein, Johann
Hermann

Schell, Jonathan

Schell, Maria

Schell, Maximilian

Schell, Ronnie

Schelling, Friedrich
Wilhelm von

Schellingianism

Schellingism

Schenck v. United
States

Schenectady

Schenectady Army
Depot

Schenectady County
Community College

Schenkel, Chris

Schering-Plough
Corporation

Schering-Plough
Foundation

Schering-Plough
HealthCare
Products, Inc.

Scherman, Thomas

Schermerhorn,
Kenneth

Schiaparelli, Elsa

Schiaparelli, Giovanni
Virginio

Schick, Béla

Schickele, Peter

Schicklgruber

Schick test

Schieffelin and
Somerset Company

Schieffer, Bob

Schiele, Ergon

Schiff, Andreas

Schiff, Hugo

Schiff's *or* Schiff
reagent

Schifrin, Lalo

Schildkraut, Joseph

Schildkraut, Rudolph

Schiller, Friedrich von

Schiller Park

Schilling, Johannes

Schipa, Tito

Schippers, Thomas

Schirra, Walter

Schism of the West

Schlafly, Phyllis

Schlatter, George

Schlegel, August
Wilhem von

Schlegel, Friedrich
von

Schleiermacher,
Friedrich Ernst
Daniel

Schlesinger,
Arthur M., Jr.

Schlesinger,
Arthur M., Sr.

Schlesinger, James

Schlesinger, John

Schlessman
Foundation

Schleswig

Schleswig-Holstein

Schliemann, Heinrich

Schlitz Playhouse of
Stars

Schlossberg, Caroline
Kennedy

Schlumberger
Foundation

Schlumberger Ltd.

Schlüter, Andreas

Schmalkaldic League

Schmaltz profile microscope

Schmeling, Max

Schmidt, Bernhardt

Schmidt, Harvey

Schmidt, Helmut

Schmidt, Mike

Schmidt system

Schmidt telescope

Schmitt, Bernadotte Everly

Schnabel, Artur

Schnabel, Stefan

Schneider, Alexander

Schneider, John R.

Schneiderman, Rose

Schnitzler, Arthur

Schoenberg, Arnold

Schoenberg, Walter

Schoenbrunn Village State Memorial

Schoendienst, Red

Schoenflies symbol

Schofield

Schofield, John McAllister

Schofield Barracks

Scholastic Aptitude Test

Scholastic Corporation

Scholastic, Inc.

Scholasticism

Schollander, Don

Schongauer, Martin

Schoolcraft, Henry Rowe

Schoolcraft College

School for International Training

School for Lifelong Learning

School for Scandal, The

School of Law

School of Metaphysics

School of Mind

School of the Art Institute of Chicago

School of the Museum of Fine Arts—Boston

School of Theology at Claremont

School of the Ozarks

School of Visual Arts

Schopenhauer, Arthur

Schopenhauerism

Schorr, Daniel

Schramm, Tex

Schreiber, Avery

Schreiner College

Schroder, Rick

Schröder-Bernstein theorem

Schrödinger, Erwin

Schrödinger equation

Schrödinger's cat

Schrödinger wave equation

Schroeder, Barbet

Schroeder, Patricia

Schubert, Franz

Schulberg, Budd

Schuller, Robert

Schultz, George P.

Schultz Company

Schulz, Charles M.

Schumacher, Joel

Schuman, Robert [French political leader; see also Schumann, Robert]

Schuman, William

Schumann, Clara

Schumann, Robert [German composer; see also Schuman, Robert]

Schumann-Heink, Ernestine

Schuman Plan

Schumpeter, Joseph Alois

Schurz, Carl

Schuschnigg, Kurt von

Schütz, Heinrich

Schuyler, James

Schuyler, Philip John

Schuylkill

Schuylkill Expressway

Schuylkill Haven

Schwan, Marvin Maynard

Schwann, Theodor

Schwann cell

Schwartz, Arthur

Schwartz, Delmore

Schwarz, Gerard

Schwarz, Hermann Amandus

Schwarzenegger, Arnold

Schwarz inequality

Schwarzkopf, Elisabeth

Schwarzkopf, H. Norman

Schwedler's maple

Schweinfurt

Schweinfurth green

Schweitzer, Albert

Schwenkfelder

Schwenkfelder Church, The

Schwenkfeldian

Schwenkfeld von Ossig, Kaspar

Schwinger, Julian

Schwinn Bicycle Company

Schwitters, Kurt

Science and Health with Key to the Scriptures

Science News

Science of Creative Intelligence

Science Service

Scientific American

Scientific-Atlanta, Inc.

Scientists Institute for Public Information

Scientologist

Scientology™

Sci-Fi Channel, The

Scilly Isles *occas.* Islands

Sciorra, Annabella

Scioto

Scipio, Publius the Elder

Scipio, Publius the Younger

Scipione

SCI Systems, Inc.

SCITREK—The Science and Technology Museum of Atlanta

Scituate

S. C. Johnson and Son, Inc.

Scobee, Dick

Scofield, Paul

Scolari, Peter

Scooby Doo

Scopas

Scopes, John Thomas

Scopes monkey trial

Scopes trial

Scorel, Jan van

Scoresby, William

Scoresby Sound

Scorpio

Scorsese, Martin

Scot

Scotch

Scotch Blackface

Scotch broom

Scotch broth

Scotch crocus

Scotch egg

Scotch foursome

Scotch furnace

Scotch Gaelic

Scotchgard™

Scotch grain

Scotch-Irish

Scotchman, *n., pl.* Scotchmen

Scotch mist

Scotch pine

Scotch Plains

Scotch rose

Scotch™ tape

Scotch terrier

Scotch thistle

Scotch verdict

Scotch whisky

Scotchwoman, *n., pl.* Scotchwomen

Scotch woodcock

Scotia

Scotia Plaza

Scotic

Scotism

Scotist

Scotland

Scotland Neck

Scotland Yard

Scots

Scots Gaelic

Scotsman, *n., pl.* Scotsmen

Scots pine

Scotswoman, *n., pl.* Scotswomen

Scott

Scott, Campbell

Scott, Cyril Meir

Scott, Dred

Scott, George C.

Scott, Sir George Gilbert

Scott, Sir Giles Gilbert

Scott, Hazel

Scott, Lizabeth

Scott, Martha

Scott, Montgomery

Scott, Randolph

Scott, Ridley

Scott, Robert F.

Scott, Sir Walter

Scott, Willard

Scott, Winfield

Scott, Zachary

Scott Air Force Base

Scott City

Scott Community College

Scottdale [* PA; *see also* Scottsdale]

Scott, Foresman and Company

Scotticism

Scottie

Scottish

Scottish Chamber Orchestra

Scottish deerhound

Scottish fold

Scottish Gaelic

Scottish National Orchestra

Scottishness

Scottish Opera

Scottish rite

Scottish terrier

Scotto, Renata

Scott Paper Company

Scott Paper Company Foundation

Scottsbluff

Scotts Bluff National Monument

Scottsboro

Scottsboro boys

Scottsboro case

Scottsburg

Scottsdale [* AZ; *see also* Scottdale]

Scottsdale Community College

Scott-Siddons, Mrs.

Scottsville

Scotty

Scouting

Scowcroft, Brent

Scrabble™

Scranton

Scranton, William

Scratch

Scream, The

Screen Actors Guild

Scriabin, Alexander *or* Aleksander

Scribe, Augustin Eugène

Scriblerus Club

Scribner, Charles, Jr.

Scribner, Charles, Sr.

Scribner's bookstore

Scripps, Edward Wyllis

Scripps College

Scripps-Howard Broadcasting Company

Scripps-Howard Foundation

Scripps-Howard Newspapers, Inc.

Scripps-Howard News Service

Scripps Institution of Oceanography

Scripture *often* Scriptures

Scritti Politti

Scrooge, Ebenezer

Scrovegni Chapel

Scruggs, Earl

Scruggs-picking

Scudder, Janet

Scudder Investor Services, Inc.

Scud missile

Sculley, John

Scully, Vin

Scylla

Scylla and Charybdis

Scythia

Scythian

Scythian lamb

Seabee

Seaborg, Glenn T.

Seabourn Cruise Line

Seabrook Nuclear Power Station

Seabury-Western Theological Seminary

Sea Cliff

Seafarers International Union of North America

Seafirst Corporation

Seafirst Foundation

Seaford

Seagate Technology, Inc.

Seagoville

Seagram Company, Ltd., The

Sea Gull, The

Sea Hunt

sea island *often* Sea Island cotton

Sea Islands

Seal Beach

Seale, Bobby

Sea Lion Legal Defense Fund, The

Seals, Dan

Seals, James

Seals and Crofts

Sealyham

Sealyham terrier

Sean

Seanad Eireann

Sea of Azov
Sea of Cortés
Sea of Galilee
Sea of Japan
Sea of Marmara
Sea of Okhotsk
Sea of Tranquility
Sea of Vapors
Searchers, The
Search for Tomorrow
Searcy
Searle, Ronald
Sears, Richard W.
Sears Canada, Inc.
Sears Financial
  Network
Sears Point
  Championship race
Sears Point
  International
  Raceway
Sears, Roebuck and
  Company
Sears Roebuck
  Foundation, The
Sears Roebuck store
Sears Savings Bank
Sears Tower
Sea Scout
Seashore, Carl
Seashore test
Seaside
Seatack
Seated Bather
Seat Pleasant
Seattle
Seattle Central
  Community College
Seattle Coliseum

Seattle Community
  College
Seattle-First National
  Bank
Seattle Kingdome
Seattle Mariners
Seattle Opera
Seattle Pacific
  University
Seattle Post-
  Intelligencer
Seattle Seafair
Seattle Seahawks
Seattle SuperSonics
Seattle Symphony
  Orchestra
Seattle-Tacoma
  International
  Airport
Seattle Times, The
Seattle University
Seattle Weekly
Seaver, Tom
Sea World
Sea World of Florida
Sebastian
Sebastian, John
Sebastian, Saint
Sebastiano del Piombo
Sebastopol *var. of*
  Sevastopol
Seberg, Jean
Sebring
Sebring International
  Raceway
Secaucus
Secchi, Angelo
Secchi disk
Seckel
Second Advent
Second Adventist

2d Air Division
  Association
Second *occas.* 2d
  Amendment [to the
  Constitution]
Second American
  Revolution
Second Balkan War
Second Birth
Second Chance Body
  Armor, Inc.
II Chronicles *or* 2
  Chronicles
Second Coming
II Corinthians *or* 2
  Corinthians
Second Council of
  Lyons
Second Council of
  Nicaea
Second Empire
Second Empire style
Second Harvest
Second International
II John *or* 2 John
Second Jungle Book,
  The
II Kings *or* 2 Kings
Second Lateran
  Council
2d of May, The
II Peter *or* 2 Peter
Second Punic War
Second Reader
Second Reich
Second Republic
II Samuel *or* 2 Samuel
Second Shepherd's
  Play
Second Sino-Japanese
  War

II Thessalonians *or* 2 Thessalonians

II Timothy *or* 2 Timothy

Second Triumvirate

Second Vatican Council

Second Viennese School

Second World War *var. of* World War II

Secord, Richard

Secretary-General of the United Nations

Secretary of Agriculture

Secretary of Commerce

Secretary of Defense

Secretary of Education

Secretary of Health and Human Services

Secretary of Housing and Urban Development

Secretary of Labor

Secretary of State

Secretary of the Air Force

Secretary of the Army

Secretary of the Interior

Secretary of the Navy

Secretary of the Treasury

Secretary of Transportation

Secretary of Veterans Affairs

Secret Garden, The

Secret Life of Walter Mitty, The

Secret Storm, The

Securities and Exchange Commission

Securities Exchange Act

Securities Industry Association

Security Pacific Bancorporation Northwest

Security Pacific Corporation

Security Pacific Foundation

Security Pacific Foundation Northwest

Security Pacific National Bank

Sedaka, Neil

Sedalia

Sedares, James

Seder, *n.*, *pl.* Sedarim *or* Seders

Sedgwick, Ellery

Sedro-Woolley

Sedwick, Jud

Seebeck, Thomas J.

Seebeck effect

Seeger, Alan

Seeger, Peggy

Seeger, Pete

Seeing Eye™ dog

See It Now

Seekonk

Seeley, Blossom

See Threepio

Seferiades, Giorgos Stylianou

Seferis, George

Segal, Erich

Segal, George

Segal, Vivienne

Segantini, Giovanni

Sega of America Inc.

Segar, Elzie C.

Seger, Bob

Seger, Hermann A.

Seger cone

Seghers, Anna

Segni, Antonio

Segovia, Andrés

Seguin

Sehna *occas.* Senna knot

Seidelman, Susan

Seidlitz powders

Seifert, Jaroslav

Seikan Tunnel

Seiko Epson Corporation

Seine

Seine-et-Marne

Seine-et-Oise

Seine-Maritime

Seine-Saint-Denis

Seinfeld, Jerry

Seistan

Seiyukai

Sclden

Selden, John

Seldes, Marian

Selective Service Commission

Selective Service System

Selec TV

Selenga

Seler, Eduard

Seles, Monica
Seleucid
Seleucidian
Seleucus
Selfridge Air Force Base
Selim
Selinsgrove
Seljuk
Seljukian
Selkirk, Alexander
Selkirk Mountains
Sellecca, Connie
Selleck, Tom
Sellers, Peter
Selma
Selma University
Selous Game Reserve
Selsam, Millicent Ellis
Selvin, Ben
Selznick, Daniel
Selznick, David O.
Selznick, Irene Mayer
Semang, n., pl. Semang or Semangs
Semenov, Nikolai
Semichastny, Vladimir
Seminary of the Immaculate Conception
Seminole
Seminole Community College
Seminole Greyhound Park
Seminole [Indian], n., pl. Seminole or Seminoles
Seminole Junior College
Seminole War

Semiramis
Semite
Semitic
Semiticist
Semitics
Semitism
Semitist
Semmering Pass
Semonides of Amorgos
Semper Fidelis
Semper Paratus
Senator, I say Senator Claghorn
Sendak, Maurice
Sender, Ramón José
Senderista
Sendero Luminoso
Send in the Clowns
Seneca
Seneca Army Depot
Seneca Falls
Seneca grass
Seneca [Indian], n., pl. Seneca or Senecas
Seneca Lake
Senecan
Seneca snakeroot
Seneca the Elder
Seneca the Younger
Senefelder, Aloys
Senegal
Senegalese, n., pl. Senegalese
Senegambia
Senegambian
Senghor, Léopold Sédar
Senior Classic PGA Golf Tournament

Senior Girl Scouts
Senior News Service
Senior World Newsmagazine
Sennacherib
Sennar
Sennett, Mack
Senor or Señor, n., pl. Senors or Señores
Senora or Señora, n., pl. Senoras or Señoras
Senorita or Señorita, n., pl. Senoritas or Señoritas
Sensormatic Electronics Corporation
Sensuous Man, The
Sensuous Woman, The
Sensurround™
Seoul
Sephardi, n., usually pl. Sephardim
Sephardic
Sephardic Jew
Sephardim, pl. of Sephardi
Sepoy Mutiny
Sepoy Rebellion
September
September Massacre
Septembrist
Septuagesima
Septuagesima Sunday
Septuagint
Septuagintal
Sequa Corporation
Sequoia National Forest
Sequoia National Park

Sequoia Systems Inc.

Serafin, Barry D.

Serapis

Serb

Serbia

Serbian

Serbian Eastern
Orthodox Church

Serbian Eastern
Orthodox Church
for the United
States of America
and Canada

Serbian Orthodox
Church

Serbian Orthodox
Church for the
United States of
America and
Canada

Serbo-Croatian

Serbonian

Serengeti

Sergeant Preston of
the Yukon

Sergius I, Saint

SER—Jobs for
Progress, Inc.

Serkin, Peter

Serkin, Rudolf

Serling, Rod

Serlio, Sebastiano

Sermon on the Mount

Serpico

Serra, Junípero

Sert, José Maria

Sertoli, Enrico

Sertoli cell

Sertoma International

Sertoman

Servetus, Michael

Servian Wall

Service, Robert W.

Service Corporation
International

Service Corps of
Retired Executives

Service Employees
International Union

Service Merchandise
Company, Inc.

Servicio Aereo de
Honduras

Servile Wars

Servite

Servite Father

Servius Tulius

Sesame Street

Sesame Street Book
Club

Sesame Street
Magazine

Sesame Street Parents'
Guide

Sesostris

Sesshu

Sessions, Roger

Seth

Seton, Anya

Seton, Ernest
Thompson

Seton, Mother

Seton Hall University

Seton Hall University
Pirates

Seton Hall University
School of Law

Seton Hill College

Seto Ohashi Bridge
Complex

Seurat, Georges

Sevareid, Eric

Sevastopol *occas.*
Sebastopol

Seven against Thebes

Seven Beauties

Seven Churches in
Asia

Seven Cities of Cibola

Seven Days battles

Seven Days of
Creation

Seven Deadly Sins

Seven Hills [* OH]

Seven Hills of Rome

700 Club

Seven Pines

Seven Sages

Seven Seas *occas.*
seven seas

Seven Sisters

Seven Sleepers of
Ephesus

Seventeen

1776 [play]

Seventeenth *occas.*
17th Amendment
[to the Constitution]

Seventh *occas.* 7th
Amendment [to the
Constitution]

Seventh Avenue

Seventh-Day
Adventist

Seventh-Day
Adventist Church

Seventh-Day Baptist

Seventh-Day Baptist
General Conference

77 Sunset Strip

7UP™ soft drink

Seven Weeks' *occas.*
Weeks War

Seven Wise Men of Greece

Seven Wonders of the Ancient World

Seven Wonders of the World

Seven Year Itch, The

Seven Years' *occas.* Years War

Severini, Gino

Severinsen, Doc

Severn

Severn, Joseph

Severna Park

Severnaya Zemla

Seversky, Alexander P.

Severus

Severus, Alexander

Sevier

Sevier, John

Sévigne, Marie de

Seville

Seville, David

Seville orange

Seville San Pablo Airport

Sévres

Sévres porcelain

Sewall, Samuel

Sewanee

Sewanee Review

Seward

Seward, William Henry

Seward County Community College

Seward Peninsula

Seward's Folly

Seward's Icebox

Sewell, Anna

Sewell, Joe

Sewell, Keith

Sewickley

Sexagesima

Sexagesima Sunday

Sex Information and Education Council of the United States

Sex Pistols

Sextans

Sexton, Anne

Seychelles

Seychelles International Airport

Seychellois

Seyfert, Carl K.

Seyfert galaxy

Seymour

Seymour, Jane

Seymour Johnson Air Force Base

Sforza, Carlo

Sforza, Francesco

Sforza, Ludovico

Shaanxi [*form.* Shensi]

Sha'ban

Shabuoth

Shackelford, Ted

Shackleton, Sir Ernest

Shadow Box, The

Shadow of a Doubt

Shadow of Your Smile, The

Shadrach

Shadwell, Thomas

Shadyside

Shaffer, Louise

Shaffer, Paul

Shaffer, Peter

Shafter

Shaftesbury, Anthony

Shahn, Ben

Shah of Iran

Shairp, John Campbell

Shaker

Shake, Rattle and Roll

Shaker Heights

Shakerism

Shakespeare, William

Shakespearean *or* Shakespearian *occas.* Shakesperean *or* Shakesperian

Shakespeareana *or* Shakespeariana

Shakespearean sonnet

Shakespeare Association of America

Shakespeare-Bacon controversy

Shaking Quaker

Shaklee Corporation

Shakopee

Shalit, Gene

Shallum

Shalmaneser

Shamir, Yitzhak

Shamokin

Shamrock

Shamu

Sha Na Na

Shandling, Garry

Shandong [*form.* Shantung]

Shandong Peninsula

Shane

Shang dynasty
Shange, Ntozake
Shanghai
Shanghai chicken
Shanghai Honqiao International Airport
Shanghai Stock Exchange
Shangri-la
Shangri-Las, The
Shang Ti
Shankar, Ravi
Shankar, Uday
Shanker, Albert
Shannon
Shannon, Claude Elwood
Shannon, Del
Shannon Airport Industrial Estate
Shannon International Airport
Shannontown
Shan Plateau
Shansi
Shan State
Shantar Islands
Shantung [now Shandong]
Shantung silk
Shapey, Ralph
Shapiro, Karl
Shapley, Harlow
Sharaku
Sharett, Moshe
Shari
Sharif, Omar
Sharkey, Jack
Sharon

Sharon, Ariel
Sharon Hill
Sharonville
Sharonwest
Sharp, Granville
Sharp, Peter Jay
Sharp, William
Sharp Corporation
Shar-pei
Sharper Image Corporation
Sharps buffalo rifle
Sharpsburg
Sharpsville
Sharra, *n.*, *pl.* Sharra or Sharras
Shasta College
Shasta cypress
Shasta daisy
Shasta Dam
Shasta Lake
Shasta-Trinity National Forest
Shastri, Lal Bahadur
Shatner, William
Shatt-al-Arab
Shavian
Shaviana
Shavianism
Shavuot
Shaw, Artie
Shaw, Bernard
Shaw, George Bernard
Shaw, Henry Wheeler
Shaw, Irwin
Shaw, Richard Norman
Shaw, Robert
Shaw, Wilbur

Shaw Air Force Base
Shawano
Shaw Industries, Inc.
Shawmut Bank
Shawmut Charitable Foundation
Shawmut National Corporation
Shawn
Shawn, Dick
Shawn, Ted
Shawn, William
Shawnee
Shawnee Community College
Shawnee [Indian], *n.*, *pl.* Shawnee or Shawnees
Shawnee National Forest
Shawnee Prophet
Shawnee salad
Shawnee State University
Shaw University
Shawwal
Shays, Daniel
Shays' Rebellion
Shazam!
Shazar, Zalman
Shea, John
Shean, Al
Shearer, Moira
Shearer, Norma
Shearing, George
Shearson Lehman Brothers Holdings Inc.
Shearson Lehman Brothers Inc.
Shearson Lehman Hutton Open

Shea Stadium

Sheba

Shebat

Sheboygan [* WI; *see also* Cheboygan]

Sheboygan Falls

Sheedy, Ally

Sheehy, Gail

Sheeler, Charles

Sheen, Charlie

Sheen, Fulton J.

Sheen, Martin

Sheepshead Bay

Sheet Metal and Air Conditioning Contractor's National Association, Inc.

Sheet Metal Workers' International Association

Sheetrock™

Sheffield

Sheffield Lake

Sheffield plate

Shehan, Lawrence Joseph Cardinal

Shelby

Shelby State Community College

Shelbyville

Sheldon

Sheldon, Sidney

Sheldon Jackson College

Shelepin, Alexandr

Shellabarger, Samuel

Shell Canada Ltd.

Shelley, Carole

Shelley, Ken

Shelley, Mary Wollstonecraft

Shelley, Percy Bysshe

Shelleyan

Shell Oil Company

Shell Oil Company Foundation

Shell Pipe Line Corporation

Shell's Wonderful World of Golf

Shelter Island

Shelton

Shelton, Ricky Van

Shelton State Community College

Shem

Shemaiah

Shenandoah

Shenandoah College and Conservatory of Music

Shenandoah National Park

Shenandoah University

Shenandoah Valley

Shensi [*now* Shaanxi]

Shenstone, William

Shenyang [*form.* Mukden]

Shenzen Stock Exchange

Shepard, Alan

Shepard, E. H.

Shepard, Sam

Shepherd, Cybill

Shepherd Boy, A

Shepherd College

Shepherd King

Sheppard, William F.

Sheppard Air Force Base

Sheppard's adjustment

Sheraton, Thomas

Sheraton City Squire

Sheraton Grand Hotel

Sheraton Nile Cruises

Sheraton-Park Avenue

Sheraton style

Sherbrooke

Sheridan

Sheridan, Ann

Sheridan, Jim

Sheridan, Philip Henry

Sheridan, Richard Brinsley

Sheridan Broadcasting Corporation

Sheridan Broadcasting Network

Sheridan College

Sheriff of Nottingham

Sherlock, Jr.

Sherman

Sherman, John

Sherman, Roger

Sherman, Stuart Pratt

Sherman, William Tecumseh

Sherman Antitrust Act

Sherman Army Air Field

Sherman College of Straight Chiropractic

Sherman House

Sherman Silver Purchase Act

Sherman tank

Sherpa, *n.*, *pl.* Sherpa *or* Sherpas

Sherriff, Robert Cedric

Sherrington, Sir Charles

Sherry, Fred

Sherwin-Williams Company, The

Sherwin-Williams Foundation

Sherwood, Robert E.

Sherwood Forest

Shetland

Shetland Islander

Shetland Islands

Shetland pony

Shetland sheepdog

Shetland wool

Shevardnadze, Eduard

Shezhen Exchange

Shield of David

Shields, Brooke

Shields, Robert

Shields and Yarnell

Shiga, Kiyoshi

Shiga bacillus

Shih Tzu

Shiite

Shikoku

Shillington

Shilluk, *n.*, *pl.* Shilluk *or* Shilluks

Shiloh

Shiloh National Military Park

Shimada, Toshiyuki

Shimazaki, Tōson

Shimer College

Shin Buddhism

Shining Path

Shinn, Everett

Shinto

Shintoism

Shintoist

Shintoistic

Shipbuilders Council of America

Ship of Fools, The

Shippensburg

Shippensburg University of Pennsylvania

Ships in Bottles Association of America

Shipton, Mother

Shire, David

Shire, Talia

Shire horse

Shirelles, The

Shirer, William L.

Shirley, James

Shirley Temple

Shiva *occas.* Siva

Shivaism

Shivaist

Shively

Shizuoka Bank Ltd.

Shkara

Shmoo

Shoals Community College

Shockley, William

Shoe

Shoemaker, Vaughn

Shoemaker, Willie

Shoes of the Fisherman

Shogun

Shoko Chukin Bank, Tokyo

Sholes, Christopher

Sholokhov, Mikhail

Shoney's, Inc.

Shoofly Pie and Apple Pan Dowdy

Shooting of Dan McGrew, The

Shopko Store

Shop Television Network

Shor, Toots

Shore, Dinah

Shore, Eddie

Shore, Jane

Shoreline Community College

Shorenstein, Walter Herbert

Shoreview

Shorewood

Short, Bobby

Short, Luke

Short, Martin

Shorter, Frank

Shorter Catechism

Shorter College

Short Happy Life of Francis Macomber, The

Short Parliament

Sh'or Yoshuv Rabbinical College

Shoshonean

Shoshone Cavern

Shoshone Dam

Shoshone Falls

Shoshone [Indian], *n.*, *pl.* Shoshone *or* Shoshones

Shoshone National Forest

Shoshone Project

Shoshoni, *n., pl.* Shoshoni *or* Shoshonis

Shostakovich, Dimitri

Shostakovich, Maxim

Shotwell, James Thomson

Showa

Showboat

Showboat Invitational PBA Bowling Tournament

Showtime Networks

Shreveport

Shrewsbury

Shrieking Sisterhood

shrimp Newburg *or* Newburgh

Shrimpton, Jean

Shriner

Shriner, Herb

Shriner, Wil

Shriners Hospital for Crippled Children

Shriver, Eunice Kennedy

Shriver, Maria

Shriver, Pam

Shriver, Robert Sargent

Shropshire

Shropshire sheep

Shroud of Turin

Shrove Monday

Shrove Sunday

Shrovetide

Shrove Tuesday

SH-60B Sea Hawk

SH-60F Ocean Hawk

SH-2 Seasprite

SH-2 Superseasprite

Shubert, Jacob

Shubert, Lee

Shubert, Sam

Shubert Alley

Shubert Brothers

Shubert Theatre

Shula, David

Shula, Don

Shull, Richard B.

Shulman, Max

Shultz, George P.

Shumway, Norman

Shure, Leonard

Shuswap

Shute, Nevil

Shydner, Ritch

Shylock

Siam [old name of Thailand]

Siamese, *n., pl.* Siamese

Siamese architecture

Siamese art

Siamese cat

Siamese fighting fish

Siamese twins

Sian [*now* Xi'an]

Sibelius, Jean

Siberia

Siberian

Siberian crab apple

Siberian high

Siberian husky

Siberian iris

Siberian larkspur

Siberian Platform

Siberian ruby

Siberian squill

Siberian tea

Siberian tiger

Siberian wallflower

Sibyline Books

Sichuan [*form.* Szechwan]

Sicilian

Siciliani, Alessandro

Sicilian Vespers

Sicily

Sickert, Walter Richard

Siddhartha

Siddons, Anne Rivers

Siddons, Sarah Kemble

Sidewinder missile

Siding Spring Mountain

Siding Spring Observatory

Sidney [given name; * British Columbia; IA; MT; NE; NY; Oh; *see also* Sydney]

Sidney, Sir Philip

Sidney, Sylvia

Sidon

Siegel, Bugsy

Siegel, Jerry

Siegel, Joel

Siege of Belfort

Siege of Leningrad

Siege of Petersburg

Siege Perilous

Siegfried

Siegfried Idyll

Siegfried line

Sieg heil
Siemaszko, Casey
Siemens, Sir Charles W.
Siemens, Werner von
Siemens, Sir William
Siemens Corporation
Siena
Siena College
Siena Heights College
Sienkiewicz, Henryk
Siepi, Cesare
Sierra
Sierra Army Depot
Sierra Blanca
Sierra Blanca Peak
Sierra Club
Sierra Club Adventure Travel Guides™, The
Sierra Club Books™
Sierra Club Foundation, The
Sierra Club John Muir Library™, The
Sierra Club Legal Defense Fund
Sierra Club Postcard Collection™, The
Sierra Community College
Sierra de Juárez
Sierra Leone
Sierra Leone Peninsula
Sierra lily
Sierra Madre
Sierra Madre del Sur
Sierra Madre Occidental
Sierra Maestra

Sierra Morena
Sierra National Forest
Sierra Nevada
Sierra Nevada College
Sierra Nevada de Mérida
Sierra Pacific Resources
Sierras, the
Sierra shooting star
Sierra Vista
Sieve of Eratosthenes
Sievers, Eduard
Sigismund
Sigma Alpha Epsilon
Sigma Alpha Mu
Sigma Chi
Sigma Corporation of America
Sigma Delta Chi [now Society of Professional Journalists]
Sigma Delta Tau
Sigma Gamma Rho
Sigma Kappa
Sigma Nu
Sigma Phi Epsilon
Sigma Phi Gamma
Sigma Phi Society
Sigma Pi
Sigma Sigma Sigma
Sigma-Tau Foundation, The
Sigma Tau Gamma
Sigma Xi
Sigmund
Signac, Paul
Signal Hill
Signal Mountain

Signed English
Signet Banking Corporation
Signet™ Books
Signet Classic™ Books
Signet Vista™ Books
Signorelli, Luca
Signoret, Simone
Sigurd
Sikeston
Sikh
Sikhism
Sikh Wars
Sikkim
Sikking, James B.
Sikorsky, Igor
Silas Marner
Silence of the Lambs, The
Silent Network, The
Silent Night
Silent Spring
Siler City
Silesia
Silhouette Books™
Silicon Graphics, Inc.
Silicon Valley
Silius
Silivas, Daniela
Silkwood, Karen
Silky terrier
Sallanpää, Frans Emil
Sillitoe, Alan
Sills, Beverly
Silly Billy
Silly Putty™
Silmarillion, The
Siloam

Siloam Springs
Silone, Ignazio
Silsbee
Silurian
Silvanus
Silver, Horace
Silver, Joan Micklin
Silver, Joe
Silver, Ron
Silver Age
Silver Bow Park
Silver City
Silver Creek
Silverheels, Jay
Silverius, Saint
Silver Lake
Silver Lake College
Silverman, Fred
Silver Purchase Act
Silvers, Phil
Silver Spring [* MD]
Silver Springs [* FL]
Silver Star Medal
Silver State
Silverstein, Joseph
Silverstein, Shel
Silverton
Sim, Alastair
Simenon, Georges
Simeon
Simeonite
Simeon Stylites, Saint
Simhat Torah
Simionato, Giuletta
Simi Valley
Simmel, George
Simmental
Simmons, Al
Simmons, Gene

Simmons, Harold
   Clark
Simmons, Jean
Simmons, Richard
Simmons College
Simms, William
   Gilmore
Simon
Simon, Carly
Simon, Herbert
   Alexander
Simon, Joe
Simon, Melvin
Simon, Neil
Simon, Norton
Simon, Paul
Simon, Saint
Simon, Théodore
Simon, William
   Edward
Simon and Garfunkel
Simon and Schuster™
   Books
Simon and Schuster,
   Inc.
Simon and Simon
Simón Bolívar
   International
   Airport
Simone, Nina
Simone, Simone
Simonides of Ceos
Simon Legree
Simon Magnus
Simon of Cyrene
Simonov,
   Konstantin M.
Simon Peter
Simon says
Simon's Rock of Bard
   College

Simon Wiesenthal
   Center for
   Holocaust Studies
Simple Simon
Simplicity Pattern
   Company, Inc.
Simplicius, Saint
Simplon Pass
Simplon Road
Simplon Tunnel
Simplot, John Richard
Simpson, Alan K.
Simpson, Bart
Simpson, Louis
Simpson, O. J.
Simpson, Thomas
Simpson, Wallis
   Warfield
Simpson College
Simpsons, The
Simpson's rule
Sims, Zoot
Simsbury
Sin, Jaime Cardinal
Sinai
Sinaiticus
Sinaloa
Sinanthropus [now
   Peking man]
Sinatra, Frank
Sinatra, Frank, Jr.
Sinatra, Nancy
Sinatra, Tina
Sinatra Society of
   America
Sinbad var. of Sindbad
Sinclair, Madge
Sinclair, May
Sinclair, Upton

Sinclair Community
  College
Sindbad *occas.* Sinbad
Sindbad the Sailor
Singapore
Singapore Airlines
  Ltd.
Singapore Changi
  Airport
Singapore Sling
Singapore Strait
Singer, Isaac Bashevis
Singer, Isaac Merrit
Singer, Israel Joshua
Singer
  Communications,
  Inc.
Singh, Ranjit
Singh, V. P.
Singhalese *or*
  Sinhalese, *n., pl.*
  Singhalese *or*
  Sinhalese
Singin' in the Rain
Single Parent, The
Singleton, Henry Earl
Singleton, John
Singleton, Penny
Singleton, Zutty
Sing Sing State Prison
  [*form.* Ossining
  Correctional
  Facility]
Sinitic
Sinkiang [*now*
  Xinjiang]
Sinn Féin
Sinn Féiner
Sinn Féinism
Sino-Japanese
Sino-Japanese War

Sinologist
Sinology
Sino-Soviet
Sino-Tibetan
Sinte Gleska College
Sinton
Sinus of Valsalva
Sion *var. of* Zion
Siouan
Sioux Center
Sioux City
Sioux Falls
Sioux Falls College
Sioux [Indian], *n., pl.*
  Sioux
Sioux Nation
Sioux State
Sioux War
SIPA News Service
Sippy, Benjamin W.
Sippy diet
Sippy regimen
Sipuncula
Siqueiros, David
  Alfaro
Siren
Siret
Sir Gawain and the
  Green Knight
Sir George Williams
  University
Sirhan, Sirhan B.
Sirica, John J.
Siricius, Saint
Sirius
Sir Mix-A-Lot
Sirocco
Sir Roger de Coverley
Sir Thomas More

Sirtis, Marina
Siskel, Gene
Siskel and Ebert
Siskiyou Mountains
Siskiyou National
  Forest
Sisler, George
Sisley, Alfred
Sismondi, Jean
  Charles de
Sisseton
Sisseton-Wahpeton
  Community College
Sister Carrie
Sister Kenny Institute
Sister Sledge
Sisters of Charity
Sisters of Charity
  Hospital School of
  Nursing
Sisters of Loretto
Sisters of Mercy
Sisters of Providence
Sister Souljah
Sistine
Sistine Chapel
Sistine Chapel ceiling
Sistine Madonna, The
Sisyphean *or*
  Sisyphian
Sisyphus
Sitka
Sitka cypress
Sitkan
Sitka National
  Historical Park
Sitka spruce
Sitter, Willem de
Sitwell, Dame Edith
Sitwell, Sir Osbert

Sitwell, Sacheverell

Siuslaw National Forest

Siva *var. of* Shivah

Sivan

Sivash Sea

Siwash

Six Dynasties

Six Flags AstroWorld

Six Flags Great Adventure

Six Flags Great America

Six Flags Magic Mountain

Six Flags over Georgia

Six Flags over Mid-America

Six Flags over Texas

Six Million Dollar Man, The

Six Nations

Six Rivers National Forest

Sixteenth *occas.* 16th Amendment [to the Constitution]

Sixth *occas.* 6th Amendment [to the Constitution]

Sixtus

Sixtus I, Saint

Sixtus II, Saint

$64,000 Challenge, The [television game show]

$64,000 question [generic big question]

$64,000 Question, The [television game show]

60 Minutes

Sizzler Buffet Court and Grill

Sizzler International, Inc. [*form.* Collins Foods, Inc.]

SJL Broadcast Management Corporation

Sjögren's syndrome

Skagerrak

Skaggs, Leonard S., Jr.

Skaggs, Ricky

Skagit

Skagit Valley College

Skagway

Skandinaviska Enskilda Banken

Skaneateles

Skaw, The

Skeat, W. W.

Skelton, John

Skelton, Red

Skerritt, Tom

Skidmore, Louis

Skidmore College

Skidmore, Owings and Merrill

Skid Row

Ski Magazine

Skin Cancer Foundation, The

Skinner, B. F.

Skinner, Cornelia Otis

Skinner, Otis

Skinner box

Skins Game

Skiros

Skoda, Emil von

Skokie

Skouras, Spyros

Skowhegan

Skowron, Bill "Moose"

Skye

Skye, Ione

Skye terrier

Skylab

Skyline College

Skyline Corporation

Skyros

Skywalker, Luke

Skywest Airlines

Slaney, Mary Decker

Slater, Christian

Slater, Helen

Slater, Samuel

Slatkin, Leonard

Slaton

Slaughter

Slaughter, Enos

Slaughter, Frank G.

Slaughterhouse Cases

Slaughter on Tenth Avenue

Slav

Slave Coast

Slavenska, Mia

Slave State

Slavey

Slavic

Slavicism

Slavicist

Slavic languages

Slavic religion

Slavik, James Donald

Slavism

Slavonia

Slavonian

Slavonic

Slavonic languages

Slavophile

Slavophobe

Slayton, Deke

Sledge, Percy

Sleeping Bear Dunes National Lakeshore

Sleeping Beauty [fairy-tale character]

Sleeping Beauty, The [ballet]

Sleeping Gypsy, The

Sleepy Eye

Sleepy Hollow

Sleepy Hollow chair

Sleuth

Slezak, Erika

Slezak, Walter

Slick, Grace

Slick, Sam

Slidell

Slide Mountain

Sligo

Slim disease

Slim Jim

Slim Whitman Appreciation Society of the United States

Slippery Rock

Slippery Rock University of Pennsylvania

Sliwa, Curtis

Sloan

Sloan, Alfred P.

Sloan, John

Sloane Ranger

Sloan Foundation

Sloatsburg

Slocum, Joshua

Sloppy Joe [sloppy man]

sloppy joe *occas.* Sloppy Joe [sandwich]

Sloppy Joe's [greasy spoon restaurant]

Slovak

Slovakia

Slovakian

Slovak literature

Slovak Socialist Republic [*now* Slovak Republic]

Slovene

Slovenia

Slovenian

Slovo, Joe

Sluggo

Sluter, Claus

Sly and the Family Stone

Small Business Administration

Small Talk

Small White

Smart, Maxwell

Smart, Richard Palmer Kaleioku

Smart and Final, Inc.

SMART Yellow Pages™

Smetana, Bedřich

Smetana Quartet

Smiley, George

Smirnoff, Yakov

Smith, Adam

Smith, A. J. M.

Smith, Alexis

Smith, Alfred E.

Smith, Allison

Smith, Bessie

Smith, Billy

Smith, Bubba

Smith, Buffalo Bob

Smith, Cal

Smith, C. Aubrey

Smith, Charles Henry

Smith, Connie

Smith, David

Smith, Delford Michael

Smith, Ethel

Smith, Frances Hopkinson

Smith, Gary

Smith, Gerald L. K.

Smith, Hale

Smith, Harry

Smith, Hoke

Smith, Howard K.

Smith, Huey

Smith, Ian Douglas

Smith, Jaclyn

Smith, James

Smith, Jedediah Strong

Smith, Jeff

Smith, Jimmy

Smith, John

Smith, John Stafford

Smith, Joseph

Smith, Julia Frances

Smith, Kate

Smith, Keely

Smith, Lane

Smith, Lawrence Leighton

Smith, Liz

Smith, Logan Pearsall

Smith, Maggie

Smith, Margaret Chase

Smith, Margo

Smith, Oliver

Smith, Patti

Smith, Pine Top

Smith, Preserved

Smith, Red

Smith, Richard Allen

Smith, Roger

Smith, Seba

Smith, Sharon

Smith, Snuffy

Smith, Stuff

Smith, Sydney

Smith, Thomas, Captain

Smith, Thorne

Smith, Tony

Smith, Vince

Smith, Walter Bedell

Smith, W. Eugene

Smith, William Kennedy

Smith, Willie the Lion

Smith Act

Smith Barney, Harris Upham and Company

Smith College

Smithereens, The

Smithfield

Smith-Hughes Act

Smith International, Inc.

SmithKline Beecham Corporation

Smith's Food and Drug Centers, Inc.

Smithson, James

Smithson, Robert

Smithsonian Institution

Smithsonian Institution Press

Smithsonian Magazine

Smithsonian World

Smithville

Smits, Jimmy

Smohalla

Smokey and the Bandit

Smokey and the Bandit II

Smokey™ bear

Smokey Robinson and the Miracles

Smoky Hill River

Smoky Mountains

Smolensk

Smollett, Tobias

Smoot, Reed

Smothers, Dick

Smothers, Tom

Smothers Brothers

Smurf™ doll

Smurfs [television series]

Smuts, Jan Christiaan

Smyrna

Smyrna fig

Smyth, Dame Ethel

Snake

Snap

Snap-on Tools Corporation

Snead, Sam

Snead State Junior College

Sneak Previews

Snel or Snell, Willebrord

Snellen's chart

Snell's law of refraction

Snerd, Mortimer

Sneva, Tom

Snider, Duke

Snipes, Wesley

Snodgrass, W. D.

Snodgress, Carrie

Snohomish

Snoopy

Snoqualmie Falls

Snoqualmie Pass

Snoqualmie River

Snorri Sturluson

Snow, Carrie

Snow, C. P.

Snow, Hank

Snowbelt occas. Snow Belt

Snow College

Snowmass Mountain

Snowmass Village

Snow-White and Rose-Red

Snow White and the Seven Dwarfs

Snowy Mountains

Snyder

Snyder, Gary

Snyder, Jimmy the Greek

Snyder, Tom

Snyders, Frans

Soane, Sir John

Soap

Soap Box Derby

Soap Opera Digest

Soap Opera Stars

Soap Opera Update

Soares, Mário

Soaring Society of America

Social Brethren

Social Credit

social Darwinism

social Darwinist

Social Democrat

Social Democratic Party

Social Distortion

Social Gospel

Socialist Labor Party

Socialist Party

Socialist Revolutionary Party

Social Security

Social Security Act

Social Security Administration

Société Generale

Société Nationale des Chemins de Fer Français

Société Nationale Elf Aquitaine

Society Center Building

Society Corporation

Society Expeditions Cruises

Society for American Baseball Research

Society for Ethnomusicology

Society for Human Resource Management

Society for Industrial and Applied Mathematics

Society for Mining, Metallurgy and Exploration

Society for Range Management

Society for Savings

Society for Technical Communication

Society for the Advancement of Material and Process Engineering

Society for the Aid of Psychological Minorities

Society for the Preservation and Encouragement of Barber Shop Quartet Singing in America

Society for the Prevention of Cruelty to Animals

Society for the Prevention of Cruelty to Children

Society for the Study of Social Biology

Society Islands

Society National Bank

Society of Actuaries

Society of American Dramatists and Composers

Society of American Florists

Society of American Foresters

Society of American Graphic Artists

Society of American Magicians

Society of American Value Engineers

Society of Architectural Historians

Society of Automotive Testers

Society of Biblical Literature

Society of Chartered Property and Casualty Underwriters

Society of Descendants of Washington's Army at Valley Forge

Society of Exploration Geophysicists

Society of Fire Protection Engineers

Society of Friends

Society of Illustrators

Society of Indexers

Society of Jesus

Society of Logistics Engineers

Society of Manufacturing Engineers

Society of Mary

Society of Mary of Paris

Society of Military Widows

Society of Mining Engineers

Society of Missionary Priests of Saint Paul the Apostle

Society of Motion Picture and Television Engineers

Society of National Association Publications

Society of Naval Architects and Marine Engineers, The

Society of Our Lady of the Cenacle

Society of Plastics Engineers

Society of Priests of Saint Sulpice

Society of Professional Journalists [*form.* Sigma Delta Chi]

Society of Saint Andrew the Apostle, The

Society of Saint Francis de Sales

Society of Saint Francis Xavier for the Foreign Missions

Society of Saint Vincent de Paul

Society of Separationists, Inc.

Society of Stage Directors and Choreographers

Society of Tammany

Society of the Cincinnati

Society of the Descendants of the Colonial Clergy

Society of the Friendly Sons of Saint Patrick

Society of the Plastics Industry

Society of the Sacred Heart

Society of the Silurians

Society of Tribologists and Lubrication Engineers

Society of Wireless Pioneers

Society of Women Engineers

Society of Women Geographers

Socorro

Socrates

Socratic

Socratic irony

Socratic method

Soddy, Frederick

Sodom

Sodom and Gomorrah

Sodoma II

Sodomite

Sofia

Sofia Vrajdebna International Airport

Software Reviews on File™

Software Toolworks™, The

Soglow, Otto

Sohio Alaska Pipeline Company

Soho [area in London]

SoHo [area in New York City]

Soho Square

Soil Conservation Service

Soil Conservation Society of America

Soil Science Society of America

Soissons

Sojourner-Douglass College

Sojourners, National

Sokoloff, Nikolai

Sokolova, Lydia

Sol

Solano Community College

Solar de la Puente Raygada, Oscar

Solarz, Stephen J.

Soldier Field

Soldier of Fortune

Soldier's Medal

Soledad

Solemn High Mass

Solemnity of Mary

Solemn League and Covenant

Solemn Mass

Solent, The

Soler, Padre Antonio

Soleri, Paolo

Solesmes

Solferino

Solheim, Karsten

Solidarity

Solid Gold

Solid South

Solimena, Francesco

Solo, Napoleon

Solo man

Solomon

Solomon, Russell

Solomonic

Solomon Islands

Solomon R. Guggenheim Foundation

Solomon R. Guggenheim Museum

Solomons Company— Dance

Solomon's lily

Solomon's-seal *or* Solomonseal [plant]

Solomon's seal [symbol]

Solon

Solonic

Solo River

Solovetski Islands

Solow, Robert M.

Solow, Sheldon Henry

Solti, Sir Georg

Solutrean

Solvang

Solvay, Ernest

Solvay process

Solway Firth

Solzhenitsyn, Aleksander *or* Alexandr

Somali [cat], *n., pl.* Somalis

Somali [people], *n., pl.* Somali *or* Somalis

Somalia

Somalian

Somali Current

Somaliland

Some Like It Hot

Somerdale

Somers, Suzanne

Somerset

Somerset, Baron Raglan

Somerset Community College

Somerset Maugham Award

Somersetshire

Somers Point

Somersworth

Somerville

Somes, Michael

Something to Think About

Somewhere out There

Sommars, Julie

Somme

Sommer, Elke

Sommer, Viola

Somnus

Somoza, Luis

Somoza Debayle, Anastasio

Somoza Debayle, Luis

Somoza García, Anastasio

Sonat Foundation

Sonat Inc.

Sondergaard, Gale

Sondheim, Stephen

Songhoy Empire

Song of Bernadette, The

Song of Hiawatha, The

Song of Roland, The

Song of Solomon, The

Song of Songs

Song of the Nibelungs

Song of the Three Children

Songs of Experience

Songs of Innocence

Songwriters Guild of America, The

Sonneck Society

Sonnets from the Portuguese

Sonnets to Orpheus

Sonny and Cher

Sonoco Products Company

son of Adam

Son of God

Son of Man

Son of Sam

Sonoma

Sonoma State University

Sonora

Sonoran Desert

Sonora Pass

Sons and Lovers

Sons of Confederate Veterans

Sons of Liberty

Sons of Norway

Sons of Sherman's March to the Sea

Sons of the American Legion

Sons of the American Revolution

Sons of the Desert

Sons of the Pioneers

Sons of the Republic of Texas, The

Sons of Union
   Veterans of the
   Civil War

Sontag, Susan

Sony Corporation

Sony Corporation of
   America

Soo, Jack

Soo Canals

Soochow [*now*
   Suzhou]

Soo Line Corporation

Soo Line Railroad
   Company

Soo Locks

Sooner

Sooner State

Soong, T. V.

Soong Ching-ling

Sophia

Sophist

Sophocles

Sophonias *var. of*
   Zephaniah

Sopwith Camel

Sorbonis

Sorbonne

Sorcerer's Apprentice,
   The

Sorel, Georges

Sorenson, James
   LeVoy

Sorolla y Bastida,
   Joaquin

Soroptimist
   International

Soroptimist
   International of the
   Americas

Soros, George

Sorrentine

Sorrento

Sorvino, Paul

Soter, Saint

Sotheby's auction
   house

Sotheby's Holdings,
   Inc.

Sothern, Ann

Sothern, E. H.

Sotho, *n., pl.* Sotho *or*
   Sothos

Souchong

Souderton

Soufflot, Jacques
   Germain

Soufrière

Soul, David

Soul, Jimmy

Soulé, Samuel W.

Soul Stirrers, The

Soul Train

Soumak rug

Sound and Fury, The

Sound of Music, The

Soupy Sales Show,
   The

Source, The

Source, Inc.

Source Perrier

Sousa, John Philip

Sousa march

Soustelle, Jacque

Souster, Raymond

Souter, David H.

South Africa

South African

South African
   Airways

South African Dutch

South African jade

South African
   literature

South African
   National Gallery

South African War

South Amboy

South America

South American

Southampton

Southampton
   Insurrection

Southampton Island

South Arabia

South Atlantic

South Australia

South Beloit

South Bend

South Bend Tribune

South Boston

South Bound Brook

Southbridge

South Broadway

South Burlington

South Carolina

South Carolina
   National Bank

South Carolina
   Network

South Carolina State
   College

South Carolina State
   College Bulldogs

South Carolinian

South Caucasian

South Central Bell
   Telephone
   Company

South Central
   Community College

South Charleston

South Chicago Heights

South China Sea

South College

South Coventry

South Dakota

South Dakotan

South Dakota School of Mines and Technology

South Dakota State University

Southdown sheep

Southeast Asia

Southeast Asian

Southeast Asian languages

Southeast Asia Resolution

Southeast Asia Treaty Organization

Southeast Bank

Southeast Banking Corporation

Southeast Banking Corporation Foundation

Southeast Community College

Southeastern Baptist College

Southeastern Baptist Theological Seminary

Southeastern Bible College

Southeastern College of the Assemblies of God

Southeastern Community College

Southeasterner

Southeastern Illinois College

Southeastern Louisiana University

Southeastern Louisiana University Lions

Southeastern Massachusetts University

Southeastern Oklahoma State University

Southeastern University

Southeastern University of the Health Sciences

Southeast Missouri State University

Southeast Vocational-Technical Institute

South El Monte

Southern Alps

Southern Arkansas University

Southern Ballet Theatre

Southern Baptist

Southern Baptist Convention

Southern Baptist Theological Seminary

Southern Bell Telephone Company

Southern California College of Chiropractic

Southern California College of Optometry

Southern California Edison Company

Southern California Gas Company

Southern California Institute of Architecture

Southern Christian Leadership Conference

Southern College

Southern College of Optometry

Southern College of Seventh-Day Adventists

Southern College of Technology

Southern Company, The

Southern Connecticut State University

Southern Cook Islands

Southern Cross

Southern Crown

Southern Democrat

Southern Educational Communications Association

Southern English

Southern Episcopal Church

Southerner

southern hemisphere *often* Southern Hemisphere

Southern Illinois University

Southern Illinois University Press

Southern Illinois University Salukis

Southern Indiana Gas and Electric Company

Southernism

Southern Junior College

Southern Living

Southern Maine Technical College

Southern Methodist Church

Southern Methodist University

Southern Methodist University Mustangs

Southern Methodist University Press

Southern Nazarene University

Southern New England Telecommunications Corporation

Southern Ohio College

Southern Oregon State College

Southern Pacific [musical group]

Southern Pacific Railroad

Southern Pacific Transportation Company

Southern Paiute

Southern Pines

Southern Poverty Law Center

Southern Rhodesia [now Zimbabwe]

Southern Seminary College

Southern Slav

Southern Sporades

Southern State Community College

Southern States

Southern T'ang dynasty

Southern Technical College

Southern Triangle

Southern Union State Junior College

Southern University

Southern University Jaguars

Southern Utah University

Southern Vermont College

Southern West Virginia Community College

South Euclid

Southey, Robert

South Farmingdale

South Fayetteville

Southfield

South Florida Community College

South Fort Mitchell

South Frigid Zone

South Gate [* CA]

Southgate [* MI]

South Georgia [island]

South Georgia College

South Georgian

South Glens Falls

South Hadley

South Haven

South Holland

South Houston

South Huntington

Southington

South Island

South Kingstown

South Korea

Southland Corporation, The

South Manchurian Railway

South Miami

South Milwaukee

South Modesto

South Mountain Community College

South Norfolk

South Ogden

South Orange

South Orkney Islands

South Pacific

South Pacific Commission

South Pacific Forum

South Pasadena

South Pass

South Plainfield

South Plains College

South Platte

South Pole

Southport

South Portland

South Puget Sound Community College

South River

South Saint Paul

South Salt Lake

South Sandwich Islands

South San Francisco

South San Gabriel

South Sea Bubble

South Sea Islander

South Sea Islands

South Seas

South Sea Scheme

South Seattle Community College

South Shetland Islands

Southside Johnny and the Asbury Jukes

Southside Virginia Community College

South Sioux City

South Suburban College of Cook County

South Temperate Zone

South Texas College of Law

South Tucson

South Vietnam [now part of Vietnam]

South West Academy of Technology

Southwest Acupuncture College

South-West Africa [now Namibia]

Southwest Agri-Radio Network

Southwest Airlines Company

Southwest Baptist University

South Westbury

Southwestern Adventist College

Southwestern Assemblies of God College

Southwestern Baptist Theological Seminary

Southwestern Bell Corporation

Southwestern Bell Foundation

Southwestern Christian College

Southwestern College

Southwestern College of Christian Ministries

Southwestern Community College

Southwesterner

Southwestern Indian Polytechnic Institute

Southwestern Life Insurance Company

Southwestern Michigan College

Southwestern Oklahoma State University

Southwestern Oregon Community College

Southwestern Public Service Company

Southwestern States

Southwestern University

Southwestern University School of Law

Southwest Federal Savings Association

Southwest Indian Foundation

Southwest Institute of Merchandising and Design

Southwest Mississippi Community College

Southwest Missouri State University

Southwest Missouri State University Bears

Southwest School of Electronics

Southwest State Technical College

Southwest State University

Southwest Territory

Southwest Texas Junior College

Southwest Texas State University

Southwest Texas State University Bobcats

Southwest Virginia Community College

Southwest Wisconsin Technical College

South Weymouth Naval Air Station

South Williamsport

South Windsor

South Yemen [now part of Republic of Yemen]

Soutine, Chaïm

Sovereign and Military Order of Malta

Sovereign Greek Order of Saint Dennis of Zante

Sovereign Order of Cyprus

Soviet

Sovietologist

Sovietology

Soviet Politburo

Soviet Socialist Republic of

Moldova [*now* Moldova]

Soviet Union

Sovran Bank

Sovran Financial Corporation

Sovran Foundation

Soweto

Soya Strait

Soyer, Isaac

Soyer, Moses

Soyer, Raphael

Soyuz

Spa

Spaak, Paul Henri

Spaatz, Carl

Space Age

Space Command

Spacek, Sissy

Spacelab

Space Needle

Spaceship Earth

Spacey, Kevin

Spad

Spada, Lionello

Spade, Sam

Spader, James

Spaeth, Sigmund

Spagna, Lo

Spahn, Warren

Spain

Spalding, Albert G.

Spalding University

Spandau

Spandau prison

Spangler, Clemmie Dixon, Jr.

Spanglish

Spaniard

Spanier, Muggsy

Spanish

Spanish America

Spanish-American, *adj.*

Spanish American, *n.*

Spanish-American literature

Spanish-American War

Spanish architecture

Spanish Armada

Spanish art

Spanish bayonet

Spanish bluebell

Spanish broom

Spanish burton

Spanish button

Spanish cedar

Spanish chestnut

Spanish Civil War

Spanish dagger

Spanish flu

Spanish fly

Spanish foot

Spanish Fork City

Spanish grippe

Spanish Guinea

Spanish heel

Spanish influenza

Spanish Information Service

Spanish Inquisition

Spanish iris

Spanish jasmine

Spanish language

Spanish lime

Spanish literature

Spanish mackerel

Spanish Main

Spanish Morocco

Spanish moss

Spanish needles

Spanishness

Spanish omelet

Spanish onion

Spanish oyster plant

Spanish paprika

Spanish plum

Spanish rice

Spanish Sahara

Spanish topaz

Spanish Town

Spanish trefoil

Spano, Joe

Spano, Vincent

Spanos, Alexander Gus

Sparbankemas Bank

Spark, Muriel

Sparkman, John

Sparks

Sparks, Jared

Sparks, Ned

Sparks State Technical College

Sparrow missile

Sparta

Spartacism

Spartacist

Spartacus

Spartacus Party

Spartan

Spartanburg

Spartanburg Methodist College

Spartanburg Technical College

Spartanism

Spassky, Boris

Speaker, Tris

Speaks, Oley

Spears, Billy Jo

Special Drawing
Rights

Special Features/
Syndication Sales

Special Forces

Special Libraries
Association

Special Olympics

Special Olympics
International

Specialty Features
Syndicate

Speck, Richard

Spector, Phil

SPECTRE

Speculum Musicae

Spee, Maxmillian von

Speech
Communication
Association

Speer, Albert

Speicher, Eugene
Edward

Speke, John Hanning

Spelling, Aaron

Spelling
Entertainment Inc.

Spellman, Francis
Joseph Cardinal

Spelman College

Spenard

Spencer

Spencer, Herbert

Spencer, John

Spencer, Platt R.

Spencer, Sir Stanley

Spencer Davis Group

Spencerian
[penmanship;
philosophy of H.
Spencer; see also
Spenserian]

Spencerianism

Spender, Sir Stephen

Spengler, Oswald

Spenglerian

Spenser, Edmund

Spenser: For Hire

Spenserian, adj. [of or
pertaining to
Edmund Spenser;
see also
Spencerian]

Spenserian sonnet

Spenserian stanza

Sperry, Elmer A.

Spertus College of
Judaica

Sphenophyta

Spica

Spice Islands

Spider-Man

Spiegel, Sam

Spiegel, Inc.

Spielberg, David

Spielberg, Steven

Spike Jones and His
City Slickers

Spike Jones
International Fan
Club

Spillane, Mickey

Spindale

Spiner, Brent

Spingarn, Joel Elias

Spingarn Medal

Spinks, Leon

Spinks, Michael

Spinners, The

Spinone Italiano

Spinoza, Benedict de

Spinozism

Spinozist

Spiral Jetty

Spirit Lake

Spirit of '76, The

Spirit of St. Louis

Spirit Wrestler

Spitalny, Phil

Spitfire

Spitsbergen

Spitteler, Carl

Spitz, Mark

Spitzweg, Karl

Spivak, Charlie

Spivey, Victoria

Spock, Benjamin

Spock baby

Spock generation

Spode, Josiah

Spohr, Ludwig

Spokane

Spokane Community
College

Spokane Falls
Community College

Spokane International
Airport

[Spokane]
Spokesman-Review,
The

[Spokane]
Spokesman-
Review/
Chronicle

Spoleto

Spoleto Festival

Spongeorama

Spooner, William Archibald

Spoon River Anthology

Spoon River College

Sporades

Sport Fishing Institute

Sporting News, The

Sport Magazine

Sports Afield

Sports Car Club of America

Sportschannel America

Sports Features Syndicate

Sports Health

Sports Illustrated

Sports Illustrated for Kids

Sportsman's Park

Sportsvision

Sportsworld

Spotsylvania Courthouse

Spotted swine

Spradlin, Brian Nolan

Spring Arbor College

Springdale

Springer, Jerry

Springer Foreign News Service

Springer Mountain

Springfield

Springfield, Dusty

Springfield, Rick

Springfield Armory National Historic Site

Springfield College

Springfield College in Illinois

Springfield Place

Springfield rifle

Springfield Technical Community College

Spring Garden College

Springhill

Spring Hill College

Spring Lake

Spring Lake Heights

Springs Foundation

Springs Industries, Inc.

Springsteen, Bruce

Spring Valley

Springville

Sprint Communications Company

Sprint Corporation [*form.* United Telecommunications, Inc.]

Sprouse-Reitz store

Sprouse-Reitz Stores Inc.

Spruance, Raymond

Spruce Goose

Sputnik

Spuyten Duyvil Creek

SPX Corporation

Spyglass Hill Golf Course

Spy Magazine

Spyri, Johanna

Spyro Gyra

Square D Company

Square D Foundation

Squaw Peak

Squaw Valley

Squeeze

Squibb Corporation

Squibob

Squirrel Nutkin

SRI International

Sri Lanka [*form.* Ceylon]

SR-71 Blackbird

SSANGYONG GROUP

SS Lusitania

S-state

Stabat Mater

Stabat Mater Dolorosa

Stacey

Stack, Robert

Stacy

Stade, Frederica von

Stadel Art Institute

Stader splint

Staël, Madame de

Stafford

Stafford, Jean

Stafford, Jim

Stafford, Jo

Stafford, Nancy

Staffordshire

Staffordshire bull terrier

Staffordshire terrier

Stage Door Canteen

stage door Johnny

Stagg, Amos Alonzo

Stahl, David

Stahl, Lesley

Stahl, Richard

Stahl, Stanley Irving

Stakhanov, Aleksey

Stakhanovism

Stakhanovite

Stalag 17

Stalin, Joseph

Stalingrad [*now* Volgograd]

Stalinism

Stalinist

Stalinoid

Stallone, Sylvester

Stambul *occas.* Stamboul

Stamford [* CT; *see also* Stanford]

Stamos, John

Stamp, Terence

Stamp Act

Stamp Act Congress

Stamping Grounds

Stampley, Joe

Standard & Poor's Corporation

Standard & Poor's Register of Corporations, Directors and Executives

Standard Brands Paint Company

Standardbred horse

Standard Commercial Corporation

Standard English

Standard Federal Bank

Standard Industrial Classification

Standard Industrial Classification Manual

Standard Motor Freight, Inc.

Standard Motor Products, Inc.

Standard Oil Company, The

Standard Products Company, The

Standard Rent-A-Car

Stander, Lionel

Standing, Guy

Standing Rock College

Standish, Miles

Standwell puppets

Standwells, The

Stanfield, Clarkson

Stanford [* KY; *see also* Stamford]

Stanford, A. Leland

Stanford, Leland

Stanford-Binet test

Stanford Court

Stanford Law Review

Stanford Linear Accelerator Center

Stanford University

Stanford University Cardinal *occas.* Cardinals

Stanford University Press

Stang, Arnold

Stanhome Inc.

Stanhope, The

Stanhope, Philip Dormer

Stanislas, Saint

Stanislaus

Stanislaus National Forest

Stanislavsky, Konstantin

Stanislavsky method

Stanislavsky system

Stankiewicz, Richard

Stanley

Stanley, Sir Henry Morton

Stanley, Kim

Stanley, Wendell M.

Stanley and Livingstone

Stanley Cup

Stanley Falls

Stanley Pool

Stanley Steamer

Stanleyville [*now* Kisangani]

Stanley Works, The

Stanley Works Foundation

Stanly Community College

Stanovoy Range

Stans, Maurice

Stansfield, Lisa

Stanton

Stanton, Edwin McMasters

Stanton, Elizabeth Cady

Stanton, Harry Dean

Stanwyck, Barbara

Stapledon, Olaf

Stapleton, Jean

Stapleton, Maureen

Stapleton International Airport

Starbuck, Jo Jo

Star Chamber

Stargell, Willie

Star Group

Stark, Koo

Stark Technical College

Starkville

Starland Vocal Band

Starlight Foundation

star of Bethlehem [bright star at the birth of Jesus]

star-of-Bethlehem [plant], *n., pl.* stars-of-Bethlehem

Star of David

star-of-Jerusalem, *n., pl.* stars-of-Jerusalem

Starr, Bart

Starr, Belle

Starr, Kay

Starr, Ringo

Starr Commonwealth Schools

Starr King School for the Ministry

Starry Night, The

Stars and Bars

Stars and Stripes [flag; newspaper]

Stars and Stripes Forever!, The [march music]

Star Search

Starship

Starship Enterprise

Starsky and Hutch

Star-Spangled Banner, The

Star Trek

Star Trek IV: The Voyage Home

Star Trek: The Motion Picture

Star Trek: The Next Generation

Star Trek: The Official Fan Club

Star Trek III: The Search for Spock

Star Trek II: The Wrath of Khan

Star Trek Welcommittee

Starved Rock

Star Wars

Stash™ tea

Stassen, Harold

State Ballet of Missouri

State Center Community College

State College

State Communities Aid Association

State Community College of East Saint Louis

State Fair Community College

State Farm Companies Foundation

State Farm Insurance

State Farm Insurance Companies

State Farm Life Insurance Company

State Farm Mutual Automobile Insurance Company

State Museums of Berlin

State Mutual Life Assurance

Company of America

Staten Island

[Staten Island] Advance

State of Franklin

State of the Union address

State of the Union message

Stater Brothers, Inc.

Stater Brothers store

Statesboro

States News Service

States' Rights Democratic Party

State Street Bank and Trust Company

State Street Boston Corporation

State Street Foundation

Statesville

State Technical Institute at Memphis

State University of New York

State University of New York at Albany

State University of New York College

State University of New York College of Agriculture and Technology

State University of New York College of Environmental Science and Forestry

State University of
New York College
of Optometry

State University of
New York College
of Technology

State University of
New York Empire
State College

State University of
New York Health
Science Center

State University of
New York Institute
of Technology

State University of
New York Maritime
College

State University of
New York Press

Stationers' Company

Stations of the Cross
occas. stations of
the cross

Statius, Publius

Statler Brothers, The

Statue of Liberty

Statue of Liberty-Ellis
Island Foundation,
Inc., The

Statue of Liberty
National Monument

Statue of Liberty play

Status Quo

Staubach, Roger

Staunton

Stead, Christina

Steadman, Hope

steamboat Gothic

Steamboat Rock

Steamboat Springs

Steamship Historical
Society of America

Steamtown National
Historic Site

Stearman Kaydet

Stedelijk Museum

Steed, John

Steel, Danielle

Steelcase Foundation

Steelcase, Inc.

Steele, Richard

Steele, Sir Richard

Steele, Wilbur Daniel

Steel Magnolias

Steely Dan

Steen, Jan

Steenburgen, Mary

Steer, Philip Wilson

Stefansson, Vilhjalmur

Steffens, Lincoln

Steger

Stegner, Wallace

Steichen, Edward

Steig, William

Steiger, Rod

Stein, Clarence

Stein, Gertrude

Steinbeck, John

Steinberg, Saul Philip

Steinberg, William

Steinbrenner, George

Steinem, Gloria

Steiner, Max

Steiner, Rudolf

Steinhem man

Steinmetz, Charles P.

Stein Roe Mutual
Funds

Steinway, Henry

Steinway and Sons
Inc.

Stella, Frank

Stella, Joseph

Steller, George W.

Steller's jay

Steller's sea cow

Steller's sea lion

St. Elsewhere

Stelvio Pass

Stempel, Ernest E.

Stempel, Robert

Stendahl

Stenerud, Jan

Stengel, Casey

Sten gun

Stenotype Academy

Stepford Wives, The

Stephanie

Stephen

Stephen I, Saint

Stephen, George

Stephen, Sir Leslie

Stephen, Saint

Stephen F. Austin
State University

Stephen F. Austin
State University
Lumberjacks

Stephen Harding,
Saint

Stephens, Jackson
Thomas

Stephens, James

Stephens, Wilton
Robert

Stephens College

Stephenson, George

Stephen the Great

Stephenville

Stepinac, Aloysius
Cardinal

St. Joe Paper Company

St. John, Jill

St. John, Michelle

St. John's, Adela Rogers

St. Johns Greyhound Park

St. Martin's Press, Inc.

Stock, Frederick

Stockbridge

Stockdale, James B.

Stockhausen, Karlheinz

Stockholm

Stockholm-Arlanda Airport

Stockholm-Bromma Airport

[Stockholm] Modern Art Museum

[Stockholm] National Museum

Stockton

Stockton, Frank R.

Stockton Naval Communications Station

Stockton State College

Stockwell, Dean

Stoic

Stoicism

Stoke-by-Nayland

Stoke-on-Trent

Stoker, Bram

Stokes, Carl

Stokes, Jonathan

Stokes-Adams disease

Stokes-Adams syndrome

Stokes aster

Stokes Law

Stokowski, Leopold

Stoller, Mike

Stolojan, Theodor

Stoltz, Eric

Stoltzman, Richard

Stolz, Mary

Stone, Edward Durell

Stone, Fred

Stone, Harlan Fiske

Stone, Irving

Stone, Lewis

Stone, Lucy

Stone, Milburn

Stone, Oliver

Stone, Robert

Stone, Sharon

Stone, Sly

Stone Age

Stone and Webster Inc.

Stone Child College

Stone Container Corporation

Stoneham

Stonehenge

Stonehill College

Stone Mountain

Stone Mountain Memorial

Stone Mountain Park

Stone of Destiny

Stone of Scone

Stone Park

Stones River National Battlefield

Stony Brook

Stony Point

Stookey, Paul

Stop & Shop Companies, Inc., The

Stop Cancer

Stoppard, Tom

Stopping by Woods on a Snowy Evening

Stop the Music

Storage Technology Corporation

Storch, Larry

Storey, David

Storm, Gale

Storm, Theodore

Stormalong, Alfred Bulltop

Storm King

Storm Lake

Storrs

Story, Joseph

Story, William Wetmore

Story of Aladdin, or the Wonderful Lamp, The

Story of Little Black Sambo, The

Story of O

Story of the Three Bears, The

Story of the Three Little Pigs, The

Storyville

Stoss, Veit

Stouffer Corporation, The

Stouffer Corporation Fund, The

Stouffer Foods Corporation

Stouffer Hotel Company

Stouffer President

Stoughton

Stout, Rex

Stowe

Stowe, Harriet Beecher

Stowe, Madeleine

St. Paul Companies, Inc.

St. Paul Federal Bank for Savings

St. Paul Fire and Marine Insurance Company

Strabo

Strachey, Lytton

Stradella, Alessandro

Stradivari

Stradivari, Antonio

Stradivarius

Straight, Beatrice

straight-A student

Strait, George

Strait of Belle Isle

Strait *occas.* Straits of Dover

Strait of Georgia

Strait of Gibraltar

Strait of Hormuz *occas.* Ormuz

Strait of Juan de Fuca

Strait of Lepanto

Strait of Macassar

Strait of Magellan

Strait of Malacca

Strait of Messina

Strait of Otranto

Strait of Singapore

Straits of Florida

Straits of Mackinac

Straits of Mackinac Bridge

Straits Settlements

Strand

Strand, Paul

Strange, Curtis

Strange Case of Dr. Jekyll and Mr. Hyde, The

Strasberg, Lee

Strasberg, Susan

Strasbourg

Strasbourg International Airport

Strasser, Robin

Strassman, Marcia

Stratas, Teresa

Strategic Arms Limitation Talks

Strategic Arms Reduction Talks

Strategic Arms Reduction Treaty

Strategic Defense Initiative

Stratemeyer, Edward

Stratemeyer, Harriet

Stratemeyer Syndicate

Stratford

Stratford-on- *occas.* Stratford-upon-Avon

Strathclyde

Stratton College

Stratus Computer, Inc.

Straub, Peter

Straus, Isidor

Straus, Jesse

Straus, Nathan

Straus, Oscar

Strauss, Eduard

Strauss, Emil

Strauss, Franz Joseph

Strauss, Johann

Strauss, Josef

Strauss, Levi

Strauss, Nathan

Strauss, Peter

Strauss, Richard

Stravinsky, Igor

Strawberry, Darryl

Strawberry Valley Project

Strawbridge, George, Jr.

Strayer College

Strayhorn, Billy

Streamwood

Streator

Streep, Meryl

street Arab

Streetcar Named Desire, A

Streets of San Francisco, The

Streicher, Julius

Streisand, Barbra

Stresemann, Gustav

Strickland, William

Stride Rite Corporation, The

Strieber, Louis Whitley

Strike It Rich

Striker, Fran

Strindberg, August

Stritch, Elaine

Stroessner, Alfredo

Stroh Brewery Company, The

Stroh Companies Inc.

Stroheim, Erich von

Stromboli

Strong/Corneliuson Capital Management, Inc.

Strongsville

Stroud, Robert

Stroudsburg

Strouse, Charles

Strozzi, Bernardo

Structural Stability Research Council

Struthers

Struthers, Sally

Stuart

Stuart, Charles Edward

Stuart, Gilbert

Stuart, James Frances Edward

Stuart, J. E. B.

Stuart, Jesse Hilton

Stuart, Marty

Stuart, Mary

Stuarti, Enzo

Stuart Little

Stuart Pimsler Dance and Theater

Stubbs, George

Stubbs, William

Studebaker

Studebaker, Clement

Studebaker, John M.

Student Loan Marketing Association

Student Nonviolent Coordinating Committee

Student Prince, The [movie]

Student Prince, [in Heidelberg], The [operetta]

Students against Driving Drunk

Students for a Democratic Society

Studio Seven Fashion Career College

Studs Lonigan

Study after Velasquez: Portrait of Pope Innocent X

Stulberg, Neal H.

Sturgeon, Theodore

Sturgeon Bay

Sturges, John Eliot

Sturges, Preston

Sturgis

Sturm und Drang

Stuttgart

Stuttgart Ballet

Stuttgart Chamber Orchestra

Stuttgart disease

Stuttgart Klossiche Philharmonie

Stutz Bearcat

Stuyvesant, Peter

S-2 Tracker

Stygian

Stylistics, The

Styne, Jule

Styrofoam™

Styron, William

Styx

Suárez, Francisco

Subaru of America Foundation

Subaru of America, Inc.

Subic Bay

Subic Bay Naval Station

Subject Was Roses, The

Sublette, William

Success Magazine

Successor of Saint Peter

Suchocka, Hanna

Suckling, Sir John

Sucre

Sucre, Antonio José de

Sudan

Sudan Airways Company Ltd.

Sudanese, n., pl. Sudanese

Sudan grass

Sudbury [* MA; Ontario; see also Sunbury]

Sudden Infant Death Syndrome Alliance

Suddenly Last Summer

Sudeck's atrophy

Sudermann, Hermann

Sudeten

Sudeten crisis

Sudetenland

Sudetes Mountains

Sudwestdeutsche Landesbank

Sue, Eugène

Sue Bennett College

Suetonius

Suez

Suez Canal
Suez Canal rudder
Suez crisis
Suffern
Suffolk
Suffolk County
  Community College
Suffolk Downs
Suffolk sheep
Suffolk University
Sufi, *n.*, *pl.* Sufis
Sufism
Sugar Babies
Sugar Bowl
Sugar Daddy
Sugaring-Off
Sugar Loaf Mountain
Sugarman, George
Suharto
Sui dynasty
Suitland
Suk, Josef
Sukarno
Sukarno-Hatta Airport
Sukkoth *or* Sukkot
Sukowa, Barbara
Sulaiman Mountains
Sulayman the
  Magnificent
Sulla, Lucius
  Cornelius
Sullavan, Margaret
Sullivan
Sullivan, Annie
Sullivan, Sir Arthur
Sullivan, Barry
Sullivan, Ed
Sullivan, Francis L.
Sullivan, Harry Stack

Sullivan, John L.
Sullivan, Kathleen
Sullivan, Leon
  Howard
Sullivan, Louis Henry
Sullivan, Maxine
Sullivan, Susan
Sullivan Award
Sullivan College
Sullivan County
  Community College
Sullivan Stadium
Sully, Thomas
Sully-Prudhomme,
  René François
  Armand
Sulphur
Sulphur Springs
Sulpician
Sul Ross State
  University
Sulu, *n.*, *pl.* Sulu *or*
  Sulus
Sulu Archipelago
Sulu Sea
Sulzberger, Arthur
  Hays
Sulzberger, Arthur
  Ochs
Sumac, Yma
Sumatra
Sumatra camphor
Sumba
Sumbawa
Sumer
Sumerian
Sumer Is Iucumen In
Sumerologist
Sumerology
Sumitomo Bank Ltd.

Sumitomo
  Corporation
Sumitomo Group
Sumitomo Trust and
  Banking Company,
  Ltd.
Summa Theologica
Summer, Donna
Summerall, Pat
Summers, Andy
Summersville Dam
Summerville
Summerville, Slim
Summit
Summit Christian
  College
Summit Hill
Summit University
  Press
Sumner, Charles
Sumner, William
  Graham
Sumner line
Sumners, Rosalynn
Sumter
Sumter Area
  Technical College
Sumter National
  Forest
Sun Also Rises, The
SunBank 24 at
  Daytona
Sunbeam
Sun Belt *occas.*
  Sunbelt
Sunbelt Savings
Sun Bowl [*now* John
  Hancock Bowl]
Sunbury [* PA; *see
  also* Sudbury]
Sun City

Sun Company, Inc.
Sunda Islands
Sundance Kid
Sunda Strait
Sunday
Sunday, Billy
Sunday Afternoon on the Island of La Grand Jatte
Sunday best
Sunday clothes
Sunday Digest
Sunday-go-to-meeting clothes
Sunday League
Sundaylike
Sunday painter
Sunday punch
Sunday School
Sun Devil Stadium
Sundstrand Corporation
Sundstrand Corporation Foundation
Sun Features, Inc.
Sunflower State
Sungari or Sunghua
Sung dynasty
Sun Life Assurance Company of Canada
Sun Life Insurance Company of America
Sun Line Cruises
Sun Microsystems, Inc.
Sunni
Sunnism
Sunnite
Sunnyside

Sunnyvale
Sun Prairie
Sun Ra
Sun Radio Network
Sunrise at Campobello
Sunrise Semester
Sunset
Sunset Books
Sunset Boulevard
Sunset Crater National Monument
Sunset Magazine
Sunset Marquis
Sunset Publishing Corporation
Sunset Strip
Sunshine Foundation
Sunshine Skyway
Sunshine Speedway
Sunshine State
SunStar Radio Network
SunTrust Banks, Inc.
Sununu, John
Sun Valley
Sun Yat-sen
Suomi College
Superadio Network
Super Bowl
Superboy
Superdome
Super 8 motel
Superfund
Superfund Act
Super Glue™
Superior
Superior National Forest
Superman

Superman IV: The Quest for Peace
Superman: The Man of Steel
Superman III
Superman II
Supermarine Spitfire
Super Mario Brothers Super Show, The
Supermarkets General Holdings Corporation
Superstars, The
Superstition Mountain
Supertramp
Super Tuesday
Super Valu Stores, Inc.
Suppé, Franz von
Supper at Emmaus, The
Supplemental Security Income for the Aged, Blind, and Disabled
Suprematism
Supreme Being
Supreme Court of the United States, The
Supreme Pontiff
Supreme Pontiff of the Universal Church
Supremes, The
Supreme Soviet
Surabaya
Surfside
Surgeon General of the United States
Suribachi
Surinam
Surinam Airways Ltd.

Surinam cherry
Suriname
Surinam toad
Surprise Symphony
Surratt, Mary
surrealism *occas.*
  Surrealism
surrealist *occas.*
  Surrealist
surrealistic *occas.*
  Surrealistic
Surrey
Surry Community
  College
Surtees, Robert Smith
Surtsey
Surveyor spacecraft
Susan
Susan, Saint
Susan B. Anthony
  Day
Susan B. Anthony
  dollar
Susann, Jacqueline
Susanville
SU-17 Flagon
Suslov, Mikhail
Susquehanna
Susquehanna
  Company
Susquehanna Depot
Susquehanna
  University
Susquehanna
  University Press
Sussex
Sussex chicken
Sussex County
  Community College
Sussex spaniel
Susskind, David

Susy-Q
Sutcliff, Rosemary
Sutherland, Donald
Sutherland, Graham
Sutherland, Dame
  Joan
Sutherland, Kiefer
Sutherland, Thomas
Sutherland Falls
Sutlej
Sutter, John
Sutter, John Augustus
Sutter's Fort
Sutter's Mill
SU-24 Fitter
SU-27 Flanker
Suu Kyi, Aung San
Suva
Suvero, Mark di
Suvorov, Aleksandr
Suwannee
Suzhou [*form.*
  Soochow]
Suzman, Janet
Suzuki, Daisetz
  Teitaro
Suzuki, Kantaro
Suzuki, Zenko
Suzuki method
Suzuki Motor
  Corporation
Svalbard
Svedberg, Theodor
Svedberg unit
Svengali
Svenska
  Handelsbanken
Sverdlovsk [*now*
  Yekaterinburg]
Swabia

Swabian
Swabian League
Swaggart, Jimmy
Swahili
Swahilian
Swahili language
Swainsboro
Swains Island
Swainson's hawk
Swainson's thrush
Swami Prabhupāda
Swammerdam, Jan
Swampscott
Swan, Billy
Swan Lake, The
Swan River daisy
Swan River
  everlasting
Swanscombe man
Swansea
Swanson, Gloria
Swanson, Howard
Swanson, Kristy
Swarthmore
Swarthmore College
Swarthout, Gladys
Swarthout, Glendon
Swartz Creek
S wave
Swayze, John
  Cameron
Swayze, Patrick
Swazi, *n., pl.* Swazi *or*
  Swazis
Swaziland
Sweat, Keith
Swede
Sweden
Swedenborg, Emanuel

Swedenborgian
Swedenborgianism
Swedenborgism
Swedish
Swedish language
Swedish literature
Swedish massage
Swedish mile
Swedish movements
Swedish Nightingale
Swedish putty
Swedish turnip
Sweelinck, Jan Pieters
Sweeney, D. B.
Sweeney Todd
Sweet, Henry
Sweet Adelines
Sweet Briar College
Sweet Home
Sweetwater
Sweetwater River
sweet William
Swenson, Inga
Swept Away
Swift, Gustavus
    Franklin
Swift, Jonathan
Swift, Tom
Swift Creek Dam or
    Swift Dam
Swift Current
Swift's disease
Swift Transportation
    Company, Inc.
Swift-Tuttle comet
Swinburne, Algernon
    Charles
Swing, The
Swinnerton, Frank

Swinnerton, James
Swire Pacific Ltd.
Swiss, *n. pl,* Swiss
Swissair
Swiss Air Transport
    Company, Ltd.
Swiss Alps
Swiss army knife
Swiss Bank
    Corporation
Swiss chard
Swiss cheese
Swiss Family
    Robinson, The
Swiss Guards
Swiss lapis
Swiss literature
Swiss muslin
Swiss steak
Swissvale
Swit, Loretta
Swithin, Saint
Switzer
Switzerland
Swope, Gerard
Sword *occas.* sword of
    Damocles
Swoyersville
Sybarite
sybaritic *occas.*
    Sybaritic
Sybaritism
Sycamore
Sydenham, Thomas
Sydenham's chorea
    [*form.* Saint Vitus'
    dance]
Sydney [* Australia;
    given name; *see
    also* Sidney]

Sydney Harbor,
    British Harbour
Sydney (Kingsford
    Smith) Airport
Sydney Opera House
Sydney Symphony
    Orchestra
Sydow, Max von
Sylacauga
Sylvania
Sylvester
Sylvester I, Saint
Sylvester, James J.
Sylvester's dialytic
    method
Sylvester the Cat
Sylvia
Sylvian fissure
Symbionese
    Liberation Army
Symbol Technologies,
    Inc.
Symington, Stuart
Symmachus, Saint
Symonds, John
    Addington
Symons, Arthur
Symphonie
    Fantastique
Syms, Sylvia
Syms Corporation
Synagogue Council of
    America
Synanon Church, The
Syndicated News
    Service
Syndicated Review
    Service
Syndicated Writers
    Group

Syndication Association, Inc.

Synge, John Millington

Synge, Richard Laurence Millington

Synoptic Gospels

Synovus Financial Corporation

Syntex Corporation

Synthetic Cubsim *occas.* synthetic cubsim

Syracuse

Syracuse Hancock International Airport

Syracuse Herald-Journal

[Syracuse] Post-Standard, The

Syracuse Symphony Orchestra

Syracuse University

Syracuse University Orange

Syracuse University Orangemen

Syracuse University Press

Syr Darya

Syria

Syriac

Syrian

Syrian Antiochan Orthodox Archdiocese [*now* Antiochan Orthodox Christian Archdiocese of North America]

Syrian Arab Airlines

Syrian Desert

Syrian hamster

Syrian Orthodox Church of Antioch (Archdiocese of the United States of America and Canada)

Syrtis Major

Sysco Corporation

Système Internationale de Unités

Szczecin

Szechwan [*now* Sichuan]

Szell, Georg

Szigeti, Joseph

Szilard, Leo

Szoka, Edmund Cardinal

Szold, Henrietta

Szymanowski, Karol

T

Taanith Esther

Tabasco

TAB Books

Tabby

Tabitha

Table Bay

Table Mountain

Tabor, Baby Doe

Tabor, Horace

Tabor College

Tabriz

Tabriz rug

Tabuchi, Shoji

Tacaná

Tachisme *occas.* tachisme

Tacitean

Tacitus, Marcus Claudius

Tacitus, Publius Cornelius

Tacna-Arica controversy

Tacoma

Tacoma Community College

[Tacoma] Morning News-Tribune

Tacoman

Taconic Mountains

Taddei, Giuseppe

TAD Technical Institute

Tadzhikistan *or* Tajik Soviet Socialist Republic [*now* Tajikistan]

Taegu

Taejon

tae kwon do *often* Tae Kwon Do

Tae-woo, Roh

Taft, Alphonso

Taft, Helen Herron

Taft, Lorado

Taft, Robert A., Jr.

Taft, Robert A., Sr.

Taft, William Howard

Taft College

Taft-Hartley Act

Tagalog language

Tagalog [people], *n.*, *pl.* Tagalog *or* Tagalogs

Taganrog

Taggard, Genevieve

Tagliabue, Paul

Taglioni, Marie

Tagore, Sir Rabindranath

Tagus

Tahiti

Tahitian

Tahitian Girl with Gardenia

Tahiti Faa'a Airport

Tahlequah

Tahoe City

Tahoe National Forest

t'ai chi chu'an *or* tai chi chuan *often* T'ai Chi Chu'an *or* Tai Chi Chuan

Tailhook Association, The

Taimyr Peninsula

Tainan

Taine, Hippolyte Adolphe

Taipei

[Taipei] National Palace Museum

Taiping

Taiping rebellion

T'ai-po

Taiwan

Taiwan Strait

Taiyuan

Tajik

Tajiki

Tajikistan [*form.*
  Tadzhikistan *or*
  Tajik Soviet
  Socialist Republic]

Taj Mahal

Tajo, Italo

Tajumulco

Takakkaw Falls

Takei, George

Take Me Out to the
  Ball Game

Takemitsu, Toru

Takeshita, Noboru

Taklimakan Desert

Takoma Park

Talbot, James Thomas

Talbot, Nita

Talbot, William Henry
  Fox

Talbot hound

Talbot School of
  Theology

Talbotype

Talca

Talcahuano

Tale of a Tub, A

Tale of Genji, The

Tale of Jemima
  Puddleduck, The

Tale of Pigling Bland,
  The

Tale of Peter Rabbit,
  The

Tale of Squirrel
  Nutkin, The

Tale of Two Cities, A

Talese, Gay

Tales from the Vienna
  Woods

Tales of Hoffmann,
  The

Tales of the South
  Pacific

Tales of Wells Fargo

Taliesin

Taliesin West

Talisman, The

Talking Heads

Talk TV Network, Inc.

Talladega

Talladega College

Talladega National
  Forest

Talladega
  Superspeedway

Tallahassee

Tallahassee
  Community College

Tallahassee Magazine

Tallapoosa

Tallchief, Maria

Tallchief, Marjorie

Talleyrand-Périgord,
  Charles Maurice de

Tallinn

Tallis, Thomas

Tallmadge

Tallmadge, Herman

Tallulah

Talmadge, Norma

Talman, William

Talman Home Federal
  Savings and Loan
  Association

Talmi, Yoav

Talmud

Talmudic

Talmudical

Talmudical Academy
  of New Jersey

Talmudical Institute of
  Upstate New York

Talmudical Seminary
  Oholei Torah

Talmudical Yeshiva of
  Philadelphia

Talmudic College of
  Florida

Talmudism

Talmudist

Talmud Torah

Taman Peninsula

Ta Matete

Tamaulipas

Tamayo, Rufino

Tambor, Jeffrey

Tambora

Tambrands, Inc.

Tamerlane

Tamil

Taming of the Shrew,
  The

Tamiroff, Akim

Tamm, Igor

Tammany

Tammany boss

Tammany Hall

Tammanyism

Tammany Society

Tammuz

Tammy

Tam O' Shanter

Tampa

Tampa Bay

Tampa Bay
  Buccaneers

Tampa Bay Downs

Tampa Bay Life

Tampa Bay Lightning

Tampa Bay Storm

Tampa College

Tampa Fronton

Tampa International Airport

Tampan

Tampa Stadium

Tampa Track

Tampa Tribune, The

Tampican

Tampico

Tampico hemp

Tamuz

Tamworth

Tan, Amy

Tana

Tanagra

Tanagra figurine

Tanaina

Tanake, Kakuei

Tanana

Tananarive

Tancred

Tandem Computers Inc.

Tandem Insurance Group

Tandy, Jessica

Tandy Beal and Company

Tandy Corporation

Taney, Roger B.

Tanganyika

Tanganyikan

T'ang dynasty

Tange, Kenzo

Tangerine Dream

Tangier

Tanglewood

Tanglewood Music Center

Tanglewood Music Festival

Tango & Cash

Tangshan

Tanguay, Eva

Tanguy, Yves

Tanimbar Islands

Tanizaki, Junichero

Tank McNamara

Tannenberg

Tanner, Henry Ossawa

Tanner, Roscoe

Tannhäuser

Tantalus

Tantra

Tantrika

Tantrism

Tantrist

Tantum ergo

Tanzania

Tanzanian

Tao

Taoism

Taoist

Taoistic

Taos

Taos [Indian], *n., pl.* Taos

Taos pueblo

TAP Air Portugal

Tapajós

Taper, Sydney Mark

Tapiloa

Tappan, Arthur

Tappan, Lewis

Tara

Tarack, Gerald

Tarack Chamber Players

Tarahumara

Taranto

Taras Bulba

Tarascan

Tarawa

Tar-baby

Tarbela Dam

Tarbell, Ida M.

Tarboro

Tarde, Gabriel

Target Center

Target store

Targhee National Forest

Tarheel

Tarheel State

Tarim

Tarim Basin

Tarkanian, Jerry

Tarkenton, Fran

Tarkington, Booth

Tarkio College

Tarleton State University

Tarmac™

Tarn

Tarn-et-Garonne

Tarnów

Tarnower, Herman

Tarpon Springs

Tarquinius

Tarrant City

Tarrant County Junior College

Tarrytown

Tarses, Jay

Tarski, Alfred

Tarsus

Tartar

Tartarean, *adj.* [of or pertaining to Tartarus]

Tartarian, *adj.* [of or
   pertaining to a
   Tartar]

Tartarian aster

Tartarian dogwood

Tartarian honeysuckle

Tartarus

Tartary

Tartikoff, Brandon

Tartini, Giuseppe

Tartuffe [play]

tartuffe *occas.* Tartuffe
   [hypocritical
   pretender to piety]

Tartuffery

Tarzan

Tasaday

Tashi

Tashi Lama

Tashkent [*now*
   Toshkent]

Tashlich

Tasman, Abel
   Janszoon

Tasman Glacier

Tasmania

Tasmanian

Tasmanian devil

Tasmanian tiger

Tasmanian wolf

Tasman Sea

Tass *occas.* TASS

Tasso, Torquato

Tata Group

Tatar

Tatarian

Tataric

Tatar Strait

Tate, Allen

Tate, Buddy

Tate, Sir Henry.

Tate, Howard

Tate, John

Tate, Nahum

Tate, Sharon

Tate Gallery

Tate Gallery Liverpool

Tatra Mountains

Tattletales

Tatum, Art

Tatum, Edward
   Lawrie

Tauber, Laszlo Nandor

Tauber, Richard

Tau Beta Pi

Taubman, A. Alfred

Tau Delta Phi

Tau Epsilon Phi

Tau Kappa Epsilon

Taunton

Taurus

Taussig, Frank W.

Taussig, Helen Brooke

Tavel wine

Tavener, John
   [English composer,
   1944–]

Taverner, John
   [English composer,
   c. 1490–1545]

Tawney, Richard
   Henry

Taxco

Tax Fairness and
   Economic Growth
   Act

Tax Foundation, The

Tax Free America

Taxi

Tax Reform Act

Tayback, Vic

Taylor

Taylor, A. J. P.

Taylor, Bayard

Taylor, Bert Leston

Taylor, Billy

Taylor, Brook

Taylor, Cecil

Taylor, Deems

Taylor, Don

Taylor, Edward

Taylor, Elizabeth

Taylor, Estelle

Taylor, Frederick
   Winslow

Taylor, Jack Crawford

Taylor, James

Taylor, James Michael

Taylor, Jeremy

Taylor, Johnnie

Taylor, Laurette

Taylor, Margaret
   Smith

Taylor, Maxwell

Taylor, Mildred

Taylor, Myron Charles

Taylor, Otis

Taylor, Paul

Taylor, Peter

Taylor, Robert

Taylor, Robert Lewis

Taylor, Rod

Taylor, Tom .

Taylor, Zachary

Taylor Business
   Institute

Taylorism

Taylorite

Taylor's series

Taylor's theorem
Taylor University
Taylorville
Taylor-Young, Leigh
Tay-Sachs disease
T-bar lift
T-bevel
T'bilisi [*form.* Tbilisi]
T-bill
T-bone steak
TBS Superstation
T cell
TCF Bank Savings
Tchaikovsky, Peter Ilich
Tchebycheff, Pafrutii L.
Tchebycheff equation
Tchebycheff polynomial
Tchelitchew, Pavel
Tcherepnin, Alexander
Tcherepnin, Nicholas
TDK Corporation
Tea Act
Tea and Sympathy
Tea Association of the United States of America
Teach, Edward
Teachers Insurance and Annuity Association of America
Teachers of English to Speakers of Other Languages
Teagarden, Charlie
Teagarden, Jack
Teague, Walter Dorwin

Teahouse of the August Moon, The
Teale, Edwin Way
Teamsters union
Teaneck
Teapot Dome
Teapot Dome scandal
Tearle, Conway
Tearle, Godfrey
Tears for Fears
Teasdale, Sara
Teatro alla Scala
Teatro di San Carlo
Teatro la Fenice
Tebaldi, Renata
Tebet
Technical Association of the Pulp and Paper Industry
Technical Career Institutes
Technical College of the Lowcountry
Technical Trades Institute
Technicolor™
Technological College of the Municipality of San Juan
Technology Institute of Milwaukee
Technoserve
TECO Energy, Inc.
Tedder, Arthur William
Teddy
Teddy boy
Teddy girl
Te Deum, *n., pl.* Te Deums
Te Deum Laudamus

Te Deum Symphony
Ted Mack's Original Amateur Hour
'TEEN
Teenage Mutant Ninja Turtles
Teenage Mutant Ninja Turtles II: The Secret of Ooze
Teflon™
Tegucigalpa
Tecucigalpa Toncontin International Airport
Tehachapi
Tehachapi Mountains
Tehran *occas.* Teheran
[Tehran] Archaeological Museum
Tehran Conference
Tehran Mehrabad International Airport
Tehuelche, *n., pl.* Tehuelche *or* Tehuelches
Tehuelchean
Teicher, Louis
Teichmann's crystals
Teichmann-Stawiarski, L.
Teikyo Post University
Teikyo Westmar University
Teilhard de Chardin, Pierre
Tekakwitha, Kateri
Tekakwitha Indian Mission
Te Kanawa, Dame Kiri

Tektronix Foundation

Tektronix, Inc.

Tel-aire Publications, Inc.

Telamon

Tel Aviv

Tel Avivan

Tel Avivian

Tel Aviv International Airport

Tel Aviv Quartet

Tel Aviv University

Tele-Communications, Inc.

Teledyne Charitable Trust Foundation

Teledyne, Inc.

Teleflora™

Telefónica de España

Teléfonos de México

Telegraph Agency of the Soviet Union

Telegraph Hill

Telemachus

Telemann, Georg Philipp

Telemundo Group, Inc.

Telephone Pioneers of America

TelePrompTer™

Teleshop

Telesphorus

Telesphorus, Saint

Telethon for Muscular Dystrophy

Teletype™

Television Bureau of Advertising

Television Program Enterprises

Television Quatre Saisons

Telex Communications, Inc.

Tell, Alma

Tell, William

Tell City

Teller, Edward

Telluride

Telluride Association

Tellus

Telshe Yeshiva— Chicago

Telstar™

Telugu, *n.*, *pl.* Telugu *or* Telugus

Tempe

Tempelhof

Temperate Zone *occas.* temperate zone

Temperature-Humidity Index

Tempest, The

Tempest, Marie

Templar

Templar, Simon

Temple [* Texas]

Temple, the [district in London, England]

Temple, Shirley

Temple, Sir William

Temple Bar

Temple City

Temple Emanu-El

Temple-Inland Foundation

Temple-Inland Inc.

Temple Junior College

Temple of Angkor Wat

Temple of Artemis

Temple of Athena Nike

Temple of Heaven

Temple of Karnak

Temple of Zeus

Temples of Abu Simbel

Temple Terrace

Templeton, Alec

Temple University

Temple University Owls

Temple University Press

Temptations, The

Tenafly

Ten Commandments

Tender Corporation

Tender Is the Night

Tenderloin

Tenebrae

Tenebrism *occas.* tenebrism

Tenebrist *occas.* tenebrist

Tenerani, Pietro

Tenerife

Teng Hsiao-ping [*now* Deng Xiaoping]

Tengri Khan

Tengri Nor

Teng Ying-chao [*now* Deng Yingchao]

Teniers, David the Elder

Teniers, David the Younger

10-K report

Tennant, Victoria
Tenneco Automotive
Tenneco Credit
 Corporation
Tenneco, Inc.
Tenneco Oil Company
Tennent, Gilbert
Tennent, William
Tennessean
Tennessee
Tennessee Agri-Net
Tennessee Barn Dance
Tennessee Institute of
 Electronics
Tennessee Magazine,
 The
Tennessee Radio
 Network
Tennessee Sportsman
Tennessee State
 University
Tennessee State
 University Tigers
Tennessee
 Technological
 University
Tennessee
 Technological
 University Golden
 Eagles
Tennessee Temple
 University
Tennessee Valley
 Authority
Tennessee walking
 horse *occas.*
 Tennessee Walking
 Horse
Tennessee warbler
Tennessee Wesleyan
 College
Tenniel, Sir John

Tennille, Toni
Tennis [magazine]
Tennstedt, Klaus
Tennyson, Alfred Lord
Tennysonian
Tenochtitlán
Ten Speed Press
Tenth *occas.* 10th
 Amendment [to the
 Constitution]
$10,000 Pyramid, The
Ten Thousand Islands
Tenure of Office Act
Tenuta, Judy
Ten Years After
Ten Years' *occas.*
 Years War
Teotihuacán
Tepes, Vlad
Terborch, Gerard
Terbrugghen,
 Hendrick
Terceira
Terek
Terence
Teresa
Teresa of Ávila, Saint
Tereshkova, Valentina
Teresian
Terex Corporation
Terhune, Albert
 Payson
Terkel, Studs
Terlingua
Terlingua International
 Championship Chili
 Cook-Off
Termagant
Terminator, The

Terminator 2:
 Judgment Day
Terms of Endearment
Tero, Lawrence
Ter-Petrosyan,
 Levon A.
Terpsichore
Terra, Daniel James
Terramycin™
Terra Nova National
 Park
Terra Technical
 College
Terre Haute
Terre Haute Ordnance
 Depot
Terrell
Terrell, Mary Church
Terrell Hills
Territoire de Belfort
Territory of the Don
 Cossacks
Terry
Terry, Bill
Terry, Clark
Terry, Eli
Terry, Dame Ellen
Terry, Paul
Terry, Sonny
Terry and the Pirates
Terry clock
Terry-Thomas
Terryville
Tertiary period
Tertullian
Tesh, John
Tesla
Tesla, Nikola
Tesla coil
Tesla induction motor

Tesla Memorial Society, Inc.

Tesla transformer

Teslin Lake

Tesoro Petroleum Corporation

Tess

Tess of the D'Urbervilles

Tet

Tet offensive

Teton

Teton [Indian], *n.*, *pl.* Teton *or* Tetons

Teton Range

Tetragrammatron

Tetrazzini, Luisa

Tetzel, Johann

Teutoburg Forest

Teuton

Teutonic

Teutonicism

Teutonic Knights

Teutonic Order

Teutonism

Teutonist

Tewes, Lauren

Tewkesbury [* England]

Tewksbury [* MA]

Tex, Joe

Texaco Inc.

Texaco Philanthropic Foundation

Texan

Texarkana

Texarkana College

Texarkana Gazette

Texas

Texas Agricultural and Mechanical University

Texas Agricultural and Mechanical University Aggies

Texas Agricultural and Mechanical University Press

Texas and Pacific Railroad

Texas armadillo

Texas buckthorn

Texas Chiropractic College

Texas Christian University

Texas Christian University Horned Frogs

Texas Christian University Press

Texas City

Texas College

Texas College of Osteopathic Medicine

Texas Commerce Bank

Texas Commerce Bank Foundation

Texas Commerce Plaza

Texas fever

Texas Highways

Texas Independence Day

Texas Industries, Inc.

Texas Instruments Foundation

Texas Instruments Inc.

Texas jujube

texas *occas.* Texas leaguer

Texas longhorn

Texas Lutheran College

Texas panhandle

Texas Raceway

Texas Ranger

Texas Ranger Hall of Fame

Texas Rangers

Texas sage

Texas Southern University

Texas Southern University Tigers

Texas Southmost College

Texas sparrow

Texas Sportsman

Texas Stadium

Texas State Genealogical Society

Texas State Network

Texas State Technical Institute

Texas Tech University

Texas Tech University Health Sciences Center

Texas Tech University Press

Texas Tommy

Texas tower *occas.* Tower

Texas Utilities Company

Texas Wesleyan University

Texas Woman's University

Tex-Mex

Tex-Mex food

Tex-Mex language
Tex-Mex music
Textron Charitable Trust
Textron Inc.
Teyve, the Milkman
T formation
T-46
T-43
T-4U Corvair
T-group
Thackeray, William Makepeace
Thackerayan
Thaddeus
Thaddeus Kosciuszko National Memorial
Thaddeus Stevens State School of Technology
Thai, n., pl. Thai or Thais
Thai Airways International Ltd.
Thailand
Thailander
Thalberg, Irving
Thale
Thales of Miletus
Thalheimer, Louis
Thames
Thames measurement
Thames tonnage
Thames Valley State Technical College
Thanatopsis
Thanatos
Thanet, Octave
Thanksgiving Day
Thanom Kittikachorn

Than Shwe, General
Thant, U
Thar Desert
Tharp, Twyla
Tharpe, Sister Rosetta
Thasian
Thásos
That Championship Season
Thatcher, Margaret
Thatcherism
Thatcherite
That Girl
That's Amore
That's What Friends Are For
That Was the Week That Was
Thaulow, Fritz
Thaves, Bob
Thaw, Harry
Thaxter, Phyllis
Thayer, Abbott Henderson
Thayer, Sylvanus
Thayer, William Roscoe
theater occas. theatre of the absurd; occas. Theater occas. Theatre of the Absurd
Theater an der Wien
Theatine
Theatre Communications Group
Theatre Development Fund
Théâtre Française
Theatre Guild, The

Theatre Library Association
Théâtre Libre
Théâtre Nationale Populaire
Theatre Row
Theatre World
Theban
Thebes
Theismann, Joe
Thelma
Thematic Apperception Test
Themis
Themistocles
Thénard, Louis Jacques
Thénard's blue
Theoblad, Lewis
Theocritan
Theocritean
Theocritus
Theodora
Theodorakis, Mikis
Theodore
Theodore of Mopsuestia
Theodore of Studium, Saint
Theodore Roosevelt Association
Theodore Roosevelt Birthplace National Historic Site
Theodore Roosevelt Inaugural National Historic Site
Theodore Roosevelt Island National Memorial
Theodore Roosevelt National Park

Theodoric

Theodoric the Great

Theodosian

Theodosian Code

Theodosius

Theodosius of
  Palestine, Saint

Theodosius the Great

Theognis

Theophrastian

Theophrastus

Theosophical Society

Theosophical Society
  in America, The

Theravada

Theresa

Theresa of Avila,
  Saint

Thérèse of Lisieux,
  Saint

Thermidor

Thermo Electron
  Corporation

Thermofax™

Thermopolis

Thermopylae

Thermos™ occas.
  thermos bottle

Theroux, Paul

Theseus

Thespis

Thessalian

Thessaly

Theta Chi

Theta Delta Chi

Theta Kappa Omega

Theta Phi Alpha

Theta Xi

Thetford Mines

Thibodaux

Thicke, Alan

Thief River Falls

Thiel College

Thierry, Augustin

Thiers, Adolphe

T hinge

Thinker, The

Thin Lizzy [musical
  group; see also Tin
  Lizzie]

Thin Man, The

Thinnes, Roy

Thiokol Corporation

Thiong'o, Ngugi Wa

Third occas. 3d
  Amendment [to the
  Constitution]

Third-Class Carriage,
  The

Third Federal Savings
  and Loan
  Association

Third International

III John or 3 John

Third Lateran Council

Third of May, The

Third Order

Third Punic War

Third Reich

Third Republic

third world often
  Third World

third world often
  Third World nation

Thirteen Colonies, the

Thirteenth occas. 13th
  Amendment [to the
  Constitution]

Thirty-Nine Articles

thirtysomething

Thirty Tyrants

Thirty Years' occas.
  Years War

Thisbe

This Is the Life

This Old House

Thistledown

This Week with David
  Brinkley

Thívai

Thoeni, Gustavo

Thoma, Hans

Thomas

Thomas, Ambroise

Thomas, Augustus

Thomas, Betty

Thomas, B. J.

Thomas, Clarence

Thomas, Danny

Thomas, Debi

Thomas, Dylan

Thomas, Earl

Thomas, George
  Henry

Thomas, Heather

Thomas, Isaiah
  [publisher]

Thomas, Isiah
  [athlete]

Thomas, John Charles

Thomas, Lowell

Thomas, Marlo

Thomas, Martha

Thomas, Norman

Thomas, Philip
  Edward

Thomas, Philip
  Michael

Thomas, Pinklon

Thomas, Richard

Thomas, Rufus

Thomas, Saint

Thomas, Seth

Thomas à Becket, Saint

Thomas A. Dooley Foundation/ Intermed-USA, Inc.

Thomas A. Edison State College

Thomas à Kempis

Thomas and Betts Corporation

Thomas Aquinas, Saint

Thomas Aquinas College

Thomas College

Thomas Gilcrease Institute of American History and Art

Thomas Jefferson Memorial

Thomas Jefferson's Birthday

Thomas Jefferson University

Thomas M. Cooley Law School

Thomas More, Saint

Thomas More College

Thomas Nelson Community College

Thomas of Celano

Thomas of Erceldoune

Thomas of Woodstock

Thomas Stone National Historic Site

Thomaston

Thomasville

Thomism

Thomist

Thompson

Thompson, Benjamin

Thompson, Butch

Thompson, David

Thompson, Dorothy

Thompson, Francis

Thompson, Hank

Thompson, Hunter S.

Thompson, Jack

Thompson, John T.

Thompson, J. Walter

Thompson, Lea

Thompson, Randall

Thompson, Sada

Thompson, Sam

Thompson, Sylvia

Thompson, William

Thompson Medical Company, Inc.

Thompson seedless grape

Thompson submachine gun

Thomsen, Christian Jürgensen

Thomson, Elihu

Thomson, Sir George Paget

Thomson, James

Thomson, Sir John Arthur

Thomson, Sir Joseph John

Thomson, Kenneth R.

Thomson, Tom

Thomson, Virgil

Thomson, Sir William

Thomson Corporation, The

Thomson effect

Thomson Newspapers Holdings Inc.

Thor

Thorazine™

Thoreau, Henry David

Thoreau Society

Thoreauvian

Thorez, Maurice

Thornburgh, Dick

Thorndike, Ashley Horace

Thorndike, Edward Lee

Thorndike, Lynn

Thorndike, Dame Sybil

Thorne, Francis

Thorne, Oakleigh Blakeman

Thorn EMI

Thorne Music Fund

Thorne-Smith, Courtney

Thornhill, Claude

Thornton

Thornton, Big Mama

Thornton, William

Thoroughbred Racing Association

Thoroughly Modern Millie

Thorpe, Jim

Thorson, Linda

Thorvaldsen *or* Thorwaldsen, Bertel

Thoth

Thousand and One Nights, The

Thousand Island dressing

Thousand Islands

Thousand Islands
International Bridge

Thousand Oaks

Thrace

Thracian

Thraco-Phrygian

Thrale, Hester Lynch

Thrasybulus

Three Affiliated
Tribes

Three Bears, The

Three Billy-Goats
Gruff

Three Blind Mice

Three Choirs Festival

3Com Corporation

Three Dog Night

311 S. Wacker Drive
building

Three Emperors'
League

Three Fires

Three Holy Children

Three Hours devotion

Three Kingdoms
period

Three Kings

Three Little Kittens,
The

Three Little Pigs, The

3 Men and a Baby

3 Men and a Little
Lady

Three Mile Island

Three Musketeers,
The

Three Pagodas Pass

Threepenny Opera,
The

Three Rivers

Three Rivers
Community College

Three Rivers
Shakespeare
Festival

Three Rivers Stadium

Three's Company

Three Signs of Being

Three Stooges, The

Three Suns, The

3-2-1 Contact

Three Wise Men

Three Women

Threlkeld, Richard

Thrift Drug, Inc.

Thriftlodge

Thrifty Corporation

Thrifty Drug Stores,
Inc.

Thrifty Rent-a-Car-
System, Inc.

Throckmorton, Sonny

Throneberry,
"Marvelous" Marv

Throop

Through the Looking-
Glass

Thr-Rift Inn

Thucydides

Thule

Thule Air Force Base

Thulin, Ingrid

Thumbelina

Thunder Bay

Thunderbirds

Thunen, Johann
Heinrich von

Thurber, James

Thuringer *occas.*
Thüringer [sausage]

Thüringer Wald

Thuringia

Thuringian

Thuringian Forest

Thurmond, Strom

Thurow, Lester

Thursday

Thursday Island

Thus Spake
Zarathustra

Thutmose

Thwaites, Reuben
Gold

Thwyng, Charles
Franklin

Thyestean banquet

Thyestes

Thyssen, Fritz

Tiahuanaco *or*
Tiahuanacu

Tiananmen Square

Tiananmen Square
massacre

Tianjin *occas.* Tientsin
or T'ien-chin

Tian Shan

Tibaldi, Pellegrino

Tibbett, Lawrence

Tibbetts, Paul W.

Tibbs, Casey

Tiber

Tiberius

Tibet [*aka* Xizang]

Tibetan

Tibetan antelope

Tibetan architecture

Tibetan art

Tibetan Buddhism

Tibetan spaniel

Tibetan terrier

Tibeto-Burman

Tibullus, Albius
Tice
Tichenor Media System
Ticketmaster Corporation
Tickner, Charles
Ticknor, George
Ticknor, William Davis
Ticknor and Fields
Ticonderoga
Ticor Corporation
Ticor Foundation
Tidewater Community College
Tidewater Inc.
Tieck, Ludwig
Tiegs, Cheryl
Tie Me Up! Tie Me Down!
Tien Shan
Tientsin *or* T'ien-chin *var. of* Tianjin
Tiepolo, Giovanni Battista
Tiepolo, Giovanni Domenico
Tiergarten
Tierney, Gene
Tierra del Fuego
Tietz, Johann Daniel
Tietze's extension theorem
Tietze's syndrome
Tiffany
Tiffany, Charles Lewis
Tiffany, Louis Comfort
Tiffany and Company
Tiffany setting

Tiffin
Tiffin University
Tiflis
Tifton
Tiger Electronics Inc.
Tiger Moth
Tiger Rag
Tiger Stadium
Tigger
Tiglathpileser
Tigrinya
Tigris
Tijuana
Tiki
Tiki Gardens
Tilden, Bill
Tilden, Samuel Jones
Tillamook
Tillamook™ cheese
Till Eulenspiegel's Merry Pranks
Tillich, Paul
Tillis, Mel
Tillis, Pam
Tillman, Floyd
Tillotson, John
Tillstrom, Burr
Tilly, Jennifer
Tilly, Meg
Tilsit cheese
Tilson Thomas, Michael
Tilton, Charlene
Tilzer, Albert von
Tilzer, Harry von
Timanthes
Timbuktu [*now* Tombouctou]
Time

Time Flies
Time Inc.
Time-Life Books, Inc.
Time Life, Inc.
Time Life Libraries Inc.
Time of Your Life, The
Times Books
Times Mirror Company, The
Times Mirror Foundation
Times Square
Time Warner Inc.
Timken Company, The
Timken Company Charitable Trust
Timon
Timon of Athens
Timon of Philius
Timor
Timor Sea
Timoshenko, Semyon
Timothy
Timothy, Saint
Timpanogos Cave National Monument
Timrod, Henry
Timucua
Timucuan
Timucuan Ecological and Historic National Preserve
Timurid dynasty
Timur the Lame
Tinbergen, Jan
Tinbergen, Nikolaas
Tindal, Matthew
Tin Drum, The

Tingley, Katherine

Tinian

Tinicum Island

Tinker, Grant

Tinker, Joe

Tinker Air Force Base

Tinker Bell

Tinkertoy™

Tinley, Scott

Tinley Park

Tin Lizzie [Ford Model T; *see also* Thin Lizzie]

Tin Pan Alley

Tinseltown

Tintagel Head

Tintern Abbey

Tintoretto

Tiny Tim

Tiomkin, Dimitri

Tippecanoe

Tippecanoe Lake

Tipperary

Tippett, Sir Michael

Tippin, Aaron

Tipton

Tiranë *occas.* Tirana

Tirich Mir

Tirol *or* Tyrol

Tirolean *or* Tyrolean

Tirolese *or* Tyrolese

Tiros

Tirpitz, Alfred von

Tirso de Molina

Tisch, Laurence Alan

Tisch, Preston Robert

Tischendorf, Lobegott

Tishah be-av

Tishri

Tisiphone

'Tis Pity She's a Whore

Tissot, James

Tisza

Titan

Titania

Titanic Historical Society

Titanism *occas.* titanism

Titian

Titianesque

Titicaca

Titius-Bode rule

Tito

Titograd

Titoism

Titoist

Titov, Vitaly

Tittle, Y. A.

Titus

Titus, Alan

Titus Andronicus

Titusville

Tiverton

Tivoli

Tivoli Gardens

T. J. Maxx store

TJX Companies, Inc., The

TJX Foundation

Tlalpan

Tlaxcala

TLC Beatrice International Holdings, Inc.

Tlingit, *n., pl.* Tlingit *or* Tlingits

T-man, *n., pl.* T-men

TMS Listing Services

Toad of Toad Hall

Toastmaster [magazine], The

Toastmasters International

Tobacco Nation

Tobacco Radio Network

Tobacco Road

Tobago

Tobe-Coburn School of Fashion Careers

Tobey, Mark

Tobias, George

Tobin, James

Tobol

Tobruk

Toby, *n., pl.* Tobys [given name]

Tocantins

Toccoa

Toccoa Falls College

Toch, Ernst

Tocharian

Tocqueville, Alexis de

Tocumen International Airport

Today

Todd, Alexander

Todd, David

Todd, Michael

Todd, Richard

Todman, Bill

Todo os Santos Bay

Toffler, Alvin

Toggenburg

Togliatti, Palmiro

Togo

Togo Heihachiro

Togolese, *n., pl.*
Togolese

Togo Shigenori

Toi, Zang

toile de Jouy

Toiyabe National
Forest

Tojo Hideki

Tokai Bank Ltd.

Tokai Bank of
California

Tokay

Tokelau

Tokelau Islands
[*form.* Union
Islands]

Tokens, The

To Kill a Mockingbird

Tokio Marine and Fire

Toklas, Alice B.

Tokugawa

Tokyo

Tokyo Bay

Tokyo Electric Power
Company, Inc., The

Tokyo International
Airport/Haneda

Tokyoite

Tokyo Rose

Tokyo Stock
Exchange

Tokyo String Quartet

Tolan, Michael

Toland, John

Toledo

Toledo Blade, The

Toler, Sidney

Tolima

Tolkien, J. R. R.

Toller, Ernst

Tolstoy, Aleksey

Tolstoy, Leo

Tolstoyan

Tolstoyism

Tolstoyist

Toltec

Toltecan

Toltec [people], *n., pl.*
Toltec *or* Toltecs

Toluca

Tom

Tomahawk

Tom and Jerry

Tombalbaye, François

Tombaugh, Clyde
William

Tombigbee

Tombigbee National
Forest

Tomb of the
Unknowns

Tombouctou [*form.*
Timbuktu]

Tombstone

Tom Collins

Tom, Dick, and Harry

Tom Jones

Tomlin, Bradley
Walker

Tomlin, Lily

Tomlinson, David

Tomlinson, Henry

Tomlinson, Michael

Tomlinson College

Tommasini, Vicenzo

Tommy, *n., pl.*
Tommys [given
name]

Tommy, *n., pl.*
Tommies [private in
British army]

Tommy gun

Tommy James and the
Shondells

Tommy Knocker, The

Tommy Tucker

Tomorrow

Tom Petty and the
Heartbreakers

Tompkins, Daniel D.

Tompkins-Cortland
Community College

Tom Sawyer

Toms River

Tom Swift

Tom Swiftie

Tom the Piper's Son

Tom Thumb

Tonawanda

Ton Duc Thang

Tone, Franchot

Tonga

Tonga Islands

Tongan

Tongass National
Forest

Tonight Show, The

Tonkin

Tonkin Gulf

Tonkin Gulf incident

Tonkin Gulf
Resolution

Tônlé Sap

Tönnies, Ferdinand

Tonto

Tonto Basin

Tonto National Forest

Tonto National
Monument

Tonton Macoute, *n.*,
  pl. Tontons
  Macoutes
Tony, *n.*, *pl.* Tonys
  occas. Tonies
  [award]
Tony, *n.*, *pl.* Tonys
  [given name]
Tony Orlando and
  Dawn
Tooele
Tooele Ordnance
  Depot
Tooke, Horne
Tooke, John Horne
Toole, John Kennedy
Toombs, Robert
Toomey, Regis
Toots and the Maytals
Tootsie
Tootsie Roll
  Industries, Inc.
Topeka
Topekan
Topelius, Zakarias
Top Gun
Top Hat
Tophet
Topkapi Palace
Topkapi Palace
  Museum
Top of the Mark
Topol
Toppenish
Topps Company, Inc.
Top 10 *or* 20 *or* 30 *or*
  40, etc.
Torah
Tor Books
Torchmark
  Corporation
Torch Song Trilogy

Toreador Song
Torelli, Giuseppe
Tork, Peter
Tormé, Mel
Torn, Rip
Torne *occas.* Tornio
  River
Torngat Mountains
Toro Company, The
Toronto
Toronto Blue Jays
Toronto-Dominion
  Bank
[Toronto] Globe and
  Mail
Toronto Life
Toronto Maple Leafs
[Toronto] SkyDome
Toronto Star, The
Toronto Star
  Syndicate
Toronto Stock
  Exchange
Toronto Stock
  Exchange Index
Toronto Sun, The
Toronto Symphony
  Orchestra
Torquemada, Tomás
  de
Torrance
Torremolinos
Torrence, Ridgely
Torrens, Sir Robert
Torrens certificate
Torrens law
Torrens system
Torreón
Torres Bodet, Jaime
Torres Strait

Torricelli, Evangelista
Torricellian
Torrid Zone
Torrigiano, Pietro
Torrijos Herrera,
  Omar
Torrington
Tors, Ivan
Tortilla Flat
Tortola
Tortuga
Torvill, Jayne
Torvill and Dean
Tory, *n.*, *pl.* Tories
Tory Democracy
Toryish
Toryism
Tosca
Toscanini, Arturo
Tosco Corporation
Toshiba America, Inc.
Toshiba Corporation
Toshkent [*form.*
  Tashkent]
TOTAL [*form.*
  TOTAL Compagnie
  Française des
  Petroles]
Total Recall
Total System Services,
  Inc.
Total Woman, The
To Tell the Truth
To the Lighthouse
Toto
Totowa
Tottenham
Touche Ross and
  Company
Touchstone Books

Touchstone Television
Tougaloo College
Tough, Dave
Toul
Toulon
Toulouse
Toulouse-Lautrec, Henri de
Toulouse-Lautrec Museum
Tour de France
Tour Du Pont
Touré, Sékou
Toure Kunda
Tourette syndrome
Tourgée, Albion W.
Tournament of Roses Parade
Tourneau Corner store
Tourneur, Cyril
Touro College
Tours
Toussaint, Allen
Toussaint L'Ouverture, François
Tovey, Sir Donald
Towanda
Tower, Joan
Tower Air, Inc.
Tower Books
Tower Bridge
Tower of Babel [biblical site]
Tower of Babel, The [painting]
Tower of London
Tower Records/Video
Towers, Constance
Town, Ithiel

Town and Country
Towneley Plays
Townes, Charles Hard
Townsend, Francis E.
Townsend, John Kirk
Townsend, John Roe
Townsend, Sir John Sealy
Townsend, Robert
Townsend, Willard
Townsend avalanche
Townsend Plan
Townsend's solitaire
Townshend, Charles
Townshend, Pete
Townshend Acts
Towson
Towson State University
Towson State University Tigers
Toye, Wendy
Toy Manufacturers of America
Toynbee, Arnold [reformer]
Toynbee, Arnold J. [historian]
Toyobo Company, Ltd.
Toyota Grand Prix of Long Beach
Toyota Monterey Grand Prix
Toyota Motor Corporation
Toyota Motor Sales, U.S.A., Inc.
Toyota Motor Sales, U.S.A., Inc. Foundation

Toyota Trucks Lime Rock Grand Prix
Toyo Trust and Banking Company Ltd.
Toys "R" Us, Inc. [company logo displays the *R* backwards]
Toy Symphony
Tracey-Warner School
Trachtenberg, Jakow
Trachtenberg system
Tractarian
Tractarianism
Tracy
Tracy, Lee
Tracy, Spencer
Trade a Book bookstore
Trade Act
Traditional Acupuncture Institute
Trafalgar Square
Trafford
Tragical History of the Life and Death of Doctor Faustus, The
Tragic Overture
Tragic Symphony
Traherne, Thomas
Traill, Thomas S.
Traill's flycatcher
Trail of Tears
Trailways™ bus
Trajan, Marcus Upius
Tralee
Trammell Crow Company
Tramp, The

Trans-Alaska Pipeline

Trans-Alpine Gaul

Trans-Amazon Highway

Transamerica Corporation

Transamerica Finance Corporation

Transamerica Life Insurance and Annuity Company

Transamerica Occidental Life Insurance Company

Transamerica Pyramid

Transandine Railway

Transantarctic Mountains

Transatlantic Holdings, Inc.

Trans-Canada Highway

Trans-Caspian Railroad

Transcaucasia

Transcaucasian

Transcendental Club

Transcendental Meditation

Transco Energy Company

Transco Tower

Transjordan [*now* Jordan]

Transkei

trans-Mississippi

TransOhio Savings Bank

Transportation Communications International Union

Transport Workers Union of America

Trans-Siberian Railroad

Transvaal

Transvaalian

Transvaal jade

Trans World Airlines, Inc.

Transworld Feature Syndicate, Inc.

Transylvania

Transylvania Company

Transylvanian

Transylvanian Alps

Transylvania University

Trapeze Artist at the Medrano Circus

Trapp, Georg von

Trapp, Maria von

Trapper John, M.D.

Trapp Family Lodge

Trapp Family Music Camp

Trapp Family Singers

Trappist

Trappist cheese

Trappistine

Traubel, Helen

Träumerei

Travalena, Fred

Travanti, Daniel J.

Travel & Leisure

Travel & Leisure Features

Travel Channel, The

Travelers Aid Association of America

Travelers Companies Foundation

Travelers Corporation, The

Travelers Indemnity Company, The

Travelers Life and Annuity Company, The

Travelers Protective Association of America

Traveler's World

Travel Holiday

Travel Industry Association of America

Travels of Jaimie McPheeters, The

Travels of Marco Polo the Venetian, The

Traven, B.

Travers, Bill

Travers, Mary

Travers, P. L.

Traverse City

Travesties

Travis

Travis, Merle

Travis, Randy

Travis, William

Travis Air Force Base

Travolta, John

Traynor, Pie

Trbovich, Thomas E.

Treacher, Arthur

Trease, Geoffrey

Treasure Chest Features

Treasure Island

Treasure Island Naval Station

Triad Society

Trials of Rosie
O'Neill, The

Triangle

Triangle Club

Triangle Publications
Inc.

Triangle Shirtwaist
factory fire

Triangle Tech

Triangulum

Triangulum Australe

Trianon

Triassic

Triathlon Federation
USA

TriBeCa *occas.*
Tribeca

Triborough Bridge

Tribune Broadcasting
Corporation

Tribune Company

Tribune Entertainment

Tribune Media
Services, Inc.

Tribune Radio
Networks

Tribute Money

Trico Products
Corporation

Tri-County
Community College

Tri-County Technical
College

Tridentine

Trident missile

Trident Technical
College

Trier

Trieste

Trigere, Pauline

Trigger

TRI-HI-Y club

Trikora Peak

Trilateral
Commission, The

Trillin, Calvin

Trilling, Lionel

Trinidad

Trinidad and Tobago

Trinidadian

Trinidad State Junior
College

Trinitarian

Trinitarianism

Trinity [book; river]

Trinity, the [belief]

Trinity Bay

Trinity Bible College

Trinity Broadcasting
Network

Trinity Christian
College

Trinity College

Trinity College of
Music

Trinity Dam

Trinity Episcopal
School for Ministry

Trinity Evangelical
Divinity School

Trinity Industries, Inc.

Trinity Lutheran
Seminary

Trinity Sunday

Trinity University

Trinity Valley
Community College

Trinova Corporation

Trinova Foundation

Trintignant, Jean
Louis

Triple Alliance

Triple Alliance and
Triple Entente

Triple Crown

Triple Entente

Triple Nine Society

Tripoli

Tripoli International
Airport

Tripolitan War

Trisha Brown
Company

Tristan

Tristan da Cunha

Tristan da Cunha
Islands

Tristano, Lennie

Tristan und Isolde

Tri-State University

Tristram

Tristram Shandy

Triton

Triton College

Tritt, Travis

Triumvirate

Trivial Pursuit™

Trobriand Islands

Trocaire College

Troccoli, Kathy

Troi, Starfleet
Counselor Deanna

Troilus

Troilus and Cressida
[legend; opera;
play]

Troilus and Criseyde
[poem]

Trois-Rivières

Trojan

Trojan asteroids

Trojan group
Trojan horse *occas.*
  Horse
Trojan War
Trojan Women, The
Trollope, Anthony
Trollope, Frances
Trollopean
Trollopian
Trombe wall
Tromsö
Trondheim
Trondheim Fjord
TR-1 aircraft
Tropical Zone
Tropic of Cancer
Tropic of Capricorn
Trotsky, Leon
Trotskyism
Trotskyist
Trotskyist
  International
Trotskyite
Trottier, Bryan
Trotwood
Troubetzkoy, Paul
Trouble in Paradise
Troup, Bobby
Trout, Robert
Trout Quintet
T. Rowe Price
  Associates, Inc.
T. Rowe Price
  Investment
  Services, Inc.
Troy
Troyanos, Tatiana
Troyes
Troyon, Constant
Troy State University

truce of God
Truce of Ulm
Trucial Coast
Trucial States [*now*
  United Arab
  Emirates]
Truckee
Truckee Meadows
  Community College
Trudeau, Garry
Trudeau, Margaret
Trudeau, Pierre Elliott
Trudy, *n., pl.* Trudys
True Confessions
True Grit
Truett McConnell
  College
Truex, Ernest
Truffaut, François
Trujillo Molina,
  Rafael
Truk
Truman, Bess
Truman, Harry S
Truman Daniel,
  Margaret
Truman Doctrine
Trumann
Trumbull
Trumbull, John
Trumbull, Jonathan
Trump, Donald J.
Trump, Ivana
Trumpeldor, Joseph
Trump Group Ltd.
Trump Tower
Trust Company Bank
Trust Company of
  Georgia Foundation

Trustees of Dartmouth
  College v.
  Woodward
Trust Territory of New
  Guinea
Trust Territory of the
  Pacific Islands
Truth, Sojourner
Truth in Lending Act
Truth or
  Consequences
Truth Seeker
  Company, Inc.
Truth That Leads to
  Eternal Light, The
TRW Foundation
TRW Inc.
Tryon, Dwight
  William
Tryon, Tom
Tsavo National Park
T-shirt
Tshisekedi wa
  Mulumba, Etienne
Tshombe, Moise K.
T sill
Tsimshian, *n., pl.*
  Tsimshian *or*
  Tsimshians
Tsinan [*now* Jinan]
Tsin dynasty
Tsingtao [*now*
  Qingdao]
Tsinling Shan [*now*
  Qinling Shan]
Tsiolkovsky,
  Konstantin
Tsiranana, Philibert
Tsitsihar [*now*
  Qiqihar]
T-6 Texan
Tsongas, Paul
T square

Tsugaru Strait
Tsushima
Tsushima current
Tsushima Strait
Tswana, *n.*, *pl.* Tswana or Tswanas
T-38 Talon
T-34 Mentor
T-37
T-33
T-28 Trojan
Tuamotu Archipelago
Tuareg, *n.*, *pl.* Tuareg or Tuaregs
Tubal-cain *occas.* Tubalcain
Tubb, Ernest
Tubbs, Tony
Tuberous Sclerosis Association of America
Tubman, Harriet
Tubman, William V. S.
Tucana
Tucci, Gabriella
Tuchman, Barbara W.
Tuckahoe
Tucker, Forrest
Tucker, Michael
Tucker, Orrin
Tucker, Richard
Tucker, Sophie
Tucker, Tanya
Tucson
Tucson International Airport
Tucson Lifestyle
Tucumcari
Tudjman, Franjo
Tudor

Tudor, Antony
Tudor, David
Tudor, Mary
Tudor, Owen
Tudor arch
Tudor style
Tuesday
Tufts University
Tu Fu
Tugboat Annie
Tugwell, Rexford Guy
Tuileries
Tuileries Gardens
Tuktoyaktuk
Tulane Law Review
Tulane University
Tulane University Green Wave
Tulare
Tulare Lake
Tularosa
Tull, Jethro
Tullahoma
Tully, Alice
Tully, Tom
Tulsa
Tulsa International Airport
Tulsa International Raceway
Tulsa Junior College
Tulsan
Tulsa Philharmonic Orchestra
Tulsa Speedway
[Tulsa] World
Tumacacori National Monument
Tumbling Tumbleweeds

Tumwater
Tunbridge Wells
Tune, Tommy
Tungting
Tungus, *n.*, *pl.* Tungus or Tunguses
Tungusic
Tunguska
Tunguska Basin
Tunguz, *n.*, *pl.* Tunguz or Tunguzes
Tunick, Jonathan
Tunis
Tunis Air
Tunis Carthage International Airport
Tunisia
Tunney, Gene
Tunxis Community College
TU-142 Bear
TU-160 Blackjack
Tupamaros
Tupelo
Tupelo National Battlefield
Tupi, *n.*, *pl.* Tupi or Tupis
Tupi-Guarania
Tupi-Guaranian
Tupolev, Andrei
Tupper, Sir Charles
Tupper Lake
Tupperware™
Tupungato
Tura, Cosimo
Turandot
Turanian

Turcoman, *n.*, *pl.*
  Turcomen

Turcophile *occas.*
  Turkophile

Turcophobe *occas.*
  Turkophobe

Turf Paradise

Turfway Park Race
  Course

Turgenev, Ivan

Turgot, Anne Robert
  Jacques

Turin

Turina, Joaquín

[Turin] Civic Museum
  of Ancient Art

Turing, Alan Mathison

Turing machine

Turk

Turkestan

Turkey

Turkey in the Straw

Turkey red

Turki

Turkic

Turkish

Turkish Airlines Inc.

Turkish and Islamic
  Art Museum

Turkish Angora

Turkish bath

Turkish carpet

Turkish coffee

Turkish crescent

Turkish delight

Turkish Empire

Turkish Islamic Holy
  War

Turkish knot

Turkish language

Turkish paste

Turkish pound

Turkish rug

Turkish tobacco

Turkish towel

Turkish tulip

Turkism

Turkman, *n.*, *pl.*
  Turkmen

Turkmen, *adj.* [of or
  pertaining to
  Turkmenistan]

Turkmenia [*aka*
  Turkmen Soviet
  Socialist Republic;
  now Turkmenistan]

Turkemenian

Turkmenistan [*form.*
  Turkmenia; *aka*
  Turkmen Soviet
  Socialist Republic]

Turkoman, *n.*, *pl.*
  Turkomen

Turkoman carpet

Turkoman rug

Turks and Caicos
  Islands

Turk's-cap lily

Turk's head

Turk's-head cactus

Turku

Turlington, Christy

Turlock

Turnberry Isle Yacht
  and Country Club

Turner, Big Joe

Turner, Frederick
  Jackson

Turner, Henry Hubert

Turner, Ike

Turner, Joe

Turner, Joseph
  Mallard William

Turner, Kathleen

Turner, Lana

Turner, Nat

Turner, Ted

Turner, Tina

Turner Air Force Base

Turner Broadcasting
  System, Inc.

Turner Entertainment
  Company

Turner Network
  Television

Turners Falls

Turner's syndrome

Turn of the Screw,
  The

Turnverein

Turpin, Ben

Turpin, Dick

Turtle Mountain
  Community College

Turtles, The

Tuscaloosa

Tuscan

Tuscan atrium

Tuscan order

Tuscany

Tuscarora, *n.*, *pl.*
  Tuscarora *or*
  Tuscaroras

Tuscola

Tuscorora Mountain

Tuscorora Mountains

Tusculum College

Tuscumbia

Tushingham, Rita

TU-16 Badger

Tuskegee

Tuskegee Airmen

Tuskegee Institute National Historic Site

Tuskegee National Forest

Tuskegee University

Tussaud, Marie

Tustin

Tustin Marine Corps Air Station

Tutankhamen *occas.* Tutankhamun *or* Tutankhamon

Tutchone

Tutsi

Tutu, Desmond

Tutuila

TU-22 Backfire

Tuva

Tuvalu [*form.* Ellice Islands]

Tuzigoot National Monument

TV Data, Inc.

TV dinner

TV Extra

TV Guide

TV Listing, Inc.

TVUpdate

Twachtman, John Henry

Twain, Mark

Twayne Publishers

Tweed, William Marcy

Tweedledum and Tweedledee

Tweed Ring

Tweetie Pie

Twelfth *occas.* 12th Amendment [to the Constitution]

Twelfth Day

Twelfth Night

Twelfthtide

Twelve Apostles

Twelve Days of Christmas, The

Twelve Disciples

12 Hours of Sebring Camel Grand Prix of Endurance

Twelve Tables, the

Twelvetrees, Helen

Twelve Tribes

Twelve Views from a Thatched Cottage

Twentieth *occas.* 20th Amendment [to the Constitution]

Twentieth Century-Fox Film Corporation

20th Century Industries

20th Century Insurance Company

Twentieth-Century Limited

Twentieth Century Mutual Funds

Twenty-fifth *occas.* 25th Amendment [to the Constitution]

Twenty-first *occas.* 21st Amendment [to the Constitution]

21st Century Casualty Company

Twenty-First Century Family Syndicate

$25,000 Pyramid, The

24 Hours of Le Mans

Twenty-fourth *occas.* 24th Amendment [to the Constitution]

Twentynine Palms Marine Corps Air Ground Combat Center

Twenty-one Demands

21 Jump Street

Twenty-second *occas.* 22d Amendment [to the Constitution]

Twenty-sixth *occas.* 26th Amendment [to the Constitution]

Twenty-third *occas.* 23d Amendment [to the Constitution]

$20,000 Pyramid, The

Twenty Thousand Leagues under the Sea

TW Holdings, Inc.

Twickenham

Twiggy

Twilight of the Gods

Twilight Zone, The

Twin Citian

Twin Cities

Twin Cities Arsenal

Twin Falls

Twining, Nathan

Twinkie defense

Twinkies™ snack cakes, *sing.* Twinkie

Twin Peaks

Twittering Machine, The

Twitty, Conway

Two Acrobats with Dog

Two Day Priority Mail™

2,4-D

2,4,5-T

Two Gentlemen of Verona, The

Two Harbors

2 Live Crew

Two Prudential Plaza

Two Rivers

Tworkov, Jack

Two Sicilies

2001: A Space Odyssey

Two Women

Two Years before the Mast

Tyche

Tyco Laboratories, Inc.

Tylenol™

Tyler

Tyler, Anne

Tyler, Bonnie

Tyler, Sir Edward Burnett

Tyler, John

Tyler, Moses Coit

Tyler, Royall

Tyler, Toby

Tyler, T. Texas

Tyler, Wat *occas.* Walter

Tyler Junior College

Tyndale, William

Tyndall, John

Tyndall, William

Tyndall Air Force Base

Tyndall beam

Tyndall effect

Tyne

Tynemouth

Tyner, McCoy

Type A personality

Type B personality

Typhoid Mary, *n., pl.* Typhoid Marys

Tyre

Tyrian

Tyrian dye

Tyrian purple

Tyrol *var. of* Tirol

Tyrolean *var. of* Tirolean

Tyrolese *var. of* Tirolese

Tyrolienne

Tyron, Thomas

Tyrone

Tyrrell, Susan

Tyrrhenian Sea

Tyrwhitt-Wilson, Gerald Hugh

Tyson, Barbara

Tyson, Cicely

Tyson, Donald John

Tyson, Mike

Tyson Foods, Inc.

Tyus, Wyomia

Tzom Gedallah

Tzu Hsi *or* Tz'O Hsi

U

UAL Corporation

Uap *var. of* Yap Islands

Ubangi

U-Bild Newspaper Syndicate

Ubiquitarian

Ubiquitarianism

U-boat

U bolt

Ucayali

Uccello, Paolo

Udall, Morris K.

Udall, Nicholas

Udall, Stewart

Ueberroth, Peter

Uecker, Bob

Ueltschi, Albert Lee

Uffizi Gallery

Uffizi Palace

Uganda

Uganda Airlines Corporation

Ugandan

Uggams, Leslie

UGI Corporation

Ugly American

Ugly Duckling, The

U-Haul International, Inc.

UH-46 Sea Knight

Uhland, Johann Ludwig

UH-1 Iroquois

UH-1 Super Huey

UH-60 Black Hawk

UH-2 Seasprite

Uhura, Lieutenant

Uinta Mountains

Uinta National Forest

UJB Financial

UJB/Hackensack

U-joint

Ukraine [nation; *form.* Ukrainian Soviet Socialist Republic]

Ukraine, the [region]

Ukranian

Ukrainian literature

Ukrainian Orthodox Church in the United States of America

Ukrainian Orthodox Church of America (Ecumenical Patriarchate)

Ukrainian Soviet Socialist Republic [*now* Ukraine]

Uladislaus

Ulan Bator

Ulanova, Galina

Ulbricht, Walter

Ulene, Art

Ul-Haq, Mohammad Zia

Ulithi

Ullman, Norm

Ullman, Tracey

Ullmann, Liv

Ulloa, Antonio de

Ulloa, Francisco de

Ulm

Ulric, Lenore

Ulric, Saint

Ulster

Ulster County Community College

Ulster cycle

Ulsterite

Ulsterman, *n., pl.* Ulstermen

Ulsterwoman, *n., pl.* Ulsterwomen

ultima Thule

Ultraquist

Ultravox

Ulysses

Ulysses S. Grant National Historic Site

Umatilla

Umatilla National Forest

Umatilla Ordnance Depot

Umayyad dynasty

Umbria

Umbrian

Umeki, Miyoshi

Umm al Qaywayn

Umnak

Umpqua

Umpqua Community College

Umpqua National Forest

Unabashed Librarian, The

Unalaska

un-American

un-Americanism

Unamuno, Miguel de

Unbearable Lightness of Being, The

Uncle Ben's Inc.

Uncle Milton Industries Inc.

Uncle Remus

Uncle Remus: His Songs and His Sayings

Uncle Sam

Uncle Tom

Uncle Tomism

Uncle Tom's Cabin

Uncle Vanya

Uncompahgre

Uncompahgre National Forest

Uncompahgre Peak

Underground Railroad

Underground Railway

Underwood, Blair

Underwood, Ron

Underwriters Laboratories Inc.

Undset, Sigrid

un-English

un-Eucharistic

un-Eucharistical

un-European

Ungava

Ungava Bay

Uniat *occas.* Uniate

Unification Church

Unification Theological Seminary

Unifi, Inc.

Uniforce Temporary Personnel, Inc.

Uniform Code of Military Justice [*form.* Articles of War]

Uniform Commercial Code

Uniform Product Code

Unigate Inc.

Unilever United States, Inc.

Unimak

Union

Union Bank Foundation

Union Bank of Switzerland

Union Camp Charitable Trust

Union Camp Corporation

Union Carbide Corporation

Union Central Life Insurance Company

Union City

Union College

Union County College

Uniondale

Union de Transports Aériéns

Union Electric Company

Union Electric Company Charitable Trust

Union Institute

Union Islands [*now* Tokelau Islands]

Union Jack

Union League Club

Union of American Hebrew Congregations

Union of American Physicians and Dentists

Union of Concerned Scientists

Union of Flight Attendants

Union of Orthodox Jewish Congregations of America

Union of Sephardic Congregations

Union of Soviet Socialist Republics

Union Pacific Corporation

Union Pacific Foundation

Union Pacific Railroad

Union Planters National Bank

Union Texas Petroleum Holdings, Inc.

Union Theological Seminary

Union Theological Seminary in Virginia

Uniontown

Union University

Union Valley Dam

Union Valley Reservoir

Unique Forms of Continuity in Space

Uniroyal Goodrich Tire Company

Unistar Radio Networks

Unisys Corporation

Unitarian

Unitarian Church

Unitarianism

Unitarian Universalist Association

Unitarian Universalist Service Committee

Unitas, John

United Action for Animals

United Activists for Animal Rights

United Airlines Foundation

United Airlines, Inc.

United Arab Emirates [*form.* Trucial States]

United Arab Republic

United Artists Entertainment Company

United Association of Journeymen and Apprentices of the Plumbing and Pipe Fitting Industry of the United States and Canada

United Auto Workers

United Bank Community Assistance Fund

United Banks of Colorado, Inc.

United Brotherhood of Carpenters and Joiners of America

United California Bank

United Cancer Council

United Cerebral Palsy Associations

United Cerebral Palsy Research and Education Foundation

United Christian Church

United Christian Missionary Society

United Church of Canada

United Church of Christ

United Colonies of New England

United Daughters of the Confederacy

United Egg Association

United Electrical, Radio and Machine Workers of America

United Electronics Institute

United Empire Loyalists

United Engineering Trustees

United Farm Workers of America

United Features Syndicate, Inc.

United Federation of Planets

United Food and Commercial Workers International Union

United Garment Workers of America

United Grocers, Inc.

United HealthCare Corporation

United Illuminating Company

United Insurance Company of America

United International Union Plant Guard Workers of America

United Investors Management Company

United Irishmen

United Irish Society

United Israel Appeal

United Jewish Appeal

United Kennel Club

United Kingdom of Great Britain and Northern Ireland

United Klans of America

United Media

United Methodist Church, The

United Mine Workers of America

United Musical Instruments U.S.A. Inc.

United Nations

United Nations Association of the United States of America

United Nations Children's Fund [*form.* United Nations International Children's Emergency Fund]

United Nations Day

United Nations Development Program

United Nations Economic and Social Commission for Asia and the Pacific

United Nations Economic and Social Commission for Western Africa

United Nations Economic and Social Council

United Nations Economic Commission for Africa

United Nations Economic Commission for Europe

United Nations Economic Commission for Latin America and the Caribbean

United Nations Educational, Scientific and Cultural Organization

United Nations General Assembly

United Nations Industrial Development Organization

United Nations Institute for Disarmament Research

United Nations Institute for Training and Research

United Nations International Children's Emergency Fund [*now* United Nations Children's Fund]

United Nations International Research and Training Institute for the Advancement of Women

United Nations Multilateral Investment Guarantee Agency

United Nations peacekeeping force

United Nations Plaza

United Nations Plaza Hotel

United Nations Relief and Rehabilitation Administration

United Nations Research Institute for Social Development

United Nations Secretariat

United Nations Security Council

United Nations Trusteeship Council

United Nations Universal Declaration of Human Rights

United Nations University

United Nations University for Peace

United Negro College Fund

United Neighborhood Centers of America

United Network for Organ Sharing

United of Omaha Life Insurance Company

United Order of True Sisters

United Ostomy Association

United Pacific Life Insurance Company

United Paperworkers International Union

United Parcel Service of America, Inc.

United Pentecostal
Church
International

United Presbyterian
Church

United Presbyterian
Church in the
U.S.A., The

United Press
International, Inc.

United Press
International
Newspictures

United Press
International Radio

United Rubber, Cork,
Linoleum and
Plastic Workers of
America

United Savings
Association of
Texas

United Seamen's
Service

United Service
Organizations

United Services
Automobile
Association

United Sports Fans of
America

United States

United States
Agricultural
Stabilization and
Conservation
Service

United States Air
Force

United States Air
Force Academy

United States Air
Force Academy
Falcons

United States Air
Force Reserve

United States Air
Force Reserve
Officers Training
Corps

United States Amateur
Confederation of
Roller Skating

United States Armor
Association

United States Army

United States Army
Command and
General Staff
College

United States Army
Ranger Association

United States Army
Reserve

United States Army
Reserve Officers
Training Corps

United States Army
Special Forces

United States Army
Warrant Officers
Association

United States Auto
Club

United States
Badminton
Association

United States Beet
Sugar Association

United States Board
on Geographic
Names

United States Botanic
Garden

United States Boxing
Association

United States Canoe
Association

United States Capitol

United States Catholic
Conference

United States Chess
Federation

United States Civil
Service
Commission

United States Coast
Guard

United States Coast
Guard Academy

United States Coast
Guard Auxiliary

United States Coast
Guard Chief Petty
Officer Association

United States Coast
Guard Chief
Warrant and
Warrant Officers'
Association

United States
Committee for
Refugees

United States
Committee for the
United Nations
Children's Fund

United States
Conference for the
World Council of
Churches

United States
Conference of
Mayors

United States
Congress

United States Council
for Energy
Awareness

United States Court of
Appeals

United States Court of
Claims

United States Court of International Trade

United States Court of Veterans Appeals

United States Customs Court

United States Customs Service

United States Cycling Federation

United States Disc Sports

United States Employment Service

United States District Court

United States Fish and Wildlife Service

United States Forest Service

United States Games Systems Inc.

United States Geological Survey

United States Golf Association

United States Government Printing Office

United States Gymnastics Federation

United States Gypsum Company

United States Handball Association

United States Hispanic Chamber of Commerce

United States Hockey Hall of Fame

United States Horse Cavalry Association

United States House of Representatives

United States Indoor Tennis Championships

United States Information Agency

United States International University

United States-Japan Security Treaty

United States Judo Association

United States League of Savings Institutions

United States Marine Corps

United States Marshals Service

United States Merchant Marine Academy

United States Merchant Marine Veterans of World War II

United States Metric Association

United States Military Academy

United States Military Academy Black Knights

United States Mint

United States National Bank

United States Naval Academy

United States Naval Academy Midshipmen

United States Naval Institute

United States Naval Observatory

United States Navy

United States of America

United States of America Catholic Charities

United States Office of Consumer Affairs

United States Olympic Committee

United States Pharmacopeia

United States Playing Card Company

United States Polo Association

United States Postal Service

United States Power Squadrons

United States Professional Cycling Federation

United States Public Interest Research Group

United States Revolver Association

United States Sanitary Commission

United States Savings Bonds

United States Secret Service

United States Senate

United States Shoe Corporation, The

United States Ski Association

United States Slo-Pitch Softball Association

United States Soccer Federation

United States Space Education Association

United States Space Foundation

United States Sports Academy

United States Steel Corporation [now USX Corporation]

United States Strategic Command

United States Submarine Veterans of World War II

United States Sugar Corporation

United States Sugar Corporation Charitable Trust

United States Surgical Corporation

United States Swimming, Inc.

United States Table Tennis Association

United States Tax Court

United States Tennis Association

United States Tobacco Company

United States Trademark Association [now International Trademark Association]

United States Trivia Association

United States Trotting Association

United States Trust Company of New York

United States Trust Company of New York Foundation

United States v. E. C. Knight Company

United States Volleyball Association

United States Water Polo

United States Weightlifting Federation

United States Yacht Racing Union

United States Youth Soccer Association

United Stations Radio Networks

United Steelworkers of America

United Synagogue of America (Conservative)

United Talmudical Academy

United Technologies Corporation

United Telecommunications, Inc. [now Sprint Corporation]

United Textile Workers of America

United Theological Seminary

United Theological Seminary of the Twin Cities

United Transportation Union (Ind.)

United Tribes Technical College

United Union of Roofers, Waterproofers and Allied Workers

United Van Lines, Inc.

United Video

United Vintners Inc.

United Way International

United Way of America

United Wesleyan College

United We Stand America

United World Atheists

United Zion Church

Unity College

Unity of the Brethren

Unity School of Christianity

Univar Corporation

Universal Autograph Collectors Club

Universal Cigar Corporation

Universal City Studios Inc.

Universal City Studios Tour

Universal Corporation

Universal Fellowship of Metropolitan

Community Churches

Universal Foods Corporation

Universalist Church of America

Universal Postal Union

Universal Press Syndicate

Universal Product Code

Universal Studios Florida

Universal Technical Institute

Universal Television

Universal Time

Universal Univis Inc.

Universidad Central del Caribe

Universidad del Turabo

Universidad Metropolitana

Universidad Politecnica de Puerto Rico

University City

University Heights

University Microfilms Inc.

University of Akron

University of Akron Zips

University of Alabama

University of Alabama Crimson Tide

University of Alabama in Birmingham

University of Alabama in Birmingham Blazers

University of Alabama Press

University of Alaska

University of Alaska Press

University of Alaska Southeast

University of Algiers

University of Arizona

University of Arizona Press, The

University of Arizona Wildcats

University of Arkansas

University of Arkansas at Little Rock

University of Arkansas at Little Rock Trojans

University of Arkansas Press, The

University of Arkansas Razorbacks

University of Baltimore

University of Bologna

University of Bridgeport

University of Bristol

University of British Columbia

University of Cairo

University of Calgary

University of California

University of California, Berkeley

University of California, Berkeley Golden Bears

University of California, Berkeley Wellness Letter

University of California, Davis

University of California, Davis Aggies

University of California, Irvine

University of California, Irvine Anteaters

University of California, Los Angeles

University of California, Los Angeles Bruins

University of California Press

University of California, Santa Barbara

University of California, Santa Barbara Gauchos

University of California v. Bakke

University of Central Arkansas

University of Central Florida

University of Central Florida Knights

University of Central Texas

University of Charleston

University of Chicago

University of Chicago Law Review

University of Chicago Press, The

University of
Cincinnati

University of
Cincinnati Bearcats

University of
Colorado

University of
Colorado Buffaloes

University of
Connecticut

University of
Connecticut
Huskies

University of Dallas

University of Dayton

University of Dayton
Flyers

University of
Delaware

University of
Delaware Fightin'
Blue Hens

University of
Delaware Press

University of Denver

University of Detroit

University of Dublin

University of
Dubuque

University of Durham

University of
Edinburgh

University of
Evansville

University of
Evansville Purple
Aces

University of Findlay

University of Florida

University of Florida
Gators

University of Georgia

University of Georgia
Bulldogs

University of Georgia
Press

University of Glasgow

University of Guam

University of Guelph

University of Hartford

University of Hartford
Hawks

University of Havana

University of Hawaii

University of Hawaii
Press

University of Hawaii
Rainbow Warriors

University of Health
Sciences, The

University of Health
Sciences—Chicago
Medical School

University of
Heidelberg

University of Houston

University of Houston
Cougars

University of Idaho

University of Idaho
Press

University of Idaho
Vandals

University of Illinois

University of Illinois
at Chicago

University of Illinois
at Chicago Flames

University of Illinois
Fighting Illini

University of Illinois
Press

University of
Indianapolis

University of Iowa

University of Iowa
Hawkeyes

University of Iowa
Press

University of Jena

University of Judaism

University of Kansas

University of Kansas
Jayhawks

University of
Kentucky

University of
Kentucky Wildcats

University of La
Verne

University of Leeds

University of Leiden

University of Leipzig

University of
Liverpool

University of London

University of
Louisville

University of
Louisville Fighting
Cardinals

University of Lowell

University of Maine

University of Maine
Black Bears

University of Maine
Press

University of
Manchester

University of
Manitoba

University of Mary

University of Mary
Hardin-Baylor

University of
Maryland

University of Maryland, Baltimore County

University of Maryland, Baltimore County Retrievers

University of Maryland, College Park

University of Maryland, College Park Terrapins

University of Maryland, Eastern Shore

University of Maryland, Eastern Shore Hawks

University of Massachusetts

University of Massachusetts Minutemen

University of Massachusetts Press

University of Medicine and Dentistry of New Jersey

University of Melbourne

University of Miami

University of Miami Hurricanes

University of Miami Law Review

University of Michigan

University of Michigan Press, The

University of Michigan Wolverines

University of Minnesota

University of Minnesota Golden Gophers

University of Minnesota Press

University of Mississippi

University of Mississippi Rebels

University of Missouri

University of Missouri Press

University of Missouri Wildcats

University of Moncton

University of Montana

University of Montana Grizzlies

University of Montevallo

University of Montpelier

University of Naples

University of Nebraska

University of Nebraska Cornhuskers

University of Nebraska Press

University of Nevada

University of Nevada at Las Vegas

University of Nevada at Las Vegas Rebels

University of Nevada at Reno

University of Nevada at Reno Wolf Pack

University of Nevada Press

University of New Brunswick

University of Newcastle

University of Newcastle-upon-Tyne

University of New England

University of New Hampshire

University of New Hampshire Wildcats

University of New Haven

University of New Jersey

University of New Mexico

University of New Mexico Lobos

University of New Mexico Press

University of New Orleans

University of New Orleans Privateers

University of North Alabama

University of North Carolina

University of North Carolina at Asheville

University of North Carolina at Asheville Bulldogs

University of North Carolina at Charlotte

University of North Carolina at Charlotte 49ers

University of North Carolina at Wilmington

University of North Carolina at Wilmington Seahawks

University of North Carolina Press, The

University of North Carolina Tar Heels

University of North Dakota

University of Northern Colorado

University of Northern Iowa

University of Northern Iowa Purple Panthers

University of North Florida

University of North Texas

University of North Texas Eagles

University of North Texas Press

University of Notre Dame

University of Notre Dame Fighting Irish

University of Notre Dame Press

University of Nottingham

University of Oklahoma

University of Oklahoma Press

University of Oklahoma Sooners

University of Oregon

University of Oregon Ducks

University of Osteopathic Medicine and Health Sciences

University of Paris

University of Pennsylvania

University of Pennsylvania Law Review

University of Pennsylvania Press

University of Pennsylvania Red and Blue

University of Pennsylvania University Museum

University of Phoenix

University of Pittsburgh

University of Pittsburgh Panthers

University of Pittsburgh Press

University of Portland

University of Portland Pilots

University of Pretoria

University of Puerto Rico

University of Puerto Rico Arecibo Technological University College

University of Puerto Rico Press

University of Puget Sound

University of Quebec

University of Quebec at Three Rivers

University of Queensland

University of Reading

University of Redlands

University of Rhode Island

University of Rhode Island Rams

University of Richmond

University of Richmond Spiders

University of Rio Grande

University of Rochester

University of Rochester Press

University of Rome

University of Saint Andrews

University of Saint Mary of the Lake Mundelein Seminary

University of Saint Thomas

University of Salamanca

University of San Diego

University of San Diego Toreros

University of San Francisco

University of San Francisco Dons

University of San Marcos

University of Santo Tomás

University of Sarasota

University of Saskatchewan

University of Science and Arts of Oklahoma

University of Scranton

University of Scranton Press

University of Sheffield

University of Sherbrooke

University of South Alabama

University of South Alabama Jaguars

University of South Carolina

University of South Carolina Fighting Gamecocks

University of South Carolina Press

University of South Dakota

University of Southern California

University of Southern California Trojans

University of Southern Colorado

University of Southern Indiana

University of Southern Maine

University of Southern Mississippi

University of Southern Mississippi Golden Eagles

University of South Florida

University of South Florida Bulls

University of Southwestern Louisiana

University of Southwestern Louisiana Ragin' Cajuns

University of Strathclyde

University of Tampa

University of Tennessee

University of Tennessee at Chattanooga

University of Tennessee at Chattanooga Moccasins

University of Tennessee Press

University of Tennessee Volunteers

University of Texas

University of Texas at Arlington

University of Texas at Arlington Mavericks

University of Texas at Austin

University of Texas at El Paso

University of Texas at El Paso Miners

University of Texas at San Antonio

University of Texas at San Antonio Roadrunners

University of Texas Health Science Center

University of Texas Longhorns

University of Texas Medical Branch

University of Texas of the Permian Basin

University of Texas—Pan American

University of Texas Press

University of Texas Southwestern Medical Center

University of the Americas

University of the Arts

University of the Bosporus

University of the District of Columbia

University of the Ozarks

University of the Pacific

University of the Pacific Tigers

University of the Philippines

University of the Sacred Heart

University of the South

University of the Virgin Islands

University of Toledo

University of Toledo Rockets

University of Toronto

University of Toronto Law Journal

University of Tulsa

University of Tulsa Golden Hurricane

University of Uppsala

University of Utah

University of Utah Press

University of Utah Utes

University of Vermont

University of Vermont Catamounts

University of Victoria

University of Virginia

University of Virginia Cavaliers

University of Virginia Wahoos

University of Wales

University of Washington

University of Washington Huskies

University of Wshington Press

University of Waterloo

University of Western Ontario

University of West Florida

University of West Los Angeles

University of West Virginia

University of Windsor

University of Winnipeg

University of Wisconsin

University of Wisconsin Badgers

University of Wisconsin—Green Bay

University of Wisconsin—Green Bay Fighting Phoenix

University of Wisconsin—Milwaukee

University of Wisconsin—Milwaukee Panthers

University of Wisconsin Press

University of Wyoming

University of Wyoming Cowboys

University Park

University Presses of Florida

University Press of America Inc.

University Press of Colorado

University Press of Kansas

University Press of Kentucky, The

University Press of Mississippi

University Press of New England

University Press of Virginia, The

University Wits

Univision

Univision Holdings, Inc.

UNIX Systems Laboratories, Inc.

Unknown American

Unknown Sea

Unknown Soldier

Unknown Youth

Unocal Corporation

Unocal Exploration Corporation

Unocal Foundation

Unser, Al, Jr.

Unser, Al, Sr.

Unser, Bobby

Unsinkable Molly Brown, The

Unsolved Mysteries

Unter den Linden

Untermeyer, Louis

Untouchables, The

U Nu

UNUM Charitable Foundation

UNUM Corporation

UNUM Life Insurance Company

UNUM Life Insurance Company of America

Upanishad

Upanishadic

Upchurch, Phil

Updike, John

UPI Cable News

UPI Radio Network

Upjohn, Richard

Upjohn, Richard Michel

Upjohn Company, The

Upjohn Company Foundation, The

Upland

Up on the Housetop

Upper Arlington

Upper Carboniferous

Upper Chinook
Upper Darby
Upper Delaware Scenic and Recreational River
Upper Iowa University
Upper Klamath Lake
Upper Peninsula
Upper Saddle River
Upper Sandusky
Upper Silesia
Upper Volta [*now* Burkina Faso]
Uppsala
Uprising, The
Upsala College
UPS Foundation
Upsilon Pi Epsilon Association
Upstairs, Downstairs
Up, Up and Away
Up with People
Ur
Ural
Ural-Altaic
Uralian
Uralian emerald
Uralic
Ural Mountains
Urals, the
Urania
Uranian
Uranium City
Uranus
Urban
Urban I, Saint
Urbana
Urban Affairs Quarterly

Urbana University
Urbandale
Urban Institute Press, The
Urban Land Institute, The
Urban League Review, The
Urdu
Ure, Mary
Urey, Harold Clayton
Uriah
Uriah Heep
Urich, Robert
Uriel
Urim and Thummim
Uris, Leon
Ur of the Chaldees
Urquhart, Robert
Urquhart, Sir Thomas
Ursa Major
Ursa Minor
Ursinus College
Ursula
Ursula, Saint
Ursuline
Ursuline College
Uruguay
Uruguayan
Us [magazine]
US *or* U.S. [United States]
USAA Casualty Insurance Company
USAA™ insurance
USA Hockey
USAir Group, Inc.
USAir, Inc.

USA/Mobil Indoor Track and Field Championships
USA/Mobil Outdoor Track and Field Championships
USA Network
USA Radio Network
U.S.A. Rail Pass
U.S.A. Today [magazine]
USA Today [newspaper]
USA Today Baseball Weekly
U.S. Bancorp
U.S. Bank of Washington
U.S. Catholic
U.S. English
USF & G Corporation
USF & G Foundation
USG Corporation
USG Foundation
US Government Product News
Ushant Island
U-shaped
U*S* Kids [magazine]
USLIFE Corporation
U.S. Naval Institute Proceedings
U.S. News & World Report
U.S. Newswire
U.S. Open
U.S. Open Championship
Uspallata Pass
U.S. Repeating Arms Company

USS or U.S.S. Abraham Lincoln

USS or U.S.S. Ainsworth

USS or U.S.S. Alabama

USS or U.S.S. Alaska

USS or U.S.S. Albany

USS or U.S.S. Albuquerque

USS or U.S.S. Alexandria

USS or U.S.S. America

USS or U.S.S. Annapolis

USS or U.S.S. Antietam

USS or U.S.S. Antrim

USS or U.S.S. Anzio

USS or U.S.S. Aquila

USS or U.S.S. Archerfish

USS or U.S.S. Aries

USS or U.S.S. Arizona

USS or U.S.S. Arizona National Memorial

USS or U.S.S. Arkansas

USS or U.S.S. Arleigh Burke

USS or U.S.S. Arthur W. Radford

USS or U.S.S. Asheville

USS or U.S.S. Aspro

USS or U.S.S. Atlanta

USS or U.S.S. Aubrey Finch

USS or U.S.S. Augusta

USS or U.S.S. Aylwin

USS or U.S.S. Bainbridge

USS or U.S.S. Baltimore

USS or U.S.S. Barry

USS or U.S.S. Batfish

USS or U.S.S. Baton Rouge

USS or U.S.S. Belknap

USS or U.S.S. Benfold

USS or U.S.S. Benjamin Franklin

USS or U.S.S. Bergall

USS or U.S.S. Berkeley

USS or U.S.S. Biddle

USS or U.S.S. Billfish

USS or U.S.S. Birmingham

USS or U.S.S. Bluefish

USS or U.S.S. Boise

USS or U.S.S. Boone

USS or U.S.S. Boston

USS or U.S.S. Bowen

USS or U.S.S. Bremerton

USS or U.S.S. Briscoe

USS or U.S.S. Buffalo

USS or U.S.S. Bunker Hill

USS or U.S.S. California

USS or U.S.S. Callaghan

USS or U.S.S. Cape Saint George

USS or U.S.S. Capodanno

USS or U.S.S. Carl Vinson

USS or U.S.S. Carney

USS or U.S.S. Caron

USS or U.S.S. Carr

USS or U.S.S. Casimir Pulaski

USS or U.S.S. Cavalla

USS or U.S.S. Chancellorsville

USS or U.S.S. Chandler

USS or U.S.S. Charlotte

USS or U.S.S. Cheyenne

USS or U.S.S. Chicago

USS or U.S.S. Chosin

USS or U.S.S. Cincinnati

USS or U.S.S. City of Corpus Christi

USS or U.S.S. Clark

USS or U.S.S. Clifton Sprague

USS or U.S.S. Cole

USS or U.S.S. Colorado

USS or U.S.S. Columbia

USS or U.S.S. Columbus

USS or U.S.S. Comte de Grasse

USS or U.S.S. Connole

USS or U.S.S. Conolly

USS or U.S.S. Constellation

USS or U.S.S. Cook

USS or U.S.S. Copeland

USS or U.S.S. Coral Sea

USS or U.S.S. Cowpens

USS or U.S.S. Crommelin

USS or U.S.S. Curtis Wilbur

USS or U.S.S. Curts

USS or U.S.S. Cushing

USS or U.S.S. Dahlgren

USS or U.S.S. Dale

USS or U.S.S. Dallas

USS or U.S.S. Daniel Boone

USS or U.S.S. David R. Ray

USS or U.S.S. De Wert

USS or U.S.S. Deyo

USS or U.S.S. Donald B. Beary

USS or U.S.S. Downes

USS or U.S.S. Doyle

USS or U.S.S. Drum

USS or U.S.S. Duncan

USS or U.S.S. Dwight D. Eisenhower

USS or U.S.S. Elliott

USS or U.S.S. Elmer Montgomery

USS or U.S.S. Elrod

USS or U.S.S. England

USS or U.S.S. Enterprise

USS or U.S.S. Estocin

USS or U.S.S. Fahrion

USS or U.S.S. Fanning

USS or U.S.S. Fife

USS or U.S.S. Finback

USS or U.S.S. Fitzgerald

USS or U.S.S. Flatley

USS or U.S.S. Fletcher

USS or U.S.S. Florida

USS or U.S.S. Flying Fish

USS or U.S.S. Ford

USS or U.S.S. Forrestal

USS or U.S.S. Fox

USS or U.S.S. Francis Hammond

USS or U.S.S. Francis Scott Key

USS or U.S.S. Gallery

USS or U.S.S. Gary

USS or U.S.S. Gemini

USS or U.S.S. George Bancroft

USS or U.S.S. George Philip

USS or U.S.S. George Washington

USS or U.S.S. Georgia

USS or U.S.S. Gettysburg

USS or U.S.S. Gonzales

USS or U.S.S. Grayling

USS or U.S.S. Greeneville

USS or U.S.S. Gridley

USS or U.S.S. Groton

USS or U.S.S. Gurnard

USS or U.S.S. Halsey

USS or U.S.S. Halyburton

USS or U.S.S. Hammerhead

USS or U.S.S. Hampton

USS or U.S.S. Harold E. Holt

USS or U.S.S. Harry E. Yarnell

USS or U.S.S. Harry W. Hill

USS or U.S.S. Hartford

USS or U.S.S. Hawes

USS or U.S.S. Hawkbill

USS or U.S.S. Hayler

USS or U.S.S. Helena

USS or U.S.S. Henry L. Stimson

USS or U.S.S. Henry M. Jackson

Ussher, James

USS or U.S.S. Hercules

USS or U.S.S. Hewitt

U.S. Shoe Corporation

USS or U.S.S. Honolulu

USS or U.S.S. Hornet

USS or U.S.S. Houston

USS or U.S.S. Hue City

USS or U.S.S. Hyman G. Rickover

USS or U.S.S. Independence

USS or U.S.S. Indianapolis

USS or U.S.S. Ingersoll

USS or U.S.S. Ingraham

USS or U.S.S. Iowa

USS or U.S.S. Jacksonville

USS or U.S.S. Jack Williams

USS or U.S.S. James K. Polk

USS or U.S.S. Jarrett

USS or U.S.S. Jefferson City

USS or U.S.S. Jesse L. Brown

USS or U.S.S. John A. Moore

USS or U.S.S. John Barry

USS or U.S.S. John C. Calhoun

USS or U.S.S. John C. Stennis

USS or U.S.S. John F. Kennedy

USS or U.S.S. John Hancock

USS or U.S.S. John H. Sides

USS or U.S.S. John L. Hall

USS or U.S.S. John Paul Jones

USS or U.S.S. John Rodgers

USS or U.S.S. John S. McCain

USS or U.S.S. John Young

USS or U.S.S. Joseph Hewes

USS or U.S.S. Josephus Daniels

USS or U.S.S. Jouett

USS or U.S.S. Kamehameha

USS or U.S.S. Kauffman

USS or U.S.S. Kentucky

USS or U.S.S. Key West

USS or U.S.S. Kidd

USS or U.S.S. Kinkaid

USS or U.S.S. Kirk

USS or U.S.S. Kitty Hawk

USS or U.S.S. Klakring

USS or U.S.S. Laboon

USS or U.S.S. La Jolla

USS or U.S.S. Lake Champlain

USS or U.S.S. Lake Erie

USS or U.S.S. Leahy

USS or U.S.S. Leftwich

USS or U.S.S. Lewis B. Puller

USS or U.S.S. Lexington

USS or U.S.S. Leyte Gulf

USS or U.S.S. L. Mendel Rivers

USS or U.S.S. Lockwood

USS or U.S.S. Long Beach

USS or U.S.S. Los Angeles

USS or U.S.S. Louisville

USS or U.S.S. MacDonough

USS or U.S.S. Mahan

USS or U.S.S. Mahlon S. Tisdale

USS or U.S.S. Maine

USS or U.S.S. Mariano G. Vallejo

USS or U.S.S. Marvin Shields

USS or U.S.S. Maryland

USS or U.S.S. McCandless

USS or U.S.S. McClusky

USS or U.S.S. McInerney

USS or U.S.S. Memphis

USS or U.S.S. Merrill

USS or U.S.S. Miami

USS or U.S.S. Michigan

USS or U.S.S. Midway

USS or U.S.S. Minneapolis-Saint Paul

USS or U.S.S. Mississippi

USS or U.S.S. Missouri

USS or U.S.S. Mitscher

USS or U.S.S. Mobile Bay

USS *or* U.S.S. Scott

USS *or* U.S.S. Scranton

USS *or* U.S.S. Seahorse

USS *or* U.S.S. Seawolf

USS *or* U.S.S. Shiloh

USS *or* U.S.S. Silversides

USS *or* U.S.S. Simon Bolivar

USS *or* U.S.S. Simpson

USS *or* U.S.S. South Carolina

USS *or* U.S.S. Spadefish

USS *or* U.S.S. Springfield

USS *or* U.S.S. Spruance

USS *or* U.S.S. Stark

USS *or* U.S.S. Stein

USS *or* U.S.S. Stephen W. Groves

USS *or* U.S.S. Sterett

USS *or* U.S.S. Stethem

USS *or* U.S.S. Stonewall Jackson

USS *or* U.S.S. Stout

USS *or* U.S.S. Stump

USS *or* U.S.S. Sturgeon

USS *or* U.S.S. Sunfish

USS *or* U.S.S. Taurus

USS *or* U.S.S. Tautog

USS *or* U.S.S. Taylor

U.S. Steel Hour, The

USS *or* U.S.S. Tennessee

USS *or* U.S.S. Texas

USS *or* U.S.S. Thach

USS *or* U.S.S. Theodore Roosevelt

USS *or* U.S.S. Thomas C. Hart

USS *or* U.S.S. Thomas S. Gates

USS *or* U.S.S. Thorn

USS *or* U.S.S. Thresher

USS *or* U.S.S. Ticonderoga

USS *or* U.S.S. Toledo

USS *or* U.S.S. Topeka

USS *or* U.S.S. Trepang

USS *or* U.S.S. Trippe

USS *or* U.S.S. Truxtun

USS *or* U.S.S. Tucson

USS *or* U.S.S. Tunny

USS *or* U.S.S. Underwood

USS *or* U.S.S. United States

Ussuri

USS *or* U.S.S. Valley Forge

USS *or* U.S.S. Vandegrift

USS *or* U.S.S. Vella Gulf

USS *or* U.S.S. Vicksburg

USS *or* U.S.S. Vincennes

USS *or* U.S.S. Virginia

USS *or* U.S.S. Von Steuben

USS *or* U.S.S. Vreeland

USS *or* U.S.S. Wadsworth

USS *or* U.S.S. Wainwright

USS *or* U.S.S. West Virginia

USS *or* U.S.S. Whale

USS *or* U.S.S. William H. Bates

USS *or* U.S.S. William H. Standley

U.S. Swimming

USS *or* U.S.S. Wisconsin

USS *or* U.S.S. Worden

USS *or* U.S.S. Wyoming

USS *or* U.S.S. Yorktown

UST Inc.

Ustinov, Sir Peter

U.S. Trust Company of California

U.S. West Foundation

U. S. West, Inc.

U.S. Women's Open Championship

USX Corporation [*form.* United States Steel Corporation]

USX Corporation—U.S. Steel Group

USX Foundation

USX Tower

Utah

Utahan

Utah Jazz

Utah Lake

Utah State University

Utah State University Aggies

Utah Valley Community College

Utah War

Utamaro, Kitigaro

Ute, *n.*, *pl.* Ute *or* Utes

Utica

Utica College of Syracuse University

Utica Cutlery Company

Utica School of Commerce

Utica Thread Company

UtiliCorp United

Utility Workers Union of America

Utley, Garrick

UTNE Reader

Uto-Aztecan

Utopia

utopian *occas.* Utopian

Utrecht

Utrillo, Maurice

Uttar Pradesh

U-turn

U2 [musical group]

U-2 [spy plane]

U-2 incident

U-235

Utzon, Jørn

Uvalde

U-value

Uwharrie National Forest

Uxbridge

Uxmal

Uzbek

Uzbekistan [*form.* Uzbek Soviet Socialist Republic]

Uzbek Soviet Socialist Republic [*now* Uzbekistan]

Uzi

V

Vaal

Vacation Bible School

Vacation Exchange
  Club

Vacation Ownership
  Council

Vacaville

Vaccaro, Brenda

Vacuum Cleaner
  Manufacturers
  Association

Vadim, Roger

Vaduz

Vagabond Inn

Vagabond King, The

Vail

Vail, Theodore N.

Vaiont Dam

Valcour Island

Valdai Hills

Val-de-Marne

Valdez

Valdez, Maximiano

Valdez Principles

Val d'Isere

Val-d'Oise

Valdosta

Valdosta State College

Vale, Jerry

Valencia

Valencia, Guillermo
  León

Valencia Community
  College

Valencian Community

Valencia orange

Valenciennes

Valenciennes lace

Valens, Flavius

Valens, Ritchie

Valente, Caterina

Valenti, Jack

Valentine, Karen

Valentine, Saint

Valentine's Day

Valentine's Day
  Massacre

Valentinian

Valentino

Valentino, Rudolph

Valenzuela, Fernando

Vale of Kashmir

Vale of Tempe

Valera, Eamon De

Valera y Alcalá
  Galiano, Juan

Valerian, Publius

Valeriani, Richard

Valerian Way

Valerie

Valerius Maximus

Valero Energy
  Corporation

Valéry, Paul

Valhalla *occas.*
  Walhalla

Valhi, Inc.

Valium™

Valjean, Jean

Valkyrian

Valkyrie *occas.*
  Walkyrie [one of
  Odin's maidens in
  opera of same name
  by Wagner]

Valkyrie, The [opera
  by Wagner]

Valladolid

Vallandigham,
  Clement

Valle d'Aosta

Vallee, Rudy

Vallejo

Vallejo, César

Vallejo, Mariano G.

Valletta

Valley Bank
  Charitable
  Foundation

614

Valley City State University

Valleyfield

Valley Forge

Valley Forge Christian College

Valley Forge Military Junior College

Valley Forge National Historical Park

Valley Girl

Valley National Corporation

Valley of Jezreel

Valley of Ten Thousand Smokes

Valley of the Dolls

Valley of the Kings

Valley of the Moon

Valley of the Tombs

Valley Station

Valley Stream

Valli, Frankie

Valli, June

Vallone, Raf

Valois

Valparaiso [* FL; IN]

Valparaíso or Valparaiso [* Chile]

Valparaiso University

Valparaiso University Fighting Crusaders

Valsalva, Antonio Maria

Valsalva maneuver

Valspar Corporation

Valspeak

Value Line Fund, Inc.

Value Line Inc.

Value Line Investment Survey, The

Valve Manufacturers Association of America

Valvoline Detroit Grand Prix

Valvoline 200

Vampire Research Center

Van Abbe Municipal Museum

Van Allen, James

Van Allen belt

van Alstyne, Egbert

Van Andel, Jay

Van Ark, Joan

Van Brocklin, Norm

Vanbrugh, Sir John

Van Buren, Abigail

Van Buren, Martin

Vance, Cyrus

Vance, Dazzy

Vance, Vivian

Vance Air Force Base

Vance-Granville Community College

Van Cleef, Lee

Van Cliburn

Vancouver

Vancouver, George

Vancouver Art Gallery

Vancouver Canucks

Vancouver Island

[Vancouver] Sun, The

Vandal

Vandalia

Vandalic

Van Damme, Jean Claude

Van de Graaf, Robert J.

Van de Graaf generator

Vandenberg, Arthur H.

Vandenberg, Hoyt S.

Vandenberg Air Force Base

Vanderbilt, Amy

Vanderbilt, Cornelius

Vanderbilt, Gloria

Vanderbilt, Harold

Vanderbilt Law Review

Vanderbilt Mansion National Historic Site

Vanderbilt University

Vanderbilt University Commodores

Vanderbilt University Press

VanderCook College of Music

Van der Goes, Hugo

Vanderlyn, John

Vanderlyn, Pieter

van der Waals, Johannes Diderik

van der Waals' equation

van der Waals' forces

Van Devere, Trish

Van Diemen's Land

Van Dine, S. S.

Van Doren, Carl

Van Doren, Charles

Van Doren, Mamie

Van Doren, Mark

Vandross, Luther

Van Druten, John

Van Dyck or Vandyke, Sir Anthony

Van Dyke, Barry

Van Dyke, Dick

Van Dyke, Jerry

Van Dyke and Company

Vandyke beard

Vandyke brown

Vandyke collar

Vane, Sir Henry

Vanessa

van Eyck, Hubert *or* Huybrecht van

Van Eyck, Jan

Van Fleet, James A.

Van Fleet, Jo

Vangelis

Van Gogh, Vincent

Van Gogh Self-Portrait with Bandaged Ear

Van Gogh Self-Portrait with Hat

Vanguard Recording Society Inc.

Van Halen

Van Halen, Alex

Van Halen, Eddie

Van Heusen, James

Van Horne, Sir William C.

Vanier, Georges

Vanilla Fudge

Vanished Children's Alliance

Vanity Fair

Van Leyden, Lucas

Van Loo, Abraham Louis

Van Loo, Carle

Van Loo, Jakob *or* Jacques

Van Loo, Jean Baptiste

Van Loo, Louis Michel

Van Loon, Hendrik Willem

Van Nostrand Reinhold™ Books

Vanocur, Sander

Van Paassen, Pierre

Van Pallandt, Nina

Van Patten, Dick

Van Patten, Joyce

Van Peebles, Mario

Van Ronk, Dave

van Ruisdael, Jacob

Van Shelton, Ricky

Vansittart, Sir Robert Gilbert

Vansittartism

Vantage Press, Inc.

Vanua Levu

Vanua Mbalavu

Vanuata [*form.* New Hebrides]

Van Vechten, Carl

Van Vleck, John

Van Vogt, A. E.

Van Wert

Van Winkle, Rip

Vanzetti, Bartolomeo

Vaphio cups

Varanasi

Varangian

Varangian guard

Vardar

Vardon, Harry

Vare, Glenna Collett

Varèse, Edgar

Variable Annuity Life Insurance Company

Varian Associates, Inc.

Variation Number 7: Full Moon

Variety

Variety Clubs International

Varig Brazilian Airlines

Varley, John

Varna

Varney, Jim

Varro, Marcus Terentius

Varsi, Diane

VASA Order of America

Vasari, Giorgio

Vaseline™

Vassar, Matthew

Vassar College

Vatican

Vatican City

Vatican City State

Vatican Council

Vatican Hill

Vaticanism

Vaticanist

Vatican Library

Vatican Museums

Vatican I

Vatican Palace

Vatican roulette

Vatican II

Vatterott College

Vaughan, Arky

Vaughan, Elizabeth

Vaughan, Frankie

Vaughan, Henry

Vaughan, Sarah
Vaughan, Stevie Ray
Vaughan Brothers
Vaughan Furniture
  Company, Inc.
Vaughan Williams,
  Ralph
Vaughn, Billy
Vaughn, Henry
Vaughn, Robert
Vaux, Calvert
Vaxholm
V block
VC-137
VCR Plus™
VC-10
Veadar
Veblen, Oswald
Veblen, Thorstein
Veblenian
Veblenism
Veblenite
Veda
Vedaic
Vedaism
Vedanta
Vedanta Press
Vedanta Society
Vedantic
Vedantism
Vedantist
V-E Day
Vedder, Elihu
Vee, Bobby
Veeck, Bill
Veep, the
Vega
Vega, Suzanne

Vega$ [movie;
  television series]
Vegetarian Journal
Vegetarian Times
Vegetius
Veidt, Conrad
V-8 *or* V-eight engine
Velasco, José Maria
Velázquez, Diego de
Velázquez, Diego
  Rodriguez
  de Silva y
Velcro™
Velcro Industries
Velcro USA Inc.
Velde, Adriaen van de
Velde, Esaias van de
Velde, Jan Jansz van
  de
Velde, Willem van de
Velo-News
Velvet Underground,
  The
Venable, Evelyn
Venantius Fortunatus,
  Saint
Vendémiaire
Vendex International
Vendôme
Vendôme, Louis
  Joseph de
Venera space probe
Veneti
Venetia
Venetian
Venetian ball
venetian *often*
  Venetian blind
Venetian dentil
Venetian door

venetian *often*
  Venetian glass
Venetian red
Venetian sumac
Venetian window
Venezia
Venezia Palace
Venezolana
  Internacional de
  Aviación
Venezuela
Venezuela Boundary
  Dispute
Venezuela Claims
Venezuelan
Venice
[Venice] Academy of
  Fine Arts
Veni Creator Spiritus
Veni Sancte Spiritus
Venizelos, Eleutherios
Venn, John
Vennard College
Venn diagram
Ventnor City
Ventôse
Ventura
Ventura, Charlie
Ventura College
Ventura County
  Community College
Ventura Educational
  Systems
Ventura Publisher™
  software
Ventura Publisher
  User's Group
Venture Clubs of the
  Americas
Ventures, The

Venturi, Giovanni
Battista
Venturi, Ken
Venturi, Robert
Venturi tube
Venus
Venus and Adonis
Venus and Cupid
Venus and Mars
Venusberg Mountains
Venus de Milo
Venus hairstone
Venusian
Venus of Melos
Venus of Urbino
Venus of Willendorf
Venus's flower basket
Venus's-flytrap *occas.*
Venus flytrap
Venus's girdle
Venus's hair
Venus's looking-glass
Venuta, Benay
Venuti, Joe
Veracruz [Mexican
state]
Veracruz Llave
[Mexican city]
Vera-Ellen
Verbatim
Vercelli
Vercelli Book
Vercingetorix
Verde
Verdi, Giuseppe
Verdon, Gwen
Verdun
Vereen, Ben
Vereschagin, Vasili
Vasilievech

Vergil *var. of* Virgil
Vergilian *var. of*
Virgilian
Verkhoyansk Range
Verlaine, Paul
Vermeer, Jan
Vermont
Vermont Business
Magazine
Vermont College
Vermonter
Vermont Law School
Vermont Life
Magazine
Vermont Magazine
Vermont Technical
College
Vermont Yankee
nuclear power
station
Vernadsky, George
Vernal Falls
Verne, Jules
Verner, Karl A.
Verner's law
Vernet, Carle
Vernet, Claude Joseph
Vernet, Émile Jean
Horace
Verneuil process
Vernier, Pierre
Vernon
Vernon, Jackie
Vernon, John
Vernon Regional
Junior College
Vero Beach
Verona
Veronese, *n., pl.*
Veronese
Veronese, Paolo

Veronica
Véronique *occas.*
Veronique
Verrazano, Giovanni
da
Verrazano-Narrows
Bridge
Verrett, Shirley
Verrius Flaccus
Verrocchio, Andrea
del
Versace, Gianni
Versace fashions
Versailles
Verschaffelt, Pieter
Anton
Vertigo
Verwoerd, Hendrik F.
Very First Books™
Very Large Array
Radio Telescope
Very light
Very pistol
Vesalius, Andreas
Vesco, Robert
Vesey, Denmark
Vespa of America
Corporation
Vespasian, Titus
Vespucci, Amerigo
Vesta
Vestalia
Vestal Virgin
Vesuvian
Vesuvius
Veteran Motor Car
Club of America
Veterans
Administration
[*now* Department of
Veterans Affairs]

Veterans *occas.*
Veterans' Day
[*form.* Armistice
Day]

Veterans for Peace

Veterans of Foreign
Wars of the United
States of America

Veterans of the Battle
of the Bulge

Veterans of the
Vietnam War

Veterans of
World War I

Veterans Stadium

Veterinary Medicine

Vezina Trophy

V.F. Corporation

VFW Auxiliary

VFW Magazine

Viacom Inc.

Viacom International
Inc.

Via del Corso

Via Dolorosa

VIA Rail Canada

Via Sacra

Vibram™ shoe soles

Vicar of Christ

Vicar of Jesus Christ

Vice President of the
United States, The

Vichy

Vichy government

Vichyite

Vichy Springs™ water

Vichy water

Vicious, Sid

Vickers, Jon

Vickers number

Vickers test

Vicksburg

Vicksburg campaign

Vicksburg National
Military Park

Vico, Giovanni
Battista

Viconian

Victor

Victor I, Saint

Victor Amadeus

Victor Emmanuel

Victoria

Victoria and Albert
Museum

Victoria College

Victoria Cross

Victoria Day

Victoria Falls

Victoria Island

Victoria Land

Victorian

Victoriana

Victorian box

Victoria Nile

Victorianism

Victorian Society in
America

Victorian style

Victoria Nyanza

Victoria Regina

Victoria University of
Manchester

Victorine

Victorinus

Victor Valley

Victor Valley College

Victor/Victoria

Victory Medal

Victory of Samothrace

Victory Optical
Manufacturing
Company

Victory ship

Vidal, Gore

Video Hits One

Video Jukebox
Network, Inc.

Video Magazine

Video Review

Video Shopping Mall

Video Software
Dealers Association

Vidmar, Peter

Vidor, King

Vien, Joseph Marie

Vienna

Vienna Airport

Vienna Boys' Choir

Vienna-Budapest
World Fair

Vienna International

Vienna Philharmonic
Orchestra

Vienna State Opera

Vienna University

Vienne

Viennese

Vientiane

Viereck, Peter

Vierendeel girder

Vierendeel truss

Viet

Vietcong, *n., pl.*
Vietcong

Vietminh, *n., pl.*
Vietminh

Vietnam

Viet Nam Buddhists

Vietnamese

Vietnamese New Year

Vietnam Veterans against the War

Vietnam Veterans Agent Orange Victims Association

Vietnam Veterans Memorial

Vietnam Veterans of America

Vietnam War

Viewer's Choice

View Near Volterra, A

View of Delft

View of Haarlem

View of Toledo

Views of Mount Juji

Vigée-Lebrun, Elisabeth

Vignola, Giacomo da

Vigny, Alfred de

Vigoda, Abe

Viking

Viking Kestrel™ Books

Viking Penguin

Viking Portable Library™

Viking Press™

Vila, Bob

Villa, Pancho

Villa Borghese

Villa d'Este

Villa Doria Pamphili

Village Blacksmith, The

Village People

Village Voice, The

Villa Giulia National Museum

Villahermosa

Villa Julie College

Villa-Lobos, Heitor

Villalpando, Catalina Vasquez

Villa Maria College of Buffalo

Villanova

Villanovan

Villanovan culture

Villanova University

Villanova University Wildcats

Villa Park

Villard, Henry

Villard, Oswald Garrison

Villard Books

Villari effect

Villars, Claude Louis Hector de

Villechaize, Herve

Villella, Edward

Villeroy and Boch

Villeroy and Boch Tableware Ltd.

Villiers, Frederic

Villiers, James

Villon, François

Villon, Jacques

Vilnius

Vilnius Airport

Vim & Vigor, America's Family Health Magazine

Viminal Hill

Viña del Mar

Vince Lombardi Award

Vincennes

Vincennes University

Vincent, Fay

Vincent, Jan Michael

Vincent, Saint

Vincent de Paul, Saint

Vincent Ferrer, Saint

Vincentian

Vincent of Beauvais

Vincent's angina

Vincent's infection

Vincent Van Gogh National Museum

Vindhya Hills

Vinegar Institute

Vineland

Vineyard Ministries International

Vining, Elizabeth

Vinland

Vinson, Carl

Vinson, Fred M.

Vinson, Helen

Vinson Massif

Vintage Books

Vinton, Bobby

Vinyon™

Violent Criminal Apprehension Program

Violle, Jules

Violle unit

Vionnet, Madeleine

Viorst, Milton

Virchow, Rudolf

Virgil *occas.* Vergil

Virgilian *occas.* Vergilian

Virgin Adoring the Christ Child

Virgin and Child with Saint Anne

Virgin Atlantic Airways Ltd.

Virgin Birth

Virgin Group

Virginia

Virginia Beach

Virginia bluebell

Virginia Cavalcade

Virginia City

Virginia College

Virginia Commonwealth University

Virginia Commonwealth University Rams

Virginia Community College

Virginia Company

Virginia cowslip

Virginia creeper

Virginia deer

Virginia Farm News

Virginia fence

Virginia ham

Virginia Highlands Community College

Virginia Intermont College

Virginia Law Review

Virginia log canoe

Virginia Marti College of Fashion and Art

Virginia Military Institute

Virginia Military Institute Keydets

Virginian

Virginian, The [novel by Wister; movie; play; television series]

Virginians, The [novel by Thackeray]

Virginia pine

Virginia Plan

Virginia Polytechnic Institute and State University

Virginia Polytechnic Institute and State University Hokies

Virginia Quarterly Review, The

Virginia rail

Virginia rail fence

Virginia reel

Virginia Resolutions

Virginia Review

Virginia Slims tennis tournaments

Virginia snakeroot

Virginia State University

Virginia stock

Virginia trumpet flower

Virginia Union University

Virginia Wesleyan College

Virginia Western Community College

Virginia willow

Virgin Islands

Virgin Islands National Park

Virgin Islands of the United States

Virginius affair

Virgin Mary

Virgin Music Group

Virgin of the Rocks

Virgin Queen

Virgin with Saint Inés and Saint Tecla, The

Virgo

Visa™ credit card

Visalia

Visayan Islands

Visayan [people], n., pl. Visayan or Visayans

Vischer, Hermann

Vischer, Peter the Elder

Vischer, Peter the Younger

Visconti, Gary

Visconti, Luchino

Viscount Melville Sound

Vishinsky, Andrei Y.

Vishnu

Vishnuism

Visible Language

Visigoth

Visigothic

Vision Council of America

Vision Interfaith Satellite Network

Visitation of Our Lady

Visit from Saint Nicholas, A

Visiting Nurse Associations of America

Vista

Vista College

Vista International

Vista/USA

Vistula

Vistula Lagoon

Visual Artist's Rights Act

Visual Education Corporation

Vita-Fore Products Company

Vitale, Dick

Vitalian, Saint

Vitalium™

vitamin A

vitamin A$_2$

vitamin B complex

vitamin B$_1$

vitamin B$_6$

vitamin B$_{12}$

vitamin B$_2$

vitamin C

vitamin D

vitamin D$_5$

vitamin D$_4$

vitamin D$_1$

vitamin D$_3$

vitamin D$_2$

vitamin E

vitamin G

vitamin H

vitamin K

vitamin K$_1$

vitamin K$_3$

vitamin K$_2$

vitamin M

vitamin P

vitamin X

Vitellius, Aulus

Viterbo College

Viti Levu

Vitim

Vitry, Philippe de

Vittadini, Adrienne

Vitu Islands

Vitus, Saint

Vivaldi, Antonio

Vivarin™

Vivarini, Alvarise

Vivarini, Antonio

Vivarini, Bartolomeo

Viva Zapata!

Vixen

Viyella™

Vizetelly, Frank

Vizsla

V-J Day

Vladimir

Vladimir I, Saint

Vladivostok

Vlad the Impaler

Vlaminck, Maurice de

Vlasic Foods Inc.

V neck, *n.*

V-necked, *adj.*

Vocal Memnon

Vocational Education Journal

Vogel, Jacqueline Mars

Vogt, William

Vogue

Vogue Patterns Magazine

Voice of America

Voice of the Turtle, The

Voight, Cynthia

Voight, Jon

Voit Sports Inc.

Volans

Volapük

Volapükist

Volcano Islands

Volcker, Paul

Volga

Volgograd [*form.* Stalingrad]

Volk, Leonard Wells

Volkslied, *n., pl.* Volkslieder

Volksturm

Volkswagen Beetle

Volkswagen Club of America

Volkswagen of America Inc.

Volkswagen Super Beetle

Volkswagenwerke

Volleyball

Volleyball Monthly

Volpone

Volstead, Andrew J.

Volstead Act

Volsunga Saga

Volta

Volta, Alessandro

Volta effect

Voltaic language

Voltaire

Voltairean

Voltairian

Volta's pile

Volterra, Daniele da

Voltsos-Vourtzis, Pericles

Volturnus

Volunteers in Service to America

Volunteers in Technical Assistance, Inc.

Volunteers of America

Volunteer State

Volunteer State Community College

VOLUNTEER—the National Center

Volvo Cars of North America

Volvo International Tennis Tournament

Volvo North America Corporation

Volvo Tennis Indoor

Volvo Tennis/Los Angeles

Volvo Tennis/San Francisco

Von Bülow, Claus

V-1 rocket

Von Furstenberg, Betsy

Vo Nguyen Giap

Von Kármán, Theodore

Vonnegut, Kurt

Von Neumann, John

Vonnoh, Bessie Potter

Vons Companies, Inc., The

Von Stade, Frederica

von Steuben, Baron

Von Stroheim, Erich

Von Sydow, Max

Von Tilzer, Harry

Von Willebrand factor

Von Willebrand's disease

Von Zell, Harry

Voorhees College

Vorster, Balthazar Johannes

Vortech Pharmaceuticals

Vos, Marten de

Vose Galleries of Boston, Inc.

Vosges

Voskhod

Vostok

Voting Rights Act

votive Mass

Voulkos, Peter

Voyager

Voyager Books

Voyager/Sun Scene

Voyageurs National Park

V-particle

Vreeland, Diana

Vries, Adriaen de

V-6 *or* V-six engine

V-22 Osprey

V-2 rocket

V-type engine

Vuchetich, Yevgeny

Vuillard, Édouard

Vuitton, Louis

Vukovich, Bill

Vukovich, Bill, Jr.

Vukovich, Bill, III

Vulcan

Vulcanalia

Vulcan cannon

Vulcan gun pod

Vulcanian

Vulcan Materials Company

Vulcan Materials Company Foundation

Vulcan Surprises Venus and Mars

Vulgar Latin

Vulgate

Vulgate Bible

Vyatka

Vychegda

W

Waban Inc.

Wabash

Wabash Cannonball

Wabash Case

Wabash College

Wabash Railroad Company

Wace, Robert

Wachovia Bank and Trust Company

Wachovia Corporation [*form.* First Wachovia Corporation]

Wachusett Dam

Wachusett Reservoir

Waco

Waddell, Rube

Wade, Sir Thomas

Wade, Virginia

Wade-Giles transliteration

Wadhams Hall Seminary and College

Wadi Hadhramaut

Wadi Mojib

Wadsworth

Wadsworth Atheneum

Wadsworth, Inc.

Wadsworth Publishing Company

Wages and Hours Act

Waggoner, Lyle

Wagner, Cyril, Jr.

Wagner, Honus

Wagner, Lindsay

Wagner, Richard

Wagner, Robert [actor]

Wagner, Robert F. [senator]

Wagner, Robert F., Jr. [*form.* mayor of New York City]

Wagner, Roger

Wagner Act

Wagner College

Wagner College Seahawks

Wagnerian

Wagoner, Porter

Wagon Train

Wahhabi *or* Wahabi

Wahhabism *or* Wahabism

Wahhabite

Wahl, Ken

Wahlberg, Donnie

Wahlburg, Marky Mark

Waianae Mountains

Waiguri

Waikato

Waikiki

Waikiki Beach

Wailing Wall

Waimea Bay

Wain, Bea

Wainwright, Jonathan

Wainwright, Loudon

Waite, John

Waite, Morrison Remick

Waite, Ralph

Waite, Terry

Waiting for Godot

Waits, Tom

Wakefield

Wake Forest

Wake Forest University

Wake Forest University Demon Deacons

Wake Forest University Press

Wake Island

Wakely, Jimmy

Wake Technical Community College

Waksman, Selman A.

Walachia *or* Wallachia

Walachian

Walburga, Saint

Walburn, Raymond

Walcott, Jersey Joe

Wald, George

Waldemar

Walden

Walden, Robert

Waldenbooks

Walden Pond

Waldenses

Waldensian

Walden University

Waldheim, Kurt

Waldo, Peter

Waldorf-Astoria Hotel

Waldorf College

Waldorf salad

Waldwick

Wales

Walesa, Lech

Waley, Arthur

Walfish *var. of* Walvis Bay

Walgreen, Charles R.

Walgreen Benefit Fund

Walgreen Company

Walgreen drug store

Walhalla *var of* Valhalla

Walken, Christopher

Walker, Alice

Walker, Chris

Walker, Clint

Walker, Herschel

Walker, Jerry Jeff

Walker, Mort

Walker, Nancy

Walker, Ralph T.

Walker, Robert

Walker, T-Bone

Walker, William

Walker Cancer Research Institute

Walker College

Walker Cup

Walker Lake

Walker State Technical College

Walking Magazine, The

Walk of Fame

Walkyrie *var. of* Valkyrie

Wallace

Wallace, Alfred Russell

Wallace, Bobby

Wallace, David

Wallace, DeWitt

Wallace, George

Wallace, Henry A.

Wallace, Irving

Wallace, Jerry

Wallace, Lew

Wallace, Mike

Wallace, Sir Richard

Wallace, Sippie

Wallace, Sir William

Wallaceburg

Wallace Collection

Wallace Computer Services, Inc.

Wallace's line

Wallace State Community College— Hanceville

Wallach, Eli

Wallachia *var. of* Walachia

Walla Walla

Walla Walla College

Walla Walla Community College

Wallcovering Manufacturers Association

Wallechinsky, David

Wallenberg, Raoul

Wallenda, Karl

Wallenstein, Albrecht von

Wallenstein, Alfred

Waller, Edmund

Waller, Fats

Wallingford

Wallington

Wallis, Hal B.

Wallis and Futuna Islands

Wallis Islands

Wall of Antoninus

Wall of Love

Walloon

Walloon sword

Wallops Flight Facility

Wallops Island

Wallowa

Wallowa Lake

Wallowa Mountains

Wallowa-Whitman National Forest

Wallraf-Richartz
 Museum

Wall Street

Wall Streeter

Wall Street Journal,
 The

Wall Street Journal/
 Europe

Wall Street Journal
 Radio Network

Wally Byam Caravan
 Club International

Wal-Mart Foundation

Wal-Mart Stores, Inc.

Walnut Canyon
 National Monument

Walnut Creek

Walnut Press

Walnut Ridge

Walpi pueblo

Walpole, Horace

Walpole, Sir Hugh

Walpole, Sir Robert

Walpole tea

Walpurgis, Saint

Walpurgis Night

Walras, Léon

Walsh, Bill

Walsh, Ed

Walsh, Joe

Walsh, M. Emmet

Walsh, Raoul

Walsh, Stella

Walsh College

Walsh College of
 Accountancy and
 Business
 Administration

Walsingham, Sir
 Francis

Walston, Ray

Walt Disney
 Company, The

Walt Disney Presents

Walt Disney
 Publishing Group,
 Inc.

Walt Disney's
 Wonderful World of
 Color

Walt Disney World

Walt Disney World
 Golf Classic

Walt Disney World's
 EPCOT Center

Walter, Bruno

Walter, Jessica

Walter, Thomas Ustick

Walter Mittyish

Walter Reed Army
 Medical Center

Walters, Barbara

Walters, Julie

Walters State
 Community College

Walter Winchell–
 Damon Runyon
 Cancer Research
 Fund

Walter W. Naumburg
 Foundation

Waltham

Walton, Alice L.

Walton, Bill

Walton, Izaak

Walton, James
 Lawrence

Walton, Jim C.

Walton, John T.

Walton, Sam

Walton, S. Robson

Walton, Sir William

Waltonian

Waltons, The

Waltrip, Darrell

Waltzing Matilda

Walvis *occas.* Walfish
 Bay

Wambaugh, Joseph

Wampanoag [Indian],
 n., pl. Wampanoag
 or Wampanoags

Wanamaker, John

Wanamaker, Sam

Wanamaker's
 department store

Wanda

Wandering Jew
 [legendary figure]

wandering *occas.*
 Wandering Jew
 [plant]

Wandering Jew, The
 [novel]

Waner, Lloyd

Waner, Paul

Wang Laboratories,
 Inc.

Wang Wei

Wank, Roland A.

Wankel, Felix

Wankel engine

Wantagh

Wapner, Joseph

Wappers, Gustave

Wappinger

Wappingers Falls

War and Peace

War between the
 States

Warburg, Otto
 Heinrich

Ward, Aaron
 Montgomery

Ward, Anita
Ward, Artemus
Ward, Barbara
Ward, Fred
Ward, Mrs. Humphry
Ward, John M.
Ward, John Quincy Adams
Ward, Sir Joseph
Ward, Lester Frank
Ward, Louis Larrick
Ward, Montgomery
Ward, Nathaniel
Ward, Rachel
Ward, Simon
Warden, Jack
Warden *occas.* warden pear
Wardian case
Ward's Auto World
Wareham
Ware Shoals
Warfield, Paul
Warfield, William
War for Independence
War for Separation in the South
War for Southern Independence
Warhol, Andy
Wariner, Steve
Waring, Fred
War in the Pacific National Historical Park
Warm Springs
Warnaco Group, Inc., The
Warner, Charles Dudley

Warner, Cheryl K.
Warner, David
Warner, H. B.
Warner, Jack, Jr.
Warner, Jack L.
Warner, Malcolm-Jamal
Warner, Pop
Warner, Seth
Warner, Sylvia Townsend
Warner Books, Inc.
Warner Brothers Inc.
Warner Brothers Television
Warner Communications Foundation
Warner Communications Inc.
Warner-Lambert Charitable Foundation
Warner-Lambert Company
Warner Pacific College
Warner Robins
Warner Southern College
Warnes, Jennifer
War of American Independence
War of 1812
War of Independence
War of Jenkins' Ear
War of Secession
War of the Austrian Succession
War of the Bavarian Succession

War of the Breton Succession
War of the Grand Alliance
War of the Nations
War of the Pacific
War of the Polish Succession
War of the Rebellion
War of the Roses
War of the Spanish Succession
War of the Toggenburg
War of the Triple Alliance
War of the Worlds, The
War Powers Act
War Powers Resolution
Warr Acres
Warren
Warren, Earl
Warren, Harry
Warren, Joseph
Warren, Lesley Ann
Warren, Robert Penn
Warren, Russell
Warren Commission
Warren County Community College
Warren report
Warrensburg
Warrensville Heights
Warrenton [* GA; MO; NC; VA; *see also* Warrington]
Warren truss
Warrenville

Warren Wilson
College

War Resisters
International

War Resisters League

Warrick, Ruth

Warrington [FL; *see
also* Warrenton]

Warsaw

Warsaw Convention

Warsaw ghetto
uprising

Warsaw Okecie
Airport

Warsaw Pact

Warsaw Treaty
Organization

Wars of Religion

Wars of the Roses

Warta

Wartburg

Wartburg College

Wartburg Theological
Seminary

War/Watch
Foundation

Warwick

Warwick, Dionne

Warwick, Robert

Warwickshire

Wasatch-Cache
National Forest

Wasatch Mountain

Wasatch Range

Wasco

Wash, The

Washburn University
of Topeka

Washington

Washington,
Booker T.

Washington, Dennis

Washington, Denzel

Washington, Desiree

Washington, Dinah

Washington, George

Washington, Grover,
Jr.

Washington, Harold

Washington, Martha

Washington and
Jefferson College

Washington and Lee
Law Review

Washington and Lee
University

Washington Bible
College

Washington Bullets

Washington Capitals

Washington Cathedral

Washington College

Washington
Conference

Washington Court
House

Washington Crossing
the Delaware

Washington, DC
[postal usage]

Washington, District
of Columbia

Washington Gas Light
Company

Washingtonian

Washingtonian
Magazine, The

Washington Institute
of Foreign Affairs

Washington Institute
of Technology

Washington Island

Washington
Journalism Review

Washington Legal
Foundation

Washington lily

Washington Marine
Barracks

Washington Monthly,
The

Washington Monthly
Company

Washington
Monument

Washington
Monument National
Memorial

Washington Mutual
Savings Bank

Washington Mutual
Savings Bank
Foundation

Washington Naval
District

Washington-on-the-
Brazos

Washington palm

Washington Park

Washington pie

Washington Post, The

Washington Post
Company, The

Washington Post
Magazine, The

Washington Post
Writers Group

Washington Square

Washington Square
Players

Washington Redskins

Washington Reports

Washington's Birthday

Washington Square
Press™ Books

Washington State

Washington State Community College

Washington State University

Washington State University Cougars

Washington State University Press

Washington Technical College

Washington Terrace

Washington Theological Union

Washington thorn

Washington University

Washington Water Power Company, The

Washington West

Washita *var. of* Ouachita River

Washo

Washtenaw Community College

Wasserman, Lew

Wassermann, August von

Wassermann, Jakob

Wassermann test

Wasserman reaction

Wasserstein, Wendy

Wassily chair

Wast, Hugo

Waste Land, The

Waste Management, Inc.

Watauga

Watauga Association

Watchtower, The

Watchtower Bible and Tract Society of New York

Watchung Mountains

Waterbed Manufacturers Association

Waterbury

Waterbury State Technical College

Wateree

Waterford

Waterford Hotel, The

Watergate

Watergate affair

Watergate scandal

Water Lilies

Waterloo

Waterloo Bridge

Waterloo campaign

Waterman, Willard

Water Pollution Control Federation

Waters, Crystal

Waters, Ethel

Waters, Joe

Waters, Muddy

Waters, Roger

Water Skier

Waterston, Sam

Waterton-Glacier International Peace Park

Waterton Lakes National Park

Water Tower Place

Watertown

Watertown Arsenal

Waterville

Watervliet

Watervliet Arsenal

WATKINS [catalog sales company]

Watkins [given name]

Watkins, Carlene

Watkins Glen

Watkins Glen International Circuit

Watkins Motor Lines, Inc.

Watley, Jody

Watling Island

Watseka

Watson, Douglass

Watson, Dr.

Watson, James Dewey

Watson, John Broadus

Watson, John Christian

Watson, Lucile

Watson, Thomas J.

Watson, Tom

Watson, Sir William

Watson and the Shark

Watson-Crick model

Watson-Guptill Book Clubs

Watson-Guptill Publications, Inc.

Watsonville

Watson-Watt, Sir Robert Alexander

Watson-Wentworth, Charles

Watt, James [Scottish inventor]

Watt, James E. [*form.* United States government official]

Watteau, Antoine

Watteau back

Watterson, Bill

Watterson, Henry

Watterson College

Watts, André

Watts, Charlie

Watts, George Frederic

Watts, Isaac

Watts-Dunton, Theodore

Watts Family Association

Watts riots

Watts Towers of Simon Rodia State Historic Park

Wat Tyler's Rebellion

Watusi *occas.* Watutsi, *n., pl.* Watusi *occas.* Watutsis

Waubonsee Community College

Wauconda

Waugh, Alec

Waugh, Arthur

Waugh, Evelyn

Waugh, Frederick Judd

Waukegan

Waukesha

Waukesha County Technical College

Wausau

Wausau Insurance Companies

Wauwatosa

Wavell, Archibald

Waverly

Waverly Novels

Wawelu Castle State Art Collections

Waxahachie

Waxman, Al

Waxman, Franz

Wayans, Damon

Wayans, Keenan Ivory

Waycross

Waycross College

Waycross Express

Wayland

Wayland the Smith

Wayland Baptist University

Wayne

Wayne, Bruce

Wayne, David

Wayne, John

Wayne, Mad Anthony

Wayne, Patrick

Wayne Community College

Wayne County Community College

Wayne National Forest

Waynesboro

Waynesburg

Waynesburg College

Wayne State College

Wayne State University

Wayne State University Press

Waynesville

Wayne's World

Way of All Flesh, The

Way of the Cross

Way of the Cross Church of Christ

Way of the World, The

Way We Were, The

Weald, The

Wealthy apple

We Are the Weird [magazine]

We Are the World [song]

Weather Channel, The

WeatherData

Weatherford

Weatherford, William

Weatherford College

Weathermen [*now* Weather Underground]

Weathers, Carl

Weather Underground [*form.* Weathermen]

Weatherwax, Rudd

Weaver, Dennis

Weaver, Doodles

Weaver, Earl

Weaver, Fritz

Weaver, Mike

Weaver, Robert C.

Weaver, Sigourney

Weavers, The

Webb, Beatrice

Webb, Chick

Webb, Clifton

Webb, Jack

Webb, Jimmy

Webb, Sidney J.

Webb, Walter Prescott

Webb City

Webber, Andrew Lloyd

Webber College

Webb Institute of Naval Architecture

Weber
Weber, Carl Maria von
Weber, Charlotte Colket
Weber, Dick
Weber, Ernst Heinrich
Weber, Joe
Weber, Max
Weber, Pete
Weber and Fields
Weberian apparatus
Webern, Anton von
Weber State College Wildcats
Weber State University
Webster
Webster, Ben
Webster, Daniel
Webster, John
Webster, Margaret
Webster, Noah
Webster, Paul Francis
Webster, William H.
Webster-Ashburton Treaty
Webster City
Webster Groves
Websterian
Webster's New World Dictionary of American English
Webster's Ninth New Collegiate Dictionary
Webster's Third New International Dictionary Unabridged
Webster University
Wechsler, David

Wechsler Adult Intelligence Scale
Wechsler-Bellevue Scale
Wechsler Intelligence Scale for Children
Weddell Sea
Wedding March
Wedekind, Frank
Wedgwood, Josiah
Wednesday
Wedtech Corporation
Wedtech scandal
Weed, Thurlow
Weehawken
Weeki Wachee
Weekley, Ernest
Weekly Reader
Weekly Reader Book Clubs
Weekly World News
Weems, Mason Locke
Weems, Ted
Weenix, Jan
Weenix, Jan Baptist
Wee Willie Winkie
Wee Wisdom
Wegener, Alfred L.
Wei
Weicker, Lowell
Weidman, Charles
Weierstrass, Karl
Weierstrass approximation theorem
Weightlifting Federation Hall of Fame
Weight Watchers International

Weight Watchers Magazine
Weil, Cynthia
Weil, Simone
Weill, Kurt
Weil's disease
Weimar
Weimaraner
Weimarian
Weimar Republic
Weinberg, Harry
Weinberg, Steven
Weinberger, Caspar
Weinberger, Jaromir
Weingarten Realty Investors
Weingartner, Felix
Weir, Julian Alden
Weir, Peter
Weirton
Weirton Steel Corporation
Weis, Robert Freeman
Weis, Sigfried
Weisgall, Hugo
Weiskopf, Tom
Weismann, August
Weismannism
Weis Markets, Inc.
Weiss, George
Weiss, Peter
Weisshorn
Weissmuller, Johnny
Weitz, Bruce
Weizmann, Chaim
Welch var. of Welsh
Welch, Kevin
Welch, Mickey
Welch, Raquel

Welch, Robert, Jr.

Welcome Back, Kotter

Welcome Wagon™

Weld, Tuesday

Welding Research Counsel

Welfare Island

Welk, Lawrence

Welland

Welland Canal

Welland Ship Canal

Welles, Gideon

Welles, Orson

Welles, Sumner

Wellesley

Wellesley, Arthur

Wellesley, Robert Colley

Wellesley College

Wellesz, Egon

Wellington

Wellington *occas.* wellington boot

Wellington International Airport

[Wellington] National Art Gallery

Wellman, William

Wellman, Inc.

Wells, H. G.

Wells, Ida Bell

Wells, Kitty

Wells, Marshall T.

Wells, Mary

Wells Cargo, Inc.

Wells College

Wells Fargo and Company

Wells Fargo Bank

Wells Fargo Foundation

Well-Tempered Clavier, The

We Love Lucy/The International Lucille Ball Fan Club

Welsbach, Carl Auer von

Welsbach burner

Welsbach mantle

Welsh *occas.* Welch

Welsh cob

Welsh corgi

Welsh dresser

Welsh language

Welsh literature

Welshman, *n., pl.* Welshmen

Welsh Marches

Welsh National Opera

Welsh pony

Welsh poppy

Welsh rabbit *occas.* rarebit

Welsh springer spaniel

Welsh terrier

Welshwoman, *n., pl.* Welshwomen

Wetzschmerz

Welty, Eudora

Wembley

Wembley Stadium

Wenatchee

Wenatchee National Forest

Wenatchee Valley College

Wenceslaus

Wenceslaus, Saint

Wendell

Wendt, George

Wendy

Wendy's International, Inc.

Wenner, Jann

Wenrich, Percy

Wensleydale cheese

Wentorth, Thomas

Wentorth, William Charles

Wentworth Institute of Technology

Wentworth Military Academy and Junior College

Wenzel, Hanni

We Remember Elvis Fan Club

Werewolf Research Center

Werfel, Franz

Werner, Oskar

Wertheim effect

Wertheimer, Max

Wescott, Glenway

Weser

Weslaco

Wesley

Wesley, Charles

Wesley, John

Wesleyan

Wesleyan Church

Wesleyan College

Wesleyanism

Wesleyan Methodist

Wesleyan University

Wesley Biblical Seminary

Wesley College

Wesley Theological Seminary

Wessex

West, Adam

West, Benjamin

West, Dottie

West, Jerry

West, Jessamyn

West, Mae

West, Morris

West, Nathaneal

West, Dame Rebecca

West, Shelly

West Africa

West African Economic Community

WestAir Commuter Airlines, Inc.

West Allis

Westar

Westark Community College

Westates Truck Equipment Corporation

West Bank

West Bend

West Bengal

West Berlin

Westborough

Westbrook

Westbrook College

Westbury

West Caldwell

West Carrollton

Westchester [* IL]

West Chester [* PA]

Westchester Business Institute

Westchester Community College

West Chester University of Pennsylvania

West Chicago

West Coast Christian College

West Coast Conference

West Coast Review of Books

West Coast Syndicate

West Coast University

West Covina

West Des Moines

Westdeutsche Landesbank Gironzentrale

Westerly

Westermarck, Edward

Western Agri-Radio Networks

Western and Southern Life Insurance Company

Western Athletic Conference

Western Australia

Western Australian

Western Auto Supply Company

Western Baptist College

Western Carolina University

Western Carolina University Catamounts

Western Chin dynasty

Western Church

Western Connecticut State University

Western Conservative Baptist Seminary

Western Dakota Vocational-Technical Institute

Western Digital Corporation

Westerner

Westerners International

Western European Union

Western Evangelical Seminary

Western Federal Savings and Loan Association

Western Ghats

Western Han dynasty

western hemisphere *often* Western Hemisphere

Western History Association

Western Illinois University

Western Illinois University Fighting Leathernecks

Western International University

Western Iowa Tech Community College

Western Islands

Western Kentucky University

Western Kentucky University Hilltoppers

Western Literature Association

Western Maryland College

Western Michigan University

Western Michigan University Broncos

Western Montana College

Western National Life Insurance Company

Western Nebraska Community College

Western Nevada Community College

Western New England College

Western New Mexico University

Western Oklahoma State College

Western Open Golf Tournament

Western Oregon State Tournament

Western Orthodox Church in America

Western Outdoors

Western Pacific Railroad

Western Piedmont Community College

Western Reserve

Western Roman Empire

western *often* Western saddle

Western Samoa

Western School of Health and Business Careers

Western Sierra Madre

Western Space and Missile Center

Western Springs

Western State College

Western States Chiropractic College

Western States Petroleum Association

Western State University College of Law

Western swing

Western Tanager Press

Western Texas College

Western Theological Seminary

Western Union Corporation [*now* New Valley Corporation]

Western Wall

Western Washington University

Western Wisconsin Technical College

Western World Avon Club

Western Writers of America

Western Wyoming College

Westerville

Westfield

Westfield State College

West 57th

West Flanders

West Florida Controversy

Westford

Westgate

West Georgia College

West Germany

West Goth

West Hartford

West Haven

Westheimer, Ruth

West Helena

West Hempstead

West Highland white terrier

West Hills Community College

Westin Crown Center, The

West Indian cedar

West Indian gherkin

West Indian kale

West Indies [*now* Caribbean Indies]

West Indies Associated States

Westinghouse, George

Westinghouse brake

Westinghouse Broadcasting Company

Westinghouse Credit Corporation

Westinghouse Electric Corporation

Westinghouse Foundation

Westin Hotel, The

Westin Hotel, Williams Center, The

Westin Saint Francis, The

West Lafayette

Westlake

Westlake, Donald E.

West Liberty State College

West Los Angeles College

West Lothian

Westmar College

West Memphis

West Midlands

West Mifflin

Westminster

Westminster Abbey

Westminster Assembly

Westminster Choir

Westminster Choir College

Westminster College

Westminster College of Salt Lake City

Westminster Conference

Westminster Confession of Faith

Westminster Hall

Westminster Kennel Club

Westminster Kennel Club Show

Westminster Palace

Westminster Theological Seminary

Westminster Theological Seminary in California

West Monroe

Westmont College

Westmoreland, William

Westmoreland Coal Company

Westmoreland County Community College

West New York

Weston

Weston, Edward

Weston, Jack

Weston, Paul

West One Bancorporation

Weston School of Theology

West Orange

Westover, Russ

Westover Air Force Base

Westpac Banking Corporation

West Pakistan [*now* Pakistan]

West Palm Beach

West Paterson [* NJ; one *t*]

Westphalia

Westphalian

Westphalian ham

West Point

West Point–Pepperell Foundation

West Point–Pepperell, Inc.

Westport

West Quoddy Head

West Riding

West Saint Paul

West Shore Community College

West Side Institute of Technology

West Side Story

West Springfield

West Suburban College of Nursing

West Texas State University

West University Place

Westvaco Corporation

Westvaco Foundation Trust

West Valley College

West Valley–Mission Community College

West Virginia

West Virginia Institute of Technology

West Virginia Metronews Radio Network

West Virginia Mountaineers

West Virginian

West Virginia Northern Community College

West Virginia School of Osteopathic Medicine

West Virginia State College

West Virginia University

West Virginia Wesleyan College

Westward, Ho!

Westways

Westwood

Westwood Lakes

Westwood Marquis Hotel and Garden

Westwood One Inc.

Westwood One Radio Network

Wethered, Joyce

Wethersfield

We Three Kings of Orient Are

Wetterhorn

We Wish You a Merry Christmas

Wexner, Bella

Wexner, Leslie
Herbert

Weyden, Rogier van
der *occas.* Roger
van der

Weyerhaeuser,
Frederick

Weyerhaeuser
Company

Weyerhaeuser
Company
Foundation

Weymouth

WFMT Fine Arts
Network

Wharton, Clifton R.,
Jr.

Wharton, Edith

Wharton County
Junior College

What a Fool Believes

Whatcom Community
College

What Kind of Fool
Am I?

What's Love Got to
Do with It?

What's My Line?

Wheat, Zack

Wheatley, Phillis

Wheaton

Wheaton, Wil

Wheaton College

Wheaton Van Lines,
Inc.

Wheat Ridge

Wheatstone, Sir
Charles

Wheatstone bridge

Wheelabrator
Technologies Inc.

Wheeler, Bert

Wheeler, Burton
Kendall

Wheeler, John
Archibald

Wheeler, Joseph

Wheeler Peak

Wheeling

Wheeling Jesuit
College

Wheeling-Pittsburgh
Corporation

Wheelock College

Wheel of Fortune

Wheels

Wheelwright, John

Wheelwright, William

When Did You Last
See Your Father?

Where Do We Come
From? What Are
We? Where Are We
Going?

Where in Europe Is
Carmen
Sandiego?™

Where in the USA Is
Carmen
Sandiego?™

Where in the World Is
Carmen
Sandiego?™

Whidbey Island

Whidbey Island Naval
Air Station

Whiffenpoof Song,
The

Whig

Whiggery

Whiggish

Whiggishness

Whiggism

Whig Party

Whirlpool Corporation

Whirlpool Foundation

Whiskey Rebellion

Whiskey Ring

Whiskeytown-Shasta-
Trinity National
Recreation Area

Whistler, James
McNeill

Whistlerian

Whistler's Mother

Whitaker

Whitaker, Forest

Whitaker, Jack

White, Barry

White, Betty

White, Bill

White, Byron R.

White, Diane

White, E. B.

White, Edward
Douglass

White, Gilbert

White, Jesse

White, Josh

White, Karyn

White, Patrick

White, Paul Dudley

White, Pearl

White, Peregrine

White, Richard Grant

White, Stanford

White, Stewart
Edward

White, Theodore H.

White, Vanna

White, Walter F.

White, William Allen

White, William Lindsay

White Aryan Resistance

White Bear Lake

Whitechapel

white cliffs of Dover

Whitefish Bay

White Friar [Carmelite friar]

Whitefriars [London district]

White Girl, The

Whitehall

Whitehall boat

Whitehall Laboratories

Whitehall Palace

Whitehead, Alfred North

Whitehorse

White House, the

White House Historical Association

White House Mountain

White Lotus Rebellion

Whiteman, Paul

Whiteman Air Force Base

White Mariposa lily

White Mountain National Forest

White Mountains

White Nile

White Oak

White Pass

White Pines College

White Plains

White River

White River National Forest

White Russia

White Russian [Byelorussian]

white or White Russian [cocktail]

White Sands

White Sands Missile Range

White Sands National Monument

White Sands Space Harbor

White Sands Test Facility

White Sea

White Settlement

White Shadow, The

White Slave Act

White-Slave Traffic Act

Whitesnake

White Sulphur Springs

Whitewater

Whiting

Whiting, Margaret

Whiting, Richard A.

Whiting Field Naval Air Station

Whitley, Keith

Whitman

Whitman, Marcus

Whitman, Narcissa

Whitman, Slim

Whitman, Stuart

Whitman, Walt

Whitman College

Whitman Corporation

Whitman Foundation

Whitman Mission National Historic Site

Whitmonday

Whitmore, James

Whitney

Whitney, Eli

Whitney, Grace Lee

Whitney, John Hay

Whitney, William Dwight

Whitney Museum of American Art

Whitsun

Whitsunday

Whitsuntide

Whittaker, Johnnie

Whittaker, Roger

Whittier

Whittier, John Greenleaf

Whittier College

Whittington, Richard

Whittle, Sir Frank

Whittredge, Worthington

Whittuesday

Whitty, Dame May

Whit Week

Whitworth, Kathy

Whitworth College

Whiz Kid occas. whiz kid

Who, The

Who Framed Roger Rabbit?

Whole Earth Catalog

Whole Earth Review

Wholesale Distributors Association

Whoopi Goldberg
Show, The

Who's Afraid of
Virginia Woolf?

Who's the Boss?

WIBC Championship
Tournament

WIBC Queens
Tournament

Wichita [* KS; *see
also* Wichita Falls]

Wichita Art Museum

Wichita Eagle, The

Wichita Eagle Beacon

Wichita Falls [* TX;
see also Wichita]

Wichita Falls Dam

Wichita [Indian]

Wichita Lineman

Wichita Mountains

Wichita State
University

Wichita State
University Shockers

Wicker, Tom

Wickes, Mary

Wickliffe [* OH]

Wickliffe *var. of*
Wyckliffe, John

Wideman, John Edgar

Widener University

Widener University
School of Law

Wider Opportunities
for Women

Wider Quaker
Fellowship

Wideworld News
Service

Widmark, Richard

Wieland, Christoph
Martin

Wieland, Heinrich

Wiener, Norbert

Wiener schnitzel

Wiesbaden

Wiesel, Elie

Wiesenthal, Simon

Wiesner, David

Weiss, Pierre

Wiest, Dianne

Wiggin, Kate Douglas

Wigglesworth,
Michael

Wigner, Eugene Paul

Wilander, Mats

Wilberforce, Samuel

Wilberforce, William

Wilberforce
University

Wilbraham

Wilbur

Wilbur, Richard

Wilburite

Wilcox, Ella Wheeler

Wilde, Cornel

Wilde, Kim

Wilde, Oscar

Wild Eights

Wilder, Billy

Wilder, Gene

Wilder, Laura Ingalls

Wilder, L. Douglas

Wilder, Thornton

Wilderness, the

Wilderness campaign

Wilderness of Zin

Wilderness Press

Wilderness Road

Wilderness Society

Wild Horse Organized
Assistance

Wild Hunt

Wild Huntsman

Wilding, Michael

Wild Kingdom

Wildlife Management
Institute

Wildlife Preservation
Trust International

Wild West

Wild West show

Wild, Wild West, The

Wildwood

Wile E. Coyote

Wiley College

Wilfred

Wilfrid

Wilfrid, Saint

Wilhelm

Wilhelm, Hoyt

Wilhelmina

Wilhelm Lehmbruck
Museum

Wilhelmshaven

Wilhelmstrasse

Wilkes, Charles

Wilkes, John

Wilkes-Barre

Wilkes Community
College

Wilkes Land

Wilkes University

Wilkie, Sir David

Wilkins,
Christopher P.

Wilkins, Sir Hubert

Wilkins, Maurice H. F.

Wilkins, Roy

Wilkinsburg

Wilkinson, Bud

Wilkinson, Sir Geoffrey

Will, George F.

Willaert, Adrian

Willamette

Willamette Industries, Inc.

Willamette National Forest

Willamette University

Willard, Archibald M.

Willard, Emma Hart

Willard, Frances E.

Willard, Frank

Willard, Jess

Willemstad

Willesdend

William

William, Warren

William Carey College

William Collins Sons and Company

William F. Farley Foundation

William Howard Taft National Historic Site

William Jennings Bryan College

William Jewell College

William Mitchell College of Law

William Morris Agency, Inc.

William Morrow and Company, Inc.

William of Auvergne

William of Auxerre

William of Champeaux

William of Conches

William of Corbeil

William of Holland

William of Malmesbury

William of Moerbeke

William of Newburgh

William of Occam or Ockham

William of Orange

William of Paris

William of Saint-Amour

William of Saint-Thierry

William of Tyre

William of Waynflete or Wainfleet

William of Wykeham or Wickham

William Paterson College

William Penn Association

William Penn College

William Rainey Harper College

William Rockhill Nelson Collection

William Rufus

Williams, Andy

Williams, Ben Ames

Williams, Bert

Williams, Billy Dee

Williams, Cindy

Williams, Cootie

Williams, Daniel Hale

Williams, Darnell

Williams, Deniece

Williams, Don

Williams, Edy

Williams, Emlyn

Williams, Esther

Williams, Hal

Williams, Hank

Williams, Hank, Jr.

Williams, JoBeth

Williams, Joe

Williams, John

Williams, J. R.

Williams, Mary Lou

Williams, Mason

Williams, Montel

Williams, Paul

Williams, Rhys

Williams, Robin

Williams, Roger

Williams, Ted

Williams, Tennessee

Williams, Tex

Williams, Thomas

Williams, Tony

Williams, Treat

Williams, Vanessa

Williams, William

Williams, William Carlos

Williams Air Force Base

Williams Baptist College

Williamsburg

Williamsburg Technical College

Williams College

Williams Companies, Inc., The

Williamson, Nicol

Williamson Free School of Technical Trades

Williamsport

Williamston [* MI; NC; SC]

Williamstown [* KY; MA; NJ; WV]

William Tell

William the Bad

William the Conqueror

William the Good

William the Lion

William the Red

William the Sailor King

William Tyndale College

William Woods College

William Wrigley Jr. Company

Willie

Willis, Bruce

Willis, Kelly

Williston

Williston Park

Willkie, Wendell

Willkie Memorial of Freedom House, Inc.

Willmar

Willmar Community College

Willmar Technical College

Willoughby

Willoughby Hills

Willow Grove Naval Air Station

Willowick

Willow Run

Will Rogers Follies, The

Will Rogers Memorial

Will Rogers Memorial Fund

Wills, Bob

Wills, Chill

Wills, Helen

Wills, Maury

Willson, Meredith

Willstätter, Richard

Willy

Wilma

Wilmette

Wilmington

Wilmington College

Wilmington News-Journal

Wilmot, David

Wilmot Proviso

Wilms, Max

Wilms' tumor

Wilshire 5000 index

Wilshire 4500 index

Wilshire Theatre

Wilson

Wilson, Alexander

Wilson, Sir Angus

Wilson, August

Wilson, Brian

Wilson, Charles E.

Wilson, Charles Thomson Rees

Wilson, Demond

Wilson, Dennis

Wilson, Dooley

Wilson, Edith

Wilson, Edmund

Wilson, Elizabeth

Wilson, Flip

Wilson, Gahan

Wilson, Hack

Wilson, Sir Harold

Wilson, Jackie

Wilson, Lanford

Wilson, Marie

Wilson, Mary

Wilson, Nancy

Wilson, Pete

Wilson, Richard

Wilson, Sloan

Wilson, Teddy

Wilson, Tom

Wilson, Woodrow

Wilson chamber

Wilson cloud chamber

Wilson College

Wilson Dam

Wilson-Gorman Tariff Act

Wilsonian

Wilsonianism

Wilson Phillips

Wilson's blackcap

Wilson's Creek National Battlefield

Wilson's disease

Wilson's petrel

Wilson's phalarope

Wilson Sporting Goods Company

Wilson's snipe

Wilson's thrush

Wilson's warbler

Wilson Technical Community College

Wilton

Wilton carpet
Wilton Diptych, The
Wilton Manors
Wilton rug
Wiltshire
Wiltshire cheese
Wimbledon
Wimbledon tennis
  championships
Wimsey, Lord Peter
Wimshurst generator
Wimshurst machine
Winchell, Paul
Winchell, Walter
Winchester
Winchester, Oliver
Winchester Arms
  Collectors
  Association
Winchester bushel
Winchester Cathedral
Winchester College
Winchester disk
Winchester Mystery
  House
Winckelmann, Johann
  Joachim
Wind beneath My
  Wings
Windbreaker™
Wind Cave National
  Park
Windermere
Windham
Windham Hill
  Records
Windhoek
Winding, Kai
Wind in the Willows,
  The
Windom, William

Window Coverings
  Association of
  America
Window Rock
Windows™ software
Wind River
Wind River Range
Windsor
Windsor, Marie
Windsor bench
Windsor Castle
Windsor chair
Windsor Court
Windsor knot
Windsor Locks
Windsor tie
Windstar Sail Cruises
Windward Channel
Windward Islands
Windward Passage
Windy City
Winebrenner
  Theological
  Seminary
Wine Enthusiast
Winema National
  Forest
Winesap apple
Winesburg, Ohio
Winfield
Winfield, Arthur
Winfield, Paul
Winfrey, Oprah
Wingate College
Wingate Ordnance
  Depot
Winged Horse
Winged Victory of
  Samothrace
Winger, Debra

Wings
Wings West Airlines
Winkler, Henry
Winn-Dixie Stores
  Foundation
Winn-Dixie Stores,
  Inc.
Winnebago [Indian],
  n., pl. Winnebago
  or Winnebagos or
  Winnebagoes
Winnebago Industries,
  Inc.
Winnemucca
Winnetka
Winnetka plan
Winnie Award
Winnie-the-Pooh
Winninger, Charles
Winningham, Mare
Winnipeg
Winnipeg Arena
Winnipeg Art Gallery
Winnipegger
Winnipeg Jets
Winnsboro
Winona
Winona State
  University
Winooski
Winslow, Edward
Winsor Dam
Winston
Winston, George
Winston 500
Winston-Salem
Winston-Salem
  · Journal
Winston-Salem State
  University
Winter Garden

Winter Garden Theater

Winterhalter, Franz

Winterhalter, Hugo

Winter Haven

Winter Olympic Games

Winter Park

Winters, Jonathan

Winters, Shelley

Winters, Yvor

Winter's bark

Winter's Tale, The

Winthrop

Winthrop, John

Winthrop College

Winthrop College Eagles

Winthrop desk

Wintun

Winwood, Steve

Wirephoto™

Wisconsin

Wisconsin Dells

Wisconsin Energy Corporation

Wisconsin Energy Corporation Foundation

Wisconsin Evangelical Lutheran Synod

Wisconsin Indianhead Technical College

Wisconsinite

Wisconsin Law Review

Wisconsin Lutheran College

Wisconsin Network, Inc.

Wisconsin Public Service Corporation

Wisconsin Public Television Network

Wisconsin Rapids

Wisconsin School of Electronics

Wisconsin School of Professional Psychology

Wise, Stephen Samuel

Wise, Thomas James

Wiseman, Joseph

Wise Men of the East

Wissler, Clark

Wister, Owen

witches' Sabbath

witch of Agnesi

Witco Corporation

Withers, Grant

Withers, Jane

Witherspoon, John

Witherspoon, Tim

Witness for Peace

Witt, Katarina

Witt, Paul Junger

Witte, Emanuel de

Witte, Sergei

Wittenberg

Wittenberg University

Wittgenstein, Ludwig

Wittgensteinian

Wittig, Georg

Witwatersrand

Wiz, The

Wizard Company, Inc.

Wizard of Id

Wizard of Oz, The [movie; see also

Wonderful Wizard of Oz, The]

WKRP in Cincinnati

Wm. Wrigley Jr. Company

Wobbly, n., pl. Wobblies

Woburn

Wodan occas. Woden

Wodehouse, Sir P. G.

Woffington, Peg

Wofford College

Wojciehowicz, Alex

Wolf, Fredrich August

Wolf, Hugo

Wolfe, Charles

Wolfe, James

Wolfe, Nero

Wolfe, Thomas [author, 1900–1938]

Wolfe, Tom [author, 1931–]

Wolfert, Ira

Wolff, Hugh

Wolff, Tobias

Wolf-Ferrari, Ermanno

Wolffian body

Wolfman Jack

Wolf Trap Farm Park for the Performing Arts

Wolf Trap Foundation for the Performing Arts

Wollaston, Hyde

Wollaston, John

Wollaston Lake

Wollaston process

Wollaston wire

Wollongong

Wollstonecraft, Mary

Wolof, *n.*, *pl.* Wolof *or* Wolofs

Wolpe, Stefan

Wolper, David L.

Wolseley, Garnet Joseph

Wolsey, Thomas Cardinal

Wolverhampton

Wolverine State

Woman Bowler

Woman's Christian Temperance Union

Woman's Day

Woman's World

Woman under the Influence, A

Woman Weeping

Woman with Suitcases

Women and Guns

Women in Communications

Women in Love

Women Marines Association

Women of Tahiti

Women on the Verge of a Nervous Breakdown

Women's Army Corps Veterans Association

Women's International Bowling Congress

Women's International League for Peace and Freedom

Women's International Tennis Association

Women's International Zionist Organization

Women's Legal Defense Fund

Women's National Republican Club

Women's Overseas Service League

Women's Rights National Historical Park

Women's Sports and Fitness

Women's Sports Foundation

Women Strike for Peace

Women's Wear Daily

Women World War Veterans

Wonder, Stevie

Wonderful Town

Wonderful Wizard of Oz, The [book; *see also* Wizard of Oz]

Wonderful World of Disney, The

Wonder Woman

Wonder Years, The

Wong, Anna May

Wong, Suzy

Wonka, Willy

Wönsan

Wood, Clement

Wood, Danny

Wood, Grant

Wood, Leonard

Wood, Natalie

Wood, Peggy

Wood, Tim

Woodall Publishing Company

Woodard, Alfre

Woodbridge

Wood Buffalo National Park

Woodbury

Woodbury University

Wooden, John

Woodhouse, Barbara

Woodhull, Victoria Claflin

Wood Junior College

Woodland

Woodlawn

Woodmen of the World

Woodmen of the World Life Insurance Society

Woodmen of the World Magazine

Woodmere

Woodner, Ian

Wood Products Manufacturers Association

Woodridge

Wood River

Woodrow

Woodruff key

Woods, Granville T.

Woods, James

Wood School

Woods Hole

Woods Hole Oceanographic Institution

Wood's light

Woodsmith

Woodson, Carter G.

Woodstock

Woodstock Music and Arts Festival

Woodville, Richard Caton

Woodward, Bob

Woodward, Edward

Woodward, Joanne

Woodward Stores

Woodworking Association of North America

Woody Woodpecker

Woolery, Chuck

Wooley, Sheb

Woolf, Leonard

Woolf, Virginia

Woollcott, Alexander

Woolley, Sir Leonard

Woolley, Monty

Wool Manufacturers Council

Woolwich

Woolworth, Charles S.

Woolworth, Frank W.

Woolworth Building

Woolworth Corporation

Woonsocket

Woosnan, Ian

Wooster

Wooster, Bertie

Wooster, David

Wopat, Tom

Worcester

Worcester, Joseph E.

Worcester china

Worcester Evening Gazette, The

Worcester Polytechnic Institute

Worcestershire

Worcestershire sauce

Worcester State College

Worcester Telegram

Worcester ware

Word Book Club

Word of Life Bible Institute

WordPerfect Corporation

WordPerfect™ software

WordPerfect: The Magazine

WordStar International Inc.

WordStar™ software

Wordsworth, Dorothy

Wordsworth, William

Wordsworthian

Wordsworthianism

Worf, Lieutenant

Workbasket, The

Workbench

Working Mother

Working Woman

Workman Publishing Company, Inc.

Workmen's Circle

Work Projects Administration

World Airways Cargo, Inc.

World Airways, Inc.

World Almanac/Bert Bell Memorial Trophy

World Almanac/George Halas Trophy

World Almanac/Jim Thorpe Trophy

World Association for Celebrating Year 2000

World Bank

World Baptist Fellowship

World Book Encyclopedia, The

World Book, Inc.

World Boxing Council

World Bridge Federation

World Championship Quarter Horse Show

World Championship Wrestling

World College West

World Communion Sunday

World Concern

World Confederation of Labor

World Conference of United Zionists

World Council of Churches

World Court

World Cup

World Day of Prayer

World Education

World Environment Policy Act

World Explorer Cruises

World Fast Draw Association

World Federalist Association

World Federation of Public Health Association

World Federation of Trade Unions

World Flying Disc Federation

World Future Society

World Health Organization

World Intellectual Property Organization

World Island

World Jewish Congress

World Medical Association

World Mercy Fund

World Meteorological Organization

World Neighbors

World News Syndicate, Ltd.

World Ocean Circulation Experiment

World Policy Institute

World Press Review

World Rehabilitation Fund

World Research

World Resources Institute

World Savings and Loan Association

World's Championship JCs Rodeo of Rodeos

World Science Fiction Society

World's Columbian Exposition

World Scout Bureau

World Series™ [baseball event]

World Series™, The [candy bar]

World Series of Poker

World's Fair Collectors Society

World Ski Championships

World Team Tennis

World Trade Center

World Trade Center, North

World Trade Center, South

World Union Press

World Vision

Worldvision Enterprises, Inc.

World War I

World War II

Worldwatch Institute

World Watch Syndicate

World Water Ski Union

World Wildlife Fund

World Woman's Christian Temperance Union

World Wrestling Federation

Worley, Jo Anne

Worms

Wormwood Scrubs Prison

Worth, Charles Frederick

Worth, Irene

Worth, Mary

Worthington

Worthington Community College

Worthington Industries, Inc.

Wor-Wic Tech Community College

Wotton, Sir Henry

Wouk, Herman

Wounded Knee

Wounded Knee Massacre

Wovoka

Wozzeck

W particle

W. P. Hobby Airport

WPIX New York

WPL Holdings, Inc.

Wrangel, Ferdinand von

Wrangel Island [island off the coast of northeastern Siberia]

Wrangell Island [island off the coast of southeastern Alaska]

Wrangell Mountains

Wrangell–Saint Elias National Park

Wrangell–Saint Elias National Preserve

Wrather, Jack

Wray, Fay

Wreck of the Hesperus, The

Wren, Sir Christopher

Wren, Percival Christopher

W. R. Grace and Company

Wright, Amy

Wright, Fanny

Wright, Frank Lloyd

Wright, George

Wright, Harold Bell

Wright, Harry
Wright, James C., Jr.
Wright, Joseph
Wright, Martha
Wright, Max
Wright, Michael
Wright, Mickey
Wright, Orville
Wright, Patience
Wright, Richard
Wright, Sewall
Wright, Steven
Wright, Teresa
Wright, Wilbur
Wright, Willard
  Huntington
Wright brothers
Wright Brothers
  National Memorial
Wright Institute
Wright–Patterson Air
  Force Base
Wright State
  University
Wright State
  University Raiders
Wrigley, William, Jr.
Wrigley Field
Wrinkle in Time, A
Wriothesley, Henry
Wriothesley, Thomas
Writer, The
Writer, Inc.
Writers Clearinghouse
Writer's Digest
Writer's Digest Book
  Club
Writer's Digest Books
Writers Guild of
  America, East

Writers Guild of
  America, West
Wronski, Jozef
Wronskian
WSM Grand Ole Opry
WTBS Atlanta
Wu dynasty
Wu-han [*now* Wuhan]
Wunderkind
Wundt, Wilhelm
Wuorinen, Charles
Wupatki National
  Monument
Wuppertal
Wurster, William
Wurtsmith Air Force
  Base
Würzburg
Wuthering Heights
W. W. Grainger, Inc.
W. W. Norton and
  Company, Inc.
Wyandot [Indian], *n.*,
  pl. Wyandot *or*
  Wyandots
Wyandotte [* MI]
Wyandotte Cave
Wyandotte [chicken],
  n., pl. Wyandotte *or*
  Wyandottes
Wyatt
Wyatt, Alexander
  Helwig
Wyatt, Jane
Wyatt, Sir Thomas
Wycherley, William
Wycliffe *occas.*
  Wyclif *or* Wickliffe
  or Wiclif, John
Wycliffism
Wycliffite

Wye
Wyeth, Andrew
Wyeth, N. C.
Wyld, Henry
Wyler, William
Wylie, Elinor
Wylie, Philip
Wyman, Bill
Wyman, Jane
Wyman–Gordon
  Company
Wyman–Gordon
  Foundation
Wymore, Patrice
Wyndham Harbour
  Island
Wynette, Tammy
Wynken, Blynken, and
  Nod
Wynn, Early
Wynn, Ed
Wynn, Keenan
Wynn, Tracy Keenan
Wynter, Dana
Wyoming
Wyomingite
Wyoming Technical
  Institute
Wyoming Valley
Wyoming Valley
  Massacre
Wyomissing
Wyss, Johann David
Wyss, Johann Rudolf
Wyszynski, Stefan
  Cardinal
Wythe, George
Wytheville
Wytheville
  Community College

X

X-Acto™ knife
Xanadu
Xanthippe [wife of Socrates]
Xanthippe *or* Xantippe [ill-tempered woman]
Xaverian Brother
Xaverian Missioners of the United States
Xavier University
Xavier University Musketeers
Xavier University of Louisiana
x-axis, *n.*, *pl.* x-axes
Xceron, John
X chromosome
XClan
x-coordinate
Xenia
Xenocrates

Xenon Entertainment
Xenophanean
Xenophanes
Xenophon
Xenophontian
Xenophontine
Xerox™
Xerox Corporation
Xerox Foundation
Xerxes
Xia Gui
Xiamen Gaoqi International Airport
Xi'an [*form.* Sian]
Xingu
Xinjiang [*form.* Sinkiang]
XIT Ranch
Xizang [*aka* Tibet]

Xmas
Xochimilco
X-ray, *adj.*
X ray, *n.*
x-ray, *v.*
X-ray astronomy
X-ray diffraction
X-ray laser
X-ray Multi-Mirror
X-ray photograph
X-ray star
X-ray technology
X-ray therapy
X-ray tube
X-30 National Aerospace Plane
x-unit
X-wave
Xylocaine™
XYZ Affair

Y

Yablonovy *or* Yablonovyy Mountains [*form.* Yablonoi Mountains]

Yablonski, Joseph A.

Yachting

Yacht Vacations Magazine

Yaddo

Yadkin

Yadkin Valley

Yaffe, James

Yagi, Hidetsugu

Yagi *or* yagi antenna

Yahgan, *n., pl.* Yahgan *or* Yahgans

Yahoo, *n., pl.* Yahoos

Yahrzeit

Yahweh *occas.* Yahveh

Yahweh ben Yahweh

Yahwism

Yahwist

Yahwistic

YAK-41 Freestyle

Yakima

Yakima Firing Range

Yakima [Indian], *n., pl.* Yakima *or* Yakimas

Yakima Valley Community College

YAK-141 Freestyle

Yakovlev, Alexander

YAK-38 Forger

Yakut [Russian autonomous province]

Yakut [people], *n., pl.* Yakut *or* Yakuts

Yakutsk [city in Yakut]

Yakuza *or* yakuza

Yale, Caroline Ardelia

Yale, Elihu

Yale, Linus

Yale Bulldogs

Yale Elis

Yale Law Journal

Yale Literary Magazine

Yale Repertory Theatre

Yale Review, The

Yale School of Drama

Yale Series of Younger Poets Competition

Yale University

Yale University Press

Yalow, Rosalyn Sussman

Yalta

Yalta Conference

Yalu

Yalung

Yamaguchi, Kristi

Yamaha Corporation [Japan-based company]

Yamaha Corporation of America

Yamaha Electronics Corporation (U.S.A.)

Yamaha Motor Company, Ltd.

Yamaha Motor Corporation, U.S.A.

Yamaha Motor Manufacturing Corporation of America (U.S.A.)

Yamamoto, Isoroku

Yamasaki, Minoru

Yamasee

Yamashita, Tomoyuki

Yamoto Bunkakan Museum

Yancey

Yancey, Jimmy

648

Yancey Action
  Networks
Yangon [*aka*
  Rangoon]
Yangon International
  Airport
Yangtze [river; *now*
  Chang]
Yangtze Gorges
Yangtze River Basin
Yangtze River Valley
Yank
Yankee
Yankee Atomic
  Electric Company
Yankee Conference
Yankeedom
Yankee Doodle
  [nursery rhyme;
  song]
Yankee Doodle Dandy
  [movie; song]
Yankeeism
Yankeeland
Yankee Rowe nuclear
  power station
Yankee Stadium
Yankovic, Weird Al
Yankton
Yaoundé *or* Yaunde
Yap *or* Uap Islands
Yaqui, *n.*, *pl.* Yaqui *or*
  Yaquis
Yar, Tasha
Yarborough, Barton
Yarborough, Cale
Yarborough, Glenn
Yarborough hand
Yarbro, Chelsea Quinn
Yarbrough, Lee Roy
Yard, Molly

Yardbirds, The
Yarkand
Yarmouth
Yarnell, Lorene
Yarrow, Peter
Yasbeck, Amy
Yastrzemski, Carl
Yasuda Trust and
  Banking Company,
  Ltd.
Yates, Cassie
Yates, Elizabeth
Yates, Peter
Yaunde *var. of*
  Yaoundé
Yavapai College
Yavapaí [Indian], *n.*,
  pl. Yavapaí *or*
  Yavapaís
Yawkey, Tom
y-axis, *n.*, *pl.* y-axes
Yazoo
Yazoo City
Yazoo land fraud
Yazoo-type river
Ybor City
Y chromosome
y-coordinate
Yeadon
Yeager, Chuck
Yeager, Jeana
Yearling, The
Year of Confusion
Yearwood, Trisha
Yeats, Jack Butler
Yeats, William Butler
Yeatsian
Yekaterinburg [*form.*
  Sverdlovsk]
Yellen, Jack

Yellow Brick Road
Yellow Cab Company
Yellow Christ, The
Yellow Emperor
Yellow Freight System
  Foundation
Yellow Freight
  System, Inc., of
  Delaware
Yellow Hats
Yellowhead Pass
Yellowknife
Yellowknife Preserve
Yellow Mountain
Yellow Newtown
  apple
Yellow Pages
  Publishers
  Association
Yellow River
Yellow Rose, The
Yellow Rose Express,
  The
Yellow Rose of Texas,
  The
Yellow Roses
Yellow Sea
Yellowstone Canyon
Yellowstone Falls
Yellowstone Lake
Yellowstone National
  Park
Yellowtail Dam
Yeltsin, Boris N.
Yeltsin, Naina
Yemen
Yemen Airways
Yemen Arab Republic
Yemeni
Yemenite

Yenisei *or* Yenisey River

Yeomen of the Guard

Yeomen Warders of the Tower of London

Yepremian, Garo

Yerba Buena Island

Yerby, Frank

Yerevan

Yergin, Daniel

Yerkes, Charles Tyson

Yerkes, Robert Mearns

Yerkes Observatory

Yertle the Turtle

Yes Clothing Company

Yesenin *occas.* Esenin, Sergey

Yeshiva and Kolel Bais Medrash Elyon

Yeshiva and Kollel Harbotzas Torah

Yeshiva and Mesivta Kol Torah

Yeshiva and Mesivta Torah Termimah Talmudical Seminary

Yeshiva Beth Moshe

Yeshiva Beth Yehuda—Yeshiva Gedolah of Greater Detroit

Yeshiva Derech Chaim

Yeshiva Gedolah Bais Yisroel

Yeshiva Gedolah Imrei Yosef D'Spinka

Yeshiva Karlin Stolin Beth Aaron V'Israel Rabbinical Institute

Yeshiva Mikdash Melech

Yeshiva of Nitra Rabbinical College

Yeshiva Ohr Elcohonon Chabad/ West Coast Talmudical Seminary

Yeshiva Shaar Hatorah-Grodno

Yeshivath Viznitz

Yeshivath Zichron Moshe

Yeshiva Toras Chaim Talmudical Seminary

Yeshiva University

Yeshiva University Press

Yesterday's Children

Yesterday, Today and Tomorrow

yeti *occas.* Yeti

Yevtushenko, Yevgeny

Yiddish

Yiddishism

Yiddishist

Yiddish language

Yin and Yang

Y-Indian Guide

Y-Indian Maiden

Y-Indian Princess

Yin dynasty

Yin-Yang School

yippie *occas.* Yippie, *n., pl.* yippies *occas.* Yippies

YMCA of the United States

Yoakam, Dwight

Yoga *occas.* yoga

Yoga Journal

Yogi, Maharishi Mahesh

Yogi Bear

Yoho National Park

Yoknapatawhpa County

Yokohama

Yokohama Rubber Company, Ltd.

Yokosuka

Yokut

Yolande

Yom Kippur

Yom Kippur War

Yong Shang-Kun

Yonkers

Yonkers Raceway

Yonsei

Yorba Linda

York

York, Sergeant Alvin Cullum

York, Dick

York, Michael

York, Susannah

York boat

York College

York College of Pennsylvania

Yorke Peninsula

Yorkin, Bud

York International Corporation

Yorkist

York rite

Yorkshire

Yorkshire bond

Yorkshire chair
Yorkshire clock
Yorkshire hog
Yorkshire pudding
Yorkshire Ripper
Yorkshire terrier
York Technical College
Yorkton [* Saskatchewan]
Yorktown [* IN; TX; VA]
Yorktown campaign
Yorktown Naval Weapons Station
York University
Yorubaland
Yoruban
Yoruba, n., pl. Yoruba or Yorubas
Yosemite Association
Yosemite Community College
Yosemite Falls
Yosemite National Park
Yosemite Park and Curry Company
Yosemite Valley
Yossarian Universal News Service
Yost, Fielding Harris
Yothers, Tina
You Are My Sunshine
You Can't Go Home Again
You Can't Take It with You
Youmans, Vincent
Young, Al [writer]
Young, Alan [actor]

Young, Andrew
Young, Art [cartoonist]
Young, Arthur [writer]
Young, Brigham
Young, Burt
Young, Charles Augustus
Young, Chic
Young, Clara Kimball
Young, Coleman
Young, Cy
Young, Edward
Young, Ella Flagg
Young, Faron
Young, Francis Brett
Young, Gig
Young, John Russell
Young, John Watts
Young, Lester Willis
Young, Karen
Young, Loretta
Young, Mahonri MacKintosh
Young, Neil
Young, Owen D.
Young, Paul
Young, Robert
Young, Roland
Young, Sean
Young, Stark
Young, Terence
Young, Thomas
Young, Victor
Young, Whitney Moore, Jr.
Young Americans for Freedom
Young and Rubicam Inc.

Young and the Restless, The
Young Audiences
Youngblood, Don
Young Communist League
Young Democrats of America
Younger, Bob
Younger, Cole
Younger, Jim
Younger, John
Younger Edda
Youngerman, Jack
Young Guns
Young Guns II
Young Hare
Young Harris College
Young Lady at the Virginals
Young Life
Young Lonigan
Youngman, Henry
Young Manhood of Studs Lonigan, The
Young Men's and Young Women's Hebrew Association
Young Men's Christian Association
Young Men's Hebrew Association
Young Person's Guide to the Orchestra, The
Young Plan
Young Pretender
Young Rascals, The
Young Republican National Federation

Youngs, Ross

Young's modulus

Young Social Democrats

Young Socialist Alliance

Youngstown

Youngstown State University

Youngstown State University Penguins

Youngstown Vindicator, The

Young *occas.* young Turk

Young Women's Christian Association

Young Women's Christian Association of the United States of America

Young Women's Hebrew Association

Young Writers

Yount, Robin

Your Cheatin' Heart

You're a Good Man Charlie Brown

Yousekevitch, Igor

Youth Ambassadors International

Youth Education Systems

Youth for Christ International

Youth for Christ/ U.S.A.

Youth for Understanding

Youth International Party

You've Got a Friend

Yo-Yo™

Y potential

Ypres

Ypsilanti

Ypsilon Mountain

Yreka

Yser

Ysonde *var. of* Iseult the Fair

Y-Teens

Yuan

Yüan Dynasty

Yuba City

Yuba College

Yuba River

Yucatán

Yucatán Channel

Yucatán Peninsula

Yucatec, *n., pl.* Yucatec *or* Yucatecs

Yucca House National Monument

Yugoslav

Yugoslav Airlines

Yugoslavia *occas.* Jugoslavia

Yugoslavian

Yugoslavic

Yugoslav literature

Yukaghir, *n., pl.* Yukaghir *or* Yukaghirs

Yukawa, Hideki

Yukon

Yukon-Charley Rivers National Preserve

Yukoner

Yukon Flats

Yukon Territory

Yukon Standard Time

Yukon Time

Yule

Yule log

Yulin, Harris

Yuma

Yuma [Indian], *n., pl.* Yumas *or* Yuma

Yuma Marine Corps Air Station

Yuman

Yuma Proving Ground

Yunnan *occas.* Yünnan

Yurok

Yvette

Yvonne

Z

Zab
ZaBach, Florian
Zabriskie Point
Zacatecas
Zach
Zachariah
Zacharias or Zachary, Saint [see also Zechariah]
Zachary
Zachary Taylor National Cemetery
Zacherle, John
Zack
Zacky Foods Company
Zadkine, Ossip
Zadora, Pia
Zagreb
Zagros
Zagut
Zaharias, Babe Didrikson
Zahn, Paula
Zaire [form. Belgian Congo]
Zairean or Zairian
Zaire River
Zale, Tony

Zale Corporation
Zambezi or Zambesi River
Zambia [form. Northern Rhodesia]
Zamboanga
Zamboanga del Norte
Zamboanga del Sur
Zamenhof, Ludwig Lejzer
Zamfir
Zanderij International Airport
Zandonai, Riccardo
Zane
Zane's Trace
Zanesville
Zangwill, Israel
Zanuck, Darryl F.
Zanuck, Richard Darryl
Zanzibar
Zanzibari
Zanzibar Island
Zapata, Carmen
Zapata, Emiliano
Zapata Corporation
Zapata mustache
Zapotec

Zapotecan
Zappa, Ahmet
Zappa, Diva
Zappa, Dweezil
Zappa, Frank
Zappa, Gail
Zappa, Moon Unit
Zaragoza [city in Mexico; province in Spain; see also Saragossa]
Zarathushtra or Zarathustra
Zardeh Kuh
z-axis, n., pl. z-axes
Zayak, Elaine
z-bar
ZCMI Department Store
ZCMI Shopping Center
z-coordinate
Zealand [* Denmark; see also Zeeland]
Zebadiah
Zebedee
Zebra Books
Zebulun
Zebulunite

653

Zechariah *or* Zacharias [Jewish prophet; *see also* Zacharias]

Zedekiah

Zeebrugge

Zeeland [* the Netherlands; *see also* Zealand]

Zeeman, Pieter

Zeeman effect

Zeff Communications Company

Zeffirelli, Franco

Zeiss Optical Inc.

Zeitgeist

Zelda

Zell, Samuel

Zemeckis, Robert

Zemlinsky, Alexander von

Zen and the Art of Motorcycle Maintenance

Zen Buddhism

Zen Buddhist

Zenger, John Peter

Zenith Electronics Corporation

Zeno

Zenobia

Zenobia, Septimia

Zenon Dance Company

Zeno of Citium

Zeno of Elea

Zeno of Sidon

Zenshinren Bank

Zen Studies Society

Zeos International, Ltd.

Zephaniah *or* Sophonias

Zephyrinus, Saint

Zephyrus

Zephyr Weather Information Service

Zeppelin *often* zeppelin [airship]

Zeppelin, Ferdinand von

Zerah

Zeravshan

Zerbe, Anthony

Zerbe, Karl

Zermatt

Zermelo's axiom

ZeroMoving Dance Company

Zeron Group

Zero Population Growth Association

Zeta Beta Tau

Zeta Phi Beta

Zeta Psi Fraternity of North America

Zeta Tau Alpha

Zetterling, Mai

Zeus

Zeuxis

Zhangjiakou [*form.* Changchiakou]

Zhao Ziyang [*form.* Chao Tzu-yang]

Zhejiang [*form.* Chekiang]

Zhengzhou [*form.* Cheng-chou]

Zhou En-lai [*form.* Chou En-lai]

Zhukov, Georgi

Zhukov, Grigory

Zia

Zia, Khaleda

Zia pueblo

Ziegfeld, Flo

Ziegfeld Club

Ziegfeld Follies

Ziegler, John

Ziegler, Karl

Ziegler, Ronald

Ziff, William Bernard

Ziff Communications Company

Ziff-Davis Press

Ziggy

Ziglar, Zig

Zillertal Alps

Zilpah

Zim, Herbert Spencer

Zimbabwe [*form.* Southern Rhodesia]

Zimbabwean

Zimbalist, Efrem, Jr.

Zimbalist, Efrem, Sr.

Zimbalist, Stephanie

Zimmer, Kim

Zimmerman, Gerhardt

Zimmerman note

Zimmerman telegram

Zindel, Paul

Zinman, David

Zinnemann, Fred

Zinsser, Hans

Zinsser, William

Zinzendorf, Nickolaus

Zion [* Illinois; Jewish homeland]

Zion *or* Sion [* Israel]

Zion Canyon

Zionism

Zionist

Zionistic

Zionist Organization
of America

Zionite

Zion National Park

Zion's Cooperative
Mercantile
Institution

ZIP Code™

ZIP+4™ barcode

Zircaloy™

Zirin Laboratories
International

Zivili Kolo Ensemble

Zmed, Adrian

Zodiac killer

Zoe

Zoeller, Fuzzy

Zoffany, Johann

Zog

Zola, Émile

Zolaesque

Zöllner, Johann

Zollner illusion

Zollverein

Zolotow, Charlotte

Zombies, The

Zond

Zondervan
Corporation, The

[Zondervan] Family
Bookstores

Zondervan Publishing
House

Zoning Improvement
Plan

Zonjic, Alexander

Zonta Club

Zonta International

Zontian

Zoological Society of
Cincinnati

Zorach, William

Zorba the Greek

Zorn, Anders

Zorn, Max August

Zorn's lemma

Zoroaster

Zoroastrian

Zoroastrian
Associations in
North America

Zoroastrianism

Zorrila y Moral, José

Zorro [television
series]

Zorro, the Gay Blade
[movie]

Zosimus, Saint

Zouave *or* zouave,
adj. [of a clothing
style]

Zouave, *n.* [soldier]

Zouaves *or* zouaves,
n., pl. or sing. [item
of clothing]

Z twist

Zuccarelli, Francesco

Zuccari *or* Zuccaro *or*
Zuccheri, Frederigo

Zuccari *or* Zuccaro *or*
Zuccheri, Taddeo

Zucker, David

Zuckerman, Mortimer
Benjamin

Zuckerman Bound

Zuckerman Unbound

Zugspitze

Zuider *occas.* Zuyder
Zee

Zukerman, Pinchas

Zukevich, Gayla

Zukor, Adolph

Zuloaga y Zabaleta,
Ignacio

Zululand

Zulu [people], *n., pl.*
Zulus

Zulu War

Zumwalt, Elmo R., Jr.

Zumwalt, Elmo R., III

Zunian *or* Zuñian

Zuni-Cibola National
Historical Park

Zuniga, Daphne

Zuni *or* Zuñi [Indian],
n., pl. Zuni *or* Zunis
or Zuñi *or* Zuñis

Zuni Mountains

Zuni *or* Zuñi pueblo

Zuni River

Zuñis

Zunz, Leopold

Zurbarán, Francisco
de

Zurich

[Zurich] Fine Arts
Museum

Zurich Insurance
Company

Zurn Industrie, Inc.

Zvereva, Natalya

Zweig, Arnold

Zweig, Stefan

Zwelithini, King
Goodwill

Zwickau

Zwilich, Ellen Taaffe

Zwingli, Huldrych *or* Ulrich

Zwinglian

Zwinglianism

Zwinglianist

Zwolle

Zworykin, Vladimir

Zylo Ware Corporation

ZZ Top

References

Sources

Three categories of sources provided entries for this book. One category was made up of lists bearing titles such as "Highest," "Longest," or "Most Notable"; these lists appear in atlases and encyclopedias. The second category consisted of headlined or highlighted items in the popular media contemporary with the period 1992 through early 1993. The list of sources in both of these categories is too extensive to be printed here. Moreover, sources in both categories contained numerous spelling errors, and were therefore not reliable enough to be considered as spelling references.

The third category of sources consisted of general and specialized reference works. These works provided entries of a technical, traditional, or historical nature. The titles of some of these references appear in the list of references used to verify spelling, below.

Principal Spelling References

Burek, Deborah M., ed. *Encyclopedia of Associations*. Detroit, Michigan: Gale Research Inc., 1992.

Elley, Derek, consulting ed. *Variety Movie Guide*. New York: Prentice-Hall, 1992.

Inman, David. *The TV Encyclopedia*. New York: Perigee Books, 1991.

Kaplan, Mike, ed. *Variety's Who's Who in Show Business*. New York: R. R. Bowker, 1989.

McNeil, Alex. *Total Television: A Comprehensive Guide to Programming from 1948 to the Present*. New York: Penguin Books, 1991.

Melton, J. Gordon. *Encyclopedia of American Religions*. Detroit: Gale Research Inc., 1989.

Neufeldt, Victoria, editor in chief. *Webster's New World Dictionary of American English*. New York: Simon and Schuster, 1988.

Random House Dictionary of the English Language. Unabridged. New York: Random House, 1987.

Standard & Poor's Register of Corporations, Directors and Executives 1992. New York: Standard & Poor's Corporation, 1992.

Torregosa, Constance Healey, ed. *The HEP Higher Education Directory*. Falls Church, Virginia: Higher Education Publications, 1990.

Trosky, Susan M., ed. *Contemporary Authors*. Detroit: Gale Research Inc., 1992.

United States Government Manual 1992–1993. Washington, D.C.: U.S. Government Printing Office, July 1, 1992.

Webster's New Biographical Dictionary. Springfield, Massachusetts: Merriam-Webster, 1983.

Webster's New Geographical Dictionary. Springfield, Massachusetts: Merriam-Webster, 1984.

Webster's Ninth New Collegiate Dictionary. Springfield, Massachusetts: Merriam-Webster, 1990.

Who's Who in America 1992–1993. New Providence, New Jersey: Marquis Who's Who, 1992.

Who's Who in Entertainment 1992–1993. Wilmette, Illinois: Marquis Who's Who, 1992.

Winklepeck, Julie, ed. *Gale Directory of Publications and Broadcast Media*. Detroit, Michigan: Gale Research Inc., 1991.

Additional Spelling References

American Book Trade Directory 1992–93. New Providence, N.J.: R. R. Bowker, 1992.

Angelucci, Enzo. *The Rand McNally Encyclopedia of Military Aircraft 1914–1980*. New York: Rand McNally & Co. 1980.

Books in Print 1992–93 Publishers. New Providence, N.J.: R. R. Bowker, 1992.

Bordman, Gerald. *The Oxford Companion to American Theatre*. New York: Oxford University Press, 1992.

Brewer, E. Cobham. *The Dictionary of Phrase and Fable*. New York: Avenel Books, 1978.

Bronson, Fred. *The Billboard Book of Number One Hits*. New York: Billboard Publications, Inc., 1988.

Drabble, Margaret, ed. *The Oxford Companion to English Literature*. New York: Oxford University Press, 1985.

Europa Publications, Ltd. *The Europa World Yearbook 1992*. London, England: Europa Publications, Ltd., 1992.

Facts on File 1992. New York: Facts on File, Inc., 1992.

Facts on File Five-Year Index 1986–1990. New York: Facts on File, Inc., 1991.

Gammond, Peter. *The Oxford Companion to Popular Music*. New York: Oxford University Press, 1991.

Gowing, Lawrence, ed. *A Biographical Dictionary of Artists*. Englewood Cliffs, N.J.: Prentice-Hall, Inc., 1983.

Hardy, Phil, and Laing, Dave. *The Faber Companion to 20th-Century Popular Music*. Boston, Faber and Faber, 1990.

Harris, William H., and Levey, Judith S., eds. *The New Columbia Encyclopedia*. New York: Columbia University Press, 1975.

Hart, James D. *The Oxford Companion to American Literature*. New York: Oxford University Press, 1983.

Katz, Bill, and Katz, Linda Sternberg. *Magazines for Libraries*. New Providence, N.J.: R. R. Bowker, 1992.

Kennedy, Michael. *The Oxford Dictionary of Music*. New York: Oxford University Press, 1985.

Kissling, Mark. *1993 Writer's Market*. Cincinnati, Ohio: Writer's Digest Books, 1992.

Lambert, Mark, editor-in-chief. *Jane's All the World's Aircraft 1992–1993*. Alexandria, Virginia: Jane's Information Group, Inc., 1992.

Lessiter, Mike. *The College Names of the Games*. New York: Contemporary Books, 1989.

LMP 1993. New Providence, N.J.: R. R. Bowker, 1992.

Mackey, Philip English. *The Givers Guide: Making Your Charity Dollars Count*. Highland Park, New Jersey: Catbird Press, 1990.

Magill, Frank N. *Magill's Cinema Annual*. Englewood Cliffs, N.J.: Salem Press, various years.

Magill, Frank N. *Magill's Survey of Cinema—English Language Films*. Englewood Cliffs, N.J.: Salem Press, 1985.

Maxfield, Dorris Morris, ed. *Charitable Organizations of the U.S. 1991–92*. Detroit: Gale Research Inc., 1991.

Mobil Travel Guide: Major Cities. New York: Prentice Hall, 1990.

Moody's Investors Service. *Moody's Bank and Finance Manual*. New York: Moody's Investors Service, 1991.

Moody's Investors Service. *Moody's International Manual*. New York: Moody's Investors Service, 1991.

Moody's Investors Service. *Moody's Transportation Manual*. New York: Moody's Investors Service, 1991.

Monush, Barry, ed. *International Television & Video Almanac*. New York: Quigley Publishing Co., 1992.

Morehead, Philip D. *The New American Dictionary of Music*. New York: New American Library, 1991.

Morgan, Bradley J., ed. *Sports Fan's Connection: An All-in-One Sports Directory*. Detroit, Michigan: Gale Research Inc., 1992.

Paxton, John, reviser. *The Penguin Dictionary of Proper Names*. New York: Viking Penguin, 1991.

Peterson's Guide to Four-Year Colleges 1992. Princeton, New Jersey: Peterson's Guides, 1991.

Pickering, David; Isaacs, Alan; and Martin, Elizabeth, eds. *Brewer's Dictionary of 20th-Century Phrase and Fable*. Boston, Massachusetts: Houghton Mifflin Company, 1992.

Roland, Tom. *The Billboard Book of Number One Country Hits*. New York: Billboard Books, 1991.

Praeger Encyclopedia of Art. New York: Praeger Publishers, 1971.

Sharpe, Richard, ed. *Jane's Fighting Ships 1992–1993.* Alexandria, Virginia: Jane's Information Group, 1992.

Stetter, Susan L., ed. *Companies and Their Brands.* Detroit: Gale Research Inc., 1992.

The 1991 World Book Year Book. Chicago: World Book, Inc., 1992.

The World Book Encyclopedia. Chicago: World Book, Inc., 1991.

Thorne, Tony. *The Dictionary of Contemporary Slang.* New York: Pantheon Books, 1990.

United States Board on Geographic Names. *Foreign Names Information Bulletin No. 1.* Washington, D.C.: Defense Mapping Agency, February 5, 1992.

Vinson, James, ed. *International Dictionary of Art and Artists.* Chicago: St. James Press, 1990.

Ward's Business Directory of U.S. Private and Public Companies. Detroit, Michigan: Gale Research Inc., 1992.

World Aviation Directory. New York: McGraw-Hill, Inc., winter 1992.

Who's Who 1992. New York: St. Martin's Press, 1992.

Wilson, Andrew, ed. *Interavia Space Directory 1992–1993.* Alexandria, Virginia: Jane's Information Group, Inc., 1992.

Appendix: Word Division*

This appendix on word division pertains not only to the dividing of capitalized terms, such as those that appear in the dictionary part of this book, but to word division in general.

Word Division—General

It is sometimes necessary to divide a word at the end of a line and to carry over part of the word to the next line. The division point is shown in dictionaries with a symbol such as a raised dot (·). In text, the division is shown with a hyphen (-) at the end of the line.

Therefore, a dictionary entry for *fas·ci·na·tion* allows divisions that

END ON ONE LINE AS   AND CONTINUE ON THE NEXT LINE AS

fas-   cination
fasci-   nation
fascina-   tion

Under ideal conditions, word division is accomplished so that the page looks neat and so that the reader is neither confused nor distracted. Unfortunately, ideal conditions do not always exist, especially when setting type on a narrow page or column.

A line can occasionally be rewritten *without changing the*

*This appendix is adapted from William C. Paxson, *The New American Spelling Dictionary* (Penguin Books, 1992).

meaning to make the line longer or shorter and thereby do away with the need for a hyphen at the end of the line. When the line cannot be rewritten, any confusion or distraction caused by an end-of-line word break is usually momentary, and context helps make the meaning clear.

For best results, careful word dividers should follow as closely as possible the guidelines given in this appendix. The guidelines are based on factors common to word division: pronunciation and appearance. Principal references are the entries in *Webster's Ninth New Collegiate Dictionary* (Merriam-Webster, 1990) and articles on word division in *Webster's Third New International Dictionary* (Merriam-Webster, 1976) and the *Chicago Manual of Style* (University of Chicago Press, 1982).

Short words. Avoid dividing short words, words of five or fewer letters. Words such as *basal*, *duty*, and *oleo* should not be broken at the end of a line even if a dictionary shows a break point.

One-syllable words. Do not divide a one-syllable word, no matter how long. A word such as *through* or *straight* is pronounced as one syllable and has no logical division point.

One-letter divisions. One-letter divisions should be avoided if at all possible. A single letter at the end of a line does not give the reader much of a clue to what follows on the next line. In addition, ending a line with a hyphen instead of a single letter is ridiculous, for if there is room at the end of the line for the hyphen, there is room for a solitary letter.

again, *not* a-gain
mighty, *not* might-y

In addition, a one-letter division should not be made immediately before or after a hyphen:

voice-over, *not* voice-o-ver
mini-camera, *not* min-i-camera

Try to avoid making a one-letter division of the suffixes *-able* and *-ably*, since *-able* and *-ably* can stand as words in their own right. That is, *considerable* should be divided as *consider-able*. If divided as *considera-ble*, the resulting *considera-* at the end of a line looks awkward.

Contractions. Do not divide contractions such as *hadn't* or *doesn't*.

Adjoining consonants. Where two adjoining consonants separate the syllables, divide between the consonants:

mis-sion
con-fuse
con-version *or* conver-sion

Exception: Do not break up a root word: *miss-ing*, not *mis-sing*.
Exception: Do not keep any combination of letters together that results in a break that looks or sounds strange: *Father* is divided as *fa-ther*, not *fat-her*.
Where three or more adjoining consonants separate the syllables, place at least one consonant with its preceding vowel, and divide the way the syllables are pronounced:

claus-trophobia, *not* claust-rophobia
mis-creant, *not* misc-reant

Adjoining vowels. Where adjoining vowels are pronounced separately, division should occur between the vowels:

cre-ation *is better than* crea-tion
re-adjust *is better than* read-just

Different usages—different divisions. Where different usages of a word exist, the word should be divided according to the pronunciations that are part of the usages:

proj-ect (*noun*) *or* pro-ject (*verb*)
microm-eter (*an instrument*) *or* micro-meter (*a unit of measurement*)

Suggestive divisions. A division should suggest the rest of the word and the word's pronunciation:

criti-cism, *not* crit-icism
offi-cial, *not* off-icial
posi-tion, *not* pos-ition
divi-sion, *not* div-ision

Consecutive lines. Try to avoid dividing words at the ends of more than two consecutive lines.

Paragraph breaks. Try to avoid dividing the last word of a paragraph. If you must divide it, carry over at least four letters to the following line.

Page breaks. Try to avoid dividing the last word on a right-hand page.

Embarrassing breaks. Avoid embarrassing word breaks:

thera-pist, *not* the-rapist
amass, *not* am-ass
fric-as-see, *not* fric-ass-ee

Division of Prefixes and Suffixes

Division of prefixes and suffixes is accomplished according to these guidelines.

Short prefixes. Divide after a short prefix:

non-taxable
post-partum
pre-arranged
un-grammatical

Long or multisyllabic prefixes. Try not to divide a long or multisyllabic prefix:

anti-depressant *is better than* an-tidepressant
multi-vitamin *is better than* mul-tivitamin
semi-trailer, *not* sem-itrailer

Suffixes—general. When the root word does *not* end with an *e*, the suffix is set off from the end of the word by using a hyphen:

moist *becomes* moist-en, moist-er, moist-est

When the root word ends with an *e*, the *e* is usually dropped, and the suffix is set off from the word by using a hyphen:

take *becomes* tak-en
white *becomes* whit-er, whit-est, whit-ish

Exceptions: *White* becomes white-ness. In addition, pronunciation sometimes dictates divisions where the hyphen is placed before the suffix: *cho-sen*, not *chos-en*; *fro-zen*, not *froz-en*.

Suffixes with one-syllable sounds. A suffix that is pronounced as one syllable is rarely divided: *-ceous*, *-cial*, *-cion*, *-cious*, *-geous*, *-gion*, *-gious*, *-sial*, *-sion*, *-tial*, *-tion*, *-tious*.

-ed suffixes. When the *-ed* suffix is pronounced, it is separated from its root word: *stat-ed*.

When the *-ed* suffix contains a silent *e*, it should not be separated from the root word:

aimed, *not* aim-ed
plugged, *not* plug-ged
stig-matized *or* stigma-tized, *not* stigmatiz-ed.

-ing **suffixes.** When the final consonant is doubled to add an *-ing* suffix, divide between the doubled consonants:

grin-ning, *not* grinn-ing

Single or double consonants that are part of the root word are usually not carried over:

forc-ing, *not* for-cing
grill-ing, *not* gril-ling

When the root word ends in *e*, the *e* is dropped to add the *-ing* suffix and division is made at the suffix:

state *becomes* stat-ing
file *becomes* fil-ing

When the root word ends in *le*, the *e* is dropped, and the *l* and sometimes one or more of the preceding consonants are carried over with the *-ing*:

chuckle *becomes* chuck-ling
twinkle *becomes* twin-kling

-le **endings.** When the word ends in the syllable *-le* that sounds like a vowel, carry over one or more of the letters that come before the *le*:

star-tle, *not* start-le
prin-ciples *or* princi-ples, *not* princip-les

Division of Compound Words

Solid compounds. A solid compound word is made up of two or more words joined without a hyphen or hyphens. *Crabgrass* is a solid compound, as is *outreach*.

A solid compound should be divided between the elements of the compound:

sales-woman *is better than* saleswom-an
news-paper (*1st choice*) *or* newspa-per (*2d choice*), *but not* new-spaper

Hyphenated compounds. A hyphenated compound is two or more words joined by a hyphen or hyphens. *Self-centered* is a hyphenated compound.

A hyphenated compound should if possible be divided at the hyphen; the idea is to avoid two hyphens close together·

self-satisfied (*1st choice*) *or* self-satis-fied (*2d choice*) *or* self-sat-isfied (*3d choice*)
self-centeredness (*1st choice*) *or* self-centered-ness (*2d choice*) *or* self-cen-teredness (*3d choice*)

A break that doesn't come at the hyphen is especially disconcerting in short compounds such as *Mason-Dixon* or with a word like *master-at-arms* that already has two hyphens.

Division of Personal Names

Every effort should be made to place on one line a person's name and any identifying titles or abbreviations. If that is not possible, the name should be broken after a middle initial. The breaks shown below are listed in descending order of acceptability:

William A. Medlich, Jr. (all on one line)
William A. -Medlich, Jr.

William A. Med-lich, Jr.
William -A. Medlich, Jr.
Wil-liam A. Medlich, Jr.
William A. Medlich, -Jr.

Although it is permissible to separate *Jr.* from the name, numerical suffixes as in *Richard III* should not be separated.

When initials are used in place of given names, break the name after the second or last initial:

T. A. -Johnson, *not* T. -A. Johnson.

Division of Abbreviations, Numerals, Dates, Headings, and Titles

Abbreviations. Do not divide short abbreviations such as *B.C.*, *M.A.*, *YWCA*. A long abbreviation may be divided as a word is: *YEE-PIE* (Youthful Energetic Elderly Person Involved in Everything).

Numerals. Try to avoid dividing closely connected numerals and their abbreviations: *$10,000* or *55 MPH*. A long string of numerals may be divided at a comma, and the comma should be retained on the first line: *(1,300,-000)*.

Dates. When writing dates, do not divide the month and the day. The year may be carried over to the next line: April 8, -1993.

Headings and titles. Do not divide words in headings and titles. Similarly, do not separate references such as *5(a)* or *4.3.* from the matter to which the references pertain.